Perception

Alfred A. Knopf Series
in Psychology

SERIES ADVISORS

Geoffrey Keppel
University of California at Berkeley

Stephen E. Glickman
University of California at Berkeley

Perception

ROBERT SEKULER
Northwestern University

RANDOLPH BLAKE
Northwestern University

Alfred A. Knopf
New York

In appreciation of their love and support,
this book is dedicated to
Susan and Elaine, Stacia, Allison,
Erica, and Geoff,
and to Mary Sekuler and Ted Blake.

First Edition

987654321

Copyright © 1985 by Alfred A. Knopf, Inc.

Library of Congress Cataloging in Publication Data

Sekuler, Robert.
  Perception.

  (Alfred A. Knopf series in psychology)
  Bibliography: p. 461
  Includes index.
  1. Perception. I. Blake, Randolph. II. Title.
III. Series.
BF311.S434 1985   153.7   84-21276
ISBN 0-394-32815-9

Text Design: Suzanne Bennett

Cover Design: Lorraine Hohman

Cover photo: Geoffrey Gove

Manufactured in the United States of America

Preface

Human beings have always wondered about how they perceived the world in which they lived. In modern times, this wonder has stimulated behavioral, biological, and medical scientists to take up a systematic study of perception. Building on the cumulative efforts of all these people, this book explains seeing, hearing, smelling, and tasting to students of perception.

The introductory chapter summarizes some of the common motivations that stimulate people to study perception, as well as the various approaches that such study can take. Chapter 1 also outlines the framework on which the text is constructed. Chapters 2 through 7 discuss seeing—the biological basis of vision and the perception of pattern, color, and depth. The treatment of seeing concludes in Chapter 8 with a discussion of the perception of visual events. The most detailed chapters in the book are Chapters 9 and 10, on hearing, and Chapter 11, on smelling

and tasting. Chapter 12 ends the text with a consideration of the various ways in which knowledge and perception can interact.

Perception has several notable features. Central topics are presented in historical context, to underscore how the contemporary study of perception is part of an ongoing intellectual process. At the same time, readers will find that our source materials are heavily biased toward recently published articles and books. Furthermore, we provide thorough coverage of "hot," rapidly developing topics. For example, one chapter provides a comprehensive treatment of visual spatial frequency analysis. Giving such special emphasis to the most recent work demonstrates that perception is a living and growing field.

The extensive program of more than 250 illustrations is another of this book's most important features. Our combined thirty years of experience as teachers have told us that students don't always see in a graph or diagram exactly what was intended. So instead of merely directing student readers to "look at the figure," we have crafted the text, figures, and figure captions to ensure accurate interpretation of the illustrative material. In addition, we have given extra care to the graphic presentation of complex ideas. Such ideas are often conveyed in this book by a short *series* of illustrations, with each illustration in a series phasing in additional concepts. This approach enables every reader to get the point—even those who are novices at interpreting graphs and diagrams. Finally, illustrations that depict previously published experimental results have been adapted and redrawn to maximize clarity and consistency of presentation.

Because the study of perception draws upon many different disciplines—physics, chemistry, anatomy, psychology, and medicine, among others—its technical vocabulary incorporates the terminology of those disciplines. Beginning students of perception are often bewildered by the flood of new terms that they must master. Recognizing this problem, we have introduced only those terms that are absolutely necessary to the discussion. Each term is carefully defined when it is first used, and all these terms appear in a Glossary at the back of the book.

We have also kept detailed, abstract descriptions of research methods to a minimum. Where appropriate, we explain particular methods in enough detail that the student reader can appreciate the methods and whatever constraints they impose on results and conclusions. Various methods for studying perception are discussed within the context of the specific problems that they were designed to solve. By integrating methods and results, we hope to facilitate the reader's genuine appreciation of both. An Appendix provides additional information about conventional behavioral methods for studying perception. The Appendix also describes some contemporary variants of those methods: forced-choice procedures, sensory decision theory, and adaptive psychophysical methods. The Appendix presents these methods within a historical framework, enabling the student to understand not only the methods but also the reasons for their development.

Since perception is not just an abstract, scientific discipline, but an integral part of everyday life, this book consistently relates scientific research on perception to the reader's own perceptual experiences. To underscore the relationship between science and everyday experience, we present many simple, interesting demonstrations that readers can perform on their own with little or no equipment. Also, in order to anchor the discussion in the reader's own experience, the text emphasizes the everyday behavioral needs that seeing, hearing, smelling, and tasting are designed to satisfy—the *functions* of perception. This functional approach to perception is highlighted in the special-topic boxes that appear throughout the text. Many of these boxes discuss clinical disorders and their fascinating perceptual consequences. Some students will be interested in learning about these disorders for personal reasons; all students should find that the study of perceptual disorders provides insight into the nature of normal perception.

We have attempted to make our treatment of perception an integrated one, in part by linking ideas across chapters. These linkages reflect the fact that different areas in perception often utilize similar techniques and related theoretical ideas. Our text is integrated in another way, blending anatomy, physiology, and psychophysics. The information and ideas from each of these three approaches have been carefully selected to ensure a coherent, complete presentation. Structure and function become more comprehensible and memorable when they are integrated.

In preparing this book, we benefitted greatly from the comments and criticisms of many people. Special credit should be given to those individuals who reviewed various chapters. These include:

Martin Banks, University of Texas at Austin

William P. Banks, Pomona College

Linda M. Bartoshuk, Pierce Foundation/Yale University

Ira H. Bernstein, University of Texas at Arlington

Irving Biederman, State University of New York at Buffalo

Richard Bowen, Loyola University of Chicago

Edward Carterette, University of California at Los Angeles

Peter Dallos, Northwestern University

David S. Emmerich, State University of New York at Stony Brook

Trygg Engen, Brown University

Robert Gesteland, Northwestern University

Lewis O. Harvey, University of Colorado

James Hillenbrand, Northwestern University

Eileen Kowler, Rutgers University

Robert M. Levy, Indiana State University

Robert Pachella, University of Michigan

Mark Perkins, University of Wisconsin

Steve Poltrock, University of Denver

James R. Pomerantz, State University of New York at Buffalo

Keith Rayner, University of Massachusetts at Amherst

Phillip Russell, Northwestern University

Allison Sekuler, Pomona College

Benjamin Wallace, Cleveland State University

Brian Wandell, Stanford University

Gerald S. Wasserman, Purdue University

David H. Westendorf, University of Arkansas

William A. Yost, Loyola University of Chicago

James L. Zacks, Michigan State University

We also thank Gregory C. Phillips of Northwestern University, who gave cheerfully of his time and talents to prepare some of the computer graphics for the book. Clare Alexander rendered invaluable help by securing obscure reference materials and ensuring that they stayed put long enough for us to use them. We are particularly grateful to Carolyn Shufeldt, whose frank comments on early drafts of each chapter were very helpful to us in revising those drafts. Thanks are owed to our students, colleagues, and, especially, our families for their tolerance during the long period of our preoccupation with this project. Finally, we thank the excellent editorial and production staff at Random House, in particular Judith Rothman, senior editor; Cecilia Gardner, project editor; Lucy Rosendahl and Leslie Carr, development editors; Evelyn Katrak, copy editor; Lorraine Hohman, designer; and David Saylor, production manager.

ROBERT SEKULER
RANDOLPH BLAKE

Contents

Chapter 1

Introduction to Perception

The world is filled with objects and events that combine to create a kaleidoscope of potential information. Though much of that information is irrelevant for people's daily needs, some of it is absolutely essential. So that they can use this information effectively, human beings are equipped with specialized machinery for capturing this information and for translating it into a language that can be understood by the nervous system. In this translated form, the selected information is digested by the brain, culminating in perceptions of the world. These perceptions then guide people's actions in the world around them.

As we've just described it, **perception** is the final link in a chain of related events. To understand perception completely, you must understand each link in the chain. To begin, you must know something about the environment in which you live, for this environment determines what there is to perceive. This first link in the chain is described

using terms borrowed from physics, because stimulation comes in various forms of physical energy: thermal, mechanical, acoustic, and electromagnetic. The physical energy that initiates the chain of events is called a **stimulus** (plural "stimuli").

Next, you have to specify how the nervous system converts these physical energies into neural events. Known as **sensory transduction,** this conversion process requires an understanding of the specialized sensory receptors such as those contained in the eye and the ear. Once this transduction has been achieved, objects and events are represented solely as patterns of neural impulses within the various sensory nerve fibers. From this point on, all further elaboration and editing of the sensory information must be performed using this neural representation.

A complete understanding of perception must include a thorough description of conscious experience, the final product in this chain of events. A great many techniques have been developed by psychologists for systematically cataloging the experiences of people and relating these experiences to patterns of physical stimulation. The enterprise of relating physical stimulation to perceptual events is known as **psychophysics.** By specifying the relation between physical and perceptual events, psychophysics provides important clues to unraveling the intervening events.

According to the view spelled out above, perception represents the final product in a chain of events stretching from events in the physical world external to the perceiver, through the translation of those events into patterns of activity within the perceiver's nervous system, culminating in the perceiver's experiential and behavioral reactions to those events. This sequence is illustrated in Figure 1.1. With this broad framework in mind, let's consider several important implications of this way of thinking about perception.

Aspects of Perception

PERCEPTION AS A BIOLOGICAL PROCESS

In this book, we approach perception as a *biological* process. In order to be perceived, *any* information about events in the world must be registered by the sensory nervous system. The noted neuroscientist Vernon Mountcastle has described this constraint very vividly:

Each of us lives within . . . the prison of his own brain. Projecting from it are millions of fragile sensory nerve fibers, in groups uniquely adapted to sample the energetic states of the world around us: heat, light, force, and chemical composition. That is all we ever know of it directly; all else is logical inference. (1975, p. 131)

In other words, Mountcastle is pointing out that sensory nerve fibers are the only

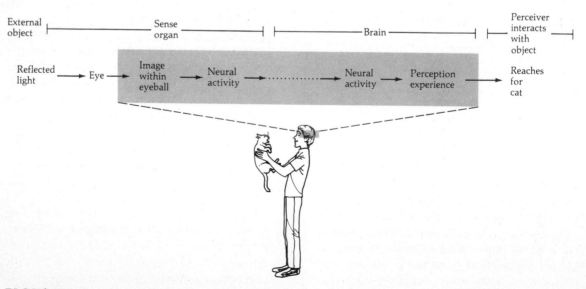

FIGURE 1.1
Sequence of major events leading to a percept.

link to the external world; they alone provide the communication channels to reality. If environmental events fall outside the range of sensitivity of the sensory channels, those events will not be experienced directly. It may be possible to detect some of these events indirectly, using specialized instruments. Such instruments work in one of two ways. Some amplify physical energy, making weak signals strong enough to stimulate the senses. For example, a microscope can magnify objects otherwise too small to be seen by the naked eye. Other instruments convert energy that is *outside* the normal bounds of the senses into a form that is within those bounds. For instance, Geiger counters can warn about the presence of radioactivity, a form of energy that cannot be sensed directly. In either case, though, such instruments are being used to extend the reach of the sensory system.

It may be difficult to accept that your rich perceptual world encompasses only a small, restricted portion of the entire universe. Because one's conception of reality is so intimately determined by one's subjective experiences, it seems unnatural to distinguish between one's "perception of the world" and the "world itself." Yet to understand perception fully, you have to make this distinction. Perhaps a few examples will enable you to appreciate what we mean by the limited scope of your perceptual world.

Consider, for instance, how various species of animals probably experience the world. It is well documented that not all animals have the same sensory systems. Consequently, various species have access to different universes of physical events. Dogs can hear sounds in regions of the frequency spectrum where humans are deaf; bees are able to navigate using a quality of light, polarization, that is outside the realm of human visual experience. And there are chemical substances that evoke no experience of odor for humans and yet elicit strong olfac-

tory responses in certain animals. In general, there is no single "environment" that all animals live in. Members of different species interact with their physical and biological world in ways that reflect their own unique requirements and capabilities. As Box 1.1 shows, although all animals inhabit the same *physical* world, their *perceptual* worlds may differ radically.

But not even all humans have equivalent sensory systems. For instance, some people have defects of the eye that prevent them from experiencing the full range of colors that other people see. There are also certain people who cannot taste one of the bitter substances in coffee because of an abnormality in their taste system. These and similar examples that we shall bring up throughout this book underscore the dependence of perception on the sensory nervous system.

Thinking about perception as a biological process highlights another important point: perceptual states are produced by brain states. If one takes this point of view, one must be careful to distinguish between the perception of an object and that object itself; the two need not correspond exactly, and sometimes the discrepancy between them is dramatic. Consider, for example, one of the so-called visual illusions. Most of you have had the experience of seeing the full moon. It looks enormous when on the horizon but appears to shrink as it climbs into the sky. Yet the actual size of the moon remains constant regardless of its position in the sky, and so does the image of the moon that strikes the back of your eye. So here's a case where *perceived* size fluctuates while *physical* size is unchanging. This illusion, which we shall consider further in Chapter 7 ("Depth Perception"), is but one of many examples demonstrating that reality and the perception of reality do not always correspond. One must regard perception as only one interpretation of reality.

BOX 1.1
Seeing the Invisible

It's hard even to imagine what it must be like to sense forms of energy that humans ordinarily cannot sense (Nagel, 1982). But one can get an inkling of this experience. Normally, humans cannot see electromagnetic radiation in the portion of the spectrum called "infrared." This form of radiation is usually associated with heat, including the body heat of living creatures. If infrared is sensed at all, it is experienced as warmth on the skin. Although some animals, notably certain snakes, have specialized sense organs that allow them to detect and respond to objects on the basis of the infrared energy radiated by those objects, humans are fairly insensitive to infrared.

To give you some idea of what it might be like to see infrared radiation we have prepared the two accompanying photographs. The photograph on the left shows a scene taken with ordinary black and white film; this film is about as *in*sensitive to infrared as the human eye is. That is why pictures taken with such film look "normal." The photograph on the right shows the same scene taken with film that is sensitive to infrared; it reveals things (areas of heat and cold) in the scene that humans ordinarily would not see. Thus, for instance, the water in the right-hand photo appears dark because it is cold.

Although the differences between these pictures are interesting, we can't really claim that the photographs provide much insight into the experiences of those infrared-sensitive snakes. In some cases, their infrared-sensitive organs are not even part of their eyes, so they probably wouldn't be *seeing* the infrared. The photographs do remind us, though, that the human perceptual world is not the only one possible.

(Glyn Cloyd)

Why do we characterize perception as an interpretive process? After all, common experience indicates that one perceives directly and immediately, without any uncertainty or guesswork. Yet if perception is a brain process, then the inference is inescapable that perception is indirect and mediated. Only through the senses can the brain acquire information about the physical world. Using this information, the brain can arrive at conclusions about the properties of objects and events (such as their size or their distance from the point of observation). The British philosopher Bertrand Russell put this succinctly: "The starry heaven that we know in visual sensation is inside us. The external starry heaven that we believe in is inferred" (1959, p. 27).

The inferences made by the brain may be accurate or they may be in error, depending on the information supplied by the senses and on the brain's predisposition to interpret information in certain ways. In effect, the brain behaves like a detective, using bits of information to piece together a solution. However, sometimes a detective can arrive at a solution that seems perfectly reasonable but turns out not to be correct. And perception, too, can be misleading, as Figure 1.2 shows. The figure is one of many extraordinary illusions devised by the Italian psychologist Gaetano Kanizsa. A well-defined, white triangle seems to be covering three black circles. But by carefully inspecting the regions where the triangle should be, you'll discover that this triangle is a figment of your imagination. Kanizsa's illusion shows that available clues can fool the brain into seeing a figure that does not really exist. In most instances, though, the clues available to perception are numerous and reliable.

To sum up, this book's viewpoint is that perception is the product of a biological process. Consequently, we believe certain qualities of perception can be explained at the biological level. In those cases, particular perceptual experiences can be related to corresponding neural events. Yet it must also be recognized that other important qualities of perception elude description in neural terms. These elusive qualities, while surely the result of brain processes, probably entail complex patterns of neural activity distributed over wide regions of the brain. Contemporary neurophysiological techniques are inadequate to illuminate the operation of

FIGURE 1.2
Subjective, or illusory, triangle. (Adapted from Kanizsa, 1976.)

these kinds of neural systems. Throughout this book we shall try to be explicit in distinguishing those aspects of perception that currently are understandable at a neural level from those that are not.

THE NEED FOR SENSORY INPUT

Although human beings live in a swarming sea of sensory information, they flourish rather than drown; human sensory machinery was designed to handle this sea of information. In fact, when deprived of sensory input, an individual's perceptual system may resort to manufacturing images with no external referent; these internally fueled images are called hallucinations. Apparently, the human perceptual system has a constant need for input from the external world. When that input is reduced or eliminated, the sensory systems lapse into a kind of disorderly conduct that yields distorted, often bizarre, perceptions (Bexton, Heron, and Scott, 1954; Siegel, 1984).

But too little input is not the only problem; overload—too much input—can be just as serious. Anyone who has tried to carry on a phone conversation while watching television and reading a homework assignment all at the same time knows the confusion and chaos that can result. Fortunately, though, most people can filter out some of this barrage through a process of selective attention. They concentrate on one set of inputs at a time, giving little heed to others. However, it seems that certain individuals—including some who are classified as schizophrenic—have trouble selecting among competing sensory inputs (Baribeau-Braun, Picton, and Gosselin, 1983). For reasons not yet understood, these people seem unable to manage the normal demands of sensory processing. They treat all inputs as equally important. Perhaps, overwhelmed by the flood of sensory information, they withdraw into a less confusing inner world (Venables, 1964). Clearly, there is an optimum range of stimulation within which most people perform best.

The demands of the environment also govern how perceptual systems are used. Probably in more primitive life styles (such as those of our primate ancestors) the lion's share of perceptual processing was devoted to survival—being on the alert to distinguish friends from foes and trying to locate the next meal. As civilization developed, these pressing demands have relaxed. As a result, civilized people enjoy the freedom to develop pastimes—the visual arts, music, cuisine—that engage their perceptual machinery in more amusing and creative ways. All of these pastimes involve stimulation of the senses. Besides their immediate aesthetic and sensual qualities, these kinds of sensory experiences play an important role in the cultural heritage of societies. Through various forms of art, people are able to share the joys and pains experienced by others and to savor vicariously the thrill of discovery that originally inspired an artist. In brief, art embodies much of a culture's wisdom; relaxed demands on our perceptual machinery allow us the luxury to create and enjoy that embodiment.

PERCEPTION INVOLVES ACTION

Perceiving usually requires some action on the part of the perceiver. Often, one must look in order to see, searching the visual environment until the desired object of regard is located. Likewise, to make a faint sound audible, one must sometimes turn an ear in its direction. When one touches an object, it is more easily identified if explored with the fingers. All of these examples are a reminder that perception is an *active* process, an idea especially championed by the American psychologist James J. Gibson (1966). This active process works to guide behavior, thereby stimulating even more activity. Once an object has been perceived, one decides whether to approach or avoid it. Hearing a noise, one might reply vocally or one might find it wiser to remain very quiet. Having identified an object by touch, one may discard it or try to keep it. In each case behavior depends on *what* is perceived.

Perception's action orientation raises an interesting distinction among the various senses that has to do with the proximity of the perceiver to the object of perception. Touch and taste require direct contact between the perceiver and the source of stimulation. Because of this restriction, taste and touch can be considered **near senses.** The sense of smell is also effectively a near sense. Volatile chemicals from an odorous substance are diluted with distance, so smell works more effectively for substances in the general vicinity of the nose. Seeing and hearing, in contrast, can be thought of as **far senses,** or **distance senses.** The eyes and ears can pick up information originating from remote sources; in this respect, they function like a ship's radar. They allow one to make perceptual contact with objects located too far away for immediate grasp: They extend one perceptually out into the world beyond the fingertips and nose. These two senses serve as able substitutes for actual locomotor exploration of the environment, enabling one to explore the surroundings vicariously. They provide early, advance warning of approaching danger, and they guide the search for friends and desired objects. In general, hearing and seeing—particularly the latter—open up to you the large world that lies outside your reach. Imagine how vulnerable you would feel if you were denied access to all information picked up by your far senses; your whole world would shrink to the area within arm's reach. You would be able to sense objects only when you touched them or when they touched you. It is not surprising, therefore, that blindness and deafness, loss of the far senses, are considered so devastating.

Incidentally, this distinction between the near and far senses has an important behavioral consequence. Any crucial reaction called for by taste or touch must be executed swiftly. There is no time to decide whether a bitter substance is toxic—you spit it out reflexively. Nor do you first try to judge what is causing a burning sensation before you remove your hand from a hot object. In these cases, you act first and then consciously think about what it was that triggered your reflex action. However, in the case of the far senses—seeing and hearing—one is usually dealing with objects located some distance away. This distance permits the luxury of evaluating the potential consequences of one's actions.

Why Study Perception?

Over the years, people have studied perception for a variety of reasons. Some of these reasons, as you will see, stem from practical considerations, such as the need to solve a particular problem. Other reasons do not reflect practical concerns but instead arise simply from intellectual curiosity about ourselves and the world we live in.

PRACTICAL REASONS FOR STUDYING PERCEPTION

The human senses evolved in an environment that was different in many ways from the one we live in now. Many of the challenges confronting the human senses today didn't exist in the more primitive environments for which these senses were designed. A few of those challenges are illustrated in Figure 1.3. It's very important to

FIGURE 1.3
Today's complex environments can stress the senses.

know just what kind of perceptual demands can reasonably be placed on the human senses without compromising safety and sanity (Russell and Ward, 1982). As already mentioned, there is an optimum range of sensory stimulation within which the majority of people work and play most effectively. Intense stimulation—such as excessive noise, glaring light, and harsh smells—can impair immediate performance as well as damage the sensory nervous system. Through the study of perception, one can identify and correct potentially hazardous environmental conditions that threaten the senses and impair the ability to make decisions.

In a related vein, studying perception enables one to design devices that ensure optimal perceptual performance. Just think how often each day you come in contact with devices designed to communicate some message to you. Traffic lights, alarm clocks, telephones, and video displays are just a few of the myriad inventions that people rely on during work, play, study, even sleep. To be effective, these devices should be tailored to human sensory systems. It would be unwise, for example, to use a high-pitched tone as a fire alarm in a hotel, because elderly people have difficulty hearing such tones. Similarly, a traffic sign with blue lettering on a green background would be inefficient since blue and green are more difficult to distinguish than other pairs of colors. In general, one wants the signs and signals in the environment to be easy to see and hear—which requires an understanding of human perceptual capacities and limitations.

Studying perception also makes it possible to design aids for individuals with impaired sensory function. Take hearing aids as an example. Most hearing aids amplify not only the sounds that the user wants to hear—such as a person's voice—but also other, unwanted sounds—such as traffic noises. Recognizing this problem, British

psychologist Richard L. Gregory developed a procedure that selectively amplifies just speech sounds (Gregory and Drysdale, 1976). This invention grew out of earlier work on the ear's ability to respond selectively to particular sounds. As you will learn in Chapter 4, research is also under way to develop artificial eyes for the blind. Designing these kinds of aids for sensory-impaired people requires understanding of mechanisms of normal perception.

Turning to another practical reason, people in consumer marketing are very interested in human perception. For instance, companies in the food and beverage industry carefully test the perceptual appeal—the taste, smell, and appearance—of their products before marketing them. Advertising, too, capitalizes on perception research to package and market products in ways that will bring those products to the attention of consumers. There are even claims that subliminal sensory messages—pictures or words presented too briefly or too faintly to be consciously seen or heard—can influence the public's buying habits (Dixon, 1981). Whether this is true or not, you can be sure that consumer marketing is very interested in human perception.

So far, our practical reasons have focused on human perception. But as the following examples show, there are solid reasons for studying animal perception too. For one thing, animals can be trained to perform jobs that are beyond the sensory limits of humans. Dogs, because of their keen sense of smell, are adept at detecting odors that are too faint for the human nose. This is why dogs are frequently employed to sniff out illegal drugs or to trace the path of a suspect. In other instances, knowledge of an animal's sensory apparatus allows one to control that animal's behavior. For instance, agriculture scientists are now controlling cotton bollworms—moth larvae that damage crops—by spraying crop fields with a chemical that fools adult males into mating with moths of a different species. The chemical works by overwhelming the smell cues that normally guide the moths. As a result, the moths engage in promiscuous and ineffective mating behavior. As a final example, scientists have recently begun studying animals whose sensory capacity is impaired as a consequence either of congenital disorders or of some experimental manipulation such as sensory deprivation (Blake, 1978). These studies, in turn, are leading to new ideas concerning the bases and treatment of comparable sensory disorders in humans.

PERCEPTION AND INTELLECTUAL CURIOSITY

Practical concerns aside, learning about perception satisfies an intellectual curiosity about ourselves and the world we live in. Perception can be thought of as each individual's personal theory of reality, a kind of knowledge-gathering process that defines our view of the world. Because this perceptual outlook guides our activities, both mental and behavioral, we naturally find it fascinating to inquire about the bases of perception.

Natural curiosity leads to a variety of conjectures about perception. When looking at a newborn child, for instance, one cannot help speculating about what that infant sees and hears. Likewise, one is curious to know if blind people really can hear sounds that escape the ears of sighted people. You may have wondered why colors seem to change depending on the time of day. As dusk approaches, greens take on a deeper richness while yellows and reds lose some of their brilliance. And why does everyone effectively become color-blind under dim light conditions? One would like to know what sensory cues enable a displaced pet to journey hundreds of miles, eventually returning to its old home. And one grudgingly marvels at how adept mosquitoes are at locating one's bare skin in total darkness.

In general, people are intrigued by their everyday experiences and curious about the basis of these experiences. This curiosity was formalized first in the discipline known today as philosophy. Throughout the ages, philosophers have argued about how human beings are able to know about the external world. Their arguments revolved around a concern for the validity, or reality, of the sense experiences. The senses tell one things about the world, and from that information one builds a concept of the world. But can the senses be relied on to tell the truth? Might we not be deceived about the world? Perhaps, as Plato suggested in *The Republic*, we see only a shadow of the real world. Some contemporary philosophers, among them Peter Unger of the University of Wisconsin, agree with Plato that our ability to know the world is inherently limited (Unger, 1971). Of course, the situation would be even worse if the world really did not exist at all. In fact, some philosophers have seriously proposed this idea, arguing that the world one experiences is but a figment of the imagination. Such a view, known as solipsism, can be fun to argue about (see Box 1.2). It is not, however, an attitude that encourages the scientific study of perception.

To avoid getting trapped by these philosophical conjectures, people who study perception sidestep such questions as "Is the world real?" They take the world's reality as a given and work from there, asking how well the human senses actually describe that world. This approach really boils down to comparing one's perceptions of the world to those descriptions of it obtained using such instruments as meter sticks, scales, and so on (Blakemore, 1979). In fact, a lot of research on human perception is concerned with just such comparisons.

Since we are discussing attitudes about

BOX 1.2
Maybe You're Only Dreaming

You think you are seeing these words, but could you not be hallucinating or dreaming or having your brain stimulated to give you the experience of seeing these marks on paper although no such thing is before you? More extremely, could you not be floating in a tank while super-psychologists stimulate your brain electrochemically to produce exactly the same experiences as you are now having, or even to produce the whole sequence of experiences you have had in your lifetime thus far? If one of these other things was happening, your experience would be exactly the same as it now is. So how can you know none of them is happening? (Nozick, 1981, p. 167)

A Harvard University philosopher, Robert Nozick, asked these questions to introduce his discussion of **epistemology,** the branch of philosophy concerned with the nature and origin of knowledge. Since the senses provide so much of one's knowledge about the world, epistemology and the study of perception share many concerns.

In fact, perceptual observations have helped to shape philosophical theories. Realizing that sensory information was not totally dependable, many philosophers became skeptical about anyone's ability to know the world as it really is. For example, the British philosopher John Locke observed that water in a bucket might feel *either* warm or cool, depending on where your hand had just been. If your hand had been in colder water, the water in the bucket would feel warm; if your hand had been in hot water, the water in the bucket would feel cool. In other words, the apparent warmth or coolness of the water does not reside in the water itself; it is a subjective quality that you attribute to the water. Since some perceived qualities of the external world seemed more subjective than others, Locke distinguished between "primary qualities" (actually present in the objects) and "secondary qualities" (present only in the perceiver). The secondary qualities, Locke said, were dependent for their existence on one's perception of them.

George Berkeley, another British philosopher, carried Locke's ideas further, asserting that objects themselves, not just their qualities, must be perceived in order to exist. This implies that if you are alone in a room with an object, that object, when you turn your back on it, should cease to exist. Berkeley found unacceptable the idea that objects could pop in and out of existence. You too probably find this notion absurd. To remedy his discomfort, Berkeley proposed that there is an omnipresent God who perceives everything everywhere. Berkeley's solution has been parodied by Ronald Knox as follows:

There was a young man who said, "God

Must think it exceedingly odd
 If he finds that this tree
 Continues to be
When there's no one about in the Quad."

  Reply
Dear Sir:
 Your astonishment's odd;
I am always about in the Quad.
 And that's why the tree
 Will continue to be,
Since observed by
  Yours faithfully,
   God.

But let's return to the questions Nozick asked at the beginning of this box. How does one deal with the skeptic who suggests that people's experiences might be delusions induced by "super-psychologists"? First, be reconciled to the fact that absolute refutation of the skeptic is impossible. You cannot prove that you are *not* floating in that tank. But all is not lost. Though you cannot prove that you are not in a tank, this doesn't prevent you from knowing other things. Take a simple analogy: If you had to take a surprise test right now on the material in this book, you might find that you did *not* know everything about perception. However, this does not preclude your knowing many other things, including your name, where you were born, or even that you are reading this book. In this way, Nozick suggests that some knowledge of the external world is possible despite the skeptic's objections. The study of perception teaches us how that knowledge is acquired and defines its limits.

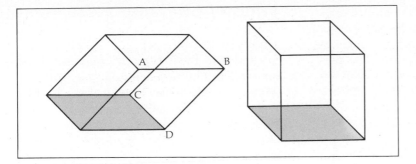

FIGURE 1.4
Transparent figures whose perspectives appear to fluctuate. The darkened surface in each figure seems sometimes to be an inner surface, and sometimes an outer surface. The fluctuations of the rhomboid (left) were first noticed by L. A. Necker about 150 years ago while he was examining some crystals. Today these figures are known as Necker's rhomboid and Necker's cube.

the relation between perception and reality, this is a good time to introduce a view that we'll mention from time to time in this book. This view, **naive realism,** is common among lay persons and beginning students of perception. "Naive realism is the view that what we know about the world is both unadulterated and unexpurgated with respect to even its most subtle details" (Shaw and Bransford, 1977, p. 18). In other words, the world *is* always exactly as it appears.

A simple test can determine if someone is a naive realist; when asked, "Why does the world look to you the way it does?" the naive realist will answer, "Because it *is* that way." In other words, the properties of experience can always be completely and easily explained by the properties of the world itself. But this simple view of perception is wrong. For one thing, it cannot explain why different people experience the same environmental event differently. And this does happen, as you'll discover throughout this book. It is known that infants cannot see small objects that adults can see; it is known that young adults can hear some sounds that older adults cannot; and it is known that certain people are completely oblivious to

odors that others have no trouble smelling. Such facts challenge naive realism. We all live in the same *physical* world. If naive realism were a valid viewpoint, wouldn't our *perceptual* worlds be identical?

There's another reason for rejecting naive realism: a single, unchanging physical stimulus can change in appearance from one moment to the next. You can see examples of this in Figure 1.4. Note how the rhomboid at the left seems to fluctuate in appearance. At one moment, line segment *AB* appears closest to you, while at another moment segment *CD* appears closest. The appearance of the figure at the right undergoes similar fluctuations. Now if perception were determined solely by the physical properties of the figures, their appearance should be stable. Such examples clearly demonstrate that one's perceptions have qualities not present in the physical attributes of the stimulus.

We've already rejected the possibility that reality itself is an illusion. And now we have rejected naive realism. So what do we propose about the relations between human perceptions and the real world? As stressed earlier, we acknowledge the existence of the real world and assert that its existence does not depend on a perceiver. At the same time, we recognize the perceiver's own contribution to the process of perception. The perceiver's view of the world is necessarily inaccurate, because the perceiver's sensory system both *limits* the information that is available and *augments* the information that is available.

To show you more exactly what we mean by the perceiver's contribution, consider a familiar question: "Does a tree falling in the forest make a sound if there is no one around to hear it?" According to a solipsist, no tree, no forest, and no sound would exist in the absence of a perceiver. But according to our view, not only would the falling tree still exist even though no perceiver happened to be around, its fall would create acoustic energy in the form of air pressure waves. But would this constitute sound? If the term "sound" means a perceptual experience, then clearly the falling tree would not produce a sound. For the tree to produce a sound would require the presence of some organism with a sensory system capable of registering the available acoustic energy. But even this does not guarantee that the resulting experience would be what is normally called sound. It's conceivable that the organism that is present might not be able to hear, because it has no ears, but instead could *feel* the energy produced by the falling tree (in the same way that you can feel the wind blowing against your skin). To qualify as sound, the energy must strike the ears of a human—or some other creature with a nervous system like that of a human. What this boils down to is that the quality of one's sensory experience depends on events within the nervous system, as is underscored in Box 1.3.

To sum up: In order to understand perception as fully as possible, one must study not only the properties of the physical world but also those of the perceiver.

Ways of Studying Perception

Traditionally, the study of perception has focused on the "typical" perceiver—the normal adult human being. Because the majority of people fall within this category, that focus is understandable and sensible. This book follows that tradition. But additional important information about perception can be discovered by studying atypical perceivers—individuals who fall outside the category of normal adult human being. Such studies might involve perceivers who are infants, or nonhuman, or physiologically abnormal. Let's consider each of these special cases in turn.

To begin, we can examine perception *developmentally*—studying newborns, infants, children, and at the life span's other end, elderly people. There are systematic and predictable changes in perception with age; and these are accompanied by developmental changes in the sense organs and central nervous system. Developmental work on perception thus offers one way to study the relation between sensory systems and perceptual experience.

Animals from nonhuman species represent another type of atypical perceiver. Although special sophisticated techniques are required to study animal perception, such work often repays the effort many times over. In this book, some of what you will learn about human perception comes from studying animals. A good deal is known about the anatomy and physiology of the sensory systems of several nonhuman species. This knowledge takes on added significance when it can be related to studies of perception in the same species.

Yet another approach to the study of perception exploits the consequences of certain disorders or diseases. Just as studying pathology illuminates the processes of health, studying the abnormal or deviant perceiver

BOX 1.3
Hearing Lightning and Seeing Thunder

Seeing and hearing are qualitatively different perceptual experiences; this is shown by the fact that people never confuse sight and sound. The same has been said for touch, taste, and smell. In fact, these qualitative differences form the basis for the classic five-part division of the senses—touch, taste, smell, hearing, and seeing. Our assumption in this book is that these subjectively different experiences are each and every one products of neural events within the brain. And yet those events, it is known, all boil down to patterns of nerve impulses within the brain. Since different experiences are represented by the same sort of events, how does the brain manage to distinguish one type of experience from another— sight from sound, and taste from smell? Let's consider this question as it applies to sight and sound.

It is tempting to answer by pointing out that sound waves, the stimulus for hearing, are fundamentally different from light energy, the stimulus for seeing. However, this argument is not adequate because the brain does not directly *receive* either sound waves or light energy—it receives only tiny electrical signals called neural impulses. In other words, from the brain's perspective, all incoming signals are equivalent. But, you might point out, although they resemble one another, those neural impulses *arise* from different sources, namely the eyes and the ears. And, you might continue, those sources *are* fundamentally different— they are specially designed to respond only to particular kinds of physical stimulation. Because of their specialized receptors, the eyes respond to light but not to sound, while the opposite is true for the ears. So, you might well conclude, the distinctiveness of seeing and hearing depends on the difference between the eyes and the ears.

This explanation is not adequate though. Sensations of light and sound can be produced without the participation of eyes and ears. One can by-pass them and stimulate the brain directly. During the course of brain surgery on awake, alert humans, neurologists sometimes need to stimulate the brain's surface electrically in order to determine exactly where they are working. Depending on the area of the brain stimulated, patients report very vivid sensations that seem quite real (Penfield and Perrot, 1963). For instance, stimulation at a point in the back of the brain can elicit sensations of light flashes, whereas stimulation at the proper spot on the side of the brain can cause the patient to hear tones. Here, then, are examples of qualitatively distinct sensations that arise from exactly the same sort of stimulation—a mild electrical current. Note, though, that the patients did not *feel* the electrical current— they "heard" it or "saw" it, depending on the brain region stimulated.

These observations force a surprising conclusion: that the critical difference between hearing and seeing depends not so much on differences between the eyes and the ears but on *where* in the brain the eyes and ears send their messages. This is actually a very old idea, dating back to Johannes Müller, a nineteenth-century German physiologist. Müller's theory, called the doctrine of **specific nerve energies,** states that the nature of a sensation depends on the particular set of nerve fibers stimulated. According to this doctrine, activity in the nerve from the eye will invariably produce visual sensations, regardless of how that activity was instigated. Nowadays, it is recognized that sensory nerves travel to specific brain areas: the nerve from the eye travels to one place, the nerve from the ear to another. Thus the emphasis has shifted from the nerves themselves to their projection sites in the brain. It is now widely believed that the distinctiveness of sight and sound is related to the unique properties of the tissue within different regions of the brain. At present, detailed information about these unique properties is lacking, although the issue has sparked lively debate (Puccetti and Dykes, 1978).

The contemporary version of Müller's doctrine suggests a provocative thought experiment. Suppose you were able to reroute the nerve from your eye, sending it to the part of your brain that normally receives input from your ear. Suppose that while you were at it, you also rerouted the nerve from your ear, sending it to that part of your brain that normally gets visual information. Now imagine that with this revised nervous system, you are caught in a thunderstorm. You should *hear* a flash of lighting and then *see* a clap of thunder. Think about it, but don't do it.

illuminates the normal processes of perception. If the physiological changes produced by some disease are known, as well as how perception is altered by that disease, it becomes possible to relate the physiological changes to the perceptual changes, thereby identifying the physiological basis for that aspect of perception. For example, current understanding of color vision's neural basis has benefited greatly from studying people whose color vision is deficient. And even when the basis for some disorder is not fully understood, one can still capitalize on its perceptual effects, especially when those effects are rather specific. In particular, one may determine which aspects of perception are affected by the disorder and which are not. This, by inference, indicates which perceptual abilities depend on shared neural structures. For example, a person with misaligned (crossed) eyes can have diminished depth perception but still be able to see objects and judge whether those objects are moving or stationary. This implies that the disorder of eye alignment has selectively affected portions of the nervous system that are concerned with the analysis of depth information. In general, this kind of selective perceptual loss indicates that the affected perceptual abilities depend on parts of the nervous system different from those mediating the unaffected perceptual abilities (Hebb, 1949; Brindley, 1970).

FIGURE 1.5
Zöllner's illusion of orientation.

The previous paragraphs described various categories of atypical perceivers. But atypical perception can also be produced in typical perceivers, by using unusual, provocative stimuli. Such stimuli provoke errors that highlight perception in ways that normal, error-free operation does not. This approach resembles the use of provocative tests in medicine, such as the stress electrocardiogram. In the case of perception, the easiest, most common provocative tests use stimuli that produce errors of perception called illusions. These errors can assume many forms: We've already mentioned the moon illusion, which involves an error in the judgment of size. Other kinds of errors can also be provoked. Take a look at Figure 1.5. The long vertical lines are actually parallel, but the central ones appear tilted with respect to one another. This figure was devised by Franz Zöllner in 1860, and it is an example of an orientation illusion. At several places in this book you'll see that illusions are more than just fascinating novelties. It may seem odd, but the special, provocative stimuli that evoke illusions can tell us much about how humans process the ordinary, mundane perceptual information encountered every day.

The Psychological and Biological Approaches to Perception

At the outset of this chapter, we characterized perception as the final link in a chain of events. Furthermore, we said that to understand perception requires knowing something about each link in the chain. This chain actually cuts across the boundaries of several different scientific disciplines, ranging from biophysics to psychology. These disciplines use different levels of analysis, ranging from the microscopic (studying the behavior of molecules) to the macroscopic (studying the behavior of whole organisms). So to get a complete picture, one needs to analyze perception at several different levels, each of which offers us a unique and invaluable perspective. To illustrate metaphorically what we mean by levels of analysis, look at Figure 1.6. It shows an aerial photograph taken over the Peruvian desert from a very great height. From this altitude, you can see a mammoth sand carving thought to be a thousand years old. The carving, made by people lost to history, is a figure nearly 1600 meters long. It is so huge that it can be recognized only from a great

height; standing on the ground, you would be unable to take in the entire carving. Thus to appreciate the carving requires a particular level of analysis, namely one a great distance above the carving. Suppose, though, that you wished to examine the details of the carving and what it was made of. Such examination would require quite a different level of analysis, one much closer to the ground.

This beautiful and mysterious desert carving dramatizes a point about perception: one must adopt different levels of analysis in order to answer all the significant questions about a subject. Consequently,

FIGURE 1.6
Aerial photograph of sand carving on Peruvian desert. (Georg Gerster/Photo Researchers)

we'll be adopting various levels of analysis in our examination of perception. The two main levels of analysis that we'll need are the *psychological* and the *biological*. Generally speaking, the psychological approach focuses on the perceptual capacities of the various senses and, in the case of humans, on the experiential aspects of perception. Returning to the metaphor of the chain, the psychological approach taps into the tail end of the sequence. The biological approach, in comparison, taps into the chain at a more intermediate point. This latter approach focuses on the anatomy and physiology of the sensory nervous system. However, the boundaries between the two approaches are sometimes unclear. Moreover, there are particularly interesting studies in which the two approaches are combined to great advantage. At various points in this book, we shall see how the understanding of perception is amplified by combining information from both approaches.

Distinguishing between the psychological and biological approaches will help organize the discussion that follows. We repeat, though, that the two approaches are not mutually exclusive but are complementary; one simply cannot learn all one wants to know about perception from either approach alone.

THE PSYCHOLOGICAL APPROACHES

First, there is no single psychological approach to perception; instead, there are many, each differing from the others in various ways. Although they all use some behavioral reaction to stimuli as a way of studying perception, they differ in terms of *what* behavioral reaction is used. For instance, one might attempt to train a bird to fly to a red perch but not to a green perch. If the bird succeeds in learning this task, one might infer that the bird can tell red

from green. (However, as indicated in Chapter 6, to justify this conclusion requires some additional tests.)

Similarly, a human being can be instructed to *push* one button whenever a red object is presented and to push another button whenever a green object is presented. For birds and humans, behavior is used to infer something about perception. There are actually many specific techniques for studying perception; and we'll describe some of those techniques as the need arises. Now, though, let's not focus on the details of particular behavioral techniques; instead, let's analyze the methods along more general lines, grouping them according to their degree of *formality*. By "formality" we mean the extent to which stimuli and reactions to them are structured or controlled.

The least formal is the phenomenal/ naturalistic method. "Phenomenal" means that the evidence used by the approach consists of one's conscious experiences. "Naturalistic" means that the evidence concerns responses to whatever stimuli occur naturally within the environment; there is no attempt to modify these stimuli or create artificial ones.

The Phenomenal/Naturalistic Approach. There are certain advantages to this least formal approach to perception. For one thing, it relies on the most easily obtainable data— experiences evoked by naturally occurring events. Such experiences might include the appearance of a sunset, the sound of a police siren, the taste of an artichoke. Everyone has untold numbers of such experiences every hour. To study perception, then, you could collect and organize these experiences. Going one step further, you could discuss your perceptual experiences with other people, for purposes of comparison. But what pitfalls would you encounter by following this program?

First, by restricting yourself to phenomenal descriptions, you would not be able to study perception in animals and preverbal infants, a real handicap. Second, even working with humans who *can* verbalize their experiences, you would need to be wary. Verbal reports can be fallible and misleading. For one thing, people don't all use words in the same way. To give an example, many people who are color-blind have learned to label colors much as color-normal people do, even though their experiences must be very different.

Because verbal reports are usually made with such confidence, one may be misled into believing that they are a direct pipeline to experience. In fact, that assumption underlies the use of verbal reports as a way to examine perceptual experience. But the assumption is probably unwarranted, for there is reason to doubt that individuals *can* accurately describe their experiences, motives, or thought processes (Nisbett and Wilson, 1977); these cannot be accessed at a conscious level. In some instances, moreover, people are motivated to avoid telling what they consider to be the truth about their experiences. Here's one instance. A malingerer is someone who pretends to have an illness or disability in order to get some special gain or avoid some responsibility. Feigned deafness is one form of malingering. Ask such a malingerer if he can hear, and you'll get no answer unless the question is communicated in writing, lip reading, or sign language. Then, the malingerer will assure you that he can't hear (a misleading verbal report). But there is a very clever, foolproof way to catch the malingerer: delayed auditory feedback. While the person is reading aloud, record his speech and, following a very short delay, play it back into his ears. If he is genuinely deaf, and not a malingerer, delayed auditory feedback will have no influence on his reading. But if he *can* hear, the delayed feedback

of his own voice will invariably disrupt his speech.*

The word "feigns" implies that someone is purposely lying or pretending. But there are instances where a person's erroneous verbal reports don't really constitute lying. One such instance is **Anton's syndrome.** This syndrome, as rare as it is bizarre, involves complete blindness coupled with denial (the blind person denies that he or she is blind). The condition supposedly arises because two different areas of the brain have been damaged—the one needed for seeing and the one needed for knowing that you're seeing (Symonds and MacKenzie, 1957). This damage to the brain occurs quite suddenly—usually as the result of a stroke—and the victim of Anton's syndrome may walk around for quite some time bumping into things and having other mishaps until he or she becomes convinced that something is wrong. But immediately following damage to the brain, victims of Anton's syndrome confidently report being able to see. Asked to describe what is seen, the victim provides a very detailed answer but one that is a complete fabrication, as evidenced by its lack of correspondence to reality.

Anton's syndrome, besides underscoring the potential unreliability of verbal reports about perception, also points up a more general fact: perceptual experiences and knowledge of those experiences are two quite separate things. Many forces that people are not aware of can influence what they perceive. These unconscious influences include expectations, prior experience, and motivations (see Figure 1.7). Although such forces are distinct from the links that form the per-

---

*This example raises an interesting issue. What if the person insists that he cannot hear, even though the auditory feedback disrupts his speech? Should one automatically label the person a "malingerer"? Should one put more faith in the delayed feedback's interference than in his verbal report? It's conceivable that delayed feedback impairs speech at a preconscious level—in which case the person might be unaware of any disruption of his speech.

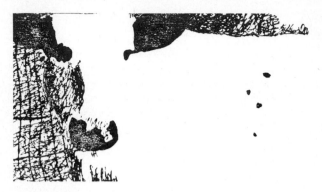

FIGURE 1.7
Look at this drawing for a while. If you cannot discern an animal, look at Figure 1.8 on page 20.

ceptual chain, the phenomenal approach would foreclose separating these two kinds of influences on perception. As you'll see in Box 1.4, other, more formal approaches *do* allow one to separate the two.

Despite its limitations, the phenomenal/naturalistic approach to perception does have an important role to play. For more than a hundred years, careful and thoughtful observers have used this informal approach as a basis upon which to build a more formal study of perception. This book will emphasize these more formal approaches; but it should not be forgotten that many of the ideas for formal study derive from this less formal method.

Experimental Approach. The psychological approach we've been discussing is naturalistic, taking stimuli as they come in nature without controlling them. The approach is simple but not entirely satisfactory. For one thing, if you want to study a particular aspect of perception, you cannot count on having the necessary stimulus; you must wait for it to occur. Moreover, you often need to use a whole series of stimuli—comparing the effect of each to the effects produced by its fellows. And the series you wanted might

never occur naturally. For example, you might want the members of the series to differ in only one attribute (such as color) with all others (such as intensity) held constant. This would make it easy to ascribe any resulting change in perception to the attribute that varied. If several attributes varied simultaneously (as is usually the case with naturally occurring stimuli) you would have trouble knowing how much each attribute contributed to perception.

Another problem with naturalistic stimuli is that often they cannot be repeated precisely. We mentioned earlier that the study of perception should be general: it should involve the perceptions of more than one person, and it should involve perceptions at more than just one moment. In order to satisfy the need to generalize, you need to measure perceptual responses repeatedly. You must be able to present the same stimuli again and again, whenever you wish.

To understand perception fully, one must be able to control and manipulate stimuli. One must often use stimuli that never occur in nature. Such stimuli are sometimes criticized as being "nonecological," because they are not the stimuli for which perceptual systems evolved (Gibson, 1966). We feel, how-

BOX 1.4
Should You Answer the Phone?

Everyone has had the following maddening experience. While taking a shower, you faintly hear what sounds like the telephone ringing. Because of the shower's steady noise, though, you're not sure it *is* the phone. So do you decide yes and run, dripping wet, to answer it? Or do you conclude that it's only your imagination?

Your behavior in this situation depends on factors other than the loudness of the ringing sound. For instance, if you are expecting an important call, you will in all likelihood scurry out of the shower to see if the phone is indeed ringing. If, in contrast, you're not expecting a call, you're more likely to attribute the ringing sound to the shower's own noises. Your decision about the reality of the sound, then, is influenced by your expectations. This example illustrates a significant principle, namely, that one's interpretation of sensory data depends significantly on nonsensory factors.

This dependence colors the way in which results from perceptual studies are interpreted. To illustrate, imagine testing a person's hearing by presenting faint sounds and having the person say whether or not she could hear the sound. Performance on such a test can vary from one person to the next, and not just because some people have better hearing than others. Some people are simply more willing to take a gamble, asserting that they heard something even if they're not 100 percent certain (these people might also want to impress the tester with their keen hearing, say if the hearing test is part of a job application). There are also more conservative people, who are not gamblers; in the hearing test, such people might require a much louder sound before they are willing to say that they heard it. Suppose that two people took a hearing test, one a conservative type, the other a gambler. On the basis of their performance on the hearing test, the tester might mistakenly conclude that the conservative had inferior hearing.

People *do* differ in the sensitivity of their sensory systems; some individuals, for instance, have a keener sense of smell than do others. But people *also* differ in their motivations, expectations, and willingness to gamble. As an aggregate these latter differences can be labeled "motivational differences." In studies of perceptual abilities, it is important to distinguish between an individual's sensitivity and motivation. Toward this end, psychologists have developed several strategies for separating the two.

To tell whether a person can *really* hear an extremely faint sound, one needs more to go on than the fact that she is constantly saying that she hears a sound. Logically, one must also ensure that she does not make exactly the same claim when no sound whatever has been presented (Goldman, 1976). Many experiments on hearing, then, randomly intermix two types of test trials. On one type of trial, a weak sound is presented; on the other, no sound is presented. After each trial, the person says whether or not she heard a sound. Someone really interested in impressing the tester might say "Yes, I hear it" after every single trial. Of course, she'd be right every trial on which a sound actually occurred, but she'd be wrong every trial on which no sound occurred. From this result, the tester should realize that this person could not discriminate the presence of sound from the absence of sound. Omitting the sound and noting the subject's failure to recognize that omission allows the tester to separate the person's sensitivity to sound from other possible factors—such as the motivation to impress.

This general strategy is not limited to the study of hearing; similar methods are used with the other senses as well. To implement the strategy, psychologists have developed a set of sophisticated statistical techniques collectively known as signal detection theory. The Appendix provides additional details of signal detection theory. For a more thorough treatment of this topic, we suggest that you consult Pastore and Scheirer (1974), McNicol (1972), or Swets, Tanner, and Birdsall (1961). Meanwhile, the next time you take a shower, take your phone off the hook.

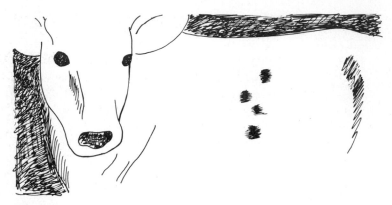

FIGURE 1.8
Outline drawing of the same animal depicted in Figure 1.7. Note how seeing this figure helps you interpret Figure 1.7. Surprisingly, this effect lasts for months.

ever, that their use can be valid since simple, artificial (nonecological) stimuli can often clarify the effects of more complex, naturally occurring stimuli. This point is well documented throughout the book. There is some merit, though, to studying perception using ecologically representative stimuli. In particular, such stimuli make it easy for one to generalize from studies in the laboratory to situations likely to be encountered every day outside the laboratory.

Control and careful manipulation of the stimulus also allow one to identify exactly *what* aspect of the stimulus underlies some perceptual experience (Stevens, 1951). To illustrate, some rare individuals are able to discriminate among thousands of different wines by taste alone. To determine the basis of this remarkable ability, you could create a series of specially constituted wines that varied in their composition, and using this set of controlled stimuli, you could isolate the cues enabling such individuals to distinguish what most people cannot.

One also needs control over the stimuli in order to conduct two kinds of experiments that are the foundation of the scientific study of perception: matching and de-

tection experiments. Matching experiments ask people to adjust one stimulus until it appears identical to another. This obviously requires stimuli that can be manipulated precisely. Detection experiments measure the weakest stimulus that a person can detect. Again, such experiments require stimuli whose intensities can be controlled. In fact, studying perception without trying to control, manipulate, and design the stimuli would be like restricting physicists to working only with objects they found lying around on the ground. They wouldn't get very far in physics by doing that, nor would we get very far in the study of perception.

As we've indicated, the psychological approach to perception uses a variety of methods, ranging from the simple and naturalistic to the highly structured and controlled. Each of these methods makes its own unique contribution. The Appendix describes some of the formal, structured methods. In addition, you'll encounter descriptions of various methods throughout the book, in the context of the research problems for which they were designed.

Although the psychological approach is useful in the study of perception, it does have distinct limits. We turn now to a complementary approach that offsets many of those limits.

THE BIOLOGICAL APPROACHES

As we have mentioned, biological approaches to perception focus on events antecedent to perceptual experience, rather than on the perceptual experience itself. The antecedent events involve neural activity. To distinguish between the antecedent neural activity and the perceptual experience itself, let's call the former Class A events and the latter Class B events. By describing an event from Class A as antecedent to one from Class B, we are implying a relation between those events. We are not saying they are identical, but we are asserting that they're importantly related.

We're interested in both classes of events because we approach perception from a mechanistic viewpoint. **Mechanism** assumes that perceptual experience depends on the operation of the nervous system. Recognizing this physiological basis for perceptual experiences, we shall often refer in this book to "mechanisms of perception." This term refers to the properties of the nervous system, both anatomical and physiological, that determine and shape the perceptual experience in question. The mechanistic viewpoint has been well expressed by Roger Sperry, the Nobel Prize–winning brain scientist from the California Institute of Technology. According to Sperry, perceptual experience is a "functional property of brain processing, constituted of neuronal and physicochemical activity, and embodied in, and inseparable from the active brain" (Sperry, 1980, p. 204).

Many people misinterpret Mechanism, believing that it reduces their mental experiences to nothing but a collection of electrical and chemical processes. Stated in this way, it's easy to see why someone might

object. However, this mischaracterizes what Mechanism intends. Although Mechanism holds that perception is based on neural events in the brain, it does not imply that one could dissect a brain and thereby locate those experiences. Again, Sperry (1980) put it quite well:

Once generated from neural events, the higher order mental patterns and programs have their own subjective qualities and progress, operate and interact by their own causal laws and principles which are different from and cannot be reduced to those of neurophysiology.
(p. 201)

To illustrate further what he had in mind, Sperry offered the example of a wheel rolling downhill. The wheel

carries its atoms and molecules through a course in time and space and to a fate determined by the overall system properties of the wheel as a whole and regardless of the inclination of individual atoms and molecules. The atoms and molecules are caught up and overpowered by the higher properties of the whole. One can compare the rolling wheel to an ongoing brain process or a progressing train of thought in which the overall organizational properties of the brain process, as a coherent organizational entity, determine the timing and spacing of the firing patterns within its neuronal infrastructure. (p. 201)

In other words, though one's experiences have a physical basis they cannot be reduced to a set of physical components; equally important are their spatial organization, what they communicate to one another, and how both spatial organization and communication change with time. If another analogy would help, consider what would happen if you took a television set completely apart and examined all its components in an effort to understand how it worked. The proper function of the television set demands a particular spatial arrangement of parts as well as a certain sequence of signals in time. The "secret" of the set's operation would have completely eluded you and could not be found in the pile of parts you'd have after the set had been dismantled.

But not everybody agrees with this Mechanistic position. Other prominent scientists, including another Nobel Prize winner, John Eccles (1979), subscribe to an alternative view. This alternative, **Dualism,** is usually associated with the seventeenth-century French philosopher René Descartes. Dualism maintains that conscious experiences exist independently of any material substrate, including the brain. In effect, Dualism assumes the existence of a mental world separate from the physical world. This idea is similar to the notion of a soul existing independent of the body. There is no way to refute Dualism by means of empirical data; efforts to discredit it on logical grounds have met with limited success (Armstrong, 1968; Churchland, 1984). Dualism fatally weakens the early links between neural events and perceptual experience. As a result, this philosophical attitude complicates and impedes the study of perception. For our purposes, then, it is more useful to pursue perception from a Mechanistic viewpoint, seeing how far that takes us.

Perception depends on many different biological processes. Consequently, people who take a biological approach to perception have to use many different methods, each one appropriate to a particular process. We postpone discussing the details of these methods until later in the book, where we will describe them as the context requires.

Why Emphasize Vision?

In this book we cover seeing, hearing, taste, and smell. But we devote more coverage to seeing than we do to the other senses. Our main reason for doing this is that more is known about vision than about the other senses. But there are other reasons, too. For example, of all the senses, vision represents the richest source of information. Recall that we talked earlier about the near and far (distance) senses; vision is king of the distance senses. Because its range is greater than that of any other sense, including hearing, the eyes at any given moment can put one in touch with a greater potential volume of information in the environment than can any other sensory organ. Incidentally, this preeminence of vision is mirrored in the proportion of the human brain that is devoted to vision.

Vision is rich in another way, too. One's visual experiences vary along many different dimensions—color, intensity, location, direction of movement, and so on. This extraordinary differentiation of experience presents the greatest challenge to one's understanding. Put simply, vision demands that one explain an awful lot of different things, including many dimensions of experience.

Vision has another claim on our attention. When pitted against the other senses, vision dominates them. Suppose, for example, you are looking at some object held in your hand. If your fingers and your eyes give you conflicting information about the shape of that object, your experience follows what your eyes have told you (Rock and Harris, 1967; Power, 1981). A ventriloquist exploits the dominance of vision to fool you into thinking that the sound originates from his dummy rather than from himself.

Finally, for psychological and social reasons, too, vision is the most important of the senses. The ability of human beings to communicate with one another depends very strongly on vision, so much so that, given a choice, people typically say that loss of vision would be the most devastating of all possible sensory losses.

Summary and Preview

We have used this chapter to lay out the framework for our analysis of perception, including the philosophical assumptions we'll be making. We have sketched in some of the practical and theoretical reasons for wanting to know more about perception.

And we have outlined two distinct though complementary ways of understanding perception: the psychological and biological approaches. Now that this general framework is in place, the next chapter will begin to fill in the pieces, starting with some fundamentals about the organ we use for seeing.

Chapter 2

The Human Eye

The visual system of any vertebrate consists of three major sections: *eyes*, which capture light and generate messages about that light; *visual pathways*, which transmit those messages from the eye; and *visual centers of the brain*, which interpret the messages in various ways. Because they all contribute to seeing, you need to understand each component's function in order to understand how you see. This chapter and the next one concentrate on the first of these components, the human eye; they discuss its anatomy (structure) and physiology (how it works). These chapters emphasize how the eye captures light and how the eye turns that light into neural messages that the brain can interpret. Chapter 4 will discuss the remaining two major sections of the mammalian visual system, the visual pathways and the brain's visual centers.

All these chapters have features that require special comment. First, we don't spend time talking about anatomy simply because we are fascinated with structure per se. We think structure is important because it influences how and what one can see. Second, though mainly interested in the *human* eye, we also consider the eyes of other animals, particularly animals whose environments and life styles differ from those of humans. Understanding the uniqueness of human vision will heighten your appreciation of the processes involved in seeing. Finally, when we discuss structure we also consider how structural defects impair vision. We have included material on dysfunction because it, too, illuminates the intimate connection between structure and function.

In writing these chapters we were very much influenced by Gordon Walls's book *The Vertebrate Eye and Its Adaptive Radiations*. He wrote eloquently about the eye, as the following statement demonstrates:

"Everything in the vertebrate eye means something." Except for the brain, there is no other organ in the body of which that can be said. It does not matter in the least whether a liver has three lobes or four, or whether a hand has five fingers or six, or whether a kidney is long and narrow or short and wide. But if we should make comparable changes in the makeup of a vertebrate eye, we should quite destroy its usefulness. Man can make optical instruments only from such materials as brass and glass. Nature has succeeded with only such things as leather and water and jelly; but the resulting instrument is so delicately balanced that it will tolerate no tampering. (Walls, 1942, pp. iii–iv)

This brief extract argues convincingly that to understand vision, one *must* understand the eye's structure. We'll begin our actual discussion of the eye with a series of general questions about the nature of vision—*why* vision took the form that it did.

Designing the Organ of Vision

WHY HAVE EYES THAT USE LIGHT?

The preceding chapter distinguished between the near and the distance senses, putting vision among the distance senses. By definition, a distance sense enables one to detect objects without having to come in immediate proximity to those objects. Hearing and seeing both endow one with this capacity. But vision enjoys a major advantage over hearing: it enables one to detect objects that make no sound. (Hearing, on the other hand, allows one to detect things that cannot be seen—but we'll get to that in Chapters 9 and 10.) Vision also provides important information about objects that hearing cannot give—for example, about an object's color, size, and shape. Such information is conveyed by light, the messenger that

bridges the distance between oneself and the objects one sees.

Light is just one form of **electromagnetic radiation;** other familiar varieties include radio waves, infrared and ultraviolet radiation, microwaves and x-rays. All these forms of energy are produced by the oscillation of electrically charged material. Since virtually all matter consists of oscillating electrical charges, electromagnetic energy exists in abundance. An animal that can sense electromagnetic radiation benefits in many ways; let's consider some.

First, electromagnetic radiation travels very rapidly (in empty space, at 186,000 miles, or approximately 300,000 kilometers, per second). Any creature that is able to detect such radiation can pick up information from distant sources with minimal delay. Thus, one sees events practically as soon as they occur. A second advantage of being able to sense electromagnetic radiation comes from its tendency to travel in straight lines. As a result of this tendency, images created by this radiation retain important geometrical characteristics of the object or objects that reflected the radiation toward the eyes. We'll come back to this point in a moment.

The frequency of electromagnetic radiation depends on the emitting material's mode of oscillation. In fact, electromagnetic radiation can be scaled or arranged along a spectrum according to the frequency of oscillation, with light occupying only a very small portion of that spectrum (see Figure 2.1). The frequency, or rate of oscillation, of light energy can be converted into units termed wavelengths. **Wavelength** is defined by how far the radiation travels between oscillations. High rates of oscillation mean that radiation will not travel very far between oscillations—hence a short wavelength. Figure 2.1 underscores an important point: light, the form of radiation on which we depend for sight, occupies only a very small portion of the electromagnetic spectrum.

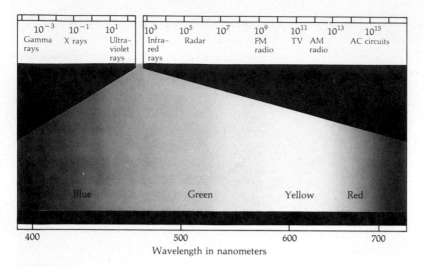

| 10^{-3} Gamma rays | 10^{-1} X rays | 10^1 Ultra-violet rays | 10^3 Infra-red rays | 10^5 Radar | 10^7 | 10^9 FM radio | 10^{11} TV | 10^{13} AM radio | 10^{15} AC circuits |

Blue   Green   Yellow   Red

400   500   600   700

Wavelength in nanometers

FIGURE 2.1

The spectrum of electromagnetic energy. The region containing visible light is shown enlarged.

Actually, radiation from other portions of this spectrum *could* have been used to bridge the distance between the perceiver and objects of visual perception. So why do the eyes depend solely on this one, very narrow portion of the entire electromagnetic spectrum, the part known as light?

One reason for using light as a medium is that there is a lot of it in the world. Light's abundance ensures that creatures will have ample opportunity to use their light-sensing apparatus. It wouldn't have made much sense for early vertebrate "eyes" to depend on radio waves, for example, since that form of electromagnetic radiation was not plentiful until quite recently. Second, light is useful as a medium of information about the world because light interacts with the surface molecules of many objects. These interactions, in the form of reflection and absorption, allow light to convey information not only about the presence and absence of objects but also about the structure of those objects and their surfaces (Gibson, 1966).

To sum up, eyes are a good idea, and eyes that use light are an even better idea.

WHERE SHOULD THE EYES GO?

Recognizing that animals would do very well to have eyes that exploit light, we must now decide *where* those eyes should be placed. Because embryologically the eyes are an outgrowth of the brain, they are constrained in their position, needing to be located in the head near the brain. But where exactly in the head should the eyes go? Nature has devised several different ways to position the eyes. In vertebrates, there are two popular designs for outfitting the head with a pair of eyes: they can be located in a *frontal* position, as are those of a human being or a cat; or they can be located in a *lateral* position as are those of the rabbit (see Figure 2.2). Each strategy carries its own advantages: frontal eyes improve depth perception, whereas lateral eyes make it possible to take in more of the visual world at one time. These advantages are considered in detail in Chapter 7, as part of our discussion of depth and distance perception. For the moment it's sufficient to recognize that there are alternative answers to the question "Where should the eyes go?"

FIGURE 2.2
The placement of the eyes in the heads of a cat (frontal eye placement) and a rabbit (lateral eye placement).

WHY SHOULD THE EYES BE ABLE TO MOVE?

With panoramic vision, an animal can take in most of its surroundings all at once. In contrast, what humans can see at any one moment is rather limited (see Figure 2.3).

And there is no guarantee that the eyes of humans will always be directed toward the things in the environment that they need to see. Fortunately, humans can compensate for their relatively narrow field of vision by being able to adjust where the eyes are directed (Gibson, 1966, p. 175). This is what you do when you look both ways before crossing a street. You also move your eyes because they are not uniformly sensitive; some parts of the eyes provide much better detail vision than do other parts. Think for a moment what you do when you notice something out of the corner of your eye. If you wish to see particular details of it, your eyes must move so that you're looking directly at those details (Walls, 1942, p. 305).

Animals use various strategies for changing their field of view: they can move their bodies, turn their heads, or move their eyes. Some animals—owls for one—can't move their eyes. This comes about because their eyes are large and fit tightly into their sock-

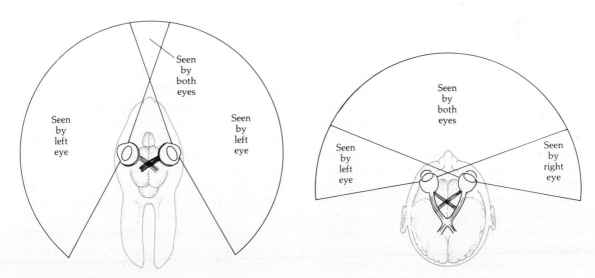

FIGURE 2.3
The extent of visual field of view for a rabbit and for a human. Note that the rabbit has almost completely panoramic vision, while the human's field of view encompasses only about 180 degrees.

ets, leaving no room for muscles that would move them (Walls, 1942, p. 212). Instead, animals such as the owl must change gaze by moving either their heads or their entire bodies. However, an animal's head and body are much larger than its eyes and thus cannot be moved as quickly. If an animal's eyes can't move, its change of gaze is slowed relative to the speed of changes that eye movements could produce.

There's another advantage to moving the eyes rather than the head when you must redirect your gaze: eye movements are less obtrusive. If a predatory animal moves only its eyes in order to search for prey, it doesn't call attention to itself as much as it would if it had to move its head or body. On a more mundane level, mobile eyes permit humans to redirect their gaze more discreetly. If you're in a boring meeting or class, you can unobtrusively shift your eyes to glance at your watch rather than turn your entire head to check the time and, thereby, broadcast your boredom. But not all the movements of your eyes are intentional, as is explained in Box 2.1.

Humans can shift the position of their eyes with enormous speed. For instance, it takes less than one-fifth of a second for the eyes to dart from their extreme leftward position to their extreme rightward position. Not only do the eyes move rapidly, they move with great accuracy too. For example, as you read these lines your eyes skip along from one place of interest to another, alighting with great precision on the desired letter or space. The cooperative interaction among the **extraocular muscles** (six for each eye) makes rapid and accurate eye movements possible. The extraocular muscles enable you to move your eye in all directions. Let's consider the mechanical arrangement that makes this possible.

How the Eyes Move. Every muscle works by contracting and thereby pulling on the structure or structures to which the muscle is attached. In the case of the extraoculars, each muscle is connected at one end to an immovable structure, the eye socket of the skull, and at the other end, to an object that is free to move, the eyeball. So when the extraocular muscle contracts, it pulls on the eyeball and moves it. The *amount* of movement depends on the strength of the muscle's contraction and on the action of the other muscles. The *direction* of movement depends on the place at which the contracting muscle is attached to the eyeball and on what the other muscles are doing. Because each extraocular muscle is attached to the eyeball at a different position, contraction of any particular muscle turns the eyeball in a characteristic direction. The following is a brief and simplified description of what the extraoculars do.

Each eye's muscles can be divided into two groups, one with four muscles and one with two. The larger group, the **rectus muscles,** run straight back from the eyeball. Muscles in the other, smaller group run obliquely back from the eyeball. The general principles of the eye's movements can be understood by looking just at muscles in the larger group.

Each rectus muscle is attached to the eyeball at a different location, in each case toward the front of the eyeball (see Figure 2.4). The other end of each rectus muscle is attached to the rear of the bony cavity holding the eyeball; this is the immovable end of the muscle. Whenever a rectus muscle contracts, it pulls the eyeball toward the place at which that muscle connects to the eyeball.

One muscle, the *medial* rectus, attaches to the side of the eyeball closest to the nose. Thus when it contracts, the medial rectus pulls the eye toward the nose. Another muscle, the *lateral* rectus, has exactly the opposite effect. Connected to the side of the eyeball farthest from the nose, its contrac-

BOX 2.1
Eyes That Never Stand Still

The extraocular muscles control the direction in which your eyes point. Contractions of these muscles pull the eyeballs, guiding their direction so you can fixate objects of interest. But even when you try to keep your eyes absolutely still, small random contractions of the extraocular muscles keep the eyes moving. These involuntary eye movements are usually so small that you are not aware of them, but they are important for seeing. Before explaining why they're important, though, we can describe a simple trick that lets you see your own eye movements.

The trick requires a pattern like the grid in the accompanying figure (Verheijen, 1963). First fixate the black dot in the center of the pattern as carefully as you can for about 30 seconds, keeping your eyes as still as possible. Then quickly move your eyes to the white dot. Again, keep your eyes as still as possible. You'll see an illusory pattern, called an **afterimage,** that jiggles slightly. The jiggling of the afterimage is caused by the movements of your eye. You can prove this to yourself by now making large, intentional eye movements; the afterimage follows your eyes.

Here's how the demonstration works. The original, 30-second period of fixation differentially fatigues the neurons over various parts of your retina. But because the black squares evoke a smaller retinal response, they fatigue your retina less than the white squares do. When you stop looking at the pattern, portions of your retina are in a state of differential, patterned adaptation. This differential adaptation produces an afterimage, such that areas that were white in the original now appear dark, while areas that were dark now appear light. Of course the fatigued neurons are fixed in place in your retina. Thus whenever you see the afterimage move, it must indicate that your eyes have moved—whether you intended them to or not. In the slight jiggling of the afterimage you are seeing the consequences of your own involuntary eye movements.

These small random eye movements are actually very important for vision; when they are eliminated, vision changes dramatically. For example, special optical systems have been developed that move whatever you're looking at in step with the movements of your eyes. This scheme produces a motionless, stabilized image on your retina. Here's one way to produce a stabilized retinal image. A small photographic transparency of some object is mounted on a special high-power contact lens. Since the contact lens moves along with the eye, the image of the transparency attached to this lens is stabilized on the retina. And the perceptual result is remarkable—after only a few seconds, the object begins to fade from view, as if the brightness on a television screen were being reduced. Eventually the object disappears entirely, leaving nothing but a homogeneous gray field. So when the effects of normal involuntary eye movements are eliminated, vision is eliminated too (Pritchard, Heron, and Hebb, 1960; Riggs et al., 1953).

The fact that stabilized retinal images fade and disappear is actually quite fortunate. If they didn't, you would be constantly annoyed by the images produced in your eyes by blood vessels. Because they are in the path of light, these blood vessels cast shadows on your retina. Since the branches move along with your eye, their shadows are stabilized

(Continued on next page)

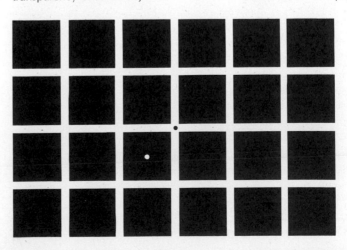

retinal images and, consequently, are invisible to you. However, you can "destabilize" them by moving a beam of light back and forth across the vessels. This causes their shadow to move back and forth slightly, enough to make them visible. The simplest way to produce this effect is with a small flashlight (a penlight). Looking straight ahead with eyes closed, place the penlight against the corner of your eye—the corner away from your nose, as is shown in the illustration at right. Gently rock the penlight back and forth. After a second or two you should begin seeing what look like the branches of a tree. These are the shadows of blood vessels in your eye. Once you get them into view, stop moving the flashlight and the branches will disappear within a few seconds, as the image returns to its normal, stabilized condition.

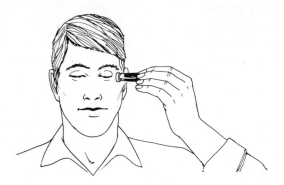

tion turns the eyeball laterally, away from the nose. The *superior* rectus muscle connects to the top of the eyeball, and its contraction elevates the eyeball, causing you to look upward. Its opposite number, the *inferior* rectus, is attached to the lower portion of the eyeball and its contraction lowers the eye, causing you to look down.

Now, let's consider how these muscles cooperate to move the eyes. Imagine that

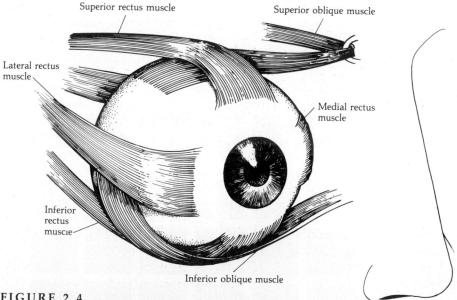

FIGURE 2.4

A view of the eye muscles attached to the right eye. The medial rectus, the muscle closest to the eye, is partially obscured by the globe.

while looking straight ahead, you decide to glance leftward. Both eyes must move to the same degree and in the same direction. To look to the left, the medial rectus of the right eye and the lateral rectus of the left eye must both contract, while the lateral rectus of the right eye and the medial rectus of the left eye must both relax. You should be able to figure out for yourself what will happen if you now decide to glance rightward.

For the eye movements just described, both eyes have moved in the same direction—upward, leftward, and so on. Eye movements of this type are called **conjunctive** eye movements. But the eyes are capable of other types of movements as well, ones in which the eyes move in opposite directions—both may turn inward or both may turn outward. These are called **vergence** eye movements. For example, the left eye can turn rightward while the right eye turns leftward. As a result, both eyes turn inward, toward the nose. This movement allows you to look at a very close object straight ahead of you. This particular type of movement is called a convergent eye movement. To accomplish it, the medial rectus muscles of both eyes contract, while the lateral rectus muscles of both eyes relax. If you are looking at an object at arm's length and bring it closer to you, your eyes converge, tracking the object. When the object moves away from you, your eye muscles will engage in the opposite behavior, resulting in a divergent eye movement.

HOW SHOULD THE EYES BE PROTECTED?

Vertebrate eyes are extremely complicated devices, occupying a very exposed position in the head. Various protective measures have evolved to compensate for their vulnerability. An outline of these protective mechanisms will provide a good introduction to the overall structure of the eye.

The eye is partially protected by virtue of its location within the **orbit,** a bony depression in the skull. Within the orbit, the eye is cushioned by heavy deposits of fat surrounding each eyeball. Without this orbital fat, blows to the head would be transmitted directly to the eye. But by absorbing such shocks, orbital fat cushions the eye against all but the most severe jolts.

The eyelids, movable folds of tissue, also protect the eye. The position of the upper lid relative to the lower one determines the opening through which the front of the eye is visible. The lids move relative to each other in various modes. For instance, they can rapidly—in a small fraction of a second—open or close. Such closures of the lids, blinks, occur voluntarily as well as involuntarily. Blinks clean and moisten the front of the eye to keep it from drying out; they also protect the eye from objects that seem to be on a collison course with it, and they reduce light when so desired (as for sleep). Box 2.2 gives more information about blinks and their function.

The lids of the eye can also change position in situations other than blinking. In conversation, the size of the opening between the lids provides a reliable clue as to how interested your listener is. Watch a friend's eyes closely; the opening between lids will average 8 millimeters (about ⅜ inch). You'll probably notice a change in that opening as your friend's attention varies. When interest is high, the opening between lids increases to about 10 millimeters. Drowsiness or boredom reduces the size of the opening (Records, 1979a, pp. 15–17). Figure 2.5 illustrates this point; you should have no trouble telling which person is listening most intently.

Tears, too, protect the eyes. Although usually associated either with emotional states or with slicing raw onions, tears are intended to protect the eyes in two different ways. Tears are secreted from a gland situ-

BOX 2.2
In the Blink of an Eye

Your body does many things that you don't notice, such as breathing and blinking. You probably know what breathing accomplishes, but perhaps you haven't thought much about why you blink.

Your eyes blink about once every 4 seconds (Records, 1979a, p. 19). The exact frequency of blinks varies from one person to another, and it also changes with environmental conditions and emotional state. When the air is very dry, the blink rate goes up, ensuring that the delicate front surface of the eye doesn't dry out. When you start a casual conversation with someone, your blink rate may double; if you become angry, your blink rate will increase even more. You can see this for yourself by observing your friends under various conditions. Just be sure they don't know you're making these observations. Otherwise, they may attempt to alter their blink rate voluntarily (Doane, 1980).

From the instant your lids begin to close until they open again, a blink takes about one-third of a second. For about half this time your lids are completely closed, cutting down the light by about 99 percent. Compare this to the dimming of room lights to 1 percent of their original intensity. If the dimming lasted only one-tenth of a second, it would have mimicked what a blink does to your vision. When lights are

actually dimmed in this way, the dimming is extremely obvious. Why is it, then, that one never notices the same blackout when it is caused by a blink?

Frances Volkmann, Lorrin Riggs, and Robert Moore, psychologists at Smith College and Brown University, tried to explain this puzzle. They believed that the part of the brain that signals the lids to close also produces a neural signal that suppresses or temporarily shuts off vision for the duration of the blink (Volkmann, Riggs, and Moore, 1980). Suppression would keep you from noticing that a blink had occurred.

This hypothesis, although intriguing, is hard to test. The appropriate test would be to measure vision during a blink without having those measurements affected by the lid closing. Volkmann and her colleagues developed the following ingenious way to stimulate the eye so that the light reaching the retina would not be affected by lid closure.

The eyes lie directly above the roof of the mouth. A strong light focused on the roof of the mouth under one eye can stimulate the retina, causing the light to be seen whether or not the lids are closed. If the room lights were off and the only light reaching your eye came through the roof of your mouth, blinking would not affect the light reaching your eye. This arrangement makes it possible to measure the ability to see a

dimming of the light at various times relative to a blink.

Volkmann and her colleagues used a bundle of transparent plastic fibers to carry light to the roof of a person's mouth. By abruptly dimming the light, they determined the smallest reduction in light intensity that was visible to the person. Remember: All the light that could be seen came through the person's mouth, by-passing the lids. At the same time, Volkmann and her associates used skin electrodes to measure when a blink occurred. Since a blink is produced by muscle contraction, it is easy to measure the electrical activity of the lid muscles and know from that activity when a blink begins and ends.

Volkmann found that dimming was much harder to see *during* a blink than *between* blinks. In order to be detected during a blink, the light had to be dimmed by an amount five times greater than it did between blinks.

This result proves that the nervous system suppresses vision just before and during each blink—keeping you from noticing visual blackouts. Without this suppression, you would be bothered ten to fifteen times per minute by profound blackouts (Riggs, Volkmann, and Moore, 1981, p. 1079). Your visual system uses a temporary, well-timed suppression to protect you from the annoying but necessary behavior of your eyelids.

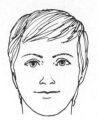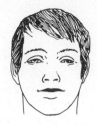

FIGURE 2.5
Can you tell which person is more attentive?

ated in the upper, front portion of each orbit (under the upper lid). From there, they pass down over the cornea, moistening it, and then drain out of the eye through small openings in the lower nasal portion of each orbit. Finally, the tears drain onto the mucous membrane lining the nose's inner surface. This nasal membrane acts as an evaporator for the tears, which explains why you have to blow your nose when you have been crying. Tears contain an antimicrobial agent that helps protect the eye from certain bacteria lurking in the environment. In addition, the regular flow of tears flushes away debris, such as dust. Tears also lubricate the surface of the eyes so that blinking won't abrade the lids or scratch the front of the eyeball. The constant, very thin film of tears over the front of the eye minimizes the wear and tear produced by constant lid movement.

Having covered its ancillary features, we are now ready to discuss the structure of the eye itself.

The Structure of the Human Eye

To enable you to understand the eye, we'll have to deal with the details of structure and function; but as an introduction, let's start with the major features. We can omit details until the second stage of our discus-

sion, by which time you'll have a good idea where those details fit into the eye's grand scheme.

The human eye is very nearly spherical, with a diameter of approximately 24 millimeters (nearly one inch), or slightly smaller than a ping-pong ball. It consists of three concentric layers, each with its own characteristic appearance, structure, and primary function. From outermost to innermost, the three layers are the **fibrous tunic,** which protects the eyeball, the **vascular tunic,** which nourishes the eyeball, and the **retina,** which detects light and initiates neural messages bound for the brain. Figure 2.6 illustrates this three-layered arrangement. Note also from this figure that the eye is partitioned into two chambers, a small anterior chamber and a larger vitreous chamber. Thus the basic layout is three concentric layers and two chambers, plus the iris, pupil, and lens.

THE OUTERMOST, FIBROUS TUNIC

Most of your experience with eyes comes from looking at your own in a mirror or from looking at other people's. Though it's useful to inspect the eye visually, doing only that gives a very limited picture of this elaborate organ. When you face someone and look directly at one eye, you can see only about one-sixth of the eye's outer surface; the rest lies hidden behind the lids and other protective structures. The "white" of the eye is part of the outermost, fibrous coat. Since this white part is made of tough, dense material, it is called the **sclera,** from a Greek root meaning "hard."*

*Most parts of the eye have names related to their character or appearance. Knowing the origin of some of these names can help you appreciate the structure of the eye. Our explanations come from a book, *On Naming the Parts of the Human Body,* written in the second century A.D. by Rufos of Euphesus, a city located in what is today Turkey. We have drawn on an excellent translation by Stephen Polyak (1941, p. 96).

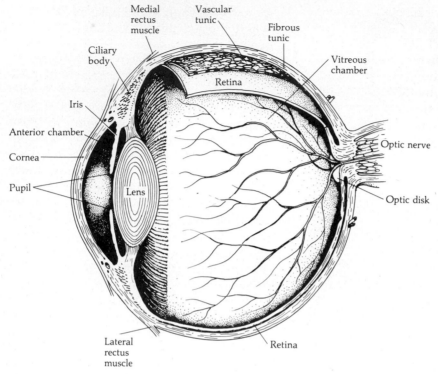

FIGURE 2.6

Cross section of human eye, showing major layers and structures. View is from above the left eye.

The sclera averages about 1 millimeter in thickness, and under a microscope, you can see that it's made of tightly packed, interwoven fibers running parallel to the sclera's surface. These densely packed fibers give the sclera its toughness. Actually, the sclera has got to be tough because pressure inside the eyeball is double that of the atmosphere. If the sclera were more elastic, that pressure could cause the eyeball to become deformed. Among other consequences, deformation would ruin the quality of one's sight. We'll return to the importance of the eyeball's shape later, when we discuss the eye as an optical instrument.

At the very front of the eye, this outer coat loses its white coloring and becomes so transparent that it's difficult to see it in the mirror. However, if you look at someone else's eye from the side, you will notice a small bulge on the front of the eye. This bulge is called the **cornea,** a term from the word for "hornlike," meaning that the cornea is composed of material similar to that in an animal's horn. If the cornea is made out of the same material as the sclera, why is the cornea transparent? The major reason is that the fibers of the cornea are arranged in a neater, more orderly fashion. In addition, greater transparency is made possible by the fact that the cornea has no internal blood supply of its own. Since blood would reduce the passage of light, the cornea draws its nourishment from the clear fluid in the anterior chamber.

Because the cornea is transparent, it permits more light to pass through. This is important because the cornea plays a crucial role in the formation of images in the eye. Anything that disturbs the cornea's transparency, therefore, will reduce the quality of these images and, hence, the quality of vision. For self-protection, the cornea has extremely high sensitivity to touch. Foreign bodies contacting the cornea trigger a sequence of protective responses, including lid closure and tear production.

THE MIDDLE, VASCULAR TUNIC

For most of its course, the vascular tunic hugs the wall of the eyeball, and only toward the front of the eyeball does it pull away from the wall. We'll begin by considering the rear two-thirds of this middle layer, the part that fits snugly against the wall of the eyeball.

Most of the middle layer consists of a dark, heavily pigmented, spongy structure called the **choroid.** The choroid averages about 0.2 millimeters in thickness and contains a network of blood vessels, including capillaries. Blood from these capillaries nourishes many cells in the retina, the innermost of the eye's three layers. Without that nourishment—oxygen and nutrients—those cells, which are vital for vision, would die.

The choroid's heavy pigmentation also reduces light scatter, the tendency for light to bounce around randomly within the eyeball, which would reduce the sharpness of images formed inside the eye. The choroid's pigmentation reduces scatter by harmlessly absorbing extra light. Incidentally, this is the same reason why the inside of a camera is painted flat black. The paint absorbs scattered light and protects the sharpness of images on the film.

THE ANTERIOR CHAMBER

Toward the front of the eye, this middle, choroidal layer no longer hugs the wall of the eyeball but instead runs more or less parallel to the front surface of the eye. Over this part of its course, the middle layer forms a long slender structure called the **ciliary body.** This spongy network of tissue manufactures **aqueous humor,** the watery fluid that fills the smaller, anterior chamber of the eye. The aqueous humor serves a number of major maintenance functions: It transports oxygen and nutrients to several of the structures it bathes, and it carries away their waste products. Elsewhere in the body, blood performs these functions, but inside the eye, blood would interfere with light transmission and make seeing difficult or impossible. Therefore, in place of blood, the crucial optical components of the eye—the cornea and lens—rely on aqueous as their source of nourishment.

The aqueous serves another function as well. Filling the anterior chamber, this fluid maintains the shape of the eyeball. If there were too little fluid in the anterior chamber, the eye would become deformed, like an underinflated basketball. It doesn't though, because cells in the ciliary body are constantly producing new aqueous to keep the supply of nutrients from becoming exhausted. The creation of new fluid also prevents the build-up of high concentrations of waste products.

There is a limit, however, to how much aqueous the anterior chamber can hold. So a balance must be achieved between the rate of creation of the fluid and the rate at which it is drained from the eye. Sometimes the balance is not maintained and too much aqueous accumulates in the eye. Excess aqueous accumulates either because of overproduction or because of improper drainage out of the anterior chamber. Drainage can be blocked or slowed down if the outlets for aqueous (which lie at the junction of ciliary body and cornea; see Figure 2.7) become squeezed shut or clogged. Pressure builds up within the eye, and if the pressure remains high for too long, vision

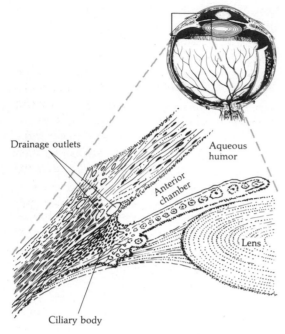

Drainage outlets

Aqueous humor

Anterior chamber

Lens

Ciliary body

FIGURE 2.7
Enlarged view of anterior chamber, showing the eye's drainage system. The small box in the inset shows the region of the eye represented in the enlarged drawing.

can be impaired permanently. This is the most common cause of blinding eye disease in North America—**glaucoma.**

THE IRIS, PUPIL, AND LENS

The Iris. As it folds inward, away from the wall of the eye, the ciliary body gives rise to the **iris,** a circular patch of tissue that gives your eye its characteristic color: brown, blue, green, gray, and at least in the case of one famous actress, violet (Howard, 1983). This variety of colors makes the name ''iris'' very appropriate, for it comes from the Greek word for ''rainbow.''

The iris actually consists of two layers, an outer layer containing pigment, and an inner layer containing blood vessels. If the outer layer is heavily pigmented, the iris will appear brown. But if this outer layer is lightly pigmented, someone looking at the iris can actually see the back layer through the front one. In this case, the iris will look blue or some other light color. The color results from a combination of the light pigmentation of the front layer and the color of the blood vessels in the back layer. If the iris's front layer had no pigment, the rear layer would become very noticeable, giving the eye a pinkish hue. This occurs in albino humans, who have greatly reduced pigmentation.

The Pupil. Looking in a mirror at the center of your own iris, you'll see a round black region, the **pupil.** The pupil is actually an opening, or gap, inside two sets of muscles. The inner set runs circularly around the pupil. When this circular band of muscles contracts, the pupil gets smaller. Another set of muscles runs radially out from the edge of the circular muscles, away from the pupillary opening. When the radial muscles contract, the pupil widens or dilates. These changes in pupil size control the amount of light reaching the back of the eye.

The size of the pupil at any given moment depends on several factors. First, it depends on the light level to which the eye is exposed: the size of the pupil decreases as the level of light increases. In young adults, the pupil diameter varies from about 8–9 millimeters down to 1.5–2 millimeters, a fourfold variation (Figure 2.8). The amount of light passing through the pupil is proportional to the pupil's *area*, which is itself proportional to the square of pupil diameter. Thus as the pupil diameter varies over a range of four to one, the amount of light the pupil admits to the eye varies over a range of sixteen to one. In older adults, the pupil responds to light by changing size, but its largest opening is less than half that of the average 20-year-old. As a result, less light gets into the eyes of very old people.

Pupil size   *Light level*

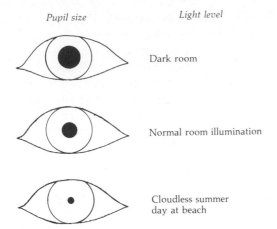

Dark room

Normal room illumination

Cloudless summer
day at beach

FIGURE 2.8
Pupil size varies with level of illumination.

Besides light level, the size of the pupil depends on other events that influence the autonomic nervous system. In particular, excitement, fear, or sexual interest can change

the size of the pupil. Some people, such as professional gamblers and jewel merchants, are quite adept at sensing emotional state on the basis of a person's pupil size (Hess, 1965). This has been appreciated for some time, and countermeasures have been developed—including dark glasses to hide the pupils.

Although large pupils allow more light into the eye, smaller pupils can sometimes offer an advantage (Cornsweet, 1970). Suppose you are looking at an object about 2 or 3 meters away. While you're looking at that object, other objects—those much closer of much farther away—will tend to appear somewhat blurred. The range of distances over which objects will appear sharp varies with the size of the pupil. This range is sometimes called the **depth of field.** The easiest way to demonstrate the depth of field is to substitute a camera for your eye. In taking the photographs shown in Figure 2.9,

FIGURE 2.9
The degree of blur in a picture depends on the size of the aperture of the camera. The sharp photo on the right was taken through a smaller aperture, thus increasing the depth of field in the photograph. (Glyn Cloyd)

the size of the camera's aperture has been varied to simulate the effects of changing pupil size. The photograph on the left was taken with a large aperture; the one on the right with a small aperture. Note that on the left, very few objects appear sharp. With a large aperture, the objects that were not precisely at the distance for which the camera was focused appear blurred. The other photograph was taken without changing the focus, only the aperture size. With a smaller aperture, more objects appear well focused—the range of distances over which objects can be situated and still be adequately focused has increased. Incidentally, this effect of pupil size on depth of field is of help to human infants. Their pupils are smaller than those of adults. As a result, although their eyes may be quite a bit misfocused, their small pupils reduce blur and help them see.

The Lens. One very important optical element of the eye, the **crystalline lens,** lies right behind the iris. The lens takes its name from its resemblance to a lentil or bean. In adults, the lens is shaped like a very large aspirin tablet, about 9 millimeters in diameter and 4 millimeters in thickness. The lens consists of three distinct parts: an elastic covering or *capsule,* an *epithelial layer* just inside the capsule, and the *lens* itself. As you might expect, each of these parts has its own job to do.

In fact, the thin, elastic capsule around the lens has two jobs. First, it moderates the flow of aqueous humor into the lens, helping the lens retain its transparency to light. Second, the elastic capsule molds the shape of the lens—varying its flatness and, thereby, the lens's optical power. This variation in optical power is called **accommodation.**

The lens never stops growing. Throughout the life span, the outer, epithelial layer of the lens continues to produce protein fibers that are added to the surface of the lens.

Consequently, those protein fibers nearest the center of the lens are the oldest (some were present at birth), while the fibers on the outside are the youngest. Between birth and age 90 years, the lens quadruples in thickness and attains a weight of 250 milligrams (Paterson, 1979). In the center of the lens the old fibers become more densely packed, producing **sclerosis,** or hardening, of the lens. We'll describe the importance of sclerosis later in this chapter.

For good vision, the lens must be transparent—light must be able to pass through it easily and with little loss. This transparency depends on the material out of which the lens is made. Of all the body's parts, the lens has the highest percentage of protein, and its protein fibers are lined up parallel to one another, maximizing the lens's transparency to light. Anything that disturbs this alignment—such as excess fluid inside the lens—reduces transparency.

An opacity (or reduced transparency) of the lens is called a **cataract.** While some cataracts are minor—barely reducing the transmission of light—others cause blindness. Cataracts are common in elderly people, but they can also occur in the young. In fact, certain populations (Arabs and Sephardic Jews, for instance) have a very high incidence of congenital cataracts—lens opacities at birth. These opacities severely degrade the stimulation received by the eye, and this can be serious. At birth, the visual nervous system is immature and its proper development depends on normal stimulation of the eye. Deprived of that proper stimulation, the immature visual nervous system will develop abnormally (Hubel, Wiesel, and LeVay, 1977). Realizing this fact, many physicians now remove congenital cataracts as early in life as possible.

Surgical removal of a cataractous lens has become more or less routine today. Since the lens contributes to the total optical power of the eye, removal of the lens must be accompanied by some form of optical compensation. Powerful spectacles or contact lenses can be worn, or alternatively, a plastic lens can be surgically inserted inside the eye, replacing the missing biological lens. None of these alternatives, however, restores the ability to accommodate.

THE VITREOUS CHAMBER

The vitreous chamber accounts for nearly two-thirds of the total volume of the eye. This larger of the eye's two chambers is bounded by the lens in front and the retina on the sides and in the rear. Like its smaller partner on the anterior side of the lens, this chamber is filled with a transparent fluid called **vitreous,** a substance with the consistency of egg white.

Encased in a thin membrane, the vitreous is anchored to the inner wall of the eyeball. Unlike the aqueous, the vitreous is not continuously renewed, which means that debris can accumulate. Sometimes you become aware of this debris, in the form of **floaters,** small opacities that float about in the vitreous (White and Levatin, 1962). If you are looking at a bright, uniform surface, the floaters cast shadows on the back of your eye, causing you to see little dark spots darting about immediately in front of you. Though floaters are usually harmless, dense or persistent floaters may be a symptom of a more serious, vision-threatening condition that requires treatment.

THE RETINA

The innermost of the eye's three layers, the **retina** resembles a very thin, fragile meshwork, which explains its name—*rete* is Latin for "fisherman's net." Although no thicker than a postage stamp, this delicate structure has a complex, layered organization. While it's hard to envision such a thin structure as being multilayered, Figure 2.10 may help you overcome this difficulty. It shows how the retina might look if you cut a section out and looked at the section from the side. The arrows represent the direction taken by incoming light. Notice that taking this view, the retina lies just below the vitreous, with the choroid underneath the retina.

To a large degree, the retina's complexity reflects its origins. Embryologically, the retina derives from the same tissue out of which the brain itself develops. So the retina is actually a direct extension of the central nervous system. This affinity with the brain has one unfortunate aspect, though: damaged retinal cells, like damaged brain cells, are not replaced. One just has to try to live with the damage.

You already know that the eye is a window through which you look outward, onto the world. But it's also a window through which someone else can look inward, into your body. In fact, the eye is the only place where the nervous system and blood supply can be viewed directly, without surgery. Hermann Helmholtz, the nineteenth-century physicist, physician, mathematician, and philosopher, is credited with the invention of the **ophthalmoscope,*** a simple device for seeing the internal structures of the living human eye, including its retina. Today, variants of Helmholtz's instrument are widely used to examine the inside of the eye and to monitor the health of the central nervous system and blood supply. Millions of examinations are made with this instrument every year, usually using a hand-held, battery-powered model with which you may be familiar.

Some Retinal Landmarks. Figure 2.11 illustrates what you would see if you looked into

---

*Actually, Charles Babbage, who developed a mechanical digital computer in the middle of the eighteenth century, made a working model of an ophthalmoscope some years before Helmholtz but didn't pursue the project (Rucker, 1971).

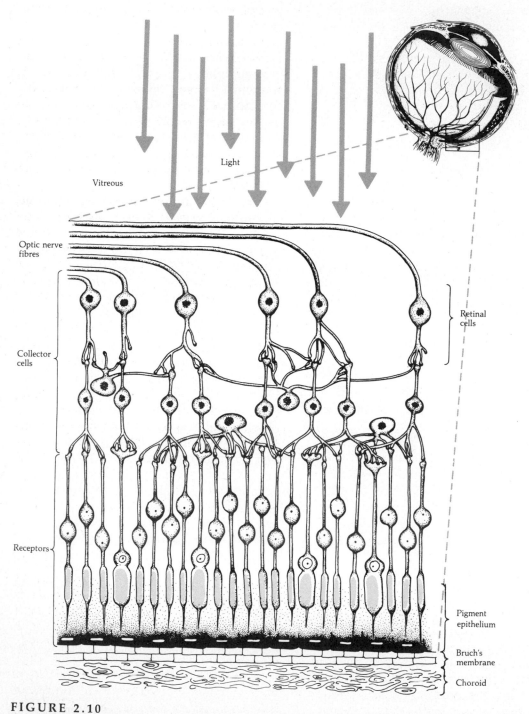

Vitreous

Light

Optic nerve fibres

Collector cells

Retinal cells

Receptors

Pigment epithelium

Bruch's membrane

Choroid

FIGURE 2.10

Cross section of the retina. The small box in the inset shows the region of the eye represented in the enlarged drawing.

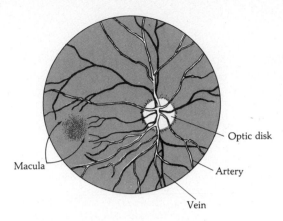

FIGURE 2.11
The inside of the back of the human eye.

a normal human eye using an ophthalmo-scope. The living retina is virtually trans-parent (Records, 1979b). As a result, what the ophthalmoscope reveals is mainly the structures lying in front of the retina—such as the central retinal artery—and structures lying behind it—such as the choroid. Al-though Figure 2.11 shows only the rearmost one-sixth of the retina, it does highlight sev-eral of the retina's most significant features. Look first at the nearly circular area indi-cated by the arrows. This region, measuring 1.5 millimeters, is called the **macula.** When you look directly at some object, the image of that object is centered within the macula of each of your eyes. Obviously, then, this part of the retina is vital for good sight. Vi-sion is most acute right in the middle of the macula.

Consider another landmark in Figure 2.11, the **optic disk.** This is the origin or "head" of the nerve that carries information from the retina to the brain. Generally, the optic disk has a pinkish color because of small blood vessels on its surface; these nourish part of the optic nerve. Loss of this pink color signifies the presence of some circu-latory problem that could eventually starve the optic nerve and impair vision. Fortu-nately, such changes in color can be de-tected quite easily with the ophthalmo-scope.

Notice also the large blood vessels that run outward from the optic disk; these are labeled "artery" and "vein." The arterial branches supply blood to a large part of the retina. Since the retina has just about the highest metabolic rate of any part of the body, its access to blood—for oxygen and nutri-tion—is vital. Box 2.3 discusses what hap-pens to vision when the retina's supply of blood is impaired.

The retina must first capture light that enters the eye and then convert, or trans-duce, that light into electrical activity that can be processed by neural elements in the eye and in the brain. To see the world around you, the pattern of light reaching your ret-ina should mirror the distribution of light in the scene you are viewing. This light distri-bution, or **retinal image** as it's called, is the raw material on which the retina works. The fidelity of the retinal image depends on a host of factors—including the way various ocular structures interact with the incoming light. Obviously then, to appreciate the workings of the retina you must first un-derstand something about the image it re-ceives.

The Eye as Optical Instrument

Light brings the eyes information about ob-jects in the environment. But how does light acquire that information in the first place? Initially, light originates from a source such as the sun or a light bulb. This is called emit-ted light. However, for purposes of seeing, the more important form of light is that which is reflected off objects and surfaces. It is this reflected light that picks up and carries in-formation about perceptually relevant ob-jects and events (Gibson, 1966).

The process is as follows. Surfaces absorb

BOX 2.3
Supplying Blood to the Retina

For its weight, the retina is one of the body's greediest consumers of oxygen. So when blood is in short supply, vision is hit very hard. To minimize its risk, most of the retina has a dual blood supply; if one supply is obstructed, the other pitches in. The inner two-thirds of the retina receives its blood from the central retinal artery and its branches. The outer one-third of the retina (including the photoreceptors) gets its blood from capillaries within the choroid.

The arteries and veins that you saw in Figure 2.11 are situated between the retina and the vitreous, in the path of incoming light. This arrangement may strike you as odd. Though the eye needs blood, too much in the wrong place blocks the passage of light, making vision difficult or impossible.

You may have noticed in Figure 2.11 that the arteries and veins seem to avoid the macula. Because they detour around the macula, blood vessels do not obstruct light on its way to that most important region for seeing. As a result of this detour, though, a tiny portion of the macula's very center does not enjoy a dual blood supply. This region gets nourishment solely from whatever nutrients seep through the retina from the choroid. Since it has only one supply of

blood, this region of the retina is particularly vulnerable to diseases and disorders that interrupt or impede the flow of blood.

But what sorts of things might interrupt the retina's blood supplies? For one thing, feeder arteries can become clogged, thereby blocking the flow of blood to and within the inner retina. This happens in arteriosclerosis ("hardening of the arteries") and sometimes in sickle cell disease, a condition common among Africans and people of African descent.

The supply of blood to the *outer* retina can be impaired as well. Look at the bottom of Figure 2.10. Note that between the outermost layer of the retina, the **pigment epithelium,** and the choroid lies a membrane, **Bruch's membrane.** Nutrients for the photoreceptors must pass through both Bruch's membrane and the pigment epithelium of the retina itself. Several diseases reduce the ease with which nutrients can penetrate these structures. When nutrients can't reach them, cells die and vision is impaired. The most common cause of this problem is aging. As one gets older, accumulated retinal debris thickens Bruch's membrane, impeding the normal penetration of nutrients. Starved for proper nutrition,

retinal cells, including photoreceptors, die. The result is senile macular degeneration, a disease that produces a progressive loss of vision. Most forms of this disease cannot yet be treated.

Diabetes is another common disease that can affect the retina's blood supply. You probably know that diabetes is marked by disordered insulin metabolism that causes too much sugar to accumulate in the diabetic's blood. By means not completely understood, the excess sugar promotes the development of a cataract in the eye's crystalline lens. The cataract then reduces vision. But diabetes has another serious consequence for vision. In some diabetics, the retina's blood supply is severely reduced. Sensing that it is being starved for oxygen (carried in the blood), the retina generates a chemical to stimulate the growth of new, large blood vessels. Growing new blood vessels may sound like an excellent solution to the problem, but it brings devastation of its own. The thick new vessels grow out of control, blocking light and causing eventual blindness. In the last ten years or so, lasers have been used very successfully to stop the growth of these new vessels.

some, but not all, of the light shining on them; the portion of light not absorbed is reflected by the surface. Objects with high reflectance usually appear "light," whereas objects with low reflectance appear "dark."

For example, this page has a reflectance of about 80 percent, while the print on this page has a reflectance of about 10 percent. Abrupt changes in reflectance usually signal discontinuities in a surface, such as those demarcating edges, corners, or the like (see the top drawing in Figure 2.12). More gradual changes in reflectance usually correspond to curved surfaces (see the middle drawing in Figure 2.12).

There are other kinds of differences in the ways in which surfaces reflect light. For example, some surfaces reflect light evenly in many different directions. Lacking highlights—areas of particularly strong reflection—such surfaces appear dull or matte. Other surfaces reflect light in only one or in very few directions, giving the surface "highlights" and making it appear glossy.

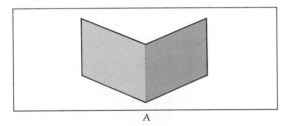

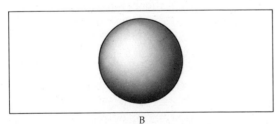

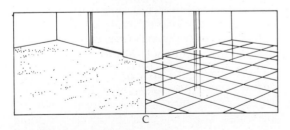

FIGURE 2.12
The top drawing illustrates how abrupt changes in reflectance signal the presence of an edge. The middle drawing illustrates how gradual changes in reflectance signal the presence of a smooth surface. The bottom drawing shows how reflected light specifies the texture of a surface.

These differences can be seen in the bottom drawing in Figure 2.12. In other words, reflected light conveys information about the texture of surfaces (Gibson, 1966).

These are just some of the ways in which objects in the environment "sculpt" light and provide potential information. But before that potential can be realized, three prerequisites must be satisfied. First, the light must be sufficiently intense to reach deep into your eyes, striking the photosensitive material in the retina. You may be surprised to learn that about 50 percent of the light striking the cornea is reflected or absorbed before reaching the retina (Cornsweet, 1970, p. 24). This can have practical consequences under conditions of very dim illumination.

Second, the distribution of light—the retinal image—must be properly focused. Think of an object as a set of very small points. To produce a sharp image of that object, light from any of its points should form a small, compact pattern on the retina. A blurred image would be created if each small point in space was imaged as a large, spread-out distribution on the retina. In this case, distributions from neighboring points on the retina would overlap, blurring one another's boundaries and making it difficult to see separate, individual points. Among other consequences, blur would make reading impossible—you couldn't tell one letter from another. Some effects of blur are illustrated in Figure 2.13.

Finally, the pattern of light falling on the retina must preserve the spatial structure of the object from which it is reflected. If that spatial structure is preserved, light arising from two adjacent points in space—from neighboring parts of an object, for instance—will fall on adjacent points of the retina. A distribution of light that preserves the spatial ordering of points in space is called an **image** (Boynton, 1974). If the light distribution on the retina were scrambled or spatially random, it would be useless as a

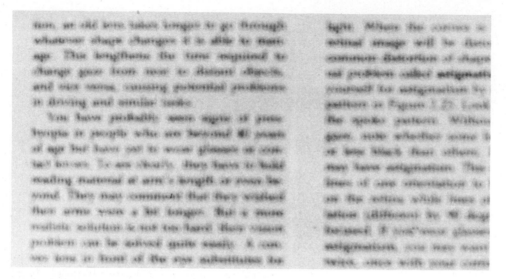

FIGURE 2.13
Effect of blur on the legibility of text. (For a legible version, see the top of page 51.)

source of information about the structure and layout of objects.

IMAGE FORMATION IN THE HUMAN EYE

The sharpness of images formed on the retina depends mainly on two factors. The first is the optical power of the cornea and crystalline lens (where "optical power" means ability to bend or refract light). The other factor controlling image sharpness is the size of the eyeball, particularly the eyeball's length from front to back. In a camera, a good picture requires that the film be just the right distance from the lens. In the eye, the same thing holds: the retina must be the right distance from the crystalline lens. Some eyes are too short, others are too long; either condition impairs vision.

The optical power of the eye is not constant, though. By changing its shape somewhat, the crystalline lens automatically changes its optical power. This automatic change, called accommodation, helps one see objects clearly, regardless of their distance

from the eye. To appreciate how these components of the eye contribute to vision, we'll have to consider the behavior of light and its interaction with these components. To simplify our analysis of image formation we'll begin with a very small object: a single point in space that emits light. The same analysis works for other, more complex visual objects, since we can think of them as consisting of a large set of points. But dealing with just one point will simplify our explanation of the rudiments of image formation.

In the eighteenth century, Thomas Young showed that light could be treated as though it consisted of waves. If you drop a pebble into a pond, you'll see wavefronts spreading out from the place where the stone hit the water. The stone corresponds to our point of light, and radiating out from the point is a set of spherical wavefronts (see Figure 2.14). Light that spreads out in this way is said to be **divergent.** Divergent light cannot form a well-focused image—a point—unless something is done to reverse its divergence. Let's examine how the eye accomplishes this feat. Certain optical devices can counteract light's

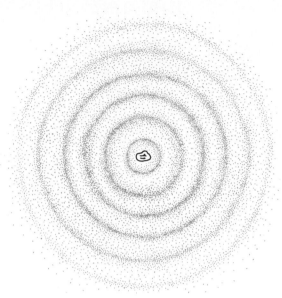

FIGURE 2.14
Light waves radiate out from a source of light in a way that resembles the ripples produced when a pebble is dropped into a pond.

tendency to diverge. One such device is a convex lens, which gets its name from its shape. Once a diverging wavefront passes through a strong convex lens, the paths of neighboring points on the wavefront get progressively closer together or converge to a single point. After passing through this point, light diverges once again. Figure 2.15 illustrates this effect of a convex lens.

Lenses differ in their ability, or power, to converge light. A highly convex lens converges light more strongly than does a mildly convex lens. As Figure 2.16 shows, rays that pass through a convex lens of high power are focused to a point very close to the lens, whereas rays that pass through a lens of lower power are focused at some distance farther from the lens. The distance at which a lens brings light to focus depends on both the power of the lens itself and the degree of divergence of the light striking the lens. In order to converge the light, a convex lens must overcome, or null, the light's divergence. This is demonstrated in Figure 2.17: a lens of constant power is shown converging light of three different degrees of divergence. The most strongly divergent light comes from the source positioned closest to

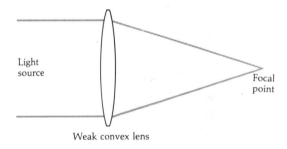

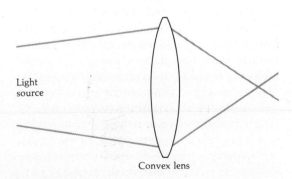

FIGURE 2.15
A convex lens focuses diverging light.

FIGURE 2.16
Convex lenses of different power bring light to focus at different distances. If the light rays striking the lens are parallel, the spot at which the light converges to a point is called the focal point.

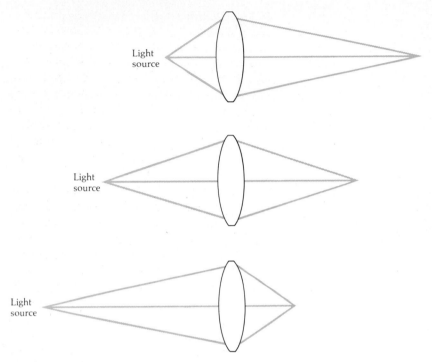

FIGURE 2.17

The spot at which a convex lens brings light to a point depends on the degree of divergence of the light arriving at the lens.

the lens, while the most weakly divergent light comes from the source farthest from the lens. In addition, each object is focused at a different distance from the lens: the most divergent light is focused farthest from the lens, and the least divergent light is focused closest to the lens.

IMAGE FORMATION IN THE HUMAN EYE

Let's begin by considering a human eye that is looking at an object sufficiently far away that light coming from that object has essentially zero divergence. As with any object, to form a useful image, light from the object must be focused on the retina. Since cornea and crystalline lens both contribute to image formation, let's lump them to-

gether, calling the combination "the optics of the eye." How powerful should those optics be in order to produce a sharp retinal image of that distant object? For the retinal image to be sharply focused, the optics' power must match the length of the eyeball—specifically, the distance from the lens to the retina.

This idea is illustrated in Figure 2.18. The top eyeball is just the right length, given the power of its optics. As a result, the distant object is brought to focus exactly on the retina. Such an eye is described as **emmetropic** (meaning "in the right measure or size").

The middle panel shows an eye that is too long, given the strength of its optics. Although an image *is* formed, that image is formed in front of the retina, rather than on it. In fact, the rays have begun to diverge

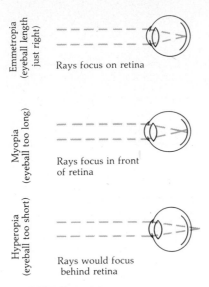

Emmetropia (eyeball length just right)

Rays focus on retina

Myopia (eyeball too long)

Rays focus in front of retina

Hyperopia (eyeball too short)

Rays would focus behind retina

FIGURE 2.18
Image formation in emmetropic, myopic, and hyperopic eyes.

again by the time they reach the retina, so the image on the retina is blurred. Such an eye is described as **myopic,** or nearsighted, because near objects will be in best focus.

The third panel in Figure 2.18 shows an eye that is too short for its optics; an image is formed on the retina, but it too is not well focused and hence the image is blurred. Actually, for this eye the best-focused image would lie behind the retina—if light were able to pass through the retina. Such an eye is described as **hyperopic,** or farsighted, because far objects will be in best focus.

What are the perceptual consequences of a mismatch between an eye's length and its optics? You've seen that in myopic or hyperopic eyes, light does reach the retina, but that it is not sharply focused. When an eye of the wrong size looks at a distant point, the resulting image on the retina will be a circular patch, not a point. Thus the point in space will appear blurred, or indistinct.

The degree of blur depends on the extent to which the eye is too short or too long: The greater the mismatch between the eye's

optics and its length, the worse the blur. The photographs in Figure 2.19 illustrate how the world might appear to a properly focused eye (panel A), to an eye that is only one-third of a millimeter too long (panel B), and to an eye that is 2 millimeters too long (panel C). Remember that when we describe an eye as "too long" or "too short," we mean this in relative terms. "Too long" and "too short" are defined relative to the power of the eye's optics.

Since about half the human race—perhaps yourself included—is afflicted with these problems, let's consider myopia and hyperopia, and what steps can be taken to correct eyes that are too long or too short.

Myopia. Suppose that we are dealing with an eye whose length and optical power match. For that eye, a distant object will be in proper focus on the retina. If we now lengthen that eye—make it myopic—by only one-third of a millimeter, the distant object will be less well focused on the retina. To be focused properly on the retina, the object must be at a distance from the eye so that wavefronts from the object will be diverging at the right rate as they strike the eye. The rate of divergence depends on the wavefront's distance from its source. In the case we're considering, we could produce a sharply focused image on the retina just by moving the object closer to the myopic person or by moving the myopic person closer to the object. But sometimes neither of these approaches is practical. Nor is it possible for this blur to be corrected by accommodation. In fact, increasing the power of the crystalline lens would increase the overall optical power of the eye, making the blur even worse. Fortunately, there is an effective solution to myopia: altering the effective optical power of the eye by placing the proper spectacle lens in front of, or the proper contact lens on, the eye. With such a lens, the total optical power of the eye will be the

A.

B.

C.

FIGURE 2.19
Focus influences the quality of the image. Panel A simulates the image formed by an emmetropic eye, panel B by a mildly myopic eye, and panel C by a more severely myopic eye. (Glyn Cloyd)

MYOPIA

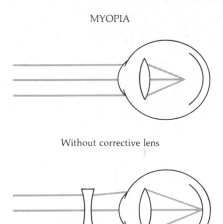

Without corrective lens

Concave lens

With corrective lens

FIGURE 2.20
A concave lens in front of the eye can correct myopia.

sum of the eye's own inherent optical power plus the power of the supplementary lens.

But what sort of corrective lens would the myopic eye need? We could correct the myopic eye by adding a concave lens (which causes light to *di*verge, combating the myopic eye's tendency to make light *con*verge too much). Figure 2.20 shows how such a lens helps to focus an otherwise misfocused target on a myope's retina. Box 2.4 discusses some of myopia's causes.

Hyperopia. Now suppose that we are dealing with an eyeball that is too short. Its best-focused image will be behind the retina, not on it (see top panel of Figure 2.21). This eye's optics are too weak even for light coming from an object so distant that it is not diverging at all. If it has to deal with light from closer objects (even more strongly diverging), the eye will misfocus the light by even more.

The hyperope can alleviate her problem by accommodating, increasing her eye's op-

BOX 2.4
Some Origins of Myopia

It's a fair bet that in advanced societies today, most people have to accommodate much more of the time than did their preliterate ancestors. Perhaps, as some claim, our culture evolved from one that demanded little close work into one that demands it almost continuously (Young, 1981). Maybe constant near work, and the accommodative effort it requires, plays some role in the development of myopia. There's some evidence to support this idea.

First, occupations requiring lots of near work are associated with an increased incidence of myopia. This is true, for instance, in the case of submariners. They are cooped up for months on end in very small quarters giving them little or no opportunity for distance vision (Kinney et al., 1980). Closer to home, several studies have documented the slow but steady development of myopia among college students (Young, 1981). Also, because myopes tend to set higher academic standards for themselves, they study more diligently and get higher grades in college. We do not mean to imply that myopia guarantees good grades. We're just noting that there is a statistical relation between myopia and academic performance.

Second, myopia can be produced intentionally in lower animals by forcing the animals to do the equivalent of close work. Francis Young, a psychologist at Washington State University, reared newborn monkeys in such a way that there was nothing for them to see more than 50 centimeters from their eyes. Over a 3-year period, these rearing conditions produced very substantial, permanent myopia (Young, 1981).

There are some weak but intriguing associations between refractive error—whether the person is hyperopic or myopic—and personality traits. No one knows how the association develops, but myopes tend to be introverted, inhibited, and conscientious; whereas hyperopes tend to be extroverted, impulsive, and carefree. Again, we're not saying that all myopes are introverted, merely that in large populations there is a statistical association (Young, Singer, and Foster, 1975).

Finally, we must emphasize that in many or most cases, myopia is not caused by too much close work; many people are simply destined by genetics to have eyeballs that are too long for the optics with which their eyeballs are equipped. Although a worldwide problem, myopia tends to be concentrated among certain populations, particularly people of Oriental descent. For example, in Hawaii nearly 80 percent of people of Chinese descent are myopic (Baldwin, 1981).

Surprisingly, many myopes go through childhood and adolescence not realizing that their vision is defective. They may have trouble seeing the blackboard clearly; but the difficulties they experience in school may be mistakenly attributed to poor learning abilities rather than to poor vision.

---

tical power. This enables her to produce focused images of objects, provided her eye is not too hyperopic and provided the objects are not too close. Accommodation makes her lens more convex, thereby increasing its power and allowing well-focused images to be formed on the retina. The middle panel of Figure 2.21 shows how accommodation helps the hyperope bring an object into better focus on the retina.

But the hyperope has to pay a price for having to accommodate constantly. First, there are limits to the amount of accommodation that the human eye can produce. As a result, if she is seriously hyperopic (her eye is much too short), she may be unable to accommodate enough to do close work, such as reading. Second, even if she can accommodate enough to read, accommodation requires maintained muscular effort. If a hyperope has to accommodate very strongly in order to read, after a while she

HYPEROPIA

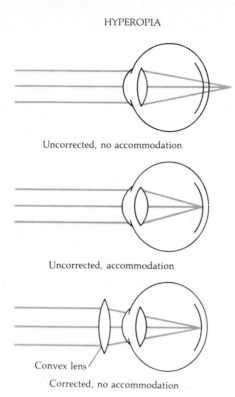

Uncorrected, no accommodation

Uncorrected, accommodation

Convex lens

Corrected, no accommodation

FIGURE 2.21

Mild hyperopia can be overcome by either accommodation or by placing a convex lens in front of the eye.

may develop eyestrain, headaches, and nausea (Daum, 1983).

Fortunately, there are alternatives. Since the hyperopic eye cannot make incoming light converge rapidly enough, the light does not come to a focus soon enough. The problem can be corrected by placing a convex lens in front of the cornea, increasing the total power of the eye. This allows distant objects to be focused properly with little or no accommodation. As a result, the hyperope will need less accommodation when doing close work and will suffer less accommodative strain. The bottom panel of Figure 2.21 illustrates how this added convex lens helps the hyperope see near objects without accommodation.

Presbyopia. Myopia and hyperopia affect many individuals. But the eye's focus can be disturbed in yet another way—a way that *everyone* will sooner or later experience. Accommodation is particularly important when one does close work such as reading. In close work, one must have sharp images of objects from which light is highly divergent, so the eyes must generate more than the usual optical power.

As people get older, though, their ability to accommodate decreases. As Figure 2.22 shows, the trend begins very early in life and continues until about age 70 (Carter, 1982). For the average 20- or 30-year-old, this loss has no practical consequence; people that age still have sufficient ability to accommodate. But upon reaching the mid-forties, the average person can no longer accommodate sufficiently to bring very close objects into focus. Reduced accommodation arises from various sources, including sclerosis of the lens and reduced elasticity of the lens's capsule (Weale, 1982). Severely diminished ability to accommodate is called **presbyopia,** meaning "old sight." In addi-

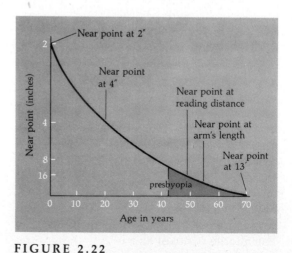

FIGURE 2.22

The near point—the closest distance at which an object can be seen without blur—increases with age.

tion, an old lens takes longer to go through whatever shape changes it is able to manage. This lengthens the time required to change gaze from near to distant objects, and vice versa, causing potential problems in driving and similar tasks.

You have probably seen signs of presbyopia in people who are beyond 40 years of age but have yet to wear glasses or contact lenses. To see clearly, they have to hold reading material at arm's length or even beyond. They may comment that they wished their arms were a bit longer. But a more realistic solution is not too hard; their vision problem can be solved quite easily. A convex lens in front of the eye substitutes for the crystalline lens's diminished ability to become sufficiently convex itself.

Benjamin Franklin was about 47 years old when he found that he could no longer read without spectacles. However, his reading glasses made distant objects too blurred. Constantly having to switch from one pair of glasses to another annoyed him, so Franklin invented bifocals—glasses having two separate lenses in front of each eye, with the more strongly convex lens filling the bottom of the frame. Looking down at reading material, Franklin could take advantage of the extra help given by that lens. Looking slightly upward, he could see the world through a less powerful convex lens, allowing him clear vision of distant objects.

Astigmatism. So far, our discussion of image formation in the eye has emphasized the role of the crystalline lens. The cornea, though, contributes more than the lens toward the formation of a sharply defined retinal image. To be more precise, the cornea contributes about two-thirds of the eye's total optical power, with the crystalline lens contributing the rest (see Box 2.5). As in the case of the lens, the cornea's shape determines its power—the more spherical the cornea, the more strongly will it converge

incoming light. When the cornea is misshapen, the retinal image will be distorted. The most common distortion of shape produces a visual problem called **astigmatism.** You can test yourself for astigmatism by using the spoke pattern in Figure 2.23. Look at the center of the spoke pattern. Without shifting your gaze, note whether some lines look lighter or less black than others. If they do, you may have astigmatism. This condition causes lines of one orientation to be well focused on the retina while lines of another orientation (different by 90 degrees) are poorly focused. If you wear glasses that correct an astigmatism, you may want to take this test twice, once with your correction and again without it. You should note a difference. You can easily determine whether your glasses correct an astigmatism. While looking through one lens, slowly rotate the glasses through a 90-degree angle and note whether the lines in the chart change in appearance. If they do, your glasses contain a correction for astigmatism.

Almost all eyes have some degree of astigmatism, because the cornea is almost never perfectly shaped. But for some people the astigmatism may be severe enough to interfere with perception. Figure 2.24 illustrates how severe astigmatism can distort the appearance of a common, everyday scene. Astigmatism can be corrected by providing a lens that compensates for the cor-

FIGURE 2.23
Chart for testing astigmatism.

BOX 2.5
Seeing Under Water

The next time you go swimming, try this experiment. Hold your hand under water and, with your head out of the water, look at you hand. Now, keeping your hand where it was, put your face into the water with eyes open. Looking at your hand, you'll notice it doesn't look as sharp and clear as it did when your eyes were out of the water. The reason is that your cornea has effectively been eliminated as part of your eyes' optical system.

When light moves from air into the cornea, the path it travels is altered. This alteration or bending of light is called **refraction.** The amount of refraction depends on the difference between air and the material out of which the cornea is made. Under water, light enters your eye not from air but from the water itself. Because of the strong similarity between water and the material out of which the cornea is constructed—a large percentage of the cornea *is* water—light from the water is bent very little as it enters your cornea. Thus when under water, your eye has effectively no cornea. Putting your face under water has reduced the optical power of your eye by about two-thirds, so no wonder you can't see so well. Of the eye's usual optical system, only the crystalline lens remains functional. But there are steps you can take to restore the effectiveness of your cornea under water. A transparent diving mask keeps water away from direct contact with your corneas, allowing them to work just as they did with your face out of water.

Other creatures also need to use their eyes under water but don't have access to face masks. How do they do it? If an animal spends all of its time under water there's no problem; its eye is designed so that the cornea contributes little optical power anyway. The lens is strong enough to do all the necessary light bending. Most fish eyes have extremely powerful convex crystalline lenses—a perfect adaptation to their aquatic world.

But what about animals who spend some time above water and some below? They face the same problem that humans do. We'll consider two particularly interesting creatures who solve this challenge in different ways. Think about the problem that a diving bird faces. Flying along, it looks for fish swimming near the surface of the water below. When it spots a fish, the bird dives into the water and tries to snatch the fish. But as soon as it enters the water, the bird's cornea will lose its optical power, handicapping the bird visually. Some diving birds avoid this effect by using the equivalent of an adjustable face mask. The cormorant, for instance, has a thick but partially transparent eyelid that closes when the bird enters the water. Keeping water from coming into contact with the bird's cornea, the lid preserves much of the cornea's optical power.

But some animals face a situation that is even more demanding optically. Instead of going into and out of the water, these creatures are simultaneously both in and out of the water. The most famous of these creatures is *Anableps anableps,* a freshwater fish found in South and Central America. Because some of its food supply consists of insects above the water, anableps swims along the surface of the river, its eyes half under water and half above water. Anableps has a rather interesting adaptation to this peculiar environmental niche. The upper portion of anableps's eye (the part that is exposed to air) is distinct from the lower portion (the part that is exposed to water). Anableps has two pupils in each eye (one below and the other above the water). In addition, the lower half of its lens is more powerful than the upper half. Anableps is commonly referred to as *cuatro ojos* (Spanish for "four eyes"), but having four eyes rather than two suits anableps's life style very well indeed.

nea's distortion by an equal and opposite distortion of its own.

The previous section detailed the optical components responsible for forming images on the back of the eye. Now we're ready to resume looking at this back portion of the eye—the retina—which serves as the screen upon which the image is cast. You'll be surprised to see that this screen is actually located *behind* a complex network of nerve cells; the carefully formed image has to run an obstacle course through this network before the image can be registered on the photo-receptors. This would be like projecting a motion picture film in a theater in which there are clumps of bushes located in front of the screen. Let's take a look at this odd but apparently successful arrangement.

A SIDEWAYS LOOK AT THE RETINA

Figure 2.25 shows a thin slice of the retina viewed from its side. To create this slice, the retina was carefully removed from the eye, stretched out on a flat surface and cut downward, through the thickness of the retina. (Chemical stains applied in the laboratory make certain types of cells or layers visually prominent.)

The cross section in Figure 2.25 was taken from the center of the retina, the region known as the macula. This cross section is arranged so that if it were actually in an animal's eye, incoming light would first pass through the *top* part of the cross section.

Notice the location of the **photoreceptors,** those specialized neurons that actually capture the light. They are situated toward the *bottom* of the drawing. This means that before light can reach them and initiate the responses that eventuate in vision, light must traverse the entire thickness of the retina. Let's think about the consequences of this seemingly backward layout.

Not all the retina is of the same thickness. Note in Figure 2.25 that the retina thins out in the center of the macula, forming a pit called the **fovea** (in Latin, *fovea* means "pit"). The fovea is not an accident, nor is it a retinal scar, as was once believed (Polyak, 1941). The retina in the foveal neighborhood is thin because some overlying structures have been peeled away. This thinness is crucial for sharp vision. The reason is that as light goes through the retina, some of it is absorbed or scattered before it can reach the photoreceptors. The thinness of the retina's fovea reduces these problems. In fact, this thinness

FIGURE 2.24
The photograph at the right was taken using a lens that simulates astigmatism.
(Glyn Cloyd)

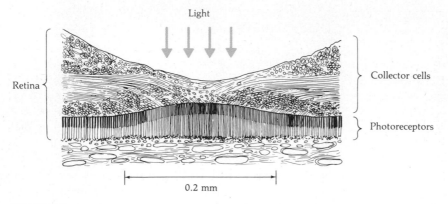

FIGURE 2.25

A sideways view of the central portion of the human retina. (Redrawn from Polyak, 1941)

may be an absolute necessity. Most regions of the retina contain not only photoreceptors but also an entire array of other neurons, **collector cells,** that gather information from the receptors and pass it along to the brain. Normally, collector cells lie directly above the receptors with which they communicate. In the fovea, though, the cell bodies of most collector cells are shunted away from the fovea. These displaced cell bodies produce a circular mound that surrounds the foveal pit.

What would happen if the collector neurons were not displaced? Every foveal photoreceptor has several collector cells associated with it. There are so many photoreceptors in the fovea that in order to accommodate the enormous number of associated collector neurons, the retina would have to be about ten times thicker than it is. Of course, light would have to pass through this heap of neurons on its way to the photoreceptors, seriously impairing one's ability to see (Hughes, 1977).

With this overview of image formation and the retina firmly in mind, let's now consider how the photoreceptor cells in the retina sense the presence of light and initiate the process of seeing.

The Photoreceptors

The human eye contains two major classes of photoreceptors: **rods** and **cones.** In humans, each eye contains about 120 million rods and approximately 8 million cones. Typical examples of the two types of photoreceptors are shown in Figure 2.26. The two types derive their names from their appearance. The tip of a cone is tapered, resembling a pine tree or an empty ice cream cone. In contrast, the tip of a rod has straighter sides and a blunt end—it is rodlike. But their differences go well beyond shape. In fact, functional differences between the two types of photoreceptors determine the life style of their owners. Creatures who have a preponderance of rods in their retinas, such as the owl, are active at night. Creatures who have a preponderance of cones, such as the squirrel, tend to be active only during daylight hours. Because human beings have duplex retinas, containing both types of photoreceptors, their activity is not limited to a fixed part of the day-night cycle.

The eye is often likened to a camera, with the eyes' photoreceptors being analogous to the camera's film. Because human eyes con-

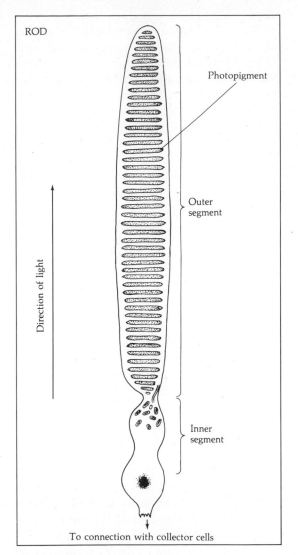

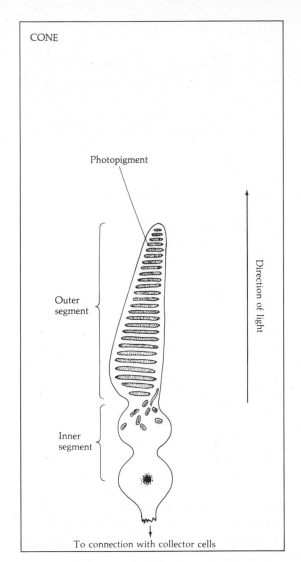

FIGURE 2.26

A single rod photoreceptor and a single cone photoreceptor, magnified approximately 1500×.

tain two types of photoreceptors, they resemble a camera that holds two different kinds of film at once. You know that the type of film you put into a camera—color versus black and white—determines what kind of pictures you get. In the eyes, two different kinds of ''film'' (rods and cones) coexist. As you might imagine, the duplex nature of the retina produces some interesting idiosyncrasies in the way humans see.

Because the kinds of photoreceptors that creatures have determine the properties of their vision—including what they can see, when they can see it, and how it looks to them—we'll have to discuss those photoreceptors before going any further.

THE GEOGRAPHY OF RODS AND CONES

Rods and cones differ not only in their shapes and numbers, but also in their geographical distributions. If you look within a very small portion of retina at the center of the macula, you will find only cones, no rods. If you look far from the macula, you will find predominantly rods, with only a scattering of cones. Our two types of "film," then, are distributed across the eye in very different ways.

Figure 2.27 shows the density of rods and cones in samples taken from various parts of the retina. A sample from the very center of the macula is represented over the center of the horizontal axis; samples taken at various distances, leftward and rightward, from the macula are represented above other points on the horizontal axis. Cones are packed densely in the very center of the human macula; about 150,000 cones occupy an area 1 millimeter square (about the size of this letter: o). Note the systematic decrease in the number and proportion of cones as you move away from the center of the macula, and a corresponding increase in the number of rods. In fact, about 7 millimeters away from the fovea—moving along the retina in a direction toward the nose—rods

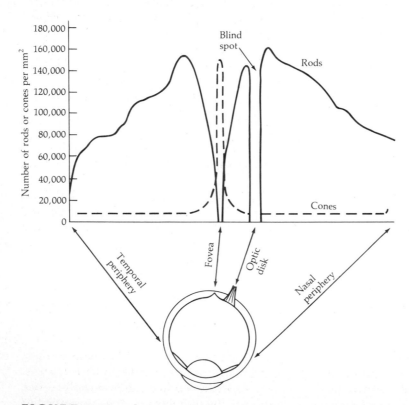

FIGURE 2.27

Distribution of rods and cones over the extent of the retina of the right eye, as seen from above. In the left eye, the nasal and temporal areas of the retina would appear reversed, but the relative distributions of rods and cones would be the same. Note the complete absence of rods within the fovea, where cones abound.

reach a density approximately the same as that found for cones in the center of the macula. Various parts of the retina make their own characteristic contributions to vision because the prevalence of rods and cones differs from one retinal region to another.

Notice the interruption in the plots shown in Figure 2.27. This gap reflects the complete absence of photoreceptors at the optic disk. Because you cannot see without photoreceptors, you are actually "blind" within that area of retina where there are no receptors. We referred earlier to an analogy between the retina and photographic film. In this analogy, the optic disk resembles a defective area of the film, on which the factory neglected to put any light-sensitive chemical. If that defective film were used in a camera and developed, the resulting picture would have a noticeable blank region. Surprisingly though, people almost never notice the large gap that the optic disks create in their retinas. Box 2.6 will help you see what you've been missing all these years.

THE FIRST STEP TOWARD SEEING

Light registers its presence on the retina by interacting with special light-sensitive molecules contained within the photoreceptors. Each of these molecules, called **photopigment,** consists of two components: a very large protein, *opsin,* and another component, derived from vitamin A. The vitamin A derivative is the same for all human photopigments, but the specific nature of the opsin varies, giving different photopigments their characteristic properties.

Normally, the two components are tightly connected, producing a stable molecule that won't break up spontaneously. But when light strikes a molecule, the molecule changes shape, or *isomerizes,* thereby releasing energy. Once this shape change occurs, the photopigment molecule is no longer stable and its two components undergo a series of changes, eventually splitting apart. This

change in shape alters the flow of electric current in and around the photoreceptor. The entire chain of events—from absorption to isomerization to current flow—occurs in less than a thousandth of a second. To appreciate how this chain of events leads to seeing, let's look more closely at the absorption of light by the photoreceptor.

By exposing a photoreceptor to light from various regions of the wavelength spectrum, it is possible to measure how much of that light is actually absorbed and, therefore, stimulates the photoreceptor. When this is done, one finds that for any given receptor there is one wavelength of light that most strongly stimulates the receptor—that is, there is one wavelength to which the receptor is most sensitive. Rods give their biggest response when stimulated with approximately 500 nanometers (the wavelength of light is measured in **nanometers,** billionths of a meter); shorter or longer wavelengths give a diminished response. This response is illustrated in Figure 2.28. In order to appreciate the stimulus to which rods are most sensitive, you should know that under daylight conditions, light of 500 nanometers looks bluish-green.

The corresponding story for cones is somewhat more complicated, since the wavelength at which sensitivity is optimum depends on *which* type of cone is being studied. There are three distinct classes of cones. One is maximally responsive to light of about 440 nanometers, a second class responds best to light of 550 nanometers, and a third class has its peak response at 570 nanometers. The responses of these three classes of cones are shown in Figure 2.29 as functions of the wavelength of stimulating light. Again, to help you understand these stimuli, under daylight conditions light of 440 nanometers looks violet, light of 550 nanometers looks yellowish-green, and light of 570 nanometers looks yellow.

The curves shown in Figures 2.28 and 2.29 underscore an important feature of human

BOX 2.6
A Gap in Your Visual Field

Optic disk is the name given to the place where the optic nerve originates, on the back of the eyeball. Because this region contains no photoreceptors, it cannot support vision—it is literally a blind spot. Note that we're distinguishing between a region defined anatomically, the optic disk, and a region defined perceptually, the blind spot. Before we go on about the blind spot, you may want some proof that it actually exists.

Of course you cannot *see* a blind spot (though you can see an optic disk, using an opthalmoscope). What you can see are the consequences of your blind spot—an object imaged within this blind region of your retina will be invisible. The figure below will help you see the consequences of having a hole in your retina. Making sure that the book is propped up at right angles to the tabletop, view the figure from a distance of about 60 centimeters. Close the left eye and, using your right eye only, stare at the fixation cross in the figure. At this viewing distance,

the black disk to the right of the cross should fall on your optic disk and therefore disappear. Since the location of the optic disk varies from one person to the next, you may have to stare at a point slightly different from the fixation cross.

The demonstration of the existence of a blind spot represented a milestone in understanding the eye. Edmé Mariotte, the French scientist who discovered the blind spot in 1668, did not simply stumble upon it by accident (Mariotte, 1668/1948). Instead, his dissection of human eyes suggested to him that vision might be impaired in the region of the optic disk. This was the first time that anyone had predicted a previously unknown perceptual phenomenon simply from an anatomical observation. From the geometry of the eyeball, including the location of the optic disk, Mariotte correctly predicted where stimuli would have to be placed relative to a fixation point in order for the image to fall on the optic disk. Mariotte also confirmed that there were individual variations

in the precise location of the blind spot, corresponding to individual variations in the optic disk itself.

While you were looking for your own blind spot, you may have noticed something strange. When the black disk disappeared, you didn't see even a shadow or other residue of the disk; the background appeared uniformly white. This is a common phenomenon called *completion* or "filling in." It's been claimed that England's "merry monarch," Charles II, exploited the retina's blind spot to "behead" symbolically members of his court who were in disfavor (Rushton, 1979). After placing them at the right distance from his throne, Charles would adjust his gaze so that the head of his "victim" was imaged on the king's optic disk. Although this is an intriguing story, the more so because Charles II's father had in fact been beheaded, Adam Reeves (1982) describes the story as "a baseless canard" against Charles II. Frankly, we're not sure who's correct.

X

Fixation cross

---

vision. The curves actually separate electromagnetic radiation that one can see ("light") from electromagnetic radiation that one cannot see. For example, one cannot see infrared radiation (wavelengths longer than 700 nanometers) because human photopigments do not respond to wavelengths that long.

The following story dramatizes how your photopigments determine what you can see. During World War II, the United States Navy wanted its sailors to be able to see infrared signal lights that would be invisible to the enemy. Normally, it is impossible to see infrared radiation because, as pointed out earlier, the wavelengths are too long for hu-

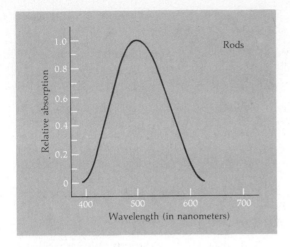

FIGURE 2.28

This graph shows how the amount of light absorbed by rod photoreceptors varies with the wavelength of the light.

man photopigments. To see infrared, the spectral sensitivity of some human photopigment would have to be changed. Vision scientists knew that a derivative of vitamin A was part of every photopigment molecule and that various forms of vitamin A existed. If the retina could be encouraged to use some

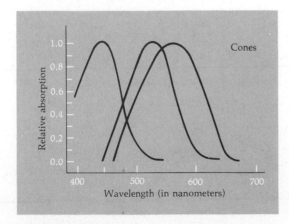

FIGURE 2.29

This graph shows how the amount of light absorbed by each of three types of cone photoreceptors varies with wavelength.

alternative form of vitamin A in its manufacture of photopigments, the spectral sensitivity of those photopigments would be abnormal, perhaps extending into infrared radiation. Human volunteers were fed diets rich in an alternative form of vitamin A but deficient in the usual form. Over several months, the volunteers' vision changed, giving them greater sensitivity to light of longer wavelengths. Though the experiment seemed to be working, it was aborted. The development of the "snooperscope," an electronic device for seeing infrared radiation, made continuation of the experiment unnecessary (Rubin and Walls, 1969). Still, the experiment demonstrates that photopigments select what one can see; changing those photopigments would change one's vision.

To actually see, though, requires more than just a change in the photoreceptors' electrical state. Messages about the presence of light must be transmitted from the receptors to their collector cells and finally to the brain. Cells in the retina communicate with one another by means of chemicals called **transmitter substances.** These transmitter substances bridge the very small gap, or **synapse,** that separates cells. Light-induced variations in the electrical state of a photoreceptor cause changes in the amount of transmitter substance that the photoreceptor secretes. Because changes in amount of transmitter substance are related to the number of isomerizations, the concentration of this chemical communicates to a collector cell how much light is falling on the photoreceptor. Figure 2.30 summarizes the chain of events that we've been describing.

Summary and Preview

With messages well on their way to the retina's collector cells, it's time to pause, take stock, and see where we are going. The

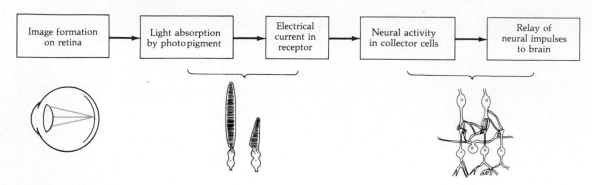

FIGURE 2.30
The chain of events discussed in this chapter.

chapter has laid out the basic design of the human eyeball, emphasizing the good fit between its structure and the job it must do. Because vision depends on an interaction between light and the eye, we also considered how light itself manages to capture information about the environment, information that is conveyed by light. This led us to a discussion of the eyeball's optical characteristics and various common imperfections in those characteristics. The chapter ended with the capture of light by photopigment molecules and the first step toward seeing—photoreceptor responses that are communicated to other neurons in the retina and eventually to the brain. The next chapter follows these messages as they pass from one retinal neuron to the next. You already know that your vision mirrors the properties of your photoreceptors; the next chapter will show you how other elements in the retina also control what you see.

Chapter 3

The Eye and Seeing

At the end of the preceding chapter, light was being absorbed by a photoreceptor, which then triggered the release of a chemical transmitter substance. We characterized these events as "the first step toward vision." This chapter picks up the story where the preceding one left off.

Each photoreceptor has a simple job to do: gauge the amount of light it is receiving. This results in about 130 million separate messages, each one specifying the light level falling on the tiny region of the eye occupied by a photoreceptor. This array of messages is then passed on to other cells in the retina, collector cells, as we called them. These collector cells have a more complicated assignment: to reorganize those millions of raw messages into a more manageable, useful form. After all, one uses one's eyes to see *objects*, including animals and people, not points of light. The collector cells facilitate this process by translating the raw messages they receive into

descriptions of visually important information about edges, textures, and thus objects.

The extraction of biologically relevant information seems like a worthwhile goal for the retina. However, before one can gauge whether the system works toward that goal one must be able to define *what* one means by "information about objects." From the standpoint of vision, what defines an object? And what must the retina do in order to reorganize the photoreceptors' raw messages into information about objects?

Think back to our discussion of image formation in the preceding chapter (p. 43). There we noted that by reflecting and absorbing light, objects "sculpt" the light that eventually falls on the retina. As a result, when it reaches the retina, the amount of light reflected from some object differs from the amount of light reflected from the object's surroundings. The key word is "differs." If one had some way of

61

identifying when neighboring retinal regions were being illuminated by *different* amounts of light, one would be on the way to identifying an object's edges or borders—places where the reflected light changes. If one is interested in objects and edges, one is *not* interested in regions of the retina over which the light level remains constant. Homogeneous or uniformly illuminated regions of the retina probably do not represent the image of an edge. To identify an edge, the retina needs to note where there are *differences* between the light levels at adjacent locations. As you'll see, many retinal cells are designed to do precisely that: respond to differences between adjacent levels of light.

Our immediate goal, then, is to understand how the retina condenses and reorganizes the multitude of messages supplied by the photoreceptors. Then we shall want to consider how the condensation and reorganization actually affect the way one sees. There are various approaches that we could take to the retina's reorganization of information. Since the network of collector cells plays a major role in this reorganization, we could work through the details of how one stage after another of collector cells alters the message it has received. However, our primary interest is in the messages sent to the brain by the retina. Therefore, let's take a more direct approach. For the moment, let's skip to those collector cells, the **retinal ganglion cells,** that are responsible for the last stage of processing within the eye itself.

During our discussion, keep in mind that although they do respond to visual stimulation, the ganglion cells themselves do not absorb light; they are not photoreceptors. Ganglion cells process neural information that other cells had collected directly from the photoreceptors. Without input from these other collector cells, the ganglion cells would be blind to everything happening in the visual world.

Moreover, you must realize that ganglion cells can signal the outcome of their processing only by generating **action potentials,** brief electrical discharges carried by the nerve fibers of the ganglion cells to more central visual stages within the brain. So whatever a ganglion cell has to "say" about a visual stimulus must be expressed using this one-"word" vocabulary. This restriction actually applies to *all* further stages of visual processing—neurons talk to one another in a language composed entirely of action potentials, or neural impulses as they are sometimes called. Particular neurons speak up with a burst of impulses only upon the appearance of particular types of visual stimuli. By virtue of their early position in this chain of visual processing, retinal ganglion cells set this neural dialogue in motion. Let's examine now what the ganglion cells have to say.

The Retinal Ganglion Cells

The human eye contains roughly 1 million retinal ganglion cells. Comparing this figure to the 130 million receptors in the eye, you know from the outset that ganglion cells must be condensing the raw messages from the receptors. Imagine you are handed a 1,000-word essay and told to reduce it to 8 words—without losing the essentials of its message. To meet this editing challenge, you must identify the essay's major points and then rephrase them, condensing so as to retain the essence of the original. The retinal ganglion cells face the same kind of problem: they must collate messages from the more numerous photoreceptors and summarize those messages in a biologically relevant way. How do the ganglion cells accomplish this job?

The most direct way to find out is to determine what kinds of visual stimuli are best able to activate these cells. Figure 3.1 illustrates how such stimuli are identified. An

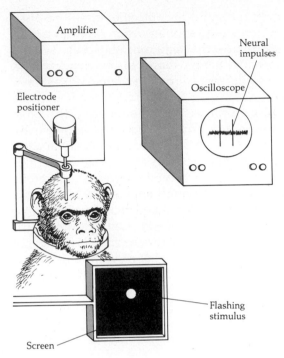

FIGURE 3.1

Laboratory setup for recording action potentials from single neurons. The placement of the recording electrode governs which stage of the visual nervous system will be examined. In the case shown, the electrode would pick up action potentials generated in the retinal ganglion cells.

experimental animal, a monkey in this case, is shown facing a screen. A tiny, fine-tipped wire called a **microelectrode** is surgically placed into the part of the visual system under study, in this case, the retina of the eye. The probe can be positioned close enough to an individual ganglion cell so that the electrode picks up the action potentials (neural impulses) from just that cell. You can then monitor the number of impulses generated by this single cell, and try to influence the cell's activity level by presenting various sorts of visual stimuli on the screen. This technique, called **single cell recording,** has been successfully employed to determine what kinds of visual stimuli it takes to

activate cells at different stages within the visual system. Here we are interested in the results found in the retina. In effect, we wish to ask the ganglion cells "What sort of visual stimulus do you like best?"—where "like best" is shorthand for "respond most strongly to." What will be the answer?

Before even getting a chance to present *anything* on the screen, you discover that the ganglion cell is already active; your electrode is picking up an irregular but persistent chatter of action potentials from the cell. This spontaneous activity continues even when the monkey is in complete darkness. To enable you to visualize this neural activity, the occurrence of individual action potentials can be plotted over time; this is done in Figure 3.2. In each of the three panels, the small vertical lines are meant to represent single action potentials from one retinal

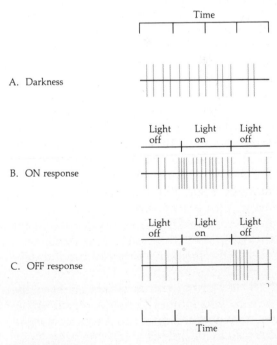

FIGURE 3.2

Neural activity (shown as vertical lines) of retinal ganglion cells. See the text for a full discussion.

ganglion cell; time is traced out along the horizontal axis. Looking at panel A, you see the impulses occurring in the absence of visual stimulation—this is the spontaneous activity of the cell.

Since it is spontaneously active when no light is present, the cell must signal the presence of light (a change from no light) by a change in its level of activity. Suppose your job is to discover what it takes to produce that *change* from spontaneous activity. Knowing that photoreceptors (the ultimate source of input to the ganglion cells) are small, you start by moving a small spot of light around over the screen. By doing this you are moving the spot of light around over the monkey's retina, stimulating photoreceptors wherever you move the spot. So in effect, your job is to search for an area of the retina where the image of the spot of light will influence the ganglion cell's level of activity.

As we proceed with our example, it is very important to keep the following in mind: different regions on the screen in front of the monkey correspond to different areas on the retina of the monkey. To maintain this correspondence, it is necessary for the monkey's eye to remain perfectly still. If the monkey moved its eye around during the experiment, you could never be certain where your spot of light would fall on its retina. By immobilizing the eye, you can specify the retinal position of your spot of light in terms of its location on the screen. You might know, for instance, that positioning the spot in the center of the screen places the image of the spot on the center of the monkey's eye, in the macula. With this in mind, let's start our experiment.

By exploring with the spot of light on the screen, you stumble upon a region of the retina where the spot causes an increase in the activity of the cell you're recording from. Concentrating on this region, you discover that the cell gives a burst of impulses when you turn the spot on within this area; when you turn the light off, the cell's activity quickly settles back to the background (spontaneous) level. This outcome is shown in panel B of Figure 3.2. Next, you test a neighboring area of the retina in the same way. Now you find just the opposite result—turning the light on causes the activity level to drop *below* the background level. But when you turn the light off, the cell emits a short, vigorous burst of impulses. This second outcome is illustrated in panel C. So this cell responds in two antagonistic ways, depending on where you place the light spot on the screen and, hence, on the retina. In one region it responds to an *increase* in light, while in the other it responds to a *decrease* in light. To distinguish these two kinds of responses, let's call the first an "ON response" and the second an "OFF response."

While still recording from this same cell, suppose you now test at other, nearby locations on the retina. You find that ON responses can be elicited from anywhere within a restricted, circular region; in fact, enlarging your spot so it just fills this circular region produces a very vigorous response. The regions giving an OFF response, however, form a ring that completely surrounds the circular ON region. So the same spot of light has opposite, or antagonistic, effects in the center and in the surround. Labeling these two regions using plus signs (ON) and minus signs (OFF), the composite looks like a small circle of plus signs surrounded by a ring of minus signs, as shown in panel A of Figure 3.3.

Light placed anywhere *outside* this donut-shaped composite has no influence whatsoever on this cell's activity. In other words, only light falling within this restricted, concentrically shaped area of the retina is registered by this ganglion cell. This area con-

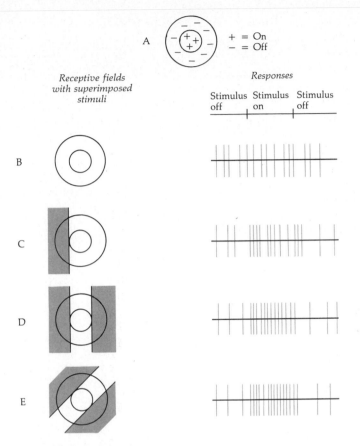

FIGURE 3.3
A single ON-center retinal ganglion cell (A) responding to uniform illumination (B), to a dark/light edge (C), to a vertical bar of light (D), and to an oblique bar of light (E).

stitutes that cell's **receptive field**—the patch of retina within which a cell's activity may be influenced.*

The concept of a receptive field is extremely important for understanding visual processing. As you will come to appreciate in this chapter and the next one, the receptive field serves as a kind of template with which a cell gauges the pattern of light falling within a restricted area of the retina. In

*The term "receptive field" was coined by H. K. Hartline (1940) in his classic work on frog retinal ganglion cells.

effect, a visual stimulus must fit into the receptive field in order to activate a cell.

To illustrate what we mean, let's consider the receptive field mapped out in panel A of Figure 3.3. Can you picture an optimal visual stimulus for this cell, one that would produce the most vigorous increase in neural activity? First, imagine illuminating the entire retina, in effect filling the cell's receptive field with light. As shown in panel B of Figure 3.3, the cell gives only a weak response to uniform illumination. This is because such a stimulus produces opposite effects in the center and surround; the two antagonistic regions compete with one another, resulting in a near stand-off. This interaction between antagonistic regions is often called **lateral inhibition.**

Now imagine what happens when an edge is positioned in the manner shown in panel C. The ON-center portion of the receptive field receives an increase in light, its preferred stimulus, while a good portion of the surround receives a reduced level of light, its preferred stimulus. The net result is a vigorous response from the cell. As panels D and E show, the cell would also respond well to bars of light positioned appropriately within the receptive field. Incidentally, because these center/surround areas are nearly always concentrically arranged, ganglion cells will respond well regardless of whether the edge is oriented vertically, horizontally, or diagonally. The orientation of an edge or bar is irrelevant so long as the edge or bar is positioned appropriately within the receptive field.

This antagonistic arrangement of center and surround within the receptive field enables the retinal ganglion cell to perform a major editing job. Lateral inhibition has enabled the cell to condense the messages from a patch of photoreceptors into a single statement: "I detect a light/dark boundary." By accenting the *difference* in light levels on adjacent areas of the retina, the cell has begun the process of extracting perceptually relevant information.

Although the cell just described does signal differences in light level, it monitors a very limited region of the retina. To learn more about the editing process initiated by retinal ganglion cells in general, you need to study other cells. You do this by moving the microelectrode, to record action potentials from another cell, and repeating the steps outlined above. We can now summarize what you will discover from studying cell after cell in this fashion.

RECEPTIVE FIELD LAYOUT

Nearly all ganglion cells will have concentrically arranged receptive fields, composed of a center and a surround that respond in an antagonistic fashion. Some of those cells will have ON centers and OFF surrounds, like the receptive field illustrated in Figure 3.3. (Box 3.1 discusses one interesting perceptual phenomenon thought to result from these cells.) Other cells will have just the opposite layout, with an OFF center and an ON surround. An example of this latter type of cell is shown in Figure 3.4.

There are about as many ON-center cells as there are OFF-center cells; both types, you can see, respond best to light/dark boundaries. The receptive fields of the ON-center cells and OFF-center cells overlap to make up a mosaic covering the entire retina. As a result, whenever light falls on a limited patch of the retina, that light is bound to affect a number of retinal ganglion cells of both types, producing opposite effects in the two. Don't imagine, though, that these opposite effects cancel one another; at higher stages of the visual system, information from ON-center and OFF-center cells remains segregated, allowing information from both types to be used (Wässle, Peichl, and Boycott, 1981).

We should mention, however, that a small percentage of ganglion cells do not exhibit separate ON and OFF regions. Instead, these cells have a *single,* large circular field that

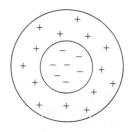

FIGURE 3.4
A receptive field of an OFF-center retinal ganglion cell.

BOX 3.1

Blacker than Black

Because of its spontaneous activity, an ON-center cell sends the brain a stronger message when no light falls in its receptive field than it does when its surround alone is illuminated. This curious state of affairs suggests the possibility that some light may actually appear darker than no light at all. In fact, surrounding a dim area with a sufficiently intense light does make that dim area appear darker than an area that contains no light whatever. Probably the intense surround drives the activity of ON-center ganglion cells *below* their spontaneous levels, signaling the brain that something blacker than black is present (Brown and Mueller, 1965).

Spontaneous activity shows up in everyday life, too. Think about what it's like to wake up in the middle of the night in an absolutely dark room. Usually the room doesn't appear totally black. In fact, many people experience dim, illusory, swirling lights, the result of spontaneous activity in the visual system (Hurvich and Jameson, 1966).

Some artists exaggerate discontinuities in intensity in order to highlight the outline of figures in their work. If an artist wants to create the deepest possible black region in some painting, he or she must do more than simply use black paint. Even if that black paint reflected no light at all (which isn't really possible with paint), receptive fields in which the black paint was imaged would still be sending spontaneous messages to the brain. To reduce those messages to a minimum, the artist surrounds the black paint with an area of white or other light-colored paint. The contrast between the two areas intensifies the blackness produced by the dark paint. Floyd Ratliff (1972) gives a good introduction to the uses of lightness illusions in art.

Mature artists are not the only people who take advantage of lightness illusions; parents and children do, too. Many children have a hard time falling asleep unless conditions are just right. Not only must it be past their appointed bedtime, but also conditions outside must confirm that it is bedtime—it must *look* sufficiently dark outside. Some wise parents take advantage of a lightness illusion to hasten bedtime—as some children realize. The Finnish-American poet Anselm Hollo captured this idea by putting the following words into the mouth of a 4-year-old:

switch on the light
so it gets dark outside
and we can go
to bed.

(Hollo, 1977, p. 30)

gives both an ON response *and* an OFF response, as though center and surround had been combined within the same area. These unusual cells seem ill-suited for edge detection and, instead, may have something to do with signaling the general level of retinal illumination.*

RECEPTIVE FIELD SIZE

The sizes of receptive fields vary systematically with retinal location (Wiesel and Hubel, 1960; de Monasterio and Gouras, 1975).

Receptive fields in the center of the retina, within the macula, are quite small, with some on the order of .01 millimeters. Cells with these centrally placed receptive fields monitor tiny areas of the visual world wherever the monkey is looking. Moving away from the macula into the periphery of the retina, the receptive fields grow increasingly larger; in fact, 10 millimeters away from the fovea, receptive field centers may be as large as 0.5 millimeters, fifty times larger than their foveal counterparts. Cells with these peripherally placed receptive fields collect information from larger areas of the retina. Figure 3.5 graphs the relation between receptive field size and retinal location. The horizon-

*As a group, these cells are arbitrarily referred to as W cells; we will consider their more conventional counterparts, X and Y cells, shortly.

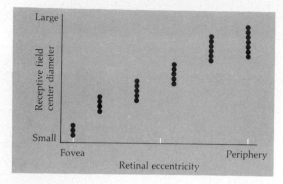

FIGURE 3.5
Graph showing how the sizes of receptive field centers increase with distance from the fovea. The size of the entire receptive field is larger than just the center diameter, since the entire receptive field consists of a center and a surround.

tal axis represents the retinal location around which the receptive field was centered; "fovea" stands for the center of the macula. The vertical axis is the diameter of the center portion of the receptive field. Note that with increasing **eccentricity**—deviation from the center of the retina—the size of receptive fields tends to increase.

The same graph actually reveals another important fact. At all eccentricities, we have data for more than just a single receptive field (more than one data point corresponding to a single location along the horizontal axis). Comparing data collected at the same eccentricity, you see that not all receptive fields at that eccentricity have exactly the same size. Because these differences occur at a single locality on the retina, the phenomenon is known as *local variation*. So the sizes of receptive fields differ in two ways: first, they vary with retinal eccentricity; second, they vary locally.

Think what this variation in receptive field size means for the sort of stimulus that would be best suited to activate a particular cell. As shown in Figure 3.6, there is one bar

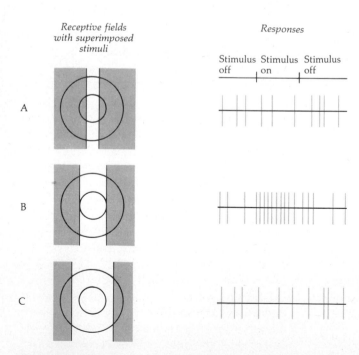

FIGURE 3.6
A single ON-center receptive field responding to bars of light of varying width.

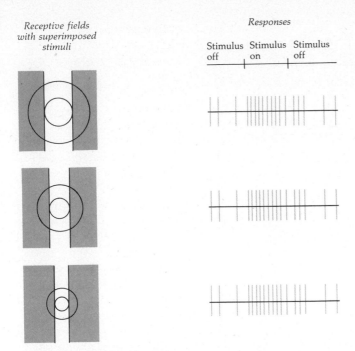

Receptive fields
with superimposed
stimuli

Responses

Stimulus Stimulus Stimulus
off   on   off

FIGURE 3.7
Three ON-center receptive fields with different-sized receptive fields responding to bars of light of matching width.

width size (panel B) that elicits the best response from that cell; bars smaller (panel A) or larger (panel C) than this produce a less than optimum response. As you can see in Figure 3.7, cells with small receptive fields will respond best to small objects, while those with large receptive fields will prefer larger objects. This principle suggests that analysis of object size may be inaugurated in the retina.

X AND Y CELLS

Some ganglion cells respond in a *sustained* manner for as long as objects remain properly positioned within their receptive fields (see the top timeline in Figure 3.8). Cells giving this kind of sustained response are sometimes called **X cells.** Other ganglion cells respond more *transiently*, giving a burst of impulses when the object is first presented and then again when it is removed (see the bottom timeline in Figure 3.8). These are called **Y cells.** The two categories of cells, X and Y, differ in several ways that are potentially important for vision. For instance, X cells tend to be concentrated in and around the fovea, where vision is the sharpest. Y cells are more uniformly distributed throughout the retina (Fukada, 1971). At any given retinal eccentricity, receptive fields of Y cells are about twice the size of the fields of X cells (Enroth-Cugell and Robson, 1966). In addition to their receptive field properties, the two types of cells look different from one another. Seen under a microscope, Y cells are larger than X cells, and the portion of the cell carrying information out of the retina, the **axon,** is thicker in Y cells (Cleland, Levick, and Wässle, 1975). This means therefore that neural impulses travel more rapidly to the brain over Y-cell axons, since the conduction velocity of neural impulses increases with axon thickness.

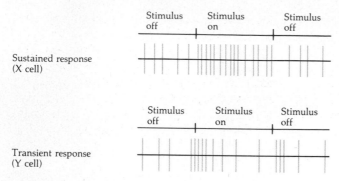

FIGURE 3.8

Response of two different retinal ganglion cells to presentation of a stimulus. One cell (upper panel) responds in a sustained fashion so long as the stimulus is present. The other cell (bottom panel) responds in a transient fashion at the onset of stimulation.

All these differences between X and Y cells—their retinal distributions, receptive field sizes, and conduction velocities—strongly suggest that the two cell types may be involved in different aspects of visual perception. Some people believe that Y cells are tailor-made to signal quick movements of objects, whereas X cells specify the texture and fine details of those objects (Woodhouse and Barlow, 1982). For instance, according to this theory, your Y cells would be able to detect a faint, dark blob scurrying across your kitchen floor. Noticing this vague event out of the corner of your eye, you would automatically direct your gaze in that direction, enabling your X cells to analyze the object's details, such as its size, shape, and number of legs.

The idea that vision divides its labors between two systems, X and Y cells, is quite popular nowadays. However, some researchers, notably Peter Lennie (1980) of the University of Rochester, are skeptical whether the division should be drawn between motion perception (Y cells) and pattern perception (X cells). So at the moment we cannot confidently assign specific functional roles to X and Y cells. Nonetheless, the very clear anatomical and physiological differences between the two cell types strongly argue that such roles do exist.

This completes, then, our abbreviated survey of the ganglion cells of the retina. By examining the workings of the retinal ganglion cells, several important things have been learned about the processing of visual information within the eye. You now know that this processing begins with the photoreceptors—they act like an array of tiny photocells, each specifying the level of light falling within the purview of the photoreceptor. These 130 million messages about light intensity are then passed on to a complex network of collector cells that integrate information from groups of neighboring photoreceptors. The results of this integration are conveyed to the retinal ganglion cells. Because of the center/surround organization of their receptive fields, the vast majority of ganglion cells are designed to detect differences in light level, or *contrast* as it is called; these cells are much less concerned with the overall level of light. This kind of local receptive field analysis is performed over the entire retina by the 1 million or so ganglion cells in the eye. Hence, everything you see must have registered its presence within this retinal machinery. The particulars of this machinery necessarily influence the *way* you see. There is no other route to visual perception but through the retinal ganglion cells.

From here on we'll be trying to relate the properties of vision to events that take place in the retina. Usually the events to which we'll refer occur at the level of the retinal ganglion cells, although sometimes these events occur earlier, in the photoreceptors themselves. It's important that you understand what we mean when we claim that some property of vision is caused by the idiosyncrasies of some retinal cell. We are *not* saying that conscious visual perception occurs in the retina. Most visual scientists think that the process called "vision" actually takes place somewhere in the brain.

Instead, we're saying that events in the retina *shape* vision by emphasizing some information (such as changes) and by de-emphasizing other information (such as uniformities). For example, because retinal ganglion cells respond very strongly to edges or discontinuities in illumination, visual experience itself reflects that bias. That's what we mean by "creating new information." Also, if no retinal cells at all responded to stimuli whose wavelengths were longer than 700 nanometers, the brain would get no information about such stimuli. That's what we mean by "excluding some information." Even though sight occurs in the brain, blindness to these wavelengths was preordained in the retina. Brindley (1970) gives a more detailed discussion of the logical basis for attributing some perceptual event to the behavior of some physiological process.

Perceptual Consequences of Center/Surround Antagonism

The preceding section emphasized the antagonism between the center and the surround of a retinal ganglion cell's receptive field. The net response of such a cell is the sum of these two opposed influences. This arrangement, which helps to reorganize the receptors' raw information, gives your perception a special flavor. Let's consider two perceptual manifestations of that antagonism between center and surround.

MACH BANDS

Ernst Mach was an Austrian physicist and philosopher who made important contributions to a number of scientific disciplines during the last part of the nineteenth century and the early part of the twentieth. (The speed of sound is given as Mach numbers.) We're concerned here with just one small part of his work. Mach was interested in the connection between light's intensity and the resulting sensation. His basic approach was to create various patterns out of paper and then to note how the perception of lightness varied from one part of the pattern to another. Many of the patterns that Mach developed produced percepts that could not easily be explained by the corresponding distribution of light reflected from those patches of paper.

Mach had the great insight that these idiosyncrasies of perception were caused by antagonistic influences within the retina.* Because we have much more information about retinal physiology and anatomy than was available to Mach, we are able to infer that these idiosyncrasies are caused by the retinal ganglion cells' center/surround antagonism.

The top portion of Figure 3.9 shows one of the kinds of patterns Mach developed. The graph below the pattern specifies the actual distribution of light intensity in the pattern. The horizontal axis of the graph

---

*Floyd Ratliff (1965) gives an excellent, highly readable account of Mach's life and work.

represents position in the pattern; the vertical axis shows how much light the pattern reflects at that position. As you move from left to right, the graph shows the level of intensity in the pattern increasing in a stepwise fashion. Thus the pattern really consists of a number of stripes, each of uniform intensity and each giving way abruptly to another level.

When you look at the pattern itself, though, you'll notice some things that are not consistent with the graph. In particular, the lightness of each stripe does not appear uniform. Take one of the stripes in the middle as an example. One edge—near the stripe's left-hand, darker neighbor—seems extra dark, while the other edge—near the stripe's right-hand, lighter neighbor—seems extra light. In other words, the *lightness* varies even though the *intensity* does not. Most people describe the edges of each stripe as having bands, extra dark and extra light regions. These bands—**Mach bands**—are named for the first person to study them systematically.

These bands, no matter how vivid they may seem, are illusory; they don't exist on the paper, only in your head. To understand where they come from, consider how your retinal ganglion cells respond to such a pattern of stripes. When you look at the pattern in the upper part of Figure 3.9, a distribution of light is produced on your retina, similar to the distribution shown by the graph in the lower part of Figure 3.9. This distribution of light is broad enough so that it extends across the receptive fields of many retinal ganglion cells. To simplify the discussion, consider only three adjacent stripes from the pattern (see Figure 3.10). Suppose that the image of the three stripes falls on some small number, say five, of ON-center receptive fields (though this assumption is not crucial to our point). These ganglion cells are each responsible for telling your brain about the intensity of light falling within their

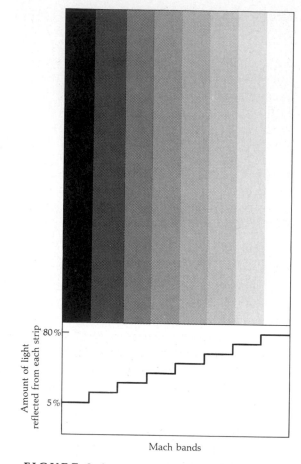

FIGURE 3.9

The lightness of each stripe in the pattern (upper portion of the figure) varies even though the intensity of each stripe is constant (lower portion of figure).

individual receptive fields. What sorts of messages would the brain get from these cells when they are stimulated by the pattern shown in the upper part of Figure 3.9?

To see what response any cell would give, we must weigh how much light falls in each of its two regions. (Remember the convention: "plus" indicates an ON region, "minus" indicates an OFF region.) Let's take the three easiest ones first. Receptive field A (leftmost ganglion cell in Figure 3.10) re-

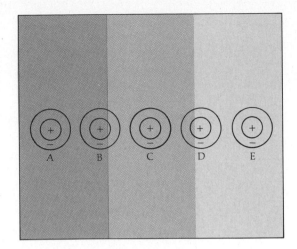

FIGURE 3.10
Possible neural explanation of Mach bands.

ceives the least light, field E the most, and field C an intermediate amount of light. The responses produced by each cell will be proportional to the amount of light falling within their receptive fields. So the stripe "seen" by A will seem the dimmest, that "seen" by E the brightest, with the stripe "seen" by C appearing intermediate to the two. That leaves B and D as the interesting cases.

Receptive field B's center is stimulated by the same level of light as A's. Their respective surrounds, however, are *differentially* stimulated. All of A's surround is dimly illuminated, thereby producing little antagonism to combat the response produced by the center. Although the left part of B's surround is similarly illuminated, the right part is stimulated by the higher light level of the middle stripe. As a result, the surround of B generates *more* antagonism than does the surround of A, *diminishing* the overall response of B to a level below that of A. Consequently, the region "seen" by B appears darker than that "seen" by A—B creates a dark Mach band.

Now consider D and E. The net response from D will be larger than that from E because D's surround is partially stimulated

by the reduced light from the center stripe, rather than by the higher level from the right-hand stripe. As a result, D's surround generates *less* antagonism to its center's response, yielding a net response that is *greater* than that from E. So the region "seen" by D will appear lighter than that "seen" by E—D creates a light Mach band.

This treatment of Mach bands just barely scratches the surface. The scientific literature on this fascinating topic is quite large and, as Mach himself suspected it would, has taught us much about the human retina. One important lesson that you should take away with you is the distinction between intensity on one hand, and lightness, on the other. **Intensity** is a physical variable, something that a light meter could measure; **lightness** is a psychological, or perceptual, variable, whose measurement requires a visual system.* Often, the two—intensity and lightness—go together, with more intense stimuli appearing lighter. But Mach bands show that the correlation is far from perfect. Although intensity changes in a stepwise fashion, lightness does not follow along. Of course, this discrepancy arises from the processing of contour information through a system that has center/surround antagonism. And there is an advantage to such a system. By intensifying the contours demarcating objects, the process that produces Mach bands makes objects more conspicuous.

*The terms "brightness" and "lightness" are sometimes used interchangeably, but technically speaking the two should be differentiated. Unfortunately, there is disagreement concerning exactly how to draw this distinction. For our purposes, the term "brightness" will be used to refer to the perceptual effect produced by looking at a source that *emits* light; for instance, we may speak of the brightness of a room light or the brightness of the sun. We will also use "brightness" to refer to the perceived level of illumination produced by an emitting source; for instance, we may speak of the brightness of the sky. "Lightness" will be used to refer to the perceptual effect produced by looking at an object or surface that *reflects* light. Thus, we may speak of the lightness of a piece of paper or the lightness of the moon. Intensity, a physical variable, can refer to either emitted or reflected light.

Mach bands are not the only way the retina's center/surround antagonism manifests itself. Let's consider another interesting manifestation.

THE HERMANN GRID

Several years ago, one of America's outstanding institutions of higher education published a particularly handsome catalog of its course offerings (Figure 3.11). When the catalog was distributed, eye doctors were deluged by callers complaining that when they looked at the cover of the university's catalog, spots mysteriously appeared before their eyes. The spots were particularly worrisome because when the people tried to look

Northwestern

Undergraduate Study 1981-83

FIGURE 3.11
The attractive cover of a catalog from one of America's outstanding institutions of higher education.

directly at one to make sure it wasn't imaginary, the dot would disappear. You can experience this for yourself. Looking at Figure 3.11, you'll see grey spots in most of the intersections between a horizontal and a vertical white stripe. Yet, when you move your eyes to look *directly* at one of these ghosts, it disappears as if it knew you were coming.

On checking into the matter, the eye doctors were able to reassure their callers. The ghostly spots are as normal as they are puzzling, a natural result of having retinal ganglion cell receptive fields with center/surround organization. Actually, the spots that had people worried were first described more than a century ago. The pattern inadvertently used by the university resembled what is known as a **Hermann grid,** first described in the nineteenth century by Ludimar Hermann, a German physiologist.

More traditional versions of Hermann's grid are shown in Figure 3.12. Looking at the left-hand grid, you'll notice dark spots located in most of the intersections of white horizontal and vertical stripes. Looking at the middle grid (a photographic negative of the other), you'll notice light spots in most of the intersections of black horizontal and vertical stripes. Looking at the right-hand grid (a smaller version of the one on the left), you'll see dark spots at *all* of the intersections. Although they are vivid, every one of these spots is illusory. Why, then, does one experience them? These illusory spots are the product of center/surround antagonism within receptive fields of retinal ganglion cells.

We'll make use of ON-center receptive fields to explain why you see spots in the left-hand grid. Two questions must be answered. First, why are the spots that you see located only at intersections between horizontal and vertical stripes, not elsewhere? Second, why do you *not* see a spot located within the intersection you look di-

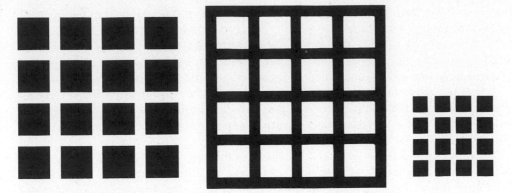

FIGURE 3.12
Several more conventional versions of Hermann grids.

rectly at? To answer the first question we've drawn receptive fields on Hermann's grid (Figure 3.13). This allows you to compare how the retinal image of the grid would affect the two receptive fields shown, one being stimulated by an intersection and the other stimulated by part of a white stripe that is not at an intersection.

To determine the response of either retinal ganglion cell, we must analyze how each of its components—center and surround—would be affected by the grid pattern. Assume that a viewer maintains her gaze on the spot labeled "fixation point." Now, note that the centers of both receptive fields receive the same amount of light, but the surrounds receive different amounts. Remember that light falling in an OFF portion of a receptive field reduces that cell's activity. This means that the cell whose receptive field is centered *on* the intersection will respond less than the cell whose receptive field is centered *between* intersections. Consequently, between intersections the white stripes will look comparatively lighter. Since the reduced response is confined to cells with re-

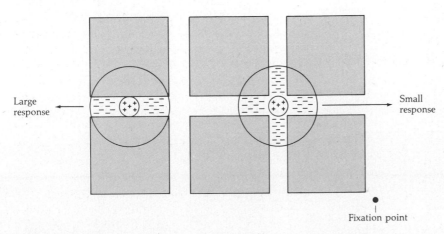

Large response ←

Small response →

Fixation point

FIGURE 3.13
A possible neural explanation of Hermann grids.

ceptive fields centered on the intersections, one experiences dimming at such locales— gray spots.

Why, though, does one not see a spot within the intersection one is looking directly at? Recall that receptive fields vary in size according to their eccentricity, the smallest receptive fields being in the macula. When you look directly at an intersection, you are using receptive fields whose centers and surrounds are so small that *both* fit completely within the width of a stripe. We've illustrated this in Figure 3.14. Assume that a person fixates the right-hand intersection of the grid. As you can see, these small receptive fields all receive the same amount of stimulation within their centers and surrounds. Consequently, all the cells around the region of fixation will give the same response—whether on the intersection or not. As a result there will not be any local dimming at the intersection.

To test your understanding of these ideas, see if you can apply this same line of reasoning to the middle grid in Figure 3.12. Now repeat this exercise using OFF-center receptive fields for both grids. Finally, see if you can explain why spots are seen at *every* intersection, including the one you are

fixating, in the right-hand grid in Figure 3.12.

Mach bands and Hermann grids, besides being entertaining, are also valuable tools for exploring human vision. Some visual scientists, most notably the German psychologist Lothar Spillmann, have cleverly exploited variations of Hermann's grid to study the characteristics of human receptive fields perceptually (Spillmann, 1971; Jung and Spillmann, 1970; Jung, 1973).

One is routinely confronted with objects in the environment that affect one's visual systems much as Mach bands and Hermann grids do (Ratliff, 1984). The borders of these objects appear similarly exaggerated, though usually not as blatantly as the ones illustrated in Figures 3.9 and 3.12. You should realize that borders set objects apart from one another, which is precisely why retinal processing concentrates on signaling information about borders. Mach bands and Hermann grids simply highlight the presence of processing machinery that one relies on all the time. This reliance is further underscored by other important visual consequences of antagonism between center and surround. To see what these are, let's perform two more experiments with retinal ganglion cells.

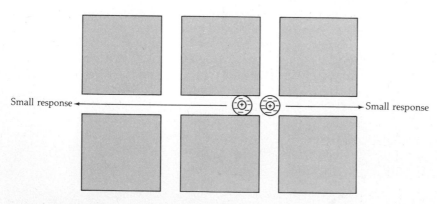

FIGURE 3.14

A possible neural explanation for the absence of Hermann grids at the point of fixation.

TWO MORE CENTER/SURROUND EXPERIMENTS

In the first experiment, let's compare how a retinal ganglion cell responds when its center is stimulated by light of different intensities while its surround is subjected, in turn, to no illumination, some illumination, and finally, intense illumination. Suppose that you are recording from a retinal ganglion cell of the ON-center variety. Finding the cell's receptive field center, you focus a small spot of light within just that area, avoiding the surround altogether. You turn the test spot on for a second and record the resulting number of impulses. After repeating this procedure with test spots of varying intensities, you plot the results as the curve labeled *A* in Figure 3.15. The graph's vertical axis represents the number of impulses; the horizontal axis represents the light intensity that evoked each response.

At the extreme left of the horizontal axis, you plot the spontaneous activity of the cell—the activity when no light is present at all. The graph reveals that several different very weak intensities of light fail to change the cell's spontaneous activity. Notice the arrow extending from curve *A* to the horizontal axis of the figure. It indicates the weakest intensity of light that will evoke a response appreciably different from that occurring with no light at all. In a sense, this is the minimum amount of light the cell can "distinguish" from complete darkness.

As the spot's intensity grows, the cell's response mirrors those increases. This steadily increasing response is important if the response of such a cell is to carry information about the intensity level of light in some scene. Finally, at some high intensity, the response of the cell *saturates:* further increases in intensity fail to produce corresponding increases in response. As far as this cell is concerned, all spots more intense than the point of saturation are indistinguishable from one another; from the cell's viewpoint, all such spots are equally light.

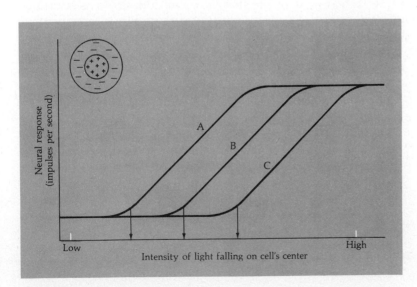

FIGURE 3.15
Graph showing the response of an ON-center ganglion cell to light of varying intensity falling on the center of the cell's receptive field. The three curves represent the effect of different intensities of surround stimulation.

Now you repeat the experiment, with one modification. The small spot again falls in the receptive field center, but now you illuminate the surround, too. The cell's response under this arrangement is shown by curve *B* in Figure 3.15. Again, you vary the intensity of the spot in the receptive field center and note the number of impulses evoked by each. What are the differences between curves *A* and *B*? For both, arrows extending to the horizontal axis indicate the dimmest intensities that will produce an appreciable change in the cell's spontaneous response rate. As you can see, when the surround is illuminated, the center must be more strongly stimulated in order to change the cell's response. More generally, adding light in the surround reduces the response produced by any given intensity of light in the center. This is another demonstration of antagonistic forces at work; light has opposite effects on the ganglion cell's activity, depending on where the light shines within its receptive field.

Before considering how these antagonistic forces might influence vision, let's repeat the same basic experiment one more time. Again, you illuminate the surround constantly, but now with a light more intense than that used before. The results—the cell's response to various intensities of light in the center—are shown by curve *C* in Figure 3.15. With this strongest light in its surround, the cell requires an even more intense light in its *center* before its response can increase noticeably.

LIGHTNESS CONTRAST AND CONSTANCY

Now let's consider how your vision is affected by ganglion cells that behave in the way shown in Figure 3.15. Assume that as its response grows, the ganglion cell is signaling your brain that light intensity is growing.* With this assumption in mind, turn to Figure 3.16. The two graphs in this figure add several features to what you saw in Figure 3.15. The left-hand graph indicates the three different intensities of light that produce the same response—a *constant response*—from the ganglion cell with various surrounds. This line of constant response is represented by a broken line parallel to the horizontal axis. The vertical arrows extending from each of the three curves to the horizontal axis point up the three different spot intensities that produce the same response from the ganglion cell. The right-hand graph of Figure 3.16 analyzes the cell's response in a different way. Now we are interested in the magnitude of response produced by a central spot of *fixed intensity*. This line of fixed intensity is represented by a broken line parallel to the vertical axis. The horizontal arrows extending from each of the three curves to the vertical axis point up the cell's response to this intensity with various surrounds.

In the left panel, the line of constant response indicates that with various lights in the receptive field's surround, different intensities of *center* stimulation are required to produce the same response. Alternatively, in the right panel, the line of fixed intensity indicates that with various lights in the surround, the same intensity of center stimulation will produce different responses. Both panels highlight the same idea: the cell's response to a stimulus falling in its receptive field center is affected by the level of stimulation in the receptive field surround. Thus the messages that the brain will get about exactly the same stimulus will vary depending on how much light is falling in the receptive field surround.

On the basis of the ganglion cell's apparent unreliability, should we dismiss such cells

---

*The following analysis holds for ON-center cells. A corresponding, separate analysis could be made for OFF-center cells.

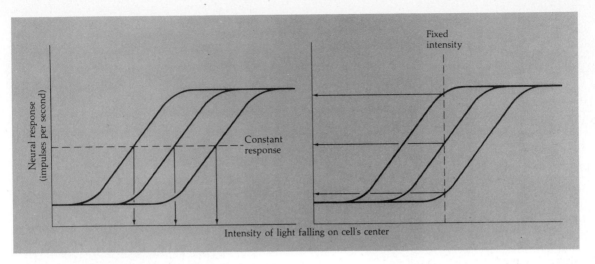

FIGURE 3.16

Two graphs showing the response of an ON-center ganglion cell to light of varying intensity falling on the center of the cell's receptive field. The left panel shows that a single, constant response (broken horizontal line) can be produced by several different intensities, depending on the amount of light falling on the cell's surround. The right panel shows that a fixed intensity of light (broken vertical line) can produce several different levels of neural response.

as possible precursors to one's experience of lightness? The answer is no. Although the cell's behavior (as represented in Figure 3.16) would certainly produce errors of perception, the errors would have two sorts of consequences, one good and one not so good. Let's consider the not so good one first.

The right-hand panel of Figure 3.16 showed that a retinal ganglion cell could send the brain very different messages about a spot of fixed intensity, depending on what other light happened to fall in the cell's surround. Translating this into perceptual terms, objects identical in intensity could appear different in lightness. Figure 3.17 demonstrates this effect, called **lightness contrast.** The two center spots are equal in *physical* intensity, but they appear different in lightness. To verify that both center spots are identical in intensity, you must eliminate the influence of their surroundings. Cut a hole

just slightly smaller than either spot in a piece of paper. Position the hole over each spot in turn, occluding the surround in each case. By looking only at the spots, without contamination by their surrounds, you will see that both are the same. This proves that the different surrounds are responsible for the differences in perceived lightness. This perceptual outcome means that one's judgments of lightness can be in error by a substantial amount—not such a good consequence.

Lightness contrast represents a case where the *same* physical intensity can yield differences in perceived lightness. The converse also occurs—*different* physical intensities can yield the *same* lightness. This routinely happens when you view an object under different levels of light. Under such conditions your perception of lightness tends to remain constant despite variations in the amount of light falling on the retina. This phenomenon

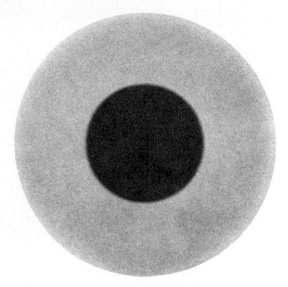

FIGURE 3.17
Demonstration of simultaneous lightness contrast.

is called **lightness constancy.** You can demonstrate lightness constancy for yourself. Hold an object, such as an aspirin tablet, under strong light, and notice how light the object looks. Then dim the lights. As the amount of light falling on the object drops, so does the amount of light that your eye receives from the object. Nonetheless, you'll notice its lightness remains unchanged over a fairly wide range of light levels. This invariance in perceived lightness is the good perceptual error we spoke of.

Why do we characterize constancy as "good"? You might argue that lightness constancy means the human visual system is a failure—your perception of light intensity fails to keep pace with the actual changes in light reflected from the aspirin tablet. But in fact, it's lucky that you have this "failing" because it allows you to recognize an object even when the conditions of illumination— the amount of light falling on it—change drastically. Because of this "failing," the perceived character of any object remains

constant even when the light level changes. After all, one is more concerned with seeing objects than with judging the level of illumination of those objects.

To understand how lightness constancy works, return once more to retinal ganglion cells. Let's measure the response of the retinal ganglion cell when a light of intensity x is flashed inside a surround several times more intense than the spot. For example, let the surround be three times the intensity of the spot, or $3x$. We now vary *both* the spot and the surround intensities, being careful to keep them in a ratio of 3 to 1. So long as this ratio remains constant, the ganglion cell will give the same neural response when the spot appears within the center. Assuming the retinal ganglion cell's response signals lightness, this invariant response means that lightness of the spot will remain constant even though the actual light from the spot is changing. The same result holds for most other ratios between the spot and its surround. This ratio explanation of light-

ERRATA

On page 80, Figure 3.17 should appear as follows:

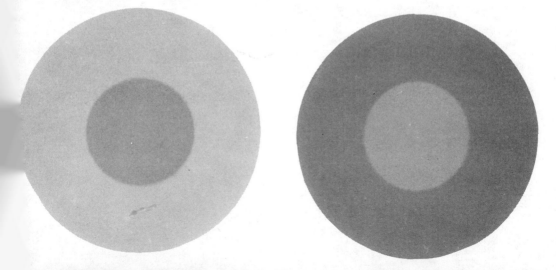

ness constancy was suggested by Hans Wallach of Swarthmore College (1963).

Now let's apply this ratio principle to the illumination of real objects, not just circular spots of light. Lay a dark-colored pen down on a piece of white paper. Because it reflects more light, the paper looks lighter than the pen. No surprise here. Using a light meter, we could actually measure the amount of light reflected by these objects. Typically, a clean piece of white paper reflects about 80 percent of the light falling on it; depending on its color, the pen might reflect about 10 percent, giving us a ratio of 8 to 1.

Now take a strong desk lamp and shine its light on both pen and paper. More light is falling on the pen than before you turned the lamp on. Consequently more light is being reflected from the pen into your eyes. But the pen looks no lighter than before (lightness constancy). The reason is that with the lamp on, more light is also being reflected from the paper. Since the ratio (8:1) of light from the paper to light from the pen is unchanged, with more light coming from *both*, perceived lightness is unchanged. Of course, if you did something to alter that ratio (such as illuminating *just* the pen), lightness constancy would fail: the lightness of the pen would change as you varied the amount of light falling on it alone. And, as Box 3.2 shows, under certain conditions, lightness constancy does indeed fail.

We've just seen how the properties of retinal ganglion cell receptive fields can account for the way vision accentuates differences between adjacent levels of illumination. Because ganglion cells collect their information from the photoreceptors, the cells' behavior reflects the preferences and peculiarities of those photoreceptors. Bearing in mind that the relation between retinal ganglion cells and the photoreceptors is particularly important for vision, we'll now turn to that relation.

Sensitivity Versus Resolution

ASPECTS OF CONVERGENCE

Earlier, we noted that over the entire retina, information from 130 million photoreceptors converges onto about 1 million retinal ganglion cells. This suggests an average convergence, over the entire retina, of about 130 to 1. But this statistic is actually a little misleading.

Suppose we examine the number of receptors and the corresponding number of ganglion cells locally, in several different small patches of retina. For each patch of retina we can calculate the degree of convergence by taking the ratio of number of receptors to number of retinal ganglion cells. This calculation reveals two important facts. First, the convergence ratio varies drastically from one part of the retina to another; second, near the center of the macula, the convergence ratio is close to unity—about one ganglion cell per receptor—whereas in the periphery of the retina, the ratio is several hundred to one. In other words, there is a strong connection between retinal eccentricity and amount of convergence. The connection is so strong that it suggests the operation of some grand plan. What might that plan be? To answer this question, we need to explain what is gained and lost by convergence.

To picture the consequences of convergence, consider an extreme form of convergence. Suppose your eye had only a single retinal ganglion cell—a convergence ratio of 130 million to 1. In effect, your entire retina would be the receptive field for this solitary cell. How would your vision differ from its present form? It's certain that your vision would be changed in two ways, one for the good, one for the bad.

We'll start with the bad. With only one retinal ganglion cell to tell your brain what

BOX 3.2
When Lightness Constancy Fails

Usually lightness constancy works and keeps you from erroneous interpretations of what you are seeing. But when constancy fails, it fails dramatically, as the following incident suggests. One of us (R.S.) woke up not long ago, looked at his wife, and was shocked. Overnight, a large patch of her hair had turned silvery white (it had been brown the night before.) He could not imagine what terrible nightmare could possibly have made her hair go white in just a few hours.

Reaching over to touch the strange patch, he discovered the silvery appearance was illusory. In fact, when he touched her hair, his hand also turned silvery. Despite this temporary disfigurement of his hand, he was relieved that he wouldn't have to break the news about her hair to his wife.

But why did this illusion occur? The partially open shutters passed a narrow beam of light into the room, illuminating part of his sleeping wife's hair though not illuminating anything else in the room. The psychologist Adhemar Gelb showed in 1929 that this sort of arrangement—illumination confined to one object with no illumination of its surround—tends to defeat constancy. Perhaps you've had a more common version of this experience while walking in a forest. Suddenly, you chance upon a large, shiny coin on the ground. Bending down to pick it up, you discover it is a leaf that had been illuminated by a narrow beam of light coming through the branches of a tree. Here, again, constancy failed; the lightness of the leaf was so much inflated that the leaf appeared to shine like silver.

Many researchers have tried to relate this breakdown of lightness constancy to the viewer's lack of knowledge, a cognitive explanation. Usually, these researchers follow the line taken by Hermann Helmholtz, namely that lightness constancy depends on an "unconscious inference" about the true conditions of stimulation. In this view, constancy breaks down when the viewer is confused about the actual level of illumination. According to this theory, lightness judgments should be corrected if the confusion is corrected. Yet incorrect unconscious inferences cannot account for the failure of lightness constancy. For instance, even after R.S. recognized its illusory nature, the silvery appearance of his wife's hair persisted. Knowledge of the correct stimulus conditions did not override the illusory perception of lightness (see also Hurvich and Jameson, 1966).

These failures of lightness constancy, and the inability of mental effort to remedy them, reinforce the idea that lightness constancy depends on lateral interactions within the visual system, interactions that are initiated by the registration of different amounts of light from adjacent areas of the field.

Although the ratio between the amounts of light reflected from two adjacent retinal areas does seem to explain many aspects of lightness constancy (and its failures), these ratios don't tell the whole story. Alan Gilchrist (1977) studied the lightness of a gray piece of paper seen against various backgrounds. When the piece of paper appeared in front of or behind the background, the paper's perceived lightness changed. These changes occurred even though the amount of light reflected from the paper and from the background were unchanged.

Here, then, lightness perception varied despite the fact that adjacent retinal areas received fixed amounts of light. Similar results have been reported by others, too (e.g., Gogel and Mershon, 1969). William Uttal (1981) discusses additional studies of lightness constancy that implicate factors other than the ratio between adjacent intensities of light.

the eye saw, you would not be able to read or watch television. In fact, you would be able to do very few of the things for which you now use your eyes. Imagine the problem faced by the brain whose only link to the visual world was this one retinal ganglion cell. The brain would have difficulty distinguishing different distributions of light. Many distributions would have the same effect on the cell. You would confuse letters of the alphabet and be unable to recognize your friends by sight. In brief, your resolution would be awful—not a good situation.

The term **resolution** refers to the ability to distinguish different parts of some image. The best-known example is visual acuity, which we shall discuss in a moment. With only one retinal ganglion cell to "describe" the image on the retina, your resolution would be nil. So long as the total light falling on the retina remained constant, you wouldn't be able to distinguish between one letter of the alphabet and another—even with extremely large, headline type. You don't need to go to the extremes of our example (a single retinal ganglion cell for the whole eye) in order to discover that convergence is incompatible with good resolution. Generally, greater degrees of convergence lead to poorer resolution. To summarize, *convergence is the enemy of resolution.*

Now for the good that convergence does. Going back to the hypothetical case, suppose again that your single retinal ganglion cell collects information from all the receptors in an eye. Before the impulse rate of any ganglion cell can be changed, the cell must receive a certain amount of transmitter substance from the cells that feed information to it. The retinal ganglion cell weighs together all the chemical influences on it, without regard to which cells they arose from. What consequences does this have for the retinal ganglion cell's ability to tell the brain about the presence of light on the retina? Take a terribly dim light and use it to cast an image on the retina. If this image was very small, only a few receptors would be affected by it and each only weakly. The messages passed along to collector cells would also be weak. As a result, the retinal ganglion cell might not receive enough transmitter substance to disturb its spike rate. Because weak messages from very few cells may not be passed along, the brain might not be informed that light was present.

However, if the same dim light were to cast a larger image on the retina, more receptors and more collector cells would be affected. This in turn would increase the number of inputs to your single retinal ganglion cell, making it more likely that the cell would be activated. As a result, the brain *would* be informed that light was present.

Generally, increasing the number of receptors contributing input to a retinal ganglion cell allows weak signals to be summed, yielding a total input strong enough to change the activity of that ganglion cell. A retinal ganglion cell sums weak signals originating from a range of retinal locations, an ability known as **spatial summation.** Spatial summation enables you to see very dim light; in other words, it enhances the sensitivity of your eyes. Because summation depends on convergence, one can say that *convergence is the ally of sensitivity.*

Note the conflict. On the one hand, convergence is a prerequisite for high sensitivity; on the other, convergence is the enemy of good resolution. To design an eye that detects very dim lights *and* possesses good spatial resolution represents a real challenge.

The Duplex Solution. How do your eyes manage to resolve the incompatibility of these two demands—resolution and sensitivity? To answer this question, let's return to an analogy we've already used, the analogy between the eye and a camera.

Cameras suffer from the problem we've been discussing. Some types of film have extremely high sensitivity to light, making them usable at very low light levels. Such types of film usually have very poor resolution—they don't produce very sharp photographs. Other types of film—such as the microfilm used by spies and librarians—produce very sharp photographs (even in huge enlargements) but work properly only at very high light levels. In film, then, as in the eye, there is a trade-off between resolution and sensitivity. The photographer can solve this dilemma simply by changing the film in the camera, matching the film to available light. Your eye, however, doesn't allow you to load and unload different types of film as needed. In fact, you don't need to; the "film" in the eye is **duplex,** consisting of two different types simultaneously. One provides high sensitivity to light, the other provides high resolution. In your eye, the two types of "film" occupy somewhat different locations along the back of the eye.

To see how this duplex arrangement works, think back to the convergence of receptors onto ganglion cells. Recall that the central region of the eye has very little convergence. Hence it has excellent resolution but only average sensitivity to light. Peripheral regions of the retina have high degrees of convergence, hence poor resolution but good light sensitivity. (For further discussion of high sensitivity, see Box 3.3.)

You learned in the preceding chapter that the center of the primate retina contains mainly cones and very few rods. As a result, retinal ganglion cells with receptive fields near the center of the retina reflect mainly the responses of cones. Because of the predominance of rods in the retinal periphery, ganglion cells with receptive fields in that region reflect mainly the influence of rods. Now as you are about to learn, rods and cones differ in numerous ways important to vision. This means that ganglion cells in the rod-dominated periphery make different contributions to vision than do those in the cone-dominated central region of the retina.*

In particular, rod-dominated ganglion cells

enable you to see even when light levels are several hundred times less than that demanded by their cone-dominated counterparts. This results from the greater sensitivity of the rods themselves (Detwiler, Hodgkin, and McNaughton, 1980), as well as their greater convergence on rod-dominated retinal ganglion cells. Vision under conditions of very little light is described as **scotopic** (from the Greek *skotos,* meaning "darkness," and *opia,* meaning "to see"). We'll use the term "scoptopic vision" to signify vision that depends on rod-dominated ganglion cells.

The cone-dominated retinal ganglion cells require higher light levels in order to function properly. Hence vision using these ganglion cells is described as **photopic** (from the Greek stem *phot,* meaning "light" or "daylight"). Figure 3.18 indicates what levels of light are considered photopic, and what

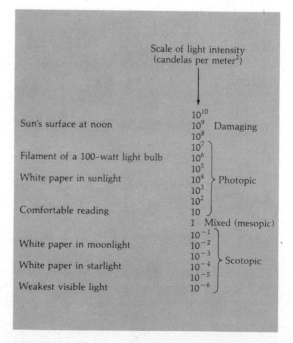

FIGURE 3.18
Scale of light intensity expressed in units called "candelas," a measure of light energy.

---

*Although some retinal ganglion cells receive inputs from both rods and cones (Enroth-Cugell, Hertz, and Lennie, 1977), for many ganglion cells the two influences are sufficiently unbalanced to justify our talking about "cone-dominated" and "rod-dominated" ganglion cells.

BOX 3.3
Adding Photons over Time and Space

Many things determine the eye's sensitivity. We've indicated some—the wavelength of light, its intensity and spatial pattern, and where on the retina the stimulus falls. But there are two other, very important variables: how long the stimulus lasts and how big it is.

To understand the importance of these variables—duration and size—we must consider exactly what events need to occur before you can detect a very weak stimulus. Suppose that seeing the stimulus requires that your photoreceptors absorb some small number of photons—a **photon** being the smallest unit of light energy. (The actual number of photons doesn't matter so long as it is greater than one.) Imagine that we split the stimulus into two installments, each intense enough to cause your receptors to absorb exactly one half the total number of photons needed for seeing. Now let's introduce one condition: allow one hour to elapse between delivery of the first and second installments of photons. Will you see the stimulus? No, because by the time the second installment of photons arrives, the effects of the first installment will have long since disappeared.

Granting that an hour's delay is unreasonable, how long can you wait between installments of photons before the effects of the first installment are completely dissipated? Photoreceptors have a limited memory—called **temporal summation**—with the rods' "memory" being somewhat longer than that of the cones. But whichever system is

stimulated, the shorter the interval between the two installments, the greater the chances that the residue of the first installment will be available to add to the effects of the second. Delivering all the photons within a very short time of one another guarantees that effects produced by the earliest photons will add to those of the later ones. If the stimulus is stretched out in time, a greater *total* number of photons must be delivered to the eye, since loss of the advantage of temporal summation makes each photon less efficient.

This fact has been formalized as **Bloch's Law,** which states that a constant product of light intensity and time will be equally detectable. Sometimes Bloch's Law is expressed as

$$I \times T = C$$

where *I* stands for intensity, *T* for time, and *C* for constant visual effect. Bloch's Law says that time can be traded for intensity. Lengthening the presentation of some weak light makes it just as visible as another, more intense light that is presented only briefly. So long as each has the same product (of intensity and time), the two stimuli contain the same total energy and will be equally detectable. These relationships are depicted in the figure on the following page. There, the vertical axis represents the stimulus intensity that is just barely detectable (*I*), and the horizontal axis represents the stimulus's duration (*T*). Two graphs are shown, one representing the behavior of the scotopic

system, the other representing the behavior of the photopic system. Bloch's Law predicts that data should fall on an oblique line, of 45 degrees slope. Note that in both graphs, this prediction is partially confirmed, at least when the durations are short.

For the rods, Bloch's Law breaks down at about one-tenth of a second; for cones, it breaks down much earlier, at about one-twentieth of a second or less (LeGrand, 1968, pp. 254–256). These values reflect the temporal memories—temporal summation—of the two systems.

There is a *spatial* analog to the *temporal* law just discussed. We mentioned before that many photoreceptors will share a single collector cell. In other words, the collector cell adds together signals from spatially separate sources—two or more photoreceptors—a capacity referred to in the text as **spatial summation.**

Suppose we take a very small stimulus and by trial and error determine how intense it must be in order to be just detectable. This stimulus causes the absorption of a minimum, or threshold, number of photons. If we distribute that same number of photons widely over the retina, seeing will not result. The spatially dispersed photons stimulate photoreceptors that do not contribute to the same collector cells. As a result, the opportunity for cooperative effect is reduced.

Within certain limits, all stimuli having the same product of

(Continued on next page)

intensity *and* area will be equally detectable. This is not completely surprising since any two stimuli having the same product of area and intensity contain identical amounts of total light. This trade-off between intensity and area is known as **Ricco's Law.** Ricco's Law holds only in the fovea; and even there, it holds only for very small stimuli. Leo Hurvich and Dorothea Jameson (1966) give a particularly clear account of both Bloch's Law and Ricco's Law.

We don't want to leave you with the idea that your visual system responds *solely* to the number of photons gathered over time and space. If your system did respond that way, you'd confuse long, weak flashes with brief, intense ones. This confusion would be particularly strong when flashes of different durations contained the same total number of photons, since according to Bloch's Law, they would be equally detectable. However, even when two flashes contain the same total number of photons (and hence are equally detectable), people can still discriminate between a long,

weak flash and a brief, intense one (Zacks, 1970). In other words, the visual system registers more than just the total number of photons; it also discriminates how those photons are packaged over time. At present, though, it is not known how the visual system manages this discrimination.

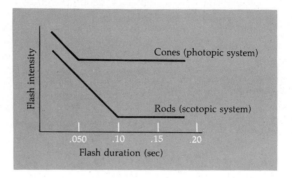

levels are considered scotopic. This is an important distinction because, as you'll see later, photopic and scotopic vision differ in a number of ways.

As noted earlier, the eyes must satisfy two competing goals, good resolution and good sensitivity. We now discuss each of these goals in turn.

RESOLUTION

Since convergence is the enemy of resolution, the photopic system, having less convergence, should have better resolution. In particular, resolution should be best in the center of the macula, where the ratio of cones to ganglion cells is about 1:1. We do not yet know precisely how the convergence of the cone system changes across the retina. The experiments required to demonstrate that physiologically would be extremely difficult to perform. Instead we have to make do with

closely related information: the density with which cones themselves are packed at various places on the retina. The heavy line in Figure 3.19, labeled "cone density," shows how the number of cones per square millimeter decreases with distance from the fovea (eccentricity). The second curve in the same graph shows visual resolution measured for various regions of the retina. This second curve, labeled "visual acuity," comes from measurements with human subjects who tried to read a well-lit eye chart while directing their gaze away from the center of the chart by various distances to the chart's side. Fixating this way causes the letters on the chart to be imaged at different, known places on the retina. Note the correspondence between the perceptual measurements of resolution (visual acuity) and the anatomical measurements (the density of cones).

You can see one consequence of the variation in acuity with eccentricity by gazing steadily at any letter on this page. You'll

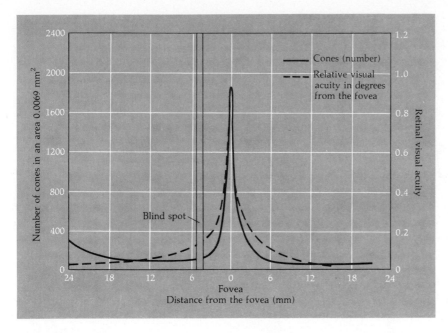

FIGURE 3.19
Graph showing how visual acuity and number of cone photoreceptors covary with retinal eccentricity. In this graph, a visual acuity of 1.0 corresponds to an image of about 0.005 millimeters on the retina. Values less than 1.0 correspond to larger images on the retina and, hence, poorer acuity.

have little trouble recognizing that letter. However, if you're careful not to move your eyes, you'll notice that letters in the periphery appear less distinct.

Stuart Anstis, a psychologist at Toronto's York University, was interested in how this ability to recognize letters varies depending on how far from the fovea the letters are imaged. With subjects seated 57 centimeters (about 22 inches) from a bright, white screen, Anstis moved a letter inward from the edge of the screen. Starting far enough away from fixation so the person could not identify the letter, Anstis brought the letter in, toward the fovea, until the person could recognize the letter. When he did this with letters of various sizes, Anstis found that small letters had to be brought much nearer to fixation than did larger letters (Anstis, 1974).

Figure 3.20 demonstrates Anstis's results. Hold the chart a little less than arm's length away from your eyes and stare fixedly

at its center. All letters should be equally legible, because the size of the letters increases at the same rate that your visual acuity decreases.

Although the data in Figure 3.19 confirm a close connection between visual acuity and the density of cones, cone density is not the entire explanation of visual acuity. Acuity decreases appreciably as the level of illumination drops (you probably already know this from your own difficulty reading a menu in a dimly lit restaurant). Yet it's obviously not the number of cones that changes with light level. The reduction in acuity with decreasing illumination is probably caused by changes in the receptive fields of the ganglion cells. For instance, the relative contribution from the centers and the surrounds of ganglion cell receptive fields depends on the overall level of illumination (Barlow, Fitzhugh, and Kuffler, 1957; Maffei and Fiorentini, 1972). Box 3.4 completes the story

FIGURE 3.20
All letters in this chart should be equally legible when the small dot in the center of the chart is fixated.

by describing additional influences on visual acuity.

SENSITIVITY

Scotopic Vision. A rod photoreceptor is at the theoretical limit of its sensitivity; it can respond to the catching of just a single photon (Baylor, Lamb, and Yau, 1979; Hecht, Shlaer, and Pirenne, 1942). But the capture of a single photon does not constitute seeing. In order to see—experience light—photons must be caught by more than one rod, though not by many more. In order for the small number of rods needed for seeing to be activated efficiently, conditions must be exactly right. The rods' own properties, together with those of their collector cells, define those right conditions. So enumerating some of the conditions gives a very good, quick introduction to scotopic vision in general. Let's consider the conditions, one at a time.

The first requirement is that the eye have a full supply of photopigment molecules. Exposure to light uses up these molecules, much as exposure to light consumes the light sensitivity of film. To restore the full supply

BOX 3.4
Visual Acuity: The Meaning of 20/20 Vision

Visual acuity has been defined in many different ways. One common definition relates acuity to the smallest target—such as a letter—that can be correctly recognized. The smaller the letters a person can recognize, the better his acuity is said to be. You may have heard someone comment with pride about having 20/20 visual acuity. What exactly do these numbers mean?

When eye doctors began quantifying acuity more than a century ago, they created eye charts—charts containing letters of various sizes. Patients tried to read ever smaller letters, until they came to letters so small that reading was not possible. One German eye doctor, Helmut Snellen, tested hundreds of people who had no eye diseases (so-called normals) and found that half these people were unable to see details smaller than a certain size. He designated this size—details whose images on the retina were about 0.005 millimeters high—as "normal." For any given detail, the viewing distance is crucial. If you move far enough away, even headlines become impossible to read. So visual acuity is expressed in relation to the distance at which the eye chart is read, usually 20 feet. Someone is said to be "normal" if, while standing 20 feet from the chart, he can read the same letters that the average healthy person can read at 20 feet. Hence the notation "20/20." The metric equivalent of 20/20 is 6/6, since testing is carried out at a viewing distance of 6 meters.

Acuity can be either better or worse than 20/20. If your eyes are poor and you can't see small print, your acuity may be only 20/60. This means that you must get as close as 20 feet in order to read what the average person can read from 60 feet. Likewise, if you have really sharp eyes, your vision may be 20/15 or even 20/10. This means that you can read letters at a distance of 20 feet that the average person cannot; he or she has to move closer, to within 15 feet of the letters (in the first case) in order to be able to read them or 10 feet (in the second) to be able to read them.

It's now appreciated that 20/20 is not good enough. A normal, healthy young person *should* be better than 20/20. This is shown in the graph below, which summarizes the manner in which visual acuity varies with age. Note that with young viewers, visual acuity is usually better than 20/20. Note also that with increasing age, acuity declines. Part of this decline is caused by the reduced light

reaching the retina because the older person's pupils are reduced in size (Owsley, Sekuler, and Siemsen, 1983).

Visual acuity varies with things other than age and light level. Some people have particular trouble reading eye charts composed of letters bunched closely together. Often, they'll be able to read smaller letters on a less crowded line of the eye chart, even though they fail with a line of larger letters that are crowded together. You can see this **crowding effect** for yourself in an eye chart prepared by Stuart Anstis, shown on the following page. Compare the legibility of this crowded chart to the legibility of the chart in Figure 3.20. They are almost the same, except that Anstis has added many extra letters. Surprisingly, manufacturers of eye charts have only recently begun to recognize the importance of the spacing between adjacent letters (Bailey and Lovie, 1976; Sloan, 1980).

(Continued on next page)

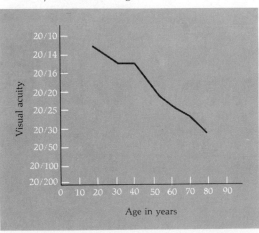

Factors other than crowding can also affect one's visual acuity score. Among these are cognitive factors, including memorization of the eye chart (by someone who is particularly anxious to ''pass'' an eye test). Sometimes these cognitive factors play a role even though neither patient nor doctor intend them to. Erica, the youngest daughter of one of the authors (R.S.) was having her eyes examined by a well-meaning though inexperienced eye doctor who, to make matters worse, was in a hurry.

Wanting to measure acuity separately for each eye, he asked her to close her left eye and read the five small letters at the bottom of the chart, using only her right eye. After she had finished a perfect rendition of the requested letters, she was told to switch eyes, now using her left eye to read the letters. Since the doctor had not bothered to change the chart, she asked him incredulously, ''Do you want me to read the *same* letters again?'' Of course, most people would have difficulty forgetting the five

letters they'd read aloud only a few seconds before. But the doctor urged her on. No surprise: her second rendition of the letters was every bit as good as her first. When the testing procedure was complete she almost—her good manners alone stood in the way—offered to read the bottom line with *both* eyes closed. The moral? Although tests of acuity are supposed to assess only one's vision, they can be influenced by other factors as well if the tester is not careful.

supply of photopigments requires keeping the person you're going to test in complete darkness for some 35 minutes. This period of adapting to the dark suffices to build the rod photopigments to maximum level.

Second, you need to deliver the photons to an area of the retina where rods are plentiful. Thus it makes no sense to image the stimulus on the fovea, where there are no rods. Rods are most plentiful in a region slightly more than 3 millimeters away from the fovea. To stimulate this retinal region, you need to know where the person is actually looking. So you ask her to fixate a small, continuously visible spot. As illustrated in Figure 3.21, knowing where she is staring, you can position the test stimulus at the right distance from that fixation spot. The test stimulus must be fairly small so that it stimulates only the desired retinal region.

Remember that you're interested in the dimmest light that is necessary for detection. The fewer the photons that are needed for vision, the higher visual sensitivity is said to be; in this way, "sensitivity" is defined by the ability to detect a very few of the photons. Not all wavelengths of light are equally effective in stimulating rods. Therefore, to find the wavelength to which the scotopic system is most sensitive, you have to stimulate the eye with various wavelengths of light, noting how many photons are needed for detection of each wavelength.

When these procedures are carried out, the data take the form shown in Figure 3.22. The horizontal axis shows the wavelength of light used to stimulate the eye. The vertical axis shows sensitivity (the reciprocal of the number of photons needed for vision). The curve represents the sensitivity of the rod-based system and is usually called the scotopic sensitivity function. The scotopic sensitivity function peaks at 500 nanometers, with the eye being less sensitive when stimulated by either shorter or longer wavelengths of light. In daylight and at sufficient intensity, light of 500 nanometers appears blue-green. To your subject, however, the faint test target will appear colorless (we'll tell you why in Chapter 6).

Photopic Vision. Though sensitivity is not the speciality of photopic vision, it's worth considering photopic sensitivity so that we can compare it against the scotopic variety. To measure *photopic* sensitivity you must image your target on a retinal area containing only cones; rods can play no role. Again, for stimuli of different wavelengths, you will want to determine the minimum number of photons required for photopic vision.

The heavy line in Figure 3.23 is the photopic sensitivity curve, with sensitivity plotted as a funtion of stimulus wavelength. (Box 3.5 discusses one very practical implication of this curve's shape.) We've used a dashed line to replot the *scotopic* sensitivity function

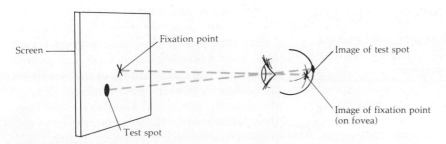

FIGURE 3.21
When fixating the X, the test spot falls in the periphery of the retina.

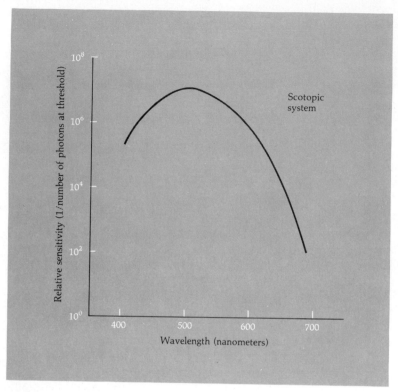

FIGURE 3.22
Visual sensitivity of rods (scotopic system) varies with wavelength of light.

in Figure 3.22. Comparing the two curves, note that scotopic sensitivity is greater than photopic sensitivity at all except the longest wavelengths, the "red" end of the spectrum. Note also that the peaks of the two curves occur at different wavelengths; maximum scotopic sensitivity occurs at 500 nanometers, whereas photopic sensitivity peaks at 550 nanometers.

The Purkinje Shift. The difference between the wavelengths at which the two curves peak has an important perceptual consequence, one that you may have experienced. This effect was first described by Johannes Evangelista von Purkinje, a Bohemian physiologist of the early nineteenth century. During the day, when vision is photopic, objects close to 550 nanometers wave-

length will tend to appear lighter than objects of 500 nanometers. As night falls, and vision becomes scotopic, the situation will be reversed; objects reflecting 500 nanometers will become lighter than those reflecting 550 nanometers. This variation in relative lightness with time of day is known as the **Purkinje shift.**

Fortunately, the Purkinje shift can be easily seen under rather pleasant conditions. Get a comfortable chair and a good book, and sit in a flower garden on a nice, warm day. Compare the lightness of the red roses to the lightness of the green foliage. During the day, the roses will look lighter because their reflected wavelengths fall closer to the peak of the photopic sensitivity curve. But as twilight falls, the foliage will appear lighter, since it reflects wavelengths closer

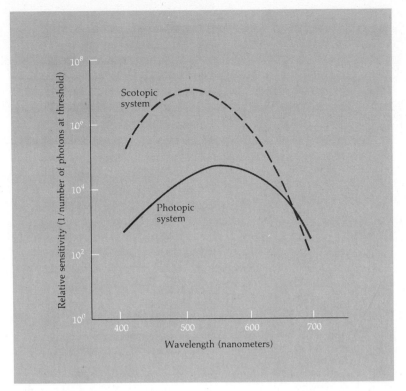

FIGURE 3.23
Visual sensitivity of cones (photopic system) varies with wavelength of light (solid line). For purposes of comparison, the scotopic curve from Figure 3.22 is included (dashed curve).

to the peak of the scotopic sensitivity curve. This is the Purkinje shift.

Dark Adaptation. The retina's duplex nature produces the differences between photopic and scotopic vision. We've already explored some of these differences. The retina's duplexity affects vision in another way, too—by controlling the recovery from exposure to light, a process called **dark adaptation.**

You're already familiar with dark adaptation from informal "experiments" of your own. Most people know about it from going to the movies. When you first enter the darkened theater from the bright lobby, you have difficulty finding a seat or seeing the faces of people around you. After a while, though, you "get used to" the dark and can see better. A small part of your improved vision can be traced to changes in your pupil. In darkness, the pupil dilates, allowing more light into the eye. But dark adaptation cannot be explained solely by pupillary dilation. For one thing, as you dark adapt, your sensitivity to light may improve by a factor of 100,000 or more, whereas the change in pupil area is relatively small, a factor of 16 at most. Moreover, your sensitivity may continue to improve for 30 to 40 minutes, whereas the pupil reaches its maximum size within a matter of seconds.

When dark adaptation is studied in the laboratory rather than in a movie theater, it

BOX 3.5

Does the Electric Company Give You Your Money's Worth?

The bill from your electric company has just arrived. Shocked by the numbers, you want to know if you're getting your money's worth. We can't put a dollar value on the pleasure you may have gotten from playing your stereo and the like, so we'll ignore those uses of electricity, sticking to one we can say something about—the use of electricity to produce light for reading.

Because only your eyes' photopic system affords you reasonable resolution, you must use that system when you read. So we can begin the analysis by looking at the photopic sensitivity curve (Figure 3.23). Since the photopic system is most sensitive to light whose wavelength is 550 nanometers, your electricity dollars would be most efficiently spent if they were used to produce radiation of only that wavelength. Electricity devoted to producing ultraviolet or infrared radiation is, of course, wasted, since you can't see either. Moreover, any electricity spent to produce visible radiation but at wavelengths other than 550 nanometers is not being used as efficiently as it could be.

Suppose you use only ordinary, tungsten light bulbs for reading. How could you determine the effectiveness of each dollar spent to power one of these bulbs? The answer depends on the spectral distribution of the light emitted by these bulbs. If they emitted only at 550 nanometers, they'd be highly efficient—putting out light precisely at the wavelength that has the greatest impact on the human visual system. The left graph in the accompanying figure shows the spectral distribution of the radiation emitted by a typical tungsten bulb. Note that most of the radiation that you pay for consists of wavelengths that you can't see, let alone use for reading. For quantification, we must turn to **Abney's Law** (named for a British physicist of the early twentieth century).

Abney's Law describes the effectiveness of a stimulus that simultaneously contains many different wavelengths—as is certainly the case for light from a tungsten bulb. For each wavelength present in such a stimulus, Abney's Law instructs one to take the product of two quantities: the amount of light present at that wavelength and how sensitive the photopic system is to that wavelength. The first of these quantities can be obtained by measuring devices (spectrum analyzers of various sorts); the second can be obtained from a table of the photopic sensitivity function's numerical value at various wavelengths (see Figure 3.23). After these products are obtained for each wavelength in the stimulus, Abney's Law requires that one sum up all the products. The resulting sum is a numerical statement of the visual effectiveness of the spectrally complex stimulus. Stated simply, Abney's Law says that one can predict the impact of a complex stimulus composed of many wavelengths by evaluating the effectiveness of each of its component wavelengths and then summing their separate effects.

To make quantitative sense of the outcome, though, we need some reference—say, some stimulus that represents 100 percent efficiency, the maximum obtainable. Since that's the best you could achieve, let's say that such a stimulus gave you a full dollar's worth of light for each dollar spent on electricity. Compared to that standard, you get only 3 cents worth of light for each dollar put into electricity for a tungsten bulb. Some tungsten bulbs do a little better—5 cents return per dollar spent—but these lamps tend to burn out quickly.

We can apply the same analysis to another common type of light used for reading—fluorescent lamps. The spectrum of a typical fluorescent lamp is shown in the right-hand graph in the accompanying figure. Compared to the tungsten bulb, the fluorescent lamp emits far more of its radiation within the visually effective band (400 to 700 nanometers) and far less in the infrared (which is experienced as heat, not light). Applying Abney's Law to the spectrum of a fluorescent lamp, we find that you get 10 cents worth of reading light for each dollar's worth of electricity, a much better buy.

Oddly, the most efficient light source for reading is one that doesn't require any electricity at all. The distinguished French vision scientist Yves LeGrand pointed out that fireflies and glowworms emit light very near the peak wavelength of the photopic sensitivity curve (LeGrand, 1968, p. 82). Because they achieve very high photopic efficiencies, a lamp full of fireflies would certainly give you your money's worth of reading light.

We don't usually tell you things that we don't want you to remember. But for your own peace of mind, the next time you have to pay an electric bill, maybe you should forget how few of your dollars are going for something you actually used.

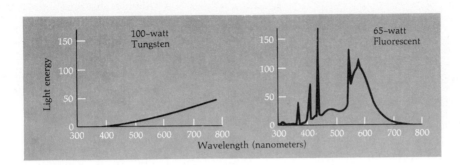

is possible to time the recovery of vision. Such experiments are numerous and have revealed a lot about vision's duplex nature. We'll present some of the highlights here; for a more extensive treatment see Bartlett (1965).

Studies of dark adaptation typically begin by exposing a subject to a strong light, called the *adaptation stimulus*. The idea is to determine how fast a person recovers from the effect of that strong light. After the adaptation stimulus has been extinguished, the person sits in complete darkness and looks for a very dim flashing light (the *test stimulus*), which is presented about once per second. The test light's intensity increases slowly until the light becomes visible to the person; then the intensity quickly decreases. This cycle is repeated over and over, perhaps for as long as 30 minutes. Each time the test stimulus becomes visible, two values are recorded: the *intensity* of that just visible stimulus and the *time* at which it was seen (that is, the time elapsed since the person was plunged into darkness). The general outcome can be described simply: the longer the person stays in the dark, the less intense

the test stimulus need be in order to be seen. To put it another way, the longer the person is in the dark, the more sensitive he or she becomes.

Now suppose that you wanted to measure the recovery of rod sensitivity separately from the recovery of cone sensitivity. How might that be done? You could capitalize on the uneven distribution of these two types of photoreceptors to isolate their separate behaviors. To measure dark adaptation using cones only, the test stimulus could be presented to the fovea; to do the same for rods, the test stimulus could be presented on the periphery.

The left-hand panel of Figure 3.24 shows how a dark adaptation experiment would turn out if the test stimulus were presented foveally. The drop in the curve over time shows an improvement in photopic sensitivity with time in darkness. The middle panel shows the results of a comparable experiment in which the test stimulus was imaged far from the fovea. Because the stimulus almost exclusively affected rods, the curve reflects the changing sensitivity over time of the scotopic system.

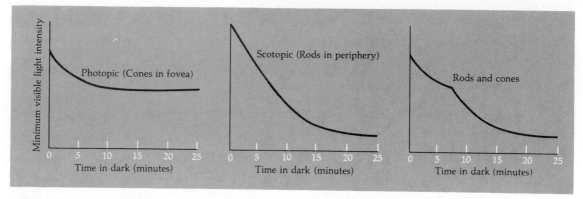

FIGURE 3.24
Graphs showing change in sensitivity with time in darkness.

Compare the two curves. Note that at the time labeled "zero," the scotopic curve (middle panel) is higher than the photopic curve (left-hand panel). Immediately after entering darkness, in other words, the scotopic system is less sensitive (needs more light to see) than the photopic system. Now compare the curves later in time, say at the points labeled "20 minutes." Here the scotopic system is more sensitive than the photopic system, the opposite of what we just saw. The greater scotopic sensitivity after prolonged darkness is consistent with the large difference between the peak sensitivities of photopic (cone) and scotopic (rod) spectral sensitivity curves (Figure 3.23).

Returning to the dark adaptation curves in Figure 3.24, note that the scotopic system starts out less sensitive than the photopic system but ends up more sensitive. After an interval of about 8 to 10 minutes, their *relative* sensitivities reverse. One other point emerges from these curves. The photopic system completes its recovery from the adaptation stimulus rather quickly (since the curve stops declining after 5 to 6 minutes). The scotopic system takes a lot longer (the curve doesn't stop declining until about 15 minutes have elapsed).

So far we have been discussing artificial conditions. Normally, to see, one must use both rods and cones rather than just one or the other. Suppose, then, that you now modify the previous study by imaging the test stimulus on a retinal region that contains both rods and cones. If you measure recovery from the same adapation stimulus as before, the outcome will resemble the curve shown in the right-hand panel of Figure 3.24.

Compare the curve in this panel to the others, noting the kink in this new curve. Things seem to go along smoothly from time "zero" until "8 minutes." In fact, recovery seems to have leveled off. Then all of a sudden, at the 8-minute mark, recovery starts over again, eventually subsiding once more at about the 15-minute mark. What is going on here? Note that the left-hand part of the kinked curve bears a striking resemblance to the early part of the photopic dark adaptation curve (left panel in Figure 3.24); the rest of the kinked curve resembles the late part of the scotopic curve (middle panel in Figure 3.24). The explanation of the kinked curve, then, is simple. Because in this case the test stimulus affects both cones and rods, you are measuring both types of adaptation simultaneously. Early in dark adaptation, the photopic system is more sensitive, so it alone determines the threshold. Later in dark adaptation, the scotopic system is more sensitive, so it alone determines the threshold.

The exact outcome of these studies depends on a number of experimental details, notably, the strength of the initial adaptation stimulus, the size of the test stimulus, and the wavelength of light used in the test stimulus. All of these variables as well as many others (including the subject's diet, as Box 3.6 indicates), change the curve of dark adaptation in ways that are predictable from one's understanding of the duplex retina (Bartlett, 1965).

BOX 3.6
Recovering from Light

When people compare the human eye to a camera, they liken the retina to the camera's film. But in one sense, the retina is more like video tape than film—both the retina and video tape are reusable. Even this analogy is inadequate, though, because unlike video tape, the retina can be used and reused millions of times. Wilhelm Kühne, a German physiologist and one of the first to study the retina's recovery, commented that,

bound together with the pigment epithelium, the retina behaves not merely like a photographic plate, but like an entire photographic workshop, in which the workman continually renews the plate by laying on new light-sensitive material, while simultaneously erasing the old image. (Translation by Wald, 1950)

How does the retina renew itself, recovering sensitivity after being exposed to light? When a photopigment molecule breaks up, it is said to have become "bleached"—a most apt term. When Franz Boll first studied this process, he noticed that the retina of the frog was usually intensely red. But when the frog's eye was exposed to light, the color of the retina disappeared—that is, it was bleached. Now we know that this loss of color is associated with the splitting apart of the retina's photopigment molecules.

In the 1880s, Kühne was struck by the analogy between the retina and the photographic plate, then still a novelty. Kühne exploited this resemblance scientifically, using retinas to make "retinal photographs," or as he called them, "optograms." An optogram treats the retina as though it were a photographic plate or piece of film, actually developing and fixing the image on the retina using special chemicals (Kühne, 1879/1977). Kühne used this approach to examine the image that various objects cast on the retina.

To make one particularly imaginative but gruesome optogram, Kühne got the cooperation of a man sentenced to die on the guillotine. The man's eyes were shielded from light for several hours before the execution, allowing light-sensitive material to accumulate in the retina. Then, just before the beheading, his eyes were uncovered. Immediately after the execution, Kühne removed the eyes and chemically treated the retinas to preserve the image of the last thing the man had seen (Wald, 1950). Unfortunately, the optogram was ambiguous, perhaps because instead of staring fixedly at just one object, the condemned man understandably moved his eyes around, taking his "last look" at one thing after another.

How does the retina manage to process millions of images over a lifetime? The secret lies in the retina's ability to restore its own sensitivity to light. Earlier we mentioned Boll's observation on bleaching in the frog's eye. He also noticed that the retina regained its normal, reddish color if the frog stayed in the dark for a short time (Boll, 1877/1977). We know now that the reddish color returns because new photopigment molecules have been created. This restoration is just as important for the visual process as is bleaching. If photopigment could not be restored, an animal would quickly become blind because all the available photopigment molecules would become bleached and thus unable to signal the presence of light.

To produce new photopigment after light has bleached part of the retina, a derivative of vitamin A diffuses through the retinal pigment ephithelium and is combined with protein available within the retina. Since all of the body's vitamin A comes from the food one eats, a serious deficiency of vitamin A in the diet slows down the restoration of the photopigments. In vitamin A

(Continued on next page)

deficiency, once a photopigment molecule is bleached, its return to the unbleached state is slowed. A person with a vitamin A deficiency is described as "night blind" because he typically experiences difficulty seeing at night or in other dim illumination (Dowling, 1966). Such people might have extreme difficulty seeing after entering a darkened theater, be unable to recognize friends on the street in a dim light, or be unable to see clearly while driving at night.

The problem of vitamin A deficiency is common in developing countries, where diet is often inadequate and vitamin supplements rare. Even people in developed countries are not immune to poor diet and night vision problems. For example, some years ago, one-third of the medical students tested showed diminished night vision that was attributable to their diet (Jeghers, 1937). These medical students were simply too busy to eat proper quantities of carrots and leafy vegetables. We should also note that night blindness can come from other causes, too, including impairment at virtually any stage of the rods' response (Ripps, 1982).

You don't need special equipment in order to verify some of these observations for yourself. Pick a night that is clear (not overcast) and just before going outside, stand for a few moments in a brightly lit room. Then quickly go outside and look at the sky. At this point you probably won't be able to see any stars. Keep looking, though, and after a while some will become visible. The first ones you'll be able to see will probably lie at the location you're fixating, because early in dark adaptation the photopic system is more sensitive than the scotopic. After a few minutes, your scotopic system will have caught up and will exceed the photopic system's sensitivity. Then you will be able to see very dim stars, using the rod-dominated periphery of your retina.

After you're dark adapted for some minutes, you can verify that the rod-dominated periphery of your retina is more sensitive than the cone-dominated central region. Glance slowly around the sky, stopping when you can *just barely* see some very dim star that lies away from the spot you're looking directly at. If the star is just barely visible using the most sensitive part of your retina (where rods are most numerous and convergence is greatest), that star will become invisible when you look directly at it (imaging it on a less sensitive part of the retina). Try it.

Summary and Preview

This chapter outlined how various aspects of your vision are shaped by the properties of your retina, notably the center/surround antagonism of retinal ganglion cells and the differences between the photoreceptors that feed the ganglion cells. Clearly, though, not all of visual perception is determined by the retina; there are lots of facts that defy explanation at this retinal level. To reduce the number of unexplained perceptual phenomena, we have to push further into the nervous system, following the messages generated by the retina back into the brain itself. There you'll see that these messages originating in the retina are further refined and reorganized in ways that account for still other properties of the way you see the world.

Chapter 4

In this chapter we continue tracing the flow of information within the visual nervous system. You'll learn how visual information about objects and events in the world is carried to the brain and distributed to different sets of cells there. You'll also see how patterns of activity within these brain cells can be related to various aspects of your visual perception. Let's begin by examining the **optic nerve,** a fragile bundle of fibers carrying information from the eyes to various processing stages in the central nervous system.

The Optic Nerve

Each eye's optic nerve is comprised of axons from all its retinal ganglion cells. Thus the optic nerve from each eye resembles a cable that contains roughly 1 million individual wires. Multiplied by two eyes, this means that the brain receives visual input from 2 million separate channels, each carrying

Central Visual Pathways

information about a small region of the visual world. That may seem like a huge number of communication lines, but it is really quite modest compared to the hundreds of millions of neurons populating the visual areas of the brain. Keep in mind that all neural processing of visual information within the brain depends on the optic nerves for input data; the optic nerves provide the brain with the raw material for visual perception.

Within the eye itself, the axons of ganglion cells are not covered by **myelin;** as you may know, myelin is a membrane that both insulates the axon from activity in neighboring axons and speeds the conduction of nerve impulses. Presumably, axons within the eye remain unmyelinated in order to reduce the clutter through which light must pass to reach the receptors—a coating of myelin could double the diameter of an axon. Once outside the eye, though, this restriction is removed, and individual axons acquire a coating of myelin.

99

Within each optic nerve, fibers from different regions of the retina congregate in an orderly fashion, with fibers carrying information from neighboring regions of the retina running adjacent to one another within the nerve. From the point at which it leaves the eye, the optic nerve travels approximately 5 centimeters (2 inches) before rendezvousing with the optic nerve from the other eye.

The optic nerves from the two eyes converge at the **optic chiasm.** The term "chiasm" comes from the Greek word meaning "cross," and a glance at Figure 4.1 shows you why this term is appropriate. At the chiasm there is a wholesale rearrangement of the constituent fibers. Using Figure 4.1, carefully trace the fibers from different regions of either eye as those fibers enter and leave the optic chiasm. You will discover that some fibers always remain on the same side of the brain—these are called uncrossed or **ipsilateral fibers** ("ipsi" means "same" and "lateral" refers to side). Regardless of which eye they come from, these ipsilateral fibers originate from that eye's temporal retina (temporal refers to that half of the retina nearest the temples). You will also find that other fibers cross to the opposite side of the brain at the optic chiasm. These are the crossed or **contralateral fibers,** and they come from the nasal retina of each eye ("contra" means "opposite"; "nasal" refers to the half of the retina closest to the nose). Thus the optic nerve from each eye branches into two segments—one crossed, the other uncrossed. Within the chiasm, crossed fibers from one eye join with uncrossed fibers from the other eye, yielding two new combinations of retinal axons. These new combina-

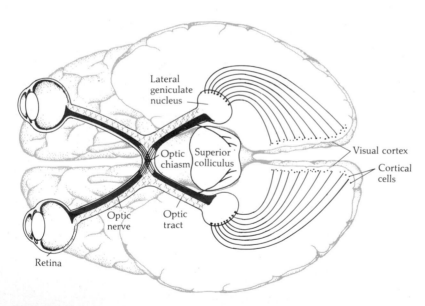

FIGURE 4.1

The projections of the optic fibers from the two eyes to the two hemispheres of the brain. The fibers represented by the solid black lines originate from the nasal retina of both eyes; they cross at the optic chiasm to the opposite hemisphere and are called contralateral fibers. The fibers represented by the hatch marks originate from the temporal retina of both eyes; they remain on the same side of the brain and are called ipsilateral fibers.

tions, which run from the chiasm to structures deeper in the brain, are known as **optic tracts.** Don't let the terminology fool you—an optic tract is still composed of axons from ganglion cells; the change in name from "nerve" to "tract" is simply a convention used by anatomists. The important thing to understand is that each optic tract contains fibers from *both* eyes, the temporal retina of one eye and the nasal retina of the other.

The proportion of crossed and uncrossed fibers in the optic tract varies among species. The percentages are not related to the species' position on the evolutionary scale; instead, they relate to the position of the animal's eyes within its head. For instance, in animals with laterally placed eyes, such as the rabbit, nearly all of the axons cross to the opposite side of the brain. In humans, about 50 percent of the axons from each eye cross at the chiasm while the other 50 percent remain uncrossed. This division between crossed and uncrossed occurs along an imaginary vertical seam bisecting the fovea.

But why should eye position in the head be related to the percentage of crossing fibers? To figure out the answer, think about the relation between the position of an object in space and the position of that object's image on your retina. The following exercise will help (see Figure 4.2). While looking at the center of this page, place your thumb on the right-hand edge of the page. The image of your thumb will now fall on the temporal retina of your left eye and nasal retina

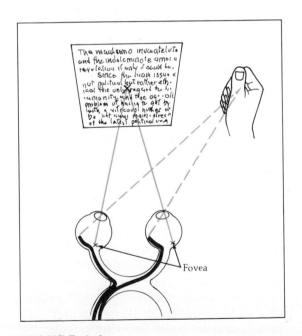
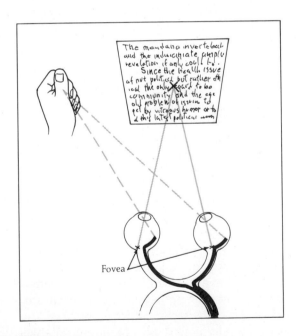

FIGURE 4.2
Objects to the right of the point of fixation cast images on the nasal retina of the right eye and the temporal retina of the left eye; fibers from these two retinal areas project to the left side of the brain (left panel). Objects to the left of the point of fixation cast images on the nasal retina of the left eye and the temporal retina of the right eye; fibers from these two retinal areas project to the right side of the brain (right panel).

of your right eye. Looking at Figures 4.1 and 4.2 you will see that fibers from these regions of the two retinas wind up together in the optic tract on the left side of the brain. Keeping your gaze on the center of the page, place your thumb on the page's left-hand edge. Now your thumb is imaged on the nasal retina of your left eye and the temporal retina of your right eye. Figures 4.1 and 4.2 show that these two regions end up sending fibers to the right side of the brain.

As this exercise demonstrates, there is a general rule to describe how information from the two halves of the visual field is distributed to the hemispheres of the brain: the right hemisphere processes information from the left visual field while the left hemisphere processes information from the right visual field. Those portions of the left and right eyes that look at the *same* area of visual space send their nerve fibers to the *same* region of the brain. The partial crossing of axons at the chiasm makes this possible. Rerouting the axons sets the stage for combining information from the two eyes, a process we'll learn more about shortly.

In animals with eyes on the side of their heads, the two eyes look at *different* areas of visual space. For these animals, it would be extremely maladaptive to mix information from the two eyes because such information specifies different objects in the world. Consequently, mixing information from the two eyes could lead to serious confusion about the location of those objects. To avoid this potential for confusion, the optic fibers from the two eyes remain strictly segregated, crossing in their entirety at the optic chiasm. This serves to route information from the two laterally placed eyes to different halves of the brain.

Let's resume tracing the destination of the fibers of the optic tract. Remember we're still talking about the axons of the ganglion cells originating in the retina. About 80 percent of the fibers project to a cluster of cell bodies known as the **lateral geniculate nucleus.** The remaining 20 percent of the optic tract projects to several neighboring structures in the midbrain, the most prominent of which is the **superior colliculus.** Since the superior colliculus and the lateral geniculate nucleus are both regions of the brain to which retinal axons project, these places are referred to as *projection areas.*

Before considering these two projection areas, it will be useful to know which classes of retinal ganglion cells project to the lateral geniculate nucleus and which to the superior colliculus. Recall that in the previous chapter we mentioned that ganglion cells in the retina fall into three categories: X, Y, and W cells. There is a method for tracing where these various cell types project in the brain. This method involves injecting a substance (an enzyme called "horseradish peroxidase") into specific sites within the brain. Axons in the vicinity of that injection then absorb the substance and transport it all the way *back* to their cell bodies. With special dyes, the cell bodies containing the transported substance can be seen under the microscope. When this enzyme is applied to the superior colliculus, it later shows up in two of the three categories of retinal ganglion cells, those with large cell bodies and those with very small cell bodies. These anatomical groups correspond to Y cells and W cells. When the substance is applied to the lateral geniculate nucleus, large- and medium-sized ganglion cells are labeled. These correspond to Y cells and X cells. So it appears that X cells project only to the lateral geniculate nucleus, W cells project only to the superior colliculus, and Y cells project to both major receiving stations.

To make it easier to follow the flow of visual information from the optic tract, we'll discuss the two branches of the optic tract separately. We'll first briefly describe the branch to the superior colliculus and then cover in more detail the other branch, to the lateral geniculate nucleus and its projection site, the visual cortex. But don't let our separate treatment of these areas of the brain mislead you. These visual centers are richly interconnected, and their functions can be carried out only when all the components work in harmony.

The Superior Colliculus

Tucked away at the top of the brainstem (see Figure 4.3), the superior colliculus is a phylogenetically older, more primitive visual area than the visual cortex. In many lower animals, such as frogs and fish, the superior colliculus represents *the* major brain center for visual processing. In human beings and other higher animals, however, the phylogenetically newer visual cortex has supplanted the superior colliculus as the more

important visual area. Nonetheless, even in these higher animals, the superior colliculus plays a prominent role in visual orienting reflexes, including the initiation and guidance of eye movements (Wurtz, Goldberg, and Robinson, 1982). The evidence pointing to this conclusion comes from several sources.

For one thing, cells in the superior colliculus have receptive fields with rather ill-defined ON and OFF regions. These cells will respond to just about any visual stimulus—edges, bars of any orientation, light flashes—falling withing their receptive fields, regardless of the shape or orientation of that simulus (Goldberg and Wurtz, 1972). These properties suggest that the colliculus is not concerned with precisely "what" the stimulus is but rather with "where" it is. For another thing, cells in the superior colliculus clearly are involved in controlling eye

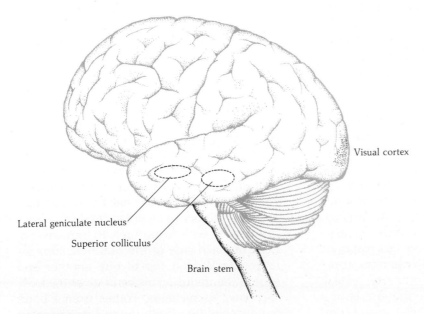

Visual cortex

Lateral geniculate nucleus

Superior colliculus

Brain stem

FIGURE 4.3
View of the left side of the brain showing the relative locations of several visual structures. The lateral geniculate nucleus and superior colliculus (drawn with dotted lines) are actually located within the brain and are not visible from its surface.

movements. Many cells in the superior colliculus emit a vigorous burst of activity just before the eyes begin to move. This burst of activity occurs, however, only if the eyes move in order to fixate a light flashed in the visual periphery; eye movements made in darkness evoke no activity in these cells. So the *intention* to move the eyes toward some object seems to be critical for the cells' responsiveness. Besides initiating eye movements, the superior colliculus also plays some role in guiding the direction and extent of those eye movements. Thus damage to the superior colliculus impairs the accuracy of visually guided eye movements in monkeys (Kurtz and Butter, 1980; Albano et al., 1982) and in humans (Heywood and Ratcliff, 1975). At present, though, there is debate about the details of how the superior colliculus actually does guide eye movements (Schiller and Koerner, 1971; Wurtz and Goldberg, 1972).

Besides receiving visual input, cells in the superior colliculus also receive auditory input from the ears, as evidenced by their responsiveness to sound stimulation (Gordon, 1972). Because they receive sensory input from the eyes *and* ears, these are called *multisensory cells*. In order for most multisensory cells to respond, auditory and visual stimulation has to originate from the same region of space. For example, if some multisensory cell responds to a light flash in the upper right portion of the visual field, that cell will respond to a sound only if it too comes from the same vicinity. Additionally, when visual and auditory inputs occur simultaneously, a multisensory cell responds more strongly than when either input occurs alone. Because of this property, a weak auditory input can amplify the effects of a weak visual input, producing a strong combined response. As a result, sight and sound can reinforce one another in these multisensory cells, enabling an animal to detect the location of feeble environmental events (Meredith and Stein, 1983).

In summary, the superior colliculus seems designed to detect and localize objects that lie away from the immediate point of fixation. It also guides the movements of the eyes as they attempt to bring that object under foveal regard. The colliculus does not, however, contain the machinery necessary for a detailed visual analysis of such objects. That job instead belongs to the other branch of the optic tract, the one projecting to the lateral geniculate nucleus and then on to the visual cortex. It is to those sites that we turn next.

The Lateral Geniculate Nucleus

In this section, we shall first consider the interesting structure of the lateral geniculate nucleus (LGN) and the way in which retinal input is distributed throughout the structure. Then we'll describe the receptive field properties of geniculate neurons and speculate on the role of these neurons in vision. Figure 4.3 gives you an idea of where in your brain the LGN can be found.

STRUCTURE OF THE LGN

The LGN has a very distinct, layered appearance, as you can see in the left panel of Figure 4.4. The layers consist of cell bodies, and the number of layers in the LGN varies from one species to another. In humans, the LGN on each side of the brain contains six layers stacked on top of one another and bent in the middle. This bend gives the LGN its name: "geniculate" comes from a Latin word meaning "with bent knee," as in "genuflect." For purposes of discussion let's number the successive layers 1, 2, 3, 4, 5, and 6, going from the bottom to the top of

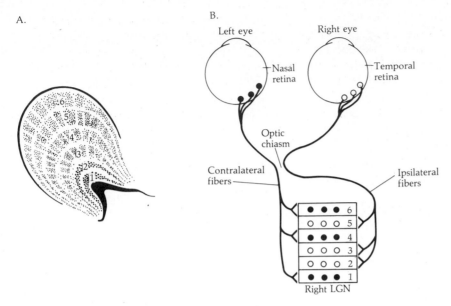

A.

B.

Left eye

Right eye

Nasal retina

Temporal retina

Optic chiasm

Contralateral fibers

Ipsilateral fibers

6
5
4
3
2
1

Right LGN

FIGURE 4.4

Cross section through the LGN showing its distinct layers (panel A). Diagram showing projections from both eyes to the right LGN (panel B); a corresponding diagram could be drawn for the projections to the left LGN.

the structure. We're now ready to consider some of the important properties of this well-organized nucleus.

To begin, let's see how fibers of the optic tract make contact with cells in the different layers of the lateral geniculate nucleus. Remember that each optic tract contains a mixture of fibers from both eyes, the temporal retina of the ipsilateral eye and the nasal retina of the contralateral eye. These fibers become very strictly segregated when they arrive at the lateral geniculate nucleus: the contralateral fibers contact only the cells in layers 1, 4, and 6, while the ipsilateral fibers contact only the cells in layers 2, 3, and 5. Take a moment to study Figure 4.4 and be sure you understand this pattern of input to the various layers. In sorting out these projections, keep in mind that the brain contains a pair of lateral geniculate nuclei, one residing in the left hemisphere and the other in the right hemisphere. This paired arrangement means that a single eye provides contralateral input to one lateral geniculate nucleus and ipsilateral input to the other. Now let's look at how retinal input is registered within these layers.

RETINAL MAPS IN THE LGN

Each layer of the LGN contains an orderly representation, or map, of the retina. This point is illustrated in Figure 4.5. As you can see, axons that carry information from neighboring regions of the retina connect with geniculate cells that are themselves neighbors. This way of distributing retinal information within any layer of the LGN creates a map of the retina within that layer. Since such a map preserves the topography of the retina, it is known as a **retinotopic map.** Each of the six layers contains its own complete retinotopic map, and these layers are stacked in such a way that comparable

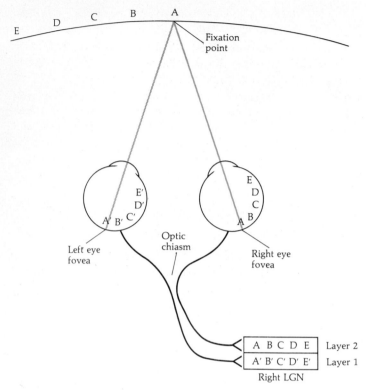

FIGURE 4.5

Drawing showing how different areas of the visual field are mapped onto the two retinas and then onto various layers of the right LGN. For simplicity, only two layers are shown.

regions of the separate maps are aligned with each other. For instance, the foveal parts of adjacent layers are situated on top of one another.

RECEPTIVE FIELD PROPERTIES OF LGN CELLS

Just like their retinal counterparts, LGN cells have circular receptive fields, subdivided into concentric center and surround components. As in the retina, these two components interact antagonistically; some cells have ON centers paired with OFF surrounds, whereas others have exactly the opposite configuration. There is an important difference, though, between LGN and ret-

ina: the surround of an LGN receptive field exerts a stronger inhibitory effect on its center than does the surround of a retinal ganglion cell (Maffei and Fiorentini, 1972). This means the LGN cells amplify or accentuate differences in illumination between neighboring retinal regions even more than do retinal ganglion cells. Incidentally, because their fields are circular in shape, LGN cells, like their retinal counterparts will respond to borders or contours of any orientation.

Within any layer of the primate LGN, receptive fields vary systematically in size, with the smallest fields devoted to foveal representation. LGN cells can be categorized as either X or Y, using the same classification scheme that we used to describe retinal ganglion cells. Interestingly, those cells classified as Y are found only in layers 1 and 2, whereas X cells are distributed throughout all six layers (Shapley, Kaplan, and Soodak, 1981). In other words, layers 1 and 2 contain both X and Y cells, whereas layers 3 through 6 contain only X cells.

There is another interesting difference between cells in the various layers, one that has to do with the processing of color information (DeValois et al., 1958; Wiesel and Hubel, 1966; Dreher, Fukada, and Rodieck, 1976). Many of the cells in layers 3 through 6 are differentially sensitive to the *color* of light shone within their receptive fields. A vigorous response can be evoked from these cells only if the center of the field is illuminated by light of one particular color (e.g., red) or if the surround is illuminated by a different, "opposite" color (e.g., green). Because of their unique response to the pairing of "opposite" colors, these cells are called *color opponent cells*. Figure 4.6 shows how one such cell responds to light in various regions of the spectrum presented to its center and to its surround. Note that when light falls in its receptive field *center*, this cell is maximally excited when that centered light is red and is inhibited when that centered light is green. When light falls in the cell's receptive field surround, just the opposite occurs: green light excites the cell whereas red light inhibits it. Because of the response of its receptive field center, the cell whose responses are shown in Figure 4.6 is called a "red-center/green-surround" cell. Other cells show exactly the opposite behavior: they respond maximally to green presented in the center or to red presented in the surround. Still other opponent-color cells respond differentially to yellow and blue. We'll consider these opponent cells in greater detail in Chapter 6.

As you might expect, opponent cells respond poorly to white light, because it is a mixture of all spectral colors (see Chapter 6)

and thereby stimulates both the center and the surround simultaneously. Instead, these cells are ideally suited for responding to the border defined by two adjacent patches of color, such as might be produced by a red insect resting on a green leaf. In layers 1 and 2 of the geniculate, however, color makes no difference in the cells' responses. Neurons in these layers respond just to lightness contrast information; they are effectively color-blind.

POSSIBLE FUNCTIONS OF THE LGN

This, then, represents a thumbnail sketch of the chief characteristics of the LGN in each hemisphere of the brain. But what do these anatomical and physiological properties suggest about the LGN's role in visual processing? As we have pointed out, the cells in the LGN are primarily concerned with differences either in illumination or in color between neighboring regions of the retina; these cells are unconcerned with the overall level of light. In other words, LGN cells are designed to detect the presence of edges in the visual environment. This alone, however, does not represent a unique contribution to vision; retinal cells have already accomplished this job of signaling the presence of edges. So we are led to ask, does the LGN seem uniquely suited for some other role, or does it merely relay messages broadcast from the retina straight on to higher brain sites with no editing or censorship? There are several reasons for thinking the LGN is considerably more than just a relay station.

For one thing, the LGN receives input not only from the retina, but from the **reticular activating system** as well (Burke and Cole, 1978). Buried in the brain stem, the reticular activating system governs an animal's general level of arousal. Hence, the flow of visual information from the LGN to higher visual centers could be modified by

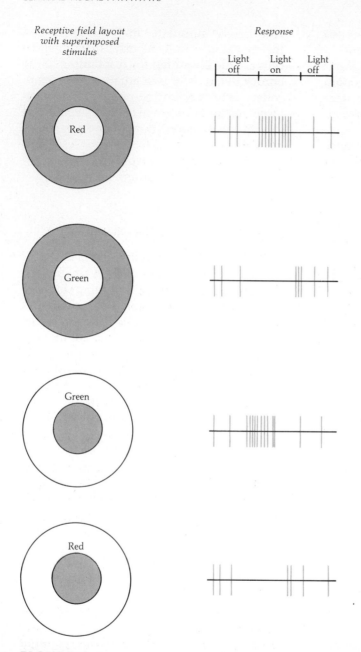

FIGURE 4.6

*Example of how one LGN cell responds to red light and to green light
presented to the center and to the surround of its receptive field.*

the animal's state of arousal. The LGN may
well operate like the volume control on a
radio, modulating the intensity of retinal in-

puts according to the animal's current state
of arousal. In support of this idea, Livingstone and Hubel (1981) found that when an

animal was in a drowsy state (as evidenced behaviorally and by brain-wave recordings) the overall level of activity in the LGN was low. The reduced level of LGN activity meant that the higher visual centers of the drowsy animal were receiving signals that were attenuated compared to those they would have received had the animal been more alert. This interplay between arousal level and the strength of signals going to the higher visual centers could promote attentiveness to visual information.

In addition to input from the reticular activating system, the LGN also receives input from the visual cortex. You may find this intriguing, since the visual cortex *receives* all its input *from* the LGN. In effect, the LGN formulates a message and transmits it to the cortex; the cortex, in turn, sends back a reply to the LGN, thereby allowing that message to be altered. This kind of arrangement is known as a *feedback loop,* and it is widely used in electronics to regulate electrical current within a circuit. At present, the biological purpose of the visual feedback between the cortex and the LGN is not known.

The highly organized arrangement of this structure suggests that the LGN may play another crucial role in visual processing. Recall that color and brightness information is segregated into different layers, as are inputs from the two eyes; moreover, each layer contains a retinotopic map. This kind of orderly sorting of visual information may set the stage for the next level of processing occurring in the visual cortex. An example should clarify what we mean.

Think for a moment about the most efficient way to assemble a complex jigsaw puzzle. You usually begin by sorting the jumble of pieces into groups, according to some shared property. You might locate and place all the pieces that make up the border into one pile, the pieces of comparable color into another pile, and so on. In general, before assembling the puzzle pieces into a pic-

ture, you will organize them so that the solution emerges with minimal trial-and-error effort. The lateral geniculate nucleus may perform an analogous sorting operation. The orderly arrangement of information within the LGN could help the next stage of visual processing to begin piecing the puzzle together. This next stage takes place in the primary visual cortex, to which we now turn.

The Visual Cortex

The visual cortex is located at the very back of the cerebral hemispheres (see Figure 4.3), in a region called the occipital lobe. If you place your cupped hand on the back of your head just above the base of your skull, your hand will be resting over this region. The visual cortex receives all of its input from the lateral geniculate nucleus. However, the visual cortex is anatomically more complex than the lateral geniculate nucleus. This anatomical complexity is paralleled by an increase in physiological complexity—particularly in the variety of receptive fields exhibited by cortical cells. But before tackling the anatomical and physiological details of this fascinating region of the brain, let's take a short break. During this time-out we shall consider some of the important findings from clinical neurology that first pointed to the cortex as a major visual center.

CORTICAL BLINDNESS

By the middle of the last century, neurologists had developed a keen interest in how the brain was subdivided. To examine its subdivisions, they removed localized regions of tissue from animals' brains and noted the behavioral consequences. Using this technique, neurologists observed that an animal *seemed* to be blind after destruction of the posterior area of its cerebral hemispheres.

At about the same time, case records began appearing in the medical literature, describing permanent loss of vision in humans who had suffered brain damage from injury. This evidence also established the occipital lobe as the visual center in man. The most thorough set of case studies was published by the Irish neurologist Sir Gordon Holmes (1944). Most of his patients were veterans of World War I with localized brain damage from gunshot wounds. Holmes measured areas of blindness within their visual fields by moving a small spot of light throughout the patient's field of view while the patient stared at a stationary point. The patient reported when the light was visible. Holmes was thus able to locate patches of blindness, or **scotomas,** within the patient's visual field. (Recall from Chapter 2 the simple demonstration of the small scotoma in *your* visual field, associated with the optic disk; also, see Box 4.1.) Holmes compared the size and location of the scotoma with the extent and position of the damage within the occipital cortex.

His results showed that the visual field (and, by extension, the retina) is represented within the cortex in a very orderly, topographic fashion. The center of the visual field maps onto the posterior region of the occipital lobe, and the periphery of the field maps onto the anterior portion. The upper portion of the visual field is represented in the lower portion of the occipital lobe, and vice versa.

Holmes found that visual disturbances always appeared in the visual field contralateral to the damaged hemisphere of the

BOX 4.1
Look Both Ways Before Crossing

Damage to different parts of the visual system produces predictable losses of vision within regions of the **visual field.** A visual field is easy to envision: while staring at some point straight ahead of you, your visual field is the entire region of space that is visible to you. Your attention is naturally focused on the center of the visual field, but you are aware of events occurring on the periphery as well.

Eye doctors and vision reseachers use a routine procedure to measure a visual field; it is called **perimetry** (from the roots *peri,* meaning "around," and *meter,* meaning "to measure"). With one eye covered and the open eye staring at a fixed point, a small, dim exploring spot is moved around slowly in front of a person's open eye and he reports when the spot disappears. The positions where the spot disappears are traced out on a map of visual space; the map shows areas of sight (unshaded regions) and areas of blindness (shaded regions). Keep in mind that a visual field map describes visual space, not the retina. To draw the map based on retinal geography requires inverting and reversing the map of visual space.

A normal visual field map for each eye looks like the pair numbered 1 in the figure opposite (for simplicity, the blind spot has been omitted). Note that the nose obscures the right portion of the left eye's view and the left portions of the right eye's view. Now suppose that because of some accident the left optic nerve were completely severed. This would totally eliminate the left eye's field, leaving the right eye's field intact; this situation is shown by the pair of maps numbered 2.

Let's consider a more complicated visual field loss. In humans, the pituitary gland lies immediately behind the middle of the optic chiasm. A tumor in the pituitary gland can squeeze this structure against the chiasm, damaging the fibers that cross through the chiasm. These fibers, you will recall from Figure 4.1, originate from the nasal portion of each retina. The resulting visual field loss will resemble that shown in the pair of maps numbered 3; the lost regions of visual space are those that are normally represented within the fibers originating from the nasal retinas.

Consider a case that is virtually the opposite of the one just described. The internal carotid arteries, branches of the prominent arteries in the neck, pass very near to the sides of the chiasm. These arteries can develop an **aneurysm,** a balloon-like bulge of the arterial wall. This bulge can push against the fibers that form the outer margin of the chiasm; recall that these are *un*crossed fibers. Thus, for example, an aneurysm of the left internal carotid artery would affect uncrossed fibers coming from the left eye—that is, fibers carrying information about the right half of the left eye's field. In this case, the visual field map would resemble the fourth pair of maps. See if you can determine for yourself the visual field loss produced when *both* left and right internal carotid arteries have developed aneurysms, a condition that does occur sometimes.

This close connection between visual field loss and disease makes perimetry a very useful diagnostic tool. But there's one very surprising aspect to visual field loss, even severe cases such as those shown here: the person exhibiting the loss is often unaware of it! Apparently, by moving the eyes around, a person's residual visual field can provide coverage that's adequate for most situations. But sometimes the coverage proves inadequate, as the following illustrates, and the outcome may be fatal.

Ella Freytag and Joel Sachs (1968) studied the records of certain traffic accidents in Baltimore. They were interested in pedestrians killed under circumstances suggesting that the victims should have seen

the vehicle that struck and killed them. Autopsies revealed that the visual systems of some accident victims had been damaged *before* the accident. In these cases, the location and extent of that damage implied a visual field loss that explained the accident. In one case, for instance, a man was struck and killed by a car approaching from his right. Autopsy showed that his right optic nerve was completely atrophied. Consequently, if this man were looking straight ahead, a car approaching from his right would fall within the blind portion of his visual field. Thus while this man's vision was probably good enough for his activities at home, his unsuspected visual deficit proved lethal when he had to cross the street.

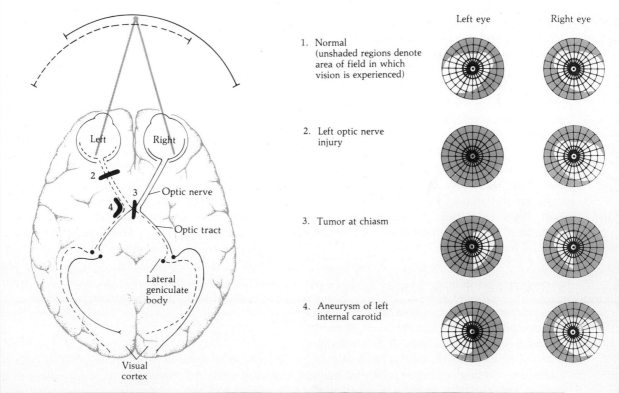

Left eye   Right eye

1. Normal
   (unshaded regions denote area of field in which vision is experienced)

2. Left optic nerve injury

3. Tumor at chiasm

4. Aneurysm of left internal carotid

Left   Right

2

3 —Optic nerve

4

—Optic tract

—Lateral geniculate body

Visual cortex

brain. Thus a wound to the left occipital lobe would be accompanied by blindness somewhere within the right visual field. Holmes also observed that the cortical map of the visual field appeared greatly distorted. The amount of cortical tissue devoted to the central portion of the field far exceeded the amount devoted to the periphery. This distortion, in which representation of the center of the field is highly exaggerated, has come to be known as **cortical magnification** (Daniel and Whitteridge, 1961). From a retinal perspective, cortical magnification means that a large portion of the cortex is devoted to a very small area of the retina. That area of the retina is the *fovea,* on which the central portion of the visual field is imaged (see Figure 4.7). Thus the lion's share of the cortex is devoted to that region of the retina responsible for your most acute vision.

Holmes's clinical work provided the earliest description of the retinotopic map on the visual cortex. Since these pioneering studies, many other neurologists have cataloged the visual deficits that result from damage to various brain centers. We shall describe some of these unusual and informative syndromes later in this chapter as well as in other chapters. In general, the victims of unfortunate accidents have greatly advanced scientific understanding of the anatomy of vision. And as Box 4.2 indicates, even the study of totally blind people has shed light on the neural basis of visual perception. Now let's look in more detail at the structures that are implicated in Holmes's clinical work.

STRUCTURE OF THE VISUAL CORTEX

The primary visual cortex is that portion of the occipital lobe receiving input from the lateral geniculate nucleus. It is sometimes referred to as Area 17, on the basis of a Zip-code-like labeling scheme, whereby neighboring areas of the brain are sequentially numbered. Others refer to this cortical region as the striate cortex, owing to the region's faintly striped appearance when seen under a low-power microscope. But the terms "Area 17," "striate cortex," and "primary visual cortex" all refer to the same portion of the brain.

Like the rest of the cerebral cortex, the visual area consists of a layered array of cells about 2 millimeters thick. In all, there are approximately 100 million cells in the Area 17 of each hemisphere. Figure 4.8 is a magnified picture of a section of brain tissue from Area 17. It shows that the various layers differ in thickness and that the concentration of cells varies from layer to layer. The million or so axons arriving from the geniculate nucleus connect with cortical cells in the layer that is fourth from the top. From here, connections within the cortex carry information to cells in other layers above and below and, eventually, to other areas within the brain.

What this picture cannot convey is the remarkable transformations of visual information occurring within this cortical area. To appreciate these transformations you must know something about the stimuli necessary to activate these cortical cells. This brings us to the research of David Hubel and Torsten Wiesel, neurobiologists whose pioneering studies of the visual cortex earned them a Nobel Prize in 1981. Their discoveries have had an enormous impact on several areas of brain science, and from their work a great deal is now known about the machinery of visual perception. The following paragraphs highlight some of their major findings. Interested students will be rewarded by reading a more detailed account of their work (Hubel and Wiesel, 1977, 1979).

RETINAL MAPS IN THE CORTEX

The first notable property of cortical cells is that each cell responds to stimulation of a restricted area of the retina—this area con-

A.

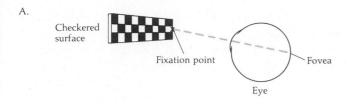

B.

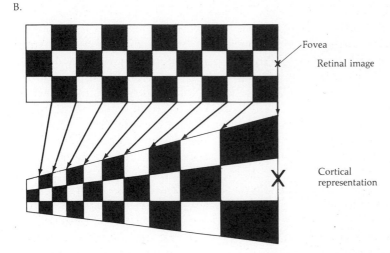

FIGURE 4.7

Imagine looking at the right-hand edge of a checkerboard pattern (see panel A). The resulting retinal image will look something like the upper portion of panel B. Notice the position of the fovea in this image. By means of the processes described in Chapters 2 and 3, this retinal image is converted into neural signals and is conveyed to the visual cortex via the LGN (represented in panel B by arrows). The bottom portion of panel B depicts how this retinal image is transcribed into neural activity within the visual cortex. The size of each square in the cortical representation is proportional to the number of cortical cells activated by any given square on the checkered surface being viewed. (This is not to imply, however, that a checkered pattern appears in the cortex.) Notice that the squares near the point of fixation are expanded in the cortical representation. This expansion reflects the disproportionately large number of cortical cells devoted to neural representation of information falling on and near the fovea. Conversely, squares located far from the point of fixation appear small in the cortical representation, reflecting the relatively small number of cortical cells devoted to the peripheral retina.

stitutes that cell's receptive field. You will recognize this property as a continuation of the processing scheme inaugurated in the retina and carried forward in the lateral geniculate nucleus: at each of these processing stages, individual cells analyze information from a limited area on the retina.

Considered as a group, the receptive fields of cells in each hemisphere of Area 17 form a topographic map of the contralateral vis-

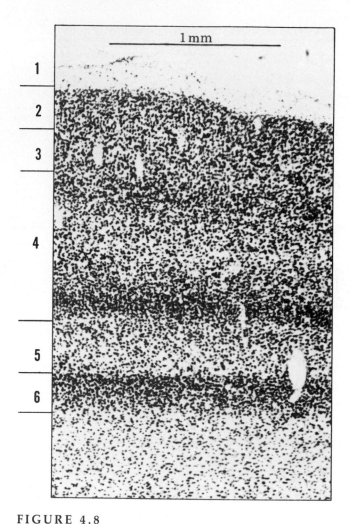

FIGURE 4.8

Magnified picture of a section of brain tissue from the visual cortex of a monkey (from Hubel and Wiesel, 1977). The top of the brain is situated just above layer 1. Below layer 6 lies the "white matter" of the brain, tissue consisting of the incoming axons from the LGN.

ual field. This cortical map, like its counterpart in the LGN, is said to be *topographic* because adjacent regions of visual space are mapped onto adjacent groups of cells in the visual cortex. The map in each hemisphere is said to represent the *contralateral* visual field because the left half of the visual field is represented in the right hemisphere, and vice versa.

Now let's consider *how* this map of the visual field is distributed over the cortex. Recall that Holmes's studies of brain-damaged people implied that a great deal of cortical area is devoted to representation of the fovea. This implication has since been confirmed by actually plotting the locations of receptive fields of cells sampled from throughout the visual cortex (Hubel and Wiesel, 1974a). It is estimated that about 80 percent of the cells in the visual cortex are

BOX 4.2
Some Illuminating Findings on Blindness

Everyone knows what the word "blindness" means—an inability to see. However, two recent developments in neurology (the branch of medicine concerned with the nervous system) and ophthalmology (the branch of medicine concerned with disorders of vision and the eye) are forcing a reconsideration of the conception of blindness. One of these developments comes from an attempt to design an artificial eye that would permit the blind to see. The second development concerns the ability of people who, despite blindness due to visual cortical damage, can still "see" in one sense. Let's consider each of these intriguing developments in more detail.

First, keep in mind that loss of sight can result from disease or injury affecting the eyes, the optic nerves, or various areas of the brain. With damage to the eyes or optic nerves, visual information cannot be relayed to higher brain centers that, in fact, may still be functional. In such cases it is the absence of input that prevents sight. Researchers are now exploring the possibility of directly stimulating the visual cortex in these blind patients, thus by-passing the defective route to the cortex. The scheme, still early in the developmental stage, would work something like this. The blind person would be outfitted with a small television camera that converted optical images of the environment into a pattern of electrical signals. This pattern of signals would then be applied directly to the person's

visual cortex, through an array of electrodes placed directly on the surface of the brain (see accompanying illustration). We already know that direct stimulation of the visual cortex does indeed generate conscious visual sensations (Dobelle and Mladejovsky, 1974; Brindley and Lewin, 1968). Called *phosphenes,* these sensations are said to resemble small, glowing spots or grains of rice. Increasing the duration of the stimulating pulse makes the phosphenes brighter; occasionally, colored phosphenes are reported, but most appear white. When several phosphenes are evoked simultaneously, patients describe seeing crude but recognizable shapes. Conceivably, this could provide the patient with useful information about the identity and location of objects in his or her environment. Before this procedure can be perfected, more work must be done to determine the number and placement of electrodes necessary to convey useful pattern information. In the meantime, this research very clearly demonstrates that the visual cortex can generate conscious visual sensations in the absence of visual input.

Perhaps even more intriguing are the residual visual abilities of some cortically blind people. In these individuals, the eyes and optic nerves remain intact; their permanent loss of sight results from injury to the visual cortex. As you will recall from the text, the extent of the region of blindness (a region called a *scotoma*) depends on the size of the damaged area of

cortex. Light flashed anywhere within this scotoma elicits no sensation of vision. Yet when asked to guess *where* a light is flashed within this blind region by *pointing* to it, these individuals can do so with reasonable accuracy. At the same time, they deny seeing any hint of the flash and describe the exercise as rather silly. This puzzling ability has been aptly named **blindsight.**

Bruce Bridgeman and David Staggs (1982) found that with practice, a cortically blind person actually became more accurate in pointing at an unseen light. Moreover, the patient they studied reported that practice on this simple pointing task in the laboratory increased his confidence in getting around outside the laboratory. He felt this training made it easier to sense approaching objects while he was walking, and this reduced his anxiety in crowded situations. More recently, the effect of practice on blindsight has also been elaborated further by others (Zihl and Werth, 1984).

By what means can a blind person accurately "guess" the location of a flash he never saw? (For a thorough discussion of possible answers, see Campion, Latto, and Smith, 1983.) Recall that earlier in this chapter we discussed the superior colliculus, a subcortical area of the brain thought to be involved in visual orienting reflexes. Because it lies below the cerebral hemispheres, the superior colliculus should be unaffected by injury to the visual cortex

(Continued on next page)

and hence remain available to provide visual information for the guidance of hand movements. The fact that accurate pointing is divorced from awareness indicates that subcortical brain regions process visual information at an unconscious level. Conscious perception may be a unique property of the phylogenetically newer visual cortex. (For an intriguing discussion of the role of consciousness in perception, see Marcel, 1983.)

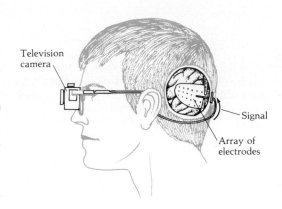

devoted to representing the central 10 degrees or so of the visual field (Drasdo, 1977). Earlier, we pointed out that this exaggerated cortical mapping of central vision is referred to as *cortical magnification.*

Some of this bias toward the central portion of the visual field is inherited from the retina and the LGN. Recall from our discussion of the retina that the number of ganglion cells subserving the fovea is considerably larger than the number devoted to the rest of the retina, even though in terms of area the periphery dwarfs the fovea. This foveal bias appears in the LGN's retinotopic map, too, where it is even further exaggerated (Malpelli and Baker, 1975). Moving on up to the cortex, the foveal representation swells to even greater proportions.

This magnified foveal representation makes sense when we consider the sizes of receptive fields of cortical cells representing different retinal eccentricities. Cells concerned with the fovea may be "looking at" a retinal area covered by no more than a few photoreceptors, whereas cells devoted to the periphery "look at" areas hundreds of times larger. Because foveal receptive fields are so small, it stands to reason that many cells may be required to cover a given patch of retina. In the representation of the periph-

ery, a comparably sized patch of retina may be monitored by relatively few cells (recall Figure 4.7). This principle explains why local damage to visual cortex (from a bullet wound, for example) may produce scotomas of different size. Damage within the foveal representation will destroy cells with small receptive fields, yielding a small scotoma in the center of vision. Damage within the peripheral representation may destroy the same number of cells, but the scotoma will be considerably larger because those cells have bigger receptive fields. This large scotoma will also, of course, be located away from the center of gaze.

So, in effect, the bulk of the machinery in your visual cortex concentrates on information about objects that you look at directly. This is why head and eye movements play such a prominent role in seeing: such movements turn your eyes toward objects of current interest. These newly fixated objects then cast their images on your fovea, ensuring that those objects will receive the most detailed visual analysis possible by your visual cortex.

So far we've considered the orderly layout of cortical receptive fields and the resulting topographic map. Our discussion focused on *where* in the visual field different cortical cells are "looking." Now let's ask *what* each cell is "looking for." Exactly what kind of visual stimulus must be present within a cell's receptive field in order to evoke activity in that cell? On the basis of your knowledge of the retina and the geniculate, you can probably anticipate one fact: cortical cells are unconcerned about overall levels of illumination. Simply increasing or decreasing the ambient illumination has no appreciable impact on a cortical cell's activity. Instead, cortical cells respond best to gradients in light intensity, such as those produced by borders, edges, and lines. In this respect cortical cells behave like their retinal and geniculate relatives from whom they inherit input. But cortical cells exhibit several notable characteristics not present in their precortical relatives. Let's examine these unique characteristics in detail.

FUNCTIONAL PROPERTIES OF CORTICAL CELLS

Orientation and Direction Selectivity. One of the most striking characteristics of cortical cells is their **orientation selectivity**. You will remember that retinal and geniculate cells, because of their circular-shaped receptive fields, respond indiscriminately to all orientations. In marked contrast, cortical cells, which are elongated, are very fussy about the orientation of a stimulus. As shown in Figure 4.9, any particular cell will respond only if the orientation of an edge or line falls somewhere within a rather narrow range. Each cortical cell has a "preferred" orientation, one to which it is maximally responsive. If a line tilts a little away from this optimum, the cell's response decreases markedly; if the line tilts even more, the cell no longer responds at all. This behavior can

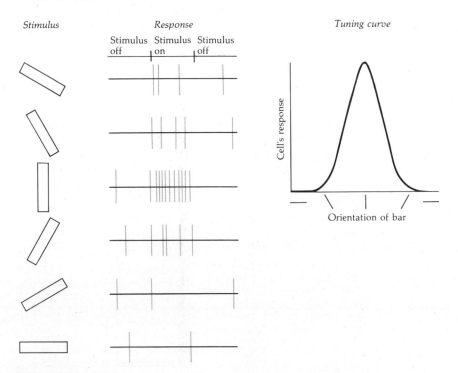

FIGURE 4.9
Response of a single cortical cell to bars presented at various orientations.

be summarized by graphing a cell's response strength as a function of orientation; the resulting "tuning curve" resembles a tepee with its peak defining the cell's preferred orientation (see the right-hand portion of Figure 4.9). The preferred orientation varies from cell to cell, such that within an ensemble of cells all orientations are represented (see Box 4.3). Usually the most effective orientation for a cell can be sharply defined. In many cells a tilt of no more than

15 degrees away from the optimum orientation is sufficient to abolish that cell's response completely. An angular deviation this small corresponds to about the difference in position of a clock's hand at 12:00 and at 12:03! Just about all cortical cells are selective for orientation, with the exception of one group. This unusual group is found in layer 4 of the cortex, where axons from geniculate cells arrive to deliver their input. In this layer, the recipient cortical cells have

BOX 4.3
The Oblique Effect

Each and every cortical cell has a preferred orientation, one that elicits the best response from the cell. Among a large sample of visual cortical cells, all possible preferred orientations are encountered—the distribution of preferred orientations covers the entire range. However, according to Richard Mansfield, a physiological psychologist at Harvard University, the distribution of preferred orientations is not uniform. Recording from many cells in the visual cortex of the monkey, Mansfield (1974) observed a distinct bias in favor of the principal axes, vertical and horizontal. The accompanying figure (adapted from Mansfield, 1974) illustrates his findings. In this polar plot, each line represents the preferred orientation of a single cortical cell. As you can see, while all orientations are represented, there is a clustering of cells that prefer vertical and another clustering of cells that prefer horizontal. Mansfield found that the unevenness of this distribution was most pronounced among cells with receptive fields close

to and within the fovea. His findings raise two intriguing questions. What are the perceptual consequences of this bias in favor of vertical and horizontal? And what factors produce this bias in the first place? Let's begin with the first question.

Long before Mansfield's physiological discoveries, scientists interested in vision had noted that horizontal and vertical lines can be detected more easily and identified more rapidly than can lines oriented obliquely. For instance, visual acuity is highest for vertical and horizontal lines, and lowest for lines oriented 45 degrees in either direction from vertical. Compared to horizontal or vertical lines, oblique lines are also more difficult to see when the contrast of the lines is faint.

You can experience the oblique effect by looking at the two bar patterns pictured opposite. Prop the book up so that you can view the pair of patterns from a distance. Backing away from the book, you should discover that at some distance the thin vertical bars remain visible while the diagonal ones blend together and are, thus,

unresolvable. By turning the book sideways, you can repeat this exercise, now comparing horizontal to diagonal.

This general superiority in the visibility of horizontal and vertical is called the **oblique effect** (Appelle, 1972). Most people experience the oblique effect, but there are some individuals who do not. In fact, some people show just the opposite bias, a tendency to see oblique lines of a particular orientation *more* clearly. Usually, those people who fail to experience the oblique effect or who show a reverse oblique effect have some degree of astigmatism. Recall from Chapter 2 that astigmatism (an irregularly curved cornea) causes contours of certain orientations to appear blurred while other orientations appear sharply focused. Depending on the direction of the astigmatism, this condition can nullify the normal oblique effect, and it can also lead to a superiority in vision for oblique lines, a sort of reverse oblique effect. Interestingly, in cases where oblique is favored, the bias endures even when the astigmatism is optically corrected, thereby making all orientations equally sharp (Mitchell et al., 1973); this condition is called **meridional amblyopia** ("amblyopia" literally means "dull vision" and refers to a visual loss that cannot be corrected optically). Apparently the astigmatism, prior to optical correction, altered the visual nervous system in a direction favoring oblique over horizontal and vertical. In fact, animals made artificially astigmatic exhibit just such alterations—cortical cells in these animals prefer orientations centered around the one most clearly focused, with very few cells responding preferentially to the blurred, astigmatic orientation (Freeman and Pettigrew, 1973). The ability of biased visual experience to alter the orientation preferences of cortical cells provides a ready explanation for meridional amblyopia: presumably people with this condition have a paucity of cortical cells tuned to the previously blurred orientation. This finding may also help us understand the neural basis of the oblique effect in people who are *not* astigmatic but who *do* see horizontal and vertical more clearly.

This brings us back to the second question raised by Mansfield's results. Why does the visual cortex exhibit a preference for horizontal and vertical over oblique? At present there are two general theories. One attributes the bias to the carpentered environment in which most people grow up (Annis and Frost, 1973). According to this idea, people are "overexposed" to horizontal and vertical contours

because these contours exist in abundance within an urban landscape of houses and buildings. This biased visual exposure, in turn, influences the development of orientation preferences among the cortical cells. This theory is supported by animal studies demonstrating that the brain *is* susceptible to biased visual experience early in life (Blakemore, 1976). The carpentered environment theory also receives support from studies testing the vision of people who grew up in noncarpentered, agrarian environments where no particular orientation predominates. These individuals *fail* to exhibit an oblique effect (Annis and Frost, 1973), presumably because their brains did not receive a heavy dose of vertical and horizontal contours. The

opposing theory ascribes the neural bias for horizontal and vertical to unspecified genetic factors that operate to favor the development of cortical cells tuned to horizontal and vertical (Timney and Muir, 1976). Those who favor this genetic theory point to the fact that infants only a few months old exhibit an oblique effect. (Leehey et al., 1975). It is hard to imagine, this theory argues, how visual experience could already have shaped the brains of infants so young.

At present this issue of the origins of the oblique effect remains unsettled. But regardless how the issue is resolved, the oblique effect represents a strong link between visual pattern perception and cortical physiology (Orban, Vandenbussche, and Vogels, 1984).

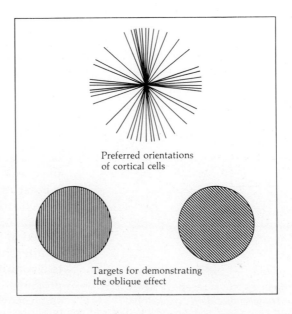

Preferred orientations
of cortical cells

Targets for demonstrating
the oblique effect

circular fields and, therefore, are responsive to all orientations. Outside of this restricted band, in the other layers of visual cortex, orientation matters very greatly.

Let's take a look at the layout of ON regions and OFF regions comprising the receptive fields of some cortical cells; from these you should be able to see why these cells are selective for orientation. Some representative cortical receptive fields are shown in Figure 4.10. There you can see that receptive fields are elongated, not circular as in retinal and geniculate cells. Notice too that the discrete zones of ON and OFF activity are arranged differently depending on the particular cell. Simply by inspecting these various arrangements, you should be able to picture what kind of oriented stimulus would evoke the best response from a given cell. For this reason cortical cells within these well-delineated zones are called **simple cells:** there is a simple relation between their re-

ceptive field layout and their preferred stimulus. For cells of this type, a properly oriented bar or edge must be exactly positioned within the receptive field to yield a large neural response. This means that simple cells are able to signal the orientation of a stimulus falling within a particular region of the visual field.

Other cortical cells do not have such well-defined ON and OFF zones, yet they also exhibit a preference for a particular orientation. Thes are called **complex cells,** because it is more complicated to predict just what stimulus will optimally activate them. Just looking at their responses to spots or bars of light does not give us a map of the best-shaped target. Unlike simple cells, complex ones will respond to an appropriately oriented stimulus falling anywhere within the boundaries of the receptive field. In other words, these cells are less particular about the precise position of the stimulus, just so long as it remains properly oriented. Incidentally, because a complex cell lacks clearly defined ON and OFF regions, it will respond quite vigorously to a bar or an edge that moves through the receptive field. In fact, most complex cells strongly prefer moving contours to stationary ones, even if the contour travels rapidly across the receptive field. Simple cells, on the other hand, respond only to stationary or slowly moving contours (Movshon, 1975).

Besides preferring contours that move, complex cells often respond to one *direction* of motion only. For instance, such a cell (like the one illustrated in Figure 4.11) might give a burst of activity when a vertical contour moved from left to right, but would remain unresponsive when that same contour moved in the opposite direction, right to left. A different complex cell might respond only to a contour moving from right to left. This property—known as **direction selectivity**—suggests that this class of cells plays an important role in motion perception (Regan,

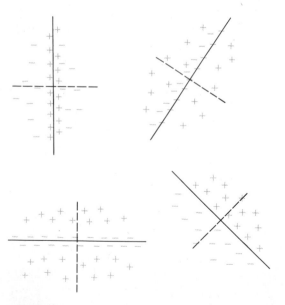

FIGURE 4.10
Layout of ON regions (+) and OFF regions (−) of several representative cortical receptive fields. The ON regions are sometimes called "excitatory zones" and the OFF regions "inhibitory zones."

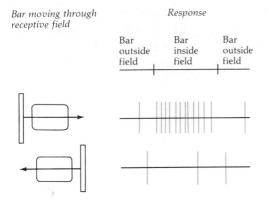

Bar moving through receptive field

Response

Bar outside field | Bar inside field | Bar outside field

FIGURE 4.11
Response of a complex cell to a bar moving through its receptive field (shown in outline).

Beverley, and Cynader, 1979). We'll return to this idea when we discuss motion perception in Chapter 8.

There are other, more subtle distinctions between simple and complex cells (for example, see Hammond and MacKay, 1977) and there are other cell types with even more complicated receptive fields. But for the present let's refocus our attention on the property that all these cell types have in common, orientation selectivity.

Columns and Hypercolumns. Earlier we mentioned that cortical cells vary in their preferred orientations, some responding best to vertical, others to horizontal, and still others to orientations in between. These orientation-selective cells are not haphazardly arranged; they are grouped in a very orderly fashion within the cortex. To envision this grouping, imagine we are able to unfold the visual cortex so that this thin, layered sheet of tissue (recall Figure 4.8) is lying flat. Now suppose we randomly select a position somewhere on the surface of this unfolded cortex. Starting here we gradually move straight downward through the various layers in a direction perpendicular to the surface of the cortex. Throughout our short, 2-millimeter journey we carefully catalogue the preferred orientation of each cell encountered. After penetrating all six cortical layers, we will discover that all cells along the path of this penetration have identical preferred orientations (except for cells in layer 4, which respond to *all* orientations). Along the way, there may be variation in the size of these cells' receptive fields, and some are likely to prefer edges while others prefer bars. But *all* cells will exhibit the same orientation preference.

Suppose we now repeat this sampling procedure, this time beginning at a position just a fraction of a millimeter away from our initial penetration. Now we will find that all cells prefer an orientation slightly different from the one encountered in the first sample. This is illustrated in Figure 4.12—note that the preferred orientation has changed by about 10 degrees from the first sample to the second one. If we repeat this sampling procedure over and over, always being careful to make such penetration perpendicular to the cortical surface, we will uncover a regular sequence of preferred orientations. Each time we make a new penetration, spacing it about .05 millimeter from the last one, the preferred orientation will change by about 10 to 15 degrees. By the time we have sampled a strip of cortex less than a millimeter in width, the sequence of preferred orientations will have progressed through one complete rotation. This regular progression through a complete set of orientations is comparable to the range of positions assumed by the second hand of a clock as it advances from vertical (at 12:00 o'clock) to horizontal (at 3:00 o'clock) and back to vertical (at 6:00 o'clock). This tidy packaging of orientation-selective cells occurs throughout the visual cortex (Hubel and Wiesel, 1974b).

At first, all these facts may overwhelm you; but taken together, they produce an interesting and coherent picture. The visual cortex appears to be composed of columns

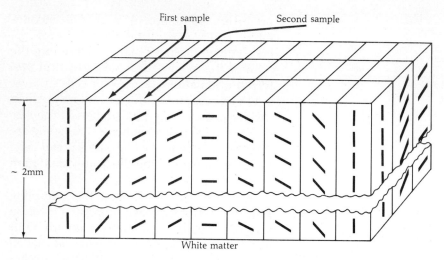

FIGURE 4.12

Orientation columns in the visual cortex. All cells in a column have the same orientation preference. An aggregate of columns representing a complete range of preferences is known as a hypercolumn.

of cells, with each column consisting of a stack of cells all preferring the same orientation. Looking back at Figure 4.8 you may be able to discern what look like vertical strings of cells, which probably represent individual columns (Frisby, 1980). Altogether, it takes roughly eighteen to twenty neighboring columns to cover a complete range of stimulus orientations. This aggregation of adjacent columns is collectively known as a **hypercolumn.** Each hypercolumn contains tens of thousands of cells whose receptive fields all overlap on the same retinal territory. The hypercolumns themselves are all uniform in size throughout the cortex, but the hypercolumns devoted to the central retina deal with a much smaller area of retina than do the hypercolumns concerned with the peripheral retina. This, of course, merely restates the principle of cortical magnification described in the previous section.

Hence each hypercolumn contains neural machinery for analyzing visual information

within a local region of the retina. Throughout the entire visual cortex there are many such hypercolumns, each receiving input from different portions of the retina. Working simultaneously, the hypercolumns analyze the entire retinal image in a local, piecemeal fashion. Each hypercolumn provides a "description" of that portion of the image falling within its own, restricted field of view. This description is embodied within the activity of cells in the constituent columns of the hypercolumn.

At the end of this chapter we shall consider just how these cells might be involved in visual perception. For the moment, though, let's consider what might transpire within the visual cortex as a person stares at a very large picture composed exclusively of, say, vertical lines (see Figure 4.13). This visual stimulus should maximally activate those cells in the cortex that prefer a vertical orientation. All other cells would respond much less vigorously or not at all. Now suppose we could look directly at the person's

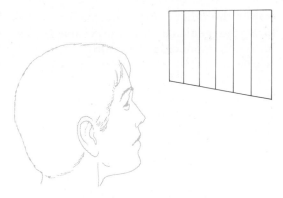

FIGURE 4.13
Imagine what goes on within the visual cortex when a person views a set of vertical lines.

cortex and visualize those cells activated by the vertical lines. On the basis of what you have just learned about the organization of the cortex, can you imagine what we would see?

Because the orientation columns are more or less evenly spaced throughout the entire cortex, we should see a regular pattern of active cells interspersed among a set of inactive ones. And in fact, this is exactly what is seen. Hubel, Wiesel, and Stryker (1978) injected monkeys with a radioactive substance, 2-deoxyglucose, that is incorporated into neurally active cells but not into inac-

tive ones. These monkeys were then exposed for 45 minutes to a visual display composed entirely of vertical bars of different widths. The display was large, and the bars moved back and forth to ensure that the visual cortex received a healthy dose of vertical visual stimulation. Following this exposure, each animal's visual cortex was viewed under a microscope, using a procedure that highlights cells containing the radioactive substance.

Figure 4.14 shows what Hubel and his colleagues saw when they took a sideways view of a slice of the visual cortex of these animals. The regularly spaced, dark, vertical bands correspond to the columns of cortical cells activated by the vertical bars. The lighter bands in between denote regions of cortex containing very little of the radioactive chemical, indicating that cells in these regions were relatively inactive during the stimulation period. The uniformly dark stripe running through the middle of the bands corresponds to layer 4; in this layer vertical contours activated all cells because these cells are not selective for orientation. Measuring the distance between the dark bands (points of maximum concentration of radioactivity) in the photograph gives a value close to half a millimeter. This corresponds nicely to the

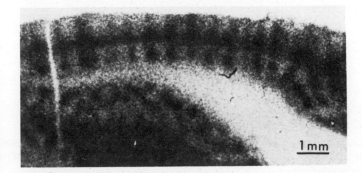

FIGURE 4.14
Magnified picture of a slice of visual cortex from a monkey who viewed a pattern like the one shown in Figure 4.13. (Hubel, Wiesel, and Stryker, 1978).

dimension of an individual hypercolumn estimated from physiological recordings from cortical cells.

These elegant anatomical experiments substantiate that orientation-selective neurons are packed in columns. To test your understanding of the material on orientation columns, suppose Hubel and his colleagues had exposed their monkeys to a set of lines that slowly rotated through all orientations. What would the distribution of radioactive substance have looked like?*

So, cortical cells respond best to contours of specific orientations, sometimes moving in a particular direction. Another unique property of cortical cells is that they are designed to piece together information from the two eyes, as we'll now see.

Binocularity. Recall that information from the two eyes is distributed in separate layers of each lateral geniculate nucleus, with individual cells receiving input from either one

*Similar techniques are being developed for visualizing patterns of neural activity in human visual cortex (Schwartz, Christman, and Wolf, 1984).

eye or the other. Once information passes from the geniculate to the visual cortex, however, **monocular** (meaning "one eye") segregation gives way to **binocular** (meaning "two eyes") integration. At the cortical level, individual cells, with few exceptions, are innervated from both eyes. Figure 4.15 shows how a typical cortical cell responds to stimulation of the two eyes. This particular cell responds moderately well to a line presented to either eye alone, but its response is even stronger when both eyes are stimulated simultaneously. Some cells respond more vigorously to stimulation of the left eye, whereas other cells favor right-eye stimulation. This variation in the relative strength of the connection with the two eyes is called **ocular dominance.** Any cell that can be excited through both eyes, regardless of its ocular dominance, is called a **binocular cell.**

Because they can be excited by either eye, all binocular cells really have two receptive fields, one for the left eye and one for the right eye. Comparing these two fields of a binocular cell, we invariably find them to be

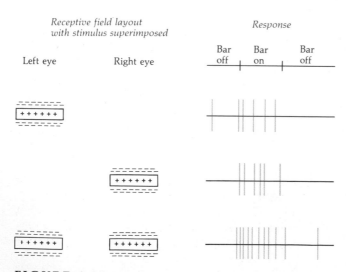

FIGURE 4.15

Response of a single cortical cell to stimulation of the left eye, right eye and both eyes. The +'s and −'s show the receptive field layout for this cell.

matched in type (simple or complex), preferred orientation, and preferred direction of motion. If, for instance, the cell responds best to a horizontal line moving upward in front of the left eye, then upward movement of a horizontal line will also evoke the largest response via the right eye.

The two receptive fields for any particular binocular cell also fall on approximately equivalent regions of the two eyes. Thus if one field is located to the right of the fovea in one eye, the other field will fall to the right of the fovea in the other eye. In general, binocular cortical cells respond most strongly when corresponding regions of each eye are stimulated by forms of corresponding size and orientation.

With this correspondence in mind, think for a moment about where a single object must be situated in the world in order to activate maximally the cell we've just described. To begin, suppose the two eyes fixate a point on the center of a viewing screen, as shown in Figure 4.16. For stimulation of the right eye to activate the binocular cell described above, an object has to be located within the area of the screen labeled "right eye" (see panel A). Note, though, that at this position the image of that object does not fall within the cell's receptive field in the left eye; so at this position stimulation of the left eye would not activate the binocular cell. To be imaged within the left eye's receptive field, and therefore activate this cell, the object must be displaced laterally on the screen, closer to the point of fixation (see panel B). Note, however, that in this location the image of the object no longer falls within the right eye's receptive field. In fact, there is no single position *on* the viewing screen where one object could simultaneously stimulate both the left and right eyes' receptive fields. But there is a position *in front of* the screen that could accomplish this—as shown in panel C: when the object is located at a particular spot in front of the screen

(and hence closer to the eyes), the two receptive fields are both stimulated.

Similarly, for each binocular cell there will be one position in three-dimensional space where the two receptive fields can be simultaneously stimulated. This position will vary, of course, from cell to cell, depending on the retinal placement of the receptive fields. Take a minute to be sure you understand why this is so. A little extra effort at this point will pay nice dividends when we talk about binocular depth perception in Chapter 7. As you will learn then, the layout of binocular receptive fields plays a fundamental role in your ability to judge the distance from one object to another. For now, though, you should appreciate two properties of binocular cells: they respond preferentially to the same type of stimulus in both eyes, and the relative positions of the two receptive fields of a cell specify the location of the stimulus that will optimally excite the cell.

So now you've encountered another important neural operation performed by cells in the primary visual cortex, binocular integration of inputs from the two eyes. This completes our overview of the receptive field properties of cells in this receiving area of the brain. As mentioned at the outset of this section, our survey just hits the highlights of this stage in visual processing. Neurophysiologists have studied cortical cells in considerably greater detail than we've gone into here. They have also begun to unravel the neural circuitry (that is, the connections between cortical cells) underlying such receptive field properties as orientation selectivity. Although fascinating, that research is not immediately germane to the questions about visual perception that will occupy our attention in the next several chapters.

Also keep in mind that we have been focusing on cells in the primary visual cortex, which is still a relatively early stage in visual

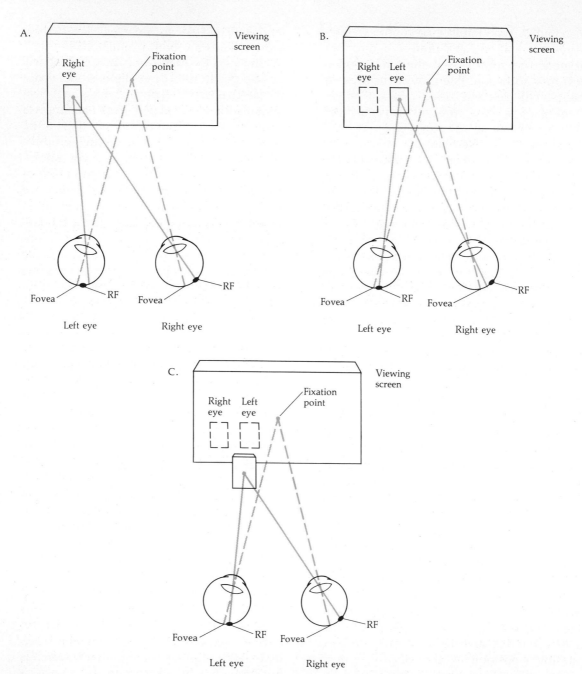

FIGURE 4.16

This series of drawings illustrates why a single object must be situated in a particular location in visual space to optimally stimulate both receptive fields (RFs) of a single binocular cell. For details, see the text.

processing. From this stage, neural information travels to a number of other visual areas of the brain (Van Essen, 1979; Van Essen and Maunsell, 1983). Within each of these subsequent projection areas there exists an orderly retinotopic map. However, these different visual areas appear to be concerned with different aspects of the visual world (Mishkin, Ungerleider, and Macko, 1983). Judging from the receptive field properties of cells in these various areas, some are specialized for analyzing information about color, whereas others are more concerned with movement (Zeki, 1978). Careful study of these other visual areas has only recently begun, and it is not known exactly how many such distinct areas there are. Nor is it known how activity in these separate areas is orchestrated to create the unitary quality of visual perception. However, the existence of these multiple areas may hold the key to understanding some perplexing visual disorders described by people with certain forms of localized brain damage (see Box 4.4, which describes one such disorder). But what was nature's reason for dividing up visual processing among several different areas of the brain? Research into the design of computers and computer programs suggests that such a scheme offers very distinct advantages:

Any large computation should be split up and implemented as a collection of small sub-parts that are as nearly independent of one another as the overall task allows. If a process is not designed in this way, a small change in one place will have consequences in many other places. This means that the process as a whole becomes extremely difficult to debug or to improve, whether by a human designer or in the course of natural evolution, because a small change to improve one part has to be accompanied by many simultaneous compensating changes elsewhere. (Marr, 1976, p. 485)

Whatever the details of this emerging picture of the multiple visual areas of the brain, it is clear that the primary visual cortex serves as the distribution center for all the subsequent stages. This is why we have concentrated in this section on the kinds of visual stimuli required to activate visual cortical neurons. In the next section we shall discuss the possible role of these cortical neurons in seeing. After all, that is a major concern of perception students.

Can Receptive Fields Explain Visual Perception?

No one seriously doubts the visual cortex's crucial involvement in visual perception. This involvement is sadly evidenced by the blindness accompanying damage to this area of the brain. It is further underscored by the fact that visual sensations are evoked whenever the visual cortex is directly stimulated, either by the application of electrical current through a probe placed on the surface of the cortex (Dobelle et al., 1976; Brindley and Lewin, 1968) or by internally generated neural activity arising within the cortex during episodes of migraine headache (Richards, 1971). In these cases of direct brain stimulation, people see flashing spots and lines, sometimes colored, at various locations in their visual fields. Because they occur even with the eyes closed or in total darkness, these **phosphenes,** as the sensations are called, must arise entirely from within the person's visual system. Visual hallucinations experienced under the influence of psychoactive drugs may also reflect the abnormal discharge of cells in the visual cortex (Gregory, 1979).

But although these observations are intriguing, they merely demonstrate that certain areas of the brain are active during visual perception; they don't prove that these cells actually cause perception. What more

BOX 4.4
Cortical Color Blindness

Information about visual processing in cortical areas beyond the primary visual cortex has come from studies of monkeys, cats, and other nonhuman species. Results from those studies indicate that these different cortical areas are concerned with specific aspects of vision, such as color, depth, or movement. Does the human brain also contain such specialized regions of visual processing? The answer to this question may well be yes. In particular, localized damage to the human brain can impair certain aspects of vision while sparing others. The nature of the impairment depends on the site of damage.

One of the most fascinating of these clinical syndromes is characterized by an acquired loss of color perception. What follows is a brief case history of an individual with this unusual disorder. This case is particularly interesting because the damaged region has been pinpointed using modern brain-scan techniques (A detailed description of this case has been given by Pearlman, Birch, and Meadows, 1979.)

The patient was a man in his mid-fifties who prior to his illness had been a customs inspector. To get that job, he had taken a color vision test, which he had passed without difficulty. Following a stroke, he was examined on several occasions, each time complaining that he couldn't see colors. He likened the problem to watching a black and white movie. Although his general health and cognitive abilities remained sound, he was forced to take another job that did not require color judgments. In addition, his deficient color vision interfered with his daily routine. For instance, he had to rely on his wife to select his clothes, so as to avoid wearing weird color combinations, and he was unable to distinguish ripe from unripe fruit.

Following his stroke, this man retained good memory for colors, as evidenced by his ability to associate objects and colors. When shown a black and white outline drawing of familiar objects, he could readily say what color each *should* be. But when he attempted to color the outline drawing using felt-tip pens, he was unable to select the appropriate colors. An example of his results are shown in Color Plate 1 (see the color insert in Chapter 6). This page from a children's coloring book was colored (8 years after his stroke) using the pens shown in the upper part of the picture. He needed 30 minutes to complete this effort, with most of his time spent comparing the various pens before selecting one. Despite the obvious color confusions evidenced in this picture, the man confidently stated that tomatoes should be red, carrots orange, and so on. He wasn't so sure, though, whether he had actually selected the appropriate colors.

Other, more formal tests confirmed that this person possessed very poor color discrimination throughout the color spectrum. In this respect, his performance differed from that of people with congenitally defective color vision. As you'll learn in Chapter 6, congenital color blindness usually involves color confusions within a restricted region of the spectrum; in all likelihood, these forms of color blindness stem from a deficiency in a particular cone photopigment. Because it is congenital, the condition is present throughout an individual's lifetime. In contrast, the person described here had perfectly normal color vision prior to his stroke. Moreover, the stroke affected only his perception of color— his acuity and depth perception remained normal. This indicates that the brain damage resulting from the stroke occurred within a region specialized for analyzing color information. Brain-scan pictures from this patient indicate that the damage occurred within a region known as the prestriate cortex. In both monkeys and humans, this region lies just in front of the primary visual cortex. In monkeys, the prestriate cortex includes a physiologically identified area containing a large number of cells that can be activated only if stimulated by lines or edges of particular colors (Zeki, 1980).

When we consider all this evidence, it is very tempting to conclude that the human brain contains a local region specialized for analyzing color, and that disorders affecting just this region are responsible for the intriguing syndrome known as acquired cortical color blindness.

can we say about the cellular events that actually mediate vision? How much of what you see can be explained by the activity of brain cells that "prefer" various kinds of visual stimuli? To answer these questions intelligently requires that you be familiar with the various aspects of visual perception—movement, color, form, and so on. Since you will read about these topics in the following chapters, it is premature for us to consider the above questions in specific detail now. However, it *is* worthwile for us to consider several arguments that limit attempts to "explain" visual perception entirely on the basis of activity within a small set of brain cells.

To begin, let's quickly reiterate the scheme of visual processing suggested by current physiological evidence. Beginning within the eye itself, the visual image is analyzed in a piecemeal fashion by the 1 million or so receptive fields distributed over the whole of the retina. Each local analysis "looks" for the presence of a contour, using a simple differencing, or center/surround, operation. The results of each local analysis pass to a second differencing operation, where contour information is further amplified; this occurs within the lateral geniculate nucleus. From the LGN the local analysis progresses to the cortex, where neurons become even more discriminating. At this level, the neural analysis focuses on the size, shape, and orientation of contours, as well as on the direction and speed of motion of those contours. This cortical analysis operates on local regions of the retina. The cortical machinery responsible for this analysis consists of an aggregate of cells grouped into what is called a hypercolumn. Each hypercolumn looks at a restricted region of visual space.

CORTICAL CELLS AS "FEATURE DETECTORS"

In view of this elaborate neural machinery, it is tempting to conclude that a cortical cell, when active, asserts something very specific about the nature of an object located at a particular region of visual space. This idea has been most thoroughly developed by Barlow (1972), who coined the term "feature detector" to characterize visual neurons with very specific stimulus requirements. According to this idea, feature-detecting neurons at higher and higher levels of visual processing become increasingly refined, to the point where they respond only to a very specific object or event (such as a red Ferrari sports car).

But this line of reasoning runs into a real stumbling block that you can probably anticipate: it requires there to be as many feature detectors as there are unique objects that you could recognize within your lifetime. These feature detectors would even have to be prepared to recognize novel objects that had never before been seen by anyone. Although enormously large, the number of brain cells available for this task hardly seems adequate to cover the repertoire of visual experiences that most people will enjoy in their lifetimes. Remember, the brain has other jobs to accomplish besides vision!

We run into another problem when talking about cortical cells as "feature detectors." Ideally such a detector would respond only when the requisite feature was present in the visual image, and in the presence of any other feature it would remain completely silent. To behave otherwise would introduce ambiguity into the detector's message, for one could never be sure which feature had activated the cell. Yet real neurons suffer from exactly this problem. Here is what we mean. As you learned earlier in this chapter, the responses of cortical cells may vary depending on such stimulus features as orientation and direction of motion. A change in any one of those features would be sufficient to reduce the level of activity in such a cell. But purely on the basis of such a reduction in the level of activity of that cell, we could never be sure *which* stimulus feature, or features, had actually changed.

Let's illustrate this problem of ambiguity with an example. Suppose a single vertical line moves slowly from left to right in front of you. Presumably this event will produce a burst of activity in those cortical cells maximally responsive both to slow rates of movement and to vertically oriented contours. Panel A of Figure 4.17 illustrates how one such cell might respond to this stimulus. We can go so far as to presume that activity in cells such as the one illustrated *causes* you to see the moving line. But now suppose the same vertical line moves more rapidly from left to right. This increased speed will reduce the neural activity within your set of cortical cells, for they prefer slower motion. Such a reduction is illustrated in panel B of Figure 4.17. But an equivalent reduction in neural activity could be produced another way as well. We could present the line at the preferred, slow rate of movement but change the orientation of the line

slightly, so that it was no longer exactly vertical. As panel C of Figure 4.17 shows, this change in orientation also reduces the cell's response. Thus changing *either* orientation *or* speed of movement would diminish the level of activity in cells such as the one illustrated. Just looking at the activity level of a small set of cells, then, we cannot tell which stimulus event actually occurred. The activity level of a cell provides an ambiguous message.

Neurons in the visual cortex cannot really be called "feature detectors," then, because individual cells cannot signal the presence of a particular visual feature with certainty. The ambiguity inherent in the response of a single cell can be overcome, however, by *collaboration* among a set of neurons (Regan, 1982). To illustrate, let's reconsider our example involving a moving line. When the line is tilted slightly away from vertical, neurons preferring vertical will show a drop in activity, just as we pointed out above. But at the same time neurons preferring the new orientation will show an increase in their level of firing. By comparing the levels of neural activity in these two sets of cells, each tuned to slightly different orientations, we could infer that the line had changed in orientation, not in speed. In other words, ambiguity within a single set of neurons can be overcome by considering the pattern of activity among sets of neurons tuned to different values along a stimulus dimension such as orientation. Box 4.5 uses this idea to explain two intriguing visual illusions involving misjudgments of the orientation of lines.

According to the scheme developed above, features are signaled within an ensemble of cells. The ensemble, in effect, would inspect the contour information within a local region of the retinal image and "vote" on the most likely feature producing the activity profile within that ensemble. These local "elections" would be occurring among a large

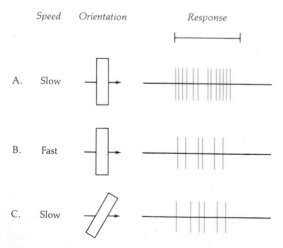

FIGURE 4.17
The response of one cortical cell to different combinations of speed and orientation of a moving bar.

BOX 4.5
The Tilt Aftereffect

Cells in the visual system, like those in other sensory systems, undergo a process called **adaptation.** When stimulated intensely for a period of time, they become temporarily fatigued and are, therefore, less responsive (Maffei and Fiorentini, 1973; Movshon and Lennie, 1979). What might be the perceptual consequences of temporarily reducing the responsiveness of orientation-selective cells of the visual cortex? One consequence may be the **tilt aftereffect,** a temporary change in the perceived orientation of lines. We'd like you first to experience this intriguing illusion for yourself; then we'll consider how it might be explained in terms of neural fatigue, or adaptation.

To begin, look at the three sets of bar patterns shown below. You should note that the bars in the middle set (the "test" pattern) are oriented straight up and down. Now stare for a minute or so at the left-hand pattern, the one composed of bars tilted slightly counter-clockwise. Let your gaze wander around the circle within the pattern while you are "adapting" to it. Finally, after this period of adaptation, quickly look back at the test

bars in the middle. You will see that the vertical bars now appear tilted slightly clockwise. This compelling illusion wears off rather quickly, so you can repeat this adaptation procedure as soon as the test bars once again look perfectly vertical. This time, adapt for a minute to the tilted bars in the right-hand pattern, again being careful to move your eyes around the circle. After you have adapted to this clockwise orientation, the bars of the test pattern will appear rotated in a counterclockwise direction. So you have learned that the apparent orientation of the test bars deviates *away* from the orientation of the adapting bars. Now let's consider how this tilt aftereffect may be explained.

In the text, we pointed out the ambiguity inherent in the response of any single cell. To get around this problem, stimulus properties such as orientation might be represented by the relative activity within a *set* of orientation-selective cells. In the case of vertical lines, this activity profile might look like that shown in the diagram on the next page (adapted from Blakemore, 1973). In the upper part of the diagram, each tepee-shaped curve represents

the orientation tuning curve for a cortical cell with a particular preferred orientation (recall Figure 4.9). The preferred orientation for each of the cells shown is represented just above the peak of the cells' tuning curve. For example, the middle tuning curve corresponds to a cell maximally responsive to vertical. When this ensemble of cells is stimulated by vertical test bars, the cells within the ensemble respond unequally. Cells with preferred orientations at vertical respond most vigorously, and those with preferred orientations removed from vertical respond less vigorously. This distribution of responses is depicted in the bar graph at the lower left of the diagram. Because this distribution of activity peaks at vertical, this is the perceived orientation of the test pattern. Suppose we now adapt this array of cells to bars tilted slightly clockwise from vertical (the pattern labeled "adapt"). With prolonged exposure, all cells activated by this orientation will be fatigued; the cells maximally responsive to the adapting orientation will be maximally fatigued and hence least responsive following adaptation.

(Continued on next page)

TILT AFTEREFFECT

Adapt

Test

Adapt

The upper right-hand portion of the diagram shows what will result when the partially adapted array of cells is again confronted with vertical. Notice that cells maximally stimulated by the tilted adaptation pattern are now fatigued and hence less able to respond to the vertical test. These fatigued cells include ones whose preferred orientation is vertical. Thus the distribution of responses produced by the vertical test pattern (lower right panel) is no longer centered around vertical. Instead, the peak of this distribution is centered on those cells whose preferred orientation is slightly counterclockwise to vertical. For this reason the test bars, though physically vertical, seem tilted counterclockwise to vertical. Evidently the fatigued cells recover quickly, since the tilt aftereffect lasts for a very short time.

See if you can apply the same reasoning to explain why adapting to an orientation counterclockwise to vertical generates a clockwise tilt aftereffect. Using this theory, see if you can also predict what will happen if you alternately adapt to both orientations by looking at one for 5 seconds and then the other for 5 seconds and so on, until a minute has elapsed. Presumably, this should fatigue cells on both sides of vertical. After you have derived your prediction, you can test it by actually adapting in that alternating fashion.

Before leaving this topic, let's consider another compelling illusion involving misjudgments of orientation, one whose neural basis may be similar to that of the tilt aftereffect. This illusion, shown opposite, does not require prior adaptation; it is induced by the simultaneous

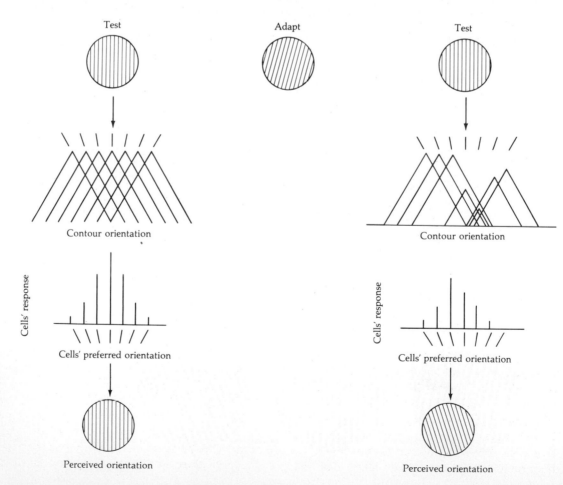

Test

Adapt

Test

Contour orientation

Contour orientation

Cells' response

Cells' response

Cells' preferred orientation

Cells' preferred orientation

Perceived orientation

Perceived orientation

presence of two different orientations. Here the bars within the two circular regions appear to be tilted in opposite directions, yet they are in fact vertical and parallel to one another. To convince yourself of this, lay a straight edge down the entire center of the figure—you'll see that the central bars line up perfectly. Blakemore, Carpenter, and Georgeson (1970) have proposed that this orientation illusion is caused by one column of cortical cells reducing the activity within another, neighboring column of cells. According to Blakemore and his colleagues, this form of neural interaction sharpens the orientation selectivity of cortical cells. Indeed, there *is* direct physiological evidence for such a sharpening mechanism (Pettigrew and Daniels, 1973; Blakemore and Tobin, 1972). Blakemore and his colleagues proposed that neural interaction also changes the activity profile produced by the bars in the central regions—a change resembling that envisioned for the tilt aftereffect. This causes the apparent twisting of the bars away from vertical. Recently, Christopher Tyler and Ken Nakayama have suggested that similar interactions among orientation-selective neurons can account for several other illusions of orientation including the Zöllner illusion pictured in Figure 1.5 (Tyler and Nakayama, 1984).

These illusions of orientation may be providing us with an indirect glimpse at the operation of orientation-selective cells in the human brain. For this reason, some visual scientists (for example, Frisby, 1980) have referred to thses phenomena as "the psychologist's microelectrode." As you will learn in the remaining chapters, aftereffects and illusions are indeed popular tools for probing the human visual system.

number of ensembles devoted to different regions of the retinal image. In fact, these ensembles could consist of the hypercolumns we described earlier. At the moment, however, we have no idea how "votes" would be tabulated within an ensemble, or hypercolumn; physiologists have not yet uncovered a cellular mechanism for reading the output of hypercolumns.

For the sake of argument, let's assume that the ambiguity inherent in the responses of individual cells can be solved by some local collaboration process such as that described above. This would mean that the primary visual cortex *does* contain a neural representation of biologically relevant features, such as oriented lines and edges. Still, such a representation could not entirely account for visual perception, for there are qualities of visual perception that have no obvious analogues within this cortical representation. Let's consider a couple of these qualities.

ASPECTS OF VISION UNEXPLAINED BY FEATURE DETECTORS

Integration of Local Features. One property of vision that you will learn about in the next chapter concerns the grouping of fragmentary impressions into organized, meaningful patterns. In vision there is a strong tendency to group bits and pieces of information into a meaningful form, even when that form is only vaguely suggested by the bits and pieces. For example, the seemingly random aggregation of black patches in Figure 4.18 eventually becomes organized into a meaningful scene. (Take a moment to study Figure 4.18 before reading on.) This percept must result from the synthesis of contour information gathered from over a large portion of the picture. Looking at only local regions of the picture, as cortical cells do, would never lead to recognition of the scene and the central object within that scene. Rather, we see the scene and the object because of some more widespread, or global, comparison of local contour information. Visual perception is replete with examples like this one, and they remind us that local feature analysis by the brain represents an early stage

FIGURE 4.18
Differentiating the elements of this picture into meaningful objects is difficult at first, and would probably be impossible if you had no previous knowledge of or experience with the objects depicted. If you cannot discern the composition of the picture after studying it, consult Figure 4.19's caption.

FIGURE 4.19
An ambiguous figure that can be seen in either of two ways. (Incidentally, Figure 4.18 depicts a Dalmatian dog walking toward a tree.)

in the sequence of neural events underlying perception.

Instability of Perception. Figure 4.19 illustrates another formidable challenge for theories of visual perception based solely on neural analyzing mechanisms in the visual cortex. Here the visual system is presented with a single figure that, although physically invariant, may be seen in two strikingly different ways. This well-known example was devised by the late E. G. Boring, a famous American psychologist (Boring, 1930). If you look at the picture for a few moments, you will see why it is sometimes called the "Wife and Mother-in-Law" figure: sometimes the figure looks like a coy young girl and other times it appears to be an ugly old woman. These fluctuations in the figure's appearance occur even though the stimulus information reaching your eyes remains unchanged. From what we know about the receptive field properties of cortical cells, the activity in your visual cortex

should not be changing over time as you stare at this picture, because the contour information contained in the picture remains the same. Presumably the neural events responsible for the spontaneous changes in the appearance of the figure arise at some higher level of visual processing beyond the visual cortex. We shall have more to say about figures of this sort in Chapter 12.

Externalization of the Visual World. Let's consider one final aspect of visual perception that has no obvious analogue within the activity of visual cortical cells—the externalization of sensed events (Blakemore, 1979). One never feels that visual sensations are localized within the eyes or the brain, yet the requisite events for seeing occur entirely within the head. Why, then, are the objects and events one sees automatically referred to the world beyond one's eyes? "Objects are externalized," you might reply, "because in fact that's where they really are." But this merely restates the observation without explaining how this aspect of perception of externality is represented within the visual nervous system. Having accepted the idea that vision evolves from the pattern of activity within areas of the brain, one cannot now treat externality as a fundamentally different aspect of vision that supersedes this level of explanation. Instead, one is obliged to view externality as a property of perception that must eventually be included within any brain-based theory of perception. At present, however, it is not known why objects are visualized outside the body, and the reason may prove as elusive as the basis of conscious experience itself.

To sum up, it would be a mistake to make the visual cortex bear the entire burden of visual perception. The cortex is elegantly designed to derive information concerning the shapes and locations of boundaries in the retinal image—an important early step in the process of seeing (Marr, 1982). But seeing involves more than this. Rather than experiencing a conglomeration of unconnected contours scattered throughout the field of view, we see these contours organized into whole objects whose sizes and shapes remain constant. This organization in perception mirrors the organization of real objects as they actually exist. The correspondence between perceptual experience and the objects represented in that experience is not accidental (Campbell, 1974; Shepard, 1981). After all, the visual system did evolve for a purpose, namely to inform one about the objects with which one needs to interact. Presumably, natural selection has sponsored this correspondence between perception and the physical world. William James put this idea succinctly: ''Mind and world . . . have evolved together, and in consequence are something of a mutual fit'' (James, 1892, p. 4).

Summary and Preview

These last two chapters have provided an overview of some of the neural machinery of visual perception. We are now ready to shift the focus to perception itself. In the next several chapters, we are going to examine different aspects, or qualities, of vision. These qualities of vision—shape, color, movement, and depth—serve to differentiate objects from one another. In discussing each of these qualities of vision, we shall treat them as the final product of the visual system's processing. We shall consider what sort of mechanism would be needed to yield this product. However, the major emphasis will be on *what* you see, rather than on *how* you see.

Chapter 5

Spatial Vision and Pattern Perception

People use sight for many different things: reading street signs, noticing when a friend has had a haircut, catching a football, flying an airplane, finding a pencil amid a desk's clutter, and many others. Though the number of tasks that depend on vision is enormous, those tasks typically involve picking out objects from their surroundings. We can call this process **detection.** Sometimes people need to go one step further, distinguishing one object from another. We can call this second, more refined process **discrimination.** In order to deal with their environment successfully, people must be able to do both: detect and discriminate.

Basically, detection tells you that objects are present. Discrimination, however, serves a more complicated purpose. For example, visual discrimination allows you to sort out important from unimportant information. Of course, what is important depends on your needs. Faced with a homework

assignment, you must be able to distinguish one book from another; when famished, you'd better be able to distinguish the edible from the inedible; when you read, you have to distinguish one letter from another.

To detect and discriminate, you depend on various sources of visual information. To make this more concrete, consider detection. An object can differ in many ways from its surroundings. For instance, the object can differ in color (a ripe, red berry against the green leaves of its bush), movement (a moving insect in a stationary environment), shape (a chocolate-covered cherry in the box of mixed chocolates), or depth (an aspirin tablet lying on a white tile floor). Most of the time, several of these sources of information are available simultaneously, facilitating detection. A breeze causes some red berries to *move* relative to the green leaves, making the berries even more conspicuous.

This chapter and the three that follow

137

deal with these sources of visual information. Although each chapter emphasizes one source (such as movement), we shall also examine how these various sources interact. The present chapter examines how an object's spatial properties influence detection and discrimination. We use the term "spatial properties" to refer to those attributes of an object that jointly determine the perceived size and shape of the object. Defined in this way, the term "spatial properties" is more or less synonymous with the often-used terms "form" and "visual pattern."

What Defines an Object?

What are the requirements for recognizing that an object is present? To answer this question, let's imagine an object that appears within uniformly illuminated surroundings. Your success in recognizing the object's presence depends not so much on the amount of light reflected by the object, as on the *difference* between that amount of light and the light reflected by the object's surroundings. Recall, from Chapters 3 and 4, that the nervous system is designed precisely to register such differences. In general, as the intensity of an object's background increases, the light reflected from that object must be even more intense in order for the object to be seen. This is why you cannot see the stars in the daytime sky even though they are present and no less intense than they are at night.*

The difference in intensity between an object and its immediate surroundings is termed **contrast.** Although there are various definitions of "contrast," for our purposes you need remember only that contrast grows with the difference between the intensity of an object and the intensity of its surroundings. It doesn't matter whether the object is

*This is but one example of a more general principle known as *Weber's Law*, which is discussed in the Appendix.

lighter or darker than its surroundings; rather it is the *difference* between object and surround that influences whether the object's presence can be recognized. Sometimes, however, it's insufficient to know merely that an object is present; the object's shape must also be known. This requires information about more than just contrast. You need to know the spatial arrangement of the contrast, since that's what defines an object's shape (see Figure 5.1). Therefore, both contrast and spatial arrangement are key elements in the perception of form.

What Are the Units of Form Perception?

You probably have some intuitive sense of what is meant by an object's "form"; typically the term refers to such attributes as size and shape. Like all other aspects of perception, perceived form results from a series of steps, most of which occur at a preconscious level. Thus simply studying the end product of this series of steps—perceived form—cannot tell you everything about how it came to be. Let us consider an analogy. The end product of cooking may be a so-

FIGURE 5.1
What specifies the shape of an object?

phisticated dish, but simply by looking at or tasting that dish, it's difficult to determine all its ingredients.

In many areas of science, progress in understanding goes hand in hand with an analytical approach—one that breaks the phenomena of that science down into appropriate components (Julesz and Schumer, 1981). This strategy has been successfully exploited by the older sciences such as physics, chemistry, and biology. In the scientific study of perception, a newer discipline, an analytical approach may be just as helpful. Therefore, we begin our discussion by trying to identify the fundamental components of form perception: the elements comprising the experience of visual form.

One's ideas about the fundamental units of form perception determine how one conceptualizes the problem and studies it. This chapter emphasizes one particular approach that explicitly identifies the components of form perception. This relatively new approach has the major virtue of unifying the results from many different experiments, both perceptual and physiological.

Before learning about this newer approach, though, you should be familiar with two important alternative approaches that played an important role in shaping the newer one. The two older views advocate diametrically opposed ideas about the units of form perception. One view assumes that the units are elementary, punctate sensations such as those evoked by single, discrete points of light. The opposing view assumes that form perception cannot be decomposed into elementary sensations; instead, the units of perception are much larger—that is, whole forms. The first approach could be described as elementary or microscopic, and the second approach as global or macroscopic. The contemporary view emphasized in this chapter falls between these extremes. We'll begin, though, with the extreme approaches.

Traditional Approaches to Form Perception

STRUCTURALISM

The structuralist tradition in perception germinated in late-nineteenth-century Europe and flowered after being transplanted to America. Its main idea is simple and attractive: complex mental processes—ideas and perceptions—are created by combining fundamental components. According to this view, simple sensations constitute the building blocks of perceived form. Given this assumption, how does one identify these simple sensations? E. B. Titchener, a leader of the structuralist movement, advocated a very simple method, called **analytic introspection.** He trained people to ignore all aspects of an object except its immediate, primary qualities. By attending only to an object's appearance and nothing else, people tried to enumerate the various sensations evoked by that object. For example, a person looking at an apple might report seeing four different colors and seventy-three different levels of lightness, with both color and lightness distributed over the apple's surface in some particular way. According to the structuralists, these ingredients constituted the sensations from which the percept of the apple was built.

After analytic introspection had been in use for a while, the number of cataloged "elementary" sensations ballooned out of control, to more than 40,000 (Boring, 1942). Compared to the number of chemical elements in the periodic table (currently, 109), 40,000 perceptual elements seemed excessive. To make matters worse, one person's reported elementary sensations often differed from those of another person. These disagreements were particularly striking because they involved people working in different laboratories. This suggests that the technique of introspection is susceptible to such nonperceptual influences as motivation and instruction. As you might imagine, what people *say* they saw depends partly on what they're encouraged to see ("Don't you think this apple has a slight tinge of green?").

Besides these problems, introspection suffers from a logical flaw, too. Even if someone can learn to recognize a particular sensation when it occurs all by itself, there's no guarantee that the person will be able to recognize it when that sensation occurs in combination with various other sensations. Taken together, these difficulties undermined the usefulness of analytic introspection. Nonetheless, one can embrace the structuralists' idea that perceptions are built from elementary units without subscribing to introspection as the method for isolating those units.

THE GESTALT SCHOOL

In Chapter 3, we saw that the neural response to even the simplest stimulus—a patch of light—depends on its surroundings. It has long been known that this dependence operates at the perceptual level. In 1920, the German psychologist Wolfgang Köhler insisted, "We do not see individual fractions of a thing; instead, the mode of appearance of each part depends not only upon the stimulation arising at *that* point but upon the conditions prevailing at other points as well" (1920/1938, p. 20). Köhler's comment relates to the lightness illusions described in Chapter 3.

Köhler's view formed the basis of the second major theory of pattern perception—a theory which rejected the idea that perception is an aggregate of simple elements somehow knitted together. Instead its adherents, called Gestalt psychologists, emphasized overall structure or pattern as the major determinant of form perception (*Gestalt* is a German word meaning "form").

Their credo is often summarized by the phrase "The whole is greater than the sum of the individual parts." Here is an analogy. Perhaps you have seen the intricate and precise formations assumed by migrating birds (see Figure 5.2). Focusing on individual members of the flock makes it impossible to capture the overall pattern of the formation. The formation itself emerges only from the coalescence of all the birds. In a similar vein, Gestalt psychologists assert that form cannot be captured by looking at discrete stimulus elements.

One important and lasting contribution of the Gestalt approach was the identification of the figural properties that cause perceptual forms to emerge and group together, segregated from their surroundings. To understand what is meant by "forms emerging and grouping together," look at Figure 5.3. You have no trouble recognizing that this is the face of a girl who is looking through a window. But consider what your visual system had to accomplish in order to arrive at this percept. At a minimum, it had to group together contours from one object (the face) and segregate them from contours belonging to another object (the window). If the visual system made errors while grouping things, you might instead experience a single, very strange object. The grouping process capitalizes on certain regularities of objects in the physical world, and the Gestalt principles attempt to summarize what those regularities are. Let's go over several of those principles now.

FIGURE 5.2
As a group flying in formation, geese form a flock.

FIGURE 5.3
Seeing an object entails segregating contours into a meaningful whole. (R. Sekuler.)

Max Wertheimer (1923/1958) described the regularities used by the visual system to group objects. He noted that when many stimulus elements are present simultaneously, they tend to become grouped or organized perceptually into distinct patterns. Although various organizations are possible, people see one particular organization or pattern. The **Gestalt principles of organization** describe how figural properties determine perceived pattern (Hochberg, 1971). Let's examine two principles that Wertheimer considered particularly important.

The principle of **proximity** describes the tendency of objects near one another to group together as a perceptual unit. As you can see in panel A of Figure 5.4, no particular organization seems to predominate when the dots are all equally spaced. Instead, the dots can be seen as forming rows, columns, di-

agonals, or simply as a collection with no pattern. None of these weak organizations persists, and none seems compelling. In fact, some effort is needed to see any of these organizations. Notice what happens, however, when the vertical distances among neighboring dots are made smaller than the horizontal distances, as in panel B of the figure. With this simple modification, a strong organization emerges: the dots form vertical strings, or columns. Panel C illustrates what happens when the horizontal distances are made smaller than the vertical: dots group into horizontal strings, or rows. Simply by varying the ratio of vertical to horizontal distances (that is, by varying the dots' proximity), we can bias the resulting percept in favor of one organization or the other. So proximity is one of the regularities that you use to organize a visual scene into distinct objects.

Wertheimer identified another major organizational tendency, known as the principle of **similarity.** "Other things being equal, if several stimuli are presented together, there is a tendency to see the form in such a way that the similar items are grouped together" (1923/1958, p. 119). The dimensions of similarity that control grouping include lightness, orientation, and size. Examples of these effects are illustrated in Figure 5.5. Notice in the left-hand figure at the top how the circles in the midst of the squares form a perceptual group. Apparently the differences between circles and squares in both

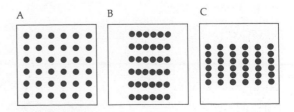

FIGURE 5.4
Objects close together tend to unite perceptually into groups.

FIGURE 5.5
Objects similar in shape and size tend to group together, although there are limits to this tendency. (Bottom panel from Julesz, 1984.)

lightness and shape contribute to this grouping. In the right-hand figure at the top, the disks form two diagonals criss-crossing the squares. Here it is shape alone that promotes grouping. But not all differences in shape are adequate to produce perceptual grouping (Julesz, 1984). In the bottom figure, you can plainly see the cluster of plus signs in the midst of the little "Ls"; but it is very hard to see the cluster of "Ts" embedded in the "Ls" in the right-hand side of the figure. Only by scrutinizing the elements individually can you discover the existence of a group of "Ts".

With these two principles—proximity and similarity—in mind, go back to Figure 5.3. You should now be able to identify what regularities your visual system may have used in order to segregate the girl's face from the window.

The Gestalt psychologists incorporated these principles into a particular theory of how the brain worked. According to their theory, visual perception is determined by the pattern of electrical activity within the brain. To illustrate this concept, imagine that you are looking at an object—such as a bottle of soda—while someone else measures the distribution of electrical activity within your brain. The Gestalt psychologists believed that this distribution would resemble the shape of the object you were seeing (see Figure 5.6). This comparability between perception and brain activity is known as **isomorphism,** and it plays a prominent role in Gestalt theory. Note that "isomorphism" doesn't imply an exact correspondence, just an approximate one.*

How does isomorphism explain the principles of figural grouping described above?

FIGURE 5.6
The Gestalt idea of isomorphism.

According to Gestalt theory, the electrical activity produced by a stimulus spreads over a restricted region of the brain. The shape assumed by this spreading activity is governed by the same forces that control other, inorganic physical systems. A drop of oil on the surface of water tends to assume a uniform, compact shape; likewise, the brain's response to some visual stimulus will *tend* to assume a uniform, compact distribution. The appearance of a visual object would be determined by the properties of this distribution of brain activity. Since, the theory holds, the distribution of brain activity tends to be uniform and compact, raggedness or small discontinuities in figures tend not to be seen. This property of brain activity would tend to obscure small breaks or gaps in figures, thereby completing them. This tendency is called the principle of **closure.** Closure also tends to unite contours that are in close proximity; Figure 5.7 illustrates this

Iso means "the same"; *morph* refers to "form." "One system is said to be isomorphic with another . . . if every point in one corresponds to a point in the other and the topological relations or spatial orders of the points are the same in the two. If a system of points is marked on a flat rubber membrane and the membrane is then stretched tightly over some irregular surface, then the points in the stretched membrane are isomorphic with the points in the flat membrane" (Boring, 1942, pp. 83–84).

FIGURE 5.7
A demonstration of closure. (Adapted from Köhler, 1969.)

tendency. At first the figure may look like a meaningless row of heartlike forms. But actually the pattern contains a handwritten version of a simple and common word—"men." In fact, the pattern contains two copies of that word, each standing in mirror-image relation to the other. Closure causes the two mirror images to cohere into a single pattern, thereby obscuring the two components.

The tendency of brain activity to form small, compact distributions would also *accentuate* figures, making them stand out from their surroundings. This accentuation is important for what the Gestaltists called **figure-ground perception**—the tendency to see parts of a scene as solid, well-defined objects (the "figure") standing out against a less distinct background (the "ground"). In addition, the apparent *location* of an object depends on where the peak activity occurs in the brain (Köhler, 1920/1938). Because of their spread, the distributions of activity produced by adjacent objects tend to be drawn together, thus explaining the tendency of adjacent objects to form perceptual groups (like the dots in Figure 5.4).

The Gestaltists made many valid points about perception, particularly ones concerning the principles of figural organization. But their overall contribution to perceptual theory has definite limitations. First, their theory of brain function (isomorphism), although reasonable in principle, turns out to be wrong. As Chapter 4 showed, the visual world is not represented as an isomorphic picture within the brain. Moreover, we now know that activity within the brain does not actually spread over the distances envisioned by the Gestaltists (Sperry, Miner, and Meyers, 1955).

So far we have considered two contrasting approaches to pattern perception. One, the structuralist approach, treated form perception as an analytical process, whereby

complex forms were decomposed into small, simple elements. While intuitively plausible, this approach floundered because of disagreement about what those simple elements might be. In part, this disagreement stemmed from the unreliability of the introspective technique. But the structuralist approach also could not account for the figural properties that the Gestaltists emphasized. The Gestaltists in turn ran into difficulties: their theory of brain function, which was crucial for explaining their demonstrations, proved to be wrong. The contribution of the Gestalt movement was limited also because of the theory not being sufficiently quantitative. The Gestalt demonstrations, though interesting and impressive, did not readily predict what would be seen in the case of other, novel stimuli. The rules required for quantitative generalization are only now being worked out (Beck, 1966; Zahn, 1971; Pomerantz, 1981; Yodogawa, 1982; Caelli and Dodwell, 1982; Julesz, 1984).

With this background in mind, we turn to an alternative approach to the problem of form perception—one that incorporates some of the good qualities of both the Gestalt and the structuralist approaches.

A Contemporary Approach to Form Perception

As Julian Hochberg has argued, the fundamental units of visual form are probably neither as small and discrete as the structuralists believed, nor as large and global as the Gestaltists claimed (Hochberg, 1971). Instead, some compromise between these extreme positions now seems reasonable. This compromise is reflected in a major contemporary approach to form perception. While still too new to evaluate thoroughly, the theory has had an enormous impact and thus deserves some detailed treatment. This contemporary approach may at first appear somewhat abstract and counterintuitive. As you'll see, no degree of introspection would disclose units of perception such as those suggested by the approach. Perhaps the best way to introduce this new theory of form perception is to describe the first, classic study that heralded it.

AN OUTLINE OF THE MODEL

In 1968, two British vision researchers, Fergus Campbell and John Robson, reported some experiments on form perception that were motivated by a novel theory based on known receptive field properties of visual neurons. Campbell and Robson (1968) hypothesized that the units of pattern perception might be those into which the visual cortex decomposes a scene, namely bars and edges of different orientations and sizes (recall Chapter 4). To test their hypothesis, Campbell and Robson needed stimuli whose orientation and size could be varied systematically. In addition, knowing that contrast is important in detection, they needed to specify and vary contrast as well. A stimulus such as the one shown in Figure 5.8 satisfies all these requirements. Such pat-

terns, called **gratings,** can be generated on a television display. The one in Figure 5.8 is called a **sinusoidal grating** because the intensity of its light and dark bars changes gradually, in a sinusoidal fashion. At sufficiently low contrast, the television screen would appear uniform and unpatterned; at higher contrasts, the pattern would be visible. For various gratings, Campbell and Robson determined the *minimum* contrast necessary to see the grating, a value called the **contrast threshold.**

Two types of gratings were used: *simple* and *compound.* Compound gratings were created by adding together several different simple sinusoidal gratings. Before describing the experiment itself, let's examine the process by which a compound grating is created. This process is illustrated in Figure 5.9—where a compound grating is constructed from three different simple sinusoidal components. The left column shows the simple components, labeled *A* through *C*. Note that as we go from top to bottom, gratings have thinner bars. Specifically, bars in grating *A* are three times as wide as those in grating *B*, and five times as wide as those in grating *C*. All three patterns have the same contrast.

The middle column of Figure 5.9 portrays the creation of a compound grating from the three simple components shown in the left column. To make it easier to visualize, we have broken the process down into steps. Grating *D* is the starting point, a replica of grating *A*. When gratings *A* and *B* are added, the result is grating *E*. When *C* is added to *E*, the result is grating *F*. Grating *F* exemplifies the compound gratings that Campbell and Robson worked with.

We'll now turn to the predictions Campbell and Robson made about the visibility and appearance of compound stimuli. According to their theory, the different components of a compound grating activate different sets of neurons in the visual cortex.

FIGURE 5.8
A sinusoidal grating pattern.

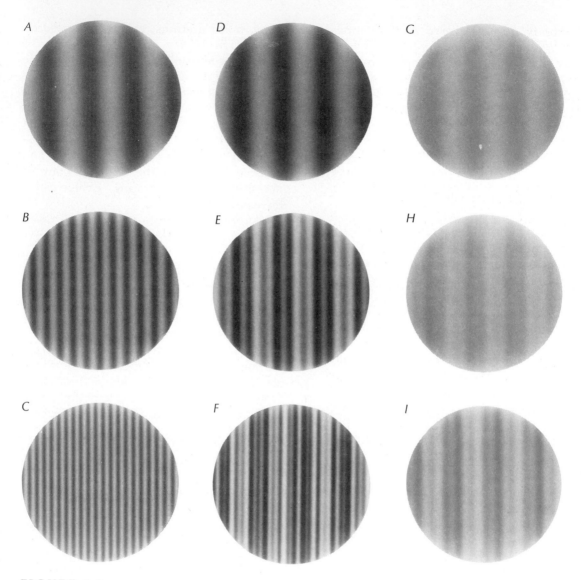

FIGURE 5.9
Steps involved in generating a complex grating from a set of simple sinusoidal patterns.

Each set of neurons would be sensitive to bars of a particular size and, hence, to only one component in the compound. In other words, Campbell and Robson thought that perception of compound gratings, such as grating *F*, was mediated by several different sets of neurons; and that each set of neurons responded to a different component in the compound. Thus although the compound grating doesn't *look* like any of its components, its appearance nonetheless depends on all of them. Neurons activated by the separate components would have to be simultaneously activated in order for the compound to appear the way it does.

If this theory is correct, it should be possible to measure the contributions made by the separate components in a compound grating. How, though, can this be accomplished? Campbell and Robson reasoned that they could do this by comparing the contrast threshold for a compound grating to the contrast thresholds of its components. From measurements with simple gratings, they already knew that the various components had different thresholds—some components required more contrast to be seen, others less.

Imagine that we set the contrast of grating *F* at a value low enough to make the pattern invisible. We then begin increasing *F's* contrast until something *is* seen on the television display. At this point, the display does not look like a compound grating; instead, it looks like one of the simple components (though at low contrast). Specifically, it resembles that component which has the lowest contrast threshold (grating *A*). In fact, the contrast of that one component in the compound is precisely equivalent to the contrast threshold of that component alone. At this low contrast, only this one component produces activity in the visual system sufficient for the component to be seen (grating *G*). Though physically present in the display, the remaining components are too weak to affect the appearance and visibility of the compound.

Now suppose we continue to increase the contrast of the compound grating. At some point, the display no longer looks like that one simple component (grating *A*) alone. Instead, the display looks like a low-contrast version of grating *E*. This is represented in grating *H*. Component *A* and component *B* now seem to be contributing to the appearance of the display. We also note that this

higher-contrast value corresponds to the threshold value for a second component of the compound, grating *B*. At this higher contrast, then, two components seem to be affecting the visual system, as evidenced by the appearance of the compound. Further increases in contrast bring an additional, predictable change in the compound's appearance. As component *C* reaches its own threshold contrast, the appearance of the compound is again altered (grating *I*).

This, then, is the essence of Campbell and Robson's classic study. Using various compound gratings, they showed that the visibility and appearance of a compound grating depends on the independent effects that each of its components has on the visual system. At high contrast, a compound grating doesn't resemble any of its components, but the visual system still treats that compound as an aggregation of several components. These results supported Campbell and Robson's hypothesis that the visual system contains sets of neurons tuned to different bar widths. They called these sets of neurons *channels,* and because their theory relates form perception to activity within many such channels, it is known as the **multichannel model.** Although it can account for Campbell and Robson's results, you may have some reservations about this model. When looking at complicated forms, you see no hint of simpler components consisting of bars of different sizes; your conscious experience doesn't point to any such process of decomposition. You might argue, therefore, that Campbell and Robson tested this model using highly artificial stimuli (but see Figure 5.10). We'll address this reservation by showing how the approach of Campbell and Robson can be extended to more natural, everyday scenes. To make this extension, though, we first need to consider grating patterns in greater detail.

FIGURE 5.10
Stripes abound in the world.

GRATINGS AS TOOLS FOR EXPLORING FORM PERCEPTION

What Exactly Are Gratings? Gratings have four properties—**spatial frequency, contrast, orientation,** and **spatial phase.** These properties are independent of one another, in the sense that any one of them can be changed without affecting the others. Since Chapter 4 described what is meant by "orientation," that term needs no explanation here. But we will have to consider the other three.

"Spatial frequency" refers to the number of pairs of bars imaged within a given distance on the retina. One-third of a milli-meter is a convenient unit of retinal distance because an image this size is said to subtend one degree of visual angle. To give an example, an image of this size is cast by your thumbnail viewed at arm's length. The size (or visual angle) of the retinal image cast by some object depends on the distance of that object from the eye (see Figure 5.11); as the distance between you and an object decreases, the object's image subtends a greater visual angle. The unit employed to express spatial frequency is the number of cycles that fall within one degree of visual angle (each cycle is one dark and one light bar). A grating of high spatial frequency—many cycles within each degree of visual angle—contains closely spaced, narrow bars. A grating of low spatial frequency—few cycles within each degree of visual angle—contains spread-out, wide bars. Because spatial frequency is defined in terms of visual angle, a grating's spatial frequency changes as your distance from it changes. As this distance decreases, each bar casts a larger image; as a result, the grating's spatial frequency decreases as the distance decreases. To give you an example, when held at arm's length, the grating in Figure 5.8 has a spatial frequency of about 1.0 cycle per degree of visual angle.

"Contrast" is related to the intensity difference between the light and dark bars of the grating. If this difference is great, the

FIGURE 5.11
Retinal image size depends on viewing distance.

On page 149, the last paragraph, beginning "Manipulating these four properties . ," should read as follows:

Manipulating these four properties of a
ting—spatial frequency, contrast, orien-
on, and phase—we can construct any
ual pattern, even a human face. To start,
s see how far we get using just two ori-
ations, oblique left and oblique right. We'll
;in with a pair of gratings, one of each
entation, and add higher-frequency pairs,
:h consisting of one oblique left and one
ique right. In part A of Figure 5.14, you
the first two gratings superimposed.
ding in the next two components (1) re-
ts in B. Adding two more components
produces the pattern shown in C. In each
e, the added components are nothing
more than a pair of obliquely oriented gratings of a particular frequency. Note two
things about C's evolution. First, from A
through C, the resemblance to a checkerboard grows. Here, interactions between
components are creating visual structures
(checks) that are not associated with individual components themselves (Kelly, 1976).
Second, from A through C, the checks become more sharply defined, even though
only unsharp, sinusoidal components went
into the checkerboard. Both facts reinforce
a point made earlier: from its appearance
alone, you cannot always tell what elementary components make up a pattern.

394-35510-5

grating's contrast is high; a small difference means the contrast is low. If the contrast is low enough, the bars of the grating may not even be visible. In this case, the grating contrast is said to be "below the threshold for visibility." Quantitatively, contrast runs from 0 percent (when there is no difference at all between the intensity of the light and dark bars) to 100 percent (when the difference between light and dark bars is maximum).* The contrast of the print you are reading is about 70 percent; the contrast in the grating shown in Figure 5.8 is about 40 percent.

"Spatial phase" refers to a grating's position relative to some landmark (such as the edge of the television display). A convenient landmark is the left edge of the display. Looking at that edge, we can say that a grating "begins" with a dark bar, a light bar, or something in between. The gratings at the top and bottom of Figure 5.12 are in opposite phase; one begins with a light bar, the other with a dark one. The phase of the middle grating is midway between those at the top and bottom.

Grating F in Figure 5.9 showed that when we add gratings together, the appearance of the resulting compound depends on what spatial frequencies are in the mixture. The compound's appearance also depends on the phases of those components. As shown in Figure 5.13, two compounds composed of the same spatial frequencies will look dramatically different if those components are placed in different phases.

Manipulating these four properties of a grating—spatial frequency, contrast, orientation, and phase—we can construct any visual pattern, even a human face. To start, let's see how far we can get using just two orientations, horizontal and vertical. Our

FIGURE 5.12
These three gratings differ in phase only.

plan is to start with a pair of gratings, one of each orientation, and add pairs of higher-frequency gratings, each additional pair consisting of a vertical and a horizontal component. Looking at Figure 5.14, in A you see the first two gratings superimposed. Adding in the next two components (1) results in B. Adding to this the next two com-

*There are many formulas for computing contrast. For gratings, though, contrast is equal to the *difference* between the light intensity of the lightest part of the grating and the light intensity of the dimmest part, divided by the *sum* of these two quantities.

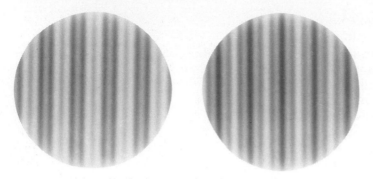

FIGURE 5.13
The same components added in different phases yield distinctly different compound gratings.

ponents (2) produces the pattern shown in C. In each case, the added components are nothing more than horizontal and vertical gratings of a particular frequency. Two things are worth noting about the evolution of C.

First, progressing from A through C, the pattern increasingly resembles a checkerboard. Second, the "squares" on the checkerboard have edges that run diagonally (Kelly, 1976). Their orientation thus seems

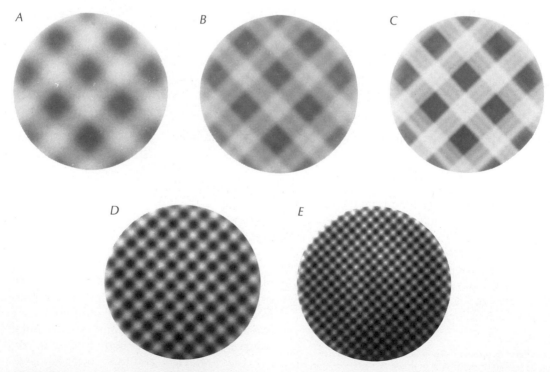

FIGURE 5.14
Steps involved in generating a "checkerboard."

to belie the fact that only horizontal and vertical components have been used to construct the checkerboard. This reinforces a point made earlier: on the basis of appearance alone, you cannot discern what elementary components make up a pattern.

Now let's try to synthesize an even more complex figure, a photograph of a natural scene. This synthesis requires that we use more than just two orientations. Because it would take a great many frequency components to synthesize the natural scene, it would be tedious to show each individual step of the process. Instead, at each stage we'll add a whole cluster of frequencies. Looking at Figure 5.15, A shows the frequency and orientation cluster with which we start. From this point, we follow the same procedure used in Figure 5.14, successively

adding the clusters shown in 1 and 2 to create B and C. Note how each cluster makes its own unique contribution to the final product, C. Bear in mind that this complex scene results from adding various simple components that differ in frequency, contrast, orientation, and phase.

As just shown, spatial frequency components can be used to create a visual scene. Because they provide a vocabulary rich enough to express important aspects of visual form, gratings have become a favorite tool for studying form perception. However, just because a scene can be synthesized from spatial frequency components does not mean that the visual system analyzes that scene into such components; evidence to that effect comes from studies that we shall consider later.

FIGURE 5.15
Steps involved in generating a natural scene, in this instance a photograph of soldiers of the Union Army taken by the famous American Civil War photographer Mathew Brady. (Computer-processed pictures courtesy of Gregory Phillips.)

Eventually, we'll show you how gratings are used to explore human pattern perception. However, since *human* vision is rather complicated, we begin with a much simpler system. As you already know from Chapter 2, there are many parallels between the eye and a camera. So as an entrée to human pattern perception, let's see how the performance of a camera's lens might be measured.

Using Gratings to Measure Performance. Measuring the lens's performance requires two steps. First we would use the lens to create an image of some target; then we would compare the image with the actual target. For example, using a lens, we would create an image of a grating of specified spatial frequency and contrast. We could then determine how good an image the lens had created. But "good" is an extremely vague term; how could we quantify it?

One approach is simply to judge the appearance of the image. But this subjective procedure can be misleading. To illustrate, look at the three gratings in Figure 5.16 and rank them in terms of their apparent contrast. Most people would rank them in the order shown, with the leftmost grating deemed lowest in contrast. But this is wrong, for all three gratings have precisely the same physical contrast. In a moment we'll con-

sider why this error in subjective judgment occurs; but first let's explore in greater detail this problem of evaluating image quality. A better, more objective way to assess the quality of images such as in Figure 5.16 is by means of some physical instrument that measures light. The following example shows how this can be accomplished.

Suppose we use an expensive, high-quality lens to cast, on a clean white paper, an image of a grating. We can use the light-measuring instrument to determine the contrast of the image produced by the lens. Let's repeat this for different spatial frequencies, always using gratings of the same contrast. We can graph the results in the following way. The horizontal axis of the graph will show spatial frequency; the vertical axis will show the image's contrast (as a percentage of the target's contrast). The resulting plot is often called a **transfer function,** because it specifies how contrast is transferred through the lens. A typical graph of this kind is shown in Figure 5.17.

Look first at the heavy line in the graph. Note that up to a certain spatial frequency the contrast in the image is identical to that of the target. For these frequencies, the lens faithfully reproduces the target. However, for still higher spatial frequencies, the contrast in the image is reduced even though the contrast in the target is constant. For

FIGURE 5.16
Which of these three gratings appears highest in contrast and which appears lowest in contrast?

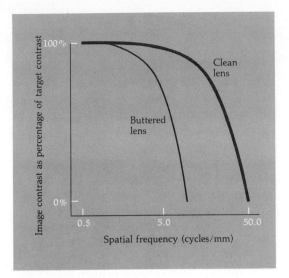

FIGURE 5.17

Two transfer functions for a lens. The curves specify how contrast in the image formed by the lens is related to contrast in the object.

these spatial frequencies, the lens reproduces the target less faithfully. The frequency at which the image contrast falls to zero is called the **cutoff frequency;** once the frequency in an actual target exceeds this value, the image will no longer contain any contrast whatsoever—the target itself might as well have zero contrast.

You will notice a second curve in Figure 5.17 (the thin line). This curve connects the points we would observe if we repeated the experiment after having made one modification: smearing the lens by running a buttery finger over its surface. At very low spatial frequencies the smear makes little difference in the performance of the lens. However, at intermediate spatial frequencies the contrast in the image is degraded by the butter on the lens. This is shown by the difference between the curves for the lens in its buttered and unbuttered states. Note also that the cutoff frequency for the buttered lens is lower than that for the clean lens.

The transfer function of a lens summarizes its performance, although in a rather abstract way. In this respect, the transfer function serves the same purpose as the United States Environmental Protection Agency's (EPA) mileage ratings for various cars tested under standard conditions. While they are useful, the EPA ratings may not specify the performance of a car under particular driving conditions. By the same token, the curves in Figure 5.17 do not indicate how any particular scene will appear on a photograph taken through that lens. They indicate only how the lens will handle one special set of "scenes"—namely, gratings. But most people want to use their cameras to photograph things other than gratings. To see how transfer functions such as those of Figure 5.17 can be applied to photographing some scene, that scene must be related to gratings.

One method for doing exactly this comes from the work of Jean Baptiste Fourier, a nineteenth-century French mathematician who, incidentally, was also a friend and associate of Napoleon. As part of a prestigious mathematics contest, Fourier was required to develop equations expressing how heat is transferred from one body to another. He recognized that extremely complex equations would be needed and that those equations would have to be general enough to apply to a wide variety of different bodies. To satisfy these requirements, Fourier developed a powerful simplification. He showed that if some quantity (such as heat) changed in a complex manner over time, that complex function of time could be approximated by a series of simple sinusoidal functions. This simplification was an enormous advantage because it allowed Fourier to break a mathematically difficult function down into simpler, mathematically more tractable components. From here the problem could be solved by working with the simple components (incidentally, he won the contest). In recognition of his accomplishment, we now refer to his technique as **Fourier analysis.**

But how does Fourier's solution enable us to relate simple sinusoidal functions to a photograph of some scene taken through a lens? First, we can consider that scene as the sum of a series of simple sinusoidal components. Then, using the transfer function of the lens, we can evaluate how the lens would image each of those components.

Consider the lens whose transfer function is given by the lighter line in Figure 5.17 (the lens smeared with butter). If we used that lens to photograph a scene containing many *very* fine details, the resulting image would be low in contrast and would appear *very* washed out. This is because "fine detail" is equivalent to "high spatial frequency." As the transfer function shows, the buttered lens does a poor job of transferring high spatial frequencies; it reduces the contrast of any high spatial frequencies contained in a scene. Though this lens could faithfully represent the general shape of a large target (such as a tree that is near the camera), it would not be adequate for fine details (such as the wrinkles in the tree's bark). This illustrates that sinusoidal targets can predict the quality of a photograph produced by a lens. To reiterate, several steps are involved. First, we determine the transfer function of the lens. Second, we analyze the visual scene into its spatial frequency components. With these pieces of information in hand, we determine which spatial frequency components will be preserved in the image of that scene and which will not. The second of these steps is beyond the scope of this book; while not terribly complicated, the calculations are tedious (Weisstein, 1980; Rzeszotarski, Royer, and Gilmore, 1983). The first step, measuring the transfer function, is straightforward in the camera. But how easy is it to measure a transfer function for a visual system such as your own? If we did know your transfer function, we could predict the visibility of any scene you might look at. As we'll describe later, these predictions confer some practical benefits. Our next goal, then, is to derive a transfer function for human vision comparable to the one we derived for a lens.

THE CONTRAST SENSITIVITY FUNCTION AS A WINDOW OF VISIBILITY

The Human Contrast Sensitivity Function. There's one major stumbling block to measuring a transfer function for human vision: we cannot duplicate with humans the procedure employed with a lens. While we can produce sinusoidal gratings of known contrast, it's difficult to measure the image such gratings produce because that image is inside the eye. Anyway, measuring this image would give only part of the visual system's complete transfer function. While describing the eye's *optical* components, this transfer function would not reflect the *neural* components of the visual system. And since we are interested in visual perception, not just the image formed in the eye, we must be concerned with the *perceptual* transfer function, which depends both on the *optical* transfer function and on the *neural* transfer function.

How then can we measure the *perceptual* transfer function? If your visual system (both its optical and its neural components) did a good job of transferring some spatial frequency, it stands to reason that you'd need little contrast to see a grating of that frequency—in other words, you'd be relatively sensitive to that frequency. However, if your visual system did a poor job of transferring that spatial frequency, you'd need more contrast to see it—you'd be relatively *in*sensitive to that frequency. In general, the sensitivity of the visual system determines the threshold contrast needed to detect a given spatial frequency. By measuring contrast thresholds for different spatial frequencies, we can derive a curve that describes the entire visual system's sensitivity to contrast. Let's call this curve the **contrast sensitivity function (CSF)**, to distinguish it from the transfer function of a lens. The term "sensitivity" is a reminder that we are dealing with a property of the visual system, not just a property of the stimulus. As you'd expect from everyday usage of the term "sensitivity," someone is said to have high sensitivity if that person requires little contrast to see a pattern. By the same token, someone is said to have low sensitivity if that person requires considerable con-

trast to see a pattern. Defined in this way, sensitivity is inversely related to threshold contrast.

Figure 5.18 shows a CSF for a human adult; this curve defines the adult's **window of visibility.** Before explaining the importance and usefulness of the CSF, let's describe how it was measured. A test grating was created electronically on a specially designed and calibrated television screen. The screen displayed a grating of fixed spatial frequency. Using a knob (like the contrast control on a television set), the contrast was adjusted until the grating was just visible. This threshold contrast was recorded by an experimenter. Typically, several estimates

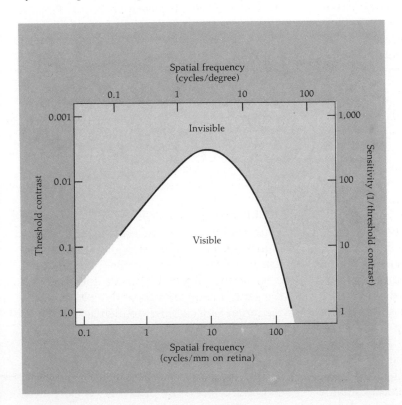

FIGURE 5.18

A contrast sensitivity function for an adult human. The upper horizontal axis is scaled in units specifying the number of pairs of light and dark bars of the grating falling within one degree of visual angle on the retina. In subsequent figures we shall refer to this scale as "cycles/degree."

of the contrast threshold were measured for that spatial frequency and these estimates were averaged. This procedure was then repeated for other spatial frequencies, and the results were finally displayed as in Figure 5.18. This curve defines a window of visibility: the region below the curve represents combinations of contrast and spatial frequency that can be seen, while the region above the curve represents combinations that cannot be seen. To clarify this idea, pick any point on the CSF curve. Because this point is the threshold contrast for seeing that pattern, decreasing the pattern's contrast (moving upward from the curve) renders the pattern invisible. Conversely, increasing the pattern's contrast (moving downward from the curve) makes the pattern more visible.

Note that in one respect the *shape* of the human CSF resembles the shape of the transfer function of a lens (Figure 5.17): each displays a high-frequency cutoff. However, in another respect the two are different. In particular, the CSF drops at low frequencies, whereas the lens's function does not. The visual system, in other words, is less sensitive to very low spatial frequencies than it is to intermediate ones. As a result, there is a range of spatial frequencies, toward the center of the horizontal axis in Figure 5.18, where humans are maximally sensitive. Gratings are less visible if they lie on either side of this optimum spatial frequency; a person requires higher contrast in order to see them. The same line of reasoning can be applied to a visual scene or photograph of that scene. If the objects in a scene have most of their spatial frequency information around the optimum point on the CSF, those objects will be clearly visible even when they are of low contrast. If those objects contain only very low spatial frequencies (very large objects) or only very high spatial frequencies (very small objects or fine details), they will be less visible and their contrast will have to be high in order for those objects to

be seen. This also explains why the gratings in Figure 5.16 *appear* different in contrast: their apparent contrast varies with your sensitivity to different spatial frequencies.

You know from experience that you are able to see better under some conditions than others. If the CSF and your ability to see are importantly related, conditions that change one should also change the other. In fact, this is precisely what happens. Let's consider one such condition.

As discussed in Chapter 3, resolution is poor under scotopic conditions. That is why it's hard to read in dim light. Since resolution involves seeing fine detail, we'd expect decreased light to affect particularly that portion of the CSF corresponding to fine detail. Indeed this happens, as the curves in Figure 5.19 illustrate. The upper curve shows a photopic (daytime) CSF; the middle curve shows a mesopic (twilight) CSF; the lowest curve represents a scotopic (nighttime) CSF. As the level of light decreases from daylight to twilight, visual sensitivity drops primarily at high spatial frequencies; lower frequencies are little affected. But when the light falls to extremely low levels (nighttime), sensitivity decreases even at low frequencies.

Think about what these curves imply for your vision under changing conditions of illumination. Driving at night, you may be unable to see the fine details (high frequencies) of the shrubs alongside the road. At the same time, you probably will be able to see larger objects (low frequencies), such as another car, just about as well as you do under daylight conditions. If you park your car in an unlit place and turn off your headlights, you will be operating under light conditions like those producing the scotopic curve. Under such conditions, even large objects will be difficult to see. Box 5.1 gives an example of a practical use of the CSF.

In summary, the CSF characterizes the ease with which people are able to detect

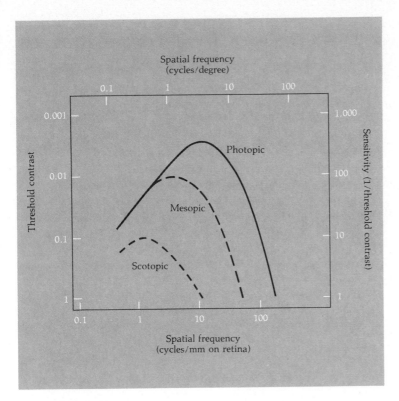

FIGURE 5.19

Contrast sensitivity functions measured at three different light levels.

objects of various sizes and perceive the structural detail, such as texture, of those objects. Conditions that alter the CSF, such as light level, change the visibility and appearance of objects. In a sense, these conditions thrust one into a different visual world. From this it follows that two creatures with different CSFs actually live in different visual worlds. The next two sections develop this intriguing possibility.

CSFs of Other Species. Cat owners sometimes notice that their pets seem to watch things their owners can't see, as if there were ghosts present. Such inexplicable behavior enhances the cat's reputation for spookiness. While we don't deny that cats can be spooky, it may well be that under certain conditions they actually do see things that

are real, though invisible to their owners (Blake, in press). We'll explain this and, in so doing, show how the CSF allows you to compare your vision to that of other animals.

Just as it does for humans, the CSF defines a window of visibility for other species. Provided they have sufficient contrast, objects producing retinal images composed of spatial frequencies falling within the range of a creature's CSF will be visible to that creature; objects producing images composed of frequencies outside that CSF will be invisible, regardless of their contrast. Thus by knowing an animal's CSF, one can predict what that animal will be able to see and what it won't be able to see. But how does one measure the CSF in a nonverbal animal such as the cat? The basic problem is to de-

BOX 5.1

Practical Uses of the CSF

The contrast sensitivity function indicates things about human vision that cannot be learned from measures such as visual acuity. **Visual acuity,** as described in Chapter 3, is a measure of the smallest detail that the visual system can resolve. When assessing visual acuity, one is interested only in the spatial (size) factors that limit vision, so other factors are optimized. For instance, if an eye chart were printed with very light gray ink on a gray card stock—rather than with very black ink on a white card stock—the letters would be harder to see. In this case, the letters' reduced contrast would limit visual acuity, preventing one from assessing performance on the basis of size alone. When measuring visual acuity, then, one tries to optimize contrast and illumination so that they do not limit performance.

When measuring visual acuity, one is interested in how size alone limits vision; when measuring the CSF, one is interested in how both contrast and size limit vision. In fact, two people can have exactly the same visual acuity but have

different contrast sensitivities, as the following demonstrates. Arthur Ginsburg of the Air Force's Aerospace Medical Research Laboratory and his associates used the CSF to predict how well pilots would be able to see objects in the air and on the ground. At least under conditions of reduced visibility—twilight or fog, for example—visual acuity gives a poor account of a pilot's visually guided performance. In fact, very fine details that might normally be seen are invisible at twilight or in fog.

Ginsburg found that under conditions of reduced visibility, the CSF of a pilot provided a very good account of his ability to see targets on the ground. He tested ten pilots in a sophisticated aircraft simulator that provided a panoramic (wraparound) view through the plane's windscreen. Pilots flew simulated missions and then "landed." On half their landings, an obstacle (another plane) blocked the runway, requiring them to abort the landing. Ginsburg determined how close each pilot came to the obstacle before aborting the landing. Even though all were

experienced jet pilots, they varied in the distance at which they could spot the obstacle; the best pilots saw the obstacle three times farther away than did the worst. Significantly, the pilots who saw the obstacle from the greatest distances were those who had the highest contrast sensitivities; pilots who had to get close to the obstacle before seeing it had the lowest contrast sensitivities. Finally, Ginsburg noted that acuity was unrelated to the performance of the pilots on this test (Ginsburg et al., 1982).

This is just one example of the usefulness of the CSF in predicting visual performance in everyday settings. Other uses include predicting how well various visually impaired people can get around in their environments (Marron and Bailey, 1982), gauging the disabling effects of glare from various types of lighting sources (Carlsson et al., 1984), and enhancing printed materials for use by the visually impaired (Pelli and Pelli, 1984). Although the CSF technique is relatively new, its popularity is growing rapidly.

termine how little contrast a cat needs to distinguish a grating from a uniform field of the same brightness. One device for doing this, developed by Mark Berkley (1970), is illustrated in Figure 5.20.

The cat faces two television screens, one displaying a grating, the second a uniformly bright field. The cat is rewarded with a morsel of food if it pushes against a small plastic switch located just in front of the television

displaying the grating. The experimenter randomly presents the grating on the left or right television screen. When the contrast of the grating is above the cat's threshold, a hungry cat will respond correctly on virtually every trial. When the contrast falls below the cat's threshold, the animal will simply guess and will be correct only half the time. The cat's threshold, then, is defined as the contrast that allows it to respond cor-

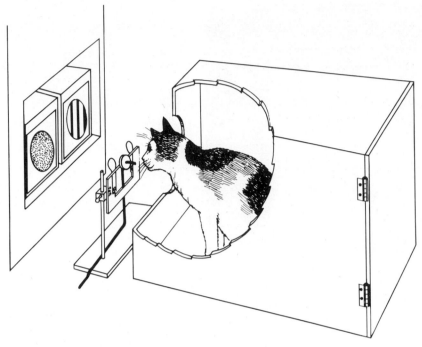

FIGURE 5.20

Apparatus for testing the cat's contrast sensitivity. (Drawing adapted by courtesy of Karin Boothroyd.)

rectly on 75 percent of the trials, a level of performance midway between chance and perfection. This threshold contrast can be measured for different spatial frequencies, and the cat's CSF can then be plotted in the same way as it is for humans.

Figure 5.21 shows a typical CSF for a cat (solid line) and for a human (dashed line) tested under comparable conditions. Note first the area common to the two CSFs. This overlapping region defines combinations of spatial frequencies and contrasts that both you and a cat can see. Next, note the regions where the two CSFs do not overlap. Within these two regions one creature—you or the cat, depending on which one has the higher sensitivity—can see patterns that are invisible to the other. At high spatial frequencies, your sensitivity is better than the cat's; at low spatial frequencies, the reverse

is true. Now suppose that a cat is sitting on your lap. If you are watching television there will be fine details in the picture (for example, Morris the Cat's whiskers) that will be seen by you but not your cat. This is because those fine details are composed of high spatial frequencies that fall outside the cat's window of visibility. But at the same time, if something large and very low-contrast appears in the room—say, an indistinct shadow on a wall—the cat may see it even though you cannot. In this instance, the shadow falls outside your window of visibility. These large, low-contrast objects could be the invisible "ghosts" that enhance the cat's reputation for spookiness.

To date, CSFs have been measured for nearly a dozen different species, and it's instructive to compare them. Figure 5.22 shows several representative curves. Look first at

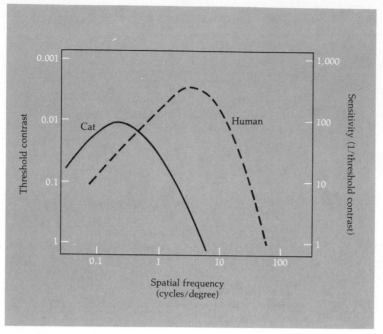

FIGURE 5.21

Contrast sensitivity functions for the cat and for the human being.

the curve labeled "human"; this is the human adult CSF that you've seen in several previous figures. Next note the curve labeled "rhesus." Like several other nonhuman primates that have been studied, the rhesus monkey's CSF is highly similar to that of a human—suggesting that the world would probably appear very similar to you and to a monkey sitting on your lap. It is certainly unlikely that you'd see things that the monkey could not, or vice versa. Next note that the goldfish's CSF is displaced toward lower spatial frequencies, a fact that makes sense considering where the goldfish lives. Its aquatic environment prevents high spatial frequencies from ever reaching the fish's eye (Uhlrich, Essock, and Lehmkuhle, 1981; Lythgoe, 1979). Like the cat, the goldfish is equipped for seeing either very large objects or smaller ones that are quite nearby. In general, there seems to be a good fit between what an animal uses its eyes for and

where its CSF lies along the spatial frequency scale.

Age and the CSF. On the basis of differences between the CSFs of various species, we've pictured what the world might look like to the owners of these CSFs. In the same way, let's consider how the world might appear to individuals at various points in their lifetimes. To begin, suppose while you are reading this book, someone puts a human infant on your lap (where previously you've had a cat and a monkey). How does your visual world compare to that of the infant? This question, incidentally, has intrigued philosophers and parents for centuries.

It is hard to know what very young, preverbal infants see. Obviously, you can't use the same methods to study infant vision that you use with cooperative, attentive adults. To get around this limitation, researchers have exploited a naturally occur-

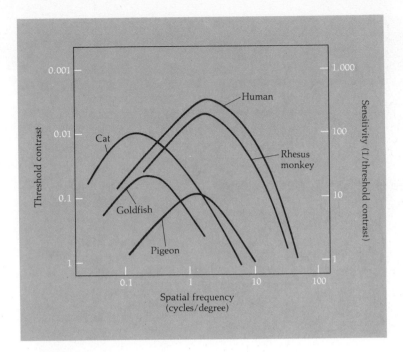

FIGURE 5.22
Contrast sensitivity functions for five different species. (Adapted from Uhlrich, Essock, and Lehmkuhle, 1981.)

ring tendency exhibited by infants. It has been known for some time that an infant prefers to look at complex rather than dull scenes (Fantz, 1961). Several research groups have exploited preferential looking to measure the infant's ability to see gratings (Atkinson, Braddick, and Moar, 1977; Banks and Salapatek, 1978; Teller, 1979; Held, 1979).

Confronted with a patch of grating and a patch of uniform brightness, an infant will prefer to look at the grating (see Figure 5.23). If the infant shows no preference for the grating over the uniform field, it is inferred that the infant cannot see the grating. This could happen for one of two reasons: either the contrast of the grating is too low or the spatial frequency of the grating falls outside the range visible to the infant.

The basic findings are summarized in Figure 5.24, which shows CSFs for an infant several months old and for a typical adult.

Note that the infant's window of visibility is very different from the adult's. An infant held on your lap will not be able to see fine spatial details visible to you (see Figure 5.25).

FIGURE 5.23
An infant's preference for looking at a pattern can be used to measure the infant's contrast sensitivity. (Drawing courtesy of Richard Held.)

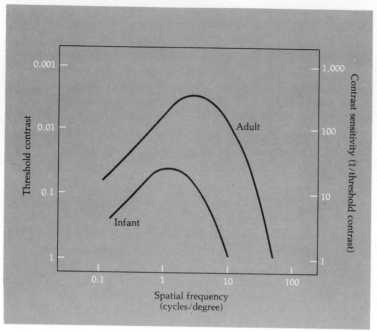

FIGURE 5.24

Contrast sensitivity functions for an infant and for an adult. (Infant data redrawn from Banks, 1982.)

In this respect, the infant more closely resembles a cat. But unlike a cat, the infant does not have an advantage over you at low frequencies: you should be able to see everything that the infant can see. Also, even for spatial frequencies visible to both of you, the infant will require more contrast than you do. In a sense, these CSFs confirm what some parents have noticed: their very young infants seem oblivious to everything except very large, high-contrast objects (Banks, 1982). Incidentally, the lack of sensitivity to high frequencies does not stem from optical causes but from the fact that the infant's immature visual nervous system fails to encode high frequencies.

The infant's CSF improves gradually over the first year or so of its life. The improvement may be arrested, though, at an immature level if the infant does not receive normal visual experiences (Jacobsen, Mo-

hindra, and Held, 1982). There are several visual disorders that can alter the quality of visual experiences received by an infant and hence keep spatial vision from its normal course of development. First of all, any condition that chronically blurs the images reaching the infant's retina will limit the information available to the visual system. Optical blur of this sort can result from myopia or hyperopia and from congenital cataracts or corneal scars (see Chapter 2). Misalignment of an infant's two eyes can also retard the development of good spatial vision. When its eyes are not properly aligned, an infant must suppress or ignore visual input from one eye in order to avoid seeing double. For reasons unknown, continuous suppression of one eye can lead to a loss in spatial vision, a condition called *amblyopia* (recall Box 4.3).

Fortunately, infants afflicted with any of

FIGURE 5.25

An infant looking at these two pictures from a distance of two meters would be unable to tell them apart, since the spatial frequency information distinguishing the two pictures is outside the window of visibility of the young infant. (© 1984 Muppets, Inc., courtesy of Children's Television Workshop; computer-processed pictures by Gregory Phillips.)

these disorders can recover normal spatial vision, providing that the disorder is corrected sometime during the first few years of life (von Noorden, 1981). But if correction is postponed until the child reaches school age, the prognosis for full recovery is much poorer. Apparently there is a critical period early in life when the visual nervous system requires normal input to mature properly. During this period, neural connections are still being formed (Hickey, 1977). This critical period of neural development ends by the time a child reaches 3 or 4 years of age. If the visual nervous system arrives at this stage not completely developed because of inadequate visual experience, any neural abnormalities are irrevocably preserved throughout the remainder of life. In view of this critical role of early visual experience, you can appreciate the importance of detecting and correcting visual disorders in infants as early as possible. One important reason for studying infant vision is to develop and refine techniques allowing early diagnosis of such disorders.

So far our discussion has focused on spatial vision in infants and young children. Let's now consider what happens to the CSF during the remainder of the life span. The CSF remains more or less stable through young adulthood; but after age 30, systematic changes in the CSF begin reappearing. Figure 5.26 shows how the CSF changes from age 20 to age 80 (Owsley, Sekuler, and Siemsen, 1983). By now you should have no trouble interpreting what a CSF implies about a person's ability to see. Suppose an elderly aunt takes the place of that infant on your lap; you should be able to predict from Figure 5.26 how her visual world might differ from yours.

Very likely, much of the loss in your aunt's sensitivity to high frequencies results from optical changes in her eyes. For example, as she has grown older, her pupil has become smaller, which means that her retina receives considerably less light than yours (Weale, 1982). This reduced illumination of her retina mimics changes that would be seen in your CSF as you went from photopic to

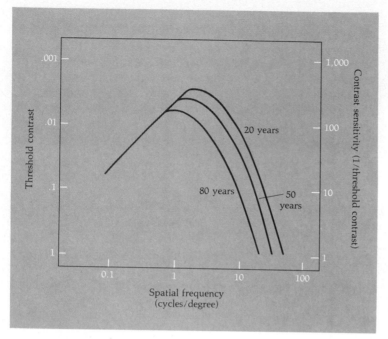

FIGURE 5.26

Contrast sensitivity functions for three different age groups.

mesopic conditions (see Figure 5.19). But whatever its origins, the variation in the CSF from birth to old age means that people experience very different visual worlds at different stages of their lives.

The Structural Basis of the CSF. Campbell and Robson, whose work we described earlier, proposed that the human visual system contains sets of neurons, each capable of responding to targets over only a narrow range of spatial frequencies. This range of "preferred" frequencies varies from one set of neurons to another. According to this hypothesis, the sensitivities of these frequency-tuned neurons, or channels, together determine the overall CSF (see Figure 5.27). Some of Campbell and Robson's own experiments (1968) support this view. But there is other evidence as well.

One reason for believing that the CSF depends on several different channels is the

fact that certain conditions can alter one portion of the CSF without affecting others. As Box 5.2 explains, diseases attacking the visual system can produce this frequency-selective change in the CSF—implying that only certain neurons are affected by the disease. But we need not wait for disease to change the CSF; we can change it intentionally, using a technique called **selective adaptation.** This procedure, mentioned in Box 4.5, produces a temporary loss of sensitivity to particular spatial frequencies.

Selective adaptation involves several stages. First you assess the person's CSF; then you have the person view a high-contrast grating for a minute or so, thereby adapting to one spatial frequency. As you might imagine, steady viewing of this adaptation grating fatigues those visual neurons that respond to its frequency (Movshon and Lennie, 1979; Albrecht, Farrar, and Hamilton, 1984). After the person has adapted to

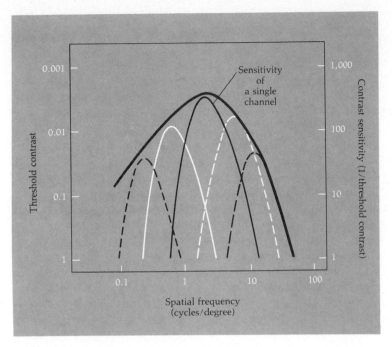

FIGURE 5.27

The overall contrast sensitivity function is determined by the individual sensitivities of neurons responsive to limited ranges of spatial frequency.

this grating for a minute or two, you redetermine his or her CSF (interspersing threshold measurements with additional adaptation to keep the level of adaptation high). The typical outcome of such experiments (e.g., Blakemore and Campbell, 1969) is shown in Figure 5.28. In each panel, the arrow on the horizontal axis indicates the frequency to which the person adapted. Note that the notch carved in each CSF is centered about the adaptation frequency. So adapting to one spatial frequency diminishes sensitivity to that frequency and neighboring ones, leaving more remote frequencies unaffected. This process of selective adaptation works even when the adaptation frequency is contained in a complex pattern such as a checkerboard (Green, 1980).

To understand how selective adaptation works, look again at Figure 5.27. If just one

of the channels is fatigued by adaptation, that channel will respond more weakly when its preferred spatial frequency is presented. This means that a grating of that preferred spatial frequency will look somewhat washed out compared to its normal appearance (Blakemore, Muncey, and Ridley, 1973). A low-contrast grating that is normally visible will stimulate the adapted channel so weakly that the grating will be below threshold. In order to attain visibility, this grating's contrast will have to be boosted—resulting in a dip in the CSF. The width of this dip depends on the selectivity of the fatigued channel. Presumably, unaffected regions of the CSF depend on channels that were not fatigued by the adaptation grating.

You can demonstrate selective adaptation for yourself. Figure 5.29 shows several different low-contrast test gratings and one

BOX 5.2
When Things Go Wrong with Pattern Vision

The way in which diseases affect vision can provide clues about the structural basis of the CSF. Ivan Bodis-Wollner, a New York City neurologist, has noted that in some of his patients, disease produces a notch in the CSF— a loss of contrast sensitivity limited to a certain range of target sizes. Moreover, the location and severity of loss of sensitivity varies from one patient to the next (Bodis-Wollner, 1972).

The loss in sensitivity was produced by damage to the visual cortex from a stroke. Other diseases can produce similar losses. The most common of these diseases is *multiple sclerosis,* a disease that attacks the insulation on nerve fibers, including fibers that make up the optic nerve. Even though their visual acuity is good, some multiple sclerosis patients complain that the world appears "washed out." Presumably, this washed-out appearance is related to the nervous system's diminished capacity to code contrast.

In addition, about 30 percent of all people who have multiple sclerosis experience *Uhthoff's symptom,* a condition first described by Wilhelm Uhthoff, an eminent turn-of-the-century ophthalmologist. For individuals with Uhthoff's symptom, exercise or emotional strain heightens their visual problems for several minutes. No one yet understands how emotional or physical strain or exercise causes these effects. But these conditions offer a unique opportunity to study the visual system under conditions of transient impairment.

In one study (Sekuler, Owsley, and Berenberg, in press) a 30-year-old accountant with Uhthoff's symptom reported that when he was emotionally upset his vision grew hazy and objects lost much of their apparent contrast. For example, during a confrontation at work, his boss's face appeared totally washed out and featureless. Surprisingly, during these episodes the patient retained his ability to read columns of small numbers, an important

part of his job. Thus he seemed to suffer a size-selective loss, retaining the ability to see fine details while losing the ability to see larger objects.

This strange set of symptoms was confirmed by comparing the patient's contrast sensitivity before and immediately after he exercised. Contrast sensitivity for high spatial frequencies was unchanged by exercise, but sensitivity for intermediate frequencies dropped. Longer periods of exercise produced an even greater loss of vision: not only was contrast sensitivity drastically reduced at all frequencies, but visual acuity was seriously impaired as well.

We do not yet understand the specific physiological basis for these restricted losses in the CSF. But such losses do imply that the CSF—and the ability to see patterns of different sizes— depends on the coordinated responses of different sets of visual cells, any one of which may be attacked and damaged by disease.

---

high-contrast adaptation grating. Before looking at the adaptation grating (in the center of the figure), note the apparent contrast of the test gratings surrounding it. Now inspect the high-contrast grating for about a minute; don't stare fixedly, but allow your eyes to roam around the circle in the grating's center. Then, without delay, look at one test grating and note its apparent contrast. After looking back at the adaptation grating for another minute, note the apparent contrast of another test grating. By adapting and then examining each test grat-

ing in turn, you'll find adapting alters the appearance of only some test gratings. Now you've seen for yourself that spatial frequency adaptation is selective.

Selective adaptation probably occurs in visual cortical cells (Albrecht, Farrar, and Hamilton, 1984). Such cells are indeed selective for spatial frequency (size); but as Chapter 4 showed, they are also selective for orientation. As a result, you might expect grating adaptation to be selective for both orientation *and* spatial frequency. The logic behind this assertion resembles that

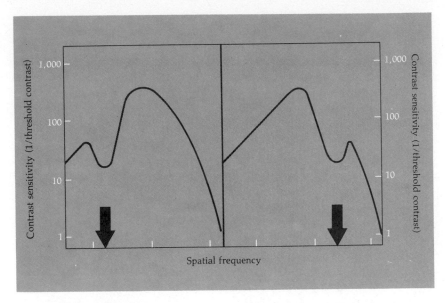

FIGURE 5.28

Adapting to a particular spatial frequency produces a temporary depression in the contrast sensitivity function at and near the adapting spatial frequency.

used to explain spatial-frequency selective adaptation.

You can demonstrate for yourself that this adaptation effect is indeed selective for orientation. Rotate this book by 90 degrees (turn it sideways) and then adapt to the high-contrast grating in Figure 5.29. This maneuver will orient the contours in that grating horizontally. After adapting for a minute, quickly return the book to its upright position and look at the vertically oriented test gratings. Unlike before, *all* of the test gratings should be as visible as they were prior to adaptation. In other words, adapting to horizontal has no effect whatsoever on vertical, regardless of similarities in spatial frequency—implying that the cells fatigued by the horizontal grating are not at all involved in seeing vertical contours.

This demonstration is a reminder of one of the properties exhibited by visual cortical cells: orientation selectivity. Recall that another characteristic of cortical cells is their binocularity: most of them receive input from

both eyes. This implies that if you adapt just one eye to a grating, you will be able to observe the consequences of adaptation while looking through either the adapted eye or the unadapted eye (Blake and Fox, 1972). You can use Figure 5.29 to verify this fact also.

These adaptation effects imply that different neural channels are used to detect different spatial frequencies, since it is possible to affect the sensitivity of one without altering the others. However, these distinct channels do interact with one another—as is evidenced by the checkerboard in Figure 5.30. In manufacturing this checkboard, Richard Kirkham purposely made some squares the wrong shade, which creates some clusters of dark squares. To find these clusters, try squinting your eyes. This should make the clusters stand out. Squinting blurs your vision, reducing the high-frequency details in the retinal image of the checkerboard. Once those details are removed, the clusters, which constitute a lower spatial

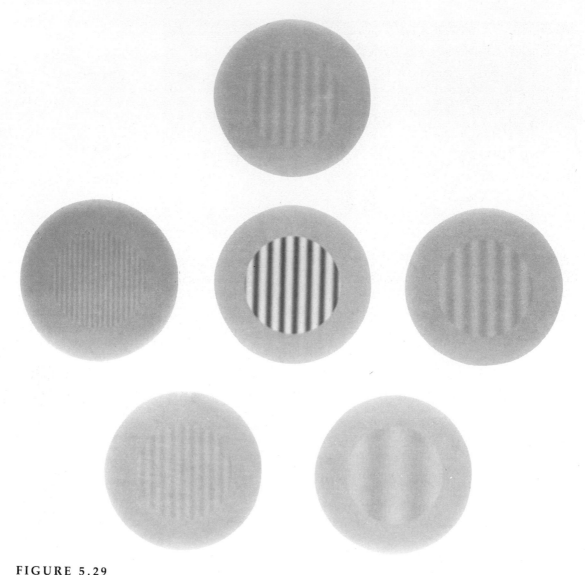

FIGURE 5.29
By following the instructions in the text, you can experience the consequences of grating adaptation.

frequency, become conspicuous. In effect, the high frequencies were camouflaging the lower-frequency clusters. Another example of this principle is shown in Figure 5.31. Again, squinting your eyes will reveal the lower-frequency pattern that otherwise is masked by the higher frequencies of the edges of the blocks. To understand how this

block portrait was created, see Figure 5.32. In this instance, strong high-frequency information camouflages and weakens low-frequency information. But when all frequencies are more nearly equal in strength they can interact more cooperatively (see Box 5.3).

To sum up, recent studies of detection

FIGURE 5.30
Checkered pattern containing a few squares incorrectly shaded. (Courtesy of Richard Kirkham.)

and pattern visibility converge on a common view of the human visual system. In this view, detection of any spatial target depends on responses generated in a set of

FIGURE 5.31
Can you tell what famous actor is pictured here? (Computer-processed photo courtesy of Gregory Phillips.)

visual cells tuned to contours of a particular size and orientation. Each set of cells is responsible for the ability to see targets over some range of sizes and orientations. In the next section, we'll see how this view provides an explanation of other aspects of form perception as well.

FORM DISCRIMINATION

So far we've described how the CSF defines a window of visibility within which objects can be seen. Our emphasis was on form detection, as determined by an observer's sensitivity to contrast and spatial frequency. Now we are ready to extend our analysis of spatial vision to form discrimination, the ability to tell one object from another. Before getting into details, though, it will be useful to specify what must go on within the visual system to make discrimination possible.

The perception of pattern, or spatial structure, depends on the responses of cells in the visual system. This dependence sets some limits on what stimuli will appear different and what stimuli will look alike. All stimuli that produce *identical* effects within the visual system will be indistinguishable from one another. But if stimuli produce different effects, potentially you have the information for telling them apart. Whether you actually can tell them apart depends on how different the neural responses are (Brindley, 1970, pp. 132–134). In Chapter 4 you learned that the response of any one cell—say a "simple" cell in the visual cortex—provides ambiguous messages about the characteristics of stimuli in the visual world. As a result, the visual appearance of objects probably depends on the pattern of activity within an *array* of cells, not just one cell alone.

Metamers. If you look at two exact duplicates of the same object, each will produce precisely the same effects on your visual system and they will look identical. But two

BOX 5.3
Not Seeing the Forest for the Trees

In this chapter, we have been developing the idea that certain mechanisms process information about fine spatial detail while others process information about coarser structure. Let's think what this idea means in terms of an everyday situation. If you were standing near a forest, one set of visual mechanisms would be responsible for allowing you to see the overall forest while another set would be responsible for your seeing individual trees. How might this neural specialization of function be helpful? According to one view (Broadbent, 1977), after the low-frequency mechanisms have defined the global structure of some object, it becomes easier to make sense of the detailed information provided by the high-frequency mechanisms. In the example at hand, once you see that you're standing in front of a forest it's easier to see its individual components.

This view is attractive for several reasons. First, it is consistent with the idea that people respond more quickly to low-frequency information than to high-frequency information (Breitmeyer, 1975; Calis and Leeuwenberg, 1981; Navon and Norman, 1983). Second, when stimuli are presented very briefly, only their low-frequency components find their way into perceptual experience—the stimuli appear like "blobs" or "blotches" (Petersik, 1978).

Normally, then, perception depends on cooperative interaction between the processing of global (low-frequency) and local (high-frequency) information. To study these interactions requires stimuli that contain both kinds of information. Ronald Kinchla, of Princeton University, and Jeremy Wolfe, of the Massachusetts Institute of Technology, used stimuli in which the relation between high and low spatial frequencies could be easily varied (Kinchla and Wolfe, 1979). Their stimuli, devised by Israeli psychologist David Navon (1977), were large letters made up of small letters; the small letters were always different from the large letter that they defined. An example is shown in the accompanying figure, where the global structure creates the letter "H" (large letter), while the local structure consists of the letter "E" (small letters).

On each trial, the observer first heard the name of a letter; then, several seconds later, one of the stimuli was briefly presented. The observer had to judge whether the stimulus contained the letter whose name had been spoken. If *either* the global or the local structure matched that spoken name, the observer was to respond yes; otherwise, no. Kinchla and Wolfe compared how long people took to respond yes when the spoken letter matched the *global* structure and how long people took to say yes when the spoken letter matched the *local* structure. They made these comparisons for stimuli of various overall size.

When the overall stimulus was very large (about the size of the retinal image cast by this book seen at arm's length), observers were quicker at detecting a match between the spoken letter and the local structure. However, when the overall stimulus was five times smaller, observers were quicker at detecting a match between the spoken letter and the global structure. To Kinchla and Wolfe, this result demonstrates that neither the lowest spatial frequencies nor the highest spatial frequencies enjoy guaranteed priority in processing. Instead, the tendency is initially to process information represented by some intermediate band of frequencies.

Returning to the example at hand, we could say that when you're standing close to a very large forest, it's easier to see the trees than the entire forest, but when the forest is small, it's easier to see the forest than the trees.

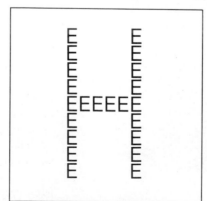

objects that are physically different can also have identical neural effects and, therefore, appear identical. In other words, things need not *be* identical to *look* identical. Two objects that are perceptually indistinguishable from one another, despite their physical differences, are called **metamers.**

We can learn much about human vision by determining which stimuli are metamers and which are not. Metamers exist because of a "blindness" to certain stimulus characteristics—characteristics that the visual nervous system fails to register. If the human visual system generates identical responses to two objects, the objects will appear identical, even if they are physically different. This might happen when two objects are identical except for one physical attribute too small or too dim to be detected (see Figure 5.33).

But the fact that two stimuli are metameric for *your* visual system does not mean

FIGURE 5.33
Stimuli that are indiscriminable are said to be metameric. (K. Bendo.)

FIGURE 5.32
The picture in the previous figure was constructed by setting the light level of each block so that it was the average intensity of the region covered by the block. Squinting (thus blurring the high frequencies) should make the detail in the two halves of the photograph equivalent. (Computer-processed photo courtesy of Gregory Phillips.)

that they will be metameric for all visual systems. In Figure 5.34, the two photographs are identical except for the presence of high spatial frequency information in the left-hand photograph. You are probably able to tell the two photos apart because from this reading distance, these high spatial frequencies are visible to you—in other words, the two photographs are not metameric for you. However, if a cat were to view this same pair of photographs from your viewing distance, the high frequencies in the left-hand photograph would be outside of its window of visibility. Thus, the two photographs would be indistinguishable to a cat,

FIGURE 5.34
While not metamers for you, these two photographs are metamers for animals unable to see high spatial frequencies, such as the cat. (Courtesy, Gregory Phillips.)

meaning the pair would be metamers for the cat.

Moreover, two stimuli that are not metameric for you under one condition (say, intense light or close viewing) might become metameric under another condition (say, dim light or distant viewing). For example, if you move away from Figure 5.34, the high frequencies in the left-hand photograph will fall outside your window of visibility, rendering the two photographs metameric for you.

But it's not only light level or distance that determines whether two stimuli are metameric; any condition that alters the response of the nervous system influences whether stimuli are metameric. One good example derives from the work of Campbell and Robson, discussed earlier. We've already seen that the appearance of a compound grating depends on the responses it evokes in visual channels tuned to different spatial frequencies. If these responses could be temporarily altered, the appearance of the grating should change. As Box 5.4 demonstrates, this is exactly what happens.

The Phenomenon of Perceived Similarity. Even when objects do not appear to be identical, they may still resemble one another to varying degrees. For instance, you may be able to judge whether the baby in the carriage looks more like its mother or its father. But how do you make these judgments? You might compare the baby's features to those of its mother and father and decide which parent looks more like the baby on the basis of which parent shares the greater number of features with the baby.

This description of how resemblance might be judged has much common-sense appeal. It relates such judgments to a check list of features. For example, if two people share many features, they are said to look alike (recall the identical twins). Presumably, the more features in common, the greater the similarity. But do people really judge the similarity of complex forms in this way? To answer, consider one class of complex forms that you are constantly judging, letters of the English alphabet. Reading would be very difficult indeed if all letters of the alphabet looked very much alike. And

BOX 5.4
The Size Aftereffect

One popular theory explains perceived size in terms of the responses in channels tuned to different spatial frequencies (Blakemore, Nachmias, and Sutton, 1970). This theory is depicted in the illustration below. In the two upper panels, the horizontal axes represent spatial frequency and the vertical axes represent sensitivity. To make the argument easier to follow, only three channels are shown. As the upper left panel indicates, channel A prefers the lowest frequency of the three, B prefers an intermediate frequency, and C prefers the highest frequency.

Suppose we present a test grating whose frequency falls halfway between the preferred frequencies of A and B. (This condition is not crucial for the argument; it merely simplifies the description.) Note that the test grating produces equal responses within channels A and B (bottom left panel). According to the theory, this neural code—equal activity in A and B—determines the way the grating looks. But if we did something to change the distribution of activity produced by that same grating, the grating's appearance would be altered. This idea was tested using an adaptation procedure much like that described in the text. First, a person looked at a grating and judged its spatial frequency. We'll refer to this as the test grating. Next, the person adapted to a high-contrast grating whose spatial frequency was lower than that of the test grating. We'll call this the adaptation grating. Finally, after one minute of adaptation, the person looked back at the test grating and

(Continued on next page)

Test grating

Channels' sensitivity — Spatial frequency

Channels' response — Channels' preferred spatial frequency

Perceived spatial frequency before adaptation

Test grating

Channels' sensitivity — Spatial frequency

Channels' response — Channels' preferred spatial frequency

Perceived spatial frequency after adaptation

again judged its spatial frequency. Did the test grating still look the same? To answer this question, let's consider how adaptation would have affected the neural code described before.

Suppose that prior to adaptation, the test grating produced equal responses in channels *A* and *B*. Suppose also that the adaptation grating is one to which *A* is highly sensitive and to which *B* is relatively less sensitive. Prolonged adaptation will thus fatigue *A* considerably but *B* very little (upper right panel). When presented again, the test grating will evoke a nearly normal response from *B* but a weakened response from *A* (lower right panel). This pattern of responses—a greater response in *B* than in *A*—is not usually produced by the test grating. Instead, this pattern of responses is usually evoked by a spatial frequency *higher* than that of the test grating. As a result, after adaptation, the spatial frequency of the test grating should *appear* higher than usual. This was the effect that Blakemore, Nachmias, and Sutton (1970) found. On the basis of the theory, can you predict what will happen if the person has adapted to a spatial frequency *higher* than that of the test grating?

You can experience this so-called **size aftereffect** for yourself. To prove that this aftereffect is not peculiar to gratings, we've borrowed from Stuart Anstis a demonstration using more familiar patterns. Still, the outcome is the same—

a temporary change in apparent size. To make the effect easier to see, this demonstration simultaneously produces two size aftereffects in opposite directions. Here's how to use the figure below. Look at the small black dot between the upper and lower panels of the left side of the figure. With your eyes fixed on the black dot, verify that the letters in the text above the line look the same size as the letters below.

We'll now explain what you must do to alter the apparent size of these letters. Because timing is important, finish reading the instructions before you execute them. First adapt, using the right side of the figure. The patch of small, tightly packed letters corresponds to high spatial frequencies, while the patch of larger, more spread out letters

corresponds to low spatial frequencies. To adapt, slowly move your eyes back and forth along the bar between the two patches of letters. Keep this up for about 90 seconds. Caution: do not look directly at either patch; keep your gaze on the horizontal bar between the two. Otherwise, you'll intermix the two types of adaptation. Finally, at the end of adaptation, look back at the dot between the patches in the left side of the figure. Keeping your eyes on the dot, note the sizes of the letters above and below. You will see that letters in the upper patch look smaller than those in the lower patch. Here, then, is a situation where stimuli that were initially metamers are rendered temporarily non-metameric by altering your visual nervous system.

in fact, sone letters do bear a strong resemblance to one another. Did you notice the substitution of one such letter for another in the preceding sentence? Since correctly recognizing letters is so important in daily life, it would be particularly interesting to know how this recognition succeeds and when it fails. To understand the process of recognition, let's consider two different accounts.

One account, the *feature* theory, uses a check list approach—it claims that letters are represented in the nervous system as a set of features, lines, and contours of various orientations (Gibson, 1965). The other account uses a spatial frequency approach derived from the work of Campbell and Robson. Lewis Harvey and his associates at the University of Colorado, Jonathon Roberts and Martin Gervais (1983), compared how well these two approaches explain the discrimination of one letter from another. Harvey and his colleagues were interested in the number of times that people confuse one letter with another. The perceptual similar-

ity of letters was defined by their tendency to be confused. The basic idea is that if two letters look a lot alike, they will often be confused with one another. A good theory of perceptual similarity should, therefore, predict which pairs of letters are confused and which are not.

In the features approach, it is necessary first to compile a check list of features—that is, to decide *what* features should make up the list. In other words, how might the nervous system represent a letter of the alphabet? One such set of features is listed in the left-hand column of Figure 5.35. For each letter the number of horizontal, vertical, and oblique lines, as well as the number of curves, can be counted. These and other features formed the check list that Harvey worked with, and each letter was evaluated against the list. The feature theory makes a very clear prediction: if two letters have many features in common, they will tend to be confused; letters that have few features in common will not be. The alternative approach hypothesizes that the spatial fre-

	A	B	C	D	E	F	G	H	I	J	K	L	M	N	O	P	Q	R	S	T	U	V	W	X	Y	Z
EXTERNAL																										
1. Horizontal					2	1						1								1						2
2. Vertical		1		1	1	1		2	1	1	1	1	2	2		1		1		1	2					
3. Slant (/)	1																					1	1		1	
4. Slant (\ )	1																					1	1		1	
5. Convex segment		2	3	2			3			1					4	1	4	1	2		1					
OPEN																										
6. Horizontal			1				1												2							
7. Vertical									1												1					
8. Wedged, horizontal		1									1							1						2	1	2
9. Wedged, vertical											2		1	2				1				1	1	2	1	
10. Internal protrusion													1								1					
11. Intersection, internal	2	1			1	1		2			1							1								
12. Bar–horizontal	1				1	1	1	1																		
13. Bar–slant, crossing																	1									
14. Symmetry, vertical	1							1	1				1		1					1	1	1	1	1		
15. Symmetry, horizontal		1	1	1	1			1	1		1				1									1		

FIGURE 5.35
A list of the features distinguishing letters of the alphabet. (Adapted from Geyer and DeWald, 1973.)

quencies of various letters account for confusions. (It should be noted that two letters can have similar spatial frequencies but differ widely in features.)

To test the two approaches, Harvey briefly flashed randomly chosen letters and asked people to name them. The flash was so short that people could correctly name the letter only half the time. When he tallied the confusions, Harvey found that some letters having several features in common, such as "K" and "N," were not confused with one another—which contradicts the feature theory. Instead, the letters that were confused tended to be those with similar spatial frequencies—which suggests that letters may be represented in the visual system in terms of their frequency content.

However, you should not conclude from Harvey's work that spatial frequency is the *only* way to describe the basis for perceived similarity. Suppose that one aspect of a complex stimulus is so striking or conspicuous that it dominates your perception of the object. In this case, you might judge the resemblance between that and other objects solely or primarily on the basis of that feature (Harmon, 1973). Not only do alternative ways exist for utilizing pattern information, but quite likely the alternatives available increase as people mature. When recognizing people's faces, young children base their judgments on isolated characteristics, such as bushy eyebrows or a large mouth; adults can base their judgments either on isolated characteristics *or* on the face's overall configuration, without reference to particular features (Carey and Diamond, 1977). As a result, children are more likely than adults to be thrown off by a change in hairdo or a new hat.

LIMITATIONS OF THE MULTICHANNEL MODEL

Though the multichannel model accounts for many important aspects of form perception,

it by no means accounts for all of them. Let's take an example. When you look at an object from different perspectives, the dimensions of the retinal image of that object differ—for instance, a coin casts a circular image when viewed head-on but an ellipsoidal image when viewed at an angle. Despite changes in image dimensions (and hence in spatial frequency content), you perceive the true, unchanging shape of the object. This constancy of perception in the face of an altered retinal image is called **shape constancy,** and its occurrence implies that form perception transcends spatial frequency information contained in the retinal image (Hochberg, 1971).

Other phenomena also defy explanation in terms of the multichannel model. Some of these involve an interplay between your knowledge about the world and what your eyes tell you. A simple example of this interaction between cognition and vision was given in Figure 4.19 (p. 135). Recall that at first the illustration appeared merely as a random collection of light and dark regions. However, when informed that a Dalmatian was pictured in the illustration, you were able to see the dog. Suddenly, the figure lost its randomness.

Even though you may not have prior knowledge about what you are looking at, you can still get useful information from the context. As a result of this contextual information, the same figure may be perceived quite differently, depending on its surroundings (Palmer, 1975). Because they are so familiar, naturalistic scenes are particularly effective in influencing the perceived form of objects. Chapter 12 will discuss these and other phenomena in which both cognition and vision play important roles.

Generally, some stored knowledge about the world is indispensable for making maximum use of sensory information. The more you *know* about some object ahead of time, the less your senses must tell you. This

BOX 5.5
It Pays to Pay Attention

This chapter has linked form perception to the behavior of channels that analyze information about size and orientation. The fact that such information is analyzed, however, does not guarantee that it will be used. Really good sight requires effort on your part, as well as judgment and attention. No complete account of vision can ignore this fact. Though not much is known about *how* attention affects spatial vision, some influences have been studied. Let's consider a few.

You know that looking directly at something makes it easier to see. But Michael Posner, a cognitive psychologist at the University of Oregon, has shown that people can shift their attention to particular places in space without moving their eyes (Posner, 1980). In one experiment, people kept their eyes fixed straight ahead and pressed a button as soon as a letter appeared. Half the time the letter appeared to their left, and half the time to their right. The person did not have to judge *where* the letter appeared but only *when* it appeared (by

pressing the button). When forewarned about which side the letter would appear on, people responded considerably faster. Seemingly, the forewarning allowed the person to distribute visual attention efficiently, thereby enhancing letter visibility (Posner, Nissen, and Ogden, 1978). This result did not depend on the person's actually shifting gaze. In fact, a special eye-movement recording apparatus allowed Posner to verify that the person's eyes had not moved; only "attention" had.

In Posner's experiment, people were uncertain about *where* a stimulus would appear. Sometimes, though, you know where something will appear but can't anticipate exactly *what* it will be. This kind of uncertainty also affects perception. Several experiments confirm this, showing that spatial vision is impaired when a person doesn't know what spatial frequency to anticipate. Suppose contrast thresholds for a grating are measured under two different conditions. In one, the *certainty* condition, testing is done with only one spatial frequency, allowing a

person to be certain about the grating that is to appear. In the other, the *uncertainty* condition, the person is kept uncertain as to what spatial frequency will appear: half the time one spatial frequency is presented and half the time another. The person merely has to judge whether a grating is visible, nothing more. The outcome of such studies is clear: gratings are far easier to see when people know *what* spatial frequency and orientation they are looking for (Thomas, Gille, and Barker, 1982; Davis and Graham, 1981).

These effects of prior knowledge are not restricted to humans. William Martens and Randolph Blake (1980) found that cats, too, detected gratings at lower contrast when the animals were certain about the frequency that would appear. At the moment we don't know for sure that all lower animals are affected by uncertainty. But this interaction between vision and cognition is obviously an important problem for study. We'll return to this interaction again in Chapter 12.

---

principle is confirmed by studies of **computer vision** (McArthur, 1982). Equipped with telelvision cameras, computers can "see" their surroundings. Such computers act as models for human vision and help to test speculations about human sight. A key question in this research concerns how much "cognitive" information the computer must be given before it can interpret what it is seeing. Without any such information, com-

puters can distinguish an object from a background and even develop a rough sketch or description of the object (Marr, 1982; Poggio, 1984). But with no information to supplement or organize what its television camera tells it, a computer cannot go much beyond this relatively early stage of visual processing. In a sense, without that additional information, the computer is much like you were before you were told that there was a Dalmatian in Figure 4.19. Normally, one takes this supplementary cognitive information for granted. But as Box 5.5 shows, such information is integral to seeing. With no hint of *what* you're looking at, you may not even be able to recognize something as familiar to you as the back of your own hand (Wuillemin and Richardson, 1982).

These are just a few of the phenomena of form perception that defy explanation by the multichannel model in its present form. It's not surprising that the model is unable to explain everything. After all, the model is based on information about only one stage in the visual system, the visual cortex. And as Chapter 4 pointed out, the visual cortex is not the only place in the brain where visual information is processed. Trying to explain all of pattern perception with concepts derived from just the visual cortex is like trying to comprehend a novel by reading only a small part of it. If you pick the right part, of course, you can learn a lot, but certainly not everything. The contributions of other neural centers and the interactions among centers are just beginning to be studied. It may well be that as these centers are explored, satisfactory explanations will de-

velop for currently inexplicable phenomena.

Summary and Preview

This chapter emphasized that visual information is used to distinguish objects from their backgrounds and to discriminate objects from one another. After presenting two traditional views of form perception, structuralism and Gestalt psychology, we described the multichannel model derived from measurements of the CSF. This model is an attempt to relate human form perception to what is known about the visual cortex. The model can account for many aspects of human and animal vision, including detection, discrimination, and certain visual illusions, but it, too, has its limitations.

As a prelude to the next three chapters, it's worth noting that the visual system uses basically the same scheme to represent many different kinds of visual information. As we've seen, pattern information is analyzed into various components and is then represented as a distribution of activity across a set of channels. As outlined in the next chapter, this same type of arrangement is used to represent information about color.

Chapter 6

Color Perception

Staying up all night studying for an examination is not much fun. There is one small consolation, though—a chance to see the beauty of sunrise. As you stare at the horizon through half-shut eyes, you realize that all through the dark night the world outdoors has been a drab, colorless collection of blacks, whites, and various grays. Then just before the sun itself becomes visible, you see a marvelous transformation. A colorless world springs to life as objects don the colors that they'll wear all day. When the world puts on its colors, you realize how bland it would appear without them.

But color gives you more than unending wonder and beauty; in fact, it influences many facets of your life. For example, color can alter the "taste" of the food and drink you consume (Duncker, 1939). You can prove this to yourself by using food coloring to create red milk or green orange juice. Color can affect your expectations about

medication, as well. One study found that people associate white tablets with the relief of pain and orange ones with increased arousal (Buckalew and Coffield, 1982). In addition, some people believe that the world's colors ebb and flow with moods—that envy can make you "green," disappointments can make you "blue," and infuriating circumstances can make you "see red." Though these are merely figures of speech, the connection between emotions and color may be more than just figurative (Sharpe, 1974). For example, some tavern owners cover their walls with colors that they expect will stimulate greater consumption of alcoholic beverages. Some people believe that color has other behavioral effects as well (Birren, 1978). For instance, certain shades of pink are reputed to calm prisoners in jail and quiet the irate fans of hapless football teams. It has been said that Knute Rockne, the great Notre Dame football coach, had his team's locker room painted red to excite his players and the opposing team's locker room painted blue to induce calm and relaxation.

People are selective not only about the colors of their walls, but about the colors they wear. In fact, it's been claimed that you can tell a lot about people—perhaps even about an entire nation—just from the colors of their clothing. One person who made such a claim was Johann Wolfgang von Goethe, the German poet-philosopher of the nineteenth century. Goethe wrote:

Lively nations, the French for instance, love intense colours . . .; sedate nations, like the English and Germans, wear straw-coloured or leather-coloured yellow accompanied with dark blue. Nations aiming at dignity of appearance, the Spaniards and Italians, for instance, suffer the red colour of their mantles to incline to the passive side. (Goethe, 1840/1970, p. 328)

But all these effects, whether real or imagined, are simply by-products of color's real purpose, to which we turn now.

Why Is It Important to See Colors?

The ability to see color facilitates detection and discrimination; in fact, this is undoubtedly why color vision has evolved. Color makes it easier to pick out an object from its background (**detection**). Manufacturers of sporting equipment exploit this fact by producing yellow tennis balls that are easier to see on the court and orange golf balls that are hard to lose on the fairway. Nature also exploits the conspicuity color affords. Many animals call attention to themselves by means of color, especially for purposes of mating: in full display, a male peacock is impossible to ignore. Plants, too, announce their availability for pollination with color. At the same time, however, nature uses color to make some creatures and plants inconspicuous (Owen, 1980). For example, the color of a praying mantis blends in so well with that of the leaves it frequents that unless the insect moves, it is invisible. Similarly, the arctic fox's white pelt provides excellent camouflage when it hunts on snow-packed land, thus giving the fox a considerable advantage over its prey.

Besides affecting your ability to see objects against a background, color helps you distinguish among various objects in the environment (**discrimination**). One shade of red tells you instantly that a vehicle is a fire truck, another tells you that an apple or tomato is ripe and ready to eat (Gibson, 1966, p. 183). One shade of yellow tells you that a vehicle is a taxi rather than a police car; another shade of yellow ensures that Kodak's photographic products will be recognized everywhere in the world merely from the color of the box. Farmers use color to identify rich soil and to tell when their crops are ready for harvest. Doctors routinely rely on color to make diagnoses: blood that is pale red indicates anemia, and a yellowish skin pallor suggests a liver disorder (Birren, 1941, p. 191). Government meat inspectors pay attention to the color of animal tissue when judging its fitness for human consumption (Collins and Worthey, 1984).

Our general point, then, is that although color does have emotional and aesthetic impact, the main purpose of color perception—as with the perception of form, motion, and depth—is to help creatures to detect and discriminate objects. To explain how color serves these goals, this chapter describes the important characteristics of color perception. The chapter also explains how color experiences depend on two factors: the light reflected from objects and the properties of the eyes and nervous system.

What Are the Units of Color Perception?

A MULTITUDE OF COLOR NAMES

The preceding chapter started out by asking about the *units* of form perception. We'll begin our discussion of color perception the same way. Most people tie their experiences of color to the names used to describe those colors. So we might expect to get some idea of the units of color perception by asking the simple question: How many color names are there? Some dictionaries list hundreds of color names, and new names are created by advertisers every year. However, common, everyday language gets along with no more than a dozen or so color names (Chapanis, 1965). This makes sense, because beyond this basic dozen, people don't really agree about what names go with what colors (Chapanis, 1965; Berlin and Kay, 1969).

Since people don't always agree on color names, perhaps it would be more useful to concentrate instead on experiences of color. One could ask: How many different colors can people see? Unfortunately, this simple question yields not just one answer but a whole series of them. If color samples are placed side by side, most people can distinguish more than a thousand different colors. You can try this for yourself the next time you're in a paint store. However, if samples are presented one at a time, performance declines (Newall, Burnham, and Clark, 1957; Nilsson and Nelson, 1981). In fact, when samples are seen one at a time—with several seconds elapsing between samples—most people can reliably recognize fewer than a dozen different colors (Halsey and Chapanis, 1951; Boyce, 1981). So how many colors *can* people see—thousands or just a dozen? The difficulty in answering this question suggests that we need to examine what people actually mean by the term

"color." To do this, let's look at early attempts to understand the nature of color.

WHAT IS COLOR? THE INSIGHTS OF ISAAC NEWTON

Not even the briefest discussion of color perception can ignore the contributions of Isaac Newton, undoubtedly one of the greatest geniuses who ever lived. During a brief retreat to his mother's farm while a plague was raging at home in Cambridge, England, Newton discovered the binomial theorem, invented the calculus, and devised a theory of gravitation. He also bought a prism that he used later to study the nature of light and color (Westfall, 1980). These studies led Newton to draw a distinction that remains fundamental to this day, a distinction between physical phenomena and perceptual phenomena. In particular, Newton observed that

the rays, to speak properly, are not coloured. In them there is nothing else than a certain Power and Disposition to stir up a Sensation of this or that Colour. (Newton, 1704/1952, pp. 124–125)

These two sentences are as difficult to accept as they are profound and true. Among other things, they imply that even the most compelling intuitions can be wrong—objects themselves have no color; nor is the light reflected from those objects colored. Instead, color is a psychological phenomenon, an entirely subjective experience. Objects *appear* colored because they reflect light from particular regions of the visible spectrum. But even that is not enough. In order for an object to appear colored, light reflected from that object must be picked by the right sort of eye or nervous system. Because many people have abnormal eyes and nervous systems, their experiences of color differ radically from those that most people enjoy.

Actually, waves in that portion of the electromagnetic spectrum that is called "light" are no more colored than waves in any other portion of the spectrum—for example, radio waves. Color arises from the capacity of particular light rays to evoke certain responses in the nervous system. To illustrate, imagine seeing someone who is wearing a red sweater. According to Newton, there is nothing inherently red about the light reflected from that sweater. No matter how firmly rooted in the sweater it may *seem*, the redness ultimately depends on your eyes and nervous system.

So to refer to a "red sweater" is incorrect, strictly speaking. To be correct you should describe it as a "sweater that when seen in daylight can evoke a sensation most humans call 'red.'" However, we don't advise going into a clothing store and using this description to ask whether the store has any red sweaters. Nor will this chapter use such cumbersome language to describe the colors evoked by objects.

While on the subject of terminology, we should further clarify the term "color." Our dictionary offers nineteen different meanings for "color" in its noun form alone. If you've ever sorted objects such as crayons or "orphan" socks, you know that colors differ from one another in various ways. Blue and green socks differ from one another but not in the same way that two green socks do—say, one brand new and another that's been washed many times. In the study of perception, the single word "color" covers three different qualities. To distinguish one quality from another, each quality is given a particular name, "hue," "brightness," and "saturation."

Hue refers to the quality that distinguishes among red, yellow, green, blue, orange, and so on. Incidentally, the word "color" is not an acceptable synonym for "hue." In fact, technically, you should refer to the "hues of the rainbow" and to Joseph's "coat of many hues" (Genesis 37:3). The second quality of color, **brightness,** is related to the amount, or intensity, of light. This quality enables you to describe an object (like a star in the sky) as "bright" or "dim." Or suppose you're dining by candlelight and find that it's hard to see with just one candle. If you increase the illumination by lighting additional candles, you'll increase the brightness of your surroundings. The third quality, **saturation,** characterizes a color as "pale," "vivid," or something between the two. After your jeans have been laundered with some bleach in the wash water, their blueness will be less saturated than when you first got them. Color Plate 2 will help you to visualize more easily what is meant by "hue," "brightness," and "saturation."

Since your color experiences vary along these three dimensions, describing a color completely requires that you specify its hue, its brightness, *and* its saturation. Moreover, an adequate theory of color perception must explain the origin of these dimensions of color experience. Having clarified what we mean by "color," we're now ready to return to the units of color perception. Let's look at the observations that led Newton to propose that color resides within oneself, not within the light rays.

What Can a Prism Reveal About Color? In one experiment, Newton allowed a beam of sunlight to pass through a small circular hole in a shutter and then through a glass prism (see Figure 6.1). After passing through the prism, the light fanned out into a rainbow of **spectral colors,** or spectrum. Newton described the spectrum as consisting of seven different colors—red, orange, yellow, green, blue, indigo, and violet. These seven colors are demarcated in the spectrum shown in Color Plate 3. In this plate, the upper scale

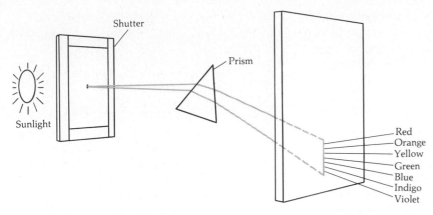

FIGURE 6.1
Newton's basic experiment.

defines the spectrum in terms of color experiences, a psychological dimension. The lower scale defines the spectrum in terms of wavelength of light, a physical dimension. The latter dimension, wavelength, was not known to Newton, which is why he had to describe color solely in psychological terms (color names).

Actually, it was known long before Newton that a prism could decompose sunlight into a spectrum of colors (Ronchi, 1970). For centuries, people had seen spectrums created by glass chandeliers, soap bubbles, and dia-

mond jewelry. Newton's contribution lay not in the observation but in the uses to which he put that observation. Two experimental techniques were particularly important in this regard. First, he developed a simple scheme for selectively blocking out or reducing the intensity of various colors in the spectrum; second, by means of a convex lens, Newton was able to collect this modified spectrum and pass it through another prism (see Figure 6.2). The combination of these two techniques allowed him to distinguish between **pure light** and light that is made up of sev-

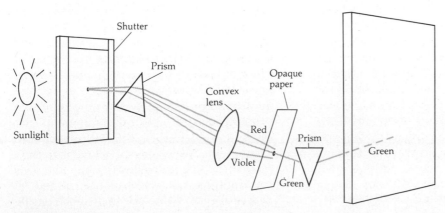

FIGURE 6.2
A modification of Newton's basic experiment.

eral different components—**composite light.** For instance, if he blocked out all the colors of the spectrum except for green and then passed the green through a second prism, the resulting light continued to be green. Because the second prism could not break green into further components, Newton deemed the green to be pure light.

To Newton these observations suggested that light from the sun was *not* pure but consisted of seven different colors that could not be decomposed. Though the first conclusion (that sunlight is not pure) is correct, the second (that sunlight contains only seven pure components) is not. Since the mistakes of geniuses can be as enlightening as their successes, let's see why Newton went wrong.

Like anyone else, scientists must be alert to the possibility that their observations can be influenced by expectation. Newton's conclusion that there were seven colors in the spectrum was influenced by just such an expectation, one based on his belief that seeing and hearing were closely related. In particular, he thought that since the musical scale included seven tones and semitones within each octave, the spectrum had to contain seven colors (Boring, 1942).*

But this error should not diminish the fact that Newton's main idea was right—light from the sun, sometimes called white light, can be decomposed into many different colors. In modern parlance, light from the sun is said to contain various amounts of energy in different regions of the electromagnetic spectrum (recall the discussion in Chapter 2). The distribution of sunlight's energy over the visible portion of the electromagnetic spectrum is shown by the heavy line in Figure 6.3. Note particularly that light from the sun consists of nearly equal amounts of energy at all the wavelengths shown.

*There is actually reason to suppose that Newton originally noticed only five different colors in the spectrum. Some claim that he later added two—orange and indigo—to bolster the analogy between spectral colors and intervals in the musical scale (Houston, cited in Helmholtz, 1909/1962, vol. 2, p. 76).

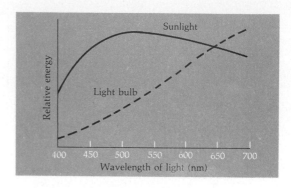

FIGURE 6.3
Energy distribution of sunlight (heavy line) and of light from an ordinary light bulb (dashed line).

Contrast this with the distribution of energy from an ordinary light bulb. As shown by the dotted line, a typical light bulb emits more energy at longer wavelengths than it does at shorter ones. This is why photographs taken with indoor lighting can have a slightly more yellowish tint than do those taken with natural light.

The idea that white light is decomposable into elementary components is universally accepted today. However, when Newton first suggested the idea, it aroused passionate disagreement that continued well after Newton's own lifetime (see Box 6.1). For example, many people were upset that their eyes couldn't be trusted—what appeared to be innocent white light actually consisted of a host of components. In reality, the situation is even worse than people imagined: using far fewer than seven components you can fool the eye into seeing white. We now know that humans experience as white a light that consists of a mixture of just two, properly chosen spectral components. Because this does not work with all pairs of components, we give a special name to those pairs for which it does work. Any two spectral components which when added together appear white are said to be **complementary.** A mixture of one component that appears blue and one that appears yellow would look just like white. Moreover, a per-

BOX 6.1
Newton Stirs Up a Hornet's Nest

Newton first presented his work on light and color in 1672, when he was 29 years old. His ideas were greeted with such fury and disdain that Newton waited more than 30 years before publishing his complete work on these topics in *Opticks*. By that time, 1704, Newton's genius was nearly universally acknowledged. Despite his eminence, his ideas about light and color continued to provoke angry rebuttals for more than a century. None of these rebuttals was more impassioned than that advanced by the German poet Goethe.

Goethe believed that he would be remembered not so much for his poetry as for his refutation of Newton (Pirenne, 1967, p. 153). Being a strong believer in the power of intuition and common sense, Goethe was shocked at the patent absurdity of Newton's prism demonstration. Goethe considered Newton a "Cossack" for denying the purity of white light (Southall, in Helmholtz, 1909/1962, vol. 2, p. 115). Since the time of Aristotle, white light had been regarded as the very essence of purity. According to this view,

color represented the contamination of white by less exalted, worldly substances. Newton's decomposition of white into colors implied that white was no more special than any other color.

In addition to these aesthetic considerations, Goethe also objected to Newton's ideas on philosophical grounds. He believed that to accept Newton's claim about white light was tantamount to treating *all* sense perception as subjective and unreliable, an idea he detested. Feeling absolutely certain that white light could *not* be a mixture of other colors, Goethe urged people to disregard the experiments performed by Newton in a darkened room in Cambridge:

Friends, escape the dark enclosure,
where they tear the light apart
and in wretched bleak exposure
twist and cripple Nature's heart.
Superstitions and confusions
are with us since ancient times—
leave the specters and delusions
in the heads of narrow minds.
(Translated by Weisskopf and Worth, in Weisskopf, 1976)

To combat Newton further, Goethe got a prism and attempted to verify some of Newton's claims. Although he did use the prism for many different experiments, Goethe never correctly repeated what Newton had done. For example, Goethe looked directly through the prism but failed to see a spectrum of colors, leading him to believe that Newton, in addition to being a Cossack, was a charlatan. Goethe went further. He enlisted the services of a young man, Arthur Schopenhauer, who would later become a famous philosopher in his own right. Goethe interested Schopenhauer in his ideas about light and color, and persuaded him to continue the assault on Newton. Using Goethe's own optical equipment, the younger man began to do experiments with light (Birren, 1941, p. 214). Unfortunately for Goethe, though, these experiments convinced Schopenhauer that Newton had been right after all: sunlight does consist of many different colors.

son would find this mixture indistinguishable from another that included orange light and greenish-blue light, which would also look like sunlight. So in effect, complementary components cancel one another, yielding a colorless or achromatic sensation.

We should stress that simple measuring instruments *can* distinguish among these various mixtures even though the human eye cannot. Hence the act of mixing com-

ponents of light does not obliterate the individual spectral components; these components are still present in the mixture. These mixtures appear equivalent because of the way the visual nervous system processes spectral information.

What Can Metamers Reveal About Color?
As we've just seen, various sets of physically different distributions of energy can

produce identical color experiences. Members of such sets are said to be **metameric,** a concept introduced in Chapter 5. For example, Newton found that orange light, alone, was metameric to a mixture of red light and yellow light. In addition, pairs of complementary colors (that yield white) are also metameric to one another. Also, those two pairs of mixtures are metameric to a mixture of Newton's seven spectral colors, which as you know, also yields the perception of white light.

Recall that metamers imply that the visual system is "blind" to certain aspects of the physical world. By identifying metamers, one learns what those aspects are. For example, suppose you have two objects that are physically identical in all respects but one. If you can't tell them apart by looking at them, your visual system must be ignoring whatever it is that makes the objects physically different. Conversely, if you can tell the two objects apart, your visual system cannot be ignoring that one distinguishing feature. The information that the system retains and the information that it discards say a lot about the workings of color perception. As a result, much of the understanding of color perception comes from the study of metameric matches. We'll turn to that topic now.

Newton's Color Circle. Newton did not have the degree of control over light that scientists enjoy today. Still, he managed to explore the perceptual results of various mixtures of light. For instance, to see what happens when two pure lights are combined, he blocked out all the other spectral components and used a convex lens to combine the remaining two. Examining the appearance of various mixtures of light, Newton developed the basic ideas of color mixture and expressed them in a graphic model of color perception. The model, known as **Newton's color circle,** is depicted in Figure

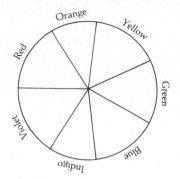

FIGURE 6.4
Newton's color circle.

6.4. Although modest in appearance, this circle represents an incredible insight on Newton's part, namely that a simple geometric form could represent the properties of something as complex as color vision (Wasserman, 1978). Each of the seven wedge-shaped sectors represents one of the spectral colors—as Newton put it, "the Circumference representing the whole series of colours from one end of the Sun's colour'd image to the other" (1704/1952, p. 154). The circle, though, is only part of the model; Newton also devised several rules that relate colors and mixtures of colors to locations on and within the circle. Let's see how the appearance of various mixtures might be predicted by this geometric model.

Suppose we were to add equal intensities of red light and yellow light. These two equal-intensity lights are represented by two equal-sized triangles in Figure 6.5. One triangle is located on the circle, in the middle of the arc for yellow; the other triangle is also located on the circle, but in the middle of the arc for red. To find the color that results from the mixture of these two, you connect the two triangles with a straight line. The color of the mixture corresponds to the line's center of gravity. (You might imagine this line as a seesaw, and the triangles as people on either end; the sizes of the triangles signify how much the people weigh.) The lo-

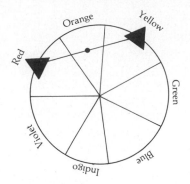

FIGURE 6.5
Newton's color circle can be used to predict the color produced by mixing equal amounts of yellow and red light.

cation of the line's center of gravity gives the predicted color of the mixture. In this case, the center of gravity lies in the middle of the orange sector. In fact, orange is what you see when equal amounts of red and yellow light are mixed. Consider what happens when *un*equal amounts are mixed, say a large quantity of red and a small quantity of yellow. This case is shown in Figure 6.6. The center of gravity of the line connecting the two unequal-sized triangles lies close to the border of the red and orange sectors, signifying that the mixture will look reddish-orange, which it does. Adding two

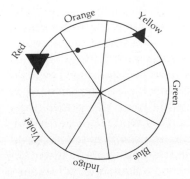

FIGURE 6.6
Newton's color circle can be used to predict the color produced by mixing unequal amounts of yellow and red light.

colors near one another on the color circle yields a mixture whose color is a compromise between the components. In fact, as one varies the proportions of the colors in the mixture, the appearance of the mixture changes correspondingly.

Adding together the appropriate components of light, Newton also discovered he could produce a color whose appearance was not like any of his seven pure lights. For example, if you add long-wavelength light (from the red end of the spectrum) and short-wavelength light (from the blue end of the spectrum) the result is purple. Today we call such colors, including purple, **nonspectral colors.** The existence of nonspectral colors reinforces the distinction between light's physical properties and its perceptual consequences. From the perceptual point of view, the physical spectrum has a gap—it does not contain all the colors that can be perceived by the human eye.

When he examined the seven colors in his spectrum, Newton noticed that they were very vivid (today we would describe them as "saturated"). But when he added these vivid components together, the resulting mixtures appeared less vivid (today we would say "washed out" or "desaturated"). This perceptual fact, that mixtures appear desaturated, is also represented in Newton's color circle. The most vivid colors lie along the circumference; less vivid colors lie away from the circumference. At the extreme, a completely desaturated color (white) is represented at the center of the circle.

As mentioned earlier, the seven pie-shaped wedges in Newton's color circle reflect his belief that there should be seven discrete pure colors. A color circle designed in this arbitrary way makes incorrect predictions about some mixtures involving colors widely separated on the color circle. In order to make correct predictions, Newton's color circle must be adjusted in two ways. First, the boundaries that divide the circle into discrete sectors must be erased, since those sectors could imply the existence of seven discrete pure colors. A circle without sectors correctly reflects the fact that color varies continuously. Second, some rational scheme for spacing the color names (or wavelengths) around the circle's circumference must be used. Complementary colors should be placed opposite each other on the circle, so that when they are connected, their balance point falls at the circle's center—white. A circle satisfying both these requirements is shown in Figure 6.7.

The circumference of the larger interrupted circle indicates the position of various spectral lights from 420 nanometers to 700 nanometers. Note that the wavelengths are not spaced uniformly; the wavelengths from 500 to 700 nanometers occupy less of the circumference than do those from 420 to 500 nanometers. In fact, the wavelengths have been positioned on the circle so that along any diameter, complementary colors stand directly opposite each other. Note that some wavelengths, such as 497 nanometers, have no single wavelength that is complementary. The inner complete circle indicates

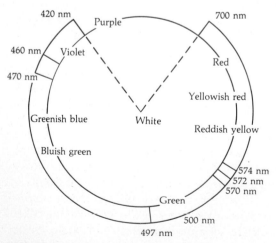

FIGURE 6.7
A revised color circle. (Adapted from Southall, 1937/1961.)

the color names an observer would give to certain of the lights.

Though this revised color circle is far more satisfactory than Newton's original, it still fails to capture some elementary facts about color. For example, Newton noted that "some colours affect the senses more strongly." He meant that yellows and greens are brighter (that is, more visible) than reds or blues. We now know that the visibility of various wavelengths of light defines the photopic sensitivity function (see Chapter 3), with maximum brightness at 550 nanometers.

There's another important fact that Newton's original circle doesn't capture: bright colors tend to look washed out or desaturated. You can see this for yourself in Color Plate 3 by comparing the colors in the middle of the spectrum (which appear relatively bright but desaturated) to those at either end (which appear less bright but more saturated). Moreover, how strongly saturated a color appears can be quantified. While someone looks at a light of a particular color, you can add white light to it, thereby desaturating that color. In this way, you can determine how much white light is needed to eliminate the color completely. The amount of white light needed depends on the color you start with. Certain colors, in other words, are more strongly saturated to begin with—they stand up better to white light. Other, less saturated colors are easily washed out by the addition of small quantities of white light. Typical results of this procedure are shown in Figure 6.8. The horizontal axis represents the wavelength of light used to produce the color; the vertical axis shows the intensity of white light needed to desaturate the color completely. This V-shaped curve shows that lights at the middle of the spectrum (yellow) appear less saturated than do lights toward the ends of the spectrum (blue or red). Adding white light to light of a given wavelength can also alter the hue produced by that wavelength. For

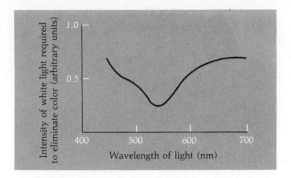

FIGURE 6.8
Intensity of white light needed to desaturate colors of various wavelengths.

instance, adding white to long-wavelength light (red) shifts its hue slightly toward yellow (Kurtenbach, Sternheim, and Spillmann, 1984).

The dependence of hue, brightness, and saturation on wavelength is not a consequence of some physical property of light. Rather, it results from the way the visual system processes information about light's wavelength. A full explanation of color experiences must, therefore, account for brightness and saturation as well as hue.

In developing the concepts of color perception, our examples have utilized simple spectral lights and their mixtures. Such lights consist of a small band of wavelengths. However, light containing only a restricted range of wavelengths is rare outside the laboratory. Ordinarily, vision depends on white light (sunlight or artificial light) that illuminates the objects one sees. But, despite the fact that the illuminating light is white, one sees most objects as colored, not white, because those objects absorb certain wavelengths in the white light and reflect the rest. The wavelengths absorbed depend on the pigments contained in the surface of those objects. For instance, "green" grass reflects a band of wavelengths more than 100 nanometers wide, nearly one-third the

width of the entire visible spectrum. This distribution of reflected wavelengths reaches the eyes, and initiates the perception of color (see Box 6.2). Surfaces containing different pigments will reflect different distributions of wavelengths and, therefore, will appear different in color. The light reflected from a surface depends also on the wavelengths with which the surface is illuminated. However, even though the wavelength distribution of illuminating light changes—thereby changing the wavelengths reflected to the eyes—the colors of objects tend to remain constant. This fact is puzzling, since it means that one's perceptions are constant even though the light stimulating the eyes is not. Let's consider how this remarkable constancy of color perception is achieved.

COLOR CONSTANCY

The light reflected from a surface depends not only on the pigments in the surface but also on the light illuminating the surface. If the spectral composition of that illumination varies, so too will the spectral distribution of the reflected light. The composition of sunlight varies with the time of day—late afternoon sunlight contains more long-wavelength light than does noonday sun. As a result, the light reflected outdoors by any object will vary from one time of day to another. Moreover, the spectral composition of ordinary indoor lights (tungsten light bulbs) differs from the spectral composition of sunlight—the indoor light contains less short-wavelength light. Thus the light reflected by objects changes when you move the objects indoors. Even though the light reaching your eye changes, you usually don't notice any change in the perceived color of objects: green grass nearly always looks green, and yellow roses yellow. **Color constancy** is the name given to the fact that an object's color tends to remain constant even though the spectrum of light falling on that

BOX 6.2
Mixing Colors

Every schoolchild knows it is possible to create a variety of shades of colors using just a few so-called primaries. Various shades of green, for example, are readily achieved simply by mixing blue and yellow inks in various proportions. This is called **subtractive color mixture,** since the component primaries each subtract a portion of the incident light, keeping that portion from reaching your eye. To illustrate this point consider the curve in panel A of the accompanying figure (adapted from Pirenne, 1976), which shows the reflectance spectrum of a typical light blue ink. The curve indicates that the ink reflects lots of light from the short-wavelength portion of the spectrum but less from the longer-wavelength portion. This happens because the ink contains a pigment that selectively absorbs light of particular wavelengths. Now look at panel B, which shows the reflectance spectrum for a typical yellow ink. Note that it reflects mainly wavelengths longer than 500 nanometers—hence its yellow appearance. Again, this is because the ink contains a pigment that absorbs light in a characteristic way. The curve in panel C shows the distribution of wavelengths reflected by a mixture of equal amounts of the two inks. How does this distribution come about, and why does it appear green?

When you mix the yellow and blue inks together, the mixture contains pigments from both components. Now suppose you view a surface that is coated with the mixture and illuminated by sunlight. The yellow pigment in the mixture will *absorb* part of the light that otherwise would have been *reflected* by the blue pigment. In other words, the yellow pigment removes much of the short wavelengths from the reflected light. Similarly, at longer wavelengths, the blue pigment will *absorb* some of the light that otherwise would have been *reflected* by the yellow pigment. Although the actual calculations are complicated, panel C reveals that the mixture of the two inks reflects light mainly around the middle of the spectrum, the only region of the spectrum at which *both* pigments reflect appreciable amounts of light. As a result, the mixture will look neither yellow nor blue but instead greenish.

The principles of subtractive color mixture were employed 25,000 years ago by the prehistoric artists who worked in the caves around Lascaux (in what is today western France). These principles have been used ever since by people to color objects in their environment; but it was nature who devised the technique: plants and animals contain pigments that selectively absorb or subtract certain wavelengths. This selective absorption gives rise to the characteristic colors one associates with those plants and animals.

Color can also be produced by a process of **additive color mixture.** This additive process is almost never used by nature and has been used by people only very recently, mainly for purposes of entertainment or research. We'll illustrate additive mixture using a familiar example, color television. The tube in a color television set contains hundreds of thousands of small spots packed very closely together. These spots light up when they are struck by an electron beam inside the set. A spot will appear red or blue or green, depending on the material of which the spot is made. Each small section of the television tube contains many closely packed spots of each type. You can verify this by putting your eye very close to the screen of a color television set. At normal viewing distances, however, the spots are too small to be seen separately and instead are blended or added together by your eye. The resulting color, then, is produced by an additive process. Because the strength of the blue, red, or green glow varies with the intensity of the electron beam at any spot, the relative proportions of the three colors in the mixture also vary. As a result, although the tube itself produces only the three colors, the properties of your own nervous system generate perceptions of a wide range of different colors according to the laws of additive color mixture.

Color Plate 4 allows you to experience additive mixture. The upper picture ("La Parade" by G. Seurat) actually consists of many dots of paint of different colors. From normal viewing distance your eye does not separate the individual dots, resulting in additive mixture of the individual colors. (Incidentally, when Newton superimposed lights of different wavelengths, he too was employing a form of additive mixture.) Shown in the lower picture is a magnified view of one small part of Seurat's painting. Here you can see the individual dots. Note that this magnified image produces less vivid colors, because the white from the background is desaturating the color of the dots.

We've seen, then, that there are two different techniques for color mixture. In one technique, the color is produced by the addition of wavelengths; in the other, by the subtraction (absorption) of wavelengths. The difference between these techniques of

color mixture has nothing to do with the nature of color vision. It shows only that light is absorbed or reflected differently under different circumstances. For both types of mixtures, the color of a surface depends on the distribution of wavelengths reaching your eye.

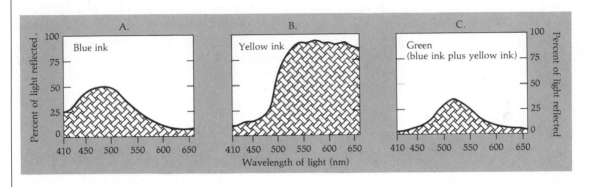

object, and thus the light reflected toward the viewer from the object, changes.

Color constancy should remind you of lightness constancy and shape constancy (discussed in Chapters 3 and 5, respectively). All of these constancies make important contributions to the stability of the environment's appearance. If visual perception changed with every change in the light reaching their eyes, people would be hopelessly confused. Color constancy allows objects to be recognized regardless of the time of day, and indoors as well as outdoors.

Suppose, for example, you are sitting outside, reading this book. It gets chilly and you go inside to read, using a lamp containing an ordinary 150-watt tungsten bulb. The light outdoors contains relatively more short-wavelength energy (blue) than the light indoors. Because it has relatively more of its energy at medium and long wavelengths, the indoor light is yellower than the light outdoors. If your color perception depend-

ed only on the light coming from a page of this book, the surface would appear somewhat yellow indoors (since indoors the page reflects more light that is normally called yellow than it does outdoors). Yet you notice no such change, for the following reason.

When any stimulus is presented for a while, the visual mechanisms it affects lose some of their sensitivity. This process, discussed in Chapters 4 and 5, is called **adaptation.** Adaptation promotes color constancy by reducing the effects of small differences among the physiological effects of various spectral distributions. After you've been exposed to the blue-rich outdoor light for a while, adaptation diminishes the visual system's response to short-wavelength light. After you've been exposed to the red- and green-rich indoor light for a while, adaptation reduces the response to long-wavelength light. Both effects "homogenize" the visual responses under sunlight and indoor light, making those responses more nearly alike than their different spectral distributions would suggest. Normally one does not notice the effect of adaptation, but there is one situation in which that effect is obvious. Suppose you are walking up to your house at night. Glancing into the window before you enter, you'll notice that the room has a yellowish cast. You're seeing the consequences of the biased spectral distribution produced by the light bulbs in the room (recall Figure 6.3). But once you enter the house, that yellowish cast disappears because your visual system has now adapted to that biased spectral distribution.

Finally, we should emphasize that this process of color constancy probably evolved in order to compensate for small variations in the broad wavelength distributions of *natural* light. As a result, when objects are illuminated by light with a restricted wavelength distribution, the compensation fails and color constancy is defeated. Color Plate 5 shows some common objects illuminated by natural sunlight and by two different lights of restricted wavelength distributions. Note how, in the later cases, the objects take on highly unnatural colors, showing that color constancy works only under conditions of broad-band illumination. Be warned that unscrupulous supermarkets exploit this limitation on color constancy. They can make their meat products look extra fresh (red) by illuminating them with light biased toward long wavelengths.

The Trichromacy of Human Vision

The preceding sections reinforce the idea that color (a psychological experience) and light (a physical quantity) are connected in complex ways. Among the complexities is the fact that different combinations of wavelengths can yield the same color experience.

Such psychologically equivalent combinations, so-called metamers, indicate that the visual system confuses certain combinations of wavelengths with one another. The number and kinds of confusions indicate how the eye analyzes the wavelength composition of the light it receives. Since this analysis is initiated by the photosensitive pigments in the cone visual receptors, color confusions depend on the number of different types of cone photopigments an eye has.* To see this connection, consider the color confusions made by an eye that possesses only one type of cone photopigment.

A DESIGN DECISION: HOW MANY CONE PIGMENTS?

What If Eyes Had Only One Cone Pigment? Every photopigment absorbs some wavelengths of light more efficiently than others. However, once absorbed, light of any wavelength initiates exactly the same train of events in the visual receptor. Thus the receptor makes no distinction as to the wavelength of the light absorbed. The response of the receptor conveys information about how much light is absorbed, but the response conveys no information about the wavelength of the absorbed light. This is called the **univariance principle,** since a receptor's response can be summarized by a single number (one variable) that specifies the amount of light absorbed (Naka and Rushton, 1966). The univariance principle is the key to understanding the photoreceptors' role in color perception. (Incidentally, the univariance principle also represents another case of the ambiguity inherent in the response of a single neuron, an issue discussed in Chapters 4 and 5.)

According to the univariance principle, an eye containing only one photopigment

---

*We are focusing on cone receptors, since color experience requires that the eyes receive sufficient light to stimulate cones.

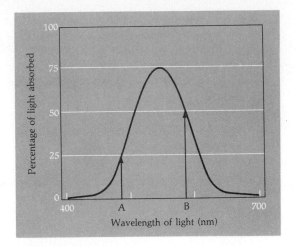

FIGURE 6.9
A one-pigment system.

type is not able to see color. Such an eye is unable to distinguish one wavelength from another because, with the proper adjustment of intensities, all wavelengths could be made to affect the receptor in exactly the same way. This is illustrated in Figure 6.9, which shows the absorption spectrum of a single, hypothetical photopigment type. The curve's height represents the amount of incident light that the pigment would absorb at each and every wavelength. Note, for example, that the pigment absorbs twice as much light (50 percent) at wavelength *B* as it does at wavelength *A* (25 percent). So, if equal amounts of *A* and *B* were incident on the photopigment, more *B* would be absorbed. However, equal amounts of *A* and *B* would be absorbed if twice as much *A* were incident on the photopigment, relative to *B*. In fact, the intensities of many different wavelengths could be adjusted such that the amount of light actually absorbed by this pigment would be the same regardless of which wavelength was incident. This means, in other words, that many wavelengths would be metameric to one another. In addition, with proper adjustment of intensities, any combination of wavelengths, in-

cluding white light, could be perfectly matched by any other wavelength or combination of wavelengths. So an eye with only one type of photopigment would treat all sorts of light mixtures as metameric, including many that the normal eye does not. A person with just one cone pigment is unable to discriminate color. Everything appears various shades of gray, hence such a person is called a **monochromat** (meaning "one-colored"). Incidentally, everyone is a monochromat under conditions of dim light, because then they are forced to rely on the rods, which contain just one type of photopigment.

What If Eyes Had Two Cone Pigments? An eye with two different photopigments would be more discriminating than the one-pigment eye just described. Consider the consequences of having two photopigments such as those whose absorption spectra are shown in Figure 6.10. Again, since each photopigment obeys the univariance principle, *on its own* a pigment cannot convey information about what wavelengths of light are present. However, when two different types of pigments act *in concert* they do provide some

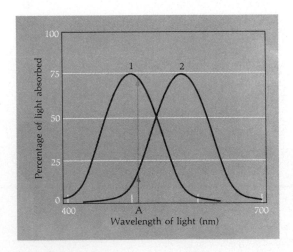

FIGURE 6.10
A two-pigment system.

information about the wavelengths that are present. Let's see how. First, note that when stimulated by light, a two-pigment system makes two statements, not one, about the amount of light energy absorbed. For any given wavelength, the statement (or response) of either pigment depends on how well that pigment absorbs light of that wavelength. Now by definition, two types of photopigments differ in how well they absorb light of various wavelengths, as summarized by their different absorption spectra (Figure 6.10). As a result, any single wavelength (for example *A* in Fig. 6.10) will generate a *pair* of responses, one from each pigment. Note in the example shown that pigment 1 generates a larger response to *A* than does pigment 2. Of course, the magnitude of each pigment's response will also vary with light intensity, since more intense lights make more energy available for absorption. However, when light gets more intense but wavelength does not change, the two responses will grow proportionately. Consequently, so long as wavelength is unchanged, the *relative* strengths of the two pigments' responses will remain constant. In summary, because the two pigment types

have different absorption spectra, an eye with two pigment types extracts some usable wavelength information from light.

This two-pigment system can nonetheless be confused about wavelength, as the following example shows. Consider the response produced by the wavelength represented in the left panel of Figure 6.11 (see arrow). Note that this wavelength stimulates both pigments and 1 and 2, yielding a small response in pigment 1 and a larger response in pigment 2. This pair of responses produced by a single wavelength can be imitated perfectly by a combination of two wavelengths. This is illustrated in the right panel of Figure 6.11, where the effects of a mixture of two wavelengths are shown. Note that the resulting pair of responses, one from each pigment, stands in the same ratio as the pair of responses elicited by the single wavelength in the left panel. The owner of this eye, therefore, would confuse that single wavelength (left panel) with the mixture (right panel).

This eye would suffer many other color confusions as well. Any wavelength or mixture of wavelengths (no matter how complex) will be represented by just a pair of

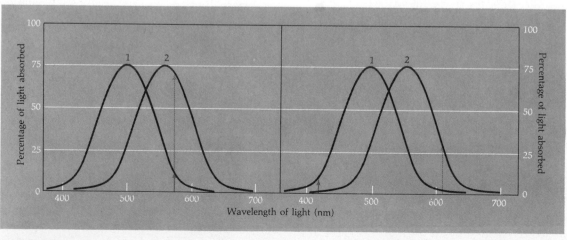

FIGURE 6.11
A two-pigment system can be confused.

signals. As a result, the effect of any wavelength or mixture of wavelengths can always be matched by just two wavelengths, provided that the two are presented in the right proportions. Moreover, such matches can be produced using any of a large number of different pairs of wavelengths. An eye exhibiting these kinds of confusions is said to be **dichromatic** (meaning "two-colored"). However, note that not all wavelengths are confused. Unlike the one-pigment eye, a dichromatic eye retains certain information about the wavelength composition of light, and this information provides a basis for color vision.

An eye with only two types of cone pigments would make one particularly interesting color confusion involving sunlight—which, as you know, consists of nearly equal amounts of all wavelengths within the visible portion of the spectrum. Like any other complex mixture of wavelengths, sunlight will be represented in this eye by a pair of responses, one from each pigment type. There also exists a single, particular wavelength of light that will produce exactly the same pair of responses. Therefore that one wavelength will be confused with sunlight. Since all other wavelengths will produce different pairs of responses, they will not be confused with sunlight. We can call the one wavelength that is confused the **neutral point** of the eye's spectral response. The existence of a single neutral point is the hallmark of a two-pigment eye. For most people, such a neutral point cannot be found, indicating that their eyes contain more than two cone pigments.

What If Eyes Had Three Cone Pigments?
So far we've seen that a one-pigment eye can match any complex combination of wavelengths using just a single wavelength. Such an eye would be wholly color blind. We've also seen that a two-pigment eye can match any complex combination of wave-

lengths using two properly selected wavelengths. Such an eye would have some ability to discriminate the wavelength composition of light. Now you should be able to anticipate what happens if an eye contains three pigments, like those represented in Figure 6.12. Note that any wavelength (such as *A*) will produce a trio of responses, one from each photopigment. Moreover, this trio of responses cannot be mimicked by any other single wavelength. To mimic these responses would require the ability to vary the intensities of up to three different wavelengths (with some exceptions, to be explained in the next paragraph). Hence, an eye containing a trio of photopigments is said to be **trichromatic** (meaning "three-colored"). Color Plate 6 illustrates the variety of colors that can be produced by mixing just three colors. Note that each projector contains a transparency that creates a beam of a different color—one blue, one red, and one green. In the center, where all the beams overlap, your eye receives the reflected light from all three, and the result is white. Where only the red and green beams overlap, the light appears yellow. If the relative intensi-

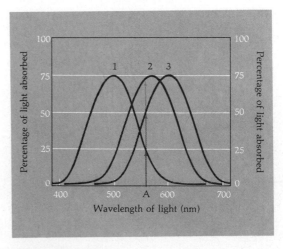

FIGURE 6.12
A three-pigment system.

ties of each beam could be adjusted, other, intermediate colors would appear.

The demonstration in Color Plate 6 does not require the particular trio of lights used there; many others would work equally well. But why *three* lights? If an eye contains three different cone photopigments, its response to any complex mixture of light can be represented by a trio of signals, one generated by each type of cone. To mimic this trio of signals, three independently adjustable lights are needed. Although any single wavelength will stimulate more than just one cone type, certain wavelengths do stimulate one type particularly well and the other types less well. A trio of wavelengths can be chosen so that each member of the trio determines *mainly* the response of one pigment. We noted earlier that there are limitations to the matches that are possible with any set of three lights. To match any light, you need independent control of the response in each cone type. Because any single wavelength will stimulate all types of cones, three lights that have been chosen to match most colors will not be able to match many extremely saturated colors. To make those matches, a different set of lights would be required.

It has been known for quite some time that normal human vision is trichromatic. The idea that color perception depends on the responses of three different pigments is also quite old. Thomas Young, a British physician, is usually credited with articulating this theory first (1801/1948). Since the German physiologist Hermann Helmholtz developed the first detailed treatment of the same idea (1909/1962), the theory is usually known by both men's names, the **Young-Helmholtz theory.** While it is true that the normal human eye does contain three types of cone pigments, it is instructive to consider the consequences of having even more types.

What If Eyes Had 300 Cone Pigments? Suppose an eye contained 300 different types of photopigments. Suppose further that each pigment type responded to only a very narrow band of wavelengths—one nanometer wide—with each pigment's response signaling the presence of one particular wavelength. Whenever the pigment sensitive to 462 nanometers signaled the capture of light energy, it would be a sure sign that the light contained that wavelength. This degree of pigment selectivity would make metamers difficult to produce, since most combinations of wavelengths would produce unique sets of responses among the 300 photopigments. Very few combinations of wavelengths would produce the same set of responses.

Since increasing the number of pigment types decreases the number of confusions (metamers), it may seem odd that the visual system uses only three. If you believe, as we do, that everything in the eye has a reason, you might ask, "Why are there not more cone pigments in our eyes?" Actually, an eye with lots of different types of cone pigments would be at a disadvantage compared to one with only a few. In order to preserve the wavelength information generated by the cones, each cone type would require its own set of collector cells. Otherwise, if different cone types shared collector cells, wavelength information would be lost (Brindley, 1970). Producing the right connections between cones and collector cells would be a nightmare for the developing visual system, like 300 mothers (collector cells) each trying to find her particular child among a mob of 300 children (the cone types). Although it may be hard to justify three cone types rather than four (Bowmaker, 1983), a very much larger number would not offer much more advantage (Barlow, 1982). Actually, with just three cone types, color vision is remarkably keen. For example, most people can appreciate extremely subtle hue differences among stimuli: they are able to discriminate more than one hundred different hues on the basis of

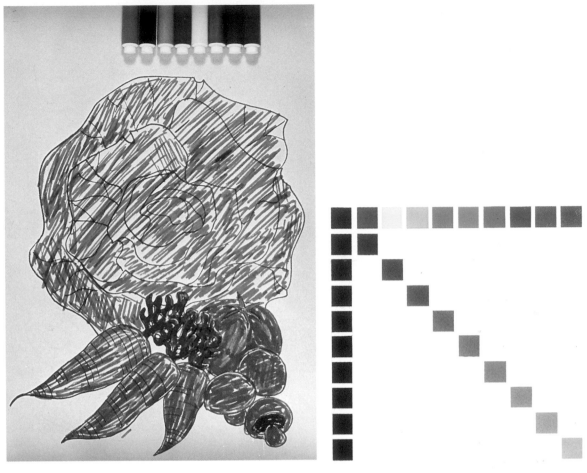

COLOR PLATE 1 See page 128. (*Courtesy of Alan J. Pearlman, M.D.*)

COLOR PLATE 2 See page 182.

COLOR PLATE 3 See pages 182 and 188.

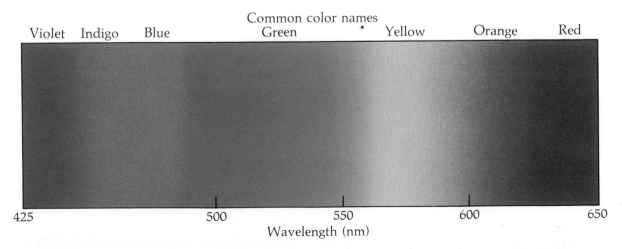

Common color names

Violet   Indigo   Blue   Green   Yellow   Orange   Red

425   500   550   600   650

Wavelength (nm)

COLOR PLATE 4 See page 190. (*Georges Pierre Seurat, "Invitation to the Sideshow/ La Parade," Metropolitan Museum of Art, bequest of Stephen C. Clark, 1960.*)

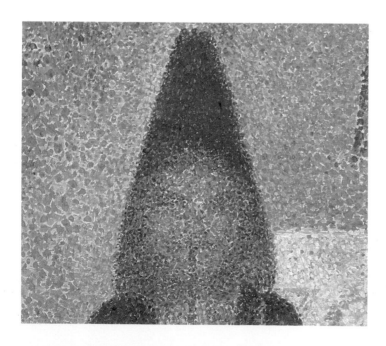

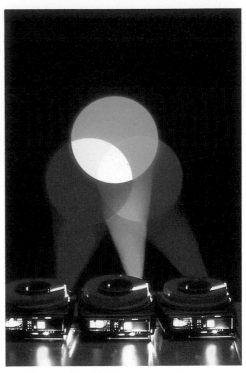

COLOR PLATE 6 See page 195.

COLOR PLATE 7 See page 200.

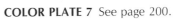

COLOR PLATE 5 See page 192. (Glyn Cloyd.)

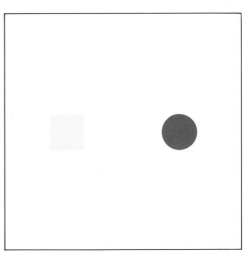

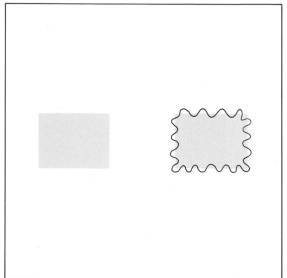

COLOR PLATE 8 See page 200.

COLOR PLATE 9 See page 201.

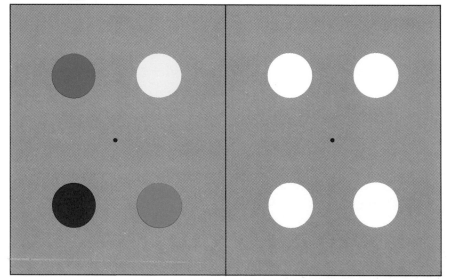

COLOR PLATE 10
See page 203.

COLOR PLATE 11
See page 211.

wavelength information alone. And if stimuli vary in brightness and saturation as well as hue, the number of discriminable colors grows to over 1,000. Of course there are some wavelength combinations that the human eye cannot discriminate from one another, as laboratory studies of metamers show. You should realize, though, that while metamers are vital for understanding color vision, they can be produced only if one has strict control over the wavelength composition of light. This kind of control never occurs in the natural environment, in which the visual system evolved, and it rarely occurs in everyday situations involving artificial illumination.

WHAT ARE THE THREE CONE TYPES?

Although psychophysical studies of color vision point to the existence of three different cone pigment types, such studies can't establish their precise characteristics (Brindley, 1970). In fact, different assumptions lead to quite different ideas about these three pigments. For example, some noted theorists believed that the three cone pigments have highly overlapping absorption spectra (like those shown in the left panel of Figure

6.13), while others proposed that the cone pigments have absorption spectra that overlap far less (like those in the right panel of Figure 6.13).

These differences of opinion suggest that psychophysical measurements alone cannot give an unequivocal answer to this physiological question. To determine the absorption spectra of cone types, direct measurements are required.

The technique for directly measuring the light absorption of photopigments has a long but descriptive name: **microspectrophotometry.** To see what the method involves, consider each part of its name. "Photometry" involves the measurement (*metry*) of light (*photo*); "spectro" indicates the spectrum (determining which wavelengths of light are present); and "micro" means "small." Hence, in the application to cone pigments, microspectrophotometry involves shining a small spot of light onto a single cone and determining, for various wavelengths, how much of that light is absorbed (MacNichol, 1964). The results obtained by studying cones in several human retinas are shown in Figure 6.14 (Dartnall, Bowmaker, and Mollon, 1983). The vertical axis portrays the amount of light absorbed, expressed as a percentage of the

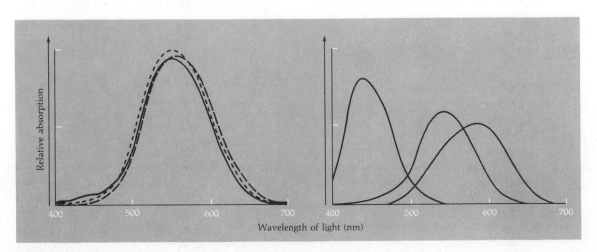

FIGURE 6.13
Pigment types as imagined by two different theorists.

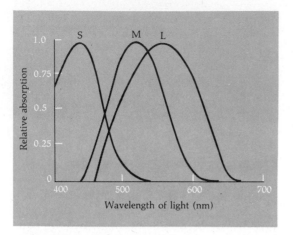

FIGURE 6.14

Microspectrophotometric records from three cone types in the human eye. (Redrawn from Dartnall, Bowmaker, and Mollon, 1983.)

light shone on the cone; the horizontal axis indicates the light's wavelength. To facilitate comparisons among pigments, each one's maximum absorption has been arbitrarily set equal to unity.

These absorption curves have several notable features. First of all, there are three different cone pigment types (one type per cone), as one would expect from experiments on color metamers. Each pigment type is most sensitive to light of a particular wavelength—approximately 420, 530, and 560 nanometers, respectively. Because of their peak sensitivities, these three cone types are referred to as short-wavelength sensitive (S cones), medium-wavelength sensitive (M cones), and long-wavelength sensitive (L cones). Notice also that each cone pigment absorbs a broad range of wavelengths. As a result of this breadth, most lights—even those that consist of only a single wavelength—stimulate more than just one class of cones. For example, stimulation in the region of 475 nanometers affects all three types. This breadth also means that the response of a single cone type provides no information about the wavelength(s) of

light being absorbed. By itself, each pigment type is "color blind" (recall the univariance principle described earlier).

You may find it puzzling that the absorption spectra of cone pigments overlap so much. Actually, this overlap has an important beneficial consequence. To appreciate this consequence, imagine an eye that had three photopigments whose absorption spectra did not overlap (like those represented in Figure 6.15). According to the univariance principle, this eye would *not* be able to discriminate among wavelengths *A*, *B*, and *C*, since all stimulate the same pigment type and only that type. However, this eye *would* be able to discriminate wavelengths *A*, *B*, and *C* from either *D* or *E*, since different pigment types would be stimulated. Thus nonoverlapping pigment spectra preclude subtle color discriminations, such as the difference between a ripe tomato and a nearly ripe one. The human eye's remarkably good color discrimination depends on the overlap among the absorption spectra of the three cone pigments.

HOW ARE THE THREE CONE TYPES DISTRIBUTED?

We've been considering the connection between color perception and the cones' absorption spectra. Let's focus now on other perceptually important facts about cone receptors. Knowing that the signals coming from three cone types are important in color perception, we need to consider how the three types are distributed across the retina. For instance, if the proportions of the three cone types varied from one retinal region to another, color perception would vary correspondingly. To ascertain the distribution of cone types, one can apply a certain chemical to a retina that has been exposed to light. This chemical stains stimulated cones, causing them to appear dark when viewed under a microscope (unstimulated cones do not

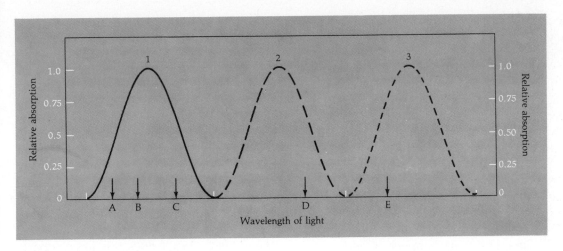

FIGURE 6.15
A system with three, nonoverlapping pigments.

appear dark). Imagine viewing a retina that had been stimulated by a weak light of a single wavelength. Simply by noting the number and location of dark spots, you can visualize the distribution of cones that had responded to that wavelength (Marc, 1982). By appropriate choice of stimulating wavelength, you can selectively stain any one of the three cone types. These measurements confirm something long suspected from psychophysical studies of color perception, namely that S cones are far less numerous than the other two types. Each of your eyes has fewer than 1 million S cones, with the other 7 million roughly evenly split between M and L cones (Gouras and Zrenner, 1981).

This chemical staining technique confirms something else long suspected from psychophysical studies: the three types of cones are unevenly distributed across the retina. S cones are scarce at the fovea (the center of the retina), sharply increase to a maximum concentration just outside the fovea, and then decline in number with increasing eccentricity. Looking at a retina whose S cones only had been stained, you'd see a concentration of cones ringing the fovea. In contrast, a retina whose M cones only had been stained would show the highest concentration of stained cones *at* the fovea and a gradual decrease in stained cones with increasing eccentricity. A similar pattern would be seen with a retina whose L cones only had been stained. What impact do these cone distributions have on your experience of color?

Since color appearance depends on the signals generated by a trio of cone types, color appearance should vary from one part of your retina to another. Indeed, this variation has long been known. To study this regional variation in color appearance requires that different, restricted regions of the retina be stimulated. When this is done, color appearance varies with the region stimulated. For example, a small light that appears greenish-blue when imaged slightly away from the fovea will appear green when imaged directly *on* the fovea. This change reflects the diminished contribution of S cones at the center of the retina. In addition, as that same light is moved into the periphery of the retina—where cones are less numerous—the light's color becomes less conspicuous. Farther out into the periphery, where cones are very sparse, vision becomes achromatic, meaning "without color." Thus when an object is seen out of the corner of your eye, you may recognize its shape, but it will appear colorless. You can see this for yourself using Color Plate 7. Looking directly at the plate, you can see that the square is yellow and the disk blue. As you fixate at points farther and farther away from the plate, however, notice how the colors become less saturated and eventually disappear. Although the composition of the light remains constant, the subjective experience of color changes. This happens because of regional variations in the machinery of color vision.

You can also use Color Plate 7 to see the consequence of having so few S cones in your fovea. Look at the center of the blue disk. At normal reading distance, the image of the blue disk not only will cover the region free of S cones (your fovea) but also will extend into regions that do contain S cones (around your fovea). Now, while continuing to fixate the blue disk, back away from the book. As you get farther from the book, the image of the blue disk will get smaller, eventually shrinking so that it falls entirely within your fovea. As this image shrinks, the disk will cease to appear blue. Notice that at the same distance, though, the square will continue to look yellow. This demonstration raises a paradox: when viewed from normal reading distance, why doesn't the blue disk appear less blue in its center? We have no ready answer for this paradoxical uniformity of perceptual experience, though it may be related to the "filling-in" process noted in Chapter 2.

The variation in color appearance with retinal region or image size has practical consequences. For example, if two stimuli containing precisely the same wavelengths differ in size or in retinal location, their color appearances will also differ. As one result,

even the most faithful photographic reproduction of a scene is bound to look different from the scene itself (Hurvich, 1981).

WHAT IS SPECIAL ABOUT SHORT-WAVELENGTH (S) CONES?

The S cones differ from the M and L types in various ways (Mollon, 1982). We've seen that the S cones are virtually absent in the central retina and that overall they are less numerous than the other types. The sparseness of S cones means that the spaces between neighboring S cones are relatively large (Marc, 1982). What does this large separation mean for perception? Recall from Chapter 3 that the distance between receptors limits the eye's resolving power (acuity). The large separation between S cones explains why acuity measured with blue targets is much poorer than acuity with either red or green targets (Pokorny, Graham, and Lanson, 1968; Green, 1968).

Because the S cones are few and far between, you may wonder why you don't see holes or gaps when looking at a large, blue-colored region. One reason is that early on, the visual system integrates signals from many different cones of the same type. Since the S cones are relatively far apart, this integration covers relatively large distances. As a result the S cones not only give poor acuity but also can distort your perception of boundaries. And since boundaries contribute to the perceived shape of an object, the S cones can distort that perceived shape. Robert Boynton of the University of California devised a strong demonstration of this fact (Boynton, 1982). One version of Boynton's demonstration is given in Color Plate 8. Note first the pale yellow rectangle at the left of the plate. The ink used to print the rectangle absorbs short-wavelength light and reflects longer wavelengths. This reflected light stimulates primarily M and L cones, hence its yellow appearance. However, the white paper around the rectangle reflects light more or less uniformly, thereby stimulating S as well as M and L cones. As a result, then, one side of the yellow-white boundary excites S cones while the other side does not. To show how poorly the S cones register contour information, we've taken the same rectangle and drawn a squiggly black line around the outline of the rectangle. This is shown at the right of Color Plate 8. Prop the book open so you can see the color plate then walk slowly backward. You'll reach a distance at which the yellow-white boundary of the right-hand figure will appear squiggly rather than straight. The region outside the squiggly boundary appears white, while the region inside appears yellow. This means that some portions in and around the boundary that used to look white now look yellow, and vice versa. It is as if the yellow had spread outward toward the black squiggly line, and the white had spread inward. This spreading does not occur for all colors, only those differentially stimulating S cones on either side of a boundary. Fortunately, the demonstration you've just experienced is a very special case. Ordinarily the two sides of a boundary do not differ only in their effect on cones of the S type. The normal involvement of M and L cones ensures that shape information is accurately registered.

Color's Opponent Character

We saw in Chapters 3 and 4 that information from the photoreceptors is transformed as it travels to the visual cortex. Messages from neighboring receptors are antagonistically organized into ON and OFF regions, which together comprise a neuron's receptive field. The characteristics of these receptive fields significantly affect the perception of visual form and brightness. So far in this chapter, we have concentrated on the initial stage of analysis of color information, an analysis performed by the three cone types. We now need to consider how messages from these three cone types are organized or linked at subsequent stages of the visual system. We can get some idea of this organization by considering several phenomena of color vision, all of which point to an opponent linkage pitting one color against another.

WHAT IS THE EVIDENCE FOR COLOR OPPONENCY?

One phenomenon that suggests some kind of opponent connection between colors is **color contrast.** Just as lightness contrast (described in Chapter 3) exaggerates lightness differences between adjacent objects, *color contrast exaggerates their color differences* (see Box 6.3). The major facts of color contrast have been known for a very long time. More than four hundred years ago, Leonardo da Vinci, a painter, scientist, and engineer, discussed color contrast in his *Treatise on Painting:*

Of different colors equally perfect, that will appear most excellent which is seen near its direct contrary . . . blue near yellow; green near red: because each color is more distinctly seen, when opposed to its contrary, than to any other similar to it. (Quoted in Birren, 1941, p. 135)

Using Color Plate 9, you can see what Leonardo had in mind. Corresponding disks in the left- and right-hand columns are identical though they do not look so. For example, look at the bottom two, blue disks. On the left, the yellow surround heightens the disk's blue appearance; on the right, the blue background diminishes the disk's blueness. (Skeptical readers, who doubt that the two blue disks are actually the same, may

BOX 6.3

Color Contrast

You've probably had the experience of purchasing an article of clothing, such as a tie or a scarf, to go with an outfit in your closet. In the store, the tie or scarf looks neutral gray; but when you get home and try on the outfit, the article acquires a distinct color other than gray. Moreover, that distinct color seems to vary, depending on what outfit you wear it with. In other words, the color of the tie or scarf depends on what color is adjacent to it. This effect, demonstrated in Color Plate 9, is called *color contrast,* and it is a powerful influence in many everyday settings. The two small colored disks on the left and right sides of the color plate are the same, though color contrast with the surrounds makes them appear different.

Some people have been able to capitalize on color contrast to enhance color perception. One such person was Michel Chevreul, director of the Gobelin tapestry works in Paris. Chevreul knew that interweaving just gray and red yarns could create tapestries that appeared to contain other colors as well—including distinct blue-green stripes—produced in the viewer's brain by color contrast. Chevreul developed a set of rules for ensuring that color contrast

would have the effect his designers and weavers wanted. He went further, though, publishing a huge volume (1839/1967) that set out the basic rules of color harmony and contrast as they related to painting, interior decoration, printing, flower gardening, and dressmaking. In fact, the French Impressionist painters of the nineteenth century used Chevreul's book as a guide.

These principles were unwittingly rediscovered by Edwin Land, the inventor of the Polaroid camera, whose published papers contain many interesting demonstrations of color contrast. Let's consider a typical one here (Land, 1959). Land took two black and white slides of the same scene. One slide (the ''red record'') was taken with a red filter in front of the camera, the other (the ''green record'') with a green filter. Using a pair of slide projectors, Land superimposed the two black and white slides on a screen. Not surprisingly, since the slides were black and white, the result was a black and white image of the original scene. The surprise came when Land placed a red filter in front of the projector containing the red record. The image on the screen now consisted of various amounts of red light (from the projector with the red filter) mixed with various amounts of

white light (from the other projector). One might expect that the only colors perceptible would be white, grays, blacks, and various shades of red. However, the image on the screen produced a wide range of colors—for example, a blond-haired girl with pale blue eyes, a red coat, blue-green collar, and natural flesh tones. Where had all these colors come from?

The major source of Land's colors was color contrast (Walls, 1960). For instance, the girl's collar appeared blue-green because it was surrounded by the red of her coat. This could be verified by examining the image of the collar through a narrow tube. When the tube blocked the surrounding region from view, the collar appeared colorless, rather than blue-green. Though Land's color demonstrations were surprising, perhaps they should not have been. More than 60 years earlier, the French photographer Ducos du Hauron had demonstrated basically the same phenomenon (Judd, 1960). Although not entirely novel, Land's color demonstrations serve one very useful purpose. They are a vivid reminder of how important contrast is in the everyday experience of the colors of objects.

wish to check out our claim. This can be done by cutting small holes in a piece of opaque white paper, positioning the holes so that when this paper is laid on top of Color Plate 9 only the blue disks will be vis-

ible.) Strong interaction between the color of an object and the color of its surround suggests some sort of antagonistic linkages within the visual machinery that processes color information.

You can use Color Plate 10 to experience another phenomenon that suggests color opponency. Stare at the left fixation point (in the center of the four colored patches) for about 60 seconds, then look at the right fixation point. The illusory colors you'll experience are called **afterimages.** Note that the afterimage produced by the yellow patch appears blue, whereas the one produced by blue appears yellow. By the same token, the afterimage of the red patch appears green, and vice versa. These color afterimages are consistent with the idea that the visual system treats certain colors as opponent pairs.

Color opponency shows up in other ways too. Consider, for example, the evolution of color perception. Many primitive animals are truly color blind, being able to distinguish only different shades of gray. Other, less primitive animals do have some degree of color vision, but it is not as refined as that of humans. Such creatures (squirrels, for example) can distinguish not only shades of gray but also short wavelengths from longer wavelengths. Roughly speaking, these animals can distinguish what is called blue from what is called yellow. More advanced creatures, such as human beings, can distinguish not only blues from yellows but also reds from greens (Ladd-Franklin 1909/1962). Commenting on the evolution of color vision, Gerald Wasserman writes:

Note the evolutionary utility of this division: One system mediates the most primitive type of vision—namely, raw sensitivity to light with no appreciation of its spectral quality. The second system refines this to permit an appreciation of the difference between sky and water versus earth and vegetation. The third system refines matters further, permitting an appreciation of much more subtle shades. There is reason to believe that the evolution of color vision in fact followed this exact sequence on several different occasions in phylogeny. (Wasserman, 1978, pp. 114–115)

You've just seen that evolution treats blue and yellow as one pair of colors, and red and green as another. Certain aspects of color experience reflect these same pairings. Blue and yellow are mutually exclusive: an object may appear blue; an object may appear yellow; but an object cannot appear *both* blue and yellow at the same time. Similarly, red and green are mutually exclusive: an object never can appear *both* red and green. Of course, other combinations of these four colors are not mutually exclusive: objects can be bluish-green or reddish-yellow. These observations suggest that the nervous system may treat red and green as one mutually antagonistic pair and blue and yellow as another such pair. These views were first articulated by Ewald Hering, a German physician. In the nineteenth century, Hering made important contributions to nerve physiology, binocular vision, the anatomy of the liver, and color vision. Unfortunately, Hering was often so far ahead of his time that his contributions could not be properly assimilated into then current scientific thought and were therefore either dismissed outright or misinterpreted (Hurvich, 1969). But Hering's views on color vision have been largely vindicated by recent discoveries.

CHROMATIC AND ACHROMATIC SYSTEMS

A combination of psychophysical and physiological studies has now established that signals from the three cone types are processed by one **achromatic system** and a pair of **chromatic systems.** The neural connections thought to underlie these three systems are sketched out in Figure 6.16. S, M, and L represent the signals generated by the short-, medium- and long-wavelength cones, respectively. A plus sign indicates that two signals are added together; a minus sign, that the difference between two signals is

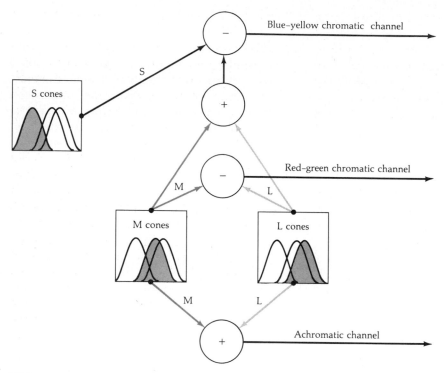

FIGURE 6.16

Chromatic and achromatic channels generated by combining the signals from three cone types.

taken. Before going further into the details of this figure, we should remind you how the nervous system adds and subtracts. Recall, from Chapter 3, that addition is accomplished via **spatial summation.** This operation is carried out when one neuron sums the messages from other neurons. Recall also that subtraction can be accomplished via an antagonism between ON and OFF signals. This operation is carried out when one neuron takes the difference between messages received from other neurons. So although the nervous system doesn't have access to a calculator, it can certainly add and subtract signals.

Let's now resume the discussion of Figure 6.16, seeing first how the achromatic system is constructed. Note that the signals generated by M and L cones are added to-

gether (as indicated by the plus sign toward the bottom of the figure). We can refer to the pathway carrying this sum to the brain as a *channel* (a set of nerve fibers bearing a common message). Activity in this *achromatic channel* depends on the total excitation of M and L cones. There are various reasons for imagining that activity in this channel determines an object's visibility. For example, the shape of the photopic sensitivity curve (closely related to visibility) can be predicted by taking a sum of M and L cone responses. Note that by adding together M and L cone signals, this achromatic channel actually discards the wavelength information that it receives.

Now let's turn to the chromatic system in Figure 6.16. Note, in the middle of the figure, that the difference between M and L cones is taken (indicated by the minus sign). This operation gives the difference between responses to light from two regions of the spectrum, one in which M cones are more sensitive and the other in which L cones are more sensitive. The difference between M and L cone signals is carried by what we can call a *red-green channel*, since the two spectral regions being compared correspond roughly to these color names.

You've probably noticed that we haven't said anything about the S cones so far. But don't think they have no role to play. Signals from S cones are involved in a second opponent, or chromatic, channel. This channel carries the difference between S cone signals, on the one hand, and the *sum* of M and L cone signals, on the other. This difference is represented by the minus sign toward the top of Figure 6.16. This channel can be referred to as the *blue-yellow channel*, because it signals the difference between short-wavelength stimulation and stimulation throughout the rest of the spectrum.

To help you understand the implications of Figure 6.16, consider how the various channels might respond when an eye is stimulated by white light, which, as you know, contains a broad spectrum of wavelengths. Such light would stimulate M and L cones to the same degree. As a result, the difference between their signals would be zero, resulting in no signal in the red-green channel. This would be true regardless of the intensity of the light. White light would be similarly ineffective for the blue-yellow channel, because such light excites both of its contributors equally well. Note however that the achromatic channel, which adds responses from M and L cones, would be excited by white light. In fact, the more intense this light, the greater the response in that achromatic channel.

The scheme outlined in Figure 6.16 gives a straightforward explanation of a puzzling observation mentioned earlier in this chapter. Recall that hues drawn from the region near the middle of the spectrum (yellow) appear less saturated than hues drawn from the ends of the spectrum (blue and red). But why should one hue look more saturated than another? The scheme in Figure 6.16 gives a simple answer. A hue will appear desaturated (washed out) if it produces a strong response in the achromatic channel and at least some response in one of the chromatic channels. Note that if light produces a response in the achromatic channel but none in either chromatic channel, it will appear completely desaturated—white. In contrast, a highly saturated hue results when a strong chromatic response is accompanied by a weak achromatic response. In general, the perceived saturation produced by light of any wavelength can be predicted straightforwardly by taking the ratio of the chromatic response it evokes to the achromatic response it evokes. For example, yellow will be relatively desaturated, because it elicits only a weak chromatic response while at the same time eliciting a strong achromatic response. It is satisfying that this scheme can account for aspects of color vision familiar to Newton—spectral brightness and saturation. We should note, however, that there are some facts for which this scheme cannot easily account (see Hood and Finkelstein, 1983). For instance, it cannot explain why stimuli of very short wavelength appear to have a distinct reddish tinge. Some alternatives to the scheme presented here can account for this fact but may be less successful in accounting for certain other observations (Jameson and Hurvich, 1968). These alternatives postulate connections that are somewhat different from those outlined in Figure 6.16.

The existence of separate chromatic and achromatic systems opens one other interesting possibility. Disease might be able to impair one of these systems while sparing the other. For example, under certain cir-

BOX 6.4
A World Seen Through Green Glasses

Imagine someone who tells you that she simply *can't* watch television if the set is black and white—she can only watch color. Usually such a claim means that someone *prefers* to watch color televison. But in one extraordinary case, a woman literally lost her ability to see black and white television while retaining perfectly normal ability to see color. How did this happen, and what does this unique case say about color vision?

Two Finnish scientists, Lea Hyvarinen and Jyrki Rovamo, made a detailed study of a 30-year-old diabetic woman who had developed seizures and partial paralysis (Hyvarinen and Rovamo, 1981). The woman found it extremely difficult to read and had very poor acuity. Using methods like those described in the previous chapter, Hyvarinen and Rovamo tested the patient's contrast sensitivity by creating gratings on a black and white television screen. They determined how much contrast she needed in order to see gratings having different-sized bars (different spatial frequencies): in order for the patient to see them, gratings

had to have approximately 100 times more contrast than normal people need.

This large loss of contrast sensitivity puzzled Hyvarinen and Rovamo. In previous cases of such poor sensitivity, the patients had been virtually blind. Yet this woman seemed to get around with relatively little difficulty. When she volunteered that she had particular trouble seeing black and white objects, they retested her contrast sensitivity while she viewed the television through a green filter. Quite remarkably, her contrast sensitivity proved to be entirely normal. A similar result was found when she viewed gratings through a red filter. An invisible black and white grating could be made highly visible simply by dropping a color filter in front of her eye.

In view of these findings, the patient began to wear glasses with deep green lenses. These had a remarkable effect: for the first time in months she could see small details—such as the tiny branches on trees. However, the colored lenses made her conspicuous and self-conscious, so she eventually stopped wearing them. Then,

over several days, her vision slowly deteriorated. Each day the tree in front of her house seemed to lose more of its branches. Small branches went first, then large ones. By the fourth day she could see only the tree's trunk (Rovamo, Hyvarinen, and Hari, 1982).

No one is sure why this strange disorder of vision occurred. Various tests and brain scans failed to reveal neural abnormalities that could explain the disorder. However, this patient's disorder does demonstrate two important features of color perception. First, it is a reminder that the nervous system uses separate channels to carry two types of information about objects— chromatic and achromatic. This woman's loss seemed to be restricted to the achromatic channel. Second, so long as she wore colored lenses her intact chromatic system apparently gave her sufficient information about objects so that she was able to get around with little difficulty. This underscores the point made at the beginning of this chapter, namely that color alone can specify the existence and location of objects.

cumstances the ability to see achromatic objects might be attacked while the ability to see chromatic objects remained normal. Box 6.4 describes an actual case that seems to confirm this idea.

THE PHYSIOLOGICAL BASIS OF OPPONENCY

Various details of the scheme in Figure 6.16 have been established by careful psycho-

physical studies (see Boynton, 1979, for a good summary). But how does the nervous system accomplish this adding and subtracting? To seek an answer to this question, let's return to the lateral geniculate nucleus, which we described in Chapter 4.

Russell DeValois, a psychologist at the University of California at Berkeley, studied cells in the lateral geniculate nucleus. Working with monkeys, he found that cells in the

LGN could be divided into two major groups: nonopponent and opponent (DeValois and DeValois, 1975). Let's consider each group in turn starting with the nonopponent.*

When light was shown on the retina, some nonopponent LGN cells responded by increasing their activity (ON cells), while others responded by decreasing their activity (OFF cells). Cells of the ON type gave ON responses to *all* wavelengths, though more strongly to some wavelengths than to others. Similarly, OFF cells gave OFF responses to all wavelengths, but again in varying strengths. Together, such cells could constitute the achromatic channel represented in Figure 6.16.

Cells of the opponent type behaved differently. In this group, any cell could give either an ON response *or* an OFF response, depending on the wavelength of light. For example, some of these cells would increase their responses when long-wavelength light was present but decrease their responses when short-wavelength was present. The opposite pattern was also found: reduced response with long-wavelength light and increased response with short-wavelength light. When light contained *both* long and short wavelengths, the ON and OFF responses tended to cancel each other and the cell gave little response. As far as the cell was concerned, the light never appeared.

If a cell gives an ON response in one portion of the spectrum and an OFF response in the other portion, there must be some transition wavelength at which the response changes from ON to OFF. DeValois found that opponent cells could be divided roughly into two groups, according to their transition wavelengths. For one group the transition occurred between the portion of the spectrum called green and the portion called red. Hence DeValois called these cells red-green cells. For the other group, the transition occurred between the portion of the spectrum called blue and the portion called yellow. DeValois called these blue-yellow cells. Note that these two groups of cells link different regions of the spectrum in an opponent fashion. Such linkages could be the realization of the red-green and blue-yellow opponent channels schematized in Figure 6.16.*

We've already seen that the interplay between opponent and nonopponent channels can account for the way in which wavelength controls brightness and saturation. The interplay between these channels can account for other important phenomena of color perception, too (DeValois and DeValois, 1975). Using DeValois's results, let's consider some of these in detail. The curves in Figure 6.17 summarize some of DeValois's data. The curve labeled *R* represents the average response of red-green opponent cells to longer-wavelength light. Note that in such cells the response begins at about 600 nanometers and grows with increasing wavelength. The *G* curve represents the average response of these same red-green opponent cells to shorter-wavelength light. Curves *Y* and *B* represent the responses of yellow-blue opponent cells to longer and shorter wavelengths, respectively. How might these curves relate to color perception?

The simplest idea is that each curve corresponds to one particular color experience.

---

*Primate retinas also contain both spectrally opponent and spectrally nonopponent cells (Gouras and Zrenner, 1981). Presumably these retinal ganglion cells are the origin of the opponent and nonopponent LGN cells studied by DeValois.

*Some researchers question whether all opponent cells can be put into just two distinct categories (Zrenner, 1983). Moreover, you should note that DeValois's experiments were performed by uniformly illuminating an LGN cell's receptive field with lights of different wavelength. Recall from Chapter 4, though, that each LGN receptive field is divisible into spatially distinct center and surround regions. More recently, physiologists have discovered that in some LGN cells, the center region of the receptive field responds best to one wavelength of light, while the surround region responds to a very different wavelength. So the color opponency derived by DeValois is really combined with the spatial opponency defined by the center/surround layout of the receptive field. Their spatially organized color opponency makes these cells ideal contributors to color contrast (Lennie, 1984).

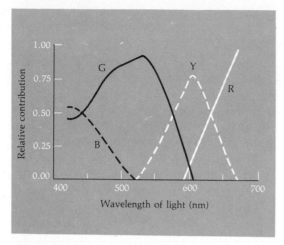

FIGURE 6.17
Responses of different LGN cells to light of various wavelengths. (Adapted from DeValois and DeValois, 1975.)

For example, the G curve might correspond to the greenness evoked by various wavelengths. To examine the possible correspondence between the curves and color experience, let's consider the results of a color-naming experiment by Robert Boynton and James Gordon (1965). People were asked to name the color of briefly flashed lights whose wavelength varied randomly across the spectrum. To help quantify these color names, people were asked to use only the names "blue," "green," "yellow," "red," and various combinations of these names—such as "yellow-red" (meaning a red that was tinged with yellow). The results are shown in Figure 6.18. The horizontal axis shows the wavelength of light, and the vertical axis shows the tendency to use a given color name in describing that wavelength. For example, the "green" curve reflects the use of the term "green" to describe color experience. Note that "green" is used to describe wavelengths ranging from about 470 to 600 nanometers. Toward the shorter-wavelength portion of this range, "green," is modified by the term "blue"; in the longer-wavelength portion of the range, "green" is mod-

ified by the term "yellow." At about 510 nanometers, the light is described solely as "green" (the "green" curve reaches its maximum at 510 nanometers). The use of "yellow" peaks at about 580 nanometers, and the use of "blue" at about 460. Note that the "red" curve consists of two segments—one at the right (longer wavelengths) and one at the left (shorter wavelengths). This is quite understandable, since very short wavelength light appears violet, a hue that can be produced by mixing blue and red.

Note the general correspondence between Boynton and Gordon's color-naming results (Figure 6.18) and DeValois's physiological results from opponent cells in the monkey (Figure 6.17). The use of the name "green" by humans seems to correspond quite well to the response of the red-green opponent cells to shorter-wavelength light—the G curve in Figure 6.17. Similarly, the use of the name "yellow" resembles the Y curve in that figure. The correspondence is suggestive, but less satisfactory, between the use of the name "blue" and the B curve. Finally, at long wavelengths, the name "red" corresponds quite well to the R curve. How-

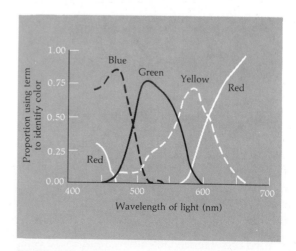

FIGURE 6.18
Proportion of trials on which different color names are assigned to various wavelengths. (Adapted from Boynton and Gordon, 1965.)

ever, the occasional use of the name "red" at short wavelengths has no counterpart in the way DeValois's cells responded. Nevertheless there is, overall, a suggestive correspondence between color naming and the responses of opponent cells.

The general correspondence that we've just seen between physiology and color naming suggests that the major color categories—blue, green, yellow, and red—may be defined by the visual nervous system. If this were true, all people with normal visual systems would agree on these four color categories. Alternatively, the correspondence between physiology and color naming could be coincidental. According to this view, the consistency of color naming might simply reflect how people learn to use the words "blue," "green," "yellow," and "red." We can decide which view is correct by examining the use of color categories by infants not old enough to have learned the association between colors and names.

COLOR "NAMING" BY INFANTS

Do infants categorize colors, and if so, how? To answer these questions, Marc Bornstein, a psychologist now at New York University, and his colleagues determined whether 4-month old infants divide up the spectrum into color categories (Bornstein, Kessen, and Weiskopf, 1976). As we've seen before, special techniques are needed to study perception in preverbal infants. The technique Bornstein and his colleagues devised capitalized on the fact that infants, like adults, get tired of looking at the same thing. When first shown some color, an infant looks at it intently. But when the same color is repeatedly presented, **habituation** occurs—the infant loses interest and looks away. Bornstein assumed that an infant would habituate not only to the very color it had been looking at but to other, similar colors as well. With this assumption in hand, Bornstein used habituation to infer whether infants

categorize colors in the same way adults do.

Each of Bornstein's tests used three different wavelengths, for example 480, 450, and 510 nanometers. In this case, the infant would first see the 480-nanometer light. After an initial period of fascination with the light, the infant would lose interest. Once the infant had habituated to this 480-nanometer light, Bornstein determined whether the infant's interest could be rekindled by either the 450- or the 510-nanometer wavelength. Note that in *physical* terms both of these lights are equally different from the 480-nanometer habituation light. However, in *perceptual* terms they are not equally different. When viewed by adults, the 450-nanometer light falls in the same color category (blue) as the 480-nanometer habituation light, whereas the 510-nanometer light (green) does not. Evidently infants have the same blue-green categories as adults: the infants showed renewed interest in the 510-nanometer light but ignored the 450-nanometer light. In other words, the infants reacted as if the 450- and 480-nanometer lights fell in the same category, and the 480- and 510-nanometer lights fell in different categories. Similar tests were made for the other color categories. In all cases, these preverbal infants categorized colors in the same way that adults do, separating colors into "blue," "green," "yellow," and "red." Apparently color categories *are* determined by the inherent nature of the nervous system, not by some arbitrary, learned scheme (Lumsden and Wilson, 1983).

Abnormalities of Color Perception

COLOR DEFICIENCY AND COLOR ANOMALY

Not everyone's experience of color is the same. On almost any test of color vision people differ from one another. These individual variations in color perception take several distinct forms. Of course, there are normal variations—small differences among individuals. But more striking, there are people whose color vision differs distinctly from the norm. Such people are described as "color deficient" (popularly called "color blind"). Finally, some people have color vision that lies between the norm and these extremes of abnormality. Because of their intermediate or odd status, their color vision is said to be "anomalous." Consideration of color deficiency and color anomaly enhances understanding of normal color vision and also reinforces Newton's idea, mentioned earlier, that "the rays are not coloured." Let's begin with color deficiency, the more bizarre of the two forms of color abnormality.

Actually **color deficiency** itself takes many different forms. And its prevalence varies among populations. For example, the incidence of color deficiency is 8 out of every 100 Caucasian males, 5 out of every 100 Asiatic males, and only 3 out of every 100 black and American Indian males. In addition, within these groups the incidence of color deficiency is much lower in females than in males—for instance, Caucasian females are ten times less likely to be color deficient than are males (Hurvich, 1981, p. 267). These statistics support the idea that color deficiency has a genetic basis. Specifically, color deficiencies are caused by defects of the chromosomes determining an individual's sex.

Although color deficiency has probably been around for thousands of years, the first recorded descriptions of the problem do not appear until the end of the eighteenth century. Among the first reports of color deficiency was one made by the English scientist John Dalton late in the eighteenth century. You may recognize Dalton's name—because he developed atomic theory, the unit of molecular weight is named in his honor.

Since he was a person of considerable distinction, his description of his own "shortcoming" was all the more interesting. Dalton wrote of himself:

I was always of the opinion, though I might not mention it, that several colours were injudiciously named. . . . All crimsons appear to me to consist chiefly of dark blue: but many of them seem to have a tinge of dark brown. I have seen specimens of crimson, claret, and mud, which were very nearly alike. Crimson has a grave appearance, being the reverse of every shewy and splendid colour. Woolen yarn dyed crimson or dark blue is the same to me. (Dalton, 1798/1948)

Though a keen observer of his own experiences, Dalton had a very mistaken idea of the origin of his abnormality. He reckoned that the vitreous humour of his eye was the wrong color, thus tinting his vision. A postmortem examination of his eyes disproved this notion. The actual cause of his disorder we'll learn about later.

There are several reasons why color deficiency such as Dalton's went unnoticed for so long. First, the common forms of color deficiency are undramatic. Rarely are people completely color blind—in the sense that they can't see colors at all. Rather, they do see color but in a way that differs from the norm. Second, many people simply don't notice that their use of color names differs from that of other people. Third, most color deficient people are able to compensate for their deficiency. For example, people who cannot distinguish reds from greens may still know when to stop or go on the basis of which light—top or bottom—is lit in a traffic signal. Also, a person who confuses reds and greens may be able to distinguish a red shirt from a green one because they differ in lightness (Jameson and Hurvich, 1978). Sometimes, though, lightness differences are not adequate substitutes for color. John Dalton, in fact, learned this to his dismay. A Quaker, Dalton was supposed to wear subdued clothing, preferably black. As a result his friends were shocked when he paraded around in his crimson academic robes, thinking that they were black.

Because color and lightness normally covary, special test materials must be designed so that lightness does not provide a clue to color. In one common type of test, which you may have seen, people are shown a numeral formed by colored dots surrounded by dots of another color. The two sets of dots differ only in hue, not in lightness. As a result, unless a person can distinguish the color of the numeral from the color of the background, the numeral will be invisible. For example, when the numeral is red and the surround is green, people with normal color vision will be able to identify the numeral but people who confuse reds and greens will not. This set of colors would only detect people who had one particular kind of color deficiency, one involving red-green confusions. To detect forms of color deficiency involving other confusions, the numeral and its surround would have to be made of some colors other than red and green. Now let's consider the origins of the deficiencies themselves.

In most forms of color deficiency the eye has the normal number of cones, but it behaves as though it had only two rather than three types of cone pigments. In fact this is exactly how Helmholtz explained color deficiency. We've already noted than an eye containing just two types of cones would be *dichromatic.* This means that the eye would require just two different wavelengths to match the appearance of virtually any other wavelength. Since the normal, trichromatic eye—one with three types of cones—requires three different wavelengths to make such matches, many matches that are satisfactory to the dichromatic eye are unsatisfactory to a trichromatic one. For example,

to a dichromat who is missing L cones, all three rectangles in Color Plate 11 appear to be of the same color. Unless you are that same type of dichromat, the rectangles won't look even vaguely alike.

Although genetic mistakes could eliminate any one of the three cone types, they more typically eliminate either M or L cones, not the S cones. When either M or L cones are missing, the red-green channel (see Figure 6.16) is also eliminated. As a result, middle and long wavelengths will tend to be confused with each other. However, all of these wavelengths will be distinguishable from short wavelengths, since a modified form of the blue-yellow system remains functional. Dichromatic color deficiencies caused by the absence of either M or L cones are lumped together under the title *red-green deficiency.* This, incidentally, is the form of dichromacy John Dalton had. In the rarer form of dichromacy, S cones are missing. This disturbs only the blue-yellow chromatic channel, leaving the red-green channel intact. The scheme in Figure 6.16 implies, and data confirm, that in this rare deficiency, lightness perception is unaffected (since S cones make no contribution to perceived lightness anyway), and discriminations among middle and long wavelengths are normal (since the red-green channel is unaffected).

People categorized as dichromats make another kind of color confusion suggestive of a two-cone eye. We pointed out earlier that eyes with only two cone types should experience a neutral point in the spectrum, a single wavelength that looks white. People with dichromatic color vision show precisely such neutral points. However, the wavelength at which the neutral point occurs varies with their form of dichromacy. To illustrate, the spectral location of the neutral point for an eye missing L cones differs from the neutral point for an eye missing S cones.

Besides these relatively rare color deficiencies, there are more common color abnormalities that we haven't mentioned yet. People with one of these common abnormalities have color vision that lies between trichromatic and dichromatic. These people are not dichromats; their spectrum shows no neutral point, and matches that satisfy dichromats fail to satisfy them. Since they require three separate lights to match virtually any hue they can see, their color perception is trichromatic. However, their color matches will not look satisfactory to someone with normal trichromatic vision. Such people are called *anomalous trichromats*. Their anomaly probably stems from the fact that one of their three cones types has an abnormal absorption curve (Dartnall, Bowmaker, and Mollon, 1983). For example, if someone's L cones were most sensitive at 550 rather than 560 nanometers, medium and long wavelengths would cause an abnormal pattern of signals to be sent to the brain. This, in turn, would affect the color matches found acceptable by the anomalous trichromat.

Figure 6.19 gives the technical names of each form of color abnormality along with the kinds of color confusions it causes and its prevalence rate (Alpern, 1981).*

ACQUIRED COLOR ABNORMALITIES

All the color abnormalities considered so far are genetic in origin. But not all color vision problems are genetic; some fairly common ones are *acquired*. We've already pointed out one case of acquired color abnormality, a man who had cortical color blindness (see Box 4.4 on p. 128). Since normal color perception depends on a whole series of neural events—starting in the retina and continuing back to the brain—disturbance in any part of the chain can alter color perception. We'll consider just a few kinds of acquired color abnormalities here; for a full discussion see Birch et al. (1979).

Some diseases—such as glaucoma and diabetes—affect the integrity of S cones, thereby disturbing color vision (Adams et al., 1982). Diabetes often changes the struc-

*There are other forms of color deficiency, too. In a few rare cases, a person seems to lack two or even all three classes of cones. Since they don't illuminate the basis of color perception any more than the cases we've already considered, we'll say no more about them.

FIGURE 6.19
Major Genetic Color Deficiencies

Name	Cause	Consequences	Prevalence
Protanomaly	Abnormal L-type pigment	Abnormal matches Poor discrimination*	M: 1.0% F: 0.02%
Deuteranomaly	Abnormal M-type pigment	Abnormal matches Poor discrimination*	M: 4.9% F: 0.4%
Protanopia	Missing L-type pigment	Confuses 520–700 Has neutral point	M: 1.0% F: 0.02%
Deuteranopia	Missing M-type pigment	Confuses 530–700 Has neutral point	M: 1.1% F: 0.01%
Tritanopia	Missing S-type pigment	Confuses 445–480 Has neutral point	Very rare

Note: "M" indicates males; "F" females. Prevalences are for North America and Western Europe. Wavelengths that are confused are given in nanometers. An asterisk (*) means that only some members of this group exhibit this problem.

ture of the eye in ways that can be seen using an ophthalmoscope. Abnormalities of color vision usually precede these structural changes in the eye. Consequently, color vision tests may be helpful in the diagnosis and treatment of diabetes (Zisman and Adams, 1982).

Diabetic changes in color vision are presumably retinal in origin. In other cases, however, acquired abnormalities of color vision can be caused by disturbances in the optic nerve rather than in the retina. For example, alcoholics frequently exhibit a reduced sensitivity to long wavelengths, causing reds to appear dark and desaturated. This change in color vision reflects a dietary deficiency—the typical alcoholic doesn't get sufficient vitamin B_{12} in his or her diet to ensure proper optic nerve function. Supplements of B_{12} restore normal color vision. Besides alcohol, certain toxins such as carbon disulfide (a substance used in the manufacture of insecticides and rubber) can disturb color vision. In each of these conditions, the onset of abnormal color vision can serve as an early warning of a threat to health.

Though the above forms of acquired color deficiency are relatively rare, there is another form that affects nearly everyone sooner or later. Once people reach about 50 years of age, the crystalline lens of the eye begins to accumulate a yellow pigment. The pigment in the lens tends to absorb short-wavelength (blue) light and transmit the rest. It may well be that this pigment serves a useful function by screening out ultraviolet radiation that could damage the already fragile retinas of older people. However, because short wavelengths have been filtered out, the color of the world appears different when seen through an older, more yellow lens. Blues look darker and they tend to be confused with greens (Weale, 1982). The tendency of older people to confuse some blues and greens can have serious consequences. For example, a yellowed crystalline lens could cause someone to mistake one type of medicine tablet or capsule for another (Hurd and Blevins, 1984).

Newton's *Opticks* ends with a series of questions that he had not been able to answer but that he hoped would one day be settled. We'll go Newton one better, ending this chapter with a set of commonly asked questions that we actually can answer (see Box 6.5). Although none of the questions is particularly profound, each is on our list of questions about color that people most often ask.

BOX 6.5
Answers to Some Common Questions About Color

• *What are the primary colors?* First, contrary to what your first-grade teacher may have said, there is no single set of primary colors. Usually the word "primary" is used to designate one member of a trio that, when properly mixed, can produce any of a large number of colors. But since many different trios all suffice for this purpose, no one of them can properly lay claim to the title "the primaries."

• *Do my dog and cat have color vision?* This question requires clarifying what is meant by "color vision." As we've seen, just because someone can tell the difference between objects of different colors is not proof of color vision; the person *might* be discriminating the objects on the basis of their differing lightness. Color vision requires that a creature be able to discriminate on the basis of wavelength alone—

regardless of lightness differences. By this definition, cats *do* have color vision, though apparently it is not as well developed as that of humans. When forced to, cats can learn to make discriminations on the basis of wavelength information. However, they seem to *prefer* to tell objects apart by their lightness differences instead. Though adequate studies of the dog's color vision have

(*Continued on next page*)

yet to be done, the organization of its retina suggests that the dog does have color vision (Jacobs, 1983).

- *Why do some black and white patterns make me see color?* Black and white patterns (like the one shown below) cause some people to experience colors (Wilkins et al., in press). This effect, sometimes called **subjective color,** has been studied for over a century, but a completely satisfactory explanation has not yet been developed. The most widely held theory assumes that the red-green and blue-yellow chromatic channels each respond best to a slightly different temporal rate of stimulation (flicker). Small involuntary eye movements cause the contours in the figure to move back and forth

on the retina. Each movement changes the pattern of light stimulation on the retina. And the rate of these changes affects the chromatic channels to different degrees, producing sensations of various colors (depending on the rate).

- *Why can't I see colors at night?* Under conditions of dim illumination, such as those prevailing at night, the eyes behave as though they had only one photopigment. At night, the light is not sufficient to stimulate the cone system; therefore vision depends exclusively on the rods. Since all rods have the same photopigment, the univariance principle prevents their conveying information about the wavelengths of light that they have absorbed. Consequently, you can see

only variations in intensity—blacks, whites, and grays. Incidentally, this is why, as the saying goes, all cats appear gray at night.

- *Why does the grass always seem greener on the other side of the fence?* Usually, this aphorism signifies that people tend to find someone else's possessions or situation more attractive than their own. Though you can debate its psychological validity, an analysis by James Pomerantz of the State University of New York at Buffalo puts the aphorism on a firm perceptual foundation. Pomerantz's argument is illustrated in the figure opposite. A person stands on a lawn (presumably his own) and views his own grass and his neighbor's on the other side of the fence. In order to view his own grass, the person must look nearly straight down. As a result he sees not only the grass, but also the ground below. The brown of the ground mixes with the green of the grass, thereby diluting the green. But when he looks on the other side of the fence, his line of sight is less nearly perpendicular to the grass and ground. As a result, he sees more grass and less ground, and the grass does seem greener on the other side of the fence. Pomerantz (1983) notes that this phenomenon depends on the height of the grass; if you don't mow your lawn, the

grass will grow high enough to flop over, obscuring the ground and thereby

equalizing the green on both sides of the fence.

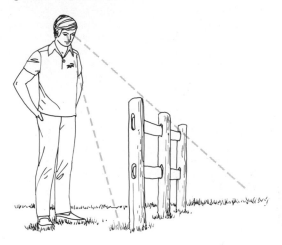

Summary and Preview

In this chapter we noted how ideas about color vision have developed over the past 300 years. We described the mechanisms of color vision, emphasizing that wavelength of light is first analyzed by three spectrally broad and widely overlapping cone photopigments and that the outcome of that analysis is then fed into chromatic and achromatic visual channels.

Unfortunately, science's success in explaining *how* people see color tends to obscure *why* they see color. Probably, the ability to perceive color developed to help creatures detect and discriminate objects in

their environment. Because objects—artificial as well as natural—have characteristic pigments, they absorb and reflect light in characteristic ways. These patterns of spectral reflection make it advantageous to have color vision. An animal whose visual system retains information about the wavelength distribution of reflected light can usually tell where one object begins and another ends. Moreover, that wavelength information enables the animal to recognize what sort of object it has encountered and what action is called for. In the next chapter we discuss depth perception, still another property of vision that helps creatures to appreciate the objects around them.

Chapter 7

Depth Perception

The previous two chapters dealt with aspects of visual perception—form and color—that define *what* an object is. In many instances, though, you need to do more than just identify an object. Often you must react to it in a specific way, such as reaching for it or avoiding it. Every time you drive a car, you're judging the distances from you to other vehicles. These judgments must be made rapidly and automatically; usually you cannot take the time to calculate these distances consciously. The same type of judgment is required numerous times a day—for instance, whenever you cross a street in traffic or reach for a pen on your desk. Reacting quickly and accurately requires that you know *where* the object is located in three-dimensional space. In other words, you need to know how far the object is from you, an ability usually referred to as **depth perception.** Some creatures, such as bats, can use their ears to pick up information about distance (Griffin, 1959); but for humans, the most reliable

sources of depth information are visual ones.

Actually, it is remarkable that human beings are able to make distance judgments at all, let alone accurate ones. The retinal images from which depth information is extracted are two-dimensional and, therefore, inherently without depth. To show you what we mean, imagine that we could take a photograph of the image falling on the back of your eye at a single instant in time. Like an individual frame in a motion picture, this photograph would consist of a complex distribution of contour and color. But this distribution would be contained in a flat, two-dimensional picture on the retina. From this two-dimensional picture, the brain extracts information about the third dimension, providing a visual world alive with depth. To accomplish this job, the brain utilizes a variety of different sources of depth information. In this chapter, we shall examine the various kinds of visual information that contribute to the perception of depth.

Sources of information about depth are sometimes referred to as *cues* to depth. Following convention, we too shall speak of "cues" to depth, but you should not misunderstand what we mean by this term. It does not mean that depth perception results from conscious deliberation on your part; to see objects in depth, you don't use cues like a detective trying to solve a mystery. On the contrary, despite its origins in a two-dimensional image on the retina, depth perception occurs automatically and effortlessly.

Accurate judgments of distance arise from the coordination of several different sources of information. In the normal environment, these various sources of depth information usually operate in harmony, yielding an unambiguous impression of three-dimensional space. But if these sources, or cues, are placed in conflict, certain kinds of errors in depth perception occur. These errors, like other errors or illusions encountered earlier in this book, provide insight into the normal operation of depth perception.

Before surveying the depth cues, we need to clarify precisely what is meant by "depth perception," because this term can be used in two quite different ways. In one case, the term refers to the distance from an observer to an object. This is sometimes called **absolute distance.** To give an example, in baseball, an outfielder attempting to throw out a base runner must judge the distance between himself and the base for which the runner is headed. Alternatively, the term "depth perception" may refer to the distance between one object and another, or between different parts of a single object. This is known as **relative distance.** When you place the cap on a ball-point pen you make a judgment involving relative distance. Distinguishing between these two types of depth perception is important because they differ markedly; the ability to judge relative depth is many times more precise than the ability to make judgments about absolute distance (Graham, 1965).

With this distinction in mind, we are now ready to explore the various cues to depth that are used by the visual system. We have divided these into two broad categories, **oculomotor cues** and **visual cues.** The oculomotor cues are actually *kinesthetic* in nature, meaning that the cue itself derives from the sensation of muscular contraction; this cue would be something like the feeling you experience when you tighten your fist. The visual cues, so called because they are genuinely visual in nature, are subdivided into those that are available only when two eyes are used (*binocular cues*) and those that are available when just one eye is used (*monocular cues*). Figure 7.1 summarizes the ways in which these types of cues to depth are related. As you will see, oculomotor cues are the only ones that provide unambiguous information about absolute distance, meaning that an oculomotor cue does not require supplementation by other cues. In contrast, any of the visual cues can provide good relative depth information, but they must be supplemented with other information in order to specify absolute distance.

Oculomotor Cues

As you learned in Chapter 2, whenever you are looking at, or fixating, an object, your eyes are focused and converged by an amount dependent on the distance between you and that object. To be seen clearly, close objects require more accommodation and convergence than do objects farther away from you. Now suppose we were able to attach tiny gauges to the two sets of muscles involved in these two reflexes, strain gauges that could tell us how much the muscles were contracted (see panel A of Figure 7.2). By monitoring the degree of muscular con-

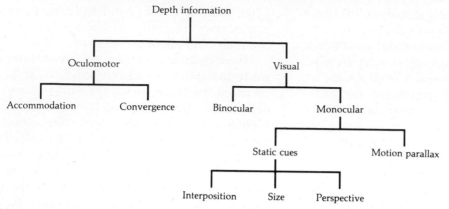

FIGURE 7.1
Major sources of depth information.

traction, we could compute either of two values: your angle of **convergence** or the amount of **accommodation** of your eyes. And because these two values are related to the distance between your eyes and the object you are viewing, we would then have a useful index of absolute distance. In other words, by monitoring your eye muscles, *we* could tell how far from you the object is that you are looking at. But before this same infor-

mation could serve as a cue to depth for *you*, your visual nervous system would have to be able to sense the contractions of your eye muscles.

It is simple to show that convergence is accompanied by a sense of muscle strain: Starting with your index finger held up at arm's length, steadily move it toward your nose while keeping both eyes focused on it. As your finger moves closer to your nose,

A.

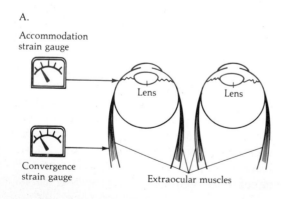

B.

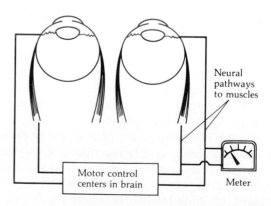

FIGURE 7.2
Two possible schemes for registering oculomotor information.

you can feel the increased strain as your eyes turn inward to maintain fixation. At the same time, your accommodation is increasing too; the lens attempts to keep the image of your finger in sharp focus on your retina. In fact, these two motor responses—accommodation and convergence—usually operate in a yoked fashion, such that changes in one are accompanied by changes in the other.

There is potentially another way for us to get information about the degree of your accommodation and convergence. We could insert some measuring instrument along the neural pathway leading to the eye muscles (see panel B of Figure 7.2). Now we would be recording the strength of the command signals being *sent* to those muscles. In effect, we would be monitoring the instructions used to steer accommodation and convergence. The signals flowing out to your muscles could furnish information about distance.

So far we have described how oculomotor cues *could* furnish information about distance. But can people accurately judge distance under conditions where accommodation and convergence provide the only cues to depth? The answer is yes—operating together, these two oculomotor cues do influence judgments of distance (Leibowitz and Moore, 1966; Wallach and Floor, 1971). But do *both* cues, accommodation and convergence, contribute equally? To answer this question, let's consider the two cues individually, starting with accommodation.

In accommodation, you have a cue whose potential effective range is necessarily limited. Whenever you focus on an object more than a few meters from you, the muscle controlling accommodation assumes its most relaxed state. So as a potential depth cue, accommodation would be useful only within the region of space immediately in front of you. Even within this small range, distance judgments based solely on accommodation are inaccurate (Heinemann, Tulving, and Nachmias, 1959; Künnapas, 1968). So we can dismiss accommodation as an effective source of depth information.

Turning next to convergence, we find that it too operates over a limited range of distance. The convergence angle formed by your two eyes vanishes to zero (your eyes are looking straight ahead) when you are looking at objects from a distance of about 20 feet and beyond. For distances less than 20 feet (about 6 meters), however, observers can use convergence angle as a reliable depth cue, in the absence of other distance information (Grant, 1942).

On their own, then, the oculomotor cues play only a restricted role in depth perception. In fact, you rely much more heavily on the so-called visual cues to depth. It is to those cues that we now turn, beginning with the cue provided by looking at the world through two separate eyes.

Binocular Visual Information: Stereopsis

In Chapter 2, we pointed out that in humans, the two eyes look at much the same region of visual space; only near the margins of the visual field do the two eyes provide exclusive monocular coverage. This overlapping binocular field of view comes about because the two eyes are located in the front of the head. Within this region of binocular overlap, the two eyes view objects from slightly different vantage points, owing to the lateral separation of the two eyes within the head. We are now ready to consider the perceptual consequences of this binocular arrangement.

To begin, why did nature position human eyes in such a way as to provide two views of the world, thereby duplicating a significant portion of those views? The answer seems clear. By virtue of the slight differences, or *disparities*, between the view seen by your left eye and the view seen by your right eye, you are able to discriminate extremely small differences in relative depth, differences that are very difficult to discriminate using either eye alone. You can demonstrate this for yourself by performing the following simple experiment.

Take two sharp pencils, one in each hand, and hold them at arm's length. Their tips should be separated by 10 centimeters or so and pointed toward one another. Now slowly bring the two pencils together in such a way that the two points are touching. First try this several times with one eye closed, each time noting by how much, if any, the two miss each other. Next repeat the exercise with both eyes open. You will probably find your accuracy much improved with binocular viewing. However, not *all* individuals benefit from using both eyes—some 5 to 10 percent of the general population do no better with two eyes than they do with one. You will learn why later in this chapter.

The ability to judge relative depth binocularly is called **stereopsis.** Besides allowing you to judge relative depth with great accuracy, stereopsis also makes it possible for you to see objects that are invisible to either eye alone. This aspect of stereopsis is described in Box 7.1. Knowing that stereopsis exists, you may wonder what sort of cues stereopsis depends on and how those cues are extracted from the two eyes by the brain. Let's consider each problem separately.

RETINAL DISPARITY

Your two eyes look at nearby objects from slightly different angles. As a result, those objects do not appear exactly the same to your left eye and to your right eye. Ordinarily, however, you are unaware of any differences between the left eye's view and the right eye's view. This is because the brain combines information from the two eyes in such a way as to obscure these differences.

Only by looking at something alternately with one eye and then the other can you actually notice the differences between the two eyes' views. You should take a moment to perform this simple exercise. Choose some object in front of you and look at it steadily, using one eye and then the other. You should be able to see more of the left side of the object with your left eye while seeing more of the right side with your right eye.

While looking alternately through your two eyes, also pay special attention to the position of the object you are looking at and compare it to the position of another, neighboring object that is located a little closer to you than the one you are looking at. To make this comparison, you may want to arrange some objects on a table. Alternatively, you can simply hold up your two index fingers in front of you, at different distances from your nose. Either way, you will now see that the lateral separation between the two objects appears to change when you switch eyes. Figure 7.3 illustrates this observation. These two photographs mimic the views seen by two eyes looking at a real scene from slightly different vantage points. These photographs were taken in succession, shifting the camera sideways by 65 millimeters (the typical distance between the two eyes) before taking the second photograph. Note that the separation between the two bottles is larger in the left-hand picture than it is in the right-hand picture. This comes about because the two bottles were located at different distances from the camera at the time these pictures were taken. The difference in lateral separation between objects as seen by the left eye and by the right eye is called **retinal disparity;** it provides information for stereoscopic depth perception.

The magnitude of the disparity, expressed in terms of lateral separation on the retina, depends on the distance between objects. If one object is much closer to the observer than the other, the resulting retinal

BOX 7.1

Cooperation Between the Eyes

Of all remarkable visual abilities, none excels the keenness of stereopsis. Using binocular disparity information, humans are able to make exceedingly fine depth judgments that are simply impossible when using just one eye. To illustrate, imagine that you are viewing a pair of pencils oriented vertically and placed side by side 1 meter away from you. At that distance, stereopsis would make it possible for you to tell whether one pencil was as little as 1 millimeter closer to you than its neighbor. From a distance of 1 meter, a 1-millimeter difference corresponds to a judgment accuracy of one-tenth of 1 percent. In this case, the resulting disparity between the two eyes' views is less than four ten-thousandths of a millimeter. This distance is many times smaller than the diameter of a single visual receptor in your eye!

Because of this extraordinary resolving power, stereopsis provides a very effective means for uncovering slight differences between a pair of pictures presented separately to the two eyes. For instance, suppose you view a pair of one-dollar bills in a stereoscope (the familiar device used for presenting two pictures, one to each eye). If the two bills are identical down to the smallest detail, the resulting percept will be a single, absolutely flat bill; there will exist no disparity to differentiate the two. But if the two bills differ, even slightly, portions of the single, combined percept will appear to stand out in relief, due to retinal disparity produced by the slight differences. This stereoscopic technique has been used for identifying counterfeit currency, as well as for comparing small details in such things as the electronic circuits in computers.

Stereopsis also provides an effective means for detecting camouflaged objects. Two views of a visual scene taken from different vantage points can reveal the presence of forms that are invisible from either vantage point alone. As an example, aerial photography of a landscape from two positions can disclose the presence and location of objects (such as military hardware) on the ground. Stereopsis can also help a predatory animal spot its next meal even when the color and texture of the meal blends into the environment.

A most dramatic example of the sleuthlike powers of stereopsis is provided by random-dot stereograms, an example of which is shown in Figure 7.7. Each eye's view consists of a random array of dots, with no hint of an object hidden therein. Yet, when the brain combines the two views, a figure in depth emerges. The technique used to create this kind of stereogram is simple (it is described in the text). In contrast, the technique used by your brain to extract depth from such a stereogram must be quite complex. For this reason, you may be surprised to learn that infants as young as 4 months of age can see the depth in random-dot stereograms (Fox et al., 1980). Moreover, this form of stereopsis is not unique to humans. Monkeys (Bough, 1970), cats (Lehmkuhle and Fox, 1977), and falcons (Fox, Lehmkuhle, and Bush, 1977) show evidence of being able to discriminate the depth portrayed in random-dot stereograms.

If you are interested in experiencing this illusion of depth for yourself, several books provide stereograms as well as special glasses to help you view the stereograms (Julesz, 1971; Frisby, 1980). The visual system seems to have to learn to see depth in these random-dot stereograms, particularly those portraying complicated surfaces, with many hills, valleys, and curlicues. Upon first viewing a stereogram, it may take you several minutes of concentrated viewing to see depth. During this time, the previously hidden surfaces appear to grow, slowly rising out of the page. Moreover, it is impossible to speed up this process by telling or showing a person what to look for (Frisby and Clatworthy, 1975). However, just as with riding a bicycle, once you learn to see depth in one of these stereograms, you never completely forget how.

FIGURE 7.3

The lateral separation between two objects as it might appear to the left eye and to the right eye. (K. Bendo.)

disparity will be large. If one object is only slightly closer to the observer than the other, the disparity will be small. Figure 7.4 illustrates this geometrical principle.

This cue to depth, retinal disparity, arises whenever objects are located in front of *or* behind the object you are looking at. Of course, you can tell visually whether an object is nearer or farther than your point of fixation, which means that your visual nervous system distinguishes between the disparities produced by these two possibilities—objects nearer versus objects farther away. If an object lies farther from you than the object you're fixating, the disparity between the two is said to be *uncrossed*. If an object is located closer to you than the one you are looking at, the disparity is said to be *crossed*. To remember this distinction easily, just keep in mind that with crossed dis-

parity you would need to converge, or *cross*, your eyes in order to look directly at the nearer object. By the same token, you would diverge, or *uncross*, your eyes to shift your fixation to a more distant object.

So the type of disparity, crossed versus uncrossed, specifies whether objects are in front of or behind the point of fixation, while the magnitude of the disparity specifies the amount by which objects are separated in depth. It is important to remember that retinal disparity specifies the *relative* depth between two or more objects; it does not provide information about absolute depth. A single small spot in an otherwise empty visual field (such as the glow of a cigarette in a dark room) cannot give rise to disparity information.

Objects in the visual field can also be situated so that they give rise to zero dispar-

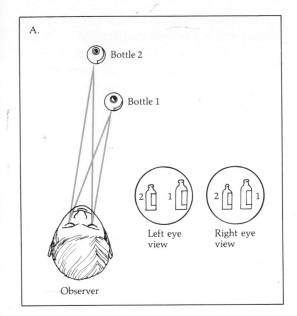

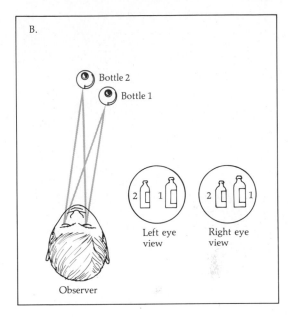

FIGURE 7.4
Retinal disparity increases with the distance, in depth, between two objects.

ity—a disparity that is neither crossed nor uncrossed. In other words, the lateral separation between the objects seen through the left eye will be identical to the separation between those objects seen through the right eye. As you should be able to deduce, zero disparity occurs when two or more objects are located at the same distance from the observer. An example of this situation is illustrated in Figure 7.5. In this case, the two bottles were located at the *same* distance from the observer. Images from such equidistant objects are said to fall on corresponding areas of the two eyes.*

The foveas of the two eyes represent one set of corresponding retinal areas. Whenever you look directly at an object, an image of that object will be formed on the fovea of your left eye and on the fovea of your right eye; in this case, we say that the images fall on corresponding retinal areas. In addition, there are numerous other sets of corresponding areas spread over the two retinas. And by definition, these areas have zero disparity with respect to the two foveas. Therefore, objects casting images on these other, nondisparate retinal areas will be seen at the same depth as the object seen by the two foveas.

To clarify this point, let's perform the following exercise. Take two pencils, one in each hand, and place one directly in front of you. While fixating that pencil, position the other one so that it is several centimeters (about an inch) to one side but located *at the same perceived distance* from you as the pencil you are looking at. To accomplish this, you may want to move the nonfixated pencil back and forth *in depth* until it appears at exactly the right distance. By so doing, you are varying retinal disparity between uncrossed and crossed until you settle on what amounts

*There are actually several alternative ways to specify retinal correspondence, but for our purposes the definition based on depth is the most appropriate.

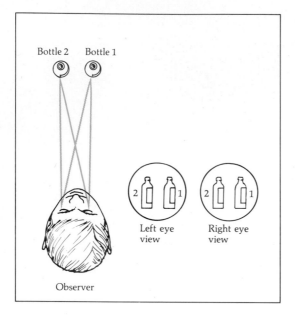

FIGURE 7.5
Zero disparity occurs when two objects are located at equal distances from the observer.

to zero disparity. If you are very careful, the second pencil will be placed so that it too casts left and right eye images on corresponding retinal areas. If you were to repeat this exercise, now repositioning the nonfixated pencil farther to one side of the point of fixation, you could generate another point at which the nonfixated pencil appeared to lie the same distance from you as the fixated pencil. In so doing, you would have established another zero-disparity location. If you repeated this exercise a number of times, all the resulting zero-disparity locations could be connected to form a curve; that curve would define an imaginary plane called the **horopter** (see Figure 7.6). So long as you maintain fixation on some point in this plane, all objects located anywhere in the plane produce images on corresponding, or nondisparate, retinal areas. Objects closer to you than this plane yield crossed disparities,

whereas objects farther from you than this plane yield uncrossed disparities.

That, then, is how retinal correspondence and retinal disparity are related to binocular depth perception. Considering that the geometry of this situation is relatively straightforward, it is surprising that prior to the last century no one fully appreciated that disparity supplied information about depth. A British physicist, Charles Wheatstone (1838/1964), first demonstrated that a vivid impression of stereoscopic depth could be created from two flat pictures (Wade, 1983). His demonstration took the following form. On two cards, Wheatstone sketched a pair of outline drawings of a three-dimensional object. One drawing depicted the view of the object as seen by the left eye and the other drawing depicted the view of the object as seen by the right eye. He then looked at this pair of two-dimensional drawings using a **stereoscope,** a device Wheatstone invented to present the two drawings (which together constitute a stereogram) separately to the two eyes. He observed that the two drawings of the object were seen as one. In addition, that one drawing conveyed an amazing sense of relief, or three-dimensionality. Thus by incorporating retinal disparity into his drawings, Wheatstone was able to recreate the three-dimensional appearance of an object—an effect that is lost in a single, two-dimensional picture. Wheatstone's novel observations demonstrated the potency of retinal disparity in producing depth perception.

So far, we have focused on stereopsis from a geometrical perspective. You have learned that objects nearer or farther than your plane of fixation project their retinal images on disparate regions of the two eyes. You have also learned that by mimicking these disparities in a stereogram (a pair of pictures), it is possible to create realistic stereoscopic depth artificially. Having defined the cues

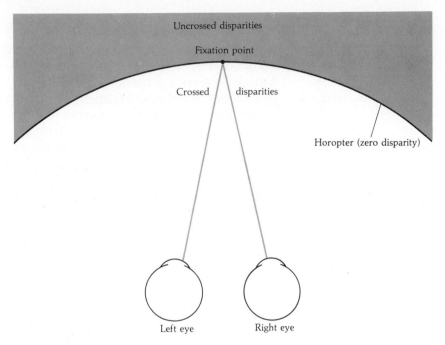

FIGURE 7.6

The horopter—an imaginary plane marking the positions of all objects located at the same perceived distance from the observer. Objects more distant than the point of fixation are said to produce uncrossed disparities (shaded area), while objects nearer than the point of fixation are said to produce crossed disparities (unshaded area).

from which stereopsis *might* arise, let's consider what the visual system would have to do in order to utilize this depth cue of retinal disparity.

MATCHING THE LEFT AND RIGHT EYES' VIEWS

Imagine for a moment that you are a brain, facing the same predicament that your brain normally encounters. Handed two slightly different pictures (retinal images) portraying various objects, you must recreate the way in which those objects are actually laid out in depth. To do this, you must use only the information contained in the two pic-

tures. How would you proceed? Since there is a connection between objects' relative distances from one another and their disparate positions in the two pictures, you might first compute these disparities. This computation requires that you compare the two pictures, noting in each where particular objects are located. Before you could perform that computation, you would have to figure out which portion of one picture matched which portion of the other. Only then would it be possible to measure the positional disparities between the two pictures.

This exercise indicates that stereopsis really involves two steps: first, matched features must be identified in the two eyes; second, the magnitude and direction (crossed versus uncrossed) of the retinal disparities between those features must be calculated. Let's consider these two steps in turn.

First, in order to match features in the two retinal images, you must decide what constitutes a feature. On the basis of intuition, the most plausible candidate would seem to be some recognizable form, or pattern, appearing in both of the pictures, For instance, if one eye's view included your roommate's face, it would be a simple matter to locate that face in the other eye's view. According to this idea, each eye's image is analyzed separately, and the two are then brought together for purposes of matching recognizable features. However, this idea cannot be entirely correct, for there are instances where stereoscopic depth can be perceived from stereograms that contain no recognizable objects whatsoever. An example of one of these **random-dot stereograms** is shown in Figure 7.7. These intriguing stereograms were first developed by Bela Julesz, a vision scientist and former engineer who works for Bell Telephone Laboratories (Julesz, 1971).

Both halves of this stereogram consist of nothing more than an array of black and white dots. The two halves are identical with one exception. In one of the halves of the stereogram, a central subset of dots has been shifted laterally by several rows, as is illustrated schematically in the middle panel of Figure 7.7. This lateral displacement creates a retinal disparity between the two halves, in much the same way as would a speckled square held in front of an identically speckled background, as depicted in the bottom panel of Figure 7.7. Because the texture in the stereogram is completely random, it is impossible to pick out from either half of the stereogram alone which area will appear in depth when the two halves are viewed simultaneously.

Think for a moment about the confusing

job confronting the brain in trying to sort out the depth in this jumble of dots. Because each half of the stereogram is made up of nothing more than a random array of tiny dots, there are numerous dots in one eye's view that would match up with any single dot in the other eye's view. Yet the brain does manage to find a satisfactory match between the two pictures, as is evidenced by the vivid illusion of depth produced by these pairs of random textures.

Thus random-dot stereograms disprove the theory that stereopsis results from an analysis of monocularly recognizable forms such as your roommate's face. But if not monocular forms, then what monocular features *do* the visual system match in order to compute disparity? Think back for a moment to Chapter 5, where you learned that form perception initially involves analyzing a figure's orientation and size, or spatial frequency. The same features are involved in stereopsis, too. The evidence favoring this idea is rather complicated, so we are going to mention just a couple of relevant studies here. John Frisby (1980) gives a more thorough discussion of feature matching and stereopsis.

It is possible to remove certain spatial frequencies from random-dot stereograms such as the one shown at the top of Figure 7.7; this process of removal is called *filtering*. When high spatial frequencies are removed from both halves of a stereogram, the dots are no longer sharply defined but instead appear blurred (recall Figures 5.15 and 5.25). Still the phantom figure is easily seen to stand out in depth. By the same token, if just low spatial frequencies are removed from both halves of a stereogram, depth may still be experienced. But if high spatial frequencies are removed from one half of the stereogram while low spatial frequencies are removed from the other, stereopsis is abolished. Instead the two halves undergo **binocular rivalry,** such that only one pic-

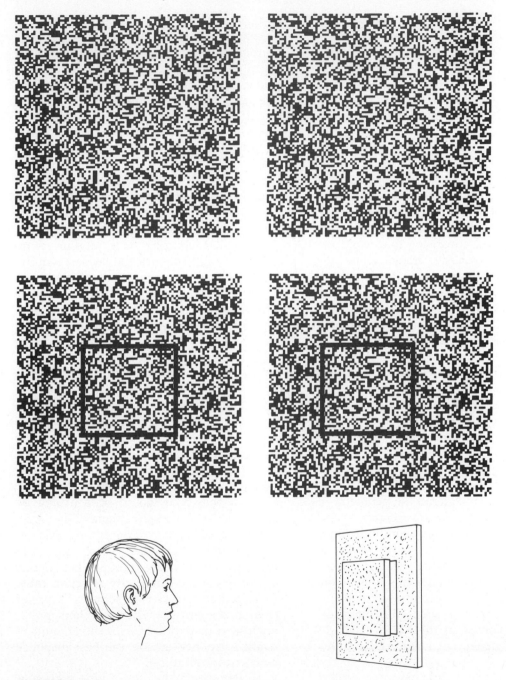

FIGURE 7.7

A random-dot stereogram. The two halves are identical, except that a central subset of dots has been shifted laterally. (The middle panel outlines the section of shifted dots.) This lateral displacement creates retinal disparity and, thus, stereoscopic depth (bottom panel). (Stereogram from Julesz, 1971.)

ture or the other is visible at any one moment (see Box 7.2). John Frisby and John Mayhew (1976) have devised several filtered stereograms of this sort, and the demonstrations are conclusive: for stereopsis to be experienced, the spatial frequency content of the two halves of a stereogram must overlap at least partially.

These and similar findings (Julesz and Miller, 1975) indicate that the brain, to match the two eyes' views, relies on channels that are responsive to limited bands of spatial frequencies. Recall from Chapter 5 that the brain relies on similar channels in form perception. It is not surprising that form perception and stereopsis should utilize the same machinery, since both form perception and stereopsis are designed to distinguish objects from their backgrounds (Marr, 1982). Because of the remarkable human ability to resolve small depth differences stereoscopically, the two eyes together can unearth objects buried in complex visual environments, objects that when viewed monocularly remain hidden from sight. In this respect, stereopsis effectively adds another dimension to form perception.

THE NEURAL BASIS OF STEREOPSIS

So far we have considered the geometry of retinal disparity (the cue for stereopsis) and the matching features that seem to be used in the analysis of retinal disparity. But how does the brain actually do its feature matching and disparity computation? Certainly the entire process is not yet understood, but something is known about the biological hardware involved in the initial stages of stereoscopic vision. Let's take a look at this hardware.

Recall from Chapter 4 that most cortical neurons receive input from both eyes, left and right. Each of these binocular neurons gives its largest response when the two eyes view the same stimulus. For instance, a par-

ticular binocular neuron that gives its most vigorous response when the left eye sees a vertical contour will respond best when the right eye sees a vertical contour, too. The same holds for contour width, or size, as well as for the direction and speed of movement of a contour. In general, binocular neurons respond best when the two eyes view matched features (Hubel and Wiesel, 1962, 1970; Nelson, Kato, and Bishop, 1977; Poggio and Fischer, 1978). This property, then, satisfies one of the requirements for the analysis of disparity information, namely the matching of monocular features.

Binocular neurons have another property, one that satisfies the second requirement for stereopsis: these neurons are sensitive to retinal disparity. In particular, some binocular cells respond only when their preferred features appear at the *same* depth plane as the point of fixation. This is because the receptive fields for these binocular neurons are located on *corresponding* areas of the two eyes. These cells, in other words, would respond best to objects giving rise to zero disparity. Activity in such cells would serve to signal the presence of stimuli located *on* the horopter. Other binocular cells respond best to stimuli that are imaged on noncorresponding, or disparate, areas of the two eyes. Cells of this type would be activated by stimuli located at depth planes other than the plane of fixation (Poggio and Fischer, 1978; Ferster, 1981). Refer back to Figure 4.16 to see the layout of the receptive field of one of these so-called **disparity-selective cells.** As noted in Chapter 4, some cells prefer crossed disparities, whereas others prefer uncrossed disparities. Also, the amount of depth (disparity) giving the best response varies from cell to cell.

So it appears that these binocular neurons perform two of the operations necessary for stereopsis, feature matching and disparity computation. But can we be sure that these binocular neurons actually play a

BOX 7.2
Competition Between the Two Eyes

Charles Wheatstone, the discoverer of stereopsis, described another intriguing aspect of binocular vision. This second discovery concerned the perceptual outcome when one eye's view differs radically from its partner's view. Wheatstone's interesting observation can best be described by reference to the figure below.

Suppose you were to view these two dissimilar patterns separately with your two eyes in such a way that your left eye saw one set of diagonal lines while your right eye saw the other set. What would be the outcome? If the two were combined by simply superimposing one on the other, the result would be a sort of checkerboard pattern. Yet when these figures are viewed stereoscopically, thereby allowing your brain to perform the combination, the two certainly do not blend into a single, stable pattern resembling a checkerboard. Instead, a person sees portions of one pattern and portions of the other, the net result resembling a mosaic of the two. Moreover, this mosaic changes over time, as regions of one eye's view replace regions of the other eye's view.

The resulting phenomenon is known as binocular rivalry, an appropriate term in view of the evident breakdown in cooperation between the two eyes. The occurrence of binocular rivalry indicates that the brain, in attempting to put together information from the two eyes, seeks to establish matches between features in the two eyes. When such matches are found, stable single vision and stereopsis result. But when satisfactory matches are impossible, the brain attends to portions of one eye's view at a time, ignoring or suppressing the corresponding portions of the other eye's view as though they were not there.

But how complete is this suppression of information during binocular rivalry? Is a person completely oblivious to new information presented to a region of the eye that is temporarily suppressed? To study this question, Robert Fox, a psychologist at Vanderbilt University, briefly flashed "probe targets," such as a word, to a suppressed region and recorded whether the person noticed the target. His results are conclusive—during suppression, a person fails to see targets that would normally be quite visible, including, for example, the person's own name.

However, the eye is not completely blind to all visual stimulation during suppression. Fox (Fox and Check, 1968) found that increasing the brightness of a suppressed stimulus or suddenly moving it will cause the stimulus to become visible. Apparently during suppression an eye's overall sensitivity, though reduced, is not totally abolished. Although vision in the suppressed eye is abolished from consciousness, some processing of information from that eye continues. This is yet another demonstration that perception is not entirely synonymous with conscious awareness (Marcel, 1983).

Left eye's view   Right eye's view

role in stereoscopic depth perception? One piece of evidence favoring such a role comes from studying cats who, while kittens, were allowed to see with only one eye at a time; the eyes were stimulated alternately by placing an opaque contact lens in one eye on one day and in the other eye on the next day. This rearing procedure effectively turns binocular neurons into monocular ones (Blakemore, 1976). When tested as adults, these animals were unable to perform binocular depth discriminations that were simple for normally reared cats (Blake and Hirsch, 1975; Packwood and Gordon, 1975). Because they lacked a normal array of binocular neurons, these cats were "blind" for stereopsis.

Recall our earlier comment that some people are stereoblind—unable to perceive depth from retinal disparity (Richards, 1970). By analogy with the stereoblind cats, we assume that this condition in humans stems from a lack of binocular neurons. Again, there is evidence to back up this assumption. For instance, when tested on the tilt aftereffect (Box 4.5, p. 131), stereoblind people show very little interocular transfer—adapting one eye has very little effect on judgments of line orientation when the non-adapted eye is tested (Mitchell and Ware, 1974). In contrast, people with good stereopsis show a substantial degree of interocular transfer, which, we assume, results from adaptation of binocular neurons. The meager degree of interocular transfer in the stereoblind individual, then, probably reflects the paucity of binocular neurons in that person's brain.

It has been estimated that the incidence of **stereoblindness** may be as high as 5 to 10 percent in the general population (Richards, 1970). As a rule, stereoblindness is associated with the presence of certain visual disorders during early childhood. The most common of these disorders is misalignment of the two eyes, a condition known as **strabismus**. People with this condition are un-

able to look at, or fixate, the same object simultaneously with both eyes. Consequently, one eye's view rarely corresponds with the other eye's view. To deal with this potentially confusing situation, the brain eventually suppresses one eye's view from visual consciousness, an outcome reminiscent of binocular rivalry. Box 7.3 describes this and similar conditions in more detail.

If left uncorrected, strabismus can lead not only to stereoblindness but also to amblyopia—which as you will recall from Box 4.3 is defined as a permanent reduction in the acuity of the eye. Both amblyopia and stereoblindness can be prevented if eye misalignment is surgically corrected early in life. If correction is postponed until school age, the chances for the attainment of normal vision are significantly reduced (von Noorden, 1981; Banks, Aslin, and Letson, 1975).

The discovery of disparity-sensitive cells represents an exciting first step toward an understanding of the neural basis of stereopsis. These important findings have been nicely summarized by Pettigrew (1972), one of the people originally involved in these studies (Barlow, Blakemore, and Pettigrew, 1967; Nikara, Bishop, and Pettigrew, 1968). This cannot be the entire story, however. For one thing, the perceived depth resulting from a given disparity depends on the absolute distance from your eyes to the object you are looking at. This can be demonstrated when an observer views a random-dot stereogram, such as the one in Figure 7.7, from different distances. The central square in the stereogram appears to move farther and farther in front of its background as viewing distance increases. This observation indicates that disparity must be supplemented by other depth information (Ritter, 1984), perhaps convergence angle (Foley, 1980).

This completes our survey of stereopsis, the major source of binocular depth information. Keen as it is, though, stereopsis cer-

BOX 7.3

Coordination Between the Two Eyes

Like any other partners, the two eyes have to share the same viewpoint in order to get along. This means that movements of the eyes must be coordinated so that both eyes are always looking in the same direction. As you learned in Chapter 2, the eyes are guided in their movements by twelve extraocular muscles—six for each eye. Because the eye movement system is complex and dependent on fallible parts, things can and do go wrong. Here, we shall consider some of the most common errors and their remedies, emphasizing extraocular dysfunctions that affect perception.

When most people look at an object, the two eyes both end up aimed at that object. For these people, the two eyes fixate together. This binocular fixation depends on the coordinated responses of the extraocular muscles that guide the two eyes. For various reasons, however, some people lack this coordination. For example, if one extraocular muscle is too short, it can exert too much pull on the eyeball, turning that eye in (toward the nose) or out (toward the ear). Chronic deviation of an eye is called **strabismus,** or *squint*. Often this is a congenital condition, which means that an infant may lack coordinated binocular vision early in life. Because strabismic eyes look in different directions, they give the brain conflicting messages,

which may result in double vision, or **diplopia** as it is called. Alternatively, the brain may simply ignore, or suppress, one eye's view altogether; in this case, only one eye contributes to vision even though both are open. This latter condition resembles a chronic form of binocular rivalry (see Box 7.2).

Various therapies have been developed for strabismus. In cases where the deviation between the positions of the two eyes is relatively small, visual exercises may help to recoordinate the eyes. In more severe cases, surgical correction may be required. This usually involves removing a small portion of one or more of the extraocular muscles and then reattaching the muscles to the eyeball, so that the eyes now line up. This procedure requires a high degree of skill, for altering the muscle by the wrong amount will leave the eyes still misaligned.

Other extraocular dysfunctions are less debilitating and less noticeable. When you do close work such as reading, your eyes must converge—each turns inward by the proper amount. Strong, constant convergence strains the muscles of the eye (Guth, 1981). Some people have difficulty converging their eyes, as you can discover for yourself. Stand facing a friend and ask him to keep his eyes on your finger as you move it slowly but directly

toward a point between his eyes. Note how well his eyes follow; some people will be able to keep both eyes fixated on the finger until it is within 1 or 2 centimeters of the nose. Others will not be able to follow the finger after it is within 5 or 6 centimeters of the nose. As the finger approaches, one of their eyes may wander off. If you try this small experiment with several people, you'll be amazed at the individual differences. In addition, when someone is tired or has consumed too much alcohol (Scott, 1979), that person's eyes may be unable to converge normally.

People who have trouble binocularly fixating close objects may experience eyestrain during prolonged reading. Eyestrain, in turn, can cause dizziness, headaches, and nausea, leading to reduced studying and hence poorer grades. Occasionally, college students suffer this kind of problem, called **convergence insufficiency,** while studying for final examinations. Amateur "psychologists" can do great harm by misdiagnosing this condition, thinking it is an aversion to studying or "a need to fail." In fact, the proper treatment is straightforward: spectacles, possibly supplemented with appropriate eye exercises. Reading will then become less of a strain, and higher grades may follow.

tainly is not the sole source of depth information. People can successfully perform visually guided tasks, such as landing an airplane (Grosslight et al., 1978), while using just one eye. And you can easily confirm that the world retains a real sense of depth even when you close one eye. Rather than collapsing into a single, depthless plane, objects in your visual field continue to appear three-dimensional. This is possible because your monocular view of the world contains many sources of information about depth. Let's consider these monocular cues.

Monocular Visual Depth Information

Some monocular depth cues are based on principles of geometry, others are based on conditions of atmosphere and illumination. In thinking about these various monocular cues, keep in mind that several of them were initially discovered by artists, in their attempt to represent depth pictorially. By the fifteenth century, artists had learned how to create an amazing impression of depth in their works, using just a handful of optical tricks. These artists managed to create two-dimensional representations that act upon the visual nervous system in much the same way as would the three-dimensional scenes being depicted. In developing the techniques of pictorial representation, artists actually discovered the cues of static monocular depth perception. The cues are called *static* because they are available to a stationary observer viewing a motionless scene.

STATIC CUES TO DEPTH

Interposition. When one object occludes, or obscures, part of another from view, as in Figure 7.8, the occluded object is automatically perceived as the more distant one. This

FIGURE 7.8
Interposition: When one object obscures part of another, the obscured object is perceived as the more distant one.

cue is called **interposition,** and from the standpoint of pictorial representation it is probably the most primitive. Young children often use interposition in their simple drawings, even though unable to reproduce any other pictorial depth cues. Actually, there is evidence that by 7 months of age human infants can judge relative distance solely on the basis of interposition (Yonas, 1984). The illusory figures created by subjective contours (see Figure 1.2) also demonstrate the effectiveness of interposition as a depth cue. In fact, interposition is so strong a depth cue that it can override retinal disparity when the two cues are in conflict (Kaufman, 1974). However, though a strong depth cue, interposition by itself can specify only "order information"—whether an object is nearer or more distant than another; it can provide no quantitative information about the amount by which objects are separated in depth. For that information, additional cues are required.

Size. Take a look at the series of squares in Figure 7.9. Note that the larger squares ap-

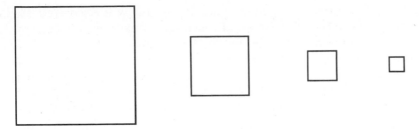

FIGURE 7.9
Size alone can influence perceived depth.

pear to be closer to you than the smaller ones. This simple demonstration indicates that size alone can influence perceived depth. Let's consider why size and distance should be related.

As the distance between you and an object varies, the size of the image of that object on your retina changes. For instance, your thumbnail viewed from arm's length casts an image on your retina that covers about three-tenths of a millimeter. As you bring your thumb closer to your face, the size of the retinal image grows. This principle is true for any object viewed from any distance. Thus if you are familiar with the

size of an object, you can judge from the size of its retinal image how far away the object is. In fact, *familiar size* has been shown to be an effective cue to distance in the absence of other information (Ittelson, 1951). But the cue of retinal image size depends crucially on knowing the correct size of the object. When you are confronted with an unfamiliar object and are provided with no clues as to its true physical size, retinal image size gives you no clear sense of the distance from you to that object. For instance, you may have trouble judging the size of the sculpture pictured in Figure 7.10 and therefore its distance from the camera. But

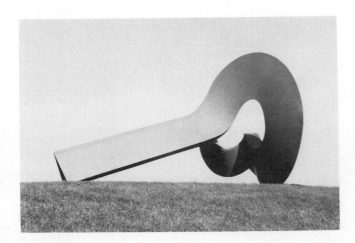

FIGURE 7.10
It is difficult to judge the size of an unfamiliar object in the absence of supporting cues.

if something familiar appears in the vicinity of that object (such as the dog in Figure 7.11), the perceived size of the unfamiliar object becomes obvious. You are also now able to judge its distance from the camera.

Interestingly, even prior knowledge about the true distance to an object may not be sufficient to support the perception of relative depth. In one study (Gruber and Dinnerstein, 1965), a person was shown a pair of squares in a lighted corridor. One square was located about 8 meters away and the other about 16 meters away. Because the farther square was physically twice as large as the nearer one, the two squares cast the same-sized images on the person's retina; but depth cues provided by the corridor and by the apparatus enabled the person to see clearly that the two squares were located at different distances. However, when the lights were extinguished, the squares (which had been outlined with luminous paint), appeared to "come together" at a common depth, completely contradicting what the person *knew* about their real locations. This demonstration underscores the point made

earlier, that depth cues are registered automatically, without conscious deliberation.

So far we have considered size as a determinant of perceived distance. But it is just as easy for perceived distance to influence apparent size. Looking at panel A of Figure 7.12, the woman on the right appears to be almost twice as big as the woman on the left. But in fact the two are really equal in size. This compelling illusion stems from the unusual construction of the room. As shown in panel B of Figure 7.12, the left corner of the room is much farther away from the observer than the right corner. The floor-to-ceiling height as well as the sizes and shapes of the windows have been distorted to make the room appear rectangular, and hence normal, when viewed from a location directly in front of the room. The back wall looks perpendicular to the line of sight, with left and right corners appearing equidistant from the viewer. Actually, though, the person on the left is farther away from the one on the right; the visual angles subtended by the two women are therefore quite different. From your perspective, this must mean

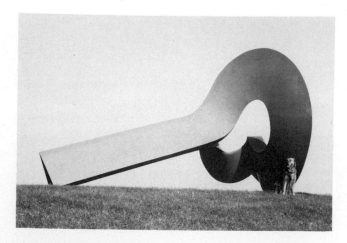

FIGURE 7.11
The size of an unfamiliar object—and therefore its distance from you—becomes obvious when you see it in the vicinity of a familiar one.

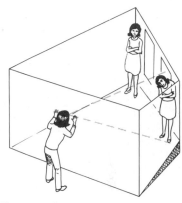

A   B

FIGURE 7.12
The Ames room: A demonstration that perceived distance influences apparent size. (Photo by Robert Berger/Science Digest © by the Hearst Corporation.)

that the woman on the right is larger, since you have been fooled into believing that the difference in visual angles is *not* due to a difference in distance. Adelbert Ames, a lawyer turned scientist, devised this clever demonstration of perceived distance's influence on apparent size; in his honor, this sort of distorted structure is called an **Ames room** (Ittelson, 1952/1968).

Besides the Ames room, there is another visual phenomenon that vividly demonstrates the interdependence of size and distance. This is the moon illusion that we mentioned in Chapter 1. You will have noticed that the moon, especially when full, appears much larger when on the horizon (see Figure 7.13) than it does when overhead at its zenith. Of course the actual size of the moon remains constant, as does its distance from the earth: the moon is 2,160 miles in diameter and 239,000 miles away. This means that regardless of its position in the sky, the full moon casts a circular image

about one-sixth of a millimeter in diameter on your retina. Why, then, does the apparent size of the moon change so strikingly?

One possible answer is that the moon's **perceived distance** varies with its heavenly

FIGURE 7.13
The moon looks larger on the horizon than higher in the sky.

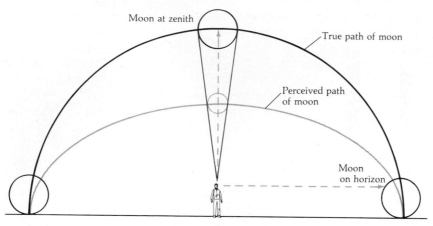

FIGURE 7.14
Explanation of the moon illusion based on perceived distance.

position. Near the horizon, where there are many depth cues, the moon seems to be farther away than when it is at its zenith. This idea is illustrated in Figure 7.14. But we know that the size of its retinal image remains constant regardless of the moon's position in the sky. This produces something of a conflict: usually, when the distance from you to a single object changes, the size of the retinal image also changes. Yet in the case of the moon, perceived distance *changes* but retinal image size *remains constant.* And the only way for image size to remain constant when distance changes is for object size to change, too. With the moon illusion, when perceived distance is great (moon on the horizon), then perceived object size must be large. But when perceived distance is reduced (moon at its zenith), perceived object size is smaller.

Support for this idea comes from some classic experiments by Lloyd Kaufman of New York University and Irvin Rock of Rutgers University (1962). They found that the normally large horizon moon shrank as soon as it was viewed through a small hole in a piece of opaque material. Looking at the moon through such a tiny hole eliminated distance cues provided by the horizon. You can easily replicate this finding by viewing the horizon moon monocularly through a small peephole made by clenching your fist. Kaufman and Rock also discovered a way to make the normally small zenith moon appear large: they had observers view the moon through an artificial horizon drawn on a large sheet of clear plastic. Thus by manipulating apparent distance, Rock and Kaufman could create the illusion or make it vanish. We should point out, however, that not everyone agrees with the theory that the moon illusion depends on perceived distance (Baird and Wagner, 1982; Baird, 1982; Iavecchia, Iavecchia, and Roscoe, 1983). Perhaps these disagreements are not surprising; after all, people have been speculating about the moon illusion for more than two thousand years.

The Ames room and the moon illusion are just two of many visual illusions involving errors in perceived distance and size. After completing the roster of monocular depth cues, we shall consider these other visual illusions in greater detail.

Perspective. The term "perspective" refers to changes in the appearance of surfaces or objects as they recede in distance away from an observer. The geometry of visual perspective was developed during the fifteenth century by Italian artists, most notably Leonardo da Vinci. Here we are concerned primarily with perspective from the perceptual, not the geometrical, standpoint, so it will not be necessary to discuss the geometry of perspective in any detail. Pirenne (1970) offers a well-illustrated account of that topic.

Let's begin with **linear perspective,** which we shall illustrate with an example. Suppose you were to look out a window at a neighboring building, as depicted in Figure 7.15A. Now imagine using a marking pen to trace the outline of the building onto the glass windowpane, being careful to hold your head still. You would be tracing the two-dimensional projection of this three-dimensional scene. The result—a perspective drawing, as it is called—would look some-thing like the outline drawing shown in Figure 7.15B. Note that the outlines of the wall of the building are drawn in such a way that the lines converge. In reality, of course, the wall's top and bottom run parallel to each other. The observer sees them as converging and draws them this way because the wall recedes in depth away from the observation point. This convergence of lines is termed "linear perspective," and when pictorially portrayed it does generate a strong impression of depth. (This technique of depicting perspective by drawing on glass was developed by Leonardo.)

As we saw in the Ames room (Figure 7.12), the impression of depth produced by linear perspective can be strong enough to cause physically similar stimuli to appear different in size. In that case, the room's distorted construction furnished perspective cues that misrepresented the actual layout of the room. Hence the sizes of the people in the room were also distorted. Figure 7.16 provides a further example of how perspective can in-

A.

B.

FIGURE 7.15
A method for generating a perspective drawing.

FIGURE 7.16
Linear perspective can cause physically identical objects to appear different in size.

fluence perceived size. By the same token, linear perspective can cause physically different stimuli to appear similar in size, as Figure 7.17 illustrates.

There is another consequence of viewing surfaces or planes that recede in depth. Most surfaces have a visible texture, such as the grain in wood or the irregularities in a sidewalk. And so long as a surface is not perpendicular to your line of sight, the density

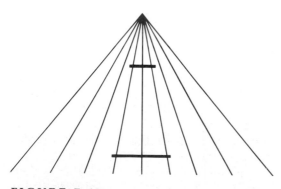

FIGURE 7.17
Linear perspective can cause objects whose sizes are genuinely different to appear identical in size.

of the surface's texture will appear to vary with distance. Examples of this are shown in Figure 7.18. This form of perspective has been called **texture gradient** by James J. Gibson, who has studied this source of depth information in the greatest detail.

According to Gibson (1950), texture gradients provide precise and unambiguous information about the distances and slants of surfaces, as well as about the sizes of objects located on those surfaces (see Figure 7.17). Gibson also proposed that abrupt changes in texture gradient signal the presence of edges or corners. In Figure 7.19, note that the texture discontinuity implies the presence of a bend, or corner, in a continuous surface.

Continuing our list of perspective cues, you've probably noticed that objects in the distance are seen less clearly than those closer to you. This effect is called **aerial perspective,** and it occurs because light is traveling through atmosphere that contains suspended particles of dirt and water. These particles scatter some of the light, thus decreasing the lightness and clarity of detail of the objects. Naturally, light reflected from more distant objects must pass through more of this atmosphere than light reflected from nearby objects. As a consequence, more distant objects appear dim and hazy (see Figure 7.20). This cue can have perceptual consequences. Upon initially encountering conditions of extremely clean air (such as in the mountains), city dwellers used to looking at the environment through congested atmosphere may seriously underestimate distances. When airline pilots are making a visual landing, they must constantly take into account the contribution of aerial perspective when judging distance because atmospheric conditions vary greatly.

Last in our list of perspective cues is the position of objects in the visual field *relative to the horizon.* As a rule, objects near the ho-

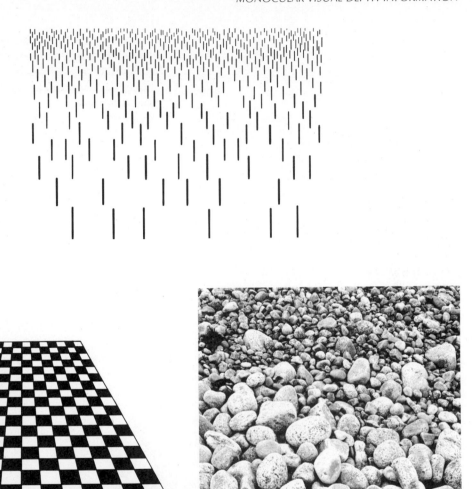

FIGURE 7.18
Texture gradients provide information about depth. (Frank Siteman/Stock, Boston.)

rizon appear more distant than objects not located near the horizon (recall the moon on the horizon). This is illustrated in Figure 7.21. Note that the tree situated closer to the horizon appears farther away than the one lower in the visual field. By the same token the airplane nearer the horizon looks more distant than the one in the upper portion of the field of view.

This completes our catalog of the static monocular cues to depth. As noted earlier, artists are able to use these cues to create an impression of three dimensionality on a flat canvas. By way of review, see if you can identify the various static depth cues as they appear in the photograph reproduced in Figure 7.22. Then look at the etching in Figure 7.23 to see the amusing outcome when

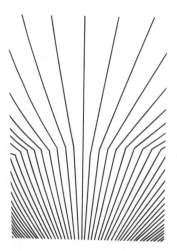

FIGURE 7.19
Texture discontinuity can signal the presence of an edge or corner.

these various cues are deliberately misused. There is, however, one monocular depth cue contained in a real scene that an artist can never capture on canvas. We shall consider that cue now.

MOTION PARALLAX

As indicated earlier, depth from static cues can be sufficiently convincing to distort the perceived size of objects. However, these distortions are experienced only so long as you are perfectly motionless. If you are allowed to move your head, the real layout of a distorted room becomes immediately apparent. Motion very quickly dispels any misperceptions that may be conveyed by

FIGURE 7.20
An example of aerial perspective. (Jan Lukas/Photo Researchers.)

FIGURE 7.21
Objects near the horizon appear more distant than those elsewhere in the field of view.

static cues. This occurs because motion introduces another, very potent source of depth information.

As you move about in the world, objects constantly shift position within your field of view. This happens whenever you are walking, traveling in a car, or simply turning your head to look at something. Next time you are a passenger in a car, notice how the world appears as you look out the window. Objects closer to you than the spot you're fixating will appear to stream past in a direction *opposite* to the car's movement. More distant objects also seem to move, but at a more gradual speed and in the *same* direction as you are traveling. This complex flow

FIGURE 7.22
Try to identify the various depth cues in this photograph, "Relative Depth" by Dennis Markley. (Courtesy of Dennis Markley.)

FIGURE 7.23

Engraving entitled "False Perspective" by William Hogarth. The artist's deliberate misuse of depth cues results in some amusing effects. (The Bettmann Archive.)

of motion, illustrated in Figure 7.24, is an example of **motion parallax**—the relative apparent motion of objects within your field of view whenever you move—which provides a very effective cue to the relative depth of objects.

To take advantage of this cue, your entire body does not have to be moving: you can perceive depth from motion parallax by moving just your head. Take a moment to demonstrate this fact to yourself. Pick out an object in front of you and look at it with one eye closed, thus eliminating the cue of retinal disparity. Now while continuing to look at this object, move your head back and forth in a sideways direction. Notice how other objects at different distances appear to move in relation to the one you are looking at. To dramatize this effect, hold your

two index fingers at different distances in front of you and perform this exercise: again with one eye closed, stare first at the nearer finger and then at the farther one, all the while moving your head back and forth. Again you will see that objects appear to move relative to your point of fixation. The direction and speed of this motion depends on the distance of those objects from the finger you are looking at.

So far we have discussed situations in which the observer moves and objects in the world remain still. However, motion parallax is also effective in the reverse situation, when a *stationary* observer views a scene in which objects themselves move. For instance, imagine looking with only one eye open at the leaves of a tree. When there is no wind, the still leaves seem to blend into

FIGURE 7.24

An illustration of a situation in which motion parallax provides potent depth information. The arrows indicate the direction of relative apparent motion.

the geometrical bases of motion parallax and binocular disparity. Figure 7.25 shows two objects, *A* and *F*, being viewed from two vantage points, *1* and *2*. Let's assume that fixation is always maintained on object *F* (for "fixation"). This means that at both vantage points the image of *F* will fall on the fovea. Because *A* is closer than *F*, the image of *A* will fall on one retinal area, *A1*, when *A* is viewed from vantage point *1*; however, when *A* is viewed from vantage point *2*, the image of *A* will fall on a different retinal area, *A2*. The distance between the retinal images produced by *A* and *F* varies from one vantage point to the other. At vantage point *1*, the retinal images are separated by the distance between *F1* and *A1*; at vantage point *2*, they are separated by a different amount, the distance between *F2* and *A2*. This variation in the retinal image distance between the images provides information about the distance between objects *A* and *F*.

a confusing array. But when stirred to life by a breeze, different groups of leaves stand out clearly in depth from one another. The movement of the leaves creates motion parallax information in the same way that movement of your head would. This creation of depth from motion has been exploited beautifully in some motion pictures. For example, many of the special effects in the *Star Wars* trilogy rely heavily on the cue of motion parallax. Myron Braunstein (1976) has described the various ways in which depth perception can be generated from displays containing movement.

Using motion parallax, observers are quite good at judging whether one object is situated in front of or behind another one. In fact relative depth judgments based on motion parallax are almost as accurate as those made using binocular disparity (Graham, 1965). This makes sense when you compare

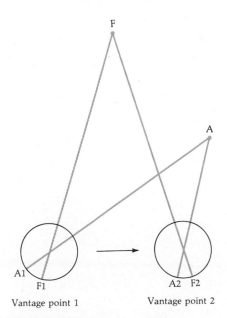

FIGURE 7.25

An illustration of the equivalence of retinal disparity and motion parallax.

There are two ways the situation shown in Figure 7.25 could arise. Vantage points *1* and *2* could represent the successive positions of a single eye as it moves from *1* to *2*. In this case, the resulting variation in retinal image distances would be called *motion parallax*. Alternatively, vantage points *1* and *2* could represent the positions of left and right eyes. In this case, the variation in retinal image distance would be called *retinal disparity*. In fact, if a single eye moves by 65 millimeters (the distance between your eyes), this movement produces a depth cue—motion parallax—that is equivalent to the cue produced by binocular viewing—retinal disparity.

There is another similarity between motion parallax and stereopsis. Recall from our discussion of random-dot stereograms how forms invisible to either eye alone could be synthesized from retinal disparity information. The same kind of synthesis of form can occur through motion parallax. In an ingenious set of experiments, Brian Rogers and

Maureen Graham (1979, 1984) of Scotland had observers view a single array of random dots with just one eye; it is important to keep in mind that their stimuli were not stereograms and that viewing was monocular. The entire display consisted of about 2,000 dots, and a subset of dots could be displaced while the rest maintained their same positions. Figure 7.26 depicts one such display. In one condition, the displacement occurred whenever just the observer's head moved. In other words, moving the head from side to side caused the predesignated subset of dots to move relative to the rest. This condition would correspond to observer-induced motion. In a second condition, the observer held still while the display itself was moved, with the predesignated region of dots moving by an amount different from the rest. Rogers and Graham found that both forms of relative motion generated a clear, immediate impression of a surface standing out in depth from its background (as in the bottom panel of Fig-

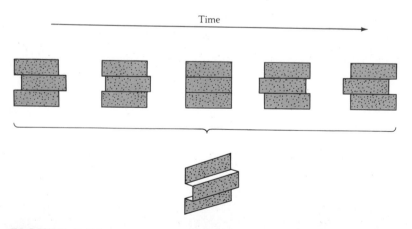

Time

FIGURE 7.26

Motion parallax, like stereopsis, can generate information about object form. The five panels in the top row depict changes over time in the position of a subset of dots in the display. These changes are produced either by the observer's head movements or by movement of the display itself. The bottom panel depicts the stable percept produced by either of these maneuvers. (Adapted from Rogers and Graham, 1979.)

ure 7.26). Moreover, so long as their heads or the display moved, observers could accurately describe the shape of this surface. But whenever both the observer's head and the display were stationary, the sensation of depth immediately vanished. Rogers and Graham's study clearly shows that motion parallax, like retinal disparity, can generate information about the shape and depth of objects, in the absence of all other cues.

We have just seen that motion of your head allows you to generate with one eye the same kind of information generated by two eyes in a stationary head. This raises an interesting question: Why is the visual system designed in such a way as to provide two equally sensitive mechanisms for seeing objects in depth, one monocular and one binocular? Wouldn't it be safer to relocate the eyes on the side of the head, thereby achieving a panoramic view of the world? The consequent loss of disparity information could be compensated for by relying on the equally effective cue of motion parallax.

The key to this puzzle may have something to do with the type of animals who possess well-developed binocular vision. As a rule, these frontal-eyed animals are predators, who rely on stealth to capture their prey. Movements of the hunter's head or body could forewarn an intended victim, thereby costing the hunter a meal. So it may have been advantageous for predators to develop the capacity for stereopsis, a quieter but equally accurate means of depth perception. For humans whose hunting is confined to the supermarket, where there is no real concern about giving away one's whereabouts, motion parallax and stereopsis provide largely redundant information.

Depth, Illusions, and Size Constancy

During our discussion of depth perception, we noted several perceptual errors that occur when people are confronted with misleading depth information. These errors involved some distortion in perceived size, such as the moon's unusually large appearance when it is on the horizon. Many other visual illusions are also characterized by misperceptions of size. Examples of two of the better-known size illusions are given in Figure 7.27. In each case, one portion of the figure appears larger than its partner, even though both are really identical in size. Almost everyone experiences these size illusions and always in the same way. For over a century psychologists have been fascinated by these illusions and have focused a great deal of research on testing various theories concerning their origins. (A good summary of these theories is Coren and Girgus, 1978). Let's consider in detail one particular

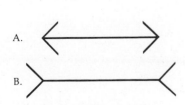

A.

B.

The Müller–Lyer illusion

The Ponzo illusion

FIGURE 7.27
Two size illusions.

theory that, although not universally accepted, has endured over the years.

The most popular theory of size illusions attributes errors in perceived size to the operation of monocular depth cues (Gregory, 1970). We'll call this the *depth theory*. Consider, for example, the left-hand illusion in Figure 7.27, the so-called *Müller-Lyer illusion*. According to the depth theory, the arrowheads on the ends of the vertical lines can be seen as angles formed by two intersecting surfaces. An example of this idea is shown in Figure 7.28. In both drawings, the vertical line represents the point of intersection, or the corner, formed by two surfaces. When the arrowheads point outward (as in A), the two surfaces are seen as slanted toward you; when they point inward (as in B), the surfaces are seen as receding away from you. Why should the "corner" formed by the receding surfaces (inward-pointing arrowheads) appear longer than the one formed by the approaching surfaces (outward-pointing arrowheads)? According to the depth theory, the answer is simple. Because of the perspective cues supplied by

the arrowheads, the receding corner appears farther away than the approaching corner. At the same time, the retinal images of the two corners are identical in size. Now there is only one way objects at *different* distances can cast images of *equal* size: the farther object must actually be larger. In the case of the two vertical lines, the height of the corner formed by the receding surfaces (inward-pointing arrowheads) would have to be longer than the height of the one that is formed by the approaching surfaces (outward-pointing arrowheads). And this is exactly how it is seen.

The same line of reasoning applies to the other size illusion illustrated in Figure 7.27, the so-called *Ponzo illusion*. In this case too, perspective cues imply that one region of the figure is located farther away than another. According to the depth theory, this distance information enters into judgments of the sizes of objects occupying these different regions. Note that the apparently larger object is situated in that portion of the figure that appears farther away.

The depth theory, then, attributes size il-

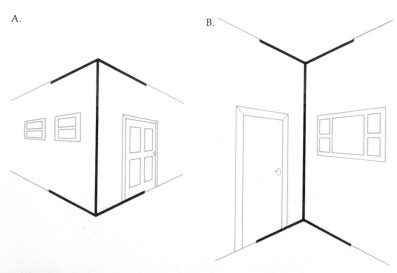

FIGURE 7.28
The Müller-Lyer illusion could arise from implied depth information.

lusions to errors in perceived distance (Gregory, 1970). The theory is based on the observation that perceived size remains constant despite differences in distance from the viewer and, hence, changes in the size of the retinal image cast. In other words, perceived size is *scaled* in terms of perceived distance, a process known as **size constancy.** We call size constancy a scaling process because one unit of measure (retinal image size) is converted, or scaled, into another (perceived size). Road maps typically include scales that transform centimeters into kilometers (or inches into miles); the visual system contains a mechanism that scales image size into object size. It's crucial that retinal image size be scaled, since the size of the image of an object depends on how far away that object is. As a result, *un*scaled *retinal* image size would be a poor index of *object* size. Without size scaling, one would always be confused about the height of people, the width of doorways, the size of cars, and so on. The fact that one rarely errs in these kinds of judgments means that the visual system utilizes depth information in making size judgments.

Just how good is the visual system at estimating the true sizes of objects? In a classic study, Holway and Boring (1941) found that an observer's accuracy at judging a circle's size was almost flawless under conditions rich with depth information. But as depth cues were progressively eliminated (for example, by requiring a person to close one eye), size judgments became increasingly dependent on retinal image size; the perceived size of the same object increased when the object was closer to the observer—a breakdown in size constancy. In an interesting extension of Holway and Boring's study, Schiffman (1967) asked at what *distance* a familiar object would appear to be if all depth cues were removed. He found that in this case, observers judged distance on the basis of their memory about the true size

of the familiar object. So in the absence of other cues, remembered size can determine perceived distance.

Size constancy seems to occur automatically. This is evidenced by the fact that people are rarely aware of the size of their retinal images. Yet with appropriate instruction people can accurately judge the retinal size of an object, in effect ignoring information about distance (Gilinsky, 1955; Epstein, 1963). You can verify this ability yourself. Hold up both thumbs with their nails facing you. Place them side by side approximately 20 centimeters (about 8 inches) from your eyes. They will look identical in size, as well they should. Next, extend one arm until that thumb is approximately 40 centimeters (about 16 inches) away, twice the distance of the other one. At first glance the two thumbs should continue to appear equivalent in size, even though the image size of the nearer one is now twice that of the farther one. This is what we mean by size constancy.

Now, while maintaining your thumbs at these different distances, move the farther one laterally until it appears just to the side of the nearer one. With one eye closed (to prevent double vision) and your head very steady, carefully compare the apparent size of the two thumbnails. Switching your attention from one to the other reveals that the closer thumbnail does look larger than the farther one. With this exercise you've managed to capture a glimpse of your retinal image. But notice how quickly this glimpse disappears once you open both eyes or move your head.

Bernice Rogowitz (1984) has described another condition where size constancy is defeated. Viewing a natural scene under stroboscopic illumination (such as that experienced at many discos), she noted that objects seemed to expand as she approached them and to shrink as she moved away from them. In the absence of continuous illumination, then, size constancy

breaks down dramatically. In a way, stroboscopic illumination is analogous to holding your head very steady with one eye
closed; both are highly artificial viewing conditions. One really has to work to
override the natural process of size constancy.

At present, it can only be guessed how
the visual system actually performs this
scaling process of size constancy. Visual
neurons, such as those described in Chapter
4, don't exhibit the properties required of
such a process. These neurons do encode
size information, by virtue of the limited
spatial extent of their receptive fields. But
this information refers to size on the retina,
not the invariant size of the object itself. If
at all involved in size perception, the activity of these neurons must somehow be integrated with depth information before size
constancy can be realized.

Of course it could be that size constancy
involves a more global, or widespread, neuronal operation that transcends individual
neurons. Eric Schwartz of New York University (1980) has proposed a theory along
these lines. His theory proposes that **cortical magnification** plays a key role in promoting size constancy. You will recall from
Chapter 4 that the retina is mapped onto the
visual cortex in a distorted manner: the
number of cortical cells devoted to a given
region of the retina varies with retinal eccentricity. The central retinal area, especially the fovea, commands a disproportionately large number of cortical cells. This
means, for instance, that a vertical line of
constant length engages fewer and fewer
cortical cells as it is imaged farther and farther into the periphery of the retina. This
relation between retinal eccentricity and
number of affected cortical cells defines cortical magnification and is illustrated in the
upper panel of Figure 7.29. If we wanted a
vertical line to engage a *constant* number of

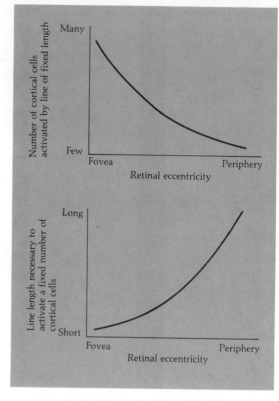

FIGURE 7.29

*Top: A line of fixed length activates fewer and
fewer cortical cells as it is imaged on more
peripheral areas of the retina. Bottom: To activate
the same number of cortical cells regardless of
where it is imaged on the retina, a line must be
made longer and longer as it is imaged farther
and farther into the peripheral retina.*

cortical cells regardless of retinal eccentricity, the length of that line would have to be
increased as eccentricity increased. This idea
is shown in the lower panel of Figure 7.29.
Putting the information in these two panels
together, for a line to engage a fixed number
of cells as it moves into the periphery, that
line must be lengthened.

Schwartz exploited the relations represented in Figure 7.29 for his novel theory of
size constancy. His arguments rest on rather

complicated geometry, but the general idea can be simply expressed. According to Schwartz, whenever you look at an object, the retinal image produced by the object's boundaries sets up a pattern of activity across your visual cortex. (You may notice a similarity between Schwartz's idea and Gestalt **isomorphism,** which we discussed in Chapter 5.) Because of the distorted way in which the retina is mapped onto the cortex, the pattern of neural activity will encompass a constant number of cortical cells, regardless of the distance between you and the object. Neural constancy, according to Schwartz, provides the actual machinery that promotes perceptual size constancy. It is important to realize that this theory stresses the contribution of the *boundaries* defining the retinal image of the object, not the total area encompassed by the image. Let's work through an example to illustrate the idea.

Imagine watching a television set with a 12-inch screen (see Figure 7.30). Suppose you begin viewing from a distance of 3 meters (about 10 feet), which means that each edge of the television screen will cast an image about 1 millimeter long on your retina. At that large viewing distance, the entire image of the telelvision screen will fall within the central portion of your retina, the portion that is magnified at the visual cortex. Now suppose you move closer to the television, say 1.5 meters (about 5 feet) away. With this move, you've doubled the length of the image of the set's vertical borders on your retina. But at the same time you've moved those borders farther into your periphery. As a result, they fall onto regions of the retina that have reduced representation in your visual cortex. As Figure 7.29 suggests, this simultaneous increase in both retinal image length and eccentricity will have an important consequence: the number of cortical cells activated by the screen's borders will be constant (as will the spatial pattern of neural activity represented by those cells). As a re-

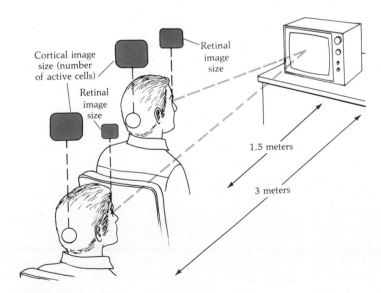

FIGURE 7.30
According to Schwartz's theory, cortical "image size" remains constant while retinal image size varies.

sult, the perceived size of the television set will be constant.

Despite its attractiveness, the current form of Schwartz's anatomical theory cannot account for all aspects of size constancy. For one thing, it is known that size constancy depends on the availability of depth cues (recall the Holway and Boring experiment). Yet Schwartz's theory does not take such cues into account. Nor is there any provision in his theory for the influence of object familiarity. But we know that size judgments are more accurate when recognizable objects are involved (Kaufman, 1974). Finally, we saw that with concentration it is possible to experience unscaled retinal image size (recall the thumbnail experiment). Hence information about retinal size must be retained in a form that is consciously accessible. In Schwartz's theory, size constancy is the unavoidable consequence of cortical anatomy—the theory contains no obvious means for temporarily defeating the process and hence experiencing size on a retinal scale. In summary, this novel theory of size constancy represents an interesting alternative to physiological models based on single-cell feature analysis (Barlow, 1972). But, in its present form, it fails to capture several important properties of size perception, as Schwartz himself (1983) and others (such as Cavanagh, 1982) have noted.

Summary and Preview

We have now examined the cues that the visual system uses to generate the experience of depth. We have emphasized that depth perception occurs automatically, with no conscious deliberation. We have also seen that depth perception influences perceived size, resulting in size constancy as well as certain illusions of size. This connection between illusion and constancy should remind you of a similar connection seen earlier, for lightness perception (Chapter 3). Although we have emphasized distance information in this chapter, the more general contribution made by depth cues should not be overlooked. As David Marr (1982) has pointed out, depth serves to define objects relative to their backgrounds—helping the viewer to distinguish those objects and appreciate their shapes. In the next chapter we take up another aspect of vision—movement—that serves the same purpose.

Chapter 8

Action and the Perception of Events

The preceding three chapters concentrated on visual experiences in a world of patterns, colors, and depth relationships. Now it's time to bring that world to life by giving objects in it the power to change and the ability to move about. As we have noted, all four of these dimensions of visual experience—pattern, color, depth, and motion—serve a common biological purpose; they all demarcate objects from their backgrounds, making those objects easier to detect and recognize. To see how this applies to motion, imagine that you're walking along in some wooded area. Suddenly a rabbit who's been sitting very still begins to scamper away from you. You realize then how inconspicuous that creature had been before it began to move.

In the example just given, motion helped you detect the presence of some creature; and moreover it helped you recognize that the creature was a rabbit. Movement, in other words, can provide information about form. This can also

be demonstrated in the laboratory, as illustrated in Figure 8.1. A wire hanger has been bent and twisted into a random three-dimensional shape. Using the arrangement shown, the bent wire casts a shadow on a piece of paper. When the wire is motionless, anyone who looks at the shadow will have no idea of the wire's twisted shape. But once the wire begins to move (rotate), its three-dimensional shape becomes obvious immediately (Wallach and O'Connell, 1953). The creation of shape from motion has since been demonstrated using more complex, electronically generated displays (Bell and Lappin, 1973; Baker and Braddick, 1982; Regan and Beverley, 1984).

Seeing an object move does more than just enhance your perception of the object's form. The ability to see motion is vital in itself. Because motion is so integral to visual experience, it is hard to imagine what seeing would be like without the experience of motion. But as a result of damage to the brain, some

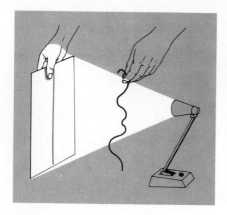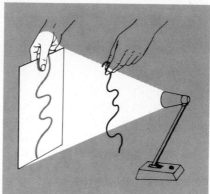

FIGURE 8.1

Movement can provide information about form.

people are deprived of the ability to see motion. To get some idea of what this would be like, consider the following description of one such person's experiences. Although her visual acuity and form perception were quite normal, she could not see movement.

She had difficulty, for example, in pouring tea or coffee into a cup because the fluid appeared to be frozen, like a glacier. In addition, she could not stop pouring at the right time since she was unable to perceive the movement in the cup (or a pot) when the fluid rose. . . . In a room where more than two other people were walking she felt very insecure and unwell, and usually left the room immediately, because "people were suddenly here or there but I have not seen them moving." . . . She could not cross the street because of her inability to judge the speed of a car, but she could identify the car itself without difficulty. "When I'm looking at the car first, it seems far away. But then, when I want to cross the road, suddenly the car is very near." (Zihl, von Cramon, and Mai, 1983, p. 315)

Obviously, being unable to see motion is frustrating and dangerous. Not only was this woman unable to see the movements of other creatures and objects, she also had difficulty seeing the consequences of her own movements and actions. Her inability to judge when enough tea had been poured is a reminder that you yourself cause many of the changes and movements that you see. Moving about among the world's objects, you see them from various perspectives. Acting on the world's objects can influence how you perceive them.

Thus while your perceptions govern your actions, your actions also influence what you perceive. We'll discuss the actions that help you explore the world in which you live. Such actions include very large movements of your body as well as very small ones. The large movements allow you to locomote about in the world; the small movements, movements of your eyes, allow you to inspect that world and search out new information. Because these actions are an integral part of visual perception, our discussion of the dynamic perceptual world has to consider what the perceiver *does* as well as what the perceiver *sees*.

What Is an Event?

Part of this chapter deals with visual events, so we had better clarify what that term means. An *event* is something that happens in both space and time. While one can talk about an object solely in terms of space—where it is or what it is—to talk about an event one needs to consider time. In fact, there are really two kinds of visual events. The simpler type involves only a change in time, not in space; the more complicated type involves changes in both time and space. Starting with the simpler type, suppose that you've managed to trap a firefly in your hand. Your closed hand will appear to emit a flickering glow as the firefly's tail blinks on and off. This simple type of visual event, involving only a change over time, is known technically as **flicker.** Box 8.1 gives some of the important findings about the way in which the human eye responds to flicker. The second, more complicated type of event is exemplified when you open your hand and see the firefly escape. This common type of event involves change not only in time but also in space. Such events constitute the various forms of visual movement that we'll be analyzing in this chapter.

BOX 8.1
Flicker

Lights that blink, flicker, or wink at you are everywhere in industrialized societies. Some of these lights—for example, the flashing lights atop a police vehicle—try to capture your attention. Others—for example, the flashing light at a railroad crossing—are designed to warn you. For a flashing light to be effective, it must flicker at a rate that can be easily seen. If it flickers too rapidly or too slowly the flicker will be imperceptible.

A lot is known about the **critical flicker frequency (CFF)**—the highest rate of flicker that can be perceived as such (Landis, 1954). When this highest frequency is exceeded, the separate flashes of light blend together to yield the perception of a light that appears to be on continuously. Under the best conditions, the human CFF is around 60 Hz. (*Hz*, short for *hertz*, is a unit of flicker rate, and is equivalent to one per second.) In fact, this is why you cannot see the flicker from a typical fluorescent lamp. Although the lamp actually does flicker on and off at a rate of 120 Hz, you can't see the flicker because its rate exceeds your CFF. However, a bee looking at the same lamp could perceive the 120-Hz flicker, since the bee's CFF is reputed to be around 300 Hz (Lythgoe, 1979).

The CFF depends on many different variables, including the light's intensity and size. In addition, CFF varies with location in the visual field. The rate of flicker of a large stimulus—such as a television set or a bank of fluorescent lights—may be too fast to be seen when you look at the stimulus directly, but may be highly visible when you look slightly away from it. You may have experienced this annoying peripheral flicker if you've been in a room where the fluorescent ceiling lights were functioning improperly.

The warning lights you encounter every day flicker at rates much lower than the CFF. Just how sensitive is the human visual system at these lower rates of flicker? Recall from Chapter 5 that human vision has an optimal spatial frequency—there is an object size that can be seen most easily. The same holds for temporal frequency—there is a rate of flicker that can be seen most easily. To determine this frequency, the intensity of a light is varied over time, usually in a sinusoidal fashion (see the insert in the figure on the next page). For various frequencies of flicker, the minimum visible fluctuation of light is assessed. At some rates, flicker can be seen even when the light's intensity fluctuates very little. At other rates, flicker can be seen only when the light's intensity fluctuates a large amount. This dependence of flicker perception on rate is

(*Continued on next page*)

shown in the main graph. The vertical axis represents "sensitivity"—how little fluctuation in intensity is needed for flicker to be detected; the horizontal axis represents the rate of flicker. Note that the visual system is most sensitive when the light flickers at around 10 Hz.

Let's continue to explore the analogy between spatial and temporal frequencies. Just as separate visual mechanisms process objects of different spatial frequencies, separate visual mechanisms process different rates of flicker. This is demonstrated by a study of flicker sensitivity in glaucoma patients (Tyler, 1981). The typical patient showed diminished sensitivity to flicker frequencies in the vicinity of 30 Hz. This impairment coexisted with normal sensitivity to other frequencies. For reasons that are not understood, the abnormal pressure within the eyeball reduces the patient's ability to perceive flicker at particular frequencies— implying that glaucoma selectively impairs neural mechanisms that process

particular rates of flicker. This impairment for particular temporal frequencies is reminiscent of selective impairment for particular spatial frequencies (discussed in Chapter 5).

We'll end this consideration of flicker with a timely warning. In some individuals, seizures can be brought on by exposure to a flickering light. Individuals

with this condition, called *photoconvulsive epilepsy*, should be aware that seizures can be triggered by a strobe light in a disco, a malfunctioning television set, or even the flashing lights of a video game (Glista, Frank, and Tracy, 1983). Obviously, such individuals would be wise to seek other, nonflickering forms of amusement.

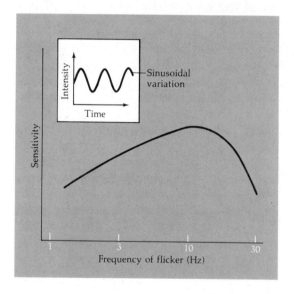

Biological Motion

Though your visual system responds to many different kinds of events, none are more important than the events that help you to distinguish animate from inanimate objects. Imagine that you're walking along the beach and you spy what looks like a clear, gooey substance. Something has probably been washed up by the tide, but you can't be sure whether it is still alive. You watch it for a while, waiting for it to move. Finally, you see some movement but not the sort that

suggests life. Instead, the gooey substance seems to be simply floating in response to the motions of incoming waves.

This seaside encounter demonstrates a couple of things. First, motion offers powerful clues about an object's biological status, whether something is living or not. The encounter is also a reminder that one kind of motion can be discriminated from another. When a creature's entire body moves en masse, the movement has a different significance than if its parts move in a certain way relative to one another.

Though you may not often examine

washed-up gooey stuff on the beach, you do regularly watch the motion of biological systems. This happens most commonly when you watch another person walk, run, or dance. The motions you see tell you much more than just whether that person is alive or not; the motions may also tell you the person's gender, perhaps even who the person is. Since this is a particularly important type of event perception, and since it provides some general lessons about motion perception, we'll begin our discussion with biological motion.

RECOGNIZING BIOLOGICAL MOTION

A friend walks across the room; what is there in her walk that allows you to recognize her just from her gait? Gunnar Johansson, at the University of Uppsala in Sweden, was the first to study this question systematically (1975). Johansson began by determining how little information is needed to recognize biological motion. Reasoning that the movement of the body's joints might convey particularly important information, Johansson attached one small light bulb to each hip, knee, ankle, shoulder, wrist, and elbow of

a person. This person was clothed entirely in black so that looking at the individual in a dark room, you would see only the small set of illuminated spots. Johansson's plan was to eliminate all the familiar, nonmotion cues that might give away the fact that the stimulus was a person.

Figure 8.2 gives you some idea of what you might have seen had you been tested by Johansson. The figure shows the lights attached to a person who is sitting quite still in a chair. The person in panel A is seated with his feet on the ground; the person in panel B is also seated, but with his legs crossed. There's really not much to give away that it's something alive you're looking at, let alone a person. The lights appear to be a random collection of spots, not unlike a constellation in the sky. Yet, Johansson found that as soon as the person began to move, viewers saw that it was a person. In other demonstrations, Johansson discovered that the same light bulbs were sufficient to reveal when a person was painting, riding a bicycle, or doing push-ups. The overall movements of the lights, and their movements relative to one another, carried this information in a most compelling way.

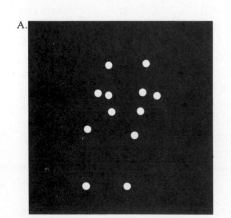 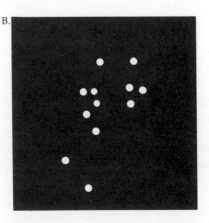

FIGURE 8.2
Each white dot is a light attached to some part of a person's body. (Drawings adapted from Johansson, 1975.)

The following is an even more impressive demonstration of the salience of biological motion. Johansson outfitted two people with light bulbs and had them dance in the dark. Figure 8.3 is a sample of frames taken from a motion picture Johansson made of the two people dancing. Since any single frame contains information only about space and none about time, examination of any one frame gives no clue as to what you're looking at. However, even the briefest section of the film, projected at the proper speed, gives an almost instantaneous impression of two people dancing. It has been found, in addition, that this minimal information enables viewers to identify the *gender* of someone walking. Viewers can recognize their own gait in such displays, as well as the gait of various friends (Cutting and Proffitt, 1981).

When people read about Johansson's demonstrations, rather than actually see them, there is a tendency to get the wrong idea. People assume that complex thought processes are required in order to resolve the complex movements of the small lights. But this assumption is wrong. Johansson's studies show that the perception of biological motion occurs automatically; people do not have to puzzle over what they are seeing. The percept is as immediate as it is in viewing any other form of motion. In fact, viewing the moving lights for just one-tenth of a second is enough to enable a person to identify familiar biological motion without having been told what to expect (Johansson, von Hofsten, and Jansson, 1980).

There's other evidence that biological motion perception does not require sophisticated thought processes—even very young infants can discriminate biological from nonbiological motion. Not only can infants tell the two types of motion apart, but they also have a distinct preference for motion that is biological in origin. Robert Fox and Cynthia McDaniel (1982) used a television screen to present two different motion patterns side by side. Infants were propped up

in front of the television screen while the biological and nonbiological motions were presented for several seconds. Following Johansson's method, each pattern consisted of several white dots against a dark background. One of the two patterns represented the joints of a human who was running; dots in the other set moved randomly in all directions. An observer sitting near the television screen noted which side of the television screen the infants preferred to look at. By 4 months of age, infants showed a clear preference for biological rather than nonbiological motion.

Fox and McDaniel were concerned that their infants might have been responding not to the biological or nonbiological character of the motion but to how random or constrained the motion was. Since arms and legs usually do not go flying in all directions, biological motion is more constrained than the random motion with which it was paired. So a second experiment was needed to verify that infants had not been responding to differences in the randomness of motion. Fox and McDaniel paired one display in which dots represented a human running in place with another display in which the same running human was presented, but upside down. Again, infants preferred the biological motion—the right-side-up human running. Though Fox and McDaniel's findings do not prove that the ability to recognize biological motion is innate (as Johansson believes), they do confirm what Johansson's work with brief exposures indicated: recognition of some forms of biological motion requires little complex intellectual processing.

SOMETHING ABOUT THE WAY YOU WALK

Now that you know how easy it is to recognize biological motion, it's natural to wonder about the basis for this ability. What information contained in these displays

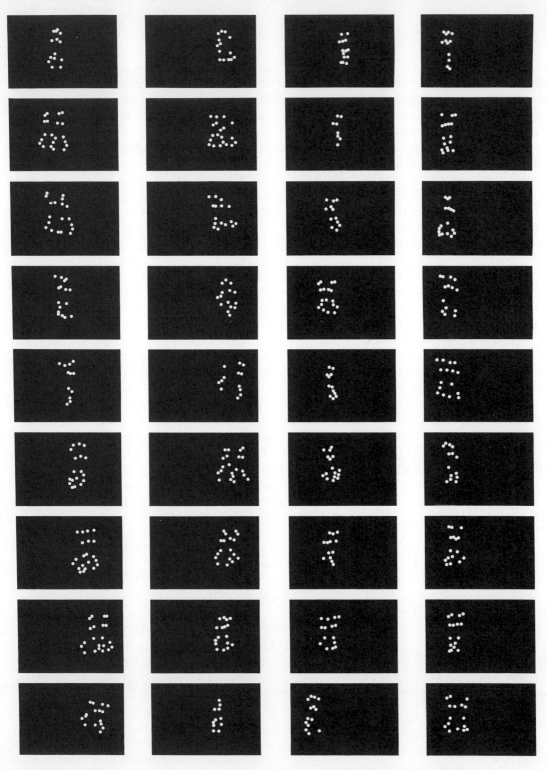

FIGURE 8.3
Frames from a movie of two dancing people with lights attached to parts of their bodies.
(Adapted from Johansson, 1975.)

makes such judgments possible? Although the answers are not known yet, one promising approach to the problem uses computer-controlled displays to isolate particular dynamic (changing) features of the gait. For example, James Cutting (1978), of Cornell University, has used computer displays of moving bright spots to simulate various types of human motion. This sort of research has enabled Cutting to identify characteristic "male" and "female" gaits. To begin, Cutting observed that the typical male adult has broader shoulders than the typical female adult, while the female's hips are broader. Because of this difference, the ratio of shoulder width to hip width is about 10 percent greater in males than in females.

But what does this have to do with gait? When you walk, your left leg and right arm swing forward together; then your right leg and left arm follow suit (see Figure 8.4). The result is a kind of oscillating, or shearing,

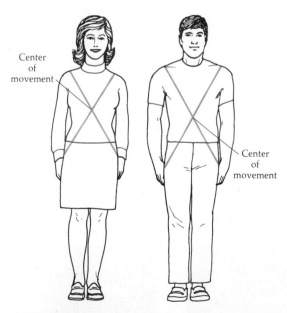

Center
of
movement

Center
of
movement

FIGURE 8.4
Males and females have different centers of movement.

motion. On each step, the body oscillates about a point that is the intersection of two lines: one connecting the left shoulder and right hip, the other connecting the right shoulder and left hip.

Recall, though, that males and females typically have different shoulder and hip widths. Consequently, as males walk, their bodies oscillate about a lower point than do the bodies of females. A computer created a display in which synthetic walkers had centers of movement calculated from the average male body or from the average female body. When viewers saw these displays, they had little trouble identifying the "gender" of the synthetic walker (Cutting, 1978). These studies presumably disclose the stimulus information utilized by the visual system to recognize biological motion (Runeson and Frykholm, 1983).

So far we've considered what happens when people see various forms of biological motion. In each case we considered the motion from the point of view of a perceiver who was stationary. But when you, as a perceiver, begin to move about, you generate motion on your own retina. This self-produced visual motion helps to guide your actions.

The Visual Guidance of Locomotion

Three centuries ago, the British philosopher George Berkeley had an intriguing idea about vision's main purpose. He wrote that vision was designed to allow animals to "foresee . . . the damage or benefit which is like to ensue, upon the application of their own bodies to this or that body which is at a distance" (Berkeley, 1709/1950, p. 39). In other words, he believed that vision keeps creatures out of trouble, which certainly is true. When you move about in the world—

walking, running, driving a car, or piloting an airplane—you'd better know *whether* you're going to collide with something, and if so, *when*. This knowledge allows you to change course, thereby avoiding harm. As Berkeley realized, vision guides movement and movement alters vision. Let's consider this interplay between vision and locomotion, starting with the visual information that allows you to steer your movements properly.

FINDING THE RIGHT DIRECTION

Most people get around easily, with a minimum number of collisions—even on sidewalks packed with people. Obviously, then, they exploit some source of information to locomote—keep on course, and, if necessary, change course appropriately. But what exactly is that source of information, and how is it used? As you move about through the world, the image on your retina changes with your movements. To take a simple example, as you move toward some stationary object, the image of that object on your retina expands. Moreover, its *rate* of expansion mirrors the rate of your approach, a point we shall detail later. James Gibson, who did im-

portant work on motion perception, pointed out that this expansion could actually guide complicated and important movements of the body and head. "To kiss someone," Gibson instructed, "magnify the face-form, if the facial expression is amiable, so as almost to fill the field of view. It is absolutely essential to keep one's eyes open so as to avoid collision. It is also wise to learn to discriminate those subtle [features] that specify amiability" (Gibson, 1979, p. 233).

Kissing isn't the only activity that produces a flow of visual information. Think about what happens when you walk toward some object such as the door to a building. To appreciate how the retinal image changes in this situation, look at Figure 8.5. Each panel in the figure represents what you might see as you move steadily toward the door. Note particularly how the view changes from one drawing to the next. Though a series of stills cannot fully capture the dynamic character of these changes, there are some important things that can be appreciated. The door you are looking at and walking toward always remains at the center of the field of view. Objects around the door—to its sides, above, and below—shift radially outward, flowing farther and farther into the periph-

FIGURE 8.5
Changes in the field of view as a person approaches a door.

ery of your visual field. The center of this flow, known as its focus, allows you to steer yourself toward the door. You will successfully reach the door by keeping the door at the center of the outward flow.

Gibson believed that people use the **focus of flow** to judge where they are going. To test this idea, he filmed the view from the cockpit of an aircraft in flight. When he showed this film to various people, they found it easy to identify the direction in which the plane was headed. Gibson believed that the focus of flow also guides other kinds of locomotion, including driving. Once a driver spots the focus of flow, he or she can steer the car by keeping the focus centered within the proper lane of the highway. In theory, the driver has only to glance at the road every now and then, relying on the stable focus to maintain course. Jokingly, Gibson complained that "when I turn around while driving our car and reply to my wife's protests that I can perfectly well see where I am going without having to look where I am going because the focus of outflow is implicit, she is not reassured" (Gibson, 1979, p. 229).

There was actually very good reason for Gibson's wife not to be reassured: he was wrong. If you shift your gaze, as Gibson apparently did while driving, the focus is *not* stable; it shifts along with your gaze. As a result, you cannot look away from the road, talk to someone along side you, and then use the center of flow to tell you in what direction you're heading. The center of flow will coincide with the direction in which you're traveling only when you're looking in that same direction.

This fact is illustrated in Figure 8.6. These pictures were made by Martin Regan and Kenneth Beverley of Dalhousie University (Regan and Beverley, 1982). Each picture is a long-duration exposure taken with the camera moving toward the woman's head. The pictures differ, though, because the camera was aimed differently for the two. To take the picture at left, the camera was aimed directly at the woman's head; to take the picture at right, the camera, though moved toward the woman's head, was aimed at the dot indicated by the arrow. The center of flow is indicated by the place where the picture is sharpest. Note that this center of

FIGURE 8.6
These two photographs illustrate how the center of flow depends on the direction of gaze.

flow differs in the two pictures, even though the camera moved straight toward the woman in both instances. In each photograph, the focus of flow reflects the direction in which the camera was aimed, rather than the direction in which it moved. The same rules hold when you substitute yourself for the camera.

But think back to the people who saw Gibson's film taken from the plane's cockpit. How *were* they able to judge the direction in which the plane was flying? They were able to do so because the camera was always aimed in the same direction the plane was headed; the focus of flow coincided with that direction. Analysis of Figure 8.6 indicates that if the camera had not been aimed straight ahead, the focus would not have coincided with the direction the plane was headed. So focus of flow is not a reliable indicator of the direction you're traveling. Fortunately, however, there is another aspect of the flow that *could* act as a beacon, keeping you on course.

Regan and Beverley (1982) found there was one property of the visual flow that always coincided with the direction a viewer was headed, regardless of where that viewer was looking. This property is related to the rate of expansion of the image. Recall that as you move toward an object, the object's image on your retina expands. Regan and Beverley noted that when a viewer approaches an object, the point where the rate of expansion is highest corresponds to the collision point.

To confirm that this source of information could actually be used, Regan and Beverley created electronic displays that simulated what a person would see while walking toward a picket fence. One display showed what the person would see if he were looking where he was going; another display showed what he would see if he were looking at some portion of the fence that was off to the side. With either display, observers could accurately identify the collision

point on the picket fence. Presumably, they were using the cue we mentioned earlier: locating the place at which the rate of expansion is most rapid.

You've just learned how visual information specifies *where* you're going. But it's equally important to know *when* you're going to arrive (or collide). Let's consider the visual information that specifies time of arrival.

JUDGING YOUR TIME OF ARRIVAL

Have you ever watched seabirds diving for food? They fly along until a fish is spotted in the water below. Then, without warning, they dive into the water at impressive speed. Usually they get their fish. The whole process is a marvel to behold, but some species of birds add one additional mystery to their performance: a split second before hitting the surface of the water, these birds fold their wings, streamlining their bodies and easing their entry into the water. Watching this performance, you'd think that somehow the bird "knew" exactly when it would hit the water. Though the bird doesn't have sophisticated navigational instruments, it performs this feat with precision and regularity (Lee and Reddish, 1981). You perform comparable, albeit less spectacular, feats whenever you walk, run, drive, or catch a ball. Let's analyze the information that enables you to do these things.

Start by considering the information that *might* be available to a creature who is approaching some stationary object in its environment. Figure 8.5 showed that as you approach an object—a door in that case— the image size of that object expands. If you are walking toward the door at a constant rate, the rate of expansion specifies the time to collision—the moment at which you will reach the door.

Suppose that at time t you're some distance, say D meters, away from the door. You probably recall formulas from physics relating the variables of time, distance, and rate. In those formulas, time is equal to distance divided by rate. So if your rate is R meters per second, and distance is D meters, then time to arrival will be D/R seconds. However, to solve this equation you must have good information about both distance and rate. How does the visual system get such information? It doesn't. Instead, as David Lee (1980) shows, it uses another, dynamic source of information about time to arrival—which makes it unnecessary to know either distance or rate.

Take a concrete example. Suppose you are 100 meters from a telephone pole when you start walking toward it at a rate of 1 meter per second. Suppose, further, that while walking, you look directly at a knothole on the pole. To simplify calculations, assume the knothole is 1 centimeter in diameter. Using simple trigonometry, we can calculate the size of the image cast by the knothole on your retina. The heavy line in Figure 8.7 portrays the results of this calculation. It will come as no surprise to you

that as you walk steadily toward the pole, the image on your retina expands, nor that because you're traveling at 1 meter per second and must cover a distance of 100 meters, you reach the pole 100 seconds after you began to walk. Note, however, that though you approach the pole at a steady rate, the image does not grow at a steady rate. Instead, its growth accelerates as you approach the pole. Hence, when you're far from the pole, its image grows slowly—signifying that you've got an appreciable time until you hit the pole. As you get very near the pole, however, the image grows rapidly—signifying an imminent collision.

This connection between imminent collision and rapid expansion of the image is not peculiar to the variables in our example; it holds in all situations. To demonstrate, the light line in Figure 8.7 summarizes calculations that would apply if you were jogging toward the telephone pole. Again, your approach begins 100 meters from the telephone pole; but because you are now jogging, not walking, your approach is five times faster than before. Since you are now going 5 meters per second, impact should be at 20 seconds—a fact confirmed by the explosion in image size at that time. The connection between imminent impact and growth in retinal image size holds for any distance, rate, or object size. It also holds for any moving creature that has its eyes open—including the diving birds with which we began this section. Incidentally, though it may take you a while to figure out your time of arrival with paper and pencil, the visual system needs only a few seconds' viewing in order to perform this computation (McLeod and Ross, 1983).

Although a cue for recognizing impending collision is available—retinal expansion—is such information *actually* used? It's hard to know, since any observer approaching an obstacle would have other cues that collision was imminent. Under these cir-

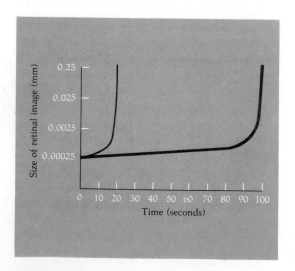

FIGURE 8.7

The retinal image size of an object expands exponentially as you walk (heavy line) or jog (light line) toward that object.

cumstances, it is impossible to specify what role retinal image expansion plays. Researchers can, however, find out whether retinal image expansion can be detected. To do this, the observer sits still and looks at displays that simulate approaching, or *looming*, objects. One such display and its behavioral effects are shown in Figure 8.8. While presenting this display, the researcher notes whether the subject responds to the simulated collision as it would to a genuine impending collision—by ducking or otherwise trying to avoid the "collision." Animals as diverse as fiddler crabs, chicks, and monkeys, as well as human infants, all try to avoid looming patterns (Schiff, 1965). This is true even for newborn infants who have never before encountered a looming stimulus. Apparently, learning plays very little role in this behavior.

What, though, is the physiological basis for these powerful, and probably innate, responses to looming? One possible candidate has been described by Martin Regan and Max Cynader. They recorded the responses of cells in the visual cortex of a cat while that animal viewed various patterns on a television screen. Of course, each neuron responded only when the pattern was displayed within the cell's receptive field. For our purposes, the most interesting neurons were those that responded strongly only to stimuli that expanded over time (Regan and Cynader, 1979). For example, if the pattern within its receptive field was a square, such a neuron would respond strongly only if the square's opposite sides were moving symmetrically away from each other—expanding (as in Figure 8.8). If the edges of the square were unchanging, the neuron would remain silent. Such neurons could signal the presence of a looming object.

Using perceptual techniques, Regan has collected evidence that these so-called **looming detectors** (or size-change detectors) exist also in the human visual system. One study made use of selective adaptation, a procedure discussed in Chapter 4. In that study, Regan and Beverley (1978) used test targets much like those used to stimulate looming-detector neurons in the cat. First, Regan and Beverley determined how sensitive an observer was to changing visual size. Using a specially modified television set, they presented a square that alternately grew and shrank. When the size of the square changed very little, people could not detect the change at all. Regan and Beverley took

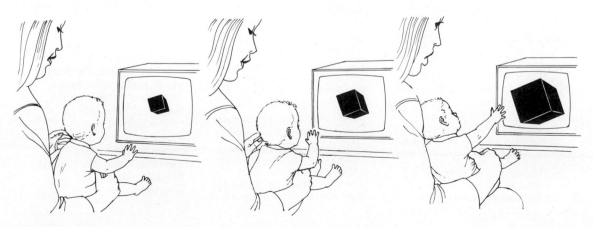

FIGURE 8.8
Most animals, including human infants, will try to avoid a looming stimulus.

advantage of this limitation to measure the threshold for changing size—the smallest change in size that could be seen. Once this threshold had been determined, the investigators proceeded to the selective adaptation phase of their experiment. Here a viewer would watch a square undergoing a large, obvious change in size—alternately growing and then shrinking. After several minutes of this exposure, Regan and Beverley remeasured the threshold for size change.

Prolonged exposure to the powerful size change made small size changes essentially impossible to see. However, this form of adaptation had no effect on the visibility of squares of constant size, including squares that moved to and fro across the field. The selectivity of this adaptation led Regan and Beverley to conclude that they had isolated detectors specific for signaling size changes.

Size-change detectors could signal a stationary observer that some object was ap-

BOX 8.2
Not Watching Where You're Going

Although vision is important for locomotion, you probably know from your own experience that locomotion can occur in the absence of vision. If you close your eyes, you can walk around with fair safety, at least for several seconds. Also, if you want to keep track of some moving object you don't have to keep your eyes fixed continuously on that object; visually sampling the object's trajectory every half second or so allows fairly accurate tracking (Thomson, 1980). Moreover, if you take a quick look at the objects on your desk, you can then close your eyes and reach fairly accurately for any one of them. You'll be able to bring your hand close to the position you had intended. But small errors will creep in during the final moments of actually trying to grasp the object; here vision seems most important.

This separation between the initial, large movements of the hand and the final, smaller

ones shows up dramatically in patients with an interesting neurological syndrome called **optic ataxia** ("ataxia" designates a disorder of movement). A neurologist, Antonio Damasio, and a neuropsychologist, Arthur Benton, have given a particularly detailed description of a patient with this disorder (Damasio and Benton, 1979). As a result of a suicide attempt, their patient had suffered localized brain lesions. One affected area, immediately in front of the visual cortex, is thought to integrate *visual* information about the hands and arms with *proprioceptive* information about the hands and arms. (**Proprioception** is the sense by which you can *feel* where your limbs are.) When the patient's eyes were open, she had great difficulty reaching for objects—a cigarette or ashtray might be missed by several inches. Her arm would begin to go in the right direction; but during the

final part of the reach, the arm and hand would go astray. She then had to grope about for the object as though she were blind.

Her difficulties with visually guided reaching were not caused by impairment of the sense of touch: with her eyes closed, she had no trouble buttoning or unbuttoning garments, or pointing to some part of her body. The impairments were also not caused by diminished vision. In fact, her visual acuity was quite normal. Moreover, she had no trouble walking with her eyes open. Her impairment seemed to be limited to fine hand movements performed under visual guidance. This rare disorder is a reminder that vision normally plays a crucial role in guiding one's movements; it is also a reminder that a complete theory of vision must include the action that vision makes possible.

proaching. Such detectors could also signal a moving observer that he or she was approaching some stationary object. In other words, such detectors could help to guide locomotion visually. (Box 8.2 discusses locomotion in the absence of vision.) Regan and his colleagues proposed that size-change detectors could also play a role in a pilot's control of an airplane. According to this proposal, pilots with particularly sensitive size-change detectors should be better able to judge their approach to the runway and should, therefore, execute smoother landings.

Regan and his associates put this proposal to a strong test in studies using U.S. Air Force pilots (Kruk et al., 1981; Kruk and Regan, 1983). First they used a cockpit simulator to test the pilots' ability to land an airplane. For each simulated landing, the researchers determined the number of corrective maneuvers a pilot had to make. This provided a quantitative index of the landing's smoothness—the fewer corrections required, the smoother the landing. They then tested the pilots' ability to detect changing size. In this test, the pilot viewed a television display of a square undergoing unpredictable changes in size. The pilot used a "joystick" (like those in arcade and home video games) to compensate for the changing size—movement of the joystick was electronically subtracted from the electrical signal that controlled the square's size. Presumably, someone very sensitive to changing size would quickly spot even the smallest change in size and null that change using the joystick. As these investigators expected, a pilot's sensitivity to changing size was strongly correlated with his landing skill. Keep these results in mind the next time a plane you're on makes an erratic landing: be charitable, and chalk up the rough landing to the pilot's subnormal sensitivity to changing size.

Eye Movements: Their Aims and Effects

There's no doubt that vision helps to control your exploration of the world around you. We've already discussed how vision guides one particular form of exploration, locomotion. Now it's time to discuss visual explorations that are made possible by small, rapid movements of the eye, rather than by larger, slower movements of limbs and the entire body.

We'll be dealing with three different kinds of eye movements. To anticipate, one type is responsible for shifting your gaze rapidly from one object to another. Such eye movements include the ones you're making right now as you read this book. A second, slower type of eye movement allows you to track a moving target—such as a golf ball that's just been putted toward the hole. Finally, a third type helps keep your eyes fixed on an object even when your head and body are moving. You can experience this last type of movement by looking at the number at the top of this page while moving your head slowly back and forth. We separate these three types of eye movements because each serves a distinct purpose and each depends on somewhat distinct neural circuits in the brain (Robinson, 1981).

Although eye movements are small and relatively fast, they play a very important role in vision (as Box 8.3 shows). To understand this role you must consider three major types of eye movements—saccades, pursuit movements, and vestibular movements.

ACQUIRING THE TARGET

Consider an unpleasant situation that you may have experienced. (We've selected this situation because it is common and also because it involves all three of the types of eye movements just mentioned.) Imagine that

BOX 8.3
No Movements, No Seeing

As you experienced for yourself in Chapter 2, your eyes are always moving. These involuntary movements are crucial for vision. To see just how important they are, consider what happens when their contribution is eliminated. This situation can be achieved by means of special optical devices that eliminate all motions of the retinal image. With these **stabilized retinal images,** objects appear to fade and, in some cases, disappear entirely (Pritchard, 1961). Such fading can also be produced by an even more drastic technique—immobilization of the eye by means of a paralyzing drug such as curare (Stevens et al., 1976).

You don't have to paralyze your eyes in order to see some of these visual consequences. Just fixate the small dot in the center of the large fuzzy bar in the photograph below. If your fixation is very steady, within 10 seconds or so the bar will fade from view. When it does fade, merely shift your gaze slightly to one side and the bar will pop back into view. Once again look at the bar until it fades. Now rather than shifting your gaze, blink your eyes once or twice. This too will restore the bar to full visibility. What do these two situations— shifting your gaze and blinking your eyes—have in common? Each of them produces a brief change in retinal stimulation. Such brief changes enhance the visibility of large, low-contrast objects (Robson, 1966). Fortunately you don't have to shift your gaze or blink your eyes consciously to enjoy this beneficial effect; the normal involuntary movements of the eyes take care of this for you.

while reading, you suddenly spot out of the corner of your eye something scurrying across the floor. Your eyes swing rapidly away from what you've been reading, toward the scurrying thing. This kind of high-speed eye movement is designed to shift the image of some interesting object (the scurrying thing) from the periphery of the retina (where resolution is poor) to the fovea (where resolution is good). About one-fifth of a second after spotting the creature, the eyes begin to move. Almost instantly, they reach a very high speed of movement (achieving velocities of almost 20 centimeters per second). Then, usually less than one-tenth of a second after they started to move, the eyes screech to a halt.

When the eyes move about in this way, they do so in abrupt jerks; as a result, eye movements of this type are called **saccades** (from the French verb *saccader,* meaning "to jerk"). The eye does not jerk, or saccade, only when it needs to fixate some object far out in the periphery. Anytime you shift your gaze from one object to another, your eye executes these jerky movements. For example, while you read this page your eyes are saccading from word to word, four or five times each second. Because you shift your gaze thousands of times each hour, saccades can certainly lay claim to being your most commonly used instrument for visual exploration. Since you need to make so many saccades, it is fortunate that the eye muscles responsible for these saccades never become fatigued (Fuchs and Binder, 1983).

There are some peculiar things, though, about this instrument of exploration. For one thing, it is usually invisible to the explorer. Stand in front of a mirror and watch the reflection of your eyes as you make saccades voluntarily; allow your eyes to jump back and forth between two points several inches apart. Though you know that your eyes have moved, you never actually see that movement. This is a puzzle. Furthermore, during the saccade you don't experience blurred vision. Yet if you took a photograph with a camera that moved at the same rate your eyes moved, you'd get a very blurred, low-contrast picture (see Figure 8.9). Why, then, do you not experience impaired vision each time you execute a saccade?

Perhaps the retinal image moves so fast that the motion can't even be perceived. After all, there is a *lower* threshold, a minimum velocity below which motion cannot be seen (Bonnet, 1982). For example, you cannot actually see the movement of a clock's minute hand even though you know that it's moving. Perhaps, then, there is also an *upper* threshold, a maximum velocity above which you can't see motion. Several people have suggested that such an upper threshold is responsible for limiting the ability to see the blur and motion accompanying saccades (see Burr and Ross, 1982, for a review).

To test this suggestion, you'd have to move some object at a rate equal to the rate at which the eye would sweep across that object during a saccade. Can an observer see an object moving at this rate? To make sure that motion was being seen, you might ask the observer to identify the direction in which the object moved. It turns out that the ability to see the moving object depends on its size and contrast. Rapidly moving objects of low contrast are impossible to see. So are small objects, regardless of their contrast. However, large, rapidly moving objects can be seen if their contrast is sufficiently great (Burr and Ross, 1982). So rapid

FIGURE 8.9
Moving a camera while the shutter is open produces a blurred picture.

movement does not in itself preclude vision.

Thus failure to see blur during a saccade cannot be due just to the rapid movement of the retinal image. Many other explanations have been offered for the omission of visual information during a saccade, including the possibility that the visual system is temporarily inactivated. But it now seems likely that **visual masking** is the major cause of saccadic omission.

Visual masking is said to occur when one stimulus reduces the visibility of another (Felsten and Wasserman, 1980). Any time two stimuli occur close together in time and are near one another in space, there is opportunity for masking interference between them (see Fox, 1978). Ordinarily, masking is studied in settings that do not involve saccades or other types of eye movements. However, visual masking during saccades may be occurring every second of your life, so it seems worthwhile to spend a few moments describing what is known about masking; then you'll be able to see how it relates to saccadic omission.

Suppose that you measure a person's threshold for seeing a brief, dim spot of light. The threshold is defined as the minimum amount of light that just permits the test spot to be seen. (By the way, such testing is done with a nonmoving eye.) The threshold is then remeasured while a larger, more intense spot is flashed immediately adjacent to the test spot and immediately *following* it in time. The threshold for seeing the first, small spot would now be higher than it was originally—the small spot would have to be more intense in order to be seen. This elevation in threshold reflects the masking influence of the larger, later stimulus, which has interfered with the perception of the first stimulus. This is known as *backward masking*, since the interference works backward in time. There is an analogous form of masking in which the more powerful masking stimulus is presented before the weaker test stimulus. This kind of masking, as you might expect, is called *forward masking*.

Ethel Matin, of Long Island University, has pointed out that in normal viewing environments each saccade produces the spatial and temporal conditions that should lead to destructive (masking) interactions (Matin, 1974). For instance, when you shift your gaze to look at a target, the sharp image of whatever you looked at before and after the saccade could mask the blurred image that was produced during the saccade. This is just a conjecture. An actual demonstration of masking's contribution to saccadic omission comes from a study by Fergus Campbell and Robert Wurtz (1978).

These investigators believed that in a well-lit environment, the retinal displacement of highly visible targets would invariably lead to the sort of masking that Matin had speculated about. According to this belief, if the environment were dark *except* when you were making an eye movement, masking could not occur because there would be no strong masking stimulus available. As a result, you should be able to see blur caused by a saccade. To test this possibility, Campbell and Wurtz used a laboratory darkened so that an observer could see only two small, red lights. The observer made a saccade from one light to the other.

Using an eye position recorder, Campbell and Wurtz were able to recognize whenever the observer initiated a saccade. The signal from the eye position recorder triggered a brief flash from a strobe light. This arrangement permitted the observer to see the room *only* during a saccade, thus minimizing masking before and after the saccade. During each saccade, observers saw that the room did indeed appear blurred, unlike the way it appeared on occasions when the strobe light was flashed while the eyes were still. This suggests that saccadic omission does indeed result from visual masking.

Incidentally, you don't need eye position recorders and strobe lights to experience at least some of what Campbell and Wurtz's observers saw. Instead, you can use a trick developed in a very early study of saccadic omission (Dodge, 1900). You'll need a small desk lamp, a piece of cardboard (about one foot square) and a room that you can darken. In the center of the cardboard cut a narrow slit about one-sixteenth of an inch wide and one inch long. With the slit oriented vertically, hold the cardboard close to your eye (see Figure 8.10). Position the slit so that when you look straight ahead in the now darkened room, you can see the light bulb. (The cardboard should be large enough so that when you look off to the side, you cannot see the bulb.) Now looking several inches to the slit's left, make a saccade large enough to carry your eye several inches to the slit's right. As your pupil swings past the slit, your eye will be momentarily illuminated by light from the bulb. You should be able to see a blurred image of the bulb, an image that would otherwise be obscured by saccadic omission. You can extend this basic observation in various ways, including repeating it with very bright room lights on. We won't tell you what will happen, since you should be able to predict that for yourself.

To sum up, saccadic omission normally works to preserve the appearance of a clear, stable, and continuous visual world, uninterrupted by saccadic blur. A similar function is served by the inability to experience the interruptions of vision that accompany blinks of the eyelid (see Chapter 2). Working together, these two forms of suppression promote the perception of a continuous world in the face of a retinal image that is distinctly intermittent and periodically blurred.

Now that you understand something about saccadic eye movements, we can return once more to the creature we left scurrying across the floor. You visually captured that creature—acquired the target—by making a saccade, but the creature is still moving, so you've now got a different problem—how to *keep* your eyes on it.

STAYING ON TARGET

Often, a saccade serves to bring the image of an object onto the observer's fovea. But if that object happens to be moving, the observer's eyes must track the object in order to keep the image on the fovea. To pursue a moving target, the eyes behave very differently from the way they do when they make a saccade: during pursuit they move smoothly, instead of with abrupt stops and starts. To guide pursuit movements by the eye, the brain must have information about the object's velocity and direction—information that may be provided by neurons that code the direction and velocity of moving objects (recall Chapter 4). With this information, the brain can send signals to the

FIGURE 8.10
Setup for experiencing the blur normally obscured by saccadic omission (see the text for details).

extraocular muscles for guidance of pursuit eye movements.

Unlike saccades, pursuit movements are not ballistic; the signals being sent to the extraocular muscles are constantly being updated and revised, thereby altering the speed and direction of the pursuit movements. Accurate pursuit is important; only if the eye's movements match some object's movement will the image of that object be relatively stationary on the retina—which will have the beneficial consequence of keeping the object sharply imaged on the fovea. If the pursuit is not accurate, the image will be smeared. But how well do pursuit movements actually match the movement of the object the eyes are pursuing? The answer depends on the speed of the moving target that the eyes have to follow (Murphy, 1978). When targets move slowly (less than one-third millimeter on the retina per second), eye movements match target movements almost perfectly. However, at higher target speeds, the eyes have increasing difficulty keeping up with target movement. This difficulty causes the target's image to slip on the retina.

Dynamic Visual Acuity. The eyes' inability to pursue rapidly moving targets helps to explain a puzzle. It has been known for quite a while that visual acuity for a *moving target* gets worse as the target moves faster. (Acuity measured with moving targets is termed **dynamic visual acuity,** to distinguish it from acuity measured with static targets.) Dynamic acuity is quite distinct from static acuity. For example, two people can have identical static acuities but one person may have dynamic acuity that is three or four times better than the other person's.

Although all early studies agreed that dynamic acuity is poorer than static acuity, they disagreed about the source of that difference. Some studies suggested that dynamic acuity is poorer simply because the eye (in attempting to pursue a target) is moving and that the eye's movement per se diminishes acuity. According to this view, no matter how well the eyes keep up with the target, dynamic acuity will still be impaired. We know now, however, that dynamic visual acuity is poorer than static not because the eyes move but because the eyes often fail to keep up with the moving target, thus producing retinal image slip. Murphy (1978) found that when the eyes do manage to keep up with the moving target, visual resolution is not impaired at all.

Murphy also found that dynamic visual acuity can be improved by practice. One of his observers showed a substantial improvement in her ability to pursue a moving target. As a consequence, the slippage of her retinal image decreased and her visual resolution improved.

With practice, dynamic acuity improves more in some observers than it does in others (Ludvigh and Miller, 1958). Since most studies of dynamic acuity have not assessed pursuit eye movements directly, we can only speculate that those who improve in dynamic acuity also improve in the accuracy of their pursuit eye movements. The effects of learning on eye movements are discussed further in Box 8.4.

It is not known whether individual differences in dynamic acuity are entirely a matter of practice. But whatever their origins, these individual differences can be quite important. Here's what we have in mind. One of the greatest baseball players who ever lived, Ted Williams, attributed part of his batting skill to his ability to see a rapidly moving baseball clearly. In fact, Williams claimed to be able to read the writing on a baseball as it hurtled toward him at better than 90 miles per hour. If true, this would be dynamic acuity of a remarkable order. Whether or not Williams's claim is true, the ability to track a moving ball certainly must be crucial for good performance in such

BOX 8.4
Learning to Move Your Eyes

The ability to move the eyes is one skill that seems to require very little practice—even newborn babies do a pretty good job of it (Wertheimer, 1961). But recent studies suggest that eye movements, like other skills, can improve with practice.

To see an object's details you must fixate the object. Otherwise, it will not be imaged on that portion of the retina where vision is sharpest. When a bright and clear fixation point is available, a young adult can fixate very well. Over several seconds, the image of a fixated point does move about on the retina, but these movements are extremely small. To what extent is this excellent control of the eyes a learned skill?

To answer this question, Eileen Kowler and Albert Martins (1982) studied eye movements and fixation stability in two cooperative children about 5 years old. In contrast to adults, the children had trouble maintaining steady fixation. During a few seconds of concerted fixation, the children's eyes jumped around, scanning an area one hundred times larger than an adult's eyes would.

This relative instability of gaze is not the only characteristic that distinguishes children's eye movements from those of adults—children's *pursuit* movements are also immature. In fact, extremely young infants can't pursue a moving target smoothly at all. Instead, their eyes try to keep up with the target by means of a series of saccades. Infants don't pursue smoothly in an adult fashion until they get to be 10 to 12 weeks old (Aslin, 1981).

Even after infants acquire the ability to pursue objects smoothly, their pursuit may still lack one important feature—the ability to anticipate. When changes in object movement are predictable, a practiced pursuit system doesn't wait for the change to happen before responding to that change. If the pursuit system did wait, neural and mechanical delays would cause the eye to lag behind the change and thereby lose the object. It's easy to demonstrate pursuit's knack for anticipating. Tie your room key to the end of a piece of string 18 inches (about 45 centimeters) long. While you swing the key back and forth like a pendulum, have a friend follow the key with her eyes. At first, each time the key changes direction, her eyes will lag slightly behind. After a few seconds, though, these pursuit eye movements, anticipating the change in direction, will move in perfect synchrony with the key.

If you were to repeat this experiment with a young child, the result would be different. According to Kowler and Martins (1982), the child's pursuit movements would never anticipate the change in direction; as a result, the image of the moving target would slip off the fovea after each change in direction, requiring one-fifth of a second to catch up again.

No one knows why children's eye movements are not like those of adults. Kowler and Martins suspect that children simply have not had an opportunity to learn efficient eye movement skills. Perhaps, as these investigators propose, adults develop their repertoire of eye movement skills over years of reading, typing, and playing various sports. According to this view, moving your eyes is just like any other skill. Though some eye movements come naturally, if you're going to use eye movements effectively to explore your world, practice is a must.

sports as baseball, cricket, tennis, football, and soccer. In fact, players are constantly being exhorted to keep their eye on the ball.

The connection between dynamic visual acuity and the quality of pursuit eye movements may explain another fascinating finding. Horner (1982) measured dynamic visual acuity in sixty-five college students, some of whom were members of the college baseball team. On average, the baseball players had considerably better dynamic acuity than the rest of the students. In addition, the better hitters among the players had better dynamic acuity. The connection between batting skill and dynamic acuity probably means that better hitters, like Ted Williams, have better pursuit eye movements. We're not saying that with practice anyone could hit as well as Williams; still, it does seem promising to try to improve athletes' pursuit eye movements.

Return one more time to the situation where you were sitting and reading when you spotted a creature scurrying across the floor. We've discussed how first you fixate it and then track it visually as the creature scurries across the floor. Now suppose you want to get up and chase it. What new problems would this create for your visual system?

VESTIBULAR EYE MOVEMENTS

Whenever your head moves, your eyes must make compensatory movements to enable you to maintain the fixation of some object. It's easy to see these compensatory eye movements. While a friend is standing directly in front of you, have him look at your nose. Now ask your friend to rotate his head

back and forth, while keeping his eyes fixed directly on your nose. During the course of all these goings on, note the position of his eyes. As illustrated in Figure 8.11, when his head is turned directly toward you, the eyes are centered in their sockets; when his head rotates toward his left, his eyes rotate rightward; when his head rotates rightward, his eyes compensate by rotating leftward. One can, of course, suppress compensatory eye movements by moving the head *and* the eyes in the same direction.

When your friend rotated his head, the rotation was sensed by structures within the **vestibule** (a chamber inside the ear). Signals from this vestibular system travel to the brainstem, which ultimately relays them to the extraocular muscles, causing compensatory eye movements (Parker, 1980). These are called **vestibular eye movements** in recognition of the anatomical site at which head movements are analyzed. Like many other functions associated with vision, vestibular eye movements are so rapid, automatic, and

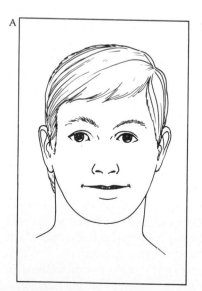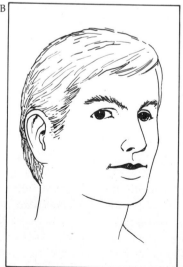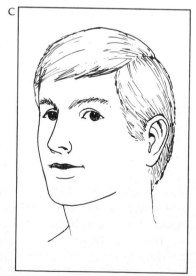

FIGURE 8.11
Your eyes move to compensate for head movements.

accurate that one virtually never notices them. Not until the vestibular mechanism fails does one become aware of how valuable they are, as the following case illustrates.

Some antibiotics have a particular affinity for the vestibular structures as well as for adjacent portions of the ear (mentioned in Chapter 9). Too heavy a dose of these antibiotics can temporarily destroy certain structures in the vestibular mechanism. A physician described his own experiences after a dose of streptomycin had rendered his vestibular mechanism inoperative. Under these conditions, no eye movements were generated to compensate for the physician's head movements. For example, when he walked about, his eyes jiggled, so that he could not read signs or recognize the faces of his friends. Every head movement, even the very smallest, disturbed his vision. When he sat perfectly still and tried to read, each tiny pulse beat in his head made the letters on the page jump about and blur (Steinman, 1976; see also Walker, 1984).

There's another situation in which vestibular eye movements can spell trouble: when you try on someone else's glasses. When you do, the glasses may cause not only blurred vision but also dizziness and, in extreme cases, nausea. The dizziness is caused by conflict between the vestibular and visual systems. There is an explanation. Suppose you are emmetropic (see Chapter 2) and thus do not need glasses, but you have borrowed some from a friend who has strong glasses. When you put them on, you notice immediately that everything appears blurred. Moreover, when you move your head the visual world appears to move. This comes about because normal compensatory eye movements produce abnormal amounts of retinal image motion, causing the world to appear to move—a disconcerting and dizzying experience.

The same kind of unpleasant and dis-orienting experience occurs when you get a new prescription for glasses. For a while, each time you move your head, the resulting vestibular eye movements are inappropriate for your new prescription. This is particularly disconcerting when there is a huge change in the prescription, such as when someone has had a cataract operation and must wear very strong lenses. In that circumstance, many people complain that when they first put their glasses on, they get dizzy when they move their heads. Fortunately, though, the vestibular system is adaptable. Within minutes, the compensatory eye movements change appropriately (Steinman, Cushman, and Martins, 1982; Collewijn, Martins, and Steinman, 1983); the movement of the retinal image is reduced, and the visual world appears stable once again. This adaptation is fortunate because otherwise no one would ever dare to get a new prescription for eyeglasses. Don't think, though, that the capacity for speedy adaptation evolved simply so that you can change your spectacles. Instead, it seems likely that this capacity evolved to compensate for growth, degeneration, or disease within the oculomotor system (Collewijn, Martins, and Steinman, 1983).

We've just discussed an unusual interaction between vision and the vestibular system, namely what happens when there's a mismatch between compensatory eye movements and movements of the retinal image. Several other kinds of unusual interactions between vision and the vestibular system are discussed by Dichgans and Brandt (1978). Though many visual-vestibular interactions promote an illusion of self-motion, this illusion can also occur under other conditions, as the following section illustrates.

ILLUSIONS OF SELF-MOTION

You are sitting in a train, next to a window. The train is waiting in the station and you are reading a newspaper. Suddenly another train moves past yours, and while it is passing, you perceive that it's *your* train that's moving. Or you are sitting in the first row of a theater that's showing a movie on a very wide screen. Even though you know better, some of the movements on the screen make you feel that *you* are moving. You feel foolish when you grab the seat to hold yourself down; you don't feel so foolish, though, when you notice that everybody around you has done exactly the same thing.

Illusions of self-motion, like the two just described, have been studied for more than a century, since Ernst Mach did the first work on them in 1875. Though these powerful illusions take many different forms, they usually depend on visual movement in the periphery of an observer's field. Before the invention of trains and wide-screen movies, movement of large expanses of the visual field occurred only when the observer moved. When motion occurs in the peripheral field of a stationary observer, the brain mistakenly attributes that visual motion to the self-produced movement of the observer's own body. This misattribution is so compelling that it can knock people out of their chairs or cause them to fall down as they try to compensate for the illusion.

Incidentally, the illusion of self-motion can be produced fairly easily, without such complex stimuli as trains or wide movie screens. Johansson (1977) found that some observers experienced self-motion when just a single bright dot moved up or down in the periphery of their visual fields. Johansson termed this the "elevator illusion," since observers felt they were standing in a moving elevator. The same bright dot that provoked the elevator illusion in the periphery produced no such illusion when it was presented in the field's center. Since the periphery of the visual field seems to play a special role in the perception of motion, we'll expand a bit on that role.

Two Visual Systems

CENTRAL VISION AND PERIPHERAL VISION

The center of your visual field, the area imaged on and around the fovea, constitutes only about 5 percent of what you can see at any one moment; simple subtraction indicates that the rest of the field, the periphery, accounts for 95 percent. Given this fact, it is surprising that most of what is known about visual function concerns the central 5 percent of the field; very little is known about the remaining 95 percent, except for vague ideas as to its importance. There are many reasons for distinguishing between center and periphery. As you learned in Chapter 3, their acuities differ; but center and periphery also differ in another way: in their responses to motion. As researchers are beginning to appreciate, this latter difference can have important consequences for safety, as we'll now explain.

Over the past hundred years or so, several different researchers (for example, Campbell and Maffei, 1981) have reported that the apparent speed of a target changes depending on where in the field it appears. You can try this for yourself. Look directly at the second hand of a clock and note its speed. Now look away from the clock so that the second hand is just barely visible in the periphery of your visual field. The second hand will appear to move more slowly. This means that the periphery and the center of vision give conflicting information about an object's speed. As people drive, both central and peripheral regions are usually being stimulated, and people's judgment of how fast they are traveling is a mixture of information from both regions. However, when visibility is reduced by fog or decreased illumination, the contribution of central vision is reduced and the judgment of speed depends primarily on peripheral vision. Under these conditions, the apparent speed of objects will be underestimated, since objects seen peripherally appear to move more slowly.

Consider the impact that fog can have on another form of travel, flying. Under conditions of good visibility, the pilot's sight of the horizon guides him through complex maneuvers. For example, when the aircraft is being banked for a turn, the image of the horizon moves appropriately. But when flying through dense fog or clouds, the pilot cannot see the horizon; instead he must rely on the plane's instruments and the responses of his own vestibular (balance) sense. This inability to see the horizon creates a conflict. When the pilot banks the plane to start a turn, the plane's instruments and the pilot's vestibular sense confirm the maneuver, but the pilot's vision denies it. The pilot's *visual* world (limited by fog or clouds to the inside of the cockpit) seems unchanged during the maneuver. Every contour in the pilot's visual field—his own knees, the edge of the instrument panel, the cockpit itself—suggest that the plane has *not* banked. This conflict between vision and vestibular information can so disorient novice pilots that they may assume their instruments are broken. Naturally, this erroneous assumption is extremely dangerous. But the dangerous disorientation can be overcome quite simply. Recent research has developed an unobtrusive artificial horizon that can be presented in the pilot's peripheral field of view. The movements of this artificial horizon, really the image of a small bar of light, mimic the movements of the real, but invisible, horizon outside, making the aircraft easier and safer to fly (Malcolm, 1984).

Obviously, there are other causes of accidents under poor visibility, but the differential involvement of the center and periphery is one intriguing possibility. Box 8.5 discusses other ways in which the erroneous perception of motion can cause accidents—but also help to prevent them. Here we have discussed several connections between safety and peripheral responses to visual movement. These examples don't exhaust the literature on the periphery and motion perception. Finlay (1982) provides a good review of this literature.

FOCAL VISION AND AMBIENT VISION

Herschel Leibowitz has modified the theme of two visual systems, characterizing one as a **focal system** concerned with object identification and discrimination, and the other as an **ambient system** concerned with spatial orientation. According to Leibowitz, the focal system utilizes just the information from the center of the retina, while the ambient system utilizes information from both the center and the periphery of the retina. He has used this distinction to account for many nighttime automobile accidents (Leibowitz et al., 1982). Briefly, his argument runs as follows. Driving requires both focal and ambient systems. Focal vision allows drivers to read traffic signs, judge distances, and watch out for pedestrians in the roadway; ambient vision allows the driver to orient the car, keeping it safely on the road. With decreasing illumination, such as that encountered at night, the focal system is selectively degraded, as shown by the decline of acuity. But the ambient system is less affected by reduced illumination—the driver can steer the car at even very low light levels. Consider what this means for the driver. Since steering ability is affected very little, the driver does not recognize that focal vision is impaired. Therefore he drives just as fast as he would during the day—a serious error and a potential hazard.

The rationale for this perceptual theory arose from a surprising source—physiological research on hamsters. Gerald Schneider (1969) was interested in the visual functions of two structures in the hamster brain, the

BOX 8.5

Perceptual Errors Can Cause or Prevent Accidents

Motion perception can literally be a matter of life or death. It can cause fatal acidents but it can also prevent them. To document this claim, we'll start with the dark side—collisions at railroad crossings.

According to the Federal Railroad Administration (1982), there are about 8,000 collisions each year between locomotives and other vehicles at railroad crossings in the United States. Most railroad crossings are protected by crossing gates and warning bells; in addition, locomotive engineers must sound a bell or horn as they approach a crossing. Because of these precautions and the ease with which motorists should be able to see these huge and conspicuous locomotives, it's a real puzzle that so many accidents occur. Herschel Leibowitz, of Pennsylvania State University, has come up with some answers to this puzzle. According to him, errors in motion perception are partly to blame (Leibowitz, 1983).

During an accident investigation, Leibowitz rode in the cab of a locomotive that retraced the route on which the accident had occurred. The trip took Leibowitz through an urban area with many gate crossings. He was astonished at the number of motorists who drove around the crossing gates and across the tracks in front of the oncoming train. The train crew, who saw this kind of thing every day, shrugged it off as ''typical.'' Since automobiles don't fare too well in collisions with railroad trains, why do people take such chances?

Leibowitz realized that

although the locomotive's bulk made it easy to see, that same bulk would cause its speed to be seriously underestimated. It has long been known that the size of an object and its apparent speed are inversely related. To study this relation, J. F. Brown (1931) asked people to adjust the speed of one square so that it appeared to move at the same speed as another square. When both squares were the same size, observers were very accurate in their adjustments. (Typically a mismatch in speed as small as 10 percent can be easily seen.) However, when the two squares differed in size, the accuracy of the matches was very low. When the squares differed in size, the larger one had to move faster than the small one in order to appear to move at the same rate. As a result, if the two squares moved at the same speed, the larger one seemed to be moving more slowly than the smaller one.

Leibowitz points out that a comparable phenomenon can be seen at just about any airport. All commercial jets, regardless of size, land at pretty much the same speed. However, the jumbo jets (DC-10s or 747s) appear to land much more slowly than the smaller jets. Leibowitz believes that the same kind of perceptual error causes motorists at railroad crossings to underestimate an oncoming train's speed, and thereby overestimate the time the train will take to reach the crossing.

Let's end on a happier note, the ability of motion perception to prevent accidents. Particularly dangerous spots in any highway

system are the intersections called rotaries (roundabouts in the United Kingdom). To navigate safely through a rotary, a driver must slow down. But since motorists often don't slow down enough, many accidents result. Because exhortations and warnings seemed to have little effect, Gordon Denton (1980) took a desperate step. He tricked motorists into believing their cars were traveling faster than they really were. His aim was to alarm the motorist into slowing down. Here's how he did it.

Imagine a road with transverse stripes painted across the pavement. A motorist passing over these stripes will get a sense of how fast she's traveling by the rate at which she passes the stripes. When the stripes are close together, she will pass them at a higher rate, causing her to overestimate her speed. Denton exploited this phenomenon by having white stripes painted across the roadway near the entrance to a rotary—the stripes near the rotary were more closely spaced than those farther away. As a result, motorists approaching the rotary erroneously perceived that they were speeding up. This misperception caused them to slow down. Preliminary tests with this simple and inexpensive scheme indicate that it works: accidents declined at over two-thirds of the rotaries on which stripes had been painted. It's nice to know that illusions of motion perception can save lives as well as take them.

visual cortex and the superior colliculus. He lesioned one structure or the other and then examined how the hamster's vision was affected. The effects of cortical lesions seemed to differ from the effects of lesions of the colliculus. In particular, destroying the cortex made it difficult for the hamster to discriminate patterns but did not affect its ability to orient its head and body toward the patterns. Conversely, destroying the colliculus made it difficult for the hamster to orient itself toward the patterns; but if Schneider helped it orient properly, the hamster had little trouble discriminating the patterns. To explain these results, Schneider suggested that many species have not just one but two visual systems. According to this idea, the cortical system helps the animal recognize *what* object is present, and the collicular system helps the animal locate *where* that object is. Presumably humans, like hamsters, have both cortical and collicular systems and can draw on both. But when one system is damaged, there may be a selective loss of function. The results of other studies support Schneider's idea of two visual systems, though there is some question about the precise anatomical correlates of these two visual systems (Mishkin, Ungerleider, and Macko, 1983). For example, Humphrey (1974b) gives an account of the visually guided behavior of a monkey whose visual cortex had been almost totally removed. Though the monkey had impaired form vision, she did develop an excellent facility for orienting toward visual objects and for walking about. Results such as Humphrey's may account for the phenomenon of **blindsight**—the ability shown by some blind people to orient toward objects that they cannot "see" (recall Box 4.2, p. 116).

Think back to that scurrying creature we mentioned earlier. As it darted across the floor, you were able to see not only that it was moving but also the direction in which it moved. When the visual system signals the presence of movement it also signals what direction that movement takes. Unlike other aspects of motion perception, the neural basis of this aspect of motion perception is fairly well understood. It is to the neural basis of direction perception that we now turn.

The Neural Basis of Motion Perception

Some cortical cells register direction of motion. Such cells respond vigorously to motion in one "preferred" direction but little if at all to motion in the opposite direction (see Figure 4.16, p. 126). Each **direction-selective cell,** then, prefers its own, characteristic direction of motion. As a result, the direction of a moving object is registered by the responses that object evokes in different cells. We can imagine an array of neurons, each "looking for" a particular range of directions of motion within the same small region of space. The direction perceived by the observer could reflect the *distribution* of activity within the set of direction-selective cells with receptive fields in that part of the visual field. You may recall that Chapter 4 proposed a comparable code for visual orientation, and Chapter 5 advanced a similar model for coding spatial frequency.* Here we will explore this hypothesis for perceived direction of motion in greater detail. One technique, **selective adaptation,** has been used to study movement perception both psychophysically and physiologically. Let's see how the two sets of results relate.

Sekuler and Ganz (1963) used selective adaptation to study motion perception be-

---

*Analogous models have also been proposed in order to account for another aspect of motion perception—the perception of a target's velocity (Orban, de Wolf, and Maes, 1984; Thompson, 1984). The plausibility of such models is enhanced by the discovery that some neurons in the visual cortex of cats and monkeys are tuned to particular ranges of stimulus velocities.

haviorally. Their stimuli were horizontal gratings that moved either upward or downward. An observer viewed an upward-moving grating of high contrast for several minutes. Exposure to this grating produced a twofold increase in the threshold for seeing upward motion. The increase was direction-selective, since the ability to see downward motion was not affected. Sekuler and Ganz proposed that adaptation fatigued cortical cells responsive to the direction of motion seen during adaptation.

This proposal has received support from physiological studies using selective adaptation. Vautin and Berkley (1977) examined single cortical cells of the cat. First they determined which direction of movement a cell preferred. Then they continuously stimulated the cell with contours moving in that preferred direction. The results from one typical cell are shown in Figure 8.12. The vertical axis shows the number of impulses the cell produced each second; the horizontal axis represents time. The leftmost one-third of this time line represents the cell's spontaneous activity—that is, its response to a uniform light, neither patterned, nor

moving. In the middle one-third of the time line, the cell was continuously stimulated by contours that moved in its preferred direction. The cell responded vigorously when the movement began; but over time, its response gradually diminished. This decline in responsiveness probably corresponds to the decline in sensitivity measured psychophysically by Sekuler and Ganz. But what about the rightmost one-third of Figure 8.12—what might be the perceptual consequence of this decline in responsiveness?

Perceptually, prolonged exposure to one direction of motion does more than merely make that direction harder to see. After viewing one direction of motion for several minutes, people experience illusory motion in the opposite direction. This is known as the **motion aftereffect** or sometimes as the **waterfall illusion,** since the illusion is often experienced after looking at a waterfall (Addams, 1834/1964). You may have already experienced this illusion. If you haven't, here is an easy way to generate a strong motion aftereffect. Many television programs have long "crawls"—the steadily moving list of people who were responsible for the show.

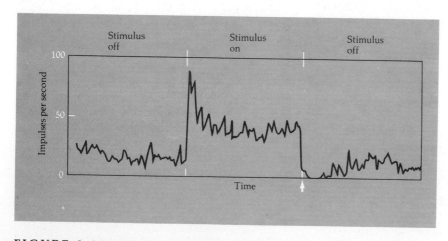

FIGURE 8.12

Response of a cat cortical cell to prolonged stimulation by motion. (Adapted from Vautin and Berkley, 1977.)

In order to read the names, your eyes have to keep up with the crawl. Next time you see a crawl, though, forget about reading the names and just keep your eyes fixed steadily on the center of the screen while the crawl goes by. Then as soon as the crawl is over, you will experience illusory motion in a direction opposite to that of the crawl—this is the motion aftereffect.

What might be the neural basis for this aftereffect? The behavior of the cell represented in Figure 8.12 gives a clue. The arrow on the horizontal axis signifies the moment at which the moving stimulus was withdrawn and the original, uniform stimulus reinstated. Immediately after the reappearance of this uniform stimulus, the cell's spontaneous response is depressed. Instead of evoking the level of spontaneous activity that it did prior to adaptation, the uniform field now causes the cell to cease firing completely. The cell usually takes 20 to 30 seconds to regain its normal level of spontaneous activity. Consider what this subnormal spontaneous activity might mean.

When the visual field is uniformly illuminated and no moving contours are present, all direction-selective cells, regardless of their direction preference, generate approximately equal levels of spontaneous activity. Following prolonged exposure to a particular direction—say downward—cells preferring downward motion will have virtually no spontaneous activity (see Figure 8.12). This produces a biased distribution of spontaneous activity: cells responsive to downward motion now show little if any spontaneous activity, while cells responsive to upward motion show a normal level of spontaneous activity. This biased distribution of spontaneous activity produced following adaptation is similar to the activity distribution evoked by actual motion upward—hence the illusory upward motion. In other words, this biased distribution of spontaneous activity could produce the mo-

tion aftereffect (Barlow and Hill, 1963; Mather and Moulden, 1980).*

We've just seen one consequence—the motion aftereffect—of a bias in the distribution of responses of direction-selective neurons. Let's examine another perceptual consequence of biased distributions, since it provides additional support for this way of thinking about the perceived direction of motion. If an object's perceived direction of motion does depend on the distribution of activity in direction-selective neurons, it should be possible to alter a moving object's perceived direction by adapting some of those neurons. Levinson and Sekuler (1976) asked observers to judge the direction in which an array of bright dots traveled across a television screen. Prior to adaptation, the judgments were accurate. After adapting for several minutes to dots moving steadily in one direction, the observers again judged the direction in which dots moved. When the dots moved steadily in a direction similar but not identical to the adaptation direction, the observers now made errors of judgment: the direction of motion of the dots always seemed to be shifted away from the adaptation direction. This phenomenon should remind you of the tilt aftereffect described in Box 4.5 (p. 131).

Apparent Motion

Ordinarily, your experience of motion is quite straightforward. You notice a small, timid rabbit standing at one spot nibbling on some weeds. Then, over the next few seconds, the rabbit hops over to another clump of

---

*The waterfall illusion is not the only case in which stationary objects appear to move. Have you ever noticed how the moon appears to move speedily across the sky as clouds pass in front of it? This is an example of **induced motion**—the real movement of the clouds causes illusory movement of the moon (Duncker, 1929/1938). Unlike the waterfall illusion, induced motion's physiological basis is not known.

weeds. Without doubt, you'll experience the changes in the rabbit's position as movement. But how does your experience arise? Obviously, the image cast on your retina by that rabbit has moved, hence the experience of motion. Conditions such as this one seem to require no explanation—you see motion because there *is* motion. But retinal image motion cannot entirely explain the perception of motion. We've already seen two cases where motion is perceived in the absence of retinal image motion—the motion aftereffect and induced motion. Now we're about to consider a third, more common case, known as **apparent motion.** This kind of motion has become an important part of our lives. As Stuart Anstis points out,

The flashing lights on a cinema marquee, which seem to move inward toward the lobby and entice us to follow them, are an example of apparent movement. If we go in and watch the movie, we experience two hours of apparent movement: each movie frame projected on the screen is actually stationary whenever the projector is open. If we stay at home and watch TV instead, we are once again experiencing apparent movement. Films and TV, as they exist today, are possible only because of a quirk in our visual systems. (Anstis, 1978, p. 656)

The visual system takes discrete and separate inputs (such as the separate frames of a movie) and knits them into an experience that is smooth and continuous. This is the "quirk" to which Anstis refers. We'll focus on apparent movement now because this quirk provides insights into how the visual system operates under conditions where there is genuine motion of the retinal image.

People have known about apparent motion for quite some time. For example, Sigmund Exner (1888) created brief but intense electrical sparks from two sources. He placed the two sources some distance apart and had observers judge which spark flashed first—

the one on the right or the one on the left. When the time delay between sparks was long, the judgment was easy; when the delay was short, the judgment became difficult. Exner found that about one-twenty-fifth of a second had to intervene between the two sparks before their order could be judged accurately. Exner next placed the two sources of sparks very close to each other. With short intervals between the two sparks, people saw apparent motion—a spark moving from one location to the other. Exner then asked people to judge the direction of that apparent motion. Although these people needed delays of one-twenty-fifth of a second to judge the order of sparks that were some distance apart, they needed less than half that delay to judge the *direction* of movement. This experience of apparent movement could not have been *derived* from judging the sequence of flashes, because the time interval separating the two flashes was too brief to allow for such a judgment. Instead, motion was experienced directly.

Next Exner brought the two sparks so close together that they appeared as a single bright spark. When the twin sparks were flashed one after the other, the observer saw apparent motion even though the sparks were too close together to be resolved. This experience of apparent movement could not have been *derived* from judging the positions of flashes, because the flashes were so close together that they couldn't be distinguished. Again, motion was experienced directly. Apparent motion between points that cannot be resolved spatially has been studied more recently by others (Thorson, Lange, and Biederman-Thorson, 1969; Foster et al., 1981).

Exner's observations led him to conclude that motion was a primary sensation in its own right, not just an inference derived from comparing temporal order or spatial position. Bearing in mind that apparent motion is not an inference, let's consider the work of Max Wertheimer, the Gestalt psychologist mentioned in Chapter 5.

In one study, Wertheimer (1912/1961) briefly presented two spatially separated vertical lines in succession. What did people *see*? The answer depended on the length of the delay that separated the two presentations. With long delays (greater than one-tenth of a second), one line appeared to succeed the other. In other words, the observer saw one line that came on and went off and then a second line that did the same. With very short delays between presentations (say one-fortieth of a second or less), the two lines appeared to come on and go off simultaneously. Perceptually there had been only a single presentation. With intermediate delays between presentation of the two lines (say, one-twentieth of a second), a single line appeared to move smoothly from one position to the other. In other words, people saw apparent motion.

To determine whether this apparent motion was retinal or central in origin, Wertheimer arranged conditions so that the first line was seen by one eye and the second line was seen by the other eye. Even under these conditions of interocular stimulation, motion was perceived. This suggests that the neural events giving rise to the perception of motion are central, lying at or beyond the site where information from the eyes has combined. Wertheimer devised a simple but effective demonstration of interocular apparent movement, one that you too can try.

Hold a thin book in both hands and lean your forehead against the book's edge, as shown in Figure 8.13. Be sure to place your head so that one eye is on each side of the book. This allows you to use the book as a separator, making it easy to present different objects to the two eyes. Now place your hands on opposite sides of the book with only the index fingers extended upward. Position the left hand so that its index finger

FIGURE 8.13
Setup for experiencing apparent motion.

can be seen by your left eye and position your right hand so that its index finger can be seen by your right eye. Don't look directly at your fingers; instead, keep your gaze directed straight ahead at a point several inches beyond the far end of the book. Your fingers should be about 6 inches from your nose. Now comes the hard part. Rhythmically open and close alternate eyes. Though it may take a little practice, at the proper speed of alternation you'll have a strange and amusing experience: your finger will appear to jump back and forth right through the book.

Wertheimer did not know what is known today about cortical function. Thus he mistakenly attributed apparent motion to a short-circuiting of current flow in the brain. Today, apparent motion is more plausibly explained by the responses of direction-selective neurons. As you've already seen, such neurons respond strongly when an object moves through the neuron's receptive field. But many of these neurons can be tricked into responding to an object that doesn't move at all. For example, one neuron may give a vigorous response when a bright bar moves through its receptive field from left to right. The same neuron may give a similar response when a *stationary* bar is briefly flashed, once at the left side of its receptive field and then at the right side. In other words, the neuron's responses to these two very different conditions are virtually identical. If neurons such as this play a role in the perception of motion, these two conditions should be indistinguishable.

ARE APPARENT MOTION AND REAL MOTION INDISTINGUISHABLE?

Several studies have tried to test the claim that apparent motion and real motion are indistinguishable; the results are mixed. Some suggest that apparent and real motion are equivalent (Frisby, 1972; Barbur, 1981); others suggest they are not (Kolers, 1972; Green, 1983). Regardless of their outcomes, most of these studies share a common flaw. When you see apparent movement you are usually aware not only of the movement but also of the shapes and positions of the targets that define the movement. So the neural signals giving rise to the experience of motion are being coordinated with signals that give rise to form and position. An unequivocal comparison of real and apparent motion would isolate motion information from information about shape and position. But how can this be done?

John Barbur, a physicist at Imperial College, London, devised an ingenious method for testing the equivalence of real and apparent motion (Barbur, 1981). The key was the use of very dim lights to produce motion of both types. Viewing dim lights, an observer could see motion but could not see the shape or precise position of the lights. Thus information about motion was uncontaminated by other visual information. An optical and electronic setup allowed Barbur to mix apparent motion and real motion. While two dim lights were producing apparent motion along some path, Barbur moved another dim light smoothly along that same path. When the smoothly moving light was intense enough, its movement was per-

ceived. When the two types of motion took the same direction and traveled at the same speed, Barbur discovered that they were perfectly interchangeable. If the light producing the real motion was dimmed appreciably (so that no motion could be seen), that dimming could be compensated by raising the intensity of the lights producing apparent motion. The perfect interchangeability of the two types of motion implies that the two types do originate from a common neural source.

Barbur's study demonstrated the visual system's ability to combine information from two different but compatible stimuli. But what happens when vision is faced with highly incompatible stimuli? In the demonstration illustrated in Figure 8.13 your visual system combined successive views of your index fingers into a single finger that appeared to pass through the book. In these circumstances, your visual system made an error that was quite understandable; it mistook two highly similar objects (your fingers) for one. But what if you made it harder for the visual system to err in this way? What would happen if you gave it an even more peculiar stimulus, such as a red index finger seen at one instant and a blue index finger seen at the next? (You may wish to try this with marking pens whose inks are washable.) Max Wertheimer (1912/1961) answered this question by alternately presenting a blue stripe and a red stripe. When this was done, observers saw a single moving stripe whose color appeared to change during the course of its travel. More recently Paul Kolers and Michael von Grunau (1975) extended Wertheimer's observation.

THE CORRESPONDENCE PROBLEM IN MOTION PERCEPTION

How does the visual system detect that an object seen at one moment corresponds to the same object seen at another moment? After all, the "finger" example demonstrates that detecting correspondence over time is a prerequisite for motion perception. We can highlight the nature of this prerequisite by comparing retinal images to photographic snapshots of the visual world. Suppose that you have two retinal "snapshots" that were taken a fraction of a second apart. Looking at the two snapshots, how would you determine whether a single object had moved? To accomplish this, you must determine which elements in one snapshot correspond to which elements in the other. Now here's the problem: potentially, any small detail in one of the snapshots *might* correspond to any number of different details in the other. This situation is illustrated by a simple display that has been widely used to study apparent motion (see Figure 8.14). Here, two displays (panel 1 and panel 2) alternate, separated by a brief uniform field (not shown). Both frames contain a trio of large dots. Note that from frame 1 to frame 2, the trio of dots has been shifted rightward. Before telling you what you would actually see, let's consider the possibilities, bearing in mind that what you'll see

depends on the correspondence that vision selects.

Panels 3 through 6 of Figure 8.14 illustrate two possible correspondences. Following the dotted lines from panel 3 to panel 4 shows that your visual system might pair dot A with dot X, dot B with dot Y, and dot C with dot Z. With these correspondences, you would see the entire group of dots moving rightward: A to X, B to Y, and C to Z. Following the dotted lines from panel 5 to panel 6 shows an alternate set of correspondences. Here, your visual system pairs dots B and X, dots C and Y, and dots A and Z. With this set of correspondences, you would see two stationary dots (since B and X occupy the same positions on successive frames as do C and Y). At the same time, you would also see a third dot (A-Z) that moves all the way from the left end of the trio to the right end.

This simple, two-frame display is interesting because its ambiguity makes possible several different percepts, depending on how the correspondence problem is solved. The apparent motion actually seen from such ambiguous displays reveals the rules used

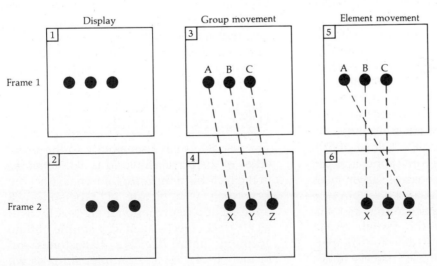

FIGURE 8.14
An illustration of the correspondence problem in motion perception.

by the visual system to establish correspondences. The percept is a choice from among the various sets of correspondences that *might* have been selected.

What, then, do observers actually see when they're shown displays such as that depicted in panels 1 and 2 of Figure 8.14? How does the visual system solve the correspondence problem? The answer is, "It depends" (Pantle and Picciano, 1976; Pantle and Petersik, 1979). Under some conditions, observers see **group movement**—all three dots seem to move *en masse* (as in panels 3 and 4). Under other conditions, observers see **element movement**—the overlapping dots of each frame appear stationary while just the third dot moves back and forth from one end to the other (as in panels 5 and 6). When the interval between displays is long, or when the two displays are shown to different eyes, observers tend to see group movement. Such conditions seem to make it difficult for the visual system to carry out detailed, point-by-point comparisons of alternate displays. When the interval is short and the two displays are shown to the same eye, observers tend to see element movement. Such conditions facilitate detailed comparisons between displays.

These results demonstrate that vision can be flexible when it has to solve a problem of correspondence. But the world in which we live contains few situations in which correspondences are as ambiguous as those represented in Figure 8.14 or as those that have been generated in other studies (Lappin, Doner, and Kottas, 1979; Ullman, 1979). The number of potential correspondences can be sharply reduced if the visual system takes advantage of regularities in the physical world (Marr, 1982; Ramachandran and Anstis, 1983). After all, the visual system evolved in a world whose objects share particular properties: natural objects don't change color suddenly; natural objects are made of parts that are connected; the surface texture of natural objects tends to be uniform; and natural objects, once in motion, tend to stay in motion. Neurons in the visual system register these and other regularities. In so doing, the visual system is biased against unnatural solutions to the correspondence problem, favoring solutions that are consistent with the properties of real-world objects.

As an example, consider one consistency between apparent motion and the motion of natural objects. Objects in either form of motion seem to obey Newton's First Law of Motion: once in motion, a body will continue in motion unless acted upon by an external force. In one demonstration of this law, Wertheimer alternated two targets at a rate that he knew would produce apparent motion between them—say, a line at the left and a line at the right. As long as the alternation continued, the line appeared to travel back and forth. Then without warning to the viewer, he occluded one of the lines but kept presenting the remaining line at its appropriate times. Surprisingly, even though only one line was being exposed, it took some time for the apparent motion to cease. For three or four repetitions, the observer continued to see motion. These findings suggest that inertia works not only in the natural world but in the world of the laboratory as well.

THE ROLE OF APPARENT MOTION IN ANIMATION

The visual system's sensitivity to the properties of the physical world is also reflected in the fact that a meaningful nonabstract object—such as a picture of a person—will undergo apparent motion more readily than an abstract object—such as a simple outline geometric figure (DeSilva, 1926; Jones and Bruner, 1954). As an example, suppose we alternately present two drawings, one a sketch of a man with his arm outstretched and the second a sketch of the same man, arm raised so that his hand touches his forehead, as in a salute (see panels 1 and 2 of Figure 8.15). When these two drawings are alternated at an appropriate rate, the viewer sees a man raising his arm to salute, dropping it, and so on. Suppose then we substitute two simple lines for the sketch of the man's arm. One line has the same orientation as the man's outstretched arm had, the other line has the orientation of the man's arm when it was raised to salute (see panels 3 and 4 of Figure 8.15). When just these two lines are alternated, it is much harder to see movement. It seems that the human context facilitates apparent movement. This conclusion has been substantiated by the finding (Sperling, 1976) that complex patterns (such as arrays of many dots) produce far more

compelling and vivid apparent movement than do simple patterns (such as just a few dots).

The susceptibility of complex patterns to apparent motion has proved very important commercially. About twenty years ago, makers of animated films began to exploit some of apparent movement's quirks (Bregman and Mills, 1982). Before then, animated films (of the Disney style) involved a succession of carefully drawn frames that approximated samples from continuous motion. To create the impression that Donald Duck is walking from one spot to another, an animator would draw and photograph a long series of individual drawings. Each drawing would portray Donald's legs in a position that was just slightly different from that of the preceding drawing. Needless to say, this

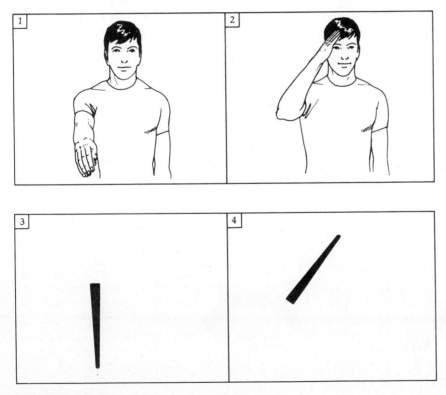

FIGURE 8.15
Stimulus complexity affects apparent motion.

was an expensive and time-consuming process.

Fred Hanna and William Barbera, creators of Fred Flintstone and other cartoon characters, took a different, more economical approach. To create the impression that Fred Flintstone is walking, drawings of Fred's legs in three different positions are made on pieces of clear plastic. To simulate walking, the three pieces of plastic are photographed alternately in combination with Fred's other parts, which are drawn on separate pieces of plastic. Because his legs can take so few different positions, Fred's gait may sometimes appear a little jerky. But he does appear to walk. Actually, though, Fred's walk is as illusory as your finger's ability to pass back and forth through a book.

Roger Shepard, of Stanford University, has developed one method that might be used to reduce the jerkiness of Fred's movements (Shepard and Zare, 1983). He presented a single black dot slightly to the left of fixation and then again to the right of

fixation. When these two dots alternated, a single dot appeared to move back and forth in a straight line. This is just apparent motion. Then a curved gray band was briefly presented, covering the region from one dot to the other (see Figure 8.16). Now instead of going along a straight line, the motion appeared to travel along the gray band. Shepard and Zare termed this *path-guided apparent motion* and noted that apparent motion could be coaxed along even more complicated paths. As these researchers have suggested, animators may be able to take advantage of path guidance to improve the quality of motion in their films. Thus by laying down some complex but unobtrusive path in the drawing of some background, Fred Flintstone's walk might be made less jerky. Incidentally, the development of computer graphics offers an ideal way to eliminate jerkiness in cartoon animation. Nowadays, once the artist has specified the beginning and ending positions of an animation sequence, computer graphics rou-

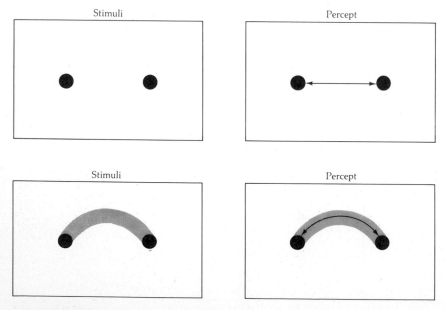

FIGURE 8.16
Path-guided apparent motion. (Adapted from Shepard and Zare, 1983.)

tines can produce the required interpolations.

For the past several pages we have focused on an error that perception makes. This error—apparent motion—is evoked under artificial conditions, including television and movies. In fact, the conditions that produce apparent motion almost never occur naturally. These artificial conditions stand in sharp contrast to the naturalistic, biological motion discussed at the beginning of this chapter. Some people question the wisdom of using apparent motion to understand a visual system that never saw such motion during the course of its evolution. However, Roger Shepard offers some wise counsel about the usefulness of exploiting unnatural conditions in order to study perception:

A recognition of the ecological foundations of perception need not entail experiments that mirror the spatiotemporal properties of the natural environment. [In fact,] the internalized constraints of this system are most clearly revealed when our experimental probings systematically depart from the patterns to which the system has evolved a complementary fit, for only then does the system lose its "transparency" and so reveal its own inner structure. (Shepard, 1981, p. 311)

Of course, Shepard's plan of attack does not rule out a complementary approach—studying motion perception under more natural conditions (Michaels and Carello, 1981). These two complementary approaches really address different aspects of perception. Studies using artificial or unnatural conditions focus on the mechanisms that underlie motion perception; here the emphasis is on the internal processes within the perceiver. Studies employing more natural or ecologically representative stimuli attempt to identify the stimulus information available in the perceiver's surroundings (see Box 8.6); here the emphasis is on the environment. We believe that a complete understanding of motion perception requires both approaches.

BOX 8.6
Looking One's Age

Some events happen so slowly that they cannot be perceived while they are happening; you perceive them only later. Despite the leisurely pace of these events, your ability to see them may involve the same processes as those discussed in relation to motion perception. One of these leisurely events is the aging process. Usually, you can judge someone's age merely by looking at that individual. But what stimulus information makes this judgment possible? Some television advertisements claim that the surest signs of age are hand wrinkles that result from washing dishes. Other commercials suggest that grayness of hair is an even surer sign of age. But might there not be some more general visual cue to age?

Examine panel A of the illustration on the next page (adapted from Pittenger, Shaw, and Mark, 1979). To create these cartoons of the human head, John Pittenger and Robert Shaw (1975) began with the head at the right. Next, they produced the remaining heads by transforming the original one according to a formula designed to capture growth's effects on the human head. Going leftward in the row of human heads, you'll probably find that the heads become younger in appearance. People's judgments of age reflect the information represented in the formula; the perceived relative ages of the faces corresponded closely to the way they had been transformed. Leonard Mark and James Todd (1983) extended this work by applying the same mathematical transformation to a three-dimensional sculpture of a 15-year-old girl's head. They used a computer to carve a new sculpture of the same girl by transforming the original. In its carving, the computer used values that were

(Continued on next page)

intended to create a sculpture of the girl at age 6. Mark and Todd took the two sculptures and asked people to judge the ages of the individuals portrayed. The age judgments averaged 14.5 years for the original and 6.3 years for the derived sculpture. This demonstrates that the formula used to create the cartoon heads also succeeds in capturing whatever information people use when they judge the age of real humans.

Pittenger and his colleagues (Pittenger, Shaw, and Mark, 1979) wondered whether the judgment of age derives from some intellectual process that is based on observers' knowledge of how faces change with age, or whether the perception of age might be more direct—like

the perception of biological motion discussed earlier in this chapter. To answer this question, they applied the same transformation to a new set of cartoon heads, this time of animals. Some of these are shown in panel B of the illustration. Again, as with human heads, the transformation used by the researchers did an excellent job of predicting the animals' ages as judged by observers. Moreover, Pittenger and his colleagues applied the same transformation (panel C) to a Volkswagen "Beetle"—an object that prior to the experiment observers could not have seen age. Even though nonbiological objects such as automobiles do not change shape as they age, observers still made consistent judgments

of the relative ages of the "Beetles"; moreover, those judgments were accurately predicted by the formula. Incidentally, Pittenger's age transformation is not restricted just to creatures from our own planet. A later study (Pittenger and Todd, 1983) found that the same transformation governs the perceived age of Martians— or what they believe Martians look like.

Pittenger suggests that people are able to see the morphological effects of aging and growth in a direct fashion, without recourse to calculation or cognition (Pittenger, Shaw, and Mark, 1979). In that view, the perception of slow events— aging and growth—may not differ qualitatively from the perception of faster ones.

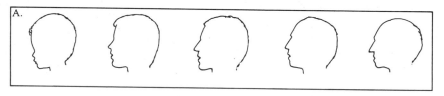

Summary and Preview

This chapter began by emphasizing how event perception defines visual objects, particularly ones that are alive and move. The chapter went on to discuss how you explore your world by means of visually guided locomotion and by means of eye movements. Next we considered the neural basis of movement perception, noting the good match between the properties of natural events and the properties of neutral mechanisms designed to register those events. Finally, some attention was given to an unnatural but common form of motion—apparent motion.

This concludes the four-chapter survey of the visual qualities that enable you to appreciate various biologically important aspects of your world. Next we turn to other senses that also provide vital information about that world. We begin with the ear and hearing.

Chapter 9

The Ear and Auditory System

Close your eyes and listen carefully to the sounds around you. Even in the quietest room, you'll be surprised how much there is to hear. As you listen, try to identify what makes one sound different from another. Undoubtedly, you will notice that sounds appear to come from sources located at different positions around you. These sources can usually be pinpointed with ease. You may also notice that sounds differ in loudness, ranging from the soft rustle of leaves on a tree to the piercing wail of a siren. You'll note that sounds vary in their complexity, too. A birdsong may be composed of just a few notes, or pitches, whereas the traffic on a busy street can generate a cacophony of sound. Besides complexity, sounds can also differ in their cadences, or rhythms. Some sounds have a regularity that makes them recognizable to you—for example, the sound of footsteps in the hallway. The tempo of those footsteps may even enable you to

tell who's coming. In contrast, other sounds you hear, such as the snap of a breaking twig, occur abruptly and without repetition.

So sounds have many features that enable you to identify and locate the objects or people from which they arise. Hearing plays a very important role in defining your perceptual world. Often, you are able to *hear* things in your environment before you can see them. You rely heavily on hearing when it is dark or when an event occurs out of your field of view. And even when a sound source *is* readily visible, your behavioral reaction to it may depend on the nature of the sound it makes. For example, some grocery shoppers believe that a melon's ripeness can be judged only from the sound made by thumping it. A similar thumping technique is sometimes used by doctors to check for fluid accumulation within a patient's chest cavity. And hearing provides the basis for many forms of social communication, the most notable being speech. Without the ability to hear voices, an individual must struggle heroically to remain in touch with the flow of social discourse. Perceptual appreciation of the world becomes substantially diminished when hearing is lost, as any deaf person will testify (Noble, 1983).

In this chapter, we shall examine the process of hearing, starting with the acoustic energy that carries auditory information, and progressing through what is known about the machinery of hearing. This coverage sets the stage for the next chapter, which considers some of the psychological aspects of hearing, such as pitch perception and sound localization. Also in that chapter we shall consider the perception of speech and music, two very important aspects of human hearing.

Aspects of Sound

WHAT IS SOUND?

Sound starts when some mechanical disturbance produces vibrations. These vibrations are transmitted through some medium (usually air) in the form of tiny collisions among the molecules in that medium. If they are sufficiently strong when they arrive at your ears, these vibrations trigger a chain of events culminating in an auditory sensation. All sounds, regardless of their nature, come to you this way. It's odd, but the strains of a symphony and the flush of a toilet share the same physical basis, a series of tiny molecular collisions. In order to understand this, let's consider sound and its properties in greater detail.

Whenever an object vibrates, or moves back and forth, it causes a disturbance within its surroundings. This disturbance takes the form of waves spreading outward from the source of vibration, and these waves constitute what is known as **acoustic energy.** They travel through the surrounding medium in a manner similar to the ripples produced when you toss a pebble into a quiet pond (see Figure 9.1); in this respect, sound waves and light waves are analogous (see Figure 2.14, p. 45). Like ripples on a pond, sound waves must have something to travel through—there can be no sound in empty space or in a perfect vacuum. This was convincingly demonstrated in the seventeenth century by Robert Boyle, a British physicist and chemist. He placed an alarm bell inside a tightly sealed jar and used a vacuum pump to suck all the air out of this jar. When the alarm went off, the bell "rang" but could not be heard. After quickly pumping air back into the jar, Boyle could hear the bell. From this simple experiment, Boyle correctly concluded that air was made up of particles and that sound involved waves of energy traveling *through* these particles. We could liken this energy to the wave of motion produced by toppling a stack of dominoes lined up in a row. In this analogy, the individual dominoes represent individual air molecules; the wave of energy is transmitted by one domino bumping into another—a chain reaction propagated the length of the row of dominoes.

Though one usually thinks of air as the medium for carrying sound, acoustic energy may also be transmitted through other media whose constituent molecules are sufficiently close together to collide with one another when they are set in motion. In fact, the more densely these molecules are packed, the faster sound will travel through them.

FIGURE 9.1
Sound waves resemble the ripples on a pond.

For instance, at room temperature airborne sound travels 340 meters per second (or 1,130 feet per second), and slightly less when the air is colder (see Box 9.1 for an account of the way the speed of sound may be computed). In the denser medium of water, sound travels about 1,500 meters per second, over four times faster than in air. And through steel, sound clips along at over 5,000 meters per second. In general, sound trav-

BOX 9.1
Clocking the Speed of Sound

You have probably had the experience of seeing a bolt of lightning before hearing the associated clap of thunder. This disparity in time between seeing and hearing the same event arises because sound travels much more slowly than light (340 meters per second versus nearly 300,000 kilometers per second). Over the centuries, there have been a number of attempts to determine the velocity of sound, all of them based on the same general principle. We shall describe a simple experiment that you can perform to demonstrate this principle.

Imagine facing a large building or a solid wall and clapping your hands together sharply. Assuming there is minimal surrounding noise, you will hear an echo as the sound from your clap bounces off the wall and travels back to your ears. The *time* elapsing between your clapping and hearing the echo will depend on the *distance* between you and the reflecting surface. Capitalizing on this fact, you could derive an estimate of the speed of sound in the following manner.

Clap your hands together twice, pausing one second between claps. Carefully note whether the echo produced by the first clap is heard before or after the second time you clap your hands together. If this first echo precedes your second clap, move farther away from the wall and repeat the test. If the first echo follows your second clap, move closer to the wall. Your aim is to find the spot where these two events—first echo and second clap— coincide. From this spot, the sound travels to the wall and back to you in one second, the time between the first and second claps. (The accuracy of this determination depends, of course, on your ability to produce a pair of handclaps exactly one second apart.)

Now you may calculate the speed of airborne sound simply by measuring the distance from you to the reflecting surface causing the echo. Doubling this value tells you the distance traveled by sound in one second. Assuming your claps were properly timed, you should find yourself 170 meters from the wall, which places the speed sound at 340 meters per second. Your estimate will depend somewhat on the air temperature, since sound travels more slowly in colder temperatures. Alternatively, *knowing* the speed of sound, you could *estimate* distance by timing how long it took a self-produced echo to return from a distant surface, such as the side of a cliff. In either case, these estimation procedures are only as reliable as your ability to gauge time accurately.

Now suppose you were to repeat the handclap experiment under water. As mentioned elsewhere in this chapter, sound travels four times faster in water than it does in air. So you would have to be located 680 meters from a reflecting surface to create a coincidence between an echo and a second handclap. As a final exercise, suppose that while standing at one end of a large swimming pool you partially submerge your head in the water so that one ear is under water while the other is not. Now let's have a person at the far end of the pool holding a toy clicker in each hand, with one in the water and the other in air. If that person operates both clickers simultaneously, what will you hear?

If the swimming pool is long enough, you should hear a pair of clicks—the first click corresponding to the one transmitted through the water, and the second corresponding to the one transmitted through the air.

els more slowly in gases than in liquids, and more slowly in liquids than in solids.

Regardless of the medium in which it is carried, sound becomes weaker as it travels farther and farther from its source, eventually disappearing altogether. Yet while it is fading in strength, sound continues to travel at a constant speed, so long as it travels in the same medium. Thus whether you whisper or shout at a nearby friend, the message will arrive at its destination in the same amount of times, albeit with a different degree of emphasis.

As sound waves spread out from their source, they interact with one another as well as with objects in their paths. These interactions can actually be more complex than those involving light. For instance, a solid object casts a shadow if exposed to light shining from one direction. But most sounds can be heard with little noticeable change if a relatively small object is situated between the source of a sound and your ears. This happens because sound, unlike light, travels around and sometimes through solid objects. Consequently, one has much more trouble excluding unwanted sounds than one does bothersome light—pulling a shade, for instance, may eliminate the glare from a nearby streetlamp, but it will not completely silence the noise of passing traffic.

When sound waves strike a surface, a portion of the acoustic energy bounces off the surface. These reflected sound waves are called **echoes,** and they can have a noticeable impact on what one hears. When echoes (reflected sound) collide with other, unreflected sound waves from the same source, these sounds interact by adding or subtracting their component energies. The result of these interactions among sounds can be particularly conspicuous in enclosed spaces such as rooms and auditoriums. Depending on an auditorium's shape and design, for example, there may be some seats where sound is unnaturally loud and other seats where sound is considerably damped. (These seats can actually be quite close to one another within an auditorium.) In an acoustically "good" auditorium, these variations in sound quality are minimal. It is a real engineering challenge to design and construct auditoriums with perfect acoustics. But great advances in the science of **acoustics** (the branch of physics concerned with audible sound) do not guarantee that even the most thoughtfully designed structure will, in fact, live up to its billing. The repeated modifications and the eventual complete reconstruction of New York's Avery Fisher Hall demonstrate how sound, particularly reflected sound, has the insidious knack of turning up where it is least expected, while avoiding where it is *supposed* to go (Bliven, 1976).

Not all sound striking a surface is reflected—some acoustic energy is absorbed. The amount of sound absorbed depends on the absorbing material. Smooth plaster, for example, absorbs only 3 percent of the sound striking its surface, reflecting the rest as an echo. This is why your singing voice invariably sounds strongest within the confines of your shower, with its hard-tiled, reflecting walls. Nylon carpet, in comparison, absorbs about 25 percent of incident sound. As you can imagine, a room containing carpet, drapes, and stuffed furniture soaks up a lot of sound energy, thereby providing a rather dead listening environment. For the same reason, the acoustics in a concert hall vary with the season, depending on whether or not the audience is dressed in heavy winter clothing that absorbs sound.

Special rooms called *anechoic chambers* have been built to create an environment devoid of echoes. The walls, floor, and ceiling of such rooms are made of porous, foam wedges that serve to absorb sound before it can be reflected to your ears. Consequently, you hear only the sounds emitted from the source itself, with no echoes. For instance, when you walk in an anechoic chamber, your footsteps sound quite unnatural, having a muffled, flat quality. This is because you are hearing the sounds of your footsteps unaccompanied by their usual echoes. In general, the dull, muted quality of sounds in an anechoic chamber underscores the contribution of echoes to the normal perception of sound.

Besides contributing to your appreciation of sound, echoes furnish information about objects from which sound is reflected. For one thing, the mere presence of an echo from sound tells you that some object must be present in your environment. And as explained in Box 9.1, by noting the time elapsing between the production of the sound and hearing its echo, you can estimate the distance from the source to the reflecting object. This information may be particularly useful if you produce the sound yourself, such as by yelling or clapping your hands. Some animals, including bats and porpoises, rely greatly on reflections of self-produced sound to navigate. While humans don't routinely put echoes to practical use, they can learn to rely on information provided by reflected sound (Griffin, 1959). Sailors claim they can hear echoes from channel-marker buoys located several hundred feet from their boat. It is well documented that blind people can use echolocation to guide their locomotion, and sighted people can learn to utilize this cue, too.

So far you have been introduced to the vibratory nature of sound waves and you have learned that these waves travel through a medium and may be reflected by surfaces. But in order to really understand hearing, you must understand the ways in which sound waves differ from one another. This entails a more complete analysis of the physical properties of sound, the topic of our next section.

THE NATURE OF SOUND WAVES

We have characterized sound, or acoustic energy, as a series of collisions caused by molecules bumping into one another. You can neither see these molecular collisions nor feel them, except in unusual cases of very strong sound waves. To help you envision the behavior of sound waves, let's imagine the following setup. Suppose you dangle a very thin, lightweight thread in front of a loudspeaker, holding the thread by one end only, so it is free to move. Now imagine that you measure the amount by which the free end of the thread is deflected as you broadcast sounds of various sorts over the loudspeaker. This setup is depicted in Figure 9.2.

The tiny dots in front of the speaker represent individual air molecules. In the absence of sound energy, air molecules are more or less evenly distributed, as illustrated in panel A. As you may know, a loudspeaker produces sound by moving back and forth, an action that physically jostles air molecules in immediate contact with the speaker cone (the round portion of the unit that actually moves). When the speaker cone moves forward, it produces an increase in air pressure that, if one could see it, involves a bunching up, or compression, of air molecules. This is shown in panel B of Figure 9.2 as a heightened concentration of dots. These compressed air molecules, in turn, collide with their immediate neighbors, thereby projecting the increase in air pressure out from the speaker itself. This miniature "breeze" eventually strikes the thin thread you are holding, causing it to bend in a direction away from the speaker. In the meantime, the loudspeaker cone has moved steadily back to its initial position. This creates a suctionlike action that spreads out, or decompresses, the air molecules, returning them to their initial density (normal air pressure). As shown in panel C, this decompression also travels outward, as air molecules are sucked into the area of de-creased pressure; eventually this de-compression pulls your thread back to its vertical position. Now suppose the speaker cone continues to move inward, further de-creasing air pressure in the immediate vicin-ity of the cone. This partial vacuum travels outward and eventually sucks the thread in a direction toward the loudspeaker. This bunching up and spreading out of air mole-cules, caused by mechanical displacement of the speaker, represent waves of high and low pressure. The air molecules themselves each move very little—it is the *wave* of pres-sure that travels steadily outward from the sound source. You might think back to the domino analogy mentioned earlier. The dominoes, like air molecules, each move only a short distance, but by colliding with their neighbors they transmit a wave of motion that can carry over great distances.

As illustrated in Figure 9.2, changes in the position of the thread reflect changes in air pressure radiating outward from the loudspeaker. Suppose we now graph the successive changes in the position of the

thread occurring over time—tracing out the sound wave produced by the loudspeaker as its cone moves in and out in a cyclic fash-ion. Such a graph is shown in Figure 9.3; the horizontal axis plots time, and the ver-tical axis plots the thread's position relative to the loudspeaker. The dotted line shows the case where the thread is perfectly ver-tical, undisturbed by sound from the loud-speaker. Deviations from this level repre-sent changes in the thread's position and, hence, changes in air pressure produced by movements of the loudspeaker. The height of the curve above or below the dotted line indicates how much the thread deviates from vertical (the amount of change in air pres-sure). This deviation of the curve from the baseline level is known as **amplitude,** and it is determined by the distance over which the speaker moves. When this movement is tiny, the air pressure change is small and the amplitude of the wave is low (the curve labeled 1 in Figure 9.3). As you might guess, small-amplitude pressure waves give rise to weak sounds. But when the loudspeaker's movements are large, the change in air pres-

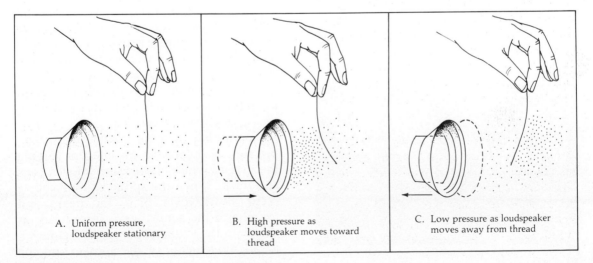

A. Uniform pressure, loudspeaker stationary

B. High pressure as loudspeaker moves toward thread

C. Low pressure as loudspeaker moves away from thread

FIGURE 9.2
Sound waves consist of changes in air pressure.

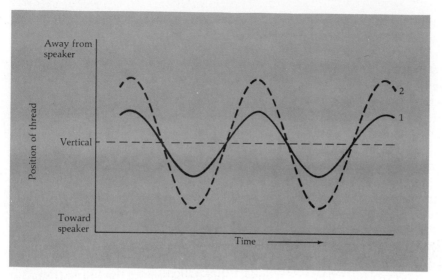

FIGURE 9.3
Change in thread position (representing air pressure) over time.

sure, and hence the wave amplitude, is great (the curve labeled 2). You would hear this as a loud sound.

As air pressure changes proceed away from the source, the amplitude gradually decreases. This principle is illustrated in Figure 9.4, a graph of wave amplitude as the function of distance from a sound source; it would be equivalent to repeating the thread

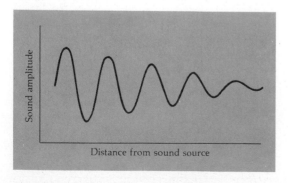

FIGURE 9.4
Sound intensity diminishes with distance from source.

experiment at different distances from the loudspeaker. This property of sound propagation explains why a sound becomes fainter, and eventually inaudible, as you move away from its source. Specifically, sound energy (just like light energy) falls off with the square of the distance between a listener and the sound source. Thus, for example, doubling the distance between your ear and a telephone receiver will produce a fourfold reduction in the sound energy reaching your ear. Sound amplitude is usually expressed in units called **decibels** (abbreviated **dB**); this unit is described in Box 9.2.

Continuing with our loudspeaker example, let's next consider the effect of varying the rate at which the speaker moves back and forth. When the speaker's movements occur slowly over time, the peaks and troughs of the sound wave spread out, as shown in the left-hand portion of Figure 9.5. Rapid movements of the speaker, on the other hand, yield bunched-up peaks and troughs, as shown in the right-hand portion of Figure 9.5. When dealing with steady, cyclic variations such as those described here, one may specify the *frequency* of the sound. This refers to the number of times per second that air pressure undergoes a complete cycle from, say, high to low and back to high, and the unit used to designate frequency is the **hertz** (abbreviated **Hz**). Thus, for instance, in the case of a 500-Hz sound, a complete cycle of air pressure change (from compression to decompression and back) occurs in two thousandths of a second, yielding 500 such cycles in one second. Think of frequency as the number of cycles of the wave passing a given point in one second. You can also consider frequency in terms of the *length* of a single wave; this refers to the distance from a point along one wave (such as its peak) to the corresponding point in the next wave. Considered in this way, a low-frequency sound wave would have a long wavelength, whereas a high-frequency wave would be short in length. Figure 9.6 illustrates the relation between wavelength and frequency. As you can see from this graph, a 400-Hz sound wave is about 3 feet in length, measuring from, say, the peak of one cycle to the peak of the next.

You will probably recognize the wave-

forms shown in Figure 9.5 as sinusoids, waveforms we discussed in Chapter 5 in relation to spatial vision. In the case of vision, recall that complex visual patterns (such as a checkerboard) can be described as the combination of certain spatial frequency components. This is why gratings of various spatial frequencies are so useful in the study of spatial vision. By the same token, complex sounds can be described as the combination of certain temporal frequencies, or **pure tones** as they are sometimes called. Analogues to sinusoidal gratings, pure tones represent sinusoidal changes in air pressure over time. Let's see how a more complicated waveform (and hence a more complicated sound) may be described as the sum of certain sinusoidal frequencies of various amplitudes. We shall develop this idea in several steps.

Think back to the loudspeaker example: what will happen when two or more tones are simultaneously broadcast over the speaker? In this case, air molecules immediately in front of the cone will be influenced by several vibratory forces. As you continue adding more and more frequencies, you create more complex sound waves.

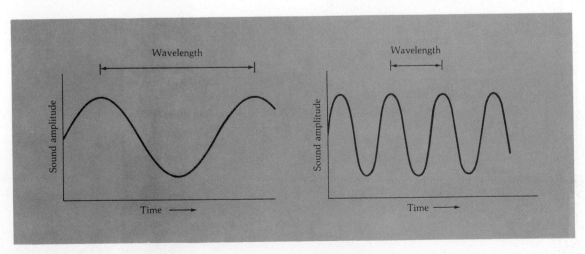

FIGURE 9.5
Rate of change in air pressure corresponds to sound's frequency.

BOX 9.2

Cries and Whispers

The human ear is able to hear and distinguish sound over an enormous range of intensities. In this respect, the ear is comparable to the eye: both manage to handle energy levels that can differ by a factor of at least 10 billion. To give you some idea of the energy levels confronted by your ears, take a look at the chart below, which lists the values of intensity characteristic of some common sounds. You will notice that these various sound intensities are scaled in units called decibels. This is a *logarithmic* scale with a particular reference level of sound. The logarithmic nature of the scale makes it much easier to show a wide range of values on a single graph. Also, the logarithmic scale specifies sound-level differences in terms of their ratio to one another, not simply in terms of their algebraic difference; this seems to describe more accurately the way one judges intensity differences. Let's consider the definition of a decibel (dB):

$$dB = 20 \log (p_1/p_0)$$

where p_1 refers to the air pressure amplitude of the sound under consideration and p_0 refers to a standard reference level of air pressure. This reference level is typically set at 0.0002 dynes/cm^2, the dyne per unit area being a measure of air pressure. To signify when amplitudes are being given relative to this particular **sound pressure level (SPL)** we'll denote such amplitudes as "dB$_{SPL}$." Under ideal conditions at that reference level, a sound in the neighborhood of 1,000 to 4,000 Hz is just barely audible. Sometimes we will use the decibel unit in a different way. Suppose that instead of expressing some sound relative to 0.0002 dynes/cm^2, we wish to compare the amplitudes of two sounds—say, a sound at 60 dB$_{SPL}$ versus a sound at 35 dB$_{SPL}$. Here we can describe amplitudes relative to each other in terms of dB, omitting the subscript $_{SPL}$. In this example, we would say that the two sounds differ by 25 dB.

With these definitions in mind, let's consider some of the entries in the chart. Note that a quiet whisper is 20 dB higher than the 0 dB$_{SPL}$ reference level. This corresponds to a 100-fold increase in sound energy. A loud scream, in contrast, can reach 100 dB$_{SPL}$ in intensity, which is 10 billion times more intense than the threshold, reference level. Sounds in excess of 130 dB$_{SPL}$ can actually lead to an experience of pain, an adaptive sensation since it causes one reflexively to cover the ears, thereby protecting them from damage. We shall discuss the consequences of exposure to loud noise in the following chapter.

The Decibel Scale

dB	Sound	
0	Threshold of hearing	
10	Normal breathing	
20	Leaves rustling in a breeze	
30	Empty movie house	
40	Residential neighborhood at night	
50	Quiet restaurant	
60	Two-person conversation	
70	Busy traffic	Beginning of danger level
80	Vacuum cleaner	Annoying
90	Water at foot of Niagara Falls	
100	Subway train	Prolonged exposure can cause hearing loss
120	Propeller plane at takeoff	
130	Machine-gun fire, close range	
140	Jet at takeoff	Threshold of pain
160	Wind tunnel	

Such waves will consist of the algebraic sum of the component frequencies, and the resulting waveform will quickly resemble a set of irregularly spaced peaks and valleys. One such example is shown in Figure 9.7. This irregular waveform depicts a complex change in air pressure over time; and if enough components are added together randomly, the resultant sound may be heard as **noise.** In a way, noise is analogous to white light, which, as you learned in Chapter 6, itself contains light energy at all wavelengths of the visible spectrum.

Actually, most of the sounds you hear in everyday life may be characterized as "complex," for very seldom does one encounter anything resembling pure tones. If events and objects in nature were to broadcast their presence using pure tones only, one's ability to identify those objects and events via hearing would be seriously limited. Because of their virtually unlimited range of unique structure, complex patterns of sound energy provide an enormous vocabulary for conveying biologically and socially relevant information. For instance, your ability to recognize a person's voice over the telephone stems from the unique "signature" provided by the package of frequencies composing that person's voice. Still, it is important to understand that all sounds, regardless of their duration or complexity, can be considered as the sum of many simple frequency components. The auditory system analyzes complex sounds into such simpler components.

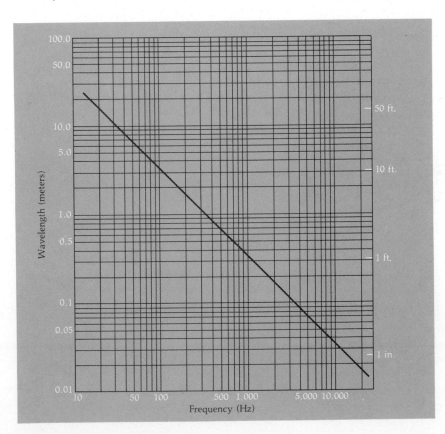

FIGURE 9.6
The relation between wavelength and frequency.

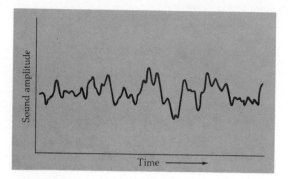

FIGURE 9.7
Many different frequencies mixed together can produce "noise."

The Auditory System: The Ear

The human auditory system consists of the ears, a pair of auditory nerves, and portions of the brain. This assembly is depicted in Figure 9.8. The top part of the figure shows a cutaway diagram of the ear, and the bottom part schematically illustrates the operations performed by the successive stages of the auditory system. In the remainder of this chapter, we shall focus on the specifics of several of these stages. As we proceed, the terms appearing in the schematic flow diagram will become clearer; you should mark this page and refer back to the diagram from time to time.

THE OUTER EAR

The most conspicuous part of the ear is the **pinna,** that shell-like flap gracing the side of your head. Some animals, such as the cat, can rotate the pinnas in order to funnel sound into their ears. Human pinnas, though, are immobile; humans must turn the entire head to orient themselves toward sound. Still, the two pinnas are not useless vestiges; their corrugations act like small reflecting surfaces that modify, or "color," the complexity of sound actually entering the ear (Bat-

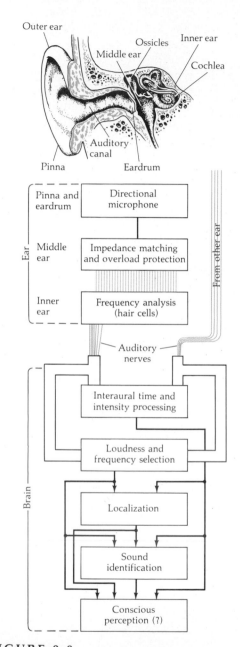

FIGURE 9.8
A schematic representation of the auditory system.

teau, 1967). The degree of coloration introduced by the pinnas depends on which direction sound is coming from. Sound originating straight ahead of you would be affected differently by the pinnas than would sound coming from a source behind you. So these ear flaps, besides providing a convenient support for eyeglasses, play a significant role in sound localization. We shall consider this role in greater detail in the next chapter.

After it is collected by each pinna, sound is channeled down the **auditory canal,** a slightly bent tube approximately 2.5 centimeters long and about 7 millimeters in diameter (the same diameter as that of a pencil, as you should never confirm). Because of its dimensions, the auditory canal has a resonant frequency (see Box 9.3) around 3,000 Hz. As a consequence, sounds containing frequencies in this neighborhood are ac-

tually amplified several decibels or more (Gulick, 1971), which is one reason why human sensitivity to barely audible sounds is best around this frequency.

At the far end of the auditory canal, sound pressure comes in contact with the **eardrum (tympanic membrane).** This thin, oval-shaped membrane vibrates when sound pressure waves strike it, and these resulting vibrations may be remarkably small. It has been estimated (Bekesy and Rosenblith, 1951) that a soft whisper—an intensity of about 20 dB$_{\text{SPL}}$—displaces the eardrum approximately 1/100-millionth of a centimeter, about the width of a single hydrogen molecule! Despite the almost infinitesimal size of this

---

BOX 9.3

Resonant Frequencies: Is It Live or Is It . . . ?

Perhaps you have seen the television commercial where Ella Fitzgerald shatters a crystal wineglass by singing a loud, high note. Or maybe you have felt the window panes in a house rattle following a loud clap of thunder. These are just a couple of illustrations of the ability of sound to produce vibrations in solid objects. Why does this happen?

All objects have a **resonant frequency,** defined as the frequency at which the object vibrates when set into motion. You are probably familiar with the high-pitched ringing sound produced by striking a glass with a spoon. This clear, pure ringing sound corresponds to the resonant frequency of the glass, and it occurs because the molecules of the glass are vibrating back and forth at that frequency. Adding water to the glass causes those molecules to vibrate at a slower rate when you strike the glass with the

spoon. You have lowered the resonant frequency of the glass. So long as the amount of water in the glass remains constant, its resonant frequency will stay the same; regardless of how you set up vibrations in the glass, it will produce the same ringing sound. In fact, sound from another source may induce vibrations in the glass, so long as that inducing sound contains energy at the resonant frequency of the glass. For instance, by whistling the right note, you could produce a faint ringing sound from the glass. And if this inducing energy is sufficiently intense (such as a loud, pure note), the vibrations set up in the glass may be sufficiently strong to shatter it. Presumably this was how the army of priests at Jericho were able to tumble that city's walls, by playing their trumpets in unison! On a less spectacular scale, these induced vibrations or *resonance,* explain why

objects in your room may tremble sometimes when you turn up the volume on your stereo. In general, the resonant frequency of an object depends on the size and rigidity of the object. This principle will become important when we consider the way in which the ear converts sound energy into neural activity.

We shall be discussing the relation between hearing and the frequency of sound in the next chapter, but at this point it would be helpful for you to have some idea of the subjective experience of different frequencies. To give a few examples, the tone called middle C has a frequency of 262 Hz; the faint, high whine produced by a television when the volume control is turned all the way down is 16,000 Hz; and adult human speech consists of frequencies ranging from 500 to 8,000 Hz.

movement, you hear the whisper. This exquisitely sensitive device, the eardrum, is actually quite sturdy; structurally it resembles an umbrella, with a framework of supporting ribs. Even when pierced, the eardrum continues to operate with only a modest reduction in efficiency.

Together, the pinna and auditory canal constitute the *outer ear*. Referring back to Figure 9.8, you can see that this portion of the auditory system functions like a directional microphone that picks up sound and modifies it, depending on its frequency content and locational source.

THE MIDDLE EAR

The eardrum forms the outer wall of a small, air-filled chamber called the *middle ear*. In the middle ear, the vibrations impinging on the eardrum are passed along to the **oval window,** which is covered by another membrane, smaller than the eardrum, that forms part of the inner wall of the middle ear. Bridging the small gap between eardrum and oval window are the **ossicles,** the three smallest bones in your body. Each of the three ossicles is about the size of a single letter on this page; their individual names reflect their shapes (see Figure 9.9). First in this chain, the **hammer** (technically called the **malleus**) is attached at one end to the center of the eardrum. The other end of the hammer is tightly bound by ligaments to the **anvil,** or **incus,** the middle link in this chain of tiny bones. The anvil, in turn, is secured to the **stirrup,** or **stapes,** whose footplate is in turn anchored against the oval window. Together the three ossicles transfer vibrations from the eardrum to the oval window.

The Role of the Ossicular Bridge. Why did nature build a delicate bridge between these two membranes, eardrum and oval window? Why not have airborne vibrations impact directly on the oval window, doing away

with this intermediate chamber, the middle ear? To appreciate the importance of the middle ear and its ossicular bridge, let's consider how things would sound to you if this chamber and series of tiny bones were eliminated from your ear.

To begin, you need to realize that the inner ear, the chamber located on the other side of the oval window, is filled with fluid; Glen Wever (1978) discusses the evolutionary significance of the fluid-filled inner ear, pointing out that it probably derives from the aquatic environment of the amphibians from which we humans inherited our ears. As land dwellers, we hear sounds that are carried to our ears by *airborne* pressure variations. Without the middle ear, these airborne pressure changes would be pushing directly against the oval window and, therefore, against the fluid contained in the inner ear. Because its constituent molecules are more densely packed, the fluid offers more resistance to movement than does air. In other words, more force is required to set up sound waves in water than in air. This explains why when you are under water you have trouble hearing sounds arising from above the water—over 97 percent of airborne sound is reflected when it strikes the water's surface; less than 3 percent is absorbed by the water (Evans, 1982a). This represents about a 30 dB loss in sound energy. Referring back to the chart in Box 9.2, you can see that lowering the intensity of sounds by 30 dB would definitely affect your hearing, wiping out altogether some routine sounds (those listed as 30 dB$_{SPL}$ or less in intensity) and reducing the intensity of all others.

So if your ear were to transfer vibrations directly from air to fluid, a great deal of sound energy would be lost. This potential loss in sound energy—or most of it—is avoided within your middle ear in two ways. First, the ossicles form a tiny lever that amplifies the force received by them at the eardrum. As you may know, it is easier to move an

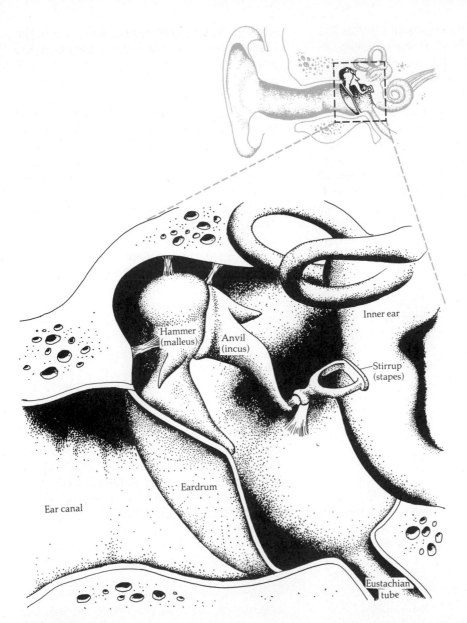

FIGURE 9.9
The middle ear.

object by applying leverage than it is to move it on your own: while you wouldn't dream of trying to lift a car, you can raise one with no great problem using the leverage provided by an automobile jack. The same principle of leverage enables the ossicles to com-

bat the resistance, or *impedance,* arising when airborne vibrations try to move water.

Actually, this leverage action of the ossicles recoups only about 3 dB of sound intensity, which still leaves about a 27 dB loss from impedance. The bulk of the rest of this loss is recovered by a kind of funneling process based on the difference in size between the eardrum and the oval window. The oval window is roughly twenty times smaller in area than the eardrum. Consequently, the force applied on the oval window exerts considerably more pressure than the same amount of force applied to the eardrum. By funneling vibrations from the large eardrum to the small oval window, sound energy is effectively amplified. This funneling effect recovers another 23 dB of the impedance loss that is caused by passing from air to water. In total, then, these two mechanisms—leverage from the ossicles and amplification due to size differences between the eardrum and the oval window—recover approximately 26 dB of the potential energy loss at the air-water interface. So the potential 30 dB loss is cut to one of just 4 dB (Lawrence, 1967). Because it operates to overcome the impedance imposed by the fluid-filled inner ear, the middle ear is sometimes referred to as an **impedance matching** device.

For this impedance matching system to work efficiently, the average air pressure within the middle ear must equal the atmospheric pressure existing in the outside environment and, hence, within the auditory canal. This equivalence is maintained by the **Eustachian tube*** connecting the middle ear and the throat. Every time you swallow, this tube opens, allowing air either to enter or to leave the middle ear, depending on the outside air pressure. You can sometimes hear the consequences of this ventilation process, such as when your ears "pop" while riding an elevator, flying in an airplane, or ascending a high mountain. Sudden increases or decreases in outside pressure (such as those experienced by scuba divers) can actually rupture the eardrum; this

occurs when the pressure differential on the two sides of the membrane becomes too great.

The Acoustic Reflex. Before we conclude our discussion of this part of the ear, we also need to draw your attention to the protective role played by the *tensor tympani*, a small muscle attached to the eardrum, and the *stapedius*, a tiny muscle attached to the stapes bone. In the presence of loud sound, these muscles contract, thereby stiffening the eardrum and restricting the movement of the ossicles (Møller, 1974). These combined actions, called the **acoustic reflex**, damp the sound vibrations passed from the outer ear to the inner ear; in this respect, the acoustic reflex acts like the damper pedal on a piano, the one that muffles the musical notes by limiting the vibrations of the piano's strings. But why should the ear contain a mechanism to damp sound?

According to one popular theory, the acoustic reflex serves to protect the inner ear from intense stimulation that could otherwise damage the delicate receptor cells within the inner ear. Considered in this way, one can draw an analogy between the acoustic reflex and the pupillary light reflex (the constriction of the pupil in response to light). It is true that the acoustic reflex *does* reduce the intensity of sound transmission by as much as 30 dB (Evans, 1982a). However, it is primarily low-frequency sounds that are damped by the acoustic reflex; high frequencies pass through the middle ear unattenuated. So as a protective device, the acoustic reflex is only partially successful. Moreover, the acoustic reflex takes about one-fiftieth of a second to exert its shielding influence. Consequently, any sudden, intense sound, like the explosion of a firecracker, can speed through the middle ear before the acoustic reflex can act to damp the force of that sound. Incidentally, abrupt sounds like this are called *transients*, and if too strong,

---

*Named after its discoverer, Bartolommeo Eustachio, a sixteenth-century Italian anatomist.

they can produce a permanent loss in hearing; this is one reason that playing with explosives such as firecrackers can be dangerous. Actually, transients are very rare in nature; aside from thunder, there are few naturally occurring auditory events that produce abrupt, strong sound levels. Most loud transients arise from man-made events such as gunshots and firecrackers. From an evolutionary standpoint, then, our precivilized ancestors had no real need for the acoustic reflex as a means to protect their ears from loud, abrupt sounds. What other role, then, might the acoustic reflex play in hearing?

Another possible role is suggested by the fact that the acoustic reflex occurs whenever you are chewing or talking—the same nerves that activate your facial muscles trigger the acoustic reflex. You can easily experience the consequences of this by listening to a steady, low-frequency sound such as the hum of a refrigerator motor while clenching and unclenching your teeth. The sound will seem fainter with your teeth clenched, because this engages the acoustic reflex. This general observation has led to the theory that the acoustic reflex reduces the ears' sensitivity to self-produced sounds such as one's own voice. These sounds *do* consist primarily of low frequencies, which as mentioned above are the ones attenuated by the acoustic reflex. We leave it to your imagination to figure out why your auditory system should want to de-emphasize self-produced sounds.

The functions of the middle ear are summarized in Figure 9.8. Basically, it serves as an impedance matching device and as a circuit overload protector. With these roles established, we are now ready to migrate to the next stage in the auditory system, the inner ear. This is where mechanical vibrations are converted into electrical nerve impulses to be carried to the brain. Within the inner ear, the auditory system really gets down to the business of hearing.

THE INNER EAR: THE COCHLEA

The *inner ear* consists of a series of hollow cavities, or labyrinths, carved into the temporal bone of the skull. One set of these cavities, the semicircular canals, is concerned with the maintenance of bodily posture and balance; we shall not consider these structures in this book. Our focus will be on the **cochlea** (meaning "snail" in Latin), a coiled, fluid-filled cavity containing the specialized receptors that place you in contact with the sounds in your environment. Vibrations of the oval window produce pressure changes in the fluid within the cochlea. These pressure changes cause movement of the sensitive receptor cells within the cochlea, providing the stimulus for their activity. To understand this process of sensory transduction, we need to look more closely at the anatomy of this small, bean-sized organ. (The cochlea depicted in Figure 9.10 is about three times larger than the one in your inner ear.)

The spiral-shaped cochlea is partitioned into three chambers, which are easier to visualize if you imagine the cochlea uncoiled, as shown in Figure 9.11. To keep track of its arrangement, we shall refer to the end nearest the middle ear as the *base* and the

FIGURE 9.10
The cochlea.

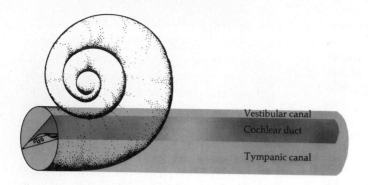

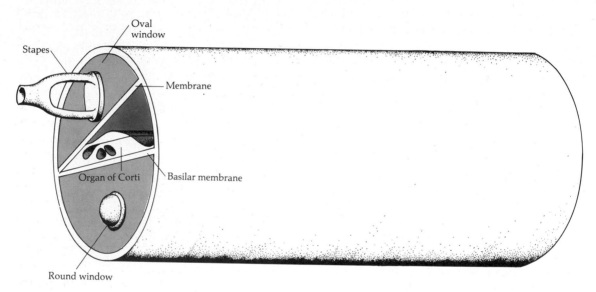

FIGURE 9.11
An uncoiled cochlea.

end normally curled up in the center as the *apex.* The three wedge-shaped chambers of the cochlea each have names: the **vestibular canal,** the **cochlear duct,** and the **tympanic canal.** The vestibular canal and cochlear duct are separated by one membrane, while the tympanic canal and the cochlear duct are separated by another membrane; this latter one is called the **basilar membrane** and it plays a crucial role in the hearing process. The three chambers run parallel to one another the entire length of the cochlea, except

right near the far end, at the apex. There the vestibular canal and the tympanic canal merge at a pinhole-sized passage. Because these two chambers are in fact continuous with each other, they contain the same fluid, similar in composition to spinal fluid. The middle chamber, the cochlear duct, contains a fluid that is chemically different from that filling the other two canals. This chemical difference between the two fluids plays a crucial role in the initial stage of hearing. For example, when the two fluids are intermixed (which can occur if the membrane separating them ruptures), hearing is impaired. Besides their apparent role in the hearing process, these fluids also take the place of blood in supplying all the nourishment for cells in the cochlea. Blood vessels, even tiny capillaries, are forbidden within this structure because their pulsations would create violent waves of sound pressure within the closed confines of the cochlea. This arrangement is reminiscent of the eye (Chapter 2), where blood vessels are routed around the fovea to avoid obstructing the image formed on this crucial part of the eye.

Except at two spots where it is covered by elastic material, the walls of the cochlea consist of hard, relatively shockproof bone. At the base of the cochlea, the vestibular canal is covered by the oval window which, you will recall, is attached to the stapes (stirrup) on the side facing the middle ear. The tympanic canal (eardrum) is likewise covered at the base by the **round window,** another thin membrane that also covers a small opening into the middle ear. These two elastic surfaces allow pressure to be distributed within the fluid-filled cochlea: when the oval window is pushed inward by the stapes, the round window bulges outward to compensate (see Figure 9.11). This compensation is possible because the two chambers, the vestibular and tympanic canals, are linked. How, though, does the fluid-borne pressure wave generated by the stapes at the oval window give rise to hearing? To answer this question, we must look more closely at the cochlear duct and, in particular, at the complex structure, the **organ of Corti,** situated inside it; the structure is named after the Italian anatomist Alfonso Corti, who first described it in 1851. The organ of Corti is the receptor organ that actually generates nerve impulses in response to vibrations passing through the fluid environment of the inner ear. The organ of Corti, in other words, transforms mechanical vibrations into neural messages that are

sent on to the brain. To understand this process of sensory transduction, let's take a close look at the organ of Corti.

The Organ of Corti. Pictured in Figure 9.12, the organ of Corti sits snugly on top of the basilar membrane (recall that this is the membrane separating the cochlear duct and the tympanic canal), and it runs the full length of the cochlear duct. The following are the major components of the organ of Corti: a layer of supporting cells resting on the basilar membrane; rows of hair cells sticking up from the supporting cells; and an awninglike membrane, the **tectorial membrane,** arching over the hair cells. Note a few things about this arrangement. First, the hair cells extend up into the fluid within the cochlear duct; second, the tectorial membrane that arches over the structure contacts the tops of some of the hair cells. Finally, note that because the tectorial membrane is attached at only one end, it can move independently of the basilar membrane. Let's focus for a moment on the hair cells, for they hold the key to the transduction of fluid vibrations into nerve impulses.

In all, there are about 15,500 hair cells, and they are lined up along the organ of Corti in two distinct groups. One group, the **inner hair cells,** is situated on the basilar membrane close to where the tectorial membrane is attached to the wall of the cochlear duct. Numbering about 3,500, these inner hair cells line up in a single row that runs the length of the basilar membrane. The 12,000 or so **outer hair cells,** in contrast, line up in anywhere from three to five rows. These rows also run the length of the basilar membrane. See Box 9.4 for more on the inner and outer hair cells.

Both the inner and the outer hair cells terminate in tiny bristles called *cilia;* these are what you see in the photograph in Box 9.4 (p. 310). Ordinarily you would be unable to look directly at the cilia of the hair cells, for they would be covered by the overlying

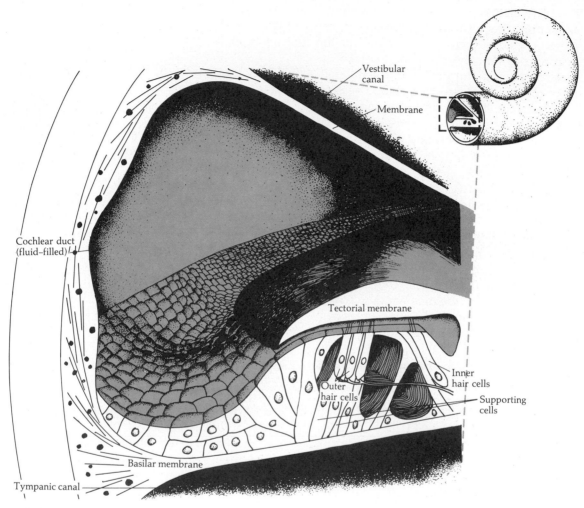

FIGURE 9.12
The organ of Corti.

tectorial membrane. It used to be thought
that cilia from *all* the hair cells actually made
contact with the tectorial membrane. Now,
however, it is generally believed that only
cilia from the outer hair cells touch the tectorial membrane (Dallos, 1981). In any event,
the cilia of both inner and outer hair cells
are extremely close to the tectorial membrane. It is widely accepted that bending of
the cilia constitutes the crucial early event

in the process that leads to hearing, for it is
this event which triggers the electrical signals that travel from the ear to the brain.
Let's take a look, then, at how airborne sound
ends up producing this crucial event, the
bending of the cilia.

As you will recall, airborne vibrations are
picked up by the external ear and converted
into a mechanical, pistonlike action by the
ossicles of the middle ear. Because it is at-

BOX 9.4
The Role of the Inner and Outer Hair Cells in Hearing

The ear is similar to the eye, in that both organs contain two different types of receptor cells. The eye, you will recall, contains rods and cones. These two classes of photoreceptors are different in shape and in retinal distribution, and they are involved in different aspects of visual perception, as we discussed in Chapters 2 and 3. The ear's receptors, the hair cells, are equally distinctive.

As the drawing below shows, each inner hair cell (IHC) is shaped like a flask, and each is surrounded by supporting cells. Each outer hair cell (OHC), in contrast, is cylindrical in shape, and each is surrounded by fluid. Not only do the IHC and OHC differ in appearance; they

also differ in number, with OHCs far outnumbering IHCs (see the text). Moreover, along the entire length of the basilar membrane, nature has carefully segregated these two cell types from each other; and within their private neighborhoods, they are arranged in distinctively different formations. This can be seen in the photograph on the next page, which was taken through an electron microscope. The brushlike structures are the cilia that stick up from the tops of the hair cells. The group of three rows at the top are cilia attached to the OHC; the single row at the bottom of the photo consists of cilia attached to the IHC. To make this photo, the

tectorial membrane that normally covers these cilia was lifted away.

Besides differing in appearance and in their distribution along the basilar membrane, these two classes of hair cells also differ in the pattern of their connections to auditory nerve fibers. The more numerous OHC are sparsely represented within the auditory nerve; only 5 to 10 percent or so of the auditory nerve fibers contact the OHC. The remaining 90 to 95 percent of the fibers contact the IHC, the smaller of the two cell populations. To draw an analogy, it is as if the telephone company took 50,000 phone lines and divided them up so that 10,000 were devoted to

(Continued on next page)

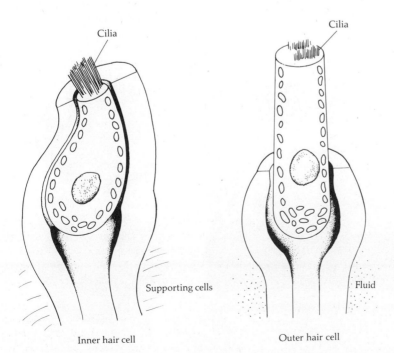

Cilia

Cilia

Supporting cells

Fluid

Inner hair cell

Outer hair cell

the entire population of Chicago while 40,000 were devoted to the much smaller population of neighboring Evanston. Again, we are reminded of the situation in the eye. Recall that the cones, although a distinct numerical minority compared to the rods, enjoy a disproportionately large share of the communication lines (optic nerve fibers) to the brain. In the case of vision, this undemocratic assignment of resources serves a purpose: it lays the groundwork for the specialized roles played by rods and cones in visual perception. There are reasons to suspect that the IHC and OHC likewise mediate different aspects of auditory perception. Let's explore those reasons.

Again, think back to our discussion of visual receptors in Chapter 3. We pointed out that convergence of many receptors onto a single nerve fiber has an advantage and a disadvantage. The advantage is that weak

signals can be detected—convergence enables the receptors to pool their responses, thereby enhancing sensitivity. The disadvantage is a loss of resolution—convergence of information from many receptors makes it impossible to specify which of those receptors were stimulated. Now how do these advantages and disadvantages apply to hearing? The nerve fibers that are fed by the OHC should be well suited for registering the presence of a sound of very weak intensity; convergence allows this OHC system to pool their responses. At the same time, the OHC system would not be able to register the precise frequency of that sound; convergence blurs the precise location along the basilar membrane where maximum displacement occurs. But what about the nerve fibers that are fed by the IHC? They exhibit far less convergence than the OHC system, so they

will be less able to register the presence of weak signals. The IHC system can, however, specify with precision the region of the basilar membrane that is maximally displaced. Thus the IHC system should be well suited for registering the frequency of sounds that are not so weak.

To summarize our reasoning so far, the OHC system seems designed for detecting weak sounds, and the IHC system seems designed for registering information about the frequency of sound. There is, in fact, evidence for this division of labor among the two classes of hair cells. Peter Dallos of Northwestern University, in collaboration with Allen Ryan and Therese McGee, has measured the hearing performance of chinchillas who were exposed to an antibiotic drug (Ryan and Dallos, 1975; Ryan, Dallos, and McGee 1979). In moderate doses, this

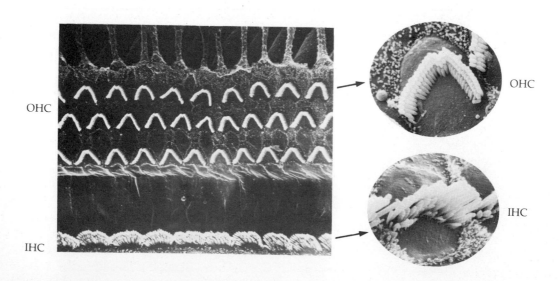

OHC

IHC

OHC

IHC

(Photograph courtesy of Dr. David Lim.)

drug destroys the OHC but leaves the IHC intact. Dallos and his colleagues found that chinchillas given this drug were no longer able to hear weak tones—intensity levels had to be about 40 dB higher than normal in order for these animals to detect tones. At the same time, the chinchillas had no trouble performing a task requiring them to discriminate among similar frequencies. These findings are consistent with the idea that the OHC (which were destroyed in these animals) are necessary for the detection of low-intensity sounds and the IHC (which were intact in these animals) are sufficient for registering information about the frequency of sounds.

There are, incidentally, humans who show the same pattern of hearing loss as the chinchillas. These are people who although not completely deaf, have difficulty hearing faint sounds. Despite this impairment, these people may have perfectly normal hearing on tests designed to measure the ear's ability to distinguish different frequencies (Pick, Evans, and Wilson, 1977). Although it is not possible in these cases to specify what has caused the hearing impairment, it is tempting to conclude on the basis of the work with chinchillas that these people have lost primarily their outer hair cells.

---

tached to the stapes, the oval window receives these mechanical displacements and passes them in the form of pressure waves into the fluids of the cochlea's vestibular and tympanic canals. As the pressure waves travel through these chambers, they cause ripples in the basilar membrane. The tectorial membrane also moves slightly in response to these pressure waves, but it tends to move in directions that are different from the movement of the basilar membrane. These opposing motions cause the cilia of the hair cells on the basilar membrane to bend, like tiny clumps of seaweed swept back and forth by invisible underwater currents. This bending triggers electrical changes within the hair cells—electrical changes that are quite complicated (Evans, 1982a) and not well understood. These electrical changes in the hair cell cause it to release a chemical transmitter substance, which is picked up by nerve endings surrounding the base of the hair cells. These endings are the terminations of nerve cells whose axons form the auditory nerve—the nerve that carries electrical impulses from the cochlea to the central nervous system. It is truly remarkable that such microscopic movements of thin membranes, tiny bones, and hairs inaugurate a process—hearing—that can have such an enormous impact on one's feelings and behaviors.

There is one important step in this sequence that we have skipped: how do the vibrations traveling within the cochlear fluid affect the basilar membrane? Because the hair cells ride on the basilar membrane, the membrane's reactions to fluid vibrations determine which hair cells are stimulated and, hence, which nerve fibers will be activated. To fill in this missing step, let's turn our attention to the basilar membrane, the thin-walled membrane separating the tympanic canal from the cochlear duct (see Figure 9.11).

The Basilar Membrane. Much of what is known today about the basilar membrane comes from work by Georg von Bekesy, a Hungarian scientist who was awarded the Nobel Prize in 1961 for his research on the ear. To appreciate Bekesy's contributions, you need to be familiar with the two major theories describing the way that pressure waves in the cochlear fluid affect the basilar membrane. Both theories were originally formulated in the nineteenth century, before anyone was able to observe the basilar membrane in action. The opposing theories, called the *frequency theory* and the *place theory*, form the background for Bekesy's important work.

The Frequency Theory. The **frequency theory** proposes that the entire basilar membrane vibrates in synchrony with the pressure changes within the cochlea. According to this idea, the stapes taps out a series of beats on the oval window, and the entire basilar membrane dances along.

Ernest Rutherford, a nineteenth-century English physiologist, was the first proponent of the frequency theory. He likened the basilar membrane to the diaphragm inside a telephone receiver. Because it is thin and light, the diaphragm moves back and forth in response to the sound waves of your voice. These movements are converted into electrical current that is carried along a telephone line; and the current eventually produces the same pattern of movements in the listening diaphragm of another person's telephone receiver, thereby reproducing the sounds of your voice. Rutherford believed that the basilar membrane behaved in a comparable fashion, vibrating as a unit at a frequency that matched the sound stimulus. In turn, this vibration produced in the auditory nerve a train of impulses whose frequency mimicked the frequency with which the entire basilar membrane was vibrating. According to Rutherford's idea, then, a 500-Hz tone would yield 500 nerve impulses per second, while a 1,200-Hz tone would yield 1,200 impulses per second.

There are several things wrong with this theory. For one thing, the basilar membrane is not like a diaphragm in a telephone. The basilar membrane varies in width and in stiffness from one end to the other. As a result, the basilar membrane, unlike a dia-

phragm, cannot vibrate uniformly over its entire length; a good description of why this is physically impossible is given by William Yost and Donald Nielsen (1977). There is another problem, too, with the frequency theory. Single auditory nerve fibers cannot match the performance of a telephone line, because neurons are incapable of firing repetitively at rates beyond 1,000 impulses per second; yet we can hear tones whose frequency greatly exceeds this value. So the neural signal required by Rutherford's theory cannot be realized by individual fibers.

This limitation in firing rate could be surmounted if separate nerve fibers fired not in unison but in a staggered fashion. For instance, two fibers each firing at 1,000 impulses per second in combination could produce 2,000 impulses per second if those impulses were appropriately interleaved (Figure 9.13). This modification of the frequency theory, known as the *volley theory*, was proposed by Wever and Bray (1937), who also described some fascinating findings in support of frequency theory (see Box 9.5). Also, the volley theory, unlike Rutherford's frequency theory, does not assume that the basilar membrane acts like a telephone diaphragm. We shall have more to say about the volley theory in our discussion of pitch

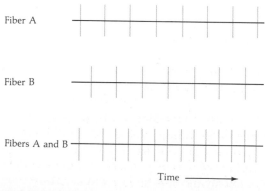

FIGURE 9.13
Two fibers firing regularly but asynchronously.

BOX 9.5
Using a Cat as a Microphone

Imagine walking into a radio studio to find a newscaster speaking into the ear of a live cat. Even more astounding, imagine *hearing* the newscaster's voice being broadcast over a loudspeaker in the room! Far-fetched as it sounds, this kind of demonstration has actually been performed (Cohen, 1969). Moreover, the demonstration works using other animals besides a cat; your own ear would work just fine. Here is how this unusual sound system works.

An electrode placed near the site where the auditory nerve exits the cochlea will pick up an electrical signal arising within the cochlea. This electrical signal results from the high concentration of certain positively charged chemicals within the cochlea's fluid. As the hair cells of the inner ear bend in response to pressure waves within those fluids, the electrical signal changes. When plotted on a graph, this change in electrical potential mirrors

the change in the amplitude of the sound wave presented to the ear. For example, playing a 500-Hz pure tone sound into the ear yields a 500-Hz sinusoidal variation in electrical potential. If this electrically recorded cochlear potential is now fed into an amplifier and then passed to a loudspeaker, you will hear the 500-Hz tone with essentially no distortion: it will be indistinguishable from the original tone played into the ear. In fact, *any* sound stimulus, such as someone's voice or a passage of music, entering the ear can be faithfully reproduced in this fashion. The ear is behaving exactly like a microphone; both devices convert airborne pressure waves into an electrical signal whose temporal waveform closely parallels the stimulus waveform. For this reason the electrical potential recorded from the cochlea has been termed the *cochlear microphonic*.

When it was first discovered by Wever and Bray in 1930, the

cochlear microphonic was thought to originate from the auditory nerve. This would have meant that the frequency of nerve impulses in the auditory nerve exactly followed the input frequency of sound. If correct, this interpretation would have provided strong support for the frequency theory described in the discussion of the basilar membrane. However, later experiments proved that the cochlear microphonic can be recorded even when the nerve itself is temporarily deadened by an anesthetic. These findings ruled out the auditory nerve as the source of the cochlear microphonic. Current evidence points instead to the outer hair cells as the generator of the cochlear microphonic. This would explain why damage to the outer hair cells severely diminishes the cochlear microphonic (Davis et al., 1958), whereas damage to the inner hair cells leaves this electrical signal unaffected (Dallos and Cheatham, 1976).

perception in the next chapter. But let's return now to the basilar membrane and consider the frequency theory's chief opponent, the *place theory*.

The Place Theory. The **place theory** maintains that different frequencies of vibration of the cochlear fluid disturb different regions of the basilar membrane. These different regions of disturbance, in turn, activate different hair cells and hence different auditory nerve fibers. You can see where this theory gets its

name—frequency information is encoded according to the location, or *place*, along the basilar membrane disturbed by fluid vibration. The most notable early proponent of the place theory was Helmholtz, whose ideas on color vision we discussed in Chapter 6. Helmholtz's theory was inspired by the fact that the basilar membrane is narrow at the base of the cochlea and broad at the apex. This layout reminded Helmholtz of the variation in the length of strings of a piano (Figure 9.14)—which led him to propose that the basilar membrane was composed of distinct fibers that individually stretched across its width. Because of the basilar membrane's tapered shape, fibers at one end would be longer than those at the other, just like piano strings. According to Helmholtz, vibrations within the cochlear fluid would set into motion only those "strings" of the basilar membrane that were tuned to the frequencies at which the fluid vibrated. In other words, fibers of the basilar membrane would vibrate in the same way that piano strings can be induced to vibrate when you sing a loud note. This is the principle of resonance discussed in Box 9.3.

While based on solid physical principles, Helmholtz's place theory was flawed in several respects. For one thing, subsequent anatomical work showed that the basilar membrane is not composed of separate fibers capable of resonating individually. Rather than a set of piano strings, the basilar membrane looks more like a continuous strip of rubber. Moreover, the basilar membrane is not under tension, like piano strings; it is

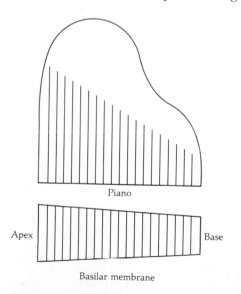

Piano

Apex   Base

Basilar membrane

FIGURE 9.14
The basilar membrane's tapered shape resembles the layout of a piano's strings.

relatively slack. So the resonance portion of Helmholtz's theory proved incorrect, but his idea that different *places* along the basilar membrane respond to different frequencies *did* survive. In fact, it is this idea that Bekesy's work so elegantly substantiated, and it is to his work that we now turn.

Traveling Waves. Bekesy realized that the essential difference between the place and frequency theories lay in how each thought the basilar membrane vibrated in response to different frequencies. Of course the simplest way to settle the issue would have been to observe the membrane's movements; but this was technically impossible in the late 1920s, when Bekesy became interested in the problem. Nonetheless, Bekesy knew that the width and thickness of the basilar membrane varied along its length, being wider and thicker at the end near the apex. Armed with these facts, he built a mechanical model of the cochlea, so he could directly observe the behavior of an enlarged replica of the basilar membrane (Bekesy, 1960).

For the tympanic and vestibular canals he used a brass tube with a small rubber cap stretched over each end; these caps represented the oval and round windows. He cut a tapered slot the length of the entire tube and covered this slot with a rubber "membrane" whose thickness increased as the slot widened; this represented the basilar membrane. For the stapes he substituted a small mallet placed against the rubber cap on one end of the tube; this mallet was vibrated by a tuning fork. A drawing of Bekesy's large-scale cochlea is shown in Figure 9.15.

To observe the behavior of his mechanical model, Bekesy lightly rested his forearm on the rubber membrane. When a pure tone was produced by striking the tuning fork, Bekesy felt the rubber membrane vibrating against his arm at one particular spot (see panel A of Figure 9.16). By testing with tuning forks that produced different frequencies, he discovered that the location of this tingling spot depended on the frequency with which the tuning fork vibrated the "oval window." With higher frequencies, this tingle occurred near his wrist, a place on the membrane corresponding to the narrow end closest to the stapes. Lower frequencies, in contrast, yielded a tingle nearer his elbow, the region of the membrane corresponding to the wide end near the apex. In panel A of the figure you can see the relation between pure-tone frequency and the point along Bekesy's mechanical model where that frequency yields its peak vibration. Translating Bekesy's results to the actual basilar membrane—a much smaller, coiled structure—yields the scaled diagram in panel B of Figure 9.16. This diagram reveals which point along the basilar membrane vibrates maximally to a particular sound frequency.

Bekesy's ingenious demonstration therefore strongly favored the place theory. In subsequent years, Bekesy went on to confirm this conclusion using other, more precise techniques, including direct visualization of the human basilar membrane, using a microscope. He explained the connection between the point of maximum vibration along the basilar membrane and sound fre-

quency in the following way. The fluctuations in fluid pressure produced by the pistonlike movements of the stapes set up a **traveling wave** along the basilar membrane itself. To envision what is meant by a "traveling wave," think what happens when you flick one end of a rope whose other end is tied to, say, a pole. You see a wave of motion traveling the length of the rope. Unlike a rope, though, the basilar membrane varies in thickness and width along its length. If you were to flick the basilar membrane, the resulting wave of motion would actually grow in amplitude as it traveled away from you. But this wave would reach a peak amplitude and then rapidly collapse, never getting to the other end. An example of this kind of traveling wave is illustrated in Figure 9.17. In this figure the basilar membrane is drawn as if uncoiled and viewed from the side. Thus in each panel the horizontal axis represents the length of the basilar membrane, with its base at the left and its apex at the right. Each separate panel shows the profile of the basilar membrane at a different instant in time. You might imagine these as successive snapshots of the basilar membrane taken just after you have flicked it as you would a rope. (Flicking it corresponds

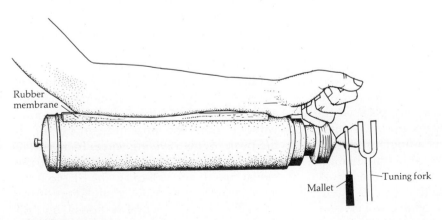

FIGURE 9.15
Bekesy's mechanical model of the cochlea.

A.

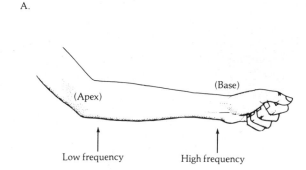

B.

FIGURE 9.16
Summary of the results of Bekesy's experiment.

to the stapes's tapping against the oval window, setting up waves of motion within the fluid in the cochlea.) As the wave progresses down the membrane over time, note how it grows in size, reaches a peak, and then rather abruptly disappears. The place along the basilar membrane where this peak occurs depends on how rapidly you flicked the basilar membrane. This idea can be seen by comparing the traveling waves depicted in the left panel of the figure to those depicted in the right panel. Note that in the series on the left, the traveling wave reaches its peak nearer the base, while in the series on the right it reaches its peak nearer the apex. The waves in the left-hand series were produced by a high-frequency tone, those in the right-hand series by a low frequency tone.

The peak of the traveling wave, you should understand, represents a place where the basilar membrane bulges upward—which is why Bekesy could feel a tingling spot on his forearm when he tested his mechanical cochlea. This upward bulge in the actual basilar membrane means that the cilia riding on this portion of the membrane will be bent more than those elsewhere along the membrane. This more pronounced bending oc-

curs because the cilia riding on the bulge come into closer contact with the tectorial membrane stretching over the top of the basilar membrane. In turn these highly bent cilia will activate their associated hair cells. In other words, any frequency of vibration will cause the basilar membrane to bulge maximally at one location, thereby maximally stimulating a characteristic group of hair cells. This arrangement is so orderly that if you were told which hair cells had been maximally stimulated, you would be able to deduce the sound frequency that had produced that stimulation. This orderly layout of frequency over the length of the basilar membrane is known as **tonotopic organization.**

The behavior of traveling waves also readily explains how intensity information is registered by the basilar membrane. For a given frequency, the intensity of the sound will determine the amplitude, or height, of the peak of the traveling wave. Increases in the amplitude of these movements of the basilar membrane will cause the cilia to bend more, leading to greater stimulation of the hair cells, a larger neural response, and ultimately an increase in perceived loudness. Increases in the amplitude of these move-

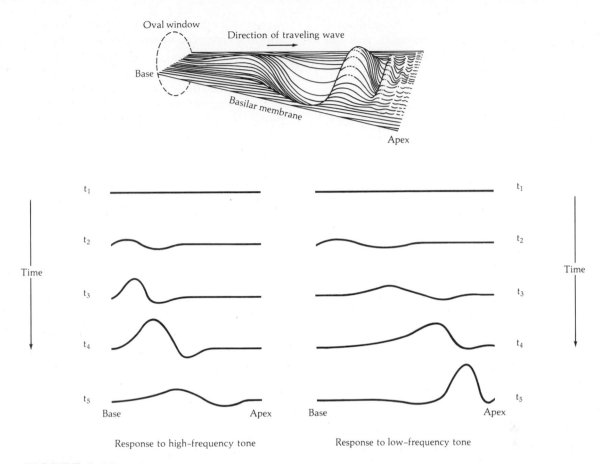

FIGURE 9.17
The top drawing shows a traveling wave deforming the basilar membrane. The set of curves below at the left represent the response of the basilar membrane over time to a high-frequency tone. The curves at the right represent the basilar membrane's response over time to a low-frequency tone.

ments also enlarge the spread of the bulge in the basilar membrane, which in turn alters the pattern of hair cells stimulated. The perceptual consequences of these changes in the basilar membrane's response to different frequencies and intensities will be discussed in the next chapter.

This gives you a bird's-eye view of the workings of the inner ear. Referring back to Figure 9.8, you can now understand why the inner ear is characterized as a frequency-

selective sound transducer. We call it "frequency-selective" because, by virtue of its mechanical properties, the inner ear breaks up incoming sound into its component frequencies. In the last section of this chapter, we will briefly survey what happens to the signals from the hair cells as they are routed to the brain via the auditory nerve. But before leaving the inner ear, we want to describe one of the cochlea's really unusual properties, its ability to *generate* sounds on its own. These so-called **cochlear emissions** represent one of the most exciting discoveries about hearing in recent years. It is still too early to say just what role, if any, these internally generated sounds play in hearing. Nonetheless, they can be readily explained in terms of the cochlea's mechanics, and for that reason they are worth considering here.

Sounds Emitted by the Cochlea. The cochlea is built to receive sound and convert it into neural impulses, and it does this exquisitely. But in addition, the cochlea is capable of actually *generating* sound energy that is transmitted back through the middle ear and into the outer ear where this sound energy can be picked up by a microphone (Kemp, 1979). First we shall describe where these "emitted sounds" come from. Then we shall tell you what they sound like and why most people cannot hear the emitted sounds from their own ears.

The chain of events stretching from the outer ear to the inner ear should be familiar to you by now:

airborne sound → movement of the eardrum → movement of the ossicles → movement of the oval window → fluid-borne pressure waves → displacement of basilar membrane → stimulation of hair cells

But there is no reason why many of these events could not occur in the reverse sequence. After all, the cochlea consists of moving parts suspended in fluid, and any time those parts move, they will create waves within the cochlear fluid. To illustrate, imagine that you are *inside* the cochlea moving your arms back and forth, splashing about as if you were in a swimming pool. Your movements would disturb the cochlear fluid, setting up waves within it that would spread throughout the volume of the fluid. Because the cochlea (your miniature swimming pool) is a sealed container, these

waves will eventually push against the oval window from the inner side. Since the oval window is attached to the stapes, this push would be felt by the stapes and passed in reverse through the other two attached bones in the ossicular chain. The hammer, as a result, would be pushed against the inner side of the eardrum. This pressure would in turn cause the eardrum to bulge outward slightly into the auditory canal, displacing air molecules within the canal. The eardrum, in other words, would behave just like the cone on a loudspeaker (recall Figure 9.2)—movements of the eardrum would create air pressure changes within the ear canal. If these air pressure changes were sufficiently robust, they could actually be *heard* by someone in the vicinity of the ear from which the sound energy was being emitted. So you can see that movements of any of the structures within the cochlea could set up the reverse chain of events, causing sound energy to be reflected back into the world.

Recent research suggests that the sequence of events just described may actually occur. Sensitive microphones placed within the auditory canal of the human ear are able to record what are called "spontaneous emissions" (Kemp, 1979; Zurek, 1981). These emissions consist of sound energy in the absence of an external stimulus—they originate from within the ear. Such spontaneous sounds can range up to 20 dB_{SPL} in intensity, a level that is certainly within the audible range (refer to Box 9.2). This is not a rare or abnormal condition; by one count (Zurek, 1981), spontaneously emitted sound could be measured from the ears of about two-thirds of the people sampled, though the measured intensity level did vary from person to person. It is generally believed that emitted sounds originate from tiny movements within the cochlea itself (analogous to your splashing about in a swimming pool). Because the middle and inner ears are so delicately designed to amplify and transduce mechanical displacements, it would take very little motion within the cochlea to trigger the chain of events leading to emitted sounds. But what could generate such motion to begin with? For an answer, you should realize that the structures within the cochlea do consist of biologically active cells that depend on metabolic events for their energy. These metabolic events, necessary for normal cell function, involve molecular movements at least as large as those capable of producing a sensation of hearing. (Recall that motion as small as the diameter of a single hydrogen atom can be heard.) It is ironic that nature has designed an ear so sensitive that it can transmit the sounds produced by its own parts!

But if our ears generate sound energy all the time, why don't we hear that sound? Shouldn't we be able to experience this self-produced hum from within our own ears? Actually, emitted sound can sometimes be heard; people able to hear their emitted sound usually suffer from a condition known as **tinnitus,** a more or less continuous ringing in the ears. This condition can be very annoying, for even though the ringing is not loud, it is persistent. In some cases, but not all, it probably results from spontaneously emitted sound (Wilson and Sutton, 1981). People who do not experience tinnitus may have adapted to their self-produced, emitted sounds, just as they adapt to a steady hum from an external source such as a refrigerator motor.

These self-produced sounds can have bizarre consequences. In some cases, although the emitted sound cannot be heard by the source (the person emitting the sound), it *can* be heard by someone else nearby (McFadden, 1982); these emitted sounds are heard as high-pitched tones. You might try listening for emitted sounds from a friend's ear. In a quiet setting, place your ear close to your friend's and notice whether you hear a steady, faint tone. If you do, have your friend move away from your ear and notice whether you still hear the tone. If the tone persists, it must be originating either from an external source or from within your own ear. But if the tone becomes inaudible when your friend moves, you very likely were hearing an emitted sound from your friend's ear. Incidentally, emitted sounds have been measured from the ears of dogs and cats (McFadden, 1982), so you need not limit your experiment to humans.

The Auditory System: The Auditory Pathways

As you have learned, the cochlea converts sound energy (pressure waves) into the only form of information understandable by the brain, neural impulses. This neural information is carried out of the inner ear by the **auditory nerve.** The auditory nerve, in turn, branches into several different pathways that eventually reconverge within the auditory cortex (the region on the side of your brain that would be covered if you put your hand over your ear). These various pathways seem designed to process different aspects of auditory information (Evans, 1974). One pathway contains neurons whose response properties enable them to specify *where* sound is coming from. Another pathway contains neurons that analyze information necessary for identifying *what* the sound is. In other words, the auditory system contains specialized neural analyzers for locating and identifying sound sources within the auditory environment.

Figure 9.18 gives you an overview of the pathways originating from the left auditory nerve and the right auditory nerve; the right ear has been omitted for clarity. For our purposes, it is unnecessary to trace the flow of information through this maze of pathways.

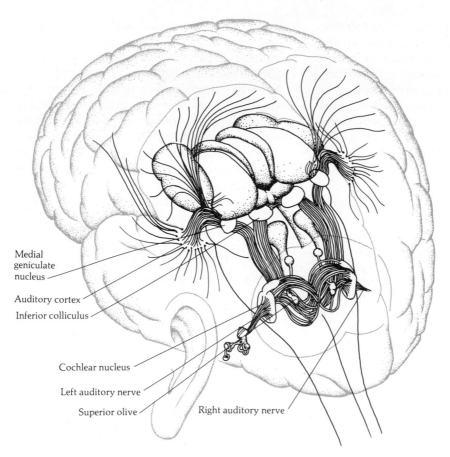

Medial
geniculate
nucleus

Auditory cortex

Inferior colliculus

Cochlear nucleus

Left auditory nerve

Superior olive

Right auditory nerve

FIGURE 9.18
An overview of the auditory pathways.

Instead, we'll summarize several aspects of auditory information that the neurons seem to be processing. Our aim is to highlight neural properties that bear on perceptual aspects of hearing to be discussed in the next chapter.

This final section of this chapter is divided into three subsections. The first summarizes the properties of neurons comprising the auditory nerve. The two remaining subsections focus on the neural analysis of the cues for sound localization (where) and the cues for sound identification (what). In the course of our discussion, you will see a

similarity between auditory neural processing and visual neural processing: at successively higher stages, individual neurons become increasingly more discriminating about the sounds that activate them.

THE AUDITORY NERVE

The auditory nerve that comes from each of your ears consists of about 50,000 individual fibers. These are the axons of nerve cells situated in the inner ear. As detailed in Box 9.4, at least 90 percent of these fibers carry information picked up from just the inner hair cells, while the remaining 10 percent or so are devoted to input from the outer hair cells. By recording the electrical impulses from many individual fibers, physiologists have determined what kinds of sound stimuli must be presented to the ear in order to activate those fibers. Let's consider some of their major findings.

First of all, fibers of the auditory nerve, like retinal ganglion cells of the eye, are active even when no stimulus is present. Therefore, in order to register its presence, a sound must alter this spontaneously occurring, random neural chatter. In auditory nerve fibers, sound is registered by a temporary increase in firing rate. However, not just any sound stimulus will do. For any given fiber, there is a limited range of pure-tone frequencies that can evoke a response. Moreover, within this limited range not all frequencies are equally effective. We shall illustrate these observations using the following example.

Suppose we measure the number of impulses that pure tones produce in a single auditory nerve fiber. Suppose further that we make such measurements for pure tones of various frequencies (Hz) and intensities (dB). (Keep in mind that a pure tone has a sinusoidal waveform.) For each frequency, we will determine the *minimum* intensity needed to produce a noticeable increase in that fiber's spontaneous level of activity; the resulting intensity value will constitute that fiber's "threshold" for detecting that frequency. We refer to this intensity as the threshold because at lower intensities the fiber behaves as if the tone were not presented at all—the fiber is "deaf" to all weaker intensities. Such a **threshold intensity** is determined for a number of frequencies. Plotting the resulting thresholds for an individual fiber would yield a graph something like the one shown in Figure 9.19.

There are a couple of points to note in this graph. At the very lowest intensity, this particular fiber responds only to a 5,000-Hz tone (abbreviated 5kHz). This value, then, constitutes this fiber's preferred, or *characteristic*, frequency. At this quiet sound level, no other tone produces activity in the fiber. But as we increase the sound intensity, previously ineffective frequencies begin to produce measurable increases in the fiber's activity. In other words, the fiber has different intensity thresholds for different frequencies. The entire curve in Figure 9.19 describes what is called the **frequency tuning curve** for that fiber.

When this sort of analysis is applied to many different auditory nerve fibers, the result is a family of tuning curves like those illustrated in Figure 9.20. Note that different fibers possess different characteristic frequencies; some respond best to low frequencies, others to medium frequencies, and still others to high frequencies. Together, these fibers cover a large range of frequencies. So in the auditory nerve, different fibers respond to different sound frequencies.

This frequency tuning of auditory nerve fibers arises from the way the fibers are connected to the basilar membrane. Recall that different sound frequencies produce traveling waves that peak at different places along the basilar membrane. As you might guess, each fiber's characteristic frequency is determined by where along the basilar membrane that fiber makes contact with hair cells. Fibers originating from the apex of the cochlea (the low-frequency region—see Figure 9.16) respond to low frequencies, whereas fibers from the base (the high-frequency region) "prefer" higher frequencies.

This idea of representing a stimulus dimension within an array of tuned neurons should be familiar to you by now. We saw the same principle at work in the visual system: visual cells are tuned for size, orientation, retinal disparity, and so on. In effect, tuned cells make a particular statement about

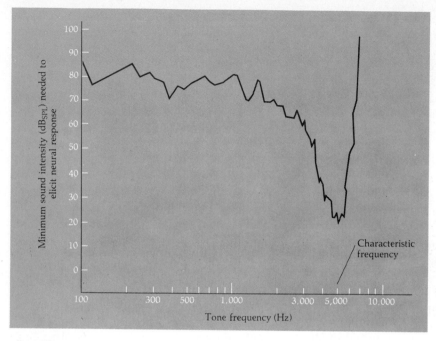

FIGURE 9.19

A graph of the threshold intensities (frequency tuning curve) for a single auditory nerve fiber. (Courtesy of Evan Relkin.)

the nature of a stimulus. In the case of the auditory nerve, individual nerve fibers are able to signal the occurrence of a tone whose frequency falls within a limited range of frequencies. Within this range, however, a fiber's activity increases with sound *intensity*, a property we shall discuss shortly. Consequently, within this limited range, the fiber's response is wholly ambiguous: any number of different frequencies could produce the same neural response if their intensities were adjusted properly. So looking just at the firing rate of a particular fiber, we could never be certain which frequency had stimulated it. (This is the same sort of ambiguity problem we talked about in Chapters 4, 5, and 6.)

We don't want to give you the impression that auditory fibers respond only to pure tones—they are considerably more versatile

than this. In fact, an auditory fiber will respond vigorously to *any* complex sound just so long as that sound contains at least some energy within the frequency range handled by that fiber. To illustrate, the sound produced when you snap your fingers is *broadband*—that is, it contains many different frequencies; so, too, is the static heard when you dial a radio between stations. Either of these broad-band sounds would activate a number of frequency-tuned fibers. Any particular fiber, however, would ''hear'' (respond to) only those frequency components of the complex sound to which it was tuned.

So far our description of auditory fibers has focused on their frequency selectivity, as reflected in their threshold response profile. Before moving to higher levels of auditory processing, let's take a look at two

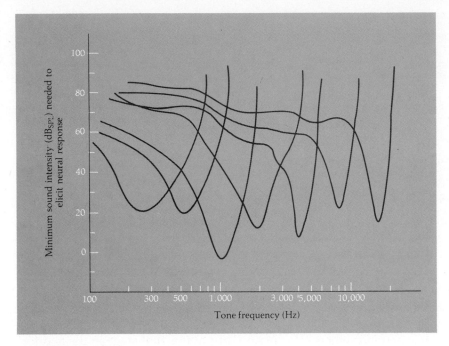

FIGURE 9.20

Frequency tuning curves for a number of different auditory nerve fibers.
(Courtesy of Evan Relkin.)

other characteristic features of auditory nerve fiber responses. One feature is the way a fiber responds to sound levels above its threshold. Imagine recording the discharge rate from the fiber whose tuning curve is shown in Figure 9.19. Suppose that we use a 5-kHz tone, that fiber's preferred frequency. As the tuning curve indicates, an intensity of 20 dB$_{SPL}$ will produce a barely discernible elevation in the fiber's activity level—this represents that cell's threshold. Now suppose we plot the discharge level produced by increasingly higher sound intensities of the 5-kHz tone. The result would be a graph like that shown in Figure 9.21. As you can see, between about 30 dB$_{SPL}$ and 70 dB$_{SPL}$, the fiber's activity steadily grows as the sound level increases. Above 70 dB$_{SPL}$, however, the fiber's activity level flattens out—higher intensities of the tone all produce the same neural response. This so-called

saturation effect, typical of auditory nerve fibers, means that the fiber has a limited range over which it can signal the intensity level of a given frequency. Hence firing rate provides an *im*perfect representation of sound level—distinguishable differences in sound intensity (for instance, 80 dB$_{SPL}$ versus 120 dB$_{SPL}$) produce indistinguishable neural responses. Clearly, some additional neural information must enter into the coding of sound intensity; we'll return to this matter of intensity coding in the following chapter.

A second significant property of auditory nerve fibers is their response to continuous, prolonged stimulation. When a sound of constant intensity is presented continuously, the level of activity evoked by that sound declines over time; this property is called **adaptation.** As described in Box 4.5 (p. 131), neural adaptation is a common property of sensory neurons. In the case of

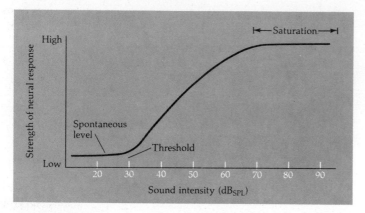

FIGURE 9.21

The neural activity of an auditory nerve fiber increases as the sound level increases, until a saturation point is reached.

hearing, this adaptation phenomenon probably has something to do with the gradual reduction in loudness you experience when listening to a steady sound, such as the hum of a refrigerator motor.

This gives you an overview of the response properties of auditory nerve fibers, your brain's sole link to the sounds in your environment. The train of neural impulses carried by the auditory nerves from your left and right ears provides the ingredients for all aspects of hearing. Subsequent auditory processing must utilize information contained within these impulses. In the two following sections, you will see how this neural information is utilized for sound localization and for sound identification.

BEYOND THE AUDITORY NERVE: SOUND LOCALIZATION

Having two ears enables you to localize sounds. This section discusses how the processing of information within the auditory system makes such localization possible.

Looking back at Figure 9.18, note that the left auditory nerve projects to the **cochlear nucleus** on the left side of the brain while

the right auditory nerve projects to the cochlear nucleus on the right side of the brain. Thus at this first stage in the auditory chain, information from the two ears remains segregated. Sound delivered to just the left ear (stimulation that is **monaural,** meaning "one ear") will activate cells in the left cochlear nucleus, but not those in the right cochlear nucleus. Exactly the opposite is true for monaural stimulation delivered to the right ear. However, at processing stages beyond the cochlear nucleus (superior olive, inferior colliculus, and higher), the auditory system becomes **binaural** ("both ears"), meaning that these higher stages receive neural input from the left ear *and* the right ear. Neurons at these stages may be activated by sound presented to *either* ear. This property should remind you of the binocular visual cells discussed in Chapter 4.

These binaural cells seem specifically designed to compare inputs from the two ears, thereby allowing you to hear where a sound originates relative to your head. To understand how these binaural cells work, you first need to be familiar with the two chief cues available for sound localization. In both of these cues, the sounds received by the two ears are compared, which is why the cues are called **binaural cues.** Let's take a moment to discuss them.

Imagine keeping your head still and listening to a sound originating from a source located at various positions in front of and to either side of your head. When the sound source lies straight ahead of you (a *midline* source), the sound energy reaching your two ears will be identical: the air pressure waves will arrive at the two ears at precisely the same time, and the intensity of the sound waves will be the same for both ears. Now suppose that a sound source is located to your left, away from the midline. In this case, the sound wave will arrive at your closer ear, the left one, slightly before reaching your farther ear, the right one. This difference in time of arrival of sound at the two ears is called **interaural time difference,** and it is a potent cue for sound localization.

Besides arriving at one ear slightly ahead of the other, sound located away from the midline will also be more intense at the ear receiving the sound first. This **interaural intensity difference** arises for two reasons. First, since sound intensity falls off with distance (recall Figure 9.4), a sound will be slightly more intense for the ear nearer to the source. Second, a portion of the source's sound energy will be blocked from reaching the farther ear because the head stands in the way. The head produces what is called a *sound shadow,* a weakening of the intensity of sound at the more distant ear. In combination, these two sources of interaural intensity difference (decline in intensity with distance and intervention of a sound shadow) provide another cue for sound localization.

So to summarize, interaural time differences and interaural intensity differences provide two sources of information for specifying the locations of sounds; both of these cues will be discussed in greater detail in the next chapter. Here we are concerned with how the auditory system processes these cues. Do neurons exist that can register time or intensity differences between

the two ears? The answer to this question is yes—neurons at several stages in the auditory chain are sensitive to small binaural time and intensity differences (Rose et al., 1966; Imig and Adrian, 1977; Knudsen and Konishi, 1978; Masterton and Imig, 1984). For example, certain cells in the **superior olivary nucleus,** often called the **superior olive** (see Figure 9.18), respond maximally when the left ear receives sound slightly before the right ear does, whereas other cells respond best when the right ear receives sound slightly before the left. The interaural time delay that gives the best response varies from cell to cell. Still other cells respond best when the two ears receive slightly different intensities, some preferring the stronger intensity in the right ear and others preferring the stronger intensity in the left ear.

As a result of these response properties, most binaural cells respond best to a sound arising from a particular location. For example, some binaural cells respond best to a source located close to the midline, while other cells respond best to sounds arising from various points to one side or the other of the midline. In effect, each binaural cell "listens" for sound within a fairly restricted region of **auditory space.** This region of space constitutes the cell's receptive field, the area in space where a sound must be located in order to stimulate the cell. As an aggregate, these cells provide a neural map of auditory space.

There are several reasons for thinking that binaural cells of this sort are involved in sound localization. For one thing, placing an earplug in one ear causes sounds to be mislocalized. Under this condition, sound seems to originate not from the actual location of the source, but from a location displaced toward the unplugged ear. This makes sense. Plugging an ear reduces sound intensity received by that ear. Plugging one ear also produces a shift in the receptive fields of binaural neurons, by an amount and direction predicted from errors in sound localization (Knudsen and Konishi, 1980). This systematic shift in the receptive field locations of binaural neurons reinforces the idea that these neurons encode the location of sound in space.

There is another reason for believing this idea, too. Not all species of mammals possess the kind of binaural neurons just described. In particular, the size of the superior olive varies greatly from one species to another. This structure is one of the brain structures containing binaural neurons. Bruce Masterton, a psychologist at Florida State University, has tested the abilities of different species to localize sound (Masterton et al., 1975). The animals were trained to listen for a short tone that came from one of two loudspeakers, one located to the animal's left and the other located to the animal's right; the tone informed the animal which way to go, left or right, in order to obtain a drink of water. Masterton found that cats and tree shrews, both of which have sizable superior olives, could perform this task with ease. However, hedgehogs and rats, who have a much smaller superior olive, made numerous errors, indicating an inability to localize sound accurately. Masterton's behavioral study reinforces the idea that binaural neurons of the superior olive are responsible for analyzing interaural cues for sound localization.

This concludes our discussion of how the auditory system processes information about *where* a sound originates. We turn now to how it processes information about *what* the sound is.

BEYOND THE AUDITORY NERVE: SOUND IDENTIFICATION

Recall that any fiber in the auditory nerve responds to a limited range of frequencies, a range that defines the fiber's frequency tuning. The responses of such fibers to more complex sounds (such as noise) can be simply predicted from each fiber's tuning curve. Moving from the auditory nerve to more central processing stages (for example, the cochlear nucleus), cells continue to respond to tones of certain frequencies, but the range of frequencies over which any given cell responds becomes narrower. Thus over the first several stages of the auditory system, tuning curves become more selective for frequency. In addition, information destined for the auditory cortex passes through the **medial geniculate nucleus** (see Figure 9.18). This structure, the analogue to the LGN in vision, also receives input from the reticular activating system (recall Chapter 4, p. 107). So again, an organism's level of arousal could modulate auditory sensitivity by means of neural influences occurring within the medial geniculate nucleus.

Once information arrives at the auditory cortex, however, temporal frequency no longer represents the crucial stimulus variable. Neurons in the auditory cortex are much less "interested" in the frequency or intensity of sounds. Instead, cortical neurons respond best to more complicated, biologically significant sounds. To give just a few examples, some cortical neurons fail to respond to any steady tone but do respond vigorously to a tone that changes in frequency. For some of these neurons, the frequency change must be in a particular direction, either up or down. One sound whose frequency goes up is the "Hmmm?" sound you make when you don't understand something (try it). A sound whose frequency goes down is the sound you make when you yawn (try it). In general, frequency changes are responsible for the inflections in your voice when you talk; speech without inflections has a flat, monotone character.

Other cortical neurons respond only to complex "kissing" sounds that resemble the noise you make when calling a dog. In animals that utilize vocalizations to communicate, the auditory cortex contains neurons specifically responsive to individual vocalizations. Such cells often fail to respond to tones, clicks, or noise and instead can be activated only by a certain "call" that forms part of that animal's natural vocabulary. For instance, in the auditory cortex of the squirrel monkey there are neurons activated exclusively by "cackles," other neurons activated only by "shrieks," and still others activated only by "trills" (Wollberg and Newman, 1972). Each of these natural vocalizations conveys a particular message within the repertoire of calls made by the squirrel monkey.

Cortical neurons, then, unlike those at lower levels of the auditory system, respond to more *abstract* features of sound—features that identify the sound source itself, not just the constituent frequencies in that sound. This is why damage to the auditory cortex impairs performance on tasks where an animal must discriminate between complex sounds but spares performance on tasks involving the detection or discrimination of simple tones. In the following chapter, we shall describe some evidence suggesting that the human brain may contain neurons selective for certain acoustic cues important for speech recognition.

Summary and Preview

This chapter has described the physical events that give rise to the experience of sound. These events are captured by the ears and ultimately are transformed into neural events. The entire chain of events was summarized in Figure 9.8. Looking back at that figure, you should be able to understand how the auditory system performs each of the functions shown in that flow diagram. Throughout this chapter we've largely avoided discussing the perceptual consequences of this sequence of events. But now that you know something about the auditory system's machinery, we're ready to consider the accomplishment that this machinery makes possible—hearing.

Chapter 10

Hearing

Do blind people hear better than sighted individuals? Does exposure to loud music impair one's hearing? How do you manage to ignore the hubbub at a noisy party while at the same time picking out and listening to a familiar voice? Why do most people cringe when fingernails are scraped across a chalkboard? These are just a few of the questions we shall consider in this chapter on hearing. Where possible, we'll relate what we say about hearing to the material presented in the previous chapter on the auditory system.

We'll start by describing your hearing abilities on tests employing simple, well-controlled sounds such as pure tones. You will learn how a tone's frequency influences the ease with which you can hear that tone. We'll also describe how frequency influences a tone's pitch and loudness. We'll outline how extraneous noise affects your ability to hear tones, and we'll consider the effects of long-term exposure to loud noise. Next, we'll discuss the ability to locate where sounds come from. Finally, we'll consider perception of particularly important sounds, human speech.

The Range and Limits of Hearing

It makes sense to begin by considering the range of sound frequencies humans can hear, for this defines the boundaries of auditory perception: you are deaf to sounds outside these boundaries. In a way, the range of audible sound frequencies is analogous to the range of visible spatial frequencies (see Chapter 5). In both instances, your eyes and ears register a fairly wide but nonetheless limited range of visual and auditory information. Because this range is limited, your perceptual world is limited.

328

In the case of hearing, the range of audible frequencies is determined by measuring the minimum intensity, or amplitude, necessary to just barely detect tones of various frequencies; these measurements are made in an otherwise quiet environment, with no other sounds present. Tones are typically delivered over earphones or through a loudspeaker. The method goes something like this. A single tone of a certain frequency is initially presented at an intensity level that can easily be heard. This familiarizes the listener with the pitch of the tone. Next, the intensity is gradually turned down until the sound can no longer be heard. At this point, the intensity is slowly turned up again until the tone is just barely audible. This resulting intensity value is referred to as the **threshold intensity;** values below this threshold intensity cannot be heard, whereas intensities higher than this can be. The same procedure is repeated for each of a number of tone frequencies, and the resulting

threshold values are plotted on a graph like the one shown in Figure 10.1; the resulting curve summarizes the range of frequencies audible to the human ear.

Curves like this, showing variations in threshold with frequency, are called **audiograms.** You should be able to see the analogy between an audiogram and a contrast-sensitivity function for spatial vision—both specify threshold performance over a range of frequencies. As the curve in Figure 10.1 indicates, the threshold of hearing varies with the frequency of sound: in the middle frequencies, far less intensity is needed to make a tone audible than in the low and high frequencies. In this figure, intensity values are expressed in terms of decibels (dB_{SPL}), with the value of 0 dB_{SPL} assigned to the weakest intensity that can be heard at any frequency (see Box 9.2). In this case, tones in the neighborhood of 2,500 Hz require least intensity to be heard. As a result, their threshold is expressed as 0 dB_{SPL} and all other

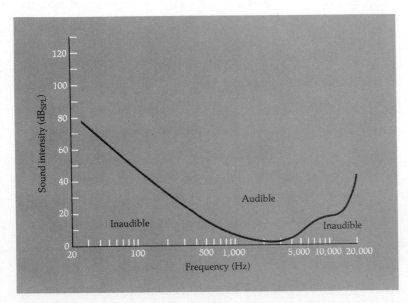

FIGURE 10.1

An audiogram showing the range of tone frequencies audible to a normal young adult.

threshold values are expressed relative to this value. Thus to hear a 250-Hz tone, its intensity must be 40 dB higher than the intensity needed to hear a 2,500-Hz tone.

To give you some points of reference, striking the lowest key on a piano produces a musical note whose primary frequency is 27.5 Hz, the note produced by middle C is 262 Hz, and the top note on the piano is 4,186 Hz. A sound of very high frequency can be produced by turning on a television set but leaving the volume turned all the way down. This generates a high-pitched whine about 16,000 Hz (16 kHz).

At its best, the human ear is extraordinarily sensitive: the intensity required to hear a 2,500-Hz tone is hardly any greater than the amplitude of vibrations associated with the random movements of air molecules! At this very low sound level the eardrum moves only about one-billionth of a centimeter, a distance less than the diameter of a single hydrogen atom (Bekesy and Rosenblith, 1951). This incredible performance testifies to what a masterpiece of engineering the ears really are—all the more remarkable in view of the fact that sounds several million times more intense will not damage the ear. And on top of this, human beings can hear a rather wide range of frequencies: most people can detect tones as low in frequency as 20 Hz, which is heard as a very low rumble; and young people can detect tones as high in frequency as 20,000 Hz. To get this much performance out of a device so sensitive represents a real design feat.

The performance summarized in Figure 10.1 represents the range of hearing for the normal young adult. This curve, the audiogram, is remarkably consistent across individuals, so much so that deviations from this norm usually signify some type of impairment in the peripheral auditory system, either in the ear or in the auditory nerve. Abnormal audiograms are *not* commonly associated with disorders of the central auditory nervous system; central neural disorders lead to other kinds of hearing loss, some of which we'll mention later in this chapter. For now, let's consider some of the conditions that can produce abnormal audiograms (higher than normal, pure-tone thresholds) and the perceptual consequences of those abnormalities.

ABNORMAL AUDIOGRAMS

Age and Other Factors Causing Hearing Loss. The most common, indeed inevitable, factor that affects the audiogram is age. In industrial societies, people gradually lose sensitivity to high frequencies, a condition known as **presbycusis** (from the Greek *presbys*, meaning "old," and *akousis*, meaning "hearing"); and this selective, high-frequency deafness begins at a surprisingly early age. According to one survey (Davis and Silverman, 1960), most people 30 years old are unable to hear frequencies above 15,000 Hz; and by 50 years of age, hearing is impossible beyond 12,000 Hz. By 70 years of age, the cutoff value drops to 6,000 Hz, a value that's within the range of normal speech. Moreover, for any given age group, men exhibit a larger degree of hearing loss than do women (Corso, 1981). These figures represent average values and therefore do not invariably apply to all people. Some researchers believe that presbycusis results, at least in part, from changes in the vasculature of the cochlea—changes that restrict the blood supply to the delicate neural elements in the inner ear, presumably leading to chronic anemia that starves these elements. Other researchers feel that cumulative exposure to loud noise may contribute to the steady loss of hearing with age.

Besides age, various pathological conditions can produce hearing loss. Chronic cigarette smokers, for instance, have slightly higher pure-tone thresholds than nonsmokers of the same age, and this loss is most pronounced at higher frequencies (Zelman, 1973). The loss may be due to the nicotine in tobacco, since that ingredient narrows the ear's blood vessels and makes the ear's blood pressure irregular. These circulatory effects could, in turn, reduce the blood supply to the cochlea.

Presbycusis and heavy cigarette smoking affect hearing at the high-frequency end of the audiogram. Other disorders, in contrast, can produce hearing loss in other regions of the audiogram, leaving high-frequency sensitivity normal. Viral infections, for instance, can lead to a loss of auditory sensitivity in limited regions anywhere throughout the audiogram. Similarly, tumors of the auditory nerve can produce hearing loss just at intermediate frequencies or just at low frequencies (Dirks, 1978). These patterns of hearing loss from tumor or infection would be quite distinct from the high-frequency loss characteristic of presbycusis and nicotine toxicity. Actually, hearing loss can take many different forms, and the nature of the particular loss provides clues as to the locus of the disorder (see Box 10.1). The audiogram, in other words, provides a useful tool for the diagnosis of ear and auditory nerve pathologies. Here again, we see a similarity between the audiogram and the spatial contrast-sensitivity function (recall Box 5.2, p. 165).

Audiologists (individuals who diagnose and treat hearing impairments) have developed a number of other sophisticated hearing tests besides audiograms. These more sophisticated tests distinguish among various types of auditory disorders. A thorough, up-to-date summary of those diagnostic tests is given by Dirks (1978). For our purposes, however, we'll concentrate on the most common sources of hearing loss.

Noise Exposure and Hearing Loss. An unfortunately common cause of hearing loss is exposure to very loud noise. For instance,

the acoustic energy from explosions—in combat or in industrial accidents—can produce sudden, permanent deafness due to trauma to the organ of Corti. Even the explosion of a single 2-inch firecracker can cause a major loss in hearing (Ward and Glorig, 1961). Comparable hearing losses have been reported in people exposed to the noise of gunfire, such as hunters (Taylor and Williams, 1966), people in the armed forces, and actors in Western movies. Included in this last group of hearing-impaired individuals is President Ronald Reagan, a former film actor.

All the cases just mentioned involve sudden, explosive noises; but this certainly is not the only type of sound that can damage your hearing. Sustained, loud noises can also lead to permanent hearing loss. And as you can imagine, chronic noise exposure represents a serious occupational hazard for individuals who work in such environments as mechanized assembly plants, airports, and construction sites. It is well documented that unprotected workers in such noisy environments suffer permanent increases in pure-tone thresholds, with the magnitude of the loss related to length of time on the job (Nixon and Glorig, 1961; Taylor, 1965). Moreover, high noise levels in industrial settings are associated with higher accident rates, presumably because noise makes it more difficult to hear warning signals such as whistles or shouts (Wilkins and Acton, 1982). Aware of these deleterious effects of noise (and their likely legal liability in such instances), more industries have begun to shield their workers from harmful noise. This shielding can consist of earplugs (which can reduce noise levels by up to 20 dB) and, where possible, sound-attenuating enclosures for workers.

But it isn't just industrial workers who receive exposure to potentially damaging levels of noise. It is now well established that the levels of loud, amplified music often

BOX 10.1

Hearing Loss

Between 17 and 20 million Americans suffer some loss of hearing, making this the most common of all physical disabilities. In its most severe form, impaired hearing means a total loss of sensitivity to sound—complete deafness. People who become completely deaf after years of normal hearing describe the experience as frightening. Since everyday sounds keep one in touch with the environment, loss of hearing isolates the totally deaf person not only from the voices of others but also from the security of life's background hum.

In legal terms, a person is said to be "totally deaf" when speech sounds cannot be heard at intensities less than 82 dB$_{SPL}$ (the intensity of ordinary speech is around 60 dB$_{SPL}$). The term "hearing impairment" refers to any loss in auditory sensitivity relative to the hearing ability of the normal young adult (see audiogram in Figure 10.1). The most common cause of impaired hearing is old age—this is the progressive form of impaired hearing, called presbycusis, discussed in the text. While more than half of those suffering from impaired hearing are over 60 years of age, hearing disorders are certainly not confined to just this age group. When college students are screened in hearing surveys, as many as 60 percent of them evidence some form of hearing problem. Medical authorities point to loud music and headphones as contributors to this disquieting statistic. In response to these

concerns, some manufacturers of headphones now include literature with each set, warning of potential hazards to hearing. One manufacturer has gone so far as to install a warning light on its portable cassette players to indicate when the volume exceeds safe listening levels.

Besides old age and exposure to excessively loud sound, other causes of hearing loss include head injuries, infections, measles, mumps, and allergies. Regardless of the cause, all hearing difficulties can be divided into two categories: conduction loss and sensory/neural loss. The first category of hearing loss, **conduction loss,** stems from some disorder within the outer ear or the middle ear, those portions of the auditory system involved in mechanically transmitting sound energy to the receptors in the inner ear. Hearing disorders originating in these peripheral stages of the auditory system typically involve an overall reduction in sensitivity to sounds of all frequencies. The second category of hearing defect, **sensory/neural loss,** originates within the inner ear or in the auditory portion of the brain; the associated hearing loss may extend over the entire range of audible frequencies or over only a portion of that range. Sensory/neural loss is irreversible, but conduction loss can be remedied in some cases. Let's consider some of those remedies.

Paradoxically, steady levels of background noise sometimes

make it easier for a person with a conduction loss to hear speech. In these instances, the background noise is too weak to be passed to the inner ear, so the hearing-impaired person doesn't hear the noise. However, people with normal hearing reflexively raise their voices in the presence of noise, and this natural amplification is sufficient to enable the hearing-impaired person to understand what is being said. Stevens and Warshofsky (1965, p. 147) relate one man's clever use of this remedy: "Legend tells of a hard-of-hearing nobleman who overcame his handicap by stationing a drummer in his audience chamber and commanding him to beat out a drum roll whenever someone spoke to him."

Sometimes conduction loss is caused by excessive build-up of ear wax in the canal of the outer ear. Simply cleaning out the plugged-up canal cures the problem. In other cases, however, the problem is more serious. Infection can cause fluid to build up in the middle ear, and if the Eustachian tube (the middle ear's pressure regulator) becomes inflamed, middle ear pressure can rupture the eardrum. Infection can also spread to the bony chamber housing the middle ear, leading to bone disease that must be treated surgically. With the advent of antibiotics, ear infections can be treated before the symptoms reach these dangerous stages.

There is another type of disorder that affects the middle ear, and this condition is not remedied by drugs. Called **otosclerosis,** this disorder involves the gradual immobilization of the stapes, the last of the tiny middle-ear bones that form the ossicular bridge between the outside world and the inner ear. Recall that the stapes (stirrup) is the bone actually responsible for tapping out sound vibrations on the oval window, which in turn sets up pressure waves within the cochlear fluids. Hence when the stapes becomes immobile, the bridge to the inner ear is destroyed. The stapes becomes immobilized by a steady accumulation of a spongy substance near the foot of this bone. This spongy substance eventually hardens, cementing the stapes in a rigid position. No one understands what triggers this disease, but it tends to occur in young adults and more often in females than in males. Fortunately, the disease can be treated. Using a surgical microscope to guide their movements, physicians can remove the immobile stapes and replace it with a plastic substitute. So long as other portions of the ear have not been affected by the disease, this form of surgery can restore hearing to normal levels.

Otosclerosis is a progressive disease that, in time, may spread to the cochlea. In these cases, surgery to replace the stapes cannot possibly improve hearing to normal levels. It is important, therefore, for the physician to know beforehand whether a candidate for stapes surgery also suffers hearing loss due to cochlear pathology. How does the physician go about determining functional status when the immobile stapes blocks sound's normal route to the cochlea? The answer is easy—there is an alternate route to the cochlea, through the bones of the skull. You have probably noticed how loud the dentist's drill sounds when it contacts one of your teeth. This is because vibrations from the drill are transmitted from your tooth to your skull. The cochlea, remember, is the coiled cavity formed within the bone of the skull. Thus when vibrations are introduced into the skull, those vibrations reach the cochlea, and if they are sufficiently strong, they set up pressure waves in the cochlear fluids. Those pressure waves behave just like the ones reaching the cochlea through the ear; they set up ripples along the basilar membrane, causing you to experience those bone-transmitted vibrations as sound. This is called hearing by **bone conduction.** Every time you speak, part of what you hear is the sound of your voice transmitted via bone conduction. That's why a tape recording of your voice sounds strange to you but not to others—listening to the recorder, you hear your voice without any contribution from bone conduction.

One wouldn't expect a sound to be as loud when carried via bone conduction as when conveyed through the ear, because this alternate route includes no mechanism like the ossicles for amplifying sound energy. For this reason, pure-tone thresholds measured through the skull of a person with good hearing are roughly 30 dB higher than those measured using tones delivered to the ear. Incidentally, to measure pure-tone thresholds for bone conduction hearing, a tuning fork is set into vibration and placed firmly against the bone just behind the ear. To return, then, to the question of whether to operate on a patient with otosclerosis: if that person's bone conduction thresholds are near normal, then the cochlea must be unaffected by the disease. Surgery should be successful in restoring the world of sound to the patient.

Finally, conduction hearing loss can be at least partially remedied by a hearing aid. Since the loss stems from the damping of sound energy, the hearing aid can counter this damping by amplifying sound. Modern hearing aids operate by converting sound into electrical signals, amplifying those signals by up to 60 dB, and then converting the amplified signals back into sound energy. Good hearing aids are designed to amplify mainly those frequencies involved in speech, 500 to 8,000 Hz. Thus other sounds, such as music, may seem distorted—much like nonspeech sounds heard over a telephone. Although not as effective as a modern electronic hearing aid, the simplest, most popular hearing aid is the hand. When the hand is cupped and placed behind the pinna, extra sound waves are funneled into the ear, raising the intensity by as much as 6 dB. Try it and listen for yourself!

encountered at rock concerts and clubs are sufficient to cause permanent hearing loss. In one study of this effect (Hanson and Fearn, 1975), pure-tone thresholds were measured in two groups of college students. One group consisted of people who attended at least one rock concert each month, while the other group consisted of people who never attended rock concerts. At all frequencies tested, which spanned the range 500–8,000 Hz, "attenders" had higher thresholds—pure tones had to be more intense in order for attenders to hear them. The differences between the groups were small, averaging just a couple of decibels, but they were consistent. The regular attenders, incidentally, were entirely unaware of their deficits, and they had no complaints about their hearing. Besides members of their audiences, pop musicians themselves can develop hearing loss from their chronic exposure to amplified music (Axelsson and Lindgren, 1978).

Even people who work and play in regular, everyday environments must tolerate such noises as the roar of a motorcycle or the wail of a siren. On an ordinary day, the sound level on a downtown Chicago street can approach 100 dB_{SPL}; and inside a subway tunnel, even this level is exceeded when trains pass through a station. But you don't need to go to a busy city to experience a noisy environment—you can do this in the "quiet" of your own home. Ordinary household appliances can generate surprising levels of noise: a dishwasher can produce 60 dB_{SPL} of sound, a vacuum cleaner 75 dB_{SPL}, and an innocent-looking garbage disposal can exceed 100 dB_{SPL} when it is working on hard objects such as bones (Stevens and Warshofsky, 1965). While these sound levels won't lead to *permanent* deafness, they are sufficiently loud to elevate your threshold for hearing *temporarily* after cessation of the noise. This transitory reduction in hearing sensitivity following noise

exposure is aptly called a **temporary threshold shift.** The phenomenon has been thoroughly studied under laboratory conditions; we'll just mention some of the highlights and implications of that work (summarized by Miller, 1978).

In general, sound levels in excess of 60 dB_{SPL} can produce temporary threshold shifts if the duration of exposure is several hours or longer. The actual size of the threshold shift can vary from just a few decibels, which for all practical purposes is unnoticeable, to complete deafness. As you might guess, the size of the shift depends strongly on the level and duration of the inducing noise. The length of time it takes for thresholds to return to normal also varies, depending on the strength and duration of noise exposure. Recovery can occur within only a few hours when the noise is modest, but it can take several days following exposure to severe noise. You may have noticed a temporary threshold shift after attending a loud party or a boisterous football game—normally audible sounds such as your own footsteps may temporarily fall below your elevated threshold. For unknown reasons, women seem to exhibit smaller threshold shifts than men when the inducing noise consists of *low* frequencies. Thus after a male and female have been listening to the romantic roar of the ocean for some time, she may be able to hear his passionate whispers, just barely, but he won't be able to make out her whispered replies. However, just the opposite is found when the inducing noise consists of *high* frequencies. Under these conditions, men exhibit smaller threshold shifts than women (Ward, 1966, 1968). So if our hypothetical couple had been listening for some time to the strains of Wagner sung by a lusty soprano, the female of the couple would be at a temporary disadvantage when it came to communicating in whispers.

Aspirin and Hearing Loss. Noise exposure is not the only thing that can temporarily shift a threshold. Large doses of the common drug aspirin may also yield a temporary hearing loss (McCabe and Dey, 1965; Myers and Bernstein, 1965). A person taking 4 to 8 grams of aspirin per day is likely to experience anywhere from a 10- to a 40-dB shift in pure-tone thresholds, with the loss often more pronounced at higher frequencies. This hearing loss persists as long as aspirin is taken, and normal hearing returns within a day or two after the person ceases to take the aspirin. Since one tablet usually contains one-fourth of a gram of aspirin, your hearing won't be affected by taking a couple of aspirin. The aspirin dose that can produce hearing loss (4 to 8 grams) is the typical prescription dose for people with rheumatoid arthritis. The temporary hearing loss induced by aspirin is often accompanied by **tinnitus,** the high-pitched ringing in the ears we described in the previous chapter. The tinnitus, too, disappears once the consumption of aspirin ceases. Some physicians instruct arthritis sufferers to adjust their aspirin intake on the basis of their experience of tinnitus. These patients are told to keep the intake of aspirin just below the level that produces the illusory high-pitched sound.

Dennis McFadden, a psychologist at the University of Texas at Austin, has found that aspirin makes people more vulnerable to the effects of noise (McFadden and Plattsmier, 1983). In his study, McFadden exposed paid volunteers to a 2,500-Hz tone for 10 minutes. The tone's intensity was adjusted to yield around a 14-dB threshold shift; the intensity of the tone required to produce such a shift was in the neighborhood of 100 dB$_{SPL}$. Dividing his volunteers into two groups, he then gave them either 1.95 or 3.9 grams every day for several days. At the end of this period, he once again exposed them to the loud tone and then retested their pure-tone thresholds. Some people who were given the higher dosage of aspirin (3.9 grams) now suffered a hearing loss that was almost twice what they had suffered initially. In addition, it took them longer to recover from the noise exposure. People who were given the smaller dosage (1.95 grams) showed neither of these effects. McFadden's results imply that people routinely exposed to loud sounds should restrict their intake of aspirin or, better yet, find a substitute pain reliever.

PERCEPTUAL CONSEQUENCES OF AN ABNORMAL AUDIOGRAM

So far, we have focused on some of the things that cause pure-tone hearing losses, either temporary or permanent. To realize the perceptual consequences of such losses, you need some idea of the frequencies and intensities of sound occurring in your everyday environment. Take, for example, the bell on a typical telephone. Its ring is a routine sound we all rely on. Suppose that the acoustic energy produced by the bell lies between 4,000 and 8,000 Hz, and that its sound level is somewhere around 70 dB$_{SPL}$. (The actual distribution of acoustic energy varies from one type of telephone to another.) Suppose also that a person with the abnormal audiogram shown in Figure 10.2 is expecting a phone call. As you can see, this person suffers about a 50-dB hearing loss in the mid- and upper-frequency range, the region where much of the bell's sound lies. Will this person be able to hear his phone ringing? As you learned in the previous chapter, sound intensity falls off with the square of the distance between the source and the listener. So our hearing-impaired person must be within about 8 meters of his phone in order to hear it ring. Beyond this distance, the sound will be too weak to be heard by his defective ears. This analysis

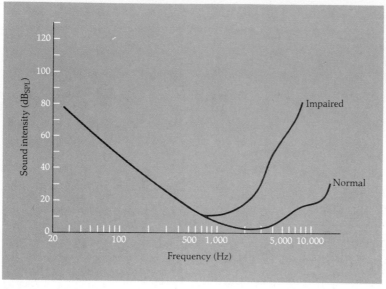

FIGURE 10.2

Audiogram of an individual with about a 50-dB hearing loss in the mid- and upper-frequency range.

assumes ideal conditions—no distracting noises and no major objects such as walls or doors to intercept the phone's acoustic energy before it reaches his ears. Incidentally, people with normal hearing would have no trouble hearing such a bell, even over distances of several hundred feet or through walls and doors.

Let's continue with this example by assuming the hearing-impaired person manages to hear his phone and now answers it. Will he have difficulty understanding the voice on the other end of the line? To find out, we must know something about the frequency content of human speech. Figure 10.3 shows the region of the frequency spectrum responsible for conveying speech sounds; note that acoustic energy in speech spans the range from 200 Hz to about 8,000 Hz. As the diagram shows, vowel sounds consist primarily of low frequencies while consonants cover very nearly the entire range. Of the consonant sounds, the nasal

ones (such as "m") are the lowest in frequency and the fricatives (such as "f") are the highest. In terms of their relative intensities, vowel sounds tend to be stronger than consonants, meaning that at normal speaking levels, vowels produce larger variations in sound-wave pressure.

Now, armed with this information, let's consider the plight of the hearing-impaired individual whose audiogram is depicted in Figure 10.2. To understand how a telephone conversation will sound to him, let's first examine how the telephone itself alters the frequency composition of the voice it transmits. Modern telephones transmit frequencies only up to about 4,000 Hz, which means that the very highest frequencies contained in normal speech are missing during a phone conversation. Since people are easily able to carry on a phone conversation, these omitted frequencies must be unnecessary for speech comprehension. For our hearing-impaired person, though, more is missing than

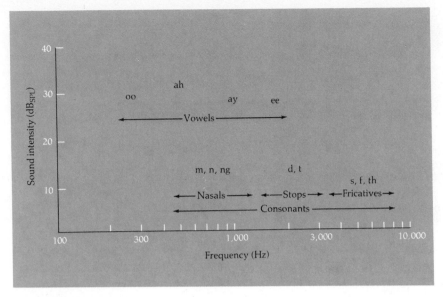

FIGURE 10.3
The region of the sound spectrum responsible for conveying speech sounds.
Vowel sounds are primarily of low frequency; consonants cover almost the
entire range.

just these high frequencies—his ears fail to pick up frequencies in speech that *are* available over the phone. His pattern of hearing loss means that some of the consonants (especially those such as /t/ and /d/) will be heard as mere whispers, if at all. (The slashes, / /, indicate that we are referring to the sounds of these characters, not to their names as letters of the alphabet.) These consonants, in fact, are some of the most important ingredients in speech (Ballantyne, 1977). So a person with an audiogram of the type shown in Figure 10.2 will have difficulty hearing some of the environment's most important sounds, those of human speech. Simple words such as "time" and "dime" may be mistaken for one another, which in turn may make whole sentences confusing. Clearly, then, a person does not need to be totally deaf in order to experience the frustrations of unintelligible speech. In a way, the plight of hearing-impaired people is par-

ticularly difficult—they hear speech sounds but are confused by the meanings. It is no wonder that some hard-of-hearing people find it easier simply to withdraw from social encounters.

THE RANGE OF HEARING IN ANIMALS

The point of discussing abnormal hearing has been to illustrate that the audiogram reveals something important about the perceptual world of an individual. The same point can be made by comparing the audiograms of different animal species. Look at Figure 10.4. Each horizontal bar shows the range of frequencies audible to a particular species, and as you can see, there is quite a diversity among animals. Members of a large part of the animal kingdom are able to hear sounds outside the limits of the human ear. Here's an example. Perhaps you're familiar with a device called a dog whistle. When

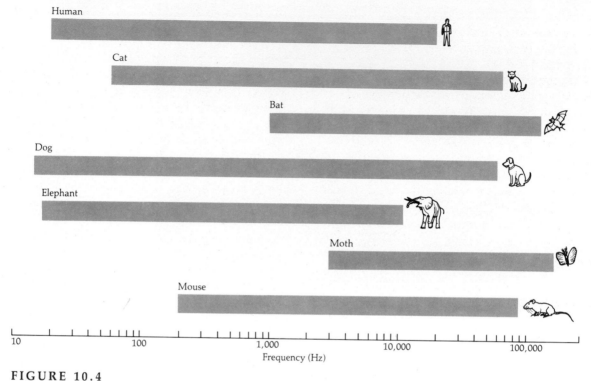

FIGURE 10.4
The range of sound frequencies audible to various species. (Data from Hefner and Hefner, 1983.)

blown, it emits frequencies around 14,000 Hz, right at the very limits of the human ear but well within the hearing range of the dog. If you've never heard a dog whistle but want to, you'd better hurry—presbycusis is bound to rob you of the opportunity.

One sound that no human will ever hear is the stream of very high frequencies emitted by bats. These emitted squeals bounce off objects in the bat's flight path and then echo back to the bat. As Figure 10.4 indicates, bats are able to hear these frequencies, and they use them to navigate (Griffin, 1959). Later on, we'll have more to say about the hearing of various species.

So far we have concentrated on the range of hearing as specified by pure-tone thresholds measured under quiet conditions. Of course, most of the sounds one usually encounters are loud enough to be easily heard, and they often occur against some background level of noise. So to understand auditory perception more fully, we need to consider these more common stimulus conditions. We will begin by discussing what determines a sound's loudness, where "loudness" refers to the perceived intensity of that sound. Note that according to this definition, *any* audible sound, whether weak or strong, has some degree of loudness.

Loudness Perception

MEASURING LOUDNESS

Everyone knows what is meant by **loudness**—one's subjective impression of the intensity of sound. And most people would have no trouble agreeing whether one sound is louder than another, indicating that they all employ the concept of "loudness" in the same way. Yet despite this agreement, there is no way to compare people's impressions of loudness directly—these are subjective experiences that cannot be measured with some instrument. One must rely on language to talk about one's perception of loudness. By the same token, there is no way to determine whether your judgment of a sound's loudness is right or wrong, for there is no right or wrong answer—a sound's loudness *is* whatever you experience. These constraints immediately raise a barrier against attempts to study loudness perception. Fortunately, psychologists have devised several effective procedures for measuring perceived sensory magnitude, including loudness. As applied to hearing, one of these procedures treats the perceiver as a measuring instrument capable of assigning numbers to sounds in proportion to their loudness; this method is generally known as **magnitude estimation.** Another method requires the person to adjust the loudness of one sound until it is equivalent to the loudness of another; this latter method is called **loudness matching.** Let's consider some of the results obtained using these two methods, starting with loudness matching.

Matching the Loudness of Tones. You've already learned that the intensity threshold for hearing tones varies with frequency. This was the relationship summarized in the audiogram of Figure 10.1. You could think of these thresholds as equal loudness values. At each point along that threshold curve, these various frequencies are *barely* audible—in other words, they all sound equal in loudness. Tones of different frequencies can also sound equal in loudness when they are *clearly* audible, well above threshold. Following is an outline of the procedure for

finding tones that match in loudness. To start, you take one frequency, say 1,000 Hz, and set its intensity to 20 dB_{SPL}. As you would expect, that tone sounds louder than it did at 0 dB_{SPL}. Next, you present a tone whose frequency is 500 Hz and adjust *its* intensity until it sounds as loud as the 1,000-Hz tone of 20 dB_{SPL}. To produce a loudness match between the two frequencies, you will need to raise the intensity of the 500-Hz tone to a level *greater* than 20 dB_{SPL}. This makes sense because, as the audiogram in Figure 10.1 shows, you were less sensitive to 500 Hz to begin with.

Now suppose you perform the same matching procedure for other frequencies. In other words, you set the physical intensity of each frequency so that the subjective loudness of that frequency matches the loudness of the 1,000-Hz, 20-dB_{SPL} tone. You could then plot, for all the frequencies, the intensity values yielding loudness matches. Connecting those points would give you a curve like the one labeled "20" in Figure 10.5. At all points along this curve, tones of different frequencies sound equivalent in loudness.

Next you could repeat this procedure, matching the loudness of other tones to the loudness of a 1,000-Hz tone whose intensity is 40 dB_{SPL}. This would yield another curve, the one labeled "40" in Figure 10.5; points along this curve specify another set of intensities at which various frequencies all sound equivalent in loudness. Repeating this maneuver for a number of different intensity values of the 1,000-Hz standard tone would yield a family of curves, each one summarizing the intensity values that make tones of different frequencies sound equal in loudness (Fletcher and Munson, 1933). Such curves are appropriately named **equal loudness contours.**

As you can see, the curves in Figure 10.5 are not parallel to one another. This means that loudness does not increase with inten-

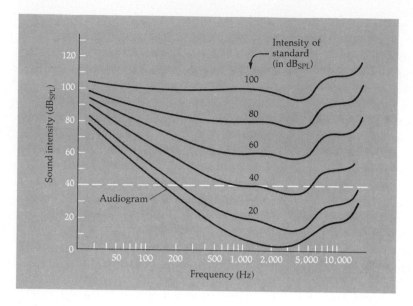

FIGURE 10.5
Equal loudness contours.

sity in the same way for all frequencies. Let's think what this implies. Suppose we draw a horizontal line straight across the graph at the point labeled "40 dB," as shown in Figure 10.5. Note that this line crosses several of the loudness contours. It enables you to compare the perceived loudness of pure tones of different frequencies, all of which have the same intensity—40 dB$_{SPL}$ in this case. Let's make a few of those comparisons.

First, note that a 50-Hz tone would not be audible at 40 dB$_{SPL}$—this intensity level is too weak to be heard at this frequency. At 50 Hz, a tone must be more than 60 dB$_{SPL}$ in order to be heard. At 200 Hz, the tone would be audible at 40 dB$_{SPL}$; but it would sound considerably weaker than, say, a 1,000-Hz tone at this same intensity. We know this because, for this sound level (40 dB$_{SPL}$), these two frequencies (200 and 1,000 Hz) lie on different equal loudness contours. In fact, to make the two tones sound equally loud, you would need to do one of

two things: either turn down the intensity of the 1,000-Hz tone or raise the intensity of the 200-Hz tone. In either case, the curves in Figure 10.5 tell you just how much you would have to change intensity in order to produce a loudness match. For instance, you could raise the intensity of the 200-Hz tone to 55 dB$_{SPL}$, thereby placing that tone on the same contour with the 40-dB$_{SPL}$, 1,000-Hz tone. See if you can figure out how much you would have to lower the 1,000-Hz tone in order for it to match the loudness of the 40-dB$_{SPL}$ tone of 200 Hz. These curves indicate that low frequencies tend to sound weaker than higher frequencies of the same intensity. Incidentally, manufacturers of audio equipment know this, and they design their amplifiers to compensate. For example, amplifiers give low frequencies a little extra boost in intensity. Some of these amplifiers even have a "loudness" switch on the front of the unit, to let the listener choose the desired amount of low-frequency boost.

You could compare the perceived loudness of other combinations of frequency and intensity. You would find that in most instances, tones of the same intensity but different frequency do not sound equally loud; to equate them for loudness requires adjusting their intensities appropriately, each to a different level. An exception to this rule occurs at very high intensity levels. As you can see in Figure 10.5, for levels approaching 100 dB$_{SPL}$, the equal contours are relatively flat—indicating that at these high intensities, all frequencies sound more or less the same in loudness. Thinking back to audio amplifiers, you can see that this has an unfortunate consequence: when sound levels are very high, amplifiers with built-in low-frequency boost will actually overemphasize low frequencies. This overemphasis can produce what stereo buffs call a "boomy" bass (bass sounds consist predominantly of low frequencies).

So far we have considered how the loudness of one tone compares to the loudness of others. Comparisons of this sort, however, say nothing about the way a sound's loudness depends on intensity. Of course, everyone knows that loudness grows with increasing intensity; but exactly how are loudness and intensity related? For example, does doubling the intensity on your stereo double the loudness of the music you're listening to? In order to answer questions such as this, you need to do more than compare the loudness of one sound to that of another. What you need is some way to measure the actual loudness of individual sounds. This brings us to magnitude estimation, a second method for assessing loudness.

Estimating the Magnitude of Loudness. Magnitude estimation seems deceptively simple: a person is instructed merely to assign numbers to sounds in proportion to their loudness. Thus if one sound seems three times louder than another, the louder sound

should be assigned a number three times larger than the number assigned to the softer sound. The person is free to select any particular numbers, just so long as those numbers faithfully reflect what the person construes as loudness. No upper or lower limits are placed on the range of acceptable numbers, although sometimes the experimenter may arbitrarily assign a given number to one particular sound intensity. For instance, you might be told to let a rating of 100 correspond to the loudness of a 60-dB$_{SPL}$ sound, but from there on your ratings would be entirely up to you.

Given this latitude in assigning numbers to loudness, you might expect the outcome to be a jumble of random numbers, but in fact this does not happen. While the particular numbers assigned to particular sound levels can vary from person to person, the order and spacing between numbers show a remarkable degree of regularity among individuals. Of course, as sound intensity increases so does loudness. However, loudness grows more slowly than does intensity. Thus, for instance, doubling sound intensity does *not* double loudness—instead, loudness increases by only about 60 percent. To double the loudness of a sound, its intensity must be approximately tripled (this corresponds to about a 10-dB increase in intensity). This means, for example, that two people singing at the top of their lungs will not sound twice as loud as one of those people singing alone; instead, the duet's singing will sound about 1.6 times louder than a solo. To double the loudness produced by one singer requires adding two additional singers.

So loudness does not grow in a simple, additive fashion, but instead grows multiplicatively (by fractional multiples of intensity). This seems to be true over the entire range of audible sound levels, and it holds for magnitude estimates of loudness obtained from just about everyone. S. S. Ste-

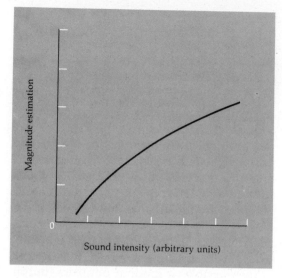

FIGURE 10.6

The growth of loudness plotted on linear axes.

vens (1960), who was among the first to think about loudness in this way, expressed this general finding in mathematical terms: loudness grows in proportion to intensity raised to the power, or exponent, 0.6. In mathematical notation:

$$L = k \cdot I^{0.6}$$

where L stands for loudness, I stands for intensity (expressed as sound pressure level) and k is a constant. This general formula has come to be known as the **power law** of loudness growth. Figure 10.6 shows what this relation between intensity and loudness looks like graphically; plotted on the horizontal axis is the sound level, or intensity, of a pure tone, while plotted on the vertical axis are the numbers (the magnitude estimates of loudness) assigned to those various intensities. Note that in this graph, intensity and loudness are scaled in linear coordinates. Plotted in this way, the resulting "loudness function" appears curved; it is described as negatively accelerating, meaning that loudness grows more slowly than intensity.

Because the relation between intensity and loudness is exponential, replotting the points on logarithmic coordinates should yield a straight line. Taking the logarithm of both sides of the above equation yields:

$$\log L = \log k + 0.6(\log I)$$

which is the formula for a straight line. To show you what this looks like graphically, the results from Figure 10.6 have been re-plotted in Figure 10.7. Note that both intensity and loudness ratings are now scaled logarithmically. (Recall from Box 9.2 that the decibel is a logarithmic unit.) As expected, the exponential curve summarizing the growth of loudness (Figure 10.6) now appears as a straight line. The constant, k, specifies where that straight line crosses, or intersects, the vertical axis; the point of intersection depends on the particular set of numbers used by the person to estimate loudness. The exponent, 0.6, specifies the slope of the straight line, or in other words, its steepness. A slope less than 1.0 means that loudness grows more slowly than intensity, as

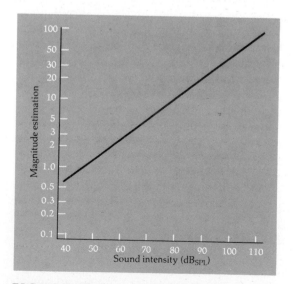

FIGURE 10.7

The growth of loudness plotted on logarithmic axes.

we described above. Box 10.2 further discusses magnitude estimation and the power law, including its application to senses other than hearing.

Loudness of Tones in Noise. The loudness function shown in Figure 10.7 was for a pure tone heard in an otherwise quiet environment—an atypical situation indeed. More often, one is called upon to listen for tones occurring against some background of sound; for practical purposes we can consider this background sound as *noise*. For instance, imagine listening for the phone to ring while taking a shower; the noise of the water makes the ring harder to hear. Using a matching procedure, it is possible to specify the loudness of a sound occurring within noise (Stevens and Guirao, 1967)—Figure 10.8 illustrates the result. These data were obtained by having a listener adjust the intensity of a tone heard in quiet to match the loudness of a tone heard against a background of noise; the different curves represent different levels of noise, ranging from moderate to very loud noise (the "100-dB" noise line). As you can see, the loudness function gets steeper as the noise level increases, implying that the exponent of the power function becomes larger—loudness grows more rapidly when sounds occur within noise. Or to put it in another way, the loudness of *intense* sounds is less affected by background noise than is the loudness of *weak* sounds.

This effect of noise on loudness has several implications, one bad and the other not so bad. To start with the bad news: weak sounds may be impossible to hear when they occur in noise. This stands to reason; we've all had the experience of being unable to hear a phone conversation when there is lots of static on the line—the noise of the static masks the sounds of the other person's voice. For sounds that are more intense, though, the situation is not so bad. Note that all the lines in Figure 10.8 converge toward the same

loudness levels at the top of the graph—intense sounds seem loud regardless of the background noise level. This is actually a fortunate circumstance. If the slope of the loudness function remained the same regardless of background noise level, we'd grossly underestimate the intensity of sounds occurring within noisy settings. To give an example, the same siren might sound faint under one condition but loud under another. This could be dangerous: imagine hearing an ambulance and trying to judge from the loudness of its siren whether it was still far enough away for you to proceed safely through an intersection. If the loudness of intense sounds were greatly affected by noise, your judgment could be fatally flawed depending on the other traffic sounds you were hearing. So it is lucky that only weak sounds are greatly affected by background noise.

The effects of noise on the detection of tones is one of the most widely studied problems in hearing. We won't go into the

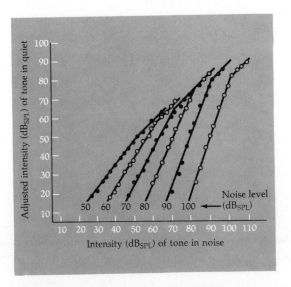

FIGURE 10.8

The intensity of a tone heard in quiet necessary to match the intensity of another tone heard against noise. (Adapted from Stevens and Guirao, 1967.)

BOX 10.2
Magnitude Estimation and the Power Law

You've probably seen judges award points to athletes, such as divers or figure skaters, as a rating of their performance. Or maybe you've watched talent shows on television where audience members register their "votes" for contestants on an applause meter, the winner being the individual who gets the loudest applause. Perhaps you've been asked to rate how well you like different songs by assigning numbers to them, higher numbers indicating greater liking. In each of these instances, the individual doing the rating behaves like a measuring gauge—that person estimates the magnitude of some quality present in a given object, person or event, where "quality" refers to some psychological factor such as gracefulness, appeal, and so forth.

This same strategy can be applied to the measurement of subjective sensory experiences such as the loudness of a sound or the brightness of a light. Used in this manner, such strategies fall under the rubric of **direct scaling techniques.** These techniques are called "direct" because the judgments people make presumably directly reflect the magnitude of some sensation they are experiencing; and those judgments, according to the advocates of direct scaling techniques, are just as valid as the reading of sound levels taken with a meter. In a way, direct scaling is similar to introspection (recall Chapter 1), in that a person's subjective report is supposed to reflect the contents of conscious

experiences such as loudness. However, in the case of direct scaling, the person's ratings are constrained in ways that make it possible to quantify the rating, thereby revealing regularities between the judgments of different people.

The person most responsible for the development of direct scaling techniques is the late S. S. Stevens, a psychologist at Harvard University. Stevens (1960) summarized the various techniques he devised for studying the intensity of sensations associated with seeing, hearing, taste, smell, and touch. His most popular technique was magnitude estimation, the technique described on page 341 as it is applied to loudness. According to Stevens, the idea of assigning numbers to gauge the strength of a sensation came from a friendly challenge:

It all started from a friendly argument with a colleague who said, "You seem to maintain that each loudness has a number and that if someone sounded a tone I should be able to tell him the number." I replied, "That's an interesting idea. Let's try it." (Stevens, 1956, p. 2)

Stevens responded to this challenge by setting up an experiment and instructing participants as follows:

You will be presented with a series of stimuli in irregular order. Your task is to tell how intense they seem by assigning numbers to them. Call the first stimulus any number that seems appropriate to you. Then assign

successive numbers in such a way that they reflect your subjective impression. There is no limit to the range of numbers that you may use. You may use whole numbers, decimals or fractions. Try to make each number match the intensity as you perceive it. (Stevens, 1975, p. 30)

As a rule, the stimuli to be rated are presented several times each, in an irregular order. No training is necessary, so it is possible to test a person in a relatively short time; this is one reason for the method's popularity. Stevens used magnitude estimation to study all the senses. He discovered that for each sense modality, the *perceived* strength of a stimulus increased in proportion to the stimulus's *physical* intensity raised to some power or exponent. (This is the power law mentioned on page 342.) Each sense modality has its own characteristic power or exponent, and some of these values are summarized in the accompanying graph. Note that the exponent for brightness is 0.3. This rather small value indicates that large increases in light intensity produce relatively small increases in brightness. In contrast, look at the exponent and graph line for electric shock—here's a sensation that grows much faster than the intensity of the stimulus. In the case of electric shock, doubling the intensity causes about a tenfold change in the perceived strength of that shock. Interestingly, perceived length has an exponent of 1.0, indicating that perceived length corresponds almost perfectly with actual length. People's ability to judge length, in other words, is very good.

Stevens and other proponents of his ideas developed methods besides magnitude estimation to measure sensation (see Gescheider, 1976). One of the more clever methods, called **cross-modality matching,** requires a person to equate the strengths of sensations arising from the stimulation of different sense modalities. To illustrate, a person might be asked to adjust the loudness of a sound until its strength matched the brightness of a light. At first glance, this kind of judgment sounds strange, but people actually have no trouble doing it. Probably, cross-modality matching is not so different from deciding how well you enjoyed a performance and clapping by an amount that reflects this enjoyment.

The matches produced across modalities conform to predictions derived from the power law. For example, to match a small increase in the

intensity of an electric shock, a person requires a large increase in the intensity of a sound; this merely reflects the fact that perceived shock intensity grows much more rapidly than loudness.

These scaling techniques, particularly magnitude estimation, have recently been applied to psychological attributes other than sensory judgments. The seriousness of various crimes, the beauty of art works, and the perceived status of various occupations—these are some of the psychological attributes that have been quantified by means

of direct scaling. Though it's still in its infancy, this approach holds great promise for helping clarify what is meant by otherwise vague concepts such as "attractiveness" or "competence." In the future, perhaps it might even be possible to dispense with the election of public officials, substituting some scaling process in its stead. In such a scheme, desirable attributes for various offices would first be identified, then different candidates scaled for those attributes. This might make no less sense than the way some public officials are now chosen.

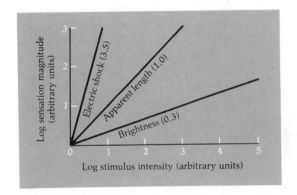

many findings but instead will refer you to the article by Patterson and Green (1978).

We've been considering how the loudness of pure tones varies with the tones' intensity and with the intensity of background noise. But the measurement of loudness is not limited to pure tones. People are also able to rate the loudness of sounds consisting of many frequencies (Zwicker and Scharf, 1965), including noise—which, as you learned in the previous chapter, consists of all audible frequencies. As a rule, the loudness of complex sounds can

be predicted by adding up the loudness contributions from the component frequencies, making allowance for the ability of one sound to reduce, or mask, the loudness of others (as shown in Figure 10.8).

INTENSITY DISCRIMINATION

Before leaving our discussion of loudness perception, we should say a word about the ability to tell whether one sound is louder than another. After all, this ability can be of considerable practical importance. Imagine, for instance, that your brother is upstairs, playing his stereo so loudly that you can't study. You holler up to him, asking him to turn it down a little, and he says he will. Just by listening, how do you tell if your brother has kept his promise? Of course, you would have no trouble hearing a large drop in intensity, but what if the drop was more subtle? How sharp is your ability to discriminate intensity changes, and what transpires within your auditory system when you make such a discrimination?

In the laboratory, intensity discrimination can be measured by varying the intensity of a tone very gradually until a person first notices that it has gotten louder. This minimum necessary increase in intensity specifies the person's **discrimination threshold.** Although the actual value of the threshold varies, depending on the details of the experiment, people typically require about a 1- to 2-dB increase in intensity to be able to notice any increase in loudness.

A listener probably achieves such keen performance by detecting an increment in the level of neural activity produced by the tone. In the example above, the most informative neural activity would arise within that subset of neurons maximally responsive to the tone's frequency; for instance, if the tone is 1,000 Hz, the listener should monitor neurons whose center frequency is 1,000 Hz (recall Figure 9.20, p. 323).

But in real life, most sounds are more complex than the pure tones used in this experiment. Sometimes you must detect a change in the intensity of one frequency component heard in the midst of many other components whose intensities are also changing. For example, an alert driver can tell that his truck's engine is malfunctioning when its high-pitched whine becomes louder than the other sounds made by the truck. In effect, he hears a change in the intensity of one set of frequencies (the high-pitched whine) in the midst of other sounds. His task is complicated. When he drives slowly, all the truck's sounds—high-pitched whine included—are weak; when he drives faster, all the sounds are louder. David Green, a hearing researcher at Harvard University, has recently offered a compelling explanation of how people detect such intensity changes in the midst of other changeable components.

Green (1982) acknowledges that if a listener only has to detect a change in the intensity of a single tone heard against an unvarying background, the traditional view is correct: only one subset of neurons need be monitored. But when other frequencies are present and their intensities are also changing from one moment to the next (as in the truck driver's situation), Green believes, a more complex process comes into play. This process uses neural information about the *relative* activity across different subsets of neurons. Green calls this process **profile analysis** because the relative neural response to various frequency bands could be represented graphically as a profile. According to Green, in an acoustically rich environment the listener picks up intensity changes by detecting a variation in the profile of activity. (This idea should be familiar to you from our discussions of orientation, spatial frequency, color, and motion perception.) To see where Green's view came from, let's consider two of his experiments.

In one experiment (Green, Kidd, and Picardi, 1983) Green created a complex sound consisting of twenty-one different tones, ranging in frequency from 300 to 3,000 Hz, all played simultaneously. He presented this set of tones twice on each trial. In one presentation, all twenty-one tones were identical in intensity; in the other presentation, the intensity of one tone (1,000 Hz) was slightly greater than the intensity of the other twenty tones. The listener's task was to identify the interval in which the 1,000-Hz tone had been incremented. Green made the task even more difficult by randomizing the *overall* intensity of the package of tones from one presentation to the next. For example, in the first presentation all the tones might be 20 dB$_{SPL}$ in intensity, while in the second presentation they might all be 50 dB$_{SPL}$. The exception, of course, was the 1,000-Hz tone, which was slightly more intense than its companions during one of the two presentations. Though the 1,000-Hz tone would be incremented *relative* to the rest, its *absolute* level of intensity would provide no clue whatever to the interval in which it had been incremented. This procedure made it impossible for the listener to base a judgment on the amount of neural activity produced by the 1,000 Hz alone; the listener was forced to compare the activity produced by the 1,000-Hz tone to the activity produced by its companions. Using these complex tones, Green determined the minimum increment of the 1,000-Hz tone that could be heard. Despite having to rely on *relative* intensity information alone, listeners were able to detect remarkably small increments in loudness. In fact, in some instances, the just detectable increment in the complex sound was about as small as that measured for the 1,000-Hz tone on its own.

In the second experiment, Green and his colleagues varied the number of different tones that accompanied the 1,000-Hz tone. Starting with a very few companion tones, Green found that adding additional tones actually *improved* a listener's ability to hear small increments in the 1,000-Hz tone. Presumably, the additional tones sharpened the definition of the neural activity profile utilized by the listener. These results and others (Green, 1982) show how useful profile analysis might be in explaining hearing performance in certain real-life situations.

Since profile analysis is so useful when you have to detect an intensity change in Green's complex stimuli, why it is still difficult to tell if your brother has turned the stereo down a little? Profile analysis itself suggests one possible answer. Most music is far more complex than the sounds used by Green; not only does the overall intensity of music change from one moment to the next, but the frequency components in the music also undergo continuous and often drastic change. As a result, it may be difficult for the listener to form a stable profile against which small intensity changes could be evaluated. Though highly speculative, this suggestion may explain the disputes about whether or not the stereo has indeed been turned down. But social strife is just one practical implication that springs from human responses to subtle increments in intensity. Let's consider another of these practical implications.

As you may know, audio amplifiers are rated in watts, an index having to do with the maximum sound output a particular amplifier can achieve. To produce a 3-dB increase in sound level (a value producing a small but noticeable increase in loudness) requires *doubling* the output wattage; and upgrading your stereo system by doubling the rating of your amplifier can be expensive. In other words, you must make a large investment in money to receive a very small return in loudness. Actually, amplifiers rarely come close to reaching their maximum output; the reproduction of most musical passages, even loud ones, requires just a few watts of output power. Mainly, it is the abrupt, loud notes that tax the limits of an amplifier. Thus in view of the infrequent occurrence of these kinds of notes and the expense of making them any louder, you're better off investing your money in more records and tapes, rather than more watts.

THE NEURAL CORRELATES OF LOUDNESS

What happens in your auditory system as the loudness of a sound varies? In other words, what is the neural code for loudness? The most obvious answer is that the discharge rate of auditory neurons increases with sound level, and this constitutes the information for loudness. After all, we did learn in the last chapter that the activity of auditory neurons increases with intensity (recall Figure 9.21). However, while discharge rate is probably involved in the coding of loudness, it alone cannot be the whole explanation. The reason is that auditory nerve fibers increase their firing rate over a limited range of sound intensities; this range typically covers only about 40 dB (Kiang, 1968). Yet one can hear variations in the loudness of sounds over a much larger range, around 120 dB. So one's range of loudness perception exceeds the range that can be coded by individual neurons.

There are two ways the nervous system may overcome the relatively limited range of responsiveness exhibited by individual neurons. First, different neurons may operate over different levels of sound intensity. One set of neurons may respond to intensity changes within the range from 20 dB_{SPL} to 60 dB_{SPL}, while another set responds to intensity changes from 60 dB_{SPL} to 100 dB_{SPL}. As you can see, each *set* covers only a 40-dB range, but as a *population* the neurons would then span an 80-dB range of intensities. Neurons responsive to different intensity ranges would be fairly simple to "construct"—it could be done by adjusting the intensity level where different neurons first start to respond. There is, in fact, physiological evidence that different auditory nerve fibers have different threshold intensities, the weakest sound level that elicits a response (Kiang, 1968). For the coding of loudness information, then, one way to overcome the limited range of individual neurons is to design them to operate within different intensity ranges. The details of such a scheme are discussed by Viemeister (1983).

There is a second possible way that increasing sound levels may produce greater and greater neural activity, and this has to do with the tuning curves for individual auditory nerve fibers. Recall that single fibers respond to just a limited range of temporal frequencies, with the preferred frequency varying from fiber to fiber (see Figure 9.21). At weak sound levels, the only fibers to respond will be those whose preferred frequencies match the frequencies contained in the sound; fibers preferring other frequencies will be unresponsive at these low sound levels. However, it is possible to recruit some of those fibers into activity by raising the sound level. At such higher levels, the sound (though it does not contain those fibers' preferred frequencies) *will* produce activity in such fibers because their tuning curves do encompass frequencies contained in the sound. We saw a hint of this spread of activity in the previous chapter, where it was noted that more intense sounds caused the traveling wave to spread out over a larger region of the basilar membrane. This is tantamount to recruiting more and more nerve fibers into action at higher and higher sound levels.

To summarize, then, the neural representation of loudness could involve both the discharge rate within individual fibers and the spread of activity among different fibers. Of course, loudness is just one component of the perceptual experience of sound, the one roughly corresponding to a sound's intensity. Loudness influences whether you are able to hear a sound; and in some instances, the loudness of a sound gives you some idea of how far away the sound source is. However, loudness alone seldom allows you to identify a sound source—for that purpose you need information about the frequencies composing that sound. This brings us to the topic of pitch perception.

Pitch Perception

DEFINING PITCH

Let's return once again to the audiogram pictured in Figure 10.1. In our discussion of loudness, we focused on the intensity dimension, the one scaled in decibels along the *vertical* axis. You learned that variations in intensity influence your perception of a sound's loudness. Now let's turn our attention to the frequency dimension, the one laid out along the *horizontal* axis. What do variations in frequency sound like? The most direct way to answer this question would be to have you listen to different frequencies. While pure-tone frequencies occur very rarely in nature, there are several relatively simple artificial ways to produce frequencies that come close to being pure tones. We'll mention a few.

Perhaps you have seen a set of tuning forks—within such a set, individual metal forks vary in size, which means that when they are struck against a hard surface, the forks vibrate at different frequencies. The term **pitch** is used to describe the perceptual quality associated with these different frequencies. A tuning fork that vibrates at a low frequency, such as 500 Hz, will sound lower in pitch than a tuning fork that vibrates at a higher frequency, say 1,000 Hz. Besides tuning forks, a set of crystal glasses filled with different amounts of water will also generate pure tones when struck lightly. In this case, a glass that is almost filled to the top with water will produce a lower-pitched tone than the same-sized glass containing just a little water. Again, these differences in pitch are associated with different frequencies of vibration, as determined

by the volume of water filling the glass. In fact, using enough glasses you can create a sufficient number of different tones to play a tune.

If you don't have access to either a set of tuning forks or crystal glasses, the notes played on a musical instrument will give you some appreciation of the relation between frequency and pitch, even though an instrument's sound is not a genuine pure tone. (We'll tell you why in a moment.) Take, for example, the piano. Each and every note on a properly tuned piano produces a sound of predominantly one frequency; that frequency is called the **fundamental frequency.** As you probably know, a musical note on the piano is produced when a small hammer strikes a string, causing it to vibrate. Strings differ in length, and the shorter ones vibrate more rapidly than the longer ones. Consequently, the shorter strings (which are struck by keys located toward the right-hand end of the keyboard) produce higher-pitched notes than the longer strings (which are struck by keys toward the left-hand end of the keyboard). Figure 10.9 shows the fundamental frequencies associated with the notes on a piano's keyboard. Moving from the low notes at the far left to the high ones at the far right, *frequency* changes in regular steps. So too does the *pitch* of the tones—your perception of the frequencies produced by those keys. Played in sequence from left to right, the notes are heard as the steps on the musical scale. As you can see in Figure 10.9, the range of frequencies produced by a piano, 27.5 Hz to 4,186 Hz, is narrower than the total range of frequencies audible to the ear of a young adult (from 20 Hz to 20,000 Hz). Still, the notes on a piano should give you some idea of how pitch changes with frequency.

Now that you know what is meant by a sound's pitch, let's consider a couple of questions about pitch, starting with its neural basis.

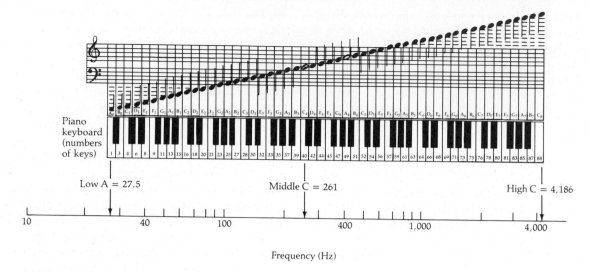

FIGURE 10.9
The fundamental frequencies associated with the notes on a piano's keyboard.

THE NEURAL CORRELATES OF PITCH

What goes on in your auditory system when you hear tones of various pitches? To answer this question, think back to the last chapter and the material on the inner ear and the auditory nerve. Recall that the basilar membrane moves up and down in response to sounds impinging on the eardrum, with the crest of this displacement depending on the sound's frequency. This displacement bends the hair cells, and this bending, in turn, triggers neural activity within the portion of the auditory nerve that innervates those hair cells. Thus when the ear is presented with a pure tone, only one portion of the basilar membrane will be displaced, only a limited set of hair cells will be disturbed and only a limited set of auditory nerve fibers will be activated. The frequency of a tone could be registered, therefore, by which set of nerve fibers is currently active. As you will recall from the last chapter, such a theory is referred to as a *place theory*. And since pitch is related to fre-

quency, the place theory represents an account of pitch perception.

The place theory has several things in its favor. First, it is known that damage to a limited portion of the basilar membrane causes a loss in the ability to hear certain frequencies. The frequencies affected depend on the region of the membrane damaged, as predicted by the place theory (Crowe, Guild, and Polvost, 1934). Also consistent with the place theory are the results from a study in which an array of small stimulating electrodes was implanted in the auditory nerve of the right ear of a 60-year-old man who was deaf in that ear because of basilar membrane damage (Simmons et al., 1965). When mild electric current was applied to a single electrode, the man described hearing a single tone; different electrodes evoked tone sensations that differed in pitch. Presumably, different electrodes were contacting different fibers in the auditory nerve. Consequently, the ability of different electrodes to evoke different pitches strengthens the presumed link between activity in individual nerve fibers and pure-tone hearing.

There are some aspects of pitch perception, however, that cannot be explained by the place theory. For instance, frequencies below 1,000 Hz produce a broad pattern of displacement along the basilar membrane. Because of this broad displacement, there is no specific place where the basilar membrane bulges maximally. Yet you have no trouble identifying the pitch of these low-frequency tones. Apparently, pitch depends on something besides place coding. As an alternative to place, the auditory system could use the firing rate of auditory nerve fibers to register low-frequency information. As you will recall from the previous chapter, this form of neural coding is known as the *frequency theory*. The idea here is that nerve fibers discharge in synchrony with the frequency of the stimulating tone. According to the frequency theory, then, the pitch of a tone corresponds to the rate of firing of nerve fibers.

Auditory physiologists have found that nerve fibers can indeed fire in rhythm with tones of moderately low frequency (Rose et al., 1967). Take one example. In response to a 500-Hz tone, a fiber might discharge once every 2 milliseconds; since a millisecond is one-thousandth of a second, this fiber would respond 500 times per second. Moreover, its discharge would be time-locked to the tone, meaning that the intervals between successive discharges would be regular. The fiber, in other words, behaves like a metronome, generating impulses in time to the frequency of the tone. Thus information about the tone's pitch can be conveyed by the pattern of fiber activity over time.

But the frequency theory has its limitations, too. The major problem is that auditory fibers cannot fire in synchrony to high-frequency tones (Rose et al., 1967). So some neural code other than frequency must be used to represent high-frequency informa-tion. As pointed out earlier, place coding would work just fine at high frequencies. It seems, then, that pitch perception may be mediated by two neural mechanisms, a frequency code at low frequencies and a place code at high frequencies. This would make pitch perception analogous to color vision. Recall from Chapter 6 that the representation of color information within the nervous system probably involves two complementary mechanisms, the trichromatic system and the opponent system. Neither system on its own can account for all aspects of color vision, but together they provide a fairly comprehensive description of how you see color. By the same token, neither the place theory nor the frequency theory alone explains pitch perception, but incorporating both enables each to cover some of the deficiencies of the other.

Having discussed the possible neural basis of pitch perception, let's now turn to another question about pitch perception, one concerning individual differences in the ability to identify the pitch of a tone.

PERFECT PITCH AND TONE DEAFNESS

Is it true that some individuals have what is called **perfect pitch**—an ability enabling them to hum any musical note they're told to or to name any note that is played? The answer is definitely yes. Such individuals are encountered in musical circles, although even among musicians the ability is quite rare (Vernon, 1977). One of the most renowned people with perfect pitch was Wolfgang Amadeus Mozart. It was claimed he could tell when the violin he was playing was tuned differently from one he had played the day before, even if those violins were mistuned by no more than "half a quarter of a tone" (Stevens and Warshofsky, 1965). Because it tends to run in families, perfect pitch used to be regarded as genetic in origin (Seashore, 1938). However, this sort of family tendency proves very little, since family members with perfect pitch are very likely to be musicians and would have received lots of exposure to musical notes, the only kind of sound in nature that allows the development of perfect pitch. Besides, there is evidence that adults can acquire perfect pitch if given extensive practice (Brady, 1970).

According to one theory, everyone has perfect pitch at one time but loses it (Ward, 1970). This theory says that all individuals are born with the ability, but that it is trained out of them early in life. This unlearning occurs because people are trained to ignore absolute pitch and to attend, instead, to the relations among various pitches. To give an example, you recognize a familiar melody such as "Pop Goes the Weasel" regardless of the key in which it is played; hence, you perceive a melody not as a specific sequence of notes but rather as a particular relation among notes (Pick, 1979). In other words, you attend to pitch relations and not to absolute pitch. While this discourages the retention of any ability for perfect pitch you may have had as a youngster, it enables you to enjoy the same musical melodies played or sung in different keys. In this regard, it is noteworthy that people with perfect pitch frequently complain that it is disquieting to listen to a piece of music played in an unusual key—the piece sounds "wrong" (Terhardt and Ward, 1982). Box 10.3 describes some additional interesting work on melody perception.

Besides perfect pitch, there is a more common ability known as **relative pitch**—people with relative pitch can identify tonal intervals very accurately, although they are not so accurate at naming the particular notes making up that interval. You can think of tonal intervals in terms of the steps of the musical scale. In particular, a tonal interval is defined by the number of steps that separate a pair of notes. For instance, the first two notes of "My Bonnie Lies over the Ocean" define a larger interval than do the first two notes of "Greensleeves." To be able to recognize and label all these various intervals means you have relative pitch. Many musicians have this ability (Siegel and Siegel, 1977).

People with perfect pitch or relative pitch are blessed with a talent. At the other extreme are people who are said to be "tone deaf." Now, these people aren't really deaf to tones. They can readily distinguish the variation in pitch associated with different notes on the piano—for instance, when two neighboring notes are struck in succession, the "tone-deaf" person can hear that the two are different. But when asked to sing a note played on the piano, such a person typically produces an ill-defined tone that bears little resemblance to the note requested. Moreover, the person usually doesn't realize the discrepancy between his or her rendition and the pitch of the note itself. So the problem is one both of sound production and of sound perception. It is as if the vocal cords and hearing apparatus were unconnected, and the consequence is that the person is unable to carry a tune. Remarkably little research has been done on this rather common and annoying problem.

PITCH VARIATIONS WITH INTENSITY

So far, we have treated pitch and frequency as though they were perfectly related. However, in reality, this relation is not so perfect. Under certain circumstances, tones of fixed frequency can sound different in pitch. For instance, the loudness of a pure tone influences that tone's pitch. You can experience this yourself by comparing the pitch of a vibrating tuning fork held at arm's length to the pitch of that same tuning fork held close to your ear. Held close to your ear, the tuning fork's note will of course sound louder, but you'll also hear that its pitch changes, too. For instance, a tuning fork vi-

BOX 10.3

What Is a Melody?

You don't have to be a musician to recognize musical melodies; that's an ability that comes naturally to just about everyone. Moreover, musicians or not, most people can recognize a familiar melody when it is played in different keys or on different instruments, or when it is sung by different voices. In these cases, the particular notes differ, but the melody remains the same. Just as different type fonts can be used to print the same sentence, different notes can produce the same melody. The implication is that people hear melodies not as specific sets of notes but as particular relations, or patterns, among those notes (Pick, 1979).

But what aspects of a melody unite musical notes into a pattern? Is it the rise and fall in the pitch of successive notes—the property known technically as **melody contour?** Does it have something to do with the size of the intervals between successive notes? One way to determine what makes a melody is to alter various properties of a familiar melody

and see if that alteration affects the ability to recognize that melody. To give an example, we mentioned that most people can recognize a melody regardless of the key in which it is played. A study by Dowling and Fujitani (1971) evaluated the effects of some other melodic alterations.

Dowling and Fujitani asked college undergraduates to identify some familiar melodies—"Yankee Doodle," "Oh, Susannah," "Twinkle, Twinkle, Little Star," "Good King Wenceslaus," and "Auld Lang Syne." Each of these tunes was tape-recorded while being performed on the same wind instrument, in the same key, and at the same tempo. When undistorted versions of these tunes were heard, listeners correctly identified the melodies 99 percent of the time—which merely confirms that the melodies were indeed well known. But how did listeners do when these melodies were distorted?

Dowling and Fujitani studied the effects of several different forms of distortion. In one

condition, the *absolute* size of the intervals between notes was altered, but the *relative* size of the intervals remained the same. To illustrate, consider the first three notes of a verse from "Oh, Susannah" (see the diagram below). In the unadulterated version, notes 1 and 2 are separated by one whole tone, as are notes 2 and 3. In the first distorted version, notes 1 and 2 are separated by two whole tones, as are notes 2 and 3. Hence in the distorted version, the absolute size of the intervals has been altered but the relative size remains unchanged. Note, too, that the pitch contour remains the same: in both versions, the second note is higher than the first, and the third note is higher than the second. Upon hearing melodies distorted in this way, listeners could correctly identify the tune 66 percent of the time. This decline in performance indicates that absolute interval size (the property distorted in this condition) does contribute to defining a melody. Still, this

(Continued on next page)

Undistorted   Distortion 1   Distortion 2

property isn't absolutely crucial—relative interval size and pitch contour provide enough information for listeners to distinguish one melody from others much of the time.

In a second condition, each melody was distorted even more severely. In this case, only the pitch contour was preserved. With this form of distortion, the sequence of notes moved up and down in pitch in the same manner as they did in the normal version, but the size of the intervals between notes in the distorted version was unrelated to the size of the intervals in the original. An example of this form of distortion, as applied to "Oh, Susannah," appears in the musical staff at the far right (distortion 2). With such distortion, listeners still managed to identify the melody 59 percent of the time. So pitch contour, all by itself, does provide some information for identifying melodies. In their final condition, Dowling and Fujitani distorted even the pitch

contour; the only thing left undistorted was the first note in each measure. With just this scant information to go on, people were not able to recognize the melodies.

In summary, the experiment by Dowling and Fujitani shows that when listeners try to recognize familiar tunes, they make use of several sources of information. These sources include absolute interval size, relative interval size, and pitch contour. Incidentally, most of the participants in Dowling and Fujitani's study had no special musical training. In another study, Dowling (1978) found that musically experienced people were better at perceiving the relative size of intervals than were musically inexperienced individuals. This is not surprising, since relative interval size is a rather subtle structural aspect of any melody. It is the sort of transformation that Bach used in many of his compositions.

There is another salient aspect of melody, and that is its

rhythm. To appreciate the salience of a melody's rhythm, have a friend select one of the five tunes mentioned above and then clap out the rhythm of that tune. You'll be surprised how easy it is to identify which of the melodies your friend is clapping. Some of the best examples of rhythm's contribution to a melody come from classical music. One is Franz Liszt's short piece for piano and orchestra, "Totentanz" ("Dance of Death"). It is an amazing example of the musical variety that can be achieved simply by altering the speed and rhythm of one theme. The piece consists of thirty variations on the same theme, the medieval "Dies Irae," and each variation makes its own unique musical statement. An attentive listener should have no trouble hearing the same melody running throughout the piece. Liszt's composition beautifully demonstrates how changes in rhythm alone can influence your perception of a melody.

brating at 300 Hz sounds lower in pitch as intensity increases, even though its frequency remains constant. In contrast, a tuning fork vibrating at 3,000 Hz sounds higher in pitch as intensity increases.

Why should the perception of pitch vary with loudness? Although this is merely a conjecture, perhaps pure tones at higher intensities produce a shift in the peak position of the mechanical wave traveling along the basilar membrane. This shift, in turn, would change the pattern of activity within auditory nerve fibers tuned to different frequencies. But why the location of peak membrane displacement should depend on intensity is an unsolved problem. In any

event, the variation in pitch with loudness underscores that pitch and frequency are not synonymous.

There is another interesting situation where pitch and frequency are partially dissociated from one another. Have you ever noticed the change in pitch produced by a sound source that moves rapidly past? One example is provided by the whine of a train's engine as it speeds past a listener standing at a railroad crossing. As the engine approaches, the pitch of the engine's sound rises steadily. Once the engine has passed, its pitch abruptly drops. The same phenomenon is experienced by spectators at an automobile race: as each car whizzes by, the

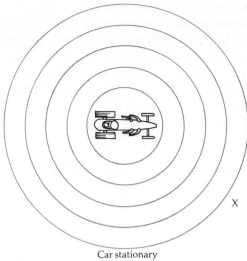

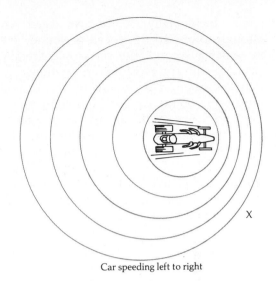

Car stationary

Car speeding left to right

FIGURE 10.10
The Doppler shift.

pitch of the sound of the engine changes. In both cases, you are hearing what is known as the **Doppler shift,** named after its discoverer, Christian Johann Doppler, a nineteenth-century Austrian physicist.

Figure 10.10 illustrates the reason for the Doppler shift, the change in pitch when a sound source moves past a listener. The circles represent sound waves spreading out from a sound source, in this case a racing car. In the left-hand panel, the car is standing still with its engine idling; the circles all share a common center (the car), and they radiate symmetrically outward. If you were standing at the position marked ''X,'' the car's engine would have a steady whine, or pitch. But suppose the car were moving rapidly from left to right; this would produce the series of circles shown in the right-hand panel. Because the car is moving, the waves no longer originate from the same location over time. Instead, the origin of successive circles moves rightward over time, as the car speeds in that direction. Note that the centers of the largest circles are located at

positions previously occupied by the moving car. The smaller circles represent more recently generated sound waves. Because the car is moving rightward, these newer, more recently generated sound waves bunch up with the older ones. Note that immediately in front of the car, the distance between waves is much less than the distance between waves trailing the car.

Now imagine you're standing at the point marked ''X'' in the right-hand panel of the figure. Just before the car passes you, you will be hearing the bunched-up sound waves; after the car passes, you will be hearing the more spread-out sound waves that trail the car. In other words, the frequency with which sound waves reach your ear is higher in the first case than in the second. And this change in frequency is heard by you as a rise in pitch. Once the car has passed, you begin hearing the more spread-out waves, which produce a decline in pitch. Of course, the frequencies actually produced by the car's engine remain constant—which is why to the driver, the engine always sounds the same. Incidentally, if the car were fast enough to exceed the speed of sound, 332 meters per second, the car would literally catch up with and pass the very sound waves it had created. This would be heard as a loud sonic boom, caused by the enormous pressure wave produced whenever a moving object breaks the sound barrier. The driver of a supersonic car (or the pilot of a supersonic jet) does not hear the shattering sound of the sonic boom, since that sound does not travel fast enough to catch up with the speeding vehicle.

By now you should be familiar with the concept of pitch and should understand its relation to the frequency of simple tones. The next step, then, is to examine what it sounds like when you listen to more complicated auditory stimuli made up of several different frequencies. Once more, let's turn to musical sounds to help us begin answering this question.

PITCH AND TIMBRE

Earlier we used musical notes to illustrate the concept of pitch. Yet a particular note played on, say, a piano is recognizably different from the same note played on another instrument, such as a clarinet. Now both notes do have the same pitch, indicating that two instruments playing the same note of the scale do produce something in common—the **fundamental frequency** produced by the piano is identical to the fundamental frequency produced by the clarinet. But besides this fundamental frequency, each instrument generates a unique set of additional frequency components. These additional components are called **overtones.** In combination with the fundamental frequency, these overtones give each musical instrument a characteristic sound called **timbre.** Your ability to identify various instruments just by hearing them rests on these differences in timbre. An example will make this clear.

Figure 10.11 shows the various frequency components produced when a guitar and an alto saxophone play the same note—one with a fundamental frequency of 196 Hz (the same note is produced on a piano by striking the G below middle C). In this figure, the horizontal axis specifies frequency and the vertical axis specifies intensity. Each vertical line in the graph means that the instrument is producing sound energy at that frequency; the height of the line indicates the amount of energy, or intensity, present in that frequency. Note that both instruments, the guitar and the alto saxophone, are producing sound energy at 196 Hz, the fundamental frequency (see the thick vertical line in Figure 10.11). Played together, these two instruments would, therefore, sound in tune. Note also, however, that the two instruments are producing different patterns of overtones (the vertical lines to the right of the fundamental); these are the frequency components that enable you to tell the guitar note from the one sounded by the saxophone. Even the same note played on two instruments of the same kind may sound slightly different. Perhaps you've heard someone claim to be able to tell the difference between a Steinway piano and a Baldwin; this is conceivable, since different versions of the same instrument produce small differences in the intensity profile of the overtones. The ear of a trained musician is amazingly keen at picking up such differences.

Incidentally, timbre depends not only on the set of frequencies produced by an instrument but also on the way those frequencies build up and decay over time. This is very clearly demonstrated if you try to identify an instrument from a tape recording played backward. Even though the profile of frequencies produced by that instrument remains the same regardless of the direction in which the tape is played, it is difficult to identify the instrument being played (Berger, 1964). The difficulty arises

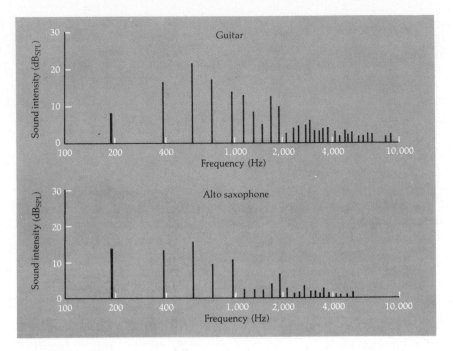

FIGURE 10.11
*The various frequency components when a guitar and an alto saxophone play
the same note. Here the note has a fundamental frequency of 196 Hz.
(Adapted from Olson, 1967.)*

because playing the tape backward has reversed the build-up and decay of the component frequencies. This is one reason why most people can easily distinguish between computer-generated music and real, acoustically produced music. Computer-generated music, while faithfully reproducing all the tones associated with a given instrument, may not contain all the other acoustic information that specifies an instrument's timbre, such as the build-up and decay of the fundamental and overtones. In the process of trying to improve the fidelity of computer-generated music, researchers are learning more about the physical correlates of the timbre of traditional musical instruments (Risset, 1978).

Our discussion of musical timbre was meant to illustrate how a sound source is defined perceptually by the profile of component frequencies that it produces. This sets the stage for our next question: why are particular frequencies grouped together, causing you to perceive them as emanating from a single sound source? An answer to this question is crucial for understanding how sounds are recognized.

Sound Recognition: Judging What the Source of a Sound Is

As we have mentioned, pure tones are rare in nature. Virtually all naturally occurring sounds consist of a number of component frequencies. You can think of these individual sounds as consisting of a unique package of frequencies. Frequency information, in other words, provides a kind of "signature'' that identifies the source of a sound. The individual frequency components that make up your voice are analogous to the letters that make up your name.

Thus to recognize a sound source, your auditory system must somehow group together the frequencies unique to that source. When you think about it, this process of grouping cannot be simple. Imagine, for instance, listening to a recording of a string trio consisting of a violin, a viola, and a cello. With a little effort, most people would have no trouble picking out any one of those instruments and following the passage of music being played by it. Although we take this ability for granted, it is really quite an amazing feat—after all, the only thing reaching your ears is a mixture of frequencies made up of all the frequency components produced by those three different instruments. Why don't you hear this combination of frequencies as a sound arising from a single instrument with its own composite timbre? How does your ear manage to identify the components arising from, say, the cello and sort them out from the component frequencies arising from the violin? Somehow this must be done, for otherwise you'd be unable to follow the musical line played by the separate instruments. And the same consideration applies to natural sounds, including speech. Suppose that you are listening to a friend and, at the same time, a dog is barking. Somehow your auditory system identifies which frequencies are associated with your friend's voice and segregates them from the frequencies that make up the sound of the barking dog. This process of identification and segregation should remind you of visual processes discussed earlier. In both stereopsis and motion perception, the visual system solves an analogous, correspondence problem—from a visual scene, it has to identify and group features representing particular objects. The auditory system is faced with a comparable correspond-

ence problem. How is the problem solved in the case of hearing?

Several acoustic features unite frequency components that arise from one source, thereby making it possible to hear that source as distinct from others (McAdams, 1981). For one thing, the intensities of a source's frequency components all wax and wane in synchrony; they all come on at the same time, they vary in intensity synchronously, and they cease simultaneously. Frequency components that grow and decay together tend to fuse into a single sound. When one frequency component within a set of frequencies is delayed slightly relative to the others, that one component tends to stand out and be heard as arising from a separate source (Bregman and Pinker, 1978). Delays as short as one-twentieth of a second are sufficient to segregate a single frequency component from an ensemble of frequencies. In effect, frequency components from the same sound source form a cohesive unit, all members following the same pattern of change. In this respect, the frequency components from a sound source are like sailors in a boat: while the individual sailors differ in size and appearance, all undergo the same up and down motions, as the boat rides the waves. This common fate links the individual sailors into a single entity called a ''crew.'' Likewise, common fate is one way that your auditory system manages to decide which sounds belong together, meaning that they come from the same source.

Another factor influencing whether frequency components seem to originate from a single sound source is the harmonic relations of those components. Frequencies that are multiples of one another are said to be harmonically related. For instance, playing the A string on a violin generates acoustic energy at the frequencies 440, 880, and 1,320 Hz; as you can see, the two higher frequencies (overtones) are multiples of the fundamental frequency, which means they are harmonically related. And, in general, harmonic tones tend to group together much more readily than do nonharmonic tones (de Boer, 1956). In this regard, it is significant that many relevant sounds in the environment, especially speech and music, are made up of harmonically related frequencies (McAdams, 1981). To give one example, automobile horns on newer model cars honk at F-sharp and A-sharp, a harmonically related pair that is judged pleasing to the ear (Garfield, 1983).

So to sum up, several factors contribute to the perceptual grouping of frequency components into a single, recognizable sound source. We could summarize the operation of these factors by saying that the auditory system picks out patterns among frequency components. These patterns could involve simultaneous changes in the intensities of certain frequency components. Or these patterns could involve a harmonic relation among certain frequency components. In both cases, these patterns unite the constituent frequencies and allow one to identify their source. At present, it is not known how the auditory nervous system actually performs this process of pattern recognition. Work on speech perception comes closest to tackling the problem, and we shall discuss some of this work in the last section of this chapter. For now, though, let's complete our coverage of sound recognition by considering an aspect of hearing that one seldom thinks about, even though it accompanies one's every movement.

AUDITORY PERCEPTION OF TEXTURE

Whenever you rub your hand over the surface of an object, your motion produces a sound that tells you something about the texture of that surface. The same thing occurs when you are walking—the sound of your feet striking pavement is different from the sound produced when you walk on a gravel surface. Normally, you don't pay much attention to those sounds, and you certainly don't rely exclusively on them to judge the texture of surfaces; vision and touch dominate judgments of texture. Yet, when those other sources of information are missing, you are still quite good at judging the roughness of a surface on the basis of sound alone. In this regard, perhaps you've seen the television commercial where a man scrapes each side of his face with a plastic credit card. From the sounds produced by this action, it is clear which side of his face has received a closer, smoother shave.

Just how accurately can you judge a surface's roughness from the sound it produces when touched? Take a few minutes to try the following exercise. While you are blindfolded, have a friend rub his hand over various objects whose surfaces differ in their degree of roughness. These objects might include the page of a book, a piece of cloth, and a fingernail file. Not only will you "hear" how rough the surface is, you'll probably have little trouble identifying the objects solely on the basis of these texture sounds. Susan Lederman, a psychologist at Queen's University in Canada, has studied auditory texture perception. She had people rate the perceived roughness of surfaces on the basis of sounds produced when someone else rubbed that surface. The surfaces consisted of metal plates with grooves cut in them, rather like the surface of corrugated cardboard. Lederman (1979) found that ratings of perceived roughness corresponded closely to the actual roughness of the surface, as gauged by the spacing of the grooves in the metal plates. One source of information for such judgments would be the pitch of the touch-produced sound: rougher surfaces tend to produce lower-pitched sounds than do smoother surfaces. Extremely smooth surfaces, such as a chalkboard, generate very high frequencies when scratched with a sharp object such as a fingernail. As you know, this sound can quite literally send chills through your body. No one knows for sure why this particular sound evokes such a universally strong reaction. It may have something to do with the fact that *any* very intense sound can be painful.

On this shrill note, we shall conclude our discussion of sound recognition, the ability to judge *what* the source of a sound is. We are now ready to consider **sound localization,** the ability to judge *where* sounds are coming from.

Sound Localization: Judging Where *a Sound Originates*

Hearing involves more than just recognizing sounds. One also has a sense of the direction from which those sounds are coming. This ability to perceive the location of sounds in space can be as important as the capacity to identify those sounds. What good is it to recognize the scream of a firetruck's siren if one cannot tell from which direction it is approaching? How frustrating it would be for a parent to hear the frightened cries of a lost child and yet be unable to pinpoint the origins of those cries. Fortunately, hearing does have a distinct spatial quality—sounds always appear to come from somewhere, although in some instances a sound's apparent location may be misleading. This section discusses the auditory information that endows sounds with this quality of spatial location.

Accurate sound localization depends crucially on having two ears. Working together, the ears, like the eyes, enable one to locate objects in three-dimensional space. As any person with unilateral deafness will tell you, sound localization using one ear is difficult. Unlike monocular vision, which has many of its own sources of information for depth perception, monaural hearing offers

little in the way of information for localization.

In the previous chapter, we mentioned that the two ears provide binaural information that specifies a sound's direction. Sound waves from the same source arriving at your two ears may differ in intensity and in time of arrival, depending on the location of that source relative to your head. We also described neurons in the auditory system that seem designed to register these differences in intensity and in time of arrival. Let's analyze both these sources of binaural information in greater detail, starting with interaural intensity differences.

INTERAURAL INTENSITY DIFFERENCES

Figure 10.12 summarizes how **interaural intensity differences** vary with the position of a sound source. These data were obtained by positioning a sound source at various points around an artificial head outfitted with microphones in each "ear" (Shaw, 1974). The vertical axis plots the intensity difference between the sounds arriving at the two ears. The horizontal axis plots the position of the sound source relative to the straight ahead position. Two curves are shown, one using a 6,000-Hz tone and the other using a 200-Hz tone. Notice that when the high-frequency (6,000 Hz) tone is located to the side of the head, the interaural intensity difference grows to almost 20 dB.

Notice also that for each and every difference in interaural intensity (values on the vertical axis), there are *two* distinct locations (on the horizontal axis) where a sound source could produce that intensity difference. Take, for example, sound originating from a location directly behind the head. As Figure 10.12 shows, this location yields an interaural intensity value of zero. Yet the same value—zero—occurs when the sound originates from a location straight in front of the head. Besides this pair of sound source lo-

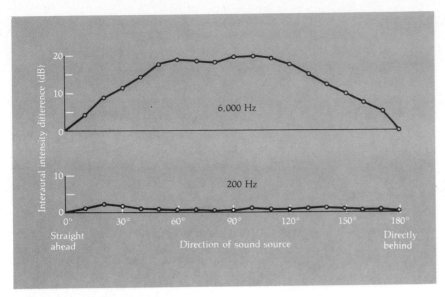

FIGURE 10.12
Sound intensity at the two ears varies with the location of the sound source.
This variation in interaural intensity difference depends on frequency. (Data
from Shaw, 1974.)

cations, there are other positions where interaural intensity provides ambiguous information. Since distinctly different spatial locations can produce the same information about interaural intensity, that ambiguous information could lead to confusions about the location of a sound source. These confusions in fact rarely occur, but we'll postpone describing why until we have completed our review of the binaural cues for sound localization. For now, let's continue our examination of Figure 10.12.

As the 200-Hz curve indicates, interaural intensity differences are much less pronounced when the sound source consists of low frequencies. This means that interaural intensity is a less potent cue for low-frequency sounds than it is for high-frequency sounds. There is a simple reason why the intensities of low frequencies are so similar at the two ears. With low-frequency sounds, the length of the sound wave (recall Figure 9.6, p. 299) is actually longer than the di-

ameter of the head, which is about 20 centimeters. For the sake of comparison, the length of a 900-Hz tone is approximately 40 centimeters, double the head's diameter. The head, in other words, is too small to get in the way of low-frequency sound waves. Because they are unimpeded by the head, these low-frequency waves lose little in the way of intensity from one side of the head to the other. High frequencies, however, are more effectively blocked by the head. Their waves are too small to leapfrog past the head, so to speak. As a result, the head more effectively blocks sound waves of high frequency from reaching the farther ear, thus weakening their intensity. Because of this physical property of sound, interaural intensity differences associated with high-frequency sounds will be larger than those associated with low-frequency sounds.

Now let's review the other source of localization information, **interaural time differences.**

INTERAURAL TIME DIFFERENCES

Figure 10.13 summarizes how the time of arrival of a sound at the two ears varies with the location of the sound source relative to the head. These measurements were made in much the same way as the ones described above, only using brief clicks as sound stimuli in this case (Shaw, 1974). The horizontal axis again plots the position of the sound source; the vertical axis, the difference in time of arrival of the sound at the two ears. As this graph shows, a sound coming from somewhere off to the side of the head strikes one ear before the other. The most pronounced difference in time of arrival occurs when the sound source is located directly to the side of the head. Notice that for this condition, the difference in time amounts to less than a millisecond (one-thousandth of a second), a tiny value indeed. In comparison, sound from a source directly ahead or behind a listener arrives at the two ears at precisely the same time. As with the case of interaural intensity differences, interaural time differences can be potentially ambiguous: the same values of time difference (vertical axis) can be produced by sources in two different locations (horizontal axis). For instance, a zero interaural time difference could arise from a source located either directly ahead of the listener or directly behind.

Using continuous tones rather than clicks, it turns out that interaural time differences are more easily registered if the tones are of low frequency than if they are of high frequency (Mills, 1958). However, this has nothing to do with head size. Instead, it has to do with the relatively large distance between the peaks and troughs of low-frequency sound waves. To be effective at all, interaural differences in time must be large enough to be registered by the auditory nervous system. If the distance between the ears were tiny, the difference in time of arrival of sound at the two ears would be too small to serve as information for localization. Of course there are lots of animal species with small heads and, therefore, closely set ears. Box 10.4 describes how these diminutive creatures may get around this problem.

THE EFFECTIVENESS OF INTERAURAL TIME AND INTENSITY DIFFERENCES

We've just seen that the two sources of information about a sound's location, time differences and intensity differences, complement each other. Intensity differences are best suited to the localization of high frequencies; time differences are best suited to the localization of low frequencies. This implies that a person listening to sounds originating from different locations in space might utilize one source of information (interaural time differences) to localize low-frequency sounds and another source of information (interaural intensity differences) to localize high-frequency sounds. An experiment by Stevens and Newman (1934) supports this idea.

For their experiment, Stevens and Newman seated a listener on the roof of a build-

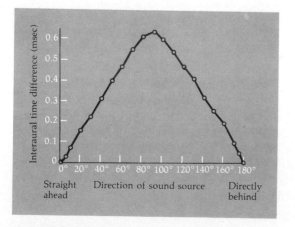

FIGURE 10.13
The time of arrival of sound at the two ears varies with the location of the sound source. (Data from Shaw, 1974.)

BOX 10.4

Nature Rewards Those Who Are Small

You've learned that sound localization depends on two sources of information: interaural time differences and interaural intensity differences. With these in mind, think about the plight of an animal, such as the mouse, whose head is considerably smaller than your own. Because its ears are so close together, there is a vanishingly tiny difference in the time of arrival of a sound at its two ears. For all practical purposes, localization information based on interaural time differences is nil for the small-headed creature. What is worse, the mouse's small head, compared to yours, represents a puny barrier to sound waves. The average mouse's head is only about 2 centimeters wide, which means that a 10,000-Hz tone will pass by the head unattenuated, as though the head weren't even there. And when sounds are not attenuated by the head, interaural intensity differences are too small to be of much help in localizing sounds. In other words, for a given sound frequency, interaural intensity is a much more potent localization cue for us big-headed humans than it is for the mouse and other small-headed creatures.

This seems like a high price to pay for being little. But nature has benevolently devised a strategy to enable small animals to overcome their handicap: these animals can hear very high sound frequencies, well above the upper limits of human ears. Look back at

Figure 10.4, which shows the range of sound frequencies heard by different species. Note the highest frequency audible for each species, and think about the size of these various animals. You will see that the upper limit of hearing, which we'll call **hearing acuity,** is related to the animal's body size. For large creatures (such as the elephant) hearing acuity is relatively low, while for small creatures (such as the mouse) it is high. This relationship between body size and hearing acuity is shown in the accompanying graph.

But how does the ability to hear sounds of very high frequency help with the problem of sound localization? The answer is simple: at very high frequencies, wavelengths are sufficiently short that even a small head will partially block

those sound waves. For example, the wavelength of an 80,000-Hz tone (which a mouse can hear) is only 5 millimeters. For a sound wave so small, the mouse's 2-centimeter-wide head represents a substantial barrier. So when that high-frequency sound originates from a source located off to the side of the animal's head, interaural intensity becomes a very useful source of information for localizing it.

The relationship between hearing acuity and head size suggests, then, that an animal's ability to hear high-frequency sounds may have to do with sound localization (Masterton, Heffner, and Ravizza, 1969). This evidence is circumstantial, but it is gratifying to think that nature watches over all creatures, great and small.

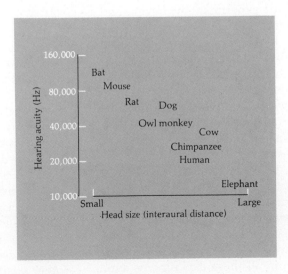

ing at Harvard University. This outdoor setting eliminated sound reflections from walls and ceilings; to minimize disturbance from extraneous sounds, data were collected during the wee hours of the morning. Extending out from the listener's chair was a long metal arm that could rotate around the listener's head. Attached to the end of this mechanical arm was a loudspeaker that could play pure tones of various frequencies. The listener sat blindfolded with his head held very still. He was instructed to point in the direction from which the sound seemed to originate. For tones below 1,000 Hz, localization accuracy was high. But for tones between 2,000 and 4,000 Hz, errors became increasingly frequent. At still higher frequencies, performance again improved, eventually becoming as good as it had been with low frequencies. Presumably, these transitions in performance corresponded to shifts in the cue used to make localization judgments. The high error rates at intermediate frequencies indicate that this is a region where neither time nor intensity is particularly effective.

Following the experiment by Stevens and Newman, there have been many other studies of sound localization. Some have used an array of loudspeakers surrounding a listener sitting in an anechoic chamber (Wightman and Kistler, 1980). Sound is played from different speakers, and the listener indicates where the sound comes from. In other experiments, listeners have been outfitted with headphones through which sounds are played (Mills, 1960; Jeffress and Taylor, 1961). Headphones have the advantage of allowing the experimenter to vary interaural time and interaural intensity independently, making it possible to examine the effectiveness of the two cues separately. In general, the results from all these experiments support the conclusions reached by Stevens and Newman: sound localization depends on in-

teraural time differences at *low* frequencies, and on interaural intensity differences at *high* frequencies. In most ordinary listening situations, sounds consist of both high and low frequencies, which means you rely on both sources of information, time differences and intensity differences, for localizing those sounds.

We should stress one point, by the way. When tested on sound localization tasks, whether with headphones or with loudspeakers, listeners never actually hear differences in intensity between the two ears. Nor can they tell that sound arrives at one ear ahead of the other. Instead, listeners hear a single sound originating from a particular direction relative to straight ahead. Perceiving a sound's location occurs effortlessly and automatically, as common experience tells you. In fact, even newborn infants will turn their eyes toward the source of a sound (Butterworth and Castillo, 1976; Wertheimer, 1961). Thus sound localization is a perceptual ability that was present from the day you were born.

ASPECTS OF SOUND LOCALIZATION AND MISLOCALIZATION

There are certain positions in space where a sound source is difficult to pinpoint accurately. As you might guess, those positions include the ones where information about interaural time and interaural intensity is ambiguous. Two such positions were mentioned earlier, straight ahead and straight behind. Sounds from either of these positions arrive at the two ears simultaneously and with equivalent intensity. So it is not surprising that sounds arising from these two positions are sometimes mislocalized. Besides these two positions, there are many other positions in space where time and intensity cues are also ambiguous (Woodworth, 1938).

Design Features That Help You Avoid Mislocalization Errors. In view of these multiple points of potential confusion, it is surprising that people don't mistake the direction of sounds more often than they do. In fact, there are two reasons why you normally are not confused about the location of sounds. The first reason has to do with *head movements.* In sound localization experiments involving an array of speakers, the listener's head remains in a fixed position. Ordinarily, though, you are free to move your head when listening to a sound, and these head movements can eliminate potential confusion arising from ambiguous localization cues. To illustrate, imagine hearing a sound from a source located directly behind your head. While interaural time and intensity information is momentarily ambiguous, you can eliminate this ambiguity simply by turning your head in either direction. The sound source will no longer be symmetrically located between your two ears, and the available localization information will now specify the sound's location unambiguously. Moving your head changes the pattern of interaural differences associated with a stationary sound source, thereby clearing up any initial confusion about where a sound comes from. Note, however, that head movements are effective in eliminating ambiguity only if the sound is of sufficient duration to allow you to listen to it while turning your head; head movements are too slow to help localize brief sounds, such as the snap of a twig (Pollack and Rose, 1967).

A second reason why you seldom make localization errors has to do with the *pinnas.* Without them, you would be poorer at judging the location of a sound (Burger, 1958). You can demonstrate this for yourself by performing the following test. While you are blindfolded, have a friend stand close enough to you that he can snap his fingers at various positions around your head. See how well you can guess where that sound comes from. Now repeat this test while wearing earmuffs or a set of headphones, either of which largely eliminate any contribution from the pinnas. While still able to hear the sound, you'll find it more difficult to pinpoint exactly where the finger-snap originates, especially when that sound originates from either directly in front of you or directly behind you. This simple exercise demonstrates that the pinnas make it easier to locate sound. But why is that so? It is thought that the pinnas aid localization because sound bounces around in the folds of the pinnas before entering the ear canals; the number and direction of the bounces depends on the direction from which the sound originated. The pinnas, in other words, mark the incoming sound wave in a way that labels the direction from which that sound arrived at the ear (Batteau, 1967). The auditory system, in turn, manages to "read" that label, thereby avoiding any ambiguity about the location of the source of that sound wave.

Because the size and shape of the pinnas vary so much from person to person (see Figure 10.14), this labeled information about a sound's direction is highly specific to one's own ears. Thus if you and a friend were to trade pinnas, your ability to localize sound might be impaired. Such an impairment has actually been demonstrated by Fred Wightman and Doris Kistler, psychologists at Northwestern University. They placed a tiny microphone inside each ear canal of a person and recorded sounds originating from speakers located at various positions around the person's head. Because of the microphone's position, the sounds it picked up had already been influenced by the person's pinna. Wightman and Kistler also had the person judge the location of the sounds, and as expected, few errors were made except for the ambiguous sound locations we men-

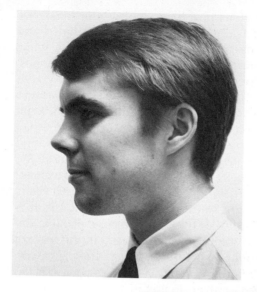

FIGURE 10.14
*Pinnas come in all sizes and shapes. (Top, left
and right: K. Bendo; bottom: courtesy of the
Lyndon Baines Johnson Library.)*

tioned earlier. Wightman and Kistler collected localization judgments and ear canal recordings from several people. They then played back those recorded sounds over headphones and had the same people once again make localization judgments. Listening to the sounds that had been recorded through their own ears, people had no trouble accurately localizing sounds. But when listening to sounds that had been recorded through someone else's ears, people were less accurate at localization. By examining the sound waveform recorded from within the ear canals of these people, Wightman and Kistler could identify the individual differences in those waveforms introduced by each person's pinnas. The individual differences in performance when listening with one's own pinnas or with someone else's implies that the auditory system does register the sound coloration introduced by the pinnas. This underscores the important role played by the pinnas in sound localization.

Mislocalization: Sound Heard Through Headphones. This discussion of the role of head movements and the pinnas in sound localization raises an interesting point. You've probably listened to music in stereophonic sound over a set of headphones. If so, you know that the sounds usually seem to originate from various places *within* your head, not from external locations. At this point you should be able to figure out why stereophonic music heard over headphones sounds the way it does. Typically, music is recorded from an array of many microphones placed at various positions around the musicians. Furthermore, technicians then combine the signals from those microphones to achieve whatever sound balance they desire. So by the time it reaches your ears over the headphones, the sound bears little resemblance to the binaural stimulus you would have heard in person.

Using just two microphones, recordings can be made that mimic what would be heard live; music recorded in this manner and heard over headphones *does* seem to emanate from out in space and not within your head (Koenig, 1950; Belendiuk and Butler, 1978). Even then, however, you must hold your head still for the illusion to be compelling. Here's why. The microphones were stationary at the time the recording was made, so the reproduced sound carries none of the changes in interaural time or intensity that would be produced by head movements. When you do move your head, the brain receives contradictory information: the vestibular system (the one responsible for signaling head orientation) informs your brain of your head movement but the auditory system does not report an associated change in interaural time or intensity. These contradictory messages reduce the otherwise compelling illusion that sounds heard over a headphone appear to come from out in space.

Mislocalization: Ears Versus Eyes. There are other instances where sound is incorrectly localized. In these instances mislocalization stems from contradictory information from the eyes and the ears. In movie theaters, for example, speakers are usually positioned on either side of the screen, yet we hear the sounds coming from the appropriate sources pictured on the screen. Another example of this kind of mislocalization is ventriloquism—speech is perceived to come from the mouth of the dummy when, of course, it comes from the still mouth of the ventriloquist. Both of these examples underscore vision's dominance over hearing when it comes to specifying the location of events (Welch and Warren, 1980).

Probably the most convincing proof of vision's dominance is provided by the *pseudophone*—the odd-looking listening device pictured in Figure 10.15. The pseudophone effectively interchanges input to the two ears, causing the left ear to hear what would normally be heard by the right, and vice versa. What this binaural swap does to sound localization depends on whether you listen with eyes open or closed (Young, 1928). Imagine that you are wearing a pseudophone and are sitting between two friends, a male to your left and a female to your right. They are arguing. With your eyes closed, the male's voice will sound as though it were coming from your right and the female's voice from your left. Although wrong, this way of hearing the two voices is not surprising; it is caused by the reversing

FIGURE 10.15

A pseudophone reverses the inputs to the two ears.

mechanism of the pseudophone. What is surprising, however, is what you hear with your eyes open. Now the male's voice will seem to originate from your left and the female's voice from your right. While this corresponds to the true seating arrangement, your brain has to *ignore* interaural time and intensity cues to arrive at this perception. Your brain, in other words, believes your eyes, not your ears.

In a way, this bias toward vision makes some sense. For one thing, sounds can bounce off solid surfaces and be reflected to your ears in the form of echoes. Hence the direction from which sound arrives at your ears may not always correspond to the actual location of the sound source. The same is not true of vision—the light reflected from an object travels in a straight line to your eye. Thus the principles of optics ensure that the light arriving at your eyes usually specifies an object's actual location. Physics offers another reason why your brain may trust your eyes more than your ears—sound travels much more slowly than light. Consequently, the sounds from a distant object (such as an airplane in flight) can belie the true position of that object, whereas the light from that object almost never lies. Considered together, these properties of light and sound may have encouraged the brain to rely more on vision for localization.

THE COCKTAIL PARTY EFFECT: MASKING AND UNMASKING SOUND

So far, our discussion of binaural hearing has focused on the role of the two ears in sound localization. There is, however, another advantage gained from binaural hearing—you are better at picking out one sound from among many in a noisy environment. Because this skill is often required at loud parties, it is aptly called the **cocktail party effect.** In the laboratory, it has been studied by having listeners detect faint sounds (called ''signals'') presented in a background of noise. Using headphones, various levels of noise may be presented to one or both ears, and signals of various intensities may likewise be presented to one or both ears. Moreover, the interval between presentation of the signal and the noise may be varied. As you can imagine from this brief description, these experiments can get rather complicated, as can the results (see Durlach and Colburn, 1978, for a review of this work). For purposes of explaining the cocktail party effect, the results can be summarized as follows.

You've already learned that background noise can interfere with your ability to hear weak sounds. This interference is called **masking,** and it is a common occurrence in everyday life. Furthermore, experience confirms that loud background noise is a more effective masker than is faint background noise—just compare what it's like to carry on a conversation at a rock concert versus in a library. However, even loud noise becomes less effective in masking a sound if the noise comes from a different location than the sound. The following observation demonstrates this point.

Imagine wearing headphones and having an audible tone delivered to your left ear only. Now suppose noise is also delivered over the headphones to that same ear, with its intensity adjusted so that you are no longer able to hear the tone; the noise, in other words, masks the tone. Finally, suppose the same amount of noise is added to the other ear as well, the one not receiving the tone. Ironically, this additional noise in the other ear actually makes the previously masked tone audible once again. This is called **binaural unmasking.** Besides unmasking the tone, adding noise to the other ear does something else, too—it seems to place that tone and the noise in different locations. With the tone and noise going to the left ear only, both are localized at that ear. But noise introduced to the right ear pairs with the noise already going to the left ear. This now causes the noise to be localized in the center of the head, no longer in the same position as the tone. In other words, when the noise and tone coincide in apparent location, masking is strong; when the two are separated, masking is weak. The neural events underlying this unmasking effect are not known, although they most probably have something to do with the neural events involved in sound localization.

Binaural unmasking enables you to focus on one person's voice in the presence of competing conversations elsewhere in a room. However, you are not totally oblivious to those other conversations. If your name happens to be mentioned in one of those conversations, your attention may be drawn to what is being said. This implies that your auditory system continues to analyze unattended sounds. Psychologists interested in selective attention have studied this phenomenon by presenting different, unrelated messages separately to the two ears (Moray, 1959). These experiments typically involve studying a listener's ability to interpret structured verbal messages. Since such tasks probably tap rather refined mental processes, most psychologists would refer to these as cognitive processes, not perceptual ones. In view of this distinction, we shall

not discuss the problem of selective attention any further here. Instead, we'll move on to the last topic of this chapter, the perception of speech sounds.

The Perception of Speech Sounds

Animals, including people, seem compelled to make sounds, and they will use just about any device at their disposal to do so. Woodpeckers drum their beaks against trees, rattlesnakes shake their tails, gorillas beat their chests, grasshoppers scrape their legs together, and termites grind their mandibles. The variety of resulting sounds is remarkable, ranging from the happy melodies of the robin to the mournful calls of the humpback whale; from the faint, rhythmic ticking of a beetle to the piercing shriek of a baboon. While some of these biological sounds may just be idle chatter to break the silence, most serve to communicate messages to friends and to foes. Obviously, then, for the sender's messages to be effective, those messages must be received by the other party. In nature, this is one of auditory perception's primary jobs, enabling animals to hear what others have to say.

Of all nature's creatures, humans have developed the largest repertoire of sounds. Human beings can make sounds using various parts of their bodies, including their hands, their feet, and of course their vocal apparatus. Not satisfied with these means, they have also invented devices to assist them in making sounds—including musical instruments, sirens, doorbells, and thousands of other noise makers. But among the many ways that humans have of producing sound, speech is undoubtedly the most important. It used to be commonly believed that the capacity to produce and to perceive speech sounds, more than anything else, set *Homo sapiens* apart from all other creatures (Blakemore, 1977). However, as we learn more about the language capabilities of nonhuman species such as the dolphin and the chimpanzee, it becomes necessary to question this belief that speech is the hallmark of the human species. Nonetheless, there is no denying that speech, the vehicle of language, has been immensely valuable in the biological and cultural evolution of the human species.

The study of speech encompasses several disciplines, ranging from neurology to linguistics. Each discipline analyzes speech from a particular perspective. For instance, the neurologist might be interested in the neuromuscular mechanisms responsible for the production of speech—here the emphasis would be on the components of the vocal tract and on the motor areas of the brain that guide the movements of those components. In contrast, a linguist might focus on the structure of grammar—the emphasis here would be less on the hardware of speech and more on the rules governing the formation and interpretation of sentences.

Where does auditory perception fit into this picture? Obviously, to understand a verbal utterance you must be able to hear the associated sounds. So speech perception must take into account the initial stages of hearing, those involved in the reception and processing of sound waves; these are the stages discussed earlier in this chapter and in the previous one. In addition, however, speech perception entails more complex auditory processing. Spoken words are composed of sounds whose acoustic properties are special. In this final section we shall summarize some of the major findings concerning the auditory processing of speech sounds.

THE SOUNDS OF SPEECH

Let's begin by considering the acoustical properties of speech sounds, since these de-

fine the relevant information that the auditory system must process in order for speech to be perceived. Speech sounds are produced when air from the lungs is forced through the vocal cords, a pair of elastic membranes stretched across the upper part of the air passage from the lungs. Air passing through the vocal cords causes them to vibrate, just like the reed on a wind instrument. Male vocal cords are slightly larger than their female counterparts, which means that the male cords vibrate at a somewhat lower frequency than do the female cords. This partially explains why the typical male voice is lower than the typical female voice.

The airborne vibrations produced by the vocal cords, in turn, are modified by changes in the shape of the throat, mouth, lips, and nasal cavity. These changes result in the vowel and consonant sounds that make up speech. Each of these sounds results from a particular positioning of the elements of the vocal tract. Take a moment to voice slowly several of the vowels and consonants, paying attention to the position of your lips, teeth, tongue, and throat. Notice how these positions differ for various vowels and consonants, which is why they sound different from one another. Not all sound differences are important, though. For example, sound differences associated with regional accents in the United States usually don't prevent people from understanding one another. Sound differences that are important are ones that actually change the meaning of an utterance. Any sound that can produce such a change is called a **phoneme.** Phonemes are considered the distinctive features of speech—together, they form the vocabulary of sounds used in a language. So the study of speech perception must concentrate on how phonemes are processed by the auditory system. To do this first requires specifying the acoustical properties of phonemes.

Any phoneme contains acoustic energy

at a number of different frequencies. It is impractical, therefore, to define phonemes the way we defined pure tones. Instead, hearing specialists use a more appropriate way to characterize speech sounds; this is called a sound **spectogram.** A spectogram is a graph showing the amount of acoustic energy at various frequencies over time. To illustrate, the spectogram shown in Figure 10.16 shows a "picture" of the speech energy produced when you utter the word "spike." The vertical axis plots sound frequency and the horizontal axis represents time. Spelled out underneath the horizontal axis is the word "spike," indicating when in time each of its phonemes was uttered. The dark portions of the graph denote the distribution of acoustic energy produced by that utterance; the degree of darkness is proportional to the amount of that energy.

Note that the hiss of the consonant "s" consists of energy distributed over a fairly wide range of frequencies, as indicated by the wide band of darkness above that letter. There is a brief period of silence between /s/ and /p/, seen in the spectogram as an absence of acoustic energy. The vowel "i" consists of several bands of acoustic energy,

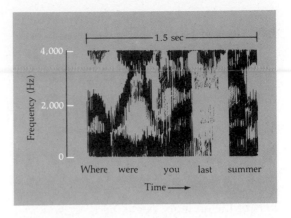

FIGURE 10.17
A sound spectogram of a sentence. Note the longer time scale in this spectogram, relative to the one in Figure 10.16.

which in the spectogram look like a group of worms located above the letter "i." Note that during the course of this utterance, one of these bands of frequencies dips down— this corresponds to the drop in the pitch of your voice when you say the phoneme /i/. (Listen to your voice as you speak this vowel.) In other words, the spectogram also depicts the intonation of your speech. The spectogram neatly summarizes the acoustic properties of speech sounds. And as Figure 10.17 illustrates, spectograms can be created for sentences as well as words. The beauty of the sound spectogram is that it depicts the entire package of frequencies making up each and every phoneme in an utterance, and it shows how those frequencies change over time. The spectogram enables you to visualize the transitions and irregularities that characterize different speech sounds. Because your voice reflects the many distinctive features of your own vocal apparatus and speech intonation, a spectogram of your voice may be as unique to you as your fingerprints (Kertsa, 1962). Incidentally, the spectographic analysis of sound can also be applied to nonspeech sounds such as those

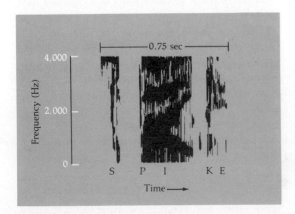

FIGURE 10.16
A sound spectogram of the utterance "spike."

made by animals, natural events, and in-animate objects (Seyfarth and Cheney, 1984).

Armed with this powerful tool for de-scribing the acoustic properties of speech sounds, let's turn to how the auditory sys-tem responds to these properties.

THE NEURAL ANALYSIS OF SPEECH SOUNDS

We'll start by thinking about how speech sounds might be represented within the fi-bers of the auditory nerve. By now, you well know that these fibers respond to narrow ranges of sound frequencies. Each fiber, in other words, "listens" for the presence of particular frequencies in the sound wave ar-riving at the ear. Different fibers "listen" for different frequencies. With this in mind, look back at the spectrogram shown in Figure 10.16. You could envision points along the axis labeled "Frequency" as representing auditory nerve fibers. Fibers that respond to low frequencies would be situated at the bottom of the axis, while fibers that respond to high frequencies would be situated at the top. Thought of in this way, distance along the vertical axis would correspond to dis-tance along the basilar membrane. The hor-izontal axis would still correspond to time. The changes in the degree of darkness within the spectogram would now correspond to the amount of neural activity within various nerve fibers.

This way of thinking about nerve fiber activity was introduced by Nelson Kiang (1975), who called the resulting plot of neural activity a **neurogram.** For a given utterance, such as the word "spike," there is a close correspondence between the pattern of acoustic energy in the sound spectogram and the pattern of neural activity in the neuro-gram. This correspondence merely confirms that the ear and the auditory nerve perform a frequency analysis on the incoming sound. This cannot be the whole story of speech

perception, though. For one thing, there are instances where speech sounds that are per-ceived as equivalent produce distinctly dif-ferent sound spectograms. To give an ex-ample, the sound spectogram representing a particular consonant can vary depending on what vowel happens to follow that con-sonant. And these variations in the sound spectogram are registered in the pattern of fiber activity. Yet despite these variations in the pattern of activity, the same consonant is heard. When it processes speech sounds, the brain somehow takes into account the transitions from consonants to vowels. These transitions, incidentally, look like the dips and rises seen in the sound spectograms of Figures 10.16 and 10.17.

There's another reason why one must look beyond the auditory nerve for the analysis of speech sounds, and this has to do with the variability of speech sounds. The pitch and speed of your speech differs from those of your friends, which is why you can iden-tify people just by hearing their voices. Yet despite these individual differences in the acoustical properties of speech, you usually have no trouble perceiving what your friends are saying. Evidently the brain uses some-thing more than just the specific frequency components making up speech sounds.

Finally, there is neurological evidence that speech perception involves more than just activity in the auditory nerve. People with damage to the temporal lobe of the brain's dominant hemisphere (the left hemisphere in the case of most right-handed individ-uals) have great difficulty recognizing speech, whereas recognition of other, nonspeech sounds is relatively unimpaired (Evans, 1982b). This implies that the dominant hemisphere, not just the auditory nerve fi-bers, contains some of the machinery essen-tial for speech perception.

To look for brain events related to the processing of speech sounds, physiologists have begun recording activity from neurons in the auditory cortex of monkeys who are listening to human speech sounds over headphones (Steinschneider, Arezzo, and Vaughan, 1982). You might wonder what neural activity in a monkey's brain could tell anyone about perception of human speech sounds. However, these physiologists feel justified in generalizing their results from monkeys to humans because monkeys can discriminate the same speech sounds as humans (Sinnott et al., 1976). Without going into details, the results can be summarized as follows. A number of perceptually significant acoustic properties of human speech affect the responses of neurons in the auditory portion of the brain. These properties include: (1) the time elapsing between the release of the lips and the start of sound production (the property enabling you to distinguish between such syllables as /pa/ and /ba/); (2) the acoustical context of a sound (such as whether a particular vowel is preceded by one consonant or another); and (3) the rate of frequency changes (an important feature distinguishing certain vowels from one another).

FACTORS THAT CONTRIBUTE TO SPEECH PERCEPTION

The Role of Feature Detection in Speech Perception. We've just seen that the auditory system of the monkey contains neurons that respond to perceptually relevant portions of human speech sounds. These neurons are located in a region of the monkey's brain that, when damaged, makes it difficult for the monkey to discriminate human speech sounds (Dewson, Pribram, and Lynch, 1969). Damage to comparable regions of the human brain also produces deficits in speech perception (Marin, 1976). This parallel between monkey and human makes it tempting to believe that the human brain also contains neurons responsive to distinctive features of speech. But how could one

go about testing this idea? Think back to Chapter 4, where we described a procedure, selective adaptation, for confirming the existence of visual neurons responsive to lines of different orientations. In that case, staring at lines of one orientation temporarily caused lines of a neighboring orientation to appear tilted away from their true orientation. This visual aftereffect presumably results from the reduced responsiveness of orientation-selective neurons.

The same line of reasoning has been applied in the search for neurons specialized for the analysis of human speech sounds. Peter Eimas and John Corbit (1973), working at Brown University, were the first to do this. Using an electronic speech synthesizer, they generated consonant sounds such as /b/, /p/, /t/ and /d/. Included among these consonant sounds were some that were ambiguous, meaning that they might sound like /t/ one time and /d/ the next. These ambiguous sounds, in other words, seemed to lie at the boundary between two unambiguous phonemic categories. Eimas and Corbit had people listen to an unambiguous consonant such as /d/ repeated over and over for several minutes. Following this period of adaptation, people listened to the previously ambiguous consonant, the one that used to sound sometimes like /t/ and other times like /d/. No longer did this consonant sound ambiguous—now it more clearly sounded like /t/ and not like the adapted consonant /d/.

Eimas and Corbit concluded that repeated exposure to one consonant had temporarily fatigued a set of detectors responsive to the distinctive features of that consonant; those feature detectors responsive to other consonants remained at full strength. Thus following adaptation, the ambiguous consonant produced more activity within the set of unadapted feature detectors than within the adapted set. Consequently, listeners heard the consonant sound signaled by the unadapted set of feature detectors. The findings of Eimas and Corbit, along with more recent results using the selective adaptation procedure (see Darwin, 1976, and Sawusch and Jusczyk, 1981), point to the existence of neural feature detectors responsive to speech sounds. But this still cannot be the entire story of speech perception. As important as they must be for registering the presence of distinctive speech sounds, these feature detectors cannot account for all aspects of speech perception. There are two other important factors that govern how the sounds of speech (the ones signaled by feature detectors) will actually be heard by a listener: the context in which those sounds occur and the perceived boundaries between speech sounds. Let's consider these two factors in turn.

The Role of Context in Speech Perception.
Figure 10.18 illustrates a well-known principle: your perception of a stimulus depends on the context in which that stimulus appears. In Figure 10.18, the two center dots circles are equal in diameter; you perceive one as larger than the other because of the surrounding dots. The same principle applies in the case of speech perception: how a given speech sound is perceived depends on the context in which it is heard (Massaro and Cohen, 1983). This context can be de-

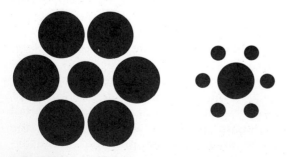

FIGURE 10.18
Context influences perception. Are the center dots in these two figures really different sizes, as they appear to be?

fined by any of several sources. For one, the *topic* of a conversation can itself provide a context for perceiving speech sounds. This form of context is amusingly illustrated by a catchy tune popular during the 1940s. Phonetically speaking, the first several measures go:

Marzi doats n doze edoats n lidul lamzey divey. . . .

Now to those of you who've never heard this song (popularized in the 1940s by Bing Crosby and the Andrews Sisters), this string of "words" may sound like make-believe speech. But in fact the words refer to the eating habits of several familiar hoofed animals. Still puzzled? Try repeating the words quickly, paying close attention to the sounds, not the letters. Once you hear the verse as it was meant to be perceived, you'll be able to hear it no other way. Knowing what the song's verses are about will influence what the words sound like to you.

In the case of the nonsense verse, context was provided by the general theme of the song. Speech perception can be influenced by other types of context, too. For instance, the same utterance can sound quite different depending on the *rapidity* with which words preceding that utterance are spoken. To give an example, a syllable may sound like /ba/ when it occurs within the context of a slowly spoken phrase but may sound like /pa/ when occurring within the same phrase rapidly spoken (Summerfield, 1975). The same thing can happen with words in a sentence, as shown by Ladefoged and Broadbent (1957). They generated sentences on tape with the words all spoken at a cadence characteristic of a particular talker. In some of the recordings, the last word was removed and replaced with the same word as it would be spoken by another person at a different cadence. People listening to these recordings would frequently misidentify the last word when its cadence differed from that of the rest of the phrase.

The experiment described above just confirms what you already know from experience: much of your ability to understand what someone is saying depends on picking up the cadence of that person's voice. Everyone has a characteristic *rhythm* to his or her speech: some people speak at a rapid clip, while others drawl. Learning the cadence of a person's speech is one key to understanding a speaker with a strong accent that differs from your own. You must accustom yourself to that individual's pronunciation before you are able to perceive effortlessly what the person is saying. So here's another instance where context (rate of speaking, in this case) influences speech perception.

In the examples just cited, the context shaping the perception of speech sounds was provided by other speech sounds. As the following experiment shows, however, *visual cues* can influence what a verbal utterance sounds like. Harry McGurk and John MacDonald, British psychologists at the University of Surrey, did an experiment in which they put auditory information about a spoken word in conflict with visual information about that word (McGurk and MacDonald, 1976). They had people watch a film of a young woman who was repeating various syllables. In some segments of the film, the audio cue (soundtrack) and the visual cue (lip movement) corresponded to the same syllable; but in other segments the soundtrack for one syllable was dubbed onto the lip movements for another syllable. People reported the syllable accurately when just the sound was heard, and they were able to name the syllable being spoken when just the lip movements were seen with no accompanying sound. (This latter observation merely confirms that people are pretty good at lip reading.) However, people made some very interesting mistakes while watching the

dubbed film. One type of mistake involved hearing entirely new syllables, ones corresponding neither to those on the soundtrack nor to those articulated by the speaker's lips. For example, when the syllable /ba/ was dubbed onto lip movements for /ga/, nearly all people reported hearing /da/. In other instances, people heard the syllable formed by the lip movements, not the one actually sounded. Moreover, this strong influence of vision on speech perception is not limited to single syllables. Again using a dubbing procedure, Barbara Dodd (1977) found that people sometimes heard the word "towel" when the sound of a voice saying "tough" was dubbed over the lip movements for "hole."

We can conclude from these dubbing experiments that speech perception depends on more than just the phonetic properties of verbal utterances. In particular, vision provides complementary information about speech. This is fortunate since people often talk to one another in noisy environments where speech sounds may be obscured. Visual information accompanying lip movements can improve speech intelligibility in these situations. You may be surprised to learn, incidentally, that infants 18 to 20 weeks old can recognize correspondence between auditory and visual components of speech (Kuhl and Meltzoff, 1982). In an experiment to test for this ability, infants viewed a pair of film sequences projected side by side at the same time. Both films depicted a woman's face as she repeated a vowel sound, one vowel for one film and a different vowel for the other. The soundtrack corresponding to one of the two faces was broadcast from a speaker located midway between the two motion pictures. By monitoring the infant's direction of gaze, it was determined that infants preferred to look at the face whose lip movements matched the sound. This indicates that by 5 months of age, infants can detect the correspondence between speech sounds and the lip movements necessary to produce those sounds.

Given vision's influence on speech perception, you might expect blind people to have difficulty in comprehending speech, especially in noisy environments. Paradoxically, just the opposite is true. When asked to discriminate spoken numbers, words, and sentences heard against a background of noise, blind high school students outperformed their sighted classmates (Niemeyer and Starlinger, 1981); this seems to imply that blind individuals hear better than sighted individuals. However, on simpler hearing tests, such as loudness discrimination, the two groups of students were comparable (Starlinger and Niemeyer, 1981). This latter result suggests that the blind students' advantage in speech comprehension reflects superior performance by their brains rather than by their ears or auditory nerves.

The experiments described so far in this section underscore that speech sounds currently cannot be wholly explained by the operation of feature detectors responsive to the acoustic properties of those sounds and the context in which those sounds occur. Now we shall look at two other important factors that govern how verbal utterances actually sound, namely the perceived boundaries between words and the intonation, or pitch, of the voice as words are spoken.

The Role of Speech Boundaries and Intonation in Speech Perception. Listening to conversational speech, one usually has no trouble distinguishing words from one another—boundaries seem to exist between words. These boundaries, however, are an illusion. Inspection of a sound spectogram of a sentence spoken at a normal, conversational speed reveals relatively few identifiable pauses. Thus the boundaries you perceive between words have no counterpart in the acoustic signals reaching your ears.

You become aware of the paucity of word boundaries when listening to a conversation in a foreign language you don't speak. In this case, it is difficult to tell where one word ends and another begins—sentences seem to consist of unbroken strings of sounds, with few demarcations to set off one word from the next. Of course, to someone familiar with that language, those individual words are as distinct as the English words you hear during ordinary conversation. What, then, causes speech sounds to be grouped into separate words?

For one thing, one relies on the context of a conversation to help one establish those boundaries. An example of this effect of context was provided by the nonsense song introduced earlier—once you discovered what the song was about, the continuous phrase "marzeydoats" sounded instead like "mares eat oats." In the absence of context information, one sometimes errs in establishing boundaries between words, leading to misperceived speech. *New York Times* columnist William Safire (1979) related a particularly amusing instance of misplaced word boundaries. Upon first hearing "the girl with kaleidoscope eyes," a phrase from a Beatles tune, someone thought that the line went "the girl with colitis goes by". Anyone not familiar with the subject of "Lucy in the Sky with Diamonds," the song in which the verse appears, could make such a mistake.

When distinct *pauses* do occur in speech, listeners naturally interpret those pauses as the completion of a clause or of a sentence. These pauses thus serve to inform a listener that it is appropriate to take a turn talking. Pauses, in other words, operate like traffic signals, controlling the flow of conversation between people. For most individuals, the arrival of an intended pause is signaled by a drop in the pitch of the voice—listen to your voice drop at the end as you speak the sentence "It's ready." Figure 10.19 illustrates this pattern of intonation. A drop in

Intonation

FIGURE 10.19
The continuous line depicts the pattern of intonation as you utter this declarative sentence.

voice pitch signals your listeners that you are through speaking. However, some individuals have a pattern of speaking in which pause signals (drops in voice pitch) occur *before* completion of a sentence. A listener hearing these extraneous pause signals may be confused—the pause signals invite the listener to become the speaker when in fact the other person may not have finished talking.

As you can imagine, people whose speech is punctuated with inappropriate pause signals are inadvertently interrupted quite frequently. One such individual is Margaret Thatcher, the prime minister of Great Britain. A trio of British psychologists, Geoffrey Beattie, Anne Cutler, and Mark Pearson (1982), were intrigued by how often Thatcher seemed to be interrupted during interviews and during debate in Parliament. By ana-

lyzing sound transcripts from a television interview with the prime minister, these psychologists discovered that the inflections in Thatcher's speaking voice included frequent drops in voice pitch in the *middle* of her sentences. In other words, Thatcher unwittingly signals listeners that she has finished talking when in fact she has more to say. Perhaps this example will make you more aware of the subtle but powerful cues that guide the flow of conversation—otherwise you're likely to misinterpret some speech interruptions as the product of rudeness.

Next let's consider the voice intonation accompanying verbalized questions. Listen to the inflection in your voice as you speak the sentence "Is it ready?" Notice how the pitch of your voice rises at the end (see Figure 10.20), in contrast to the falling pitch

Intonation

FIGURE 10.20
The continuous line depicts the pattern of intonation as you utter this question.

that characterizes the end of a declarative sentence. Besides signaling the end of a sentence, then, the voice intonation at the end indicates whether that sentence was declarative or interrogative.

Voice intonation indicates even more than this. In speech perception, one also relies on voice intonation to serve as an index of the speaker's mood. Excitement, whether from enthusiasm or anger, is characterized by marked swings in intonation, whereas calm and boredom are typically signaled by flat, relatively unchanging intonation of the voice. You would be surprised how much information can be conveyed just by humming your sentences—in other words, using only pitch changes to convey a message. Next time you answer the phone, see how long you can carry on a "conversation" using hummed speech. You'll gain an appreciation of intonation's role in speech perception.

Summary and Preview

These last two chapters have merely scratched the surface of one of perception's most highly developed areas of research, hearing. Acoustics and hearing were among the first fields of study to develop quantitative measures for describing their subject. These developments date back to the early Greeks, who showed experimentally that pitch was related to the length of a vibrating string. Hearing researchers were also among the first to come up with experimental techniques (such as direct scaling) for measuring perceptual reactions to sensory stimulation. These measurements were necessary in order to know what acoustic events actually sound like in terms of loudness, pitch, and so forth. Contemporary research in hearing has made possible a very sophisticated understanding of the initial mechanical and neural events that eventually culminate in auditory perception. Still many of hearing's mysteries remain to be solved, including that very special case of hearing, speech perception.

We are now ready to consider a pair of senses, taste and smell, that play subtle but important roles in your everyday life.

Chapter 11

Smell and Taste

Taste and smell are sometimes called the minor senses, probably out of respect for seeing and hearing. But this designation is rather arbitrary. Though you do rely heavily on your eyes and ears to guide your everyday activities, your "minor senses" often provide you with crucially important information. The smell of smoke, for instance, can alert you to a dangerous fire, and the foul taste of spoiled food can save you from ingesting harmful substances. In fact, many animal species depend almost exclusively on taste and smell to tell them about their world. The mole's very keen sense of smell, to take just one example, allows the mole to live in the dark, safe confines of underground burrows, with virtually no need for eyes. Although as a human being you don't rely as much on taste and smell as other creatures do, you should not underestimate your capacity to use these senses to detect and recognize objects in the environment. In fact one of the things you are likely to gain from reading this chapter is a healthy respect for your nose and tongue.

As we mentioned above, taste and smell are called the minor senses. They are also sometimes referred to by their technical names, *gustation* (from the Latin *gustare,* meaning "to taste") and *olfaction* (from the Latin *olfacere,* meaning "to smell"). Taste and smell are also sometimes lumped together as the "chemical senses" because the receptors housed in the nose and on the tongue register the presence of chemical substances. In this respect, chemical substances are analogous to light energy that strikes the photoreceptors of the eye. But as this book has emphasized, you see objects, not light; by the same token, you taste and smell objects and substances, not chemicals. So from the standpoint of an organism concerned with its environment, the term "chemical senses" is a bit misleading. In fact, taste and smell serve precisely the same purposes as vision and hearing; all of them provide behaviorally relevant information about the environment.

Although all the senses work for one

common goal, something sets taste and smell apart: the sensations arising from stimulation of the tongue and nose can take on a uniquely pleasurable, sometimes sensual, quality. Sunsets may look beautiful and symphonies may sound enrapturing; but their pleasures are less compelling than the aroma and taste of, say, freshly baked chocolate chip cookies. On the other hand, few sights or sounds are as repulsive as a really putrid smell or foul taste. When there's an annoying song on the radio, you can usually succeed in ignoring it. But it is much harder to ignore the stench of a stopped-up toilet. Similarly, just thinking about the taste of some food that once made you sick can make you nauseous all over again. Thus in addition to their roles as sources of information, taste and smell wield a powerful emotional impact.

There is a sizable and growing body of data—both perceptual and physiological— concerning taste and smell, and in this chapter we shall discuss some of these findings. We shall consider taste and smell separately, although the two are intimately bound up with each other. Let's begin with smell.

The Sense of Smell

Smells are with you all the time. From the aroma of your first cup of coffee in the morning to the smell of clean sheets as you doze off at night, you are constantly immersed in a sea of odors. Smells enhance your enjoyment of food (which is why your appetite decreases when a cold stops up your nose). You can verify this for yourself. Compare the taste of a piece of apple and a piece of raw potato while holding your nose so that you cannot smell them—you'll be astonished to find that on the basis of taste alone, the two are very similar. Odors also influence the ways you spend your money.

How often have you passed by a bakery and been enticed in by the smells wafting onto the street? It is said that some bakeries vent their ovens onto the sidewalk, using the aroma of fresh bread purposely to lure customers inside (Winter, 1976). Besides the natural smells of the bakery, some businesses also use artificially created odors to influence people's buying habits. For example, plastic briefcases are impregnated with leather scents to enhance their appeal to prospective buyers, and the market value of a second-hand car increases if it's been sprayed with ''new car'' smell.

Besides the odors of foods, cars, and briefcases, there are other smells that influence you. TV commercials constantly remind you that you are yourself an important source of odors and exhort you to buy products that will modify your existing body odors as well as create new ones. In this pursuit, vast amounts of money are spent every year. Such products include deodorants, perfumes, aftershave lotions, mouthwashes, and antiflatulence medications. Nonetheless, every individual continually gives off a unique though invisible cloud of smells. Your odors constitute a smell signature so distinctive that a trained scenthound can trace your tracks amid the ''noise'' of odors from many other people. Only the scents of identical twins seem to confuse good scent-hounds (Kalmus, 1955). But these hounds are not the only creatures that can use scent for tracking. Some humans—the Botocudos of Brazil and members of some aboriginal tribes in the Malay peninsula— can hunt by following their prey's scent (Titchener, 1915). Though not many people in industrialized societies perform similar feats, they do have some primitive abilities to use scents for distinguishing people from one another (see Box 11.1).

Odors also possess the remarkable ability to call up long-ago memories. A whiff of cedar triggers remembrance of the chest in

BOX 11.1
Gender-Related Odors

If you had to judge whether another person was male or female on the basis of smell alone, do you think you could? Of course human beings rarely need to make such judgments. By comparison, animals in nature—primates included—rely heavily on natural, gender-related smells to identify potential mates. But have humans retained any of this ability to judge sex from smell? The answer appears to be yes.

Patricia Wallace, a psychologist at Clarion College in Pennsylvania, tested whether college students could discriminate male from female just by smelling a person's hand (Wallace, 1977). While blindfolded, a student would sniff a hand held one-half inch from the student's nose. The male and female individuals whose hands served as test stimuli had washed thoroughly before the test session and then worn a disposable plastic glove for 15 minutes prior to testing, to promote perspiration. Wallace found that subjects could tell male from female hands, with over 80 percent accuracy. Wallace further found that female sniffers were better at the task than were male sniffers.

In addition to the smell from sweaty hands, people are also able to make accurate judgments of gender on the basis of breath odor. Working at the Clinical Smell and Taste Research Center at the University of Pennsylvania, Richard Doty and his co-workers had male and female judges (college students) assess the breath odor of student donors who sat on the other side of a partition (see the drawing below). By inserting their noses into a plastic funnel, the judges were able to smell the breath of the "donors," who were exhaling through a glass tube connected to the funnel. Donors had been instructed to refrain from eating spicy food the day before testing and were not permitted to wear any odorous cosmetic products. Most judges scored better than chance (50 percent) at identifying the sex of the donor, and again female judges outperformed male judges (Doty et al., 1982). Doty also had judges rate breath odors for pleasantness and intensity. The breath odors of men were rated on the average as less pleasant and more intense than the breath odors of females. In interpreting their results, Doty and his colleagues noted that fluctuations in reproductive hormones during a female's menstrual cycle cause changes in oral bacteria, which in turn can affect breath odor.

Probably the most remarkable example of acuity for body

(Continued on next page)

odor is the case described by William James (1890, Vol 1, pp. 509–510) of a blind woman who worked in the laundry of the Hartford asylum. She would sort the laundry of individual inmates on the basis of smell only, after the clothes had been washed. Less dramatic but impressive nonetheless is the performance of people in the dirty shirt study by Mark Russel, a British psychologist (1976). He had twenty-nine freshmen bathe with clear water and then don T-shirts that they wore for the next 24 hours, during which

they used no perfume or deodorant. At the end of this period, the T-shirts were collected and individually placed in sealed containers. The same freshmen were now presented with three containers, one with their own shirt, one with the T-shirt worn by an unknown female, and one with the T-shirt worn by an unknown male. Of the twenty-nine people, twenty-two were able to pick out their own T-shirt—a level of performance well above chance. Moreover, twenty-two out of the twenty-nine were also able to identify

which of the remaining two T-shirts belonged to a male and which belonged to a female. Male odors were described as "musky," while female odors were described as "sweet."

Considered together, these findings amply demonstrate that people *can* judge gender using only their noses, if forced to. (You might want to arrange a test to discover how well you would do at such a task.) Whether people do rely unconsciously on gender-related odor cues remains a mystery.

which your grandmother kept her blankets; scent from a carnation vividly recalls your senior prom; and the smell of clove brings back memories of a dentist's office. Some people have developed a huge repertoire of odor memories and rely on them for their profession. Perfume makers, for example, can discriminate hundreds of aromas, many quite subtle. Astute physicians rely on the nose as a diagnostic tool, using a patient's odors as clues for detecting disease. In fact, any number of disorders have characteristic odors. To give some examples, typhoid creates a smell like that of freshly baked, brown bread; yellow fever creates a smell like that in a butcher shop; and kidney failure creates a smell of ammonia. (For a complete table of diseases and odors, see Smith, Smith, and Levinson, 1982.)

As you probably know, smell plays an enormously important role in the social lives of many animals. For many species, mate identification and selection are entirely governed by odor. The females of these species emit sensuous scents, called **pheromones,** from specialized glands, and these scents can be detected by potential mates. Among

such species is the male cabbage moth, an insect whose antennae can sense minute concentrations of the scent released from a sexually receptive female cabbage moth many miles away. In fact, the cabbage moth's keen sense of smell may explain this insect's suicidal tendency to fly into candle flames (Figure 11.1). According to Philip S. Callahan, a biologist with the U.S. Department of Agriculture, the moth mistakes the candle flame for a potential mate. Callahan noted that this self-destructive behavior is far more common among the males of the moth species. Callahan's measurements showed that part of the electromagnetic energy from the candle flame stimulates the male moth's nervous system much the same way as does the chemical signals emitted by the female moth. It's thought that as a result of this mimicry, the male moth dies trying to mate with the flame (Callahan, 1977).

The understanding of chemical sex signals has allowed scientists to exploit other species' pheromones. For example, agricultural biologists use pheromones to control some harmful insects. With sex attractants as bait, unsuspecting harmful insects can be

FIGURE 11.1
Male moths mistake a candle flame for a female moth. (Drawing courtesy of P. S. Callahan.)

secretions are also used to mark an animal's territory (one reason why dogs spend so much time sniffing their surroundings) and to establish social rank among individuals of the same species. Odors also guide animals in their search for food, whether it is the bee attracted to the fragrance of flowering plants or the vulture picking up the scent of a dead animal. In fact, the human reliance on eyes and ears to guide vital activities may be unique, since other animals depend primarily on their noses for such guidance. Indeed, if we were writing this perception book for a nonhuman audience, we'd have to revise it drastically. Instead of emphasizing seeing and hearing, the vast bulk of the book would have to address the most pressing concern of the nonhuman world—the sense of smell.

THE STIMULUS FOR SMELL

Let's start with the basics, asking what physical properties give various substances the power to evoke sensations of odor. As you'll see, the answers are complex. First, to be odorous, a substance must be *volatile*—that is, it must give off vapors (invisible molecules of gas). This requirement has some practical consequences. For example, because heated soup gives off more vapors than cold soup, hot soup invariably smells more inviting. It used to be thought that these volatile molecules had to be airborne in order to be smelled; according to this view, substances suspended in liquid would be odorless even when they were in direct contact with the sensitive receptors in the nose. Thus if you were to submerge yourself in a pool of perfume you would smell nothing. Ernst Weber, the nineteenth-century physiologist, actually performed an equivalent experiment: while holding his head upside down, he poured perfume into his nostrils—whereupon he smelled nothing (Boring, 1942). It's now thought, however, that

lured to their deaths in traps. Pheromones can also be exploited for the eating pleasure of humans. Certain female pigs are trained to hunt truffles, a fungus highly prized by many gourmets. These sows can sniff out truffles buried as much as a meter below ground, and once the truffles are located, the animals root furiously to unearth them. The reason the sows expend all that energy, rooting so furiously for a piece of fungus, is that truffles contain a chemical with a distinct, musklike odor that is highly similar to the scent secreted by male pigs during mating behavior. So it appears that the sow's intense interest in truffles is sexually motivated (Claus, Hoppen, and Karg, 1981).

Besides promoting sexual arousal in animals, smells are often employed as defensive weapons. Everyone can testify to the rank odor of a skunk's discharge and can well appreciate how that odor would ward off enemies (and friends as well). Chemical the perfume may have damaged the receptors in Weber's nose, preventing him from smelling anything.

A genuine prerequisite for smell is that the volatile molecules be soluble in fat, because the receptor cells in the nose that capture volatile molecules are surrounded by fatlike materials. When odorous molecules are fat-soluble, they can be absorbed by substances containing fat. This explains why uncovered butter on one shelf of your refrigerator takes on the smell of uncovered tuna fish sitting on another shelf. At the same time, not all volatile and fat-soluble substances are odorous. Additional chemical properties, such as atomic weight, common to all odorous substances must surely exist; but no one has yet been able to determine all these properties (Wright, 1966). The difficulty is closely related to the problem of odor classification, a topic we consider next.

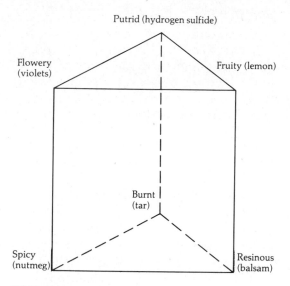

FIGURE 11.2
Henning's smell prism.

THE CLASSIFICATION OF ODORS

As you learned in Chapter 6, the understanding of color vision was really launched when Newton devised a scheme (his color circle) for describing the relations among different colors. Following Newton's work, there emerged some consensus about the categories of color. It has been widely assumed that odors, too, fall into a distinct set of categories, comparable in their uniqueness to blue, green, yellow, and red. Knowledge of these odor categories would pave the way for determining the chemical properties shared by members of the various categories. But attempts to identify odor categories have led to much disagreement. We'll consider several of the better-known odor categorization schemes and point out their shortcomings.

Most similar in spirit to Newton's color circle is Hans Henning's (1916) smell prism.

This geometric model (see Figure 11.2) is meant to depict the "principal" odors from which all other odors can be generated. To determine the number of principal odors, Henning used two procedures. First, he instructed people to use verbal labels to describe various scents presented one at a time. Second, he gave people sets of odorous substances and instructed them to line up the substances according to the similarity of their smells (Gamble, 1921). In all, Henning tested well over 400 different odorous substances. Using these sets of judgments, Henning constructed a three-dimensional form—a triangular prism (shown in Figure 11.2)—whose surfaces were meant to reflect people's judgments of odor similarity. Particular odors corresponded to points on the surface of the prism, with nearby points corresponding to odors that were judged similar. Odors were confined to the surfaces and edges of the prism; its interior was considered hollow, meaning that points inside the prism were not used to describe an odor.

Odors near the corners of his prism seemed to Henning to have unique qualities—they could be described using a single verbal label (shown in Figure 11.2). To give you some idea of substances that evoke these six principal odors, we have included in parentheses a substance representative of each. Odors located other than at the corners of the prism (either or an edge or on the plane of one surface) could not be described using a single verbal label. But they could be described by some *combination* of principal qualities represented by the labels at the prism's corners. For example, the smell associated with pine was located along the edge midway between "fruity" and "resinous"—implying that the odor of pine possesses both of those qualities. Pine was located where it is on the prism because of its similarity to lemon and balsam. Similarly, the smell of garlic was located on the surface bounded by "flowery/fruity/resinous/spicy," implying that the odor of garlic possesses all four of those qualities. Again, garlic was placed at that point on the prism because its odor bears at least some similarity to the odors of violet, lemon, balsam, and nutmeg.

Henning's scheme purported to show how odors on the edges or surfaces of the smell prism resemble odors at the prism's corners. This does not mean, however, that a mixture of odors from the corners could produce odors on other parts of the prism. Although it is similar in smell to both balsam and lemon, pine cannot be synthesized by a mixture of those two. In fact, "the resulting odor tends to be a unique percept blend in which both components can be smelled" (Engen, 1982). In this sense, odor shares the analytic character of pitch perception rather than the synthetic character of color perception. For example, if you simultaneously sound a D and an F on the piano, you can hear the separate components in the chord; however, if you mix red and green lights, the result is a synthesis (yellow) in which each component's identity is lost.

Henning's model is appealing for precisely the same reason that Newton's color circle is appealing: both provide a simple, geometric description of sensory experiences. The accuracy of geometric models is easy to test because they make clear predictions. However, in the case of Henning's smell prism, the predictions have not been confirmed, as William Cain (1978) documents. One major problem is that most people find it impossible to classify odors using just six categories—which implies that Henning may have underestimated the number of principal odors. Critics have also faulted Henning for using a small number of highly trained subjects and for eschewing quantitative analysis of his data. In defense of his procedures, Henning bragged that "the critical introspection of trained psychologists is more valuable than statistics taken on all the students in the University, and the statistical procedure, about which science in America has raved so much, has by no means the precision of a *qualitative* analysis" (Henning, 1916; from a translation by Gamble, 1921).

Following Henning's work, other researchers have also tried to group odors according to qualitative similarities (for example, Crocker and Henderson, 1927). Most of these categorization schemes have started out by identifying a series of semantic descriptors to be used as odor qualities—descriptors such as "sweet," "flowery," "fruity," "burned," and so forth. Whatever odor categories may emerge, therefore, are constrained right from the start; they've got to conform to the specific descriptors chosen by the researcher in the first place. Moreover, there are reasons to question how reliably people can use verbal labels to describe their olfactory sensations (Davis, 1977). The constraints imposed by the descriptors, as well as the difficulty of using any label at all, would distort any classification scheme based on predefined verbal labels.

There is a technique, however, called **multidimensional scaling (MDS),** that sidesteps these problems. This technique has been used by Duke University psychologist Susan Schiffman (1974) to study odor classification. Instead of using descriptor terms for various odors, a person merely compares different odors, rating their similarity to one another. These similarity ratings are then used to place odors within a geometric framework called an odor space. Odors are arranged within the odor space in such a way that the distances separating odors reflect the rated similarity or dissimilarity of those odors. Odors rated as highly similar (such as cinnamon and ginger) would be placed near each other in an odor space, while odors judged to be dissimilar (such as vanillin and turpentine) would be located far apart (see Box 11.2 for additional details of multidimensional scaling). As you can see, the idea of an odor space is reminiscent of Henning's smell prism—both arrange odorous substances in a geometric form based on perceptual similarity. However, the rules for generating an odor space by means of multidimensional scaling differ from those used by Henning. In multidimensional scaling, objective numerical procedures create the geometric arrangement of odors; Henning used his own subjective impressions of data to create his geometric arrangement.

The procedures used in multidimensional scaling offer another advantage. The experimenter does not constrain the number of possible dimensions ahead of time; instead, statistical treatment of the similarity ratings determines the number of dimensions needed to place odors in the odor space. (You can think of the dimensions as axes defining the coordinates of a geometrical space, like the Cartesian coordinates used to define the two-dimensional space you're familiar with from plane geometry.)

In using multidimensional scaling, Schiffman found that just two dimensions adequately described the relations among a wide variety of odorous substances. Figure 11.3 replots some of the data from Schiffman's analysis. Look at the various odors in this odor space, and note their relative positions. You'll probably agree that the nearby entries smell more alike than do the widely separated ones. How can the two dimensions that Schiffman's work uncovered be interpreted? To answer this question, Schiffman examined the adjectives people use to describe the various odors she tested. She found that proceeding from left to right in Figure 11.3, odors tended to shade from pleasant (such as vanillin) to unpleasant (such as hydrogen sulfide). Proceeding from top to bottom, however, Schiffman was unable to find any systematic progression in the adjectives used to describe the odors. Thus although objective, numerical judgments of similarity change systematically from top to bottom of the odor space, there is no corresponding pattern to the adjectives people use to label the odors running from top to bottom. The finding suggests that this dimension of odor experience does not correlate with any simple psychological dimension for which there are descriptors. To what, then, might the ordering in the odor space correspond?

Schiffman (1974) asked whether perceptually similar odors might have some molecular property in common, such as the size or shape of the molecules making up the odorous substances. The discovery of molecular similarities among perceptually comparable odors might furnish important clues about how odorous substances affect receptor cells in the nose. Schiffman considered several molecular characteristics in an at-

BOX 11.2
Introducing Multidimensional Scaling

Multidimensional scaling is a mathematical tool for making a pictorial representation of the similarities among stimuli. This pictorial representation is a kind of map (Schiffman, Reynolds, and Young, 1981). The stimuli in an MDS study can be almost anything— perfumes, cola drinks, beers, taste chemicals, colors, U.S. senators, food flavors, and so on. Regardless of what the stimuli are, though, an MDS study begins by asking people to judge how similar the stimuli are to one another.

Sometimes, a researcher does not know what basis people will use to make their similarity judgments. For example, if they're judging the similarity of a Chevrolet Corvette and a Mazda RX7 they might respond to the fact that both are sports cars (and judge them ''similar'') or to the fact that they come from different countries (and judge them ''dissimilar''). This can be a problem if the researcher wants to avoid biasing people's judgments. With taste and smell it's very hard to know the basis for perceptions of similarity and dissimiliarity. Here MDS comes in extra handy, helping to define the perceptual basis for the judgments (even though the researcher doesn't know that basis ahead of time).

Let's start with a simple experiment. Suppose we concoct four different concentrations of sodium chloride (salt) in water. We give them two at a time to people who sip them and then make a numerical judgment of

how similar the two are. Suppose they rate similarity on a scale from 100 meaning ''perfect identity between the two,'' all the way to 0 for ''absolutely no similarity whatever'' (other judgment schemes can also be used; see Schiffman, Reynolds, and Young, 1981).

In our hypothetical study, salt solutions A and C are judged most similar, solutions A and B least similar, and the other pairs are judged as somewhere in between. How does one make a spatial map that corresponds to these judgments? The goal is to make a map with four points, A, B, C and D; the distances between the points should correspond to the judgments of similarity—similar salt solutions should be close together and dissimilar ones far apart. For convenience, we start with the

pair A and B. Since these two solutions are judged least alike, their corresponding spots on the map should be far apart. Arbitrarily, we can position A at the left and B way to the right. Since D is judged equally similar to C and B, D should go about halfway between C and B. Finally, because A and C are judged quite similar, we know that C goes somewhere close to A; but we don't know whether to left or right. We get the answer by comparing judgments of A and B, on the one hand, with judgments of B and C, on the other. Since C and B are judged more similar than A and B, we know that C must lie somewhere between A and B. The complete arrangement is shown in panel 1 of the diagram below. To validate our map, we can look at similarity

(Continued on next page)

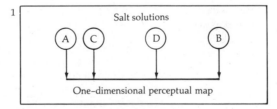

1   Salt solutions

A   C   D   B

One–dimensional perceptual map

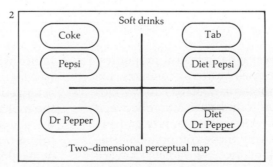

2   Soft drinks

Coke   Tab

Pepsi   Diet Pepsi

Dr Pepper   Diet Dr Pepper

Two–dimensional perceptual map

judgments and corresponding points that we haven't used thus far. On the map, C is closer to A than to D; this is consistent with the fact that C is judged more similar to A than it is to D.

When the stimuli can be represented along a single straight line, it indicates judgments were made on the basis of a single aspect or "dimension" of the stimuli—in this case probably the intensity of the salt taste. Thus the study with salt solutions led to a map that was a one-dimensional representation. However, a one-dimensional map is impossible whenever people use more than just one aspect of the stimuli as a basis for their similarity judgments. In such cases, a map of two or three dimensions might be needed. Let's take a simple example, based on an actual experiment (Schiffman, Reynolds, and Young, 1981).

Suppose we take six brands of carbonated soft drinks (with brand identifications hidden): Coca-Cola, Pepsi-Cola, Dr Pepper, Tab (a diet cola similar to Coca-Cola), Diet Pepsi-Cola, and Diet Dr Pepper. As before, we allow people to sip pairs of the drinks and then ask for numerical judgments of how

similar the two are. These similarity judgments are the data from which we will try to produce our perceptual map. Here are the hypothetical results. Coke and Pepsi are judged highly similar in taste, but each one is judged quite dissimilar from Dr Pepper. In addition, Coke, Pepsi, and Dr Pepper are each judged dissimilar to their respective diet versions. Finally, some pairs are judged to be particularly dissimilar: Coke (or Pepsi) versus Diet Dr Pepper, and Dr Pepper versus Diet Pepsi or Tab.

With these results in hand, we proceed to produce an appropriate one-dimensional map. Again, we start by putting the most dissimilar stimuli at the ends of the line. For example, we place Coke and Pepsi at one end (close to each other) and Diet Dr Pepper at the other—because these were judged extremely dissimilar. Now we've got a problem; other soft drinks were also judged extremely dissimilar— Dr Pepper versus the diet versions of Coke and Pepsi. If we try to place these on the same line we used for Diet Dr Pepper, Coke, and Pepsi, the map will necessarily contradict some of the similarity judgment data we collected. Try it for

yourself. The solution is to make a two-dimensional map such as the one shown in panel 2 of the diagram. The arrangement of the stimuli on this map is consistent with the idea that people were judging sodas on the basis of two criteria—whether they had a *cherry* taste (like Dr Pepper) and whether they had a *diet* taste. Note that the data themselves forced us to describe the perceptions in two dimensions.

Incidentally, it was fairly easy to create the maps in our two examples because both examples involved a small number of stimuli. Most real MDS experiments, though, use a dozen or more stimuli, making it quite difficult to produce the right map "by hand." In those cases, the researcher could use a computer program containing sophisticated trial-and-error schemes for making the map. Programs available for this task are described in the excellent introduction to MDS by Schiffman and her colleagues (Schiffman, Reynolds, and Young, 1981). These researchers also describe a whole series of uses of MDS, including the development of new consumer products.

---

tempt to uncover what physical properties, if any, similar smells have in common. Examining the molecular shapes of various substances, she found no relation between the shapes of various compounds and the odors produced by those compounds. This finding, incidentally, contradicts a very popular theory of odor perception. John Amoore (1970), a noted olfactory scientist, proposed that a molecule's shape deter-

mines which receptor it is able to stimulate (see Figure 11.4). This theory has been characterized as the lock-and-key model, since the molecule "unlocks" the receptor only if the shape of the molecule matches that of the receptor. According to this theory, molecules that look alike (in terms of the arrangement of their constituent atoms) should also smell alike. However, Schiffman's analysis fails to support this simple

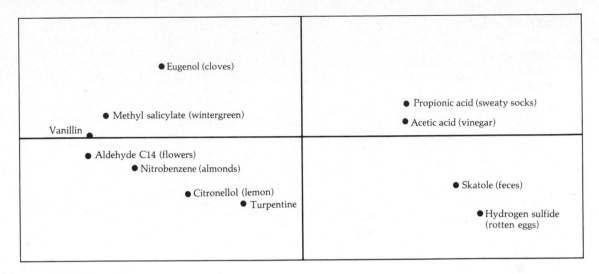

FIGURE 11.3
An odor space, showing the relations among various odors as defined by multidimensional scaling. (Adapted from Schiffman, 1974.)

idea; she finds no relation between the shapes of molecules and the similarity of the odors they produce.

Besides molecular shape, Schiffman also examined a number of other chemical characteristics of compounds that smell alike, such as their molecular weight and their solubility in water. However, she found no single characteristic that could explain odor similarity. At the moment, then, the relation between odor quality and molecular structure remains a mystery. Somehow it

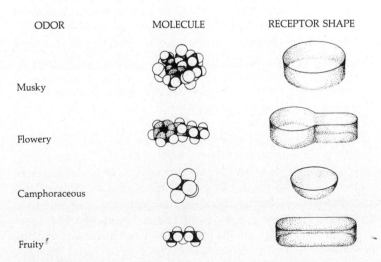

FIGURE 11.4
The clusters of spheres represent four odorous molecules, and the receptacles beside each molecule represent olfactory receptors. Note how each molecule fits best into one particular receptor.

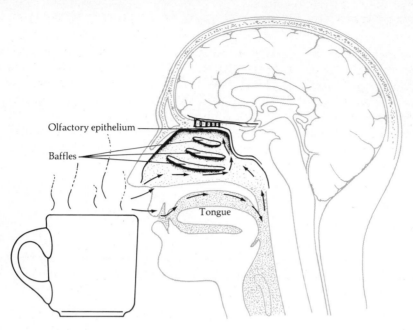

FIGURE 11.5
A cutaway section of a human head, showing the routes taken by air inhaled into the mouth and nasal cavity.

seems ironic that of all the senses, smell, nature's oldest and most primitive sense, has a stimulus that is one of the most complicated and baffling.

Before continuing our discussion of odor perception, we should first present the major components of the olfactory system, in particular the olfactory receptors that capture the volatile molecules from odorous substances. The properties of these receptors, after all, shape your world of smell.

THE ANATOMY AND PHYSIOLOGY OF SMELL

As noted in the previous section, the stimulus for smell consists of airborne molecules, or vapors. As you inhale, these vapors are pulled into your nostrils and then circulate through your nasal cavity, a hollow region inside your nose where the olfactory (smell) receptors are located (see Figure 11.5). As you exhale, the vapors are

expelled back into the air. You can hasten these processes by sniffing or sneezing. Sniffing is your way of drawing more odorous vapors into your nose and speeding their circulation through the nasal cavity.* In this respect, sniffing is comparable to cupping your ear to help you hear a faint sound. Sneezing, in contrast, represents a reflexive clearing of the nostrils, an action comparable to covering your ears to muffle a loud sound.

Odor-bearing vapors can also reach the nasal cavity through the mouth, circulating up the throat through a chimneylike passage leading to the smell receptors. Both routes, then—the nostrils and the throat—lead to the same place, the olfactory receptors in the nasal cavity. However, vapors

*Optimum odor detection occurs when the odorant flows through the nose at a rate of about 30 liters per minute. Interestingly, whenever you try to sniff some odor in your environment, you produce this optimal flow rate without having to think about it (Laing, 1983).

from a substance in the mouth may smell different from the same vapors brought in through the nostrils. This odd disparity is described in Box 11.3.

Most of the air entering the nostrils and mouth flows down the throat to your lungs. However, wisps of air do rise up into the nasal cavity, where they circulate around a series of baffles formed by three bones lo-cated in the nasal cavity (see Figure 11.5). As it circulates through this series of baffles, the air is warmed and humidified, and de-bris such as dust is removed by tiny hairs lining the nasal cavity. The entire process has been likened to an air-conditioning sys-tem that improves smell acuity (Negus, 1956). As you can imagine, when your nose is con-gested, the passages of the nasal cavity are

---

BOX 11.3

Is Olfaction a Dual Sense?

Have you noticed that some foods smell almost repulsive before you get them into your mouth, but once you start eating them they are enjoyable? Certain strong cheeses, such as Limburger and Roquefort, are good examples of this disparity between odor and flavor. Yet what is referred to as "flavor" is largely the smell associated with the food as it is chewed. This is known from the fact that foods lose their flavor when olfactory cues are eliminated during eating (such as when you have a head cold). How is it, then, that the same food can generate two distinct odor experiences, depending on whether you are sniffing the food or eating it?

Paul Rozin, a psychologist at the University of Pennsylvania, thinks this happens because olfaction is a dual sense—that is, one used to acquire two sets of information: information about objects in the external world and information about objects within the mouth. According to Rozin (1982), these two types of information have different behavioral consequences. Airborne odors arriving through the nostrils can come from a host of objects and events—other people, animals, plants, fire, and so on—only some of which have anything to do with eating. Behavioral reactions to these odors depend on identifying the source of the odor (Gibson, 1966). In this sense, olfaction serves the same interests as vision and hearing, identifying relevant objects and events in the environment. But olfaction's role changes during eating, after food has been selected and introduced into the mouth. Now odors become part of the flavor complex that also includes taste, temperature, and palatability. Rozin believes that these two different contexts (odor in the mouth versus odor out there) are registered by the olfactory nervous system and give rise to distinctly different perceptual experiences.

Rozin figured that if odor does indeed have different perceptual properties in the mouth versus outside the mouth, people should have trouble recognizing odor through the mouth if their previous experience with the odor was just through the nose. To test this hypothesis, Rozin came up with a set of unfamiliar odors and flavors by mixing together various exotic fruit juices and soups. He then taught blindfolded people to identify these various mixtures on the basis of their odors; each mixture was assigned a number for purposes of identification. Once his subjects had learned to do this, Rozin asked them to identify the same mixtures delivered directly to the mouth through a plastic tube. In this way, any contribution of odor inhaled through the nostrils was eliminated; odor information came entirely from aromas passing up the throat to the olfactory receptors. The results were clear—people made many errors in identifying the mixtures, and they reported that the flavors were impossible to recognize. Evidently, the same substance smells different, depending on whether it is in the external world or in the mouth. This would explain why you may dislike the flavor of things (such as coffee) that smell appealing and also why you can enjoy eating foods that smell foul. Without encouragement, most people would never get around to eating foul-smelling foods in the first place.

narrowed, limiting the amount of odorous vapors that can reach the smell receptors. This is why your sense of smell is dulled when a cold clogs up your nasal cavities.

Incidentally, have you ever wondered why you have two nasal cavities, rather than just one? As you learned in earlier chapters, there are compelling reasons for having two eyes and two ears: to facilitate the accurate localization of objects on the basis of *differences* between the information reaching the two eyes or the two ears. Georg von Bekesy, whose work on cochlear mechanics was described in Chapter 9, believed that the source of a smell is localized in an analogous fashion—by comparing the intensity of vapors entering the separate nostrils (Bekesy, 1964). In one of his experiments, Bekesy simultaneously injected slightly different concentrations of an odorant into the two nostrils. The apparent location of the smell source shifted in the direction of the nostril receiving the stronger concentration. Apparently, then, people *can* use internasal concentration differences to localize the source of a smell. Whether they *ordinarily* use this potential cue for smell localization is uncertain.

So far we've described how vapors are introduced into the nose and how they circulate inside the nasal cavities. Now let's consider how neural elements turn these vapors into the perception of an odor. The receptor cells that register the presence of odorous molecules sit on a patch of tissue called the **olfactory epithelium.** As you can see in Figure 11.5, the olfactory epithelium forms part of the ceiling of the nasal cavity. There are actually two patches of olfactory epithelium, one at the top of each nasal cavity. Each patch of tissue is about the diameter of a dime, but much thinner.

Figure 11.6 shows an enlarged drawing of an olfactory epithelium. Note that the structure labeled **olfactory receptor cell** is embedded in a layer of supporting cells; a tuft of hairs (called **cilia**) from each receptor cell projects down into the mucus that lines the bottom of the olfactory epithelium. The nose contains roughly 10 million olfactory receptor cells. Dogs, in comparison, have about 200 million olfactory receptor cells, which accounts for their legendary ability to track the path of a person hours after the individual has trodden that path. Notice also in Figure 11.6 the structure labeled **free nerve**

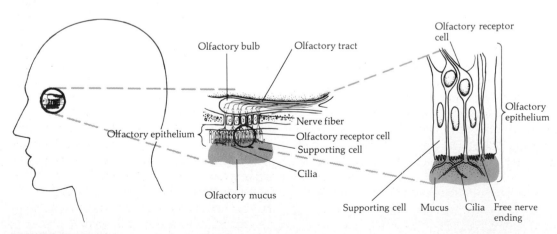

FIGURE 11.6
The olfactory epithelium (enlarged to show detail).

ending. Although these nerve fibers do not themselves give rise to odor sensations, they do significantly influence the perception of odors. We shall consider the role played by these nerve endings shortly, but for now let's continue focusing on the olfactory receptor cells.

There are a couple of things very special about olfactory receptors that set them apart from receptors in the eye and ear. For one, olfactory receptors, unlike photoreceptors and hair cells, are genuine *brain* cells, possessing all the paraphernalia of such cells—cell bodies, dendrites, and axons. Therefore, olfactory receptors are able to perform two jobs at once: they transduce chemical stimulation into neural impulses, while at the same time they carry those impulses up to the brain along their axons, which make up the **olfactory nerve.** In vision, hearing, and taste, these jobs are assigned to different types of cells. This means, incidentally, that the only neurons in the brain that actually come in contact with the outside world are the olfactory cells in the ceiling of the nose.

Even more remarkable, olfactory receptor cells/neurons are constantly dying and being replaced (Graziadei, 1973; Moulton, 1974). Nowhere else are neurons capable of reproducing. Once in place, neurons elsewhere in the brain are there for life; when those neurons die, the loss is irrevocable. But olfactory cells live for only about 5 to 8 weeks. As a result, the olfactory cells currently at work in your nose have been on the job no more than a few months at most, and already in your lifetime you've gone through hundreds of generations of olfactory receptor neurons. This turnover of neurons is all the more remarkable when you realize that as each new olfactory cell matures, its axon must grow an appreciable distance to reach its target site in the brain. And once there, each axon must form connections that duplicate the wiring pattern undone by the death of its predecessor—otherwise odors

would not smell the same from one month to the next. This is an amazing developmental feat.

Some people believe that this cyclical turnover of cells may have something important to do with reduced sensitivity to an odor following prolonged exposure to that odor. But in order to appreciate how this might come about, you'll need to know a little more about the structure of the olfactory receptors, in particular the parts that actually extend into the mucous lining of the nose.

Attached to each receptor cell is a clump of several cilia—thin, hairlike growths that extend through the mucous layer into the nasal cavity. Robert Gesteland, a neurobiologist at Northwestern University, has performed some elegant experiments that allowed him to observe the activities of these cilia in frogs. Viewed under a microscope, these cilia were seen to sway leisurely to and fro in a haphazard, unsynchronized way. However, immediately after blowing an odorous vapor across the olfactory epithelium, Gesteland could see that the supporting cells were secreting mucus that engulfed the odorous molecules. At the same time, the cilia began to sway vigorously and in unison. This swaying action sweeps the mucus and its captive odorant off the epithelium—a broomlike action that probably readies the olfactory epithelium for the arrival of new odorous vapors (Gesteland, 1982).

Besides housecleaning, the cilia also play a crucial role in the process of sensory transduction. It is generally accepted that the receptor sites themselves are situated on the cilia. At these sites, odorous molecules trigger electrical changes in the cell. This would explain why the sense of smell is temporarily lost whenever the cilia are damaged, as they are by certain drugs, including some anesthetics. Once new cilia grow, smell returns. At present, though, it is not known how the cilia actually capture odorous molecules, nor how such a capture triggers neural impulses in the cell (Lancet, 1984). Setting aside this question of sensory transduction, let's consider the neural coding of odor quality. How are the various qualities of odor represented within the olfactory nervous system? How are you able to discriminate, say, the smell of lemons from that of limes?

Odor Quality: Selectivity of Olfactory Fibers. You've already learned something about how quality is represented in other senses. Recall from Chapter 9 that each fiber in the auditory nerve prefers a particular sound frequency, with the preferred frequency varying from fiber to fiber. Likewise, each fiber in the optic nerve prefers contours of a particular size and, for some, a particular color. Again, the preferred size or color varies from fiber to fiber. As a group, olfactory nerve fibers (the axons of the olfactory receptors) do not behave in this discriminating fashion. Many olfactory nerve fibers respond to *any* of a whole host of different odors. As a result, these fibers can signal that an odorous substance is present, but they cannot provide information about the identity of that substance. A mere fraction of the olfactory nerve fibers respond to only a limited set of odorous substances (Gesteland, 1978); these are the only fibers that can provide information about the presence of particular odorous substances. This predominance of nonselective fibers has led to the theory that odor quality is coded by the *pattern* of neural activity across a large group of olfactory nerve fibers (Keverne, 1982)—an idea similar to the ensemble theory described in Chapter 4.

Until now, the idea that odor quality depends on the pattern of neural activity seemed to be the only viable explanation of odor perception—in view of the preponderance of nonselective olfactory neurons. However, recent work by Gesteland and his colleagues has shed new light on the neural coding of odor quality (Gesteland, Yancey,

and Farbman, 1982; Mair, Gesteland, and Blank, 1982). It now appears that the nonselective olfactory neurons, the ones that respond to a wide range of odors, are in fact immature cells still in the process of developing. Their axons have yet to grow all the way to the brain—they haven't made connections with their target site. These nonselective cells, in other words, are unable to forward their ambiguous messages about odors to the brain. The selective cells, in contrast, are full-fledged, mature neurons that have already made their hookups to the brain. And as the work of Gesteland and his colleagues shows, these mature neurons make specific statements about what odors stimulate them. The specificity of these statements could allow the olfactory system to represent odor quality by means of the activity in particular olfactory neurons.

The Olfactory Pathways. So far our discussion of smell has focused on the olfactory epithelium and the receptor neurons embedded in that tissue. The rest of the olfactory system consists of the **olfactory bulb** (which receives all the input from the olfactory nerve) and the **olfactory brain** (a cluster of neural structures receiving projections from the olfactory bulb). Structurally, the olfactory bulb resembles the retina, in that it has several layers of cells laterally interconnected, but the consequences of these connections in the bulb are not well understood. Very little is known also about the behavior of neurons in various structures of the olfactory brain. It is known, though, that patients with damage to certain regions of the olfactory brain exhibit severe difficulty in detecting and recognizing odors (Mair and Engen, 1976; Rausch and Serafetinides, 1975; Eichenbaum et al., 1983; Abraham and Mathai, 1983). Apparently, then, these higher brain centers are involved in sensory decisions concerning olfactory information.

This overview of the olfactory system sets

the stage for considering the perception of odors.

SENSITIVITY TO ODORS

Detection and Identification. It is often said that the human sense of smell is rather dull compared to that of other species such as the dog (Moulton, 1976). While this is true, the human nose is remarkably sensitive nonetheless. For instance, people can detect ethyl mercaptan (a foul-smelling substance) in concentrations as minute as 1 part per 50 billion parts of air. This performance rivals that of the most sensitive laboratory instruments available for measuring tiny concentrations of molecules. Such sensitivity is all the more impressive when you realize that only a small fraction of the odor molecules in this minute concentration actually reaches the olfactory receptors in the top of the nasal cavity. It has been estimated that during normal breathing, only about 2 percent of the odorous molecules entering the nostrils actually make it to the receptors; the remaining molecules are absorbed by the lining inside the nose. Olfactory sensitivity varies greatly from odor to odor. For example, the substance mentioned above, mercaptan, can be detected at a concentration 10 million times less than that needed to smell carbon tetrachloride, a liquid sometimes used in dry-cleaning fluid (Wenger, Jones, and Jones, 1956). Because people are so sensitive to mercaptan, it is often added to natural gas, itself odorless but toxic, to warn of gas leaks (Engen, 1982).

Having bragged about the sensitivity of the human nose, we must qualify what we mean by "sensitivity." The remarkable performance described above refers to the ability to *detect* the presence of a faint odor; this does not mean that you could *identify* the odor. In fact, at near threshold concentrations, people can smell an odor but not tell what odor they are smelling. The following experiment illustrates this point (Engen,

1960). When given three empty test tubes and a fourth test tube containing an extremely dilute odor, people can accurately select the tube that "smells different" from the others. But using the same set of stimuli, people make many errors when instructed to pick the test tube that contains some named odor ("pick the tube containing menthol"). So people behave as if they have two thresholds, one for detecting the presence of an odor and a second, higher threshold for identifying what that odor is.

Odor sensitivity depends on a number of factors, including time of day, age, and sex. In particular, people are generally able to detect weak odors better in the morning than in the evening (Stone and Pryor, 1967); elderly people are less sensitive than young adults (Schemper, Voss, and Cain, 1980; Schiffman, 1983); and females are more sensitive, on the average, than males (Koelega and Koster, 1974). Because of these age and gender differences in smell acuity, some people may be put off by body odors that others are not even aware of. Your own experiences in social settings probably confirm this observation. Your experiences may also lead you to believe that your sensitivity to odors increases when you are hungry. But this belief is questionable—some experiments say yes (Schneider and Wolf, 1955), others say no (Furchtgott and Friedman, 1960). Also, contrary to popular belief, smokers seem about as sensitive to most odors as do nonsmokers (Pangborn, Trabue, and Barylko-Pikielna, 1967).

Odor Concentrations. Another misconception about the sense of smell concerns people's alleged poor ability to judge differences in odor concentrations. Until recently, it was generally assumed that people require about a 25 percent difference in odor concentration before they can tell that one sample of an odor is stronger than another sample of that same odor. (This assumption implies that a bouquet of five flowers would smell no stronger than a bouquet of four flowers, since they differ by only 20 percent.) Compared to vision and hearing (where difference thresholds are on the order of 10 percent), this represents dull sensitivity indeed. However, William Cain of Yale University has shown that this dismal performance does not reflect an inferiority on the part of the olfactory nervous system (Cain, 1977); instead, the poor performance stems from the *variability* in the amount of odor vapor delivered to the olfactory receptors from trial to trial. But where does this variability come from?

As mentioned earlier, most of the odorous molecules entering the nostrils never make it to the olfactory epithelium, and at any given moment it is difficult to specify exactly the effective odor concentration (the amount of odorous vapor reaching the receptors). So in effect, the stimulus in a typical experiment on discrimination of odor intensity is unpredictable owing to its variability. Cain used an improved technique to control effective odor concentration and actually measured trial-to-trial variability of the odor vapor with a gas chromatograph, an instrument for measuring the concentration of molecules in gas. Taking account of variability in effective odor concentration, Cain found that concentration differences as small as 7 percent are discriminable. This places the nose in the same league with the eye and the ear as a judge of intensity differences. (Thus if their fragrance was delivered through Cain's apparatus, five flowers *would* smell stronger than four.)

Remember the description of loudness scaling in Chapter 10, where people assigned numbers to sounds according to how loud they seemed? Comparable scaling measurements have been made of perceived odor intensity. As with loudness, odor intensity grows as a power function of concentration. With some exceptions, most odors give exponents in the neighborhood of 0.6,

indicating that perceived odor intensity grows somewhat gradually relative to increasing concentration. To illustrate, doubling odor concentration produces only about a 50 percent increase in perceived intensity, not 100 percent (the value associated with an exponent of 1.0). As a result, a bouquet of ten flowers will not smell twice as strong as a bouquet of five flowers; to smell twice as strong as five flowers, a bouquet would have to consist of seventeen flowers. Magnitude scaling of odor intensity has practical uses. People interested in pollution control have used this scaling technique to assess the strength of odors produced by smokestack emissions, food processing plants, and animal manure (Engen, 1982).

Now you know that your ability to discriminate differences in odor concentration is better than previously thought. But when might this ability actually be useful? Suppose you walk into your house and smell some foul odor. You can't see where it's coming from so you have to rely on your sense of smell to guide you to the source. You move around trying to locate where the smell becomes stronger. Since odor concentration varies with distance, this strategy will ultimately bring you to the source.

While tracking the odor, you might also sniff, thereby pulling more of the odorous vapors into your nose. You might expect that perceived odor intensity will vary depending on the vigor of the sniff. A deep sniff, after all, pulls more odorous vapors into the nose than does a weak, shallow sniff. And since more odorous molecules will be available for stimulating the olfactory receptors, the resulting smell seemingly should be stronger the deeper the sniff. Yet this may not always happen—some investigators have reported that odor intensity remains constant regardless of the vigor of a sniff (Teghtsoonian et al., 1978). This finding is especially surprising since when sniffs are produced artificially, by blowing odorous air into the nose, perceived intensity *does* depend on the rate of air flow (Rehn, 1978). Why would artificial sniffs and natural ones have different effects on perceived odor intensity? After all, with both types of sniffs the flow rate of the odorant varies comparably. According to Teghtsoonian et al. (1978), the olfactory system may recognize when the increase in flow rate results from a natural sniff, and it may then calibrate the perception of intensity to take this factor into account. These investigators have dubbed the phenomenon **odor constancy,** since perceived strength of an odor remains constant despite variations in flow rate. You can see the similarity between this phenomenon and form constancy (Chapter 5), color constancy (Chapter 6), and size constancy (Chapter 7). In all these instances, perception of objects in the world remains constant despite changes in the energy impinging on the receptors. We should note in passing that others have suggested alternative mechanisms by which odor constancy may be achieved (Laing, 1983).

The Common Chemical Sense. While on the subject of odor concentrations, we should note that most odors judged pleasant at moderate concentrations lose some of their attractiveness at high concentrations. This is why a sales clerk in a cosmetics department always urges customers to allow a dab of perfume time to dilute before smelling it. One reason intense odors can be overpowering has to do with those free nerve endings we pointed out when discussing the olfactory epithelium (a look back at Figure 11.6 will refresh your memory). Those nerve endings are chemical-sensitive cells that are stimulated by just about any volatile substance of moderately high concentration, and they make up what is known as the **common chemical sense.** It is the common chemical sense that is responsible for the *feeling* that accompanies certain "smells"—

such as the coolness of menthol or the tingle in your nose when you burp. Even the crisp, invigorating "smell" of fresh mountain air (which itself has no odor) comes from stimulation of the common chemical sense by ozone in the air. In fact, just about any volatile substance can elicit this "feeling" in your nose if the concentration of that substance is high enough. In the case of some substances, stimulation of the common chemical sense produces a burning sensation that causes you to hold your breath and turn your head away from the source of stimulation. Those of you who have inhaled ammonia fumes know what this feeling is like. Incidentally, cigarette smokers are less sensitive to stimulation of the common chemical sense; for them, the inhaled concentration of an irritating substance must be about 25 percent higher, as compared to nonsmokers, to elicit a reflexive change in breathing pattern (Cometto-Muniz and Cain, 1982). There are people who have completely lost their common chemical sense, due to damage to the nerve carrying information from the nose's free nerve endings to the brain. In these individuals, harsh chemical substances elicit *no* reaction when inhaled.

The common chemical sense serves as a warning system to alert you to the presence of potentially irritating substances. However, its operation is not limited to dangerous concentration levels; in fact, even at relatively low, safe levels of stimulation the common chemical sense influences the perception of odor, as an experiment by Cain and Murphy (1980) demonstrates. In their study, people sniffed amyl butyrate (a fruity-smelling substance) and rated the perceived intensity of the odor. Mixed in with the odorant were various amounts of carbon dioxide. (Carbon dioxide is a gas that does *not* stimulate olfactory receptors but *does* stimulate the free nerve endings in the nose. Hence it has no odor; but because it stimulates the common chemical sense, it elicits a pungent sensation when inhaled.) Cain and Murphy wanted to know whether stimulation of the common chemical sense would influence people's judgments of odor intensity. Some of the results from their experiment are summarized in Figure 11.7; the vertical axis plots the perceived odor intensity of the amyl butyrate and the horizontal axis shows the concentration of the odorless carbon dioxide. Note that increasing the concentration of carbon dioxide, which itself could not be smelled, reduced the perceived intensity of the amyl butyrate. Even though the actual concentration of amyl butyrate remained constant, its smell changed from pleasant and fruity (at low levels of carbon dioxide) to pungent and irritating (at high levels of carbon dioxide). People also rated how irritating the "smell" seemed. As expected, higher concentrations of the odorless carbon dioxide gas were judged more irritating. However, the pungency of the carbon dioxide was lessened when more

amyl butyrate was mixed in with it. We see, then, that the interaction between odor and the common chemical sense works both ways, with each influencing the perception associated with the other. Clearly, the common chemical sense adds an important ingredient to your experience of odorous substances.

Let's continue our discussion of odor perception and consider **anosmia,** a term referring to a loss in the ability to perceive odors.

Disorders of Smell. Deficiencies in hearing and seeing are usually easy to detect because people depend so much on sight and sound to guide their everyday activities. Deficiencies in odor perception, in comparison, can easily go unnoticed. Though it's hard to imagine, some individuals are completely unable to distinguish odorless, pure air from strong concentrations of odorous substances. One frequent cause of this "odor blindness," or anosmia, is a blow to the head; in such cases, the anosmia often proves to be temporary, suggesting that the olfactory receptors or their axons had been damaged (recall that these neurons can regenerate). Anosmia may also be acquired from inhaling such caustic agents as lead, zinc sulfate, or cocaine. These, too, are believed to injure the olfactory receptors, which is why recovery of smell sensitivity often occurs once the caustic agent has been removed. Schiffman (1983) reviews the various causes of anosmia.

Sometimes anosmia does not involve a total loss of the sense of smell but is instead specific to particular substances. In these cases, a person shows normal sensitivity to some odors but abnormally poor sensitivity to others. These so-called **specific anosmias** are more common than you might think. For example, 3 percent of the population have trouble smelling the odor of sweat, 12 percent have diminished sensitivity to musky

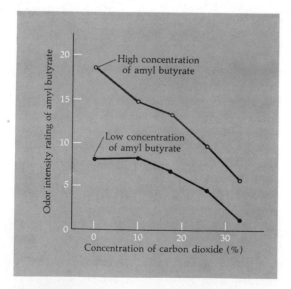

FIGURE 11.7
Stimulation of the common chemical sense (carbon dioxide) affects perceived odor (amyl butyrate).

odors, and 47 percent have trouble smelling the odor of urine (Amoore, 1977).

Specific anosmias are thought to be genetic in origin. Amoore (1977), the odor scientist who has studied this problem in the greatest detail, believes that specific anosmias result from the absence of certain classes of olfactory receptors. His theory hinges on the idea that different odorous substances stimulate different groups of olfactory receptor cells (recall Figure 11.4). According to his theory, specific anosmias are analogous to the various types of color blindness, each of which results from the absence of one or more of the three types of cone photopigments in the eye. Amoore's theory is not completely accepted, in part because of skepticism about the "lock-and-key" theory of odor perception upon which his theory is based.

Regardless of its cause, losing one's sense of smell can have serious consequences. Individuals with acquired anosmia often claim that eating is no longer pleasurable, and these people show a loss of both appetite and weight (Schechter and Henkin, 1974). There is even speculation that anosmia may dull one's sexual drive (Bobrow, Money, and Lewis, 1971). This possibility is not entirely far-fetched. Animals rely very heavily on odor to motivate and guide their sexual behavior. And certainly, the large sums of money spent on perfume, not to mention the erotic nature of many perfume commercials, suggest a connection between the nose and sexual behavior.

Before leaving our discussion of disorders of smell, this seems a good place to mention **odor hallucinations**—the experiencing of odors for which there is no physical stimulus. Odor hallucinations are sometimes associated with brain tumors (Douek, 1974); they are also a common complaint of people diagnosed as mentally ill (Rubert, Hollender, and Mehrhof, 1961). But don't assume that odor hallucinations necessarily indicate brain damage or mental illness. People sometimes describe sensing strange, metallic-like odors when they have the flu or other viral diseases (Schiffman, 1983). This effect is thought to result from a virus having damaged cells in the olfactory epithelium. In any event, you needn't become immediately alarmed when you experience some olfactory hallucination; it is often difficult to distinguish real odors from imaginary ones, since the source of an odor may not be obvious. How many times have you searched your house trying to discover where that "funny smell" was coming from?

Adaptation to Odors. You have undoubtedly had the experience of walking into the lobby of a movie theater and smelling the aroma of fresh popcorn. Driven by this lovely smell, you stand in line to buy some, but by the time you reach the counter the aroma has faded considerably. This is just one example of how exposure to an odor decreases sensitivity to that odor—a phenomenon called **odor adaptation.** Certain occupations depend crucially on odor adaptation—sewer workers, for instance, can carry out their jobs without being bothered by the stench of their surroundings. Odor adaptation also means that people cease to be aware of their own body odors or of the odors permeating their immediate surroundings; sometimes one must rely on other people for such information—a theme that is widely exploited in deodorant and soap commercials.

Odor adaptation has been studied in the laboratory, and the results confirm what experience suggests (see Halpern, 1983). Following even prolonged exposure to an odor, one never *completely* loses the sensitivity to that odor. Instead, its perceived intensity steadily decreases with continued exposure, eventually falling to about 30 percent of its initial level (Cain, 1978). (This is why some people can "tolerate" wearing an overpowering amount of perfume or aftershave—their noses have adapted to the strong fragrance that others wince at.) If an odor's concentration is weak to begin with, it may be impossible to detect that weak odor following adaptation to a strong concentration of the same odor.

Recovery from exposure to an odor takes just a few minutes unless the adaptation odor was quite strong, in which case an hour or more may be required for complete recovery (Berglund et al., 1971). There is also anecdotal evidence for an ultralong-term adaptation effect, whereby individuals develop a chronic insensitivity to odors common to their work environment. Even when they report to work first thing in the morning, they fail to smell odors that visitors readily sense. The adaptation of these workers carries over from one day to the next. At the same time, these individuals exhibit normal sensitivity for odors not peculiar to their workplace; so they have not completely lost their sense of smell. Moreover, upon returning to work following a short vacation, they are initially able to sense the odors that their colleagues on the job cannot sense; after a few days on the job, however, they again become insensitive to those odors. Gesteland (1982) has speculated that these long-term losses in odor sensitivity may be related to the growth processes in the olfactory receptor cells that we described earlier. Perhaps chronic exposure to a limited set of odors strips the nose of receptors that are responsive to that set of odors, and several weeks away from that environment are needed to allow the spoiled cells to be replaced with fresh ones.

This explanation of long-term adaptation probably does not apply, however, to short-term adaptation, where brief exposure to an odor temporarily lessens your sensitivity to it. In this latter case, the process responsible for adaptation probably occurs within the brain, not in the nose. One reason for believing this is that you can adapt one nostril

to an odor (keeping the other one closed) and then measure a loss in odor sensitivity using just the unadapted nostril (Zwaardemaker, 1895, cited in Engen, 1982). Since this nostril was closed during adaptation, the olfactory receptors associated with the nostril must have received no stimulation. Nonetheless, your perception of odors introduced into this nostril are still dulled, indicating that the process underlying the loss in sensitivity occurs in the brain, not in the receptor cells. However, the physiology of postreceptor adaptation is poorly understood.

So far we have considered situations where the perceived strength of an odor is reduced by prior exposure to strong concentrations of that same odor. In some cases, though, a temporary loss in sensitivity to one odor can be produced by exposure to a different odor—a phenomenon called **cross-adaptation**. As you might expect, odors that tend to smell alike (such as nail polish remover and airplane glue) usually show a large degree of cross-adaptation: exposure to one reduces your sensitivity to the other. If you spend several minutes sniffing perfume samples at the cosmetic counter, don't be surprised if the fragrance you're already wearing seems temporarily to have worn off; sniffing perfumes similar to your own has lessened your sensitivity to the one you're wearing. Dissimilar odors, in contrast, do not influence each other nearly so much (Moncrieff, 1956). Thus sniffing perfume samples will not subsequently affect your ability to appreciate the aroma of coffee.

You can experience cross-adaptation by performing the following simple experiment. First, take a sniff of a lemon and get an idea of the intensity of its aroma. Now hold a spoon of peanut butter close to your nose for a minute or so, adapting to its smell. Then quickly take another whiff of the lemon—you will find the lemon's fragrance just as strong as before. Next adapt for a minute to a lime held under your nose, and then again sniff the lemon. This time you will find the lemon's fragrance noticeably weakened. A lesson to learn from this exercise is that your appreciation of food during a multicourse meal depends on the order in which the foods are served. This is particularly true for foods with similar aromas. For instance, cheese with a strong, overpowering smell (such as Roquefort) should not be served before one with a more delicate aroma (such as Gouda).

Initially, it was hoped that cross-adaptation would provide a method for odor classification. Presumably, odors stimulating the same receptors should exhibit maximum cross-adaptation, while odors stimulating different receptors should show little or no cross-adaptation. While this sounds reasonable, the results are confusing. In particular, cross-adaptation is sometimes asymmetrical: adaptation to odor *A* may strongly influence your perception of odor *B*, but adaptation to odor *B* may exert hardly any effect on the smell of odor *A* (Cain and Engen, 1969). This outcome seems to indicate that cross-adaptation is not strictly due to receptor adaptation. Moreover, odors that exhibit marked cross-adaptation sometimes bear no resemblance to each other chemically. Cross-adaptation, like short-term adaptation in general, then, does not appear to result from fatigue of the olfactory receptors.

Odor Mixtures. Besides cross-adaptation, different odors can affect one another when they are mixed together in the air you inhale. In fact, this occurs quite commonly, as the following examples illustrate. Most meals you eat consist of a bouquet of aromas that when properly mixed can generate a very pleasing experience. Mixing fragrances is the essence of the perfume maker's job; it is also a concern of people who bathe only with a soap that will complement their cologne. Odor mixture also underlies the success of

commercial air fresheners sold to cover up house odors. In effect, these products exploit the ability of one odor to mask another, by "swamping" the offensive odor with an even stronger pine or floral scent. These products should be distinguished from true deodorizers, which act by actually removing odorous molecules from the air or by preventing the production of odorous molecules in the first place (the mechanism employed in some underarm deodorants).

In general, the nose seems able to sort out and identify the various odors that are in a mixture. This is why you can identify many of the food ingredients that went into some complex dish simply from the smell of that dish. In this sense, the nose's behavior resembles the ear's ability to single out one pitch from a musical chord; the nose does not behave like the eye, which sometimes loses track of the individual hues making up a mixture. (For a full discussion of odor mixture, see Engen, 1982).

Practice in Odor Identification. During your lifetime, you have been exposed to thousands of different odors—to some, many times over and over. Most of those odors were associated with information from your other senses, information that unambiguously identified the source of those odors. For instance, a citruslike aroma is usually accompanied by the sight of a lemon. But how good do you think you might be at identifying odors if they were presented in the absence of other information? Probably not very good—if you are like most people. In experiments, people usually get fewer than half the items correct (Engen and Pfaffman, 1960; Desor and Beauchamp, 1974; Cain, 1979). This seems puzzling. People certainly have the ability to *distinguish* among a large number of odors; their difficulty is in *naming* them. Odor identification involves something besides discrimination—one must be able to attach a verbal label to the odor. And this seems to be the hard part about identifying odors: an odor may be familiar to you, yet you cannot quite come up with its proper label. This inability to name a familiar odor has been aptly termed the *tip of the nose* phenomenon (Lawless and Engen, 1977)—a variation on the phrase typically used when one blocks on a term or a name. If the problem is indeed one of retrieving odor names from memory, prompting with clues as to an odor's identity should help. And it does. Richard Davis (1981) found that merely providing people with a color name related to an odor (such as "yellow" when lemon was being sniffed) was sufficient to trigger correct identification.

Besides cues, practice with feedback also improves the ability to identify odors. Desor and Beauchamp (1974) tested people's ability to name thirty-two common odorous objects contained in individual opaque jars. After sniffing the jar, the person guessed what the object was and rated the familiarity of the odor. Some smells—such as coffee, paint, and banana—were readily identified and were also rated as highly familiar. Other smells—including ham, cigar, and crayon—were incorrectly identified by most people; these odors were also rated as less familiar. Desor and Beauchamp then went through the series again, this time providing people with the correct answer when they made errors. With this practice, everyone was able to learn to name each of the thirty-two odors correctly. Furthermore, the same people were trained on an additional set of thirty-two new odors, and with practice they were able to identify all sixty-four odors with few errors.

FIGURE 11.8

Odor identification performance for eighty common stimuli, arranged from top to bottom in order of ease of identification. Unshaded bars indicate the superior ability of female subjects to identify a particular stimulus; shaded bars indicate superior ability of male subjects. (Redrawn with permission from Cain, 1982.)

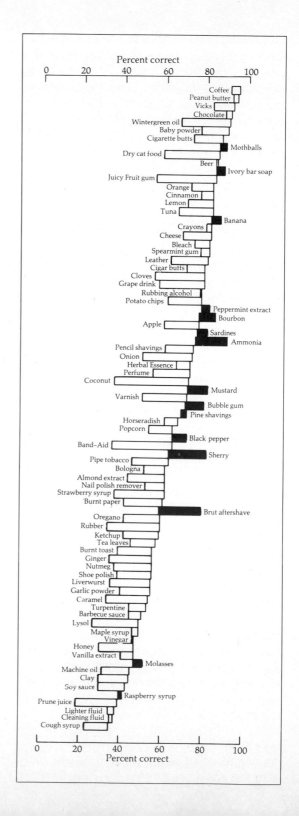

Although practice improves odor identification, it does not help everybody to the same degree. For example, practice seems to benefit females more than males, as Figure 11.8 shows. The graph summarizes results from an experiment performed by William Cain, whose work on the common chemical sense we described earlier. In this odor study, Cain (1982) asked male and female college students to identify each of the eighty common odorous stimuli listed in the figure. Each person went through the set of stimuli several times, with feedback provided after every trial. Students of both sexes improved with practice on this task, but the females consistently outperformed the males on just about every odorous stimulus. Each bar in Figure 11.8 summarizes identification performance for a particular stimulus. Stimuli in the upper portion of the figure (for instance, coffee) were readily identified, while stimuli toward the lower portion (such as cough syrup) were difficult to identify. Unshaded bars indicate female superiority at identifying that odorant, while shaded bars indicate male superiority. The length of the bar denotes the size of the sex difference in odor identification. For instance, males were much better than females at identifying Brut aftershave lotion, but only marginally better at identifying the smell of mothballs. Females were much better than males at identifying coconut, but only slightly better at identifying peanut butter. As the overwhelming number of unshaded bars indicates, females are generally better at this task than are males. This outcome goes along with the results described in Box 11.1, showing female superiority on odor identification tasks that don't involve actual naming. The origin of these sex differences is not yet known; nonetheless, it is clear that both sexes do benefit from practice.

Odors and Memory. Even when people cannot identify some odor, they are often able to say with confidence whether or not they have smelled it before—which suggests that odors can reach back into memory (see Box 11.4). For Helen Keller, who was blind and deaf from infancy, smell was

a potent wizard that transports us across thousands of miles and all the years we have lived. The odors of fruits waft to me in my southern home, to my childhood frolics in the peach orchard. Other odors, instantaneous and fleeting, cause my heart to dilate joyously or contract with remembered grief. (1908, p. 574)

Odors can certainly call up memories. But can memories call up odors? The answer seems to be no. Most people have great difficulty *imagining* what an odor smells like, even a very familiar one. Can you, for instance, conjure up the smell of a rose? Of course you recognize its fragrance when you actually encounter a rose, but recalling such a smell seems very difficult. Isn't it odd that one can readily hum tunes in one's head, can vividly picture a scene in the mind's eye, but cannot re-create in the mind a remembered smell? Perhaps, during the course of evolution, the sense of smell became fully developed before consciousness came on the scene. And perhaps, as a result, the olfactory system does not have access to the neural machinery needed to imagine odors consciously in the absence of the objects that normally evoke them.

On this speculative note we'll end our discussion of smell and move on to its sister sense, taste.

The Sense of Taste

You say of food, "This tastes good" or "I like the taste of that." But taste determines not only how much you like or dislike some food, but also whether you will eat it at all. In effect, the tongue and mouth (assisted by the nose) are designed to ensure that nutritious substances are eaten while noxious ones

BOX 11.4
Smell, Taste, and Literature

Languages have limited vocabularies for describing smell and taste experiences. Though it's fairly easy to describe what you see and what you hear, smell and taste are another matter (Bedichek, 1960). This works a special hardship on authors who must communicate their character's smell and taste experiences. Fortunately, good writers rise above the apparent limitations of language. When you read a work in which smell and taste play a key part you are reminded how important these "inarticulate senses" really are. To show you what we mean, let's consider some samples of writing in which authors have managed to give these inarticulate senses a voice of their own.

Smell can evoke memories long-buried and obscure; the same thing can happen in the case of taste. Probably the best-known literary description of this phenomenon comes from Marcel Proust's *Swann's Way*. In the book's overture, the narrator muses that it's impossible to recapture one's past merely by trying to think about it. True recapture requires that you re-experience the *sensations* that you felt originally. And he then goes on to provide an eloquent example of this idea. While he is visiting her, the narrator's mother sees that he is cold and gives him a cup of tea and some little cakes called *petites madeleines*. Without thinking, he drinks some of the tea, into which cake crumbs have fallen. Immediately, he finds himself overcome with an "all-powerful joy," but he doesn't understand why. Then it strikes him: the taste was one he had experienced years before, as a young boy in the little French village of Combray.

In that moment all the flowers in our garden and in M. Swann's park, and the water-lilies on the Vivonne and the good folk of the village and their little dwellings and the parish church and the whole of Combray and of its surroundings, taking their proper shapes and growing solid, sprang into being, town and gardens alike, from my cup of tea. (Proust, 1928, p. 58)

Since the next two hundred pages of Proust's novel deal with his remembrances of things that happened in Combray, the entire novel actually springs from the taste of those few tea-soaked cake crumbs. They must have been a powerful jolt to the memory.

One lesson from Proust is that any writer who wants to create truly convincing and complete lives cannot ignore smell and taste. James Joyce understood this as well as any writer of the past hundred years. In his masterpiece, *Ulysses*, Joyce frequently used smells to reach into the minds of various characters. You probably know that various episodes in *Ulysses* emphasize different organs of the human body, with the so-called "Nausicaa" episode highlighting the eye and the nose. This episode takes place just after sunset on a June evening in 1904. Leopold Bloom, the middle-aged Dubliner around whose comings and goings the book revolves, is walking along the beach, trying to clear his head. Bloom finds himself attracted to Gerty MacDowell, a young girl who's sitting on some rocks near the beach. Although they never even speak, Bloom is smitten. When she leaves, Gerty waves her perfumed handkerchief at Bloom. The scent reaches Bloom, triggering thoughts of Gerty and of his wife, Molly, too.

Wait. Hm. Hm. Yes. That's her perfume. Why she waved her hand. I leave you to think of me when I'm far away on the pillow. What is it? Heliotrope? No, hyacinth? Hm. Roses, I think. She'd like scent of that with a little jessamine mixed. Her high notes and her low notes. At the dance night she met him, dance of the hours. Heat brought it out. She was wearing her black and it had the perfume of the time before . . . Mysterious thing too. Why did I smell it only now? Took its time in coming like herself, slow but sure. Suppose it's ever so many millions of tiny grains blown across . . . Clings to everything she takes off. Vamp of her stockings. Warm shoe. Stays. Drawers: little kick, taking them off. Byby till next time. Also the cat likes to sniff in her shift on the bed. Know her smell in a thousand. Bathwater too. Reminds me of strawberries and cream. (Joyce, 1922/1934, p. 368)

Many people consider James Joyce to be the greatest writer in English of the twentieth century. For contrast, we'll end with Joris Karl Huysman, a

French writer who richly deserves the obscurity that enshrouds him today. Published about one hundred years ago, Huysman's novel, *Against the Grain*, has more discussions of smell and taste than any other we know of. For example, one chapter consists entirely of smell hallucinations so vivid that they exhaust the book's central character, Des Esseintes, a bizarre, depraved aristocrat. A student of the perfumer's art, Esseintes has developed several devices for titillating his jaded senses. Besides special instruments for re-creating any conceivable odor, he has constructed a special "mouth organ," designed to stimulate his palate rather than his ears. The organ's regular pipes have been replaced by rows of little barrels, each containing a different liqueur. In Esseintes's mind, the taste of each liqueur corresponded with the sound of a particular instrument.

Dry curaçao, for instance, was like the clarinet with its shrill, velvety note: kümmel like the oboe, whose timbre is sonorous and nasal; crème de menthe and anisette like the flute, at one and the same time sweet and poignant, whining and soft. Then to complete the orchestra, comes kirsch, blowing a wild trumpet blast; gin and whisky, deafening the palate with their harsh outbursts of cornets and trombones: liqueur brandy, blaring with the overwhelming crash of the tubas. (Huysman, 1884/1931, p. 132)

By careful and persistent experimentation, Esseintes learned to "execute on his tongue a succession of voiceless melodies; noiseless funeral marches, solemn and stately; could hear in his mouth solos of crème de menthe, duets of vespertro and rum." Though this sounds like an interesting idea, frankly, we prefer our music the old-fashioned way—heard through the ears.

These few samples give you some idea of how writers of varying backgrounds and literary significance have worked with smell and taste. These samples, and others we could have mentioned, are a reminder of how impoverished one's own perceptual world would be without these "inarticulate senses."

---

are not. Living in a civilized environment, you seldom need to judge on the basis of its taste whether a food is edible—rather, you assume that if the grocer sells it or the restaurant serves it, it must be safe to eat. For you, then, taste serves mainly to define your preferences among a large group of commercially available edible foods. Still, taste provides you with a bounty of perceptual experiences and therefore deserves to be studied.

Technically, the term "taste" is used to refer to sensations caused when various substances dissolved in saliva penetrate the taste buds on the tongue and surfaces of the mouth. If you were to drop a pinch of sugar onto the tip of your tongue, the resulting sensation would constitute what most people call "taste." But when you actually eat something, you learn much more than this about the substances in your mouth—besides taste, you have an immediate appreciation of the food's temperature, texture, and consistency (Gibson, 1966). All these sources of information combine with the substance's taste to form a complex of sensations that is known as **flavor**. While the remainder of this chapter is concerned with the taste component of flavor, keep in mind that these other sources of information also contribute to your enjoyment of food.

In our discussion of taste, we shall follow the same general outline used in the section on smell: we'll describe the stimulus for taste, consider the question of taste categories, provide a brief overview of the anatomy and physiology of the gustatory system, and then take up the question of taste sensitivity. Finally, we'll explore the interaction between taste and smell.

THE STIMULUS FOR TASTE

In order to be tasted, a substance must be *soluble*—that is, it must dissolve when it comes in contact with saliva. This is why you cannot tell the difference between a plastic spoon and a stainless steel spoon simply on the basis of their taste—neither material will dissolve in saliva. Incidentally, saliva closely resembles salt water, although the sodium content of saliva varies from one person to the next. It is claimed that you can actually detect this difference in sodium content when you taste someone else's saliva (Bartoshuk, 1980), but we'll leave it to the intellectually curious to confirm this claim.

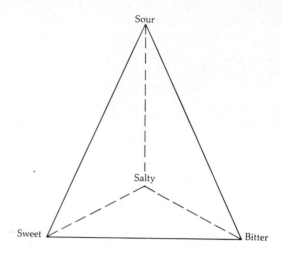

FIGURE 11.9
Henning's taste tetrahedron.

THE CLASSIFICATION OF TASTES

Nowadays it is widely believed that tastes can be grouped into four distinct categories: sweet, sour, salty, and bitter. However, this particular idea is still controversial. Earlier lists of the basic taste qualities contained more entries. For example, Aristotle believed there were seven basic tastes, the four listed above plus pungent, harsh, and astringent. In the centuries following Aristotle's time, new tastes were added to the list (such as viscous and fatty) while others were dropped (Bartoshuk, 1978). It wasn't until the early part of the nineteenth century that the list dwindled to the four categories most people are now familiar with. The person who formalized the four-taste idea is Henning (1916), the same man who was responsible for the odor classification scheme shown in Figure 11.2. Once again, Henning relied on geometry to represent the relations among the various taste categories. In this case his model, shown in Figure 11.9, took the form of a tetrahedron, with each of the four taste qualities located at one of the four corners.

Henning wanted his geometric model to emphasize the unity of the four taste qualities; he emphatically rejected the idea that these four taste qualities could be *separately* experienced in any complex mixture of tastes. More recently, however, Donald McBurney (1974) has argued that one *can* pick out and judge the relative contributions of these four primaries, or "basics," as he calls them. He believes this is possible because the tongue analyzes substances into these four distinct categories. While it is commonly recognized that the tongue is indeed differentially sensitive to these four tastes (Collings, 1974), some taste experts nonetheless oppose the idea that there are genuinely separate taste qualities. Two of these notable opponents, Susan Schiffman and Robert Erickson (1980), have questioned much of the evidence for the existence of distinct taste primaries. Besides challenging this evidence, Schiffman and Erickson have also performed their own experiments on this topic. Let's consider the results from a couple of their studies.

Schiffman (whose work on odor categories we described earlier) used multidimensional scaling to analyze people's ratings of taste similarity. (Recall from Box 11.2

that this procedure establishes the number of dimensions required to account for similarity ratings.) Her analysis disclosed that taste judgments could not be contained within a "taste space" defined by just four components. (Henning's tetrahedron is one possible taste space utilizing four components.) Schiffman obtained evidence for more than four components even when taste judgments were obtained from anosmic individuals. Because these people could not smell, Schiffman could be certain that the extra dimensions uncovered in her analysis were not the product of olfaction. This led her to conclude that four primaries are inadequate to account for the entire range of taste (Schiffman and Dackis, 1975).

Robert Erickson, a physiological psychologist at Duke University, approached the notion of taste primaries in a different way. He presented people with taste solutions consisting of one or more of the so-called primary tastes and asked those people to judge whether they perceived "one" or "more than one" taste quality. For comparison, Erickson asked for the same judgment about auditory tones presented either alone or in a chord. As expected, a single tone was always judged as one whereas multiple tones were always judged as more than one. This merely confirms the analytical nature of pitch perception: identification of one tone is possible in the presence of another. The results with the taste solutions were quite different. Solutions composed of a single component were sometimes judged as more than one, whereas multicomponent solutions were sometimes judged as one. Moreover, people were often unable to identify whether a mixture contained a particular component, even when they could reliably identify that component in isolation. For instance, quinine (a bitter-tasting substance) was easily recognized on its own; but when mixed with sucrose (which as you know is sweet), the quinine in the mixture was unrecognizable.

These findings led Erickson to conclude that complex tastes are *not* analyzed into primary components but instead take on their own, unique quality, which may give little hint of their ingredients (Erickson, 1982).

This issue of taste categories is by no means settled (see, for example, McBurney and Gent, 1979); at present, the weight of opinion is probably still on the side of four taste primaries. There is a good reason why some taste researchers are reluctant to give up the idea of four primaries. In particular, some progress has been made in identifying chemical similarities among substances belonging to the same taste group (Beidler, 1978). Establishing the molecular basis of taste quality is a goal that taste experts have been striving toward for decades. Abandoning the categorization scheme that has guided this search would be a bitter pill to swallow. For the moment we'll set aside the question of primaries and proceed to a less controversial topic, the neural mechanisms of taste perception.

THE ANATOMY AND PHYSIOLOGY OF TASTE

The Taste Receptors. Let's begin by taking a tour of your tongue and the inside of your mouth. The tongue itself consists of muscle covered with mucous membrane. To picture the terrain we'll be discussing, take a careful look at your tongue in a mirror (stick your tongue way out). Notice that it is covered with little bumps. These bumps are called **papillae** (from the Latin *papula*, meaning "pimple"). When viewed from the side (see Figure 11.10), they resemble regularly spaced columns separated by channels. The walls of the papillae are lined with tiny structures, called **taste buds,** that are shaped like garlic bulbs. These taste buds house the receptor cells responsible for registering the presence of chemical substances. Not all the papillae scattered over your tongue contain taste

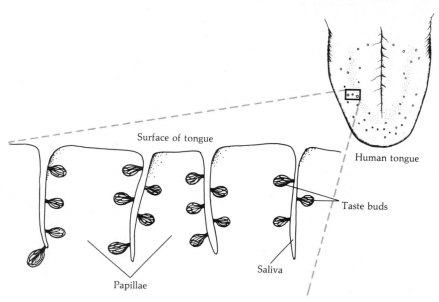

FIGURE 11.10
A side view of the tongue's papillae.

buds—those in the center of the tongue have none, which is why food confined to this area has no taste. The center of your tongue is analogous to the blind spot in your eye, in that both are devoid of receptors. You also have some taste buds in the roof of your mouth, inside your cheeks, and in your throat. Some animals have structures similar to taste buds on parts of their bodies other than the tongue and inside of the mouth. Fish, which live in a watery equivalent of saliva, have taste receptors scattered over the surface of their bodies; and some insects have them on their feet, enabling them to taste the surfaces they walk over.

Human papillae that do contain taste buds have anywhere from several hundred buds down to just a single bud (Bradley, 1979), with a grand total of something like 10,000 taste buds distributed throughout the inside of your mouth. But the total number of buds varies with age (Cowart, 1981). Infants start out with relatively few taste buds, but dur-

ing childhood the number steadily increases to the number cited above. Around age 40, the trend reverses and the overall number of taste buds declines. Ludel (1978) has speculated that this decline in the taste bud population may account for the documented fact that the elderly generally exhibit lower taste sensitivity (Schiffman, 1983).

Like the olfactory receptors, taste buds are constantly degenerating and being replaced by new ones (Beidler and Smallman, 1965). The life expectancy of an individual taste bud is only about 10 days. Hence throughout your lifetime there is a continuous, rapid turnover within the large population of taste buds. Unlike olfactory cells, however, taste buds are not true neurons, meaning that they do not have axons that project to the brain. In a moment, we'll see how taste information is carried to the brain; for now, though, let's take a closer look at an individual taste bud.

Figure 11.11 illustrates what an individ-

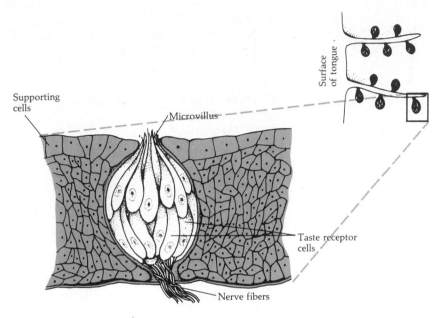

Supporting
cells

Surface
of tongue

Microvillus

Taste receptor
cells

Nerve fibers

FIGURE 11.11
An individual taste bud.

ual taste bud looks like under the micro-scope (buds are too small for the unaided eye to see). Each bud contains an average of fifty individual taste receptor cells, ar-ranged within the bud like the cloves of a garlic. Sprouting out of the end of each taste receptor cell is a slender, threadlike struc-ture (labeled microvillus in the figure). A clump of these threads juts into a tiny open-ing in the wall of the taste bud. It is here that taste solutions actually touch the taste receptor cells, causing a change in electrical potential within them. Mucous secretions from supporting cells carry the solution away from the vicinity of the taste bud. This cleaning action is analogous to that de-scribed in the case of the olfactory epithe-lium. But because the tongue's rinsing process is relatively slow, aftertastes can lin-ger after you have swallowed or spit out what was in your mouth.

Back inside a papilla, the taste receptor cells make contact with nerve fibers inner-vating the tongue. Remember that taste re-ceptors themselves do not have axons to send messages to the brain; like photoreceptors, they must pass their messages on to neu-rons that in turn carry neural impulses to higher centers. Taste buds in the tongue and mouth are innervated by no less than three distinct cranial nerves, and the same taste bud may be innervated by more than one nerve (Keverne, 1982). We'll not go into which nerves innervate which regions of the tongue and mouth; but keep in mind that taste information arrives at the brain over several different communication lines. Moreover, these communication lines are hooked to a population of receptor cells whose members are constantly dying and being replaced. It is remarkable, then, that your taste experiences remain as stable over time as they do.

So far we've considered the tongue's re-ceptors; but we have not tried to relate the responses of specific receptors to specific taste

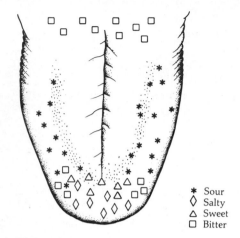

* Sour
◇ Salty
△ Sweet
□ Bitter

FIGURE 11.12
Regions of taste sensitivity on the human tongue.

qualities. Apparently, taste qualities are somehow related to particular receptors, since not all regions of the tongue are equally sensitive to all taste qualities. To locate the various taste regions, Virginia Collings (1974) used weak concentrations of different solutions (sweet, sour, salty, and bitter). She soaked a tiny piece of paper in one of the solutions and applied it to a person's tongue. Since the paper was quite small, it stimulated only a very limited region of the tongue. Papers soaked in different solutions were applied to various regions of the tongue, and for each a person had to name the taste quality produced. As Figure 11.12 indicates, both sweet and salty sensations are produced toward the front of the tongue, while sour is associated with the sides of the tongue. Bitter is evoked from the front of the tongue, just like sour and sweet. But bitter is also elicited by stimulation of the throat just above the back of the tongue.

Keep in mind, though, that these regional variations refer to taste sensitivity—the ability to detect *weak* solutions. At higher concentrations, any of the four taste sensations can be elicited from any place on the tongue where there are taste buds. Moreover, several different distinct taste qualities can be evoked by applying different substances to a single papilla (McCutcheon and Saunders, 1972). This finding further underscores the intermingling of taste qualities over the tongue.

This concludes our discussion of taste receptors. Now let's consider how messages generated by those receptors are represented in nerve fibers carrying information from the taste receptors to the brain.

The Taste Pathways. Individual taste fibers exhibit a low, sustained discharge even when no taste substances are on the tongue. When such a substance is introduced, a fiber's activity increases by an amount that depends both on the nature of the substance and on its concentration (Erickson, 1963; Ogawa, Yamashita, and Sato, 1974). With respect to the nature of the substance, most individual fibers respond to several different taste substances—for instance, one particular fiber might respond to both acids and salts. If individual fibers are indeed not selective for a particular taste, an individual fiber cannot unambiguously specify a certain taste quality.* How, then, could the brain know which taste substance was actually present?

Carl Pfaffmann, a physiologist now at Rockefeller University, proposed that taste quality is represented in the *pattern* of activity across a population of taste fibers (Pfaffmann, 1955). This **cross-fiber theory** of taste quality has also been championed by Erickson (1968, 1984). Of course, for such a pattern theory to work, taste fibers must respond better to some substances than to others—if they responded to the same extent to *all* taste substances, the cross-fiber pattern of activity would be equivalent for

*You should be aware that some people now believe the taste fibers to be more selective than previously thought. If correct, the activity in a single fiber *could* uniquely specify taste quality (Bartoshuk, 1980).

all substances as well. In fact, although most neurons in the taste system are responsive to several taste stimuli, each responds best to a particular taste substance (Frank, 1973). These neurons, in other words, respond selectively to different taste substances. This selective response within a given fiber means that information about taste quality may be coded by the pattern of activity within an ensemble of fibers, as the cross-fiber theory requires.

Besides differing in quality, the tastes of substances also vary in intensity, depending on the concentration of the substance. Let's consider, then, how taste intensity might be represented within the taste fibers. Most taste experts believe that intensity is signaled by the level of activity within individual fibers, since firing rate increases with the concentration of the stimulating solution. Moreover, if the same solution remains present on the tongue for several seconds, a fiber's activity quickly decreases from the level initially evoked, to a somewhat lower one. You might suspect that this drop in neural activity explains why your sense of taste is dulled by repeated sampling of the same food or drink. However, this can't be the entire story, for adaptation of taste sensations may take anywhere from several seconds to a few minutes. Instead of adaptation, the decreased response of taste fibers probably serves a specific function—getting the tongue ready for new tastes. We'll explain why this is important.

Recall that taste judgments allow you to gauge the edibility of food. Taste judgments can be made with astonishing speed: you can identify the taste of what you're eating within the first second of tasting it (Kelling and Halpern, 1983). So after this initial identification, it's less important to continue tasting what you've been tasting than it is to get ready for new tastes. And getting ready for new tastes requires letting the activity in the nerve fibers settle back to a level where they can once again signal the presence of a new substance. Neural adaptation of the kind exhibited by nerve fibers thus makes detection of these changes in taste quality possible (Ludel, 1978). This property of adaptation is particularly important in such sensory modalities as taste, where one fiber may carry information about several different stimulus qualities.

Fibers carrying taste information from the tongue project to two different regions of the brain, with these two regions mediating different aspects of taste perception. One region, the *parietal cortex*, is the taste analogue to the visual cortex and the auditory cortex. Your conscious experience of tastes presumably arises from activity within this area of the brain, as evidenced by the losses in taste perception occasioned by damage to the parietal region (Bornstein, 1940). The other taste region of the brain is part of the *limbic system*, a set of subcortical brain structures thought to be involved in emotional reactions. People who have *only* this subcortical pathway intact cannot identify taste substances verbally but still show characteristic facial reactions to sour and bitter solutions. These subcortical taste areas, then, appear to register at least some behaviorally relevant information about taste. It is speculated that this subcortical taste center mediates learned taste aversion, a phenomenon we shall discuss later in this chapter.

SENSITIVITY TO TASTE

Detection and Identification. You've already seen that taste sensitivity varies across the tongue (Figure 11.12). Now we shall consider some other factors that influence your ability to taste substances in weak concentrations. Actually, right at the limit of your sensitivity, where you are barely able to detect that a solution contains some substance, you would have great difficulty saying exactly what it is you are tasting. As with odors, your *identification* threshold for taste is considerably higher than your *detection* threshold for taste (McBurney, 1978). Try the following experiment to confirm this point. Fill three identical glasses with equal amounts of water. (The water should be at room temperature.) Place a few grains of sugar in one and a few grains of salt in another and stir both thoroughly. Don't add anything to the water in the third glass. While you keep your eyes closed, have a friend hand you each glass one at a time. Take a sip from each and see if you can pick out the one containing plain water—to do this requires merely *detecting* that the other two contain "something." Next, try to pick the glass containing sugar and the one containing salt. This task requires *identifying* the tastes; if you were sufficiently frugal in the amounts you added to each glass, this task should be difficult if not impossible. Realizing that you can succeed just by guessing, see how many times you are correct over a series of ten trials. For this demonstration to work, you may need to use less salt than sugar in producing the solutions. The reason is that a salt solution can be detected at one-third the concentration necessary for the detection of sugar, when the solutions are at room temperature. For most people, the highest sensitivity is to bitter, so if you were to repeat the above demonstration using quinine you'd have to add just a minute quantity to the water. As Box 11.5 indicates, however, there are some people whose sensitivity to bitter is not so great.

In the preceding demonstration, we specified that the water should be at room temperature because taste sensitivity varies greatly with temperature. Moreover, not all substances are affected alike by temperature changes. Salty and bitter become more difficult to detect as temperature increases, but sugar becomes easier to detect; sour is relatively unaffected by temperature. Figure 11.13 summarizes the effect of a substance's temperature on its taste; it also tells you something about the effect of temperature on the taste of various foods and drinks. For instance, wine advertisements that urge you to serve their product well chilled are probably trying to hide its acid taste (a combination of sour and bitter), a common problem with cheap wines. The variations in sensitivity shown in Figure 11.13 also underscore an important guideline in cooking: if you season food on the basis of taste, the final seasoning should be done only after the dish has reached serving temperature.

Is there anything to the adage that your ability to taste is better when you're hungry? From the results of one study (Moore, Linker, and Purcell, 1965), the answer appears to be no—if by "ability to taste" one means detecting very weak solutions. The study did find, though, that taste sensitivity was better in the afternoon than in the morning, which may explain why people *think* their sense of taste is keener when they're hungry. Another misconception about taste concerns the dulling effects of smoking on a person's sensitivity to taste. Here, too, the evidence is to the contrary—regular smokers are just as good as nonsmokers at correctly identifying taste solutions. (Pangborn, Trabue, and Barylko-Pikielna, 1967; McBurney and Moskat, 1975). Why, then, are ex-smokers always claiming

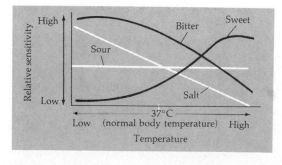

FIGURE 11.13
The effect of temperature on taste.

BOX 11.5

Some Like It Bitter Better Than Others

There is probably universal agreement about what is meant by "bitter"—it's the taste that makes you wrinkle your nose and spit out the offensive substance. Even newborn infants show a characteristic reaction to substances that taste bitter to adults, so those substances very likely taste bitter to them too. What you might not realize, though, is that not all people are equally sensitive to bitter substances. For example, the chemical phenylthiocarbamide (PTC) tastes quite bitter to about two-thirds of all Americans, whereas the remaining one-third are barely able to detect any taste at all from PTC. (Inexpensive paper strips impregnated with PTC are readily available from science supply firms; you might want to purchase some to test yourself and friends.) Studies of families show that sensitivity to the bitterness of PTC is genetically determined. Individuals to whom PTC doesn't taste bitter ("nontasters," we can call

them) have two recessive genes for this trait; those who are sensitive to the bitter ("tasters") have one or two dominant genes for the trait.

PTC is not commonly found in things you put into your mouth, so the inability to taste it is inconsequential. However, Linda Bartoshuk and her colleagues at Yale University have found that tasters and nontasters of PTC also show reliable differences in their judgments of the bitterness of some very common substances. One of those substances is saccharin, an ingredient in many diet sodas. As you may know, saccharin can have a bitter taste in addition to its sweet one. When tasters are given solutions of saccharin in concentrations comparable to those found in commercial beverages, they rate the solutions two to three times more bitter than do nontasters (Bartoshuk, 1979). The same outcome obtains for caffeine, one of the bitter ingredients in coffee. Tasters rate caffeine as more bitter than do nontasters.

In fact, the caffeine in a typical cup of coffee is not perceived as bitter by nontasters although it is by tasters (Hall et al., 1975). This means, then, that a cup of black coffee will taste more bitter to some people than to others. Perhaps individuals who add lots of sugar and cream to their coffee are PTC tasters trying to tone down a degree of bitterness that nontasters never even experience.

There are lots of common bitter substances yet to be tested on tasters and nontasters, and many of these may turn out to be perceived differently by the two groups of people. Bartoshuk's finding underscores a theme running throughout this book: it cannot be taken for granted that all individuals share the same perceptual experiences. Instead, each person lives in a perceptual world that is constrained by the workings of his or her own, individual sensory nervous system.

---

that food tastes better since they quit? Remember that flavor consists of several mouth-related sensations, taste being just one. Perhaps the reformed smoker's enhanced pleasure from food comes from one of these other sources. For example, smokers are less able to appreciate the pungency of odors (Cometto-Muniz and Cain, 1982), and pungency is a sensation produced by a number of spices used in cooking (Rozin, 1978).

As in the case of odor identification, it has been found that females are better at taste identification than males (Meiselman

and Dzendolet, 1967). Though the reasons for female superiority are not yet understood, there seems no doubt that females are better equipped taste- and smell-wise to appreciate food.

Discriminating Taste Intensity. So far we've focused on various aspects of the ability to detect and identify different solutions. Now let's consider how good people are at judging differences in concentration of a single taste substance—another kind of judgment needed in the preparation of food. To get some idea of the difficulty of such judgments, you should try a modification of the taste experiment used to introduce this section. This time fill three large glasses with clear water and place one teaspoon of sugar in the first glass, one and one-quarter teaspoons of sugar in the second, and one and one-half teaspoons of sugar in the third. After stirring, have someone else rearrange the glasses so that you don't know which is which but the other person does. Now try to rank them in order of sugar concentration. This task measures your ability to judge differences in taste concentration. Although the problem has not been thoroughly studied, available results indicate that people require about 15 to 25 percent difference to be able to judge that one solution is stronger than another (McBurney, 1978). On the basis of these numbers, you should be just barely able to pick out the weakest of the three sugar solutions but will probably be unable to discriminate between the remaining two. The fact that people can discriminate concentration changes in the neighborhood of 15 to 25 percent has implications for cooking: to improve a dish's taste by adding more of some ingredient, add just enough to increase the total amount by about 25 percent each time. This will ensure that you don't suddenly add too much.

Taste Adaptation and Modification. Outside the taste laboratory, people rarely ingest substances in very weak, near threshold concentrations, and moreover, hardly ever are those substances encountered in isolation. When you eat, your palate is typically bathed in a complex of taste substances. So it is of interest to study how the taste of one substance is influenced by the presence of other substances. Such influences can take two forms: (1) the taste of a substance may be weakened by prior exposure to that same substance—the familiar process of **adaptation;** (2) the taste of a sub-

stance may be altered in quality by another substance—a process called **modification.** Let's start with adaptation.

You can demonstrate taste adaptation for yourself in the following way. Fill four glasses with equal amounts of water. Now take a freshly sliced lemon and carefully squeeze one drop of juice into one glass, two drops into the second, and the remaining juice into the third (this is the adaptation solution). Thoroughly stir all three solutions. Keep the fourth glass free of lemon—it should contain water only. In this demonstration you should be aware which glass is which (you may want to number them). Now take a sip of the first solution, the one containing a single drop of lemon juice. You should be able to detect a slightly sour taste (sour is the predominant taste of pure lemon juice), especially in comparison to the neutral taste of water only. Next sip the two-drop solution and compare it to water only. As it is twice as strong, this solution should taste more sour than the one-drop one, and certainly different from water only.

Now adapt your tongue to sour—take enough of the concentrated solution into your mouth to cover your tongue. Don't swallow it; instead roll it around in your mouth for about 30 seconds, then spit it out. Now once again sip the two dilute solutions, again comparing them to water only. You should find that the sour taste of both is considerably weaker—perhaps too weak to distinguish from the taste of water only. Wait a few minutes and then repeat this part of the test. You'll find that your sensitivity recovers rather quickly.

This demonstration merely confirms that taste—just like vision, hearing, and smell—shows adaptation. As pointed out in the previous section, this decline in taste sensitivity cannot be caused entirely by the reduced responsiveness of taste fibers; the time course of fiber adaptation is much too short to account for the adaptation of taste sensations. This latter form of adaptation must take place along one of the neural pathways discussed earlier, but exactly where is a mystery (see Gillan, 1984).

Suppose you had adapted to a strong solution of *salt* water and then were tested on the dilute solutions of lemon. Recall that cross-adaptation provides a way to test whether different substances stimulate the same neural elements (look back at page 400 to refresh your memory about the logic of the procedure). You would find that adaptation to salty has essentially no effect on your ability to taste sour. The same would be true if you were to adapt to sweet and then test your sensitivity to sour. In general, cross-adaptation works only when the adapting substance is similar in quality to the test substance (McBurney and Gent, 1979; Bartoshuk, 1974). Thus you'd find your sensitivity to dilute solutions of lemon temporarily reduced if you were first to eat a sour pickle, since these two share the quality "sour." The quality "bitter" seems to be an exception to this rule: sensitivity to bitter substances can be reduced by adaptation to a different taste, sour (McBurney, Smith, and Shick, 1972). In all, though, the results from cross-adaptation studies generally point to the existence of distinct taste qualities.

Modification, the second form of taste interaction, occurs when exposure to one substance subsequently alters the taste of another substance. Several of these so-called "taste illusions" have been described by Linda Bartoshuk of Yale University (1974; Bartoshuk et al., 1969). One that might be familiar to you involves fresh artichokes—after eating this delicacy, people find that other foods and drinks, including plain water, tend to have a sweet taste. (Actually, this is but one example of taste aftereffects involving water; Box 11.6 describes others that you can easily experience.) Another intriguing taste illusion is produced by the leaves of the *Gymnema sylvestre* plant, found

in India and Africa. Eating the leaves, or drinking tea made from those leaves, temporarily abolishes the sweet taste of sugar. In fact, following exposure to *Gymnema sylvestre*, sugar crystals on the tongue are indistinguishable from grains of sand; salt, in contrast, retains its taste—proof that *Gymnema sylvestre* doesn't simply wipe out the entire sense of taste.

Another, equally exotic taste modifier comes from the *Synsepalum dulcificum* bush. Popularly called "miracle fruit," the berries from this bush impart an intensely sweet taste to even the sourest foods, such as lemons. Moreover, this sweetening aftereffect lasts about an hour after eating just a small amount of miracle fruit. This could provide a novel way to reduce your intake of sugar—you could fool your tongue into believing that food was sweet without adding sugar. While it's not known exactly how miracle fruit works, it is known that it alters the responsiveness of taste fibers (Brouwer et al., 1983). Following exposure of the tongue to miracle fruit's active ingredient, fibers normally responsive to sweet substances but not to sour ones develop a temporary sensitivity to sour. In other words, these nerve fibers temporarily behave as though sour were sweet. After about an hour, these fibers return to their normal state, once again ignoring sour. Recall that an hour is also about how long the taste illusion persists. Incidentally, the sweet taste caused by miracle fruit can be abruptly abolished by tasting *Gymnema sylvestre*, the leaf that destroys the taste of sugar. Here's an interesting case where one illusion can be used to combat another.

There's one taste modifier that you're all familiar with: toothpaste. You've probably had the annoying experience of finding that the taste of your morning fruit juice has been ruined because you had just brushed your teeth. This cross-adaptation occurs because toothpaste contains an ingredient that tem-

BOX 11.6

The Taste of Water: An Aftereffect

You would probably agree that water doesn't seem to have any particular taste, aside from the faint mineral taste found in tap water. Yet by adapting your tongue to different substances, you can make water take on various distinct tastes. This phenomenon—"water taste"—is somewhat similar to the negative color afterimages described in Chapter 6. In the case of water, however, the taste aftereffect is not organized in an opponent fashion. This will become apparent when you perform the following experiment.

You should obtain a bottle of distilled water for this experiment, for distilled water has no mineral taste whatsoever (you should confirm this for yourself). Pour a glass full of distilled water—this will be the test stimulus. Next, fill three other glasses with water (the tap variety will do) and add a teaspoon of salt to one, a teaspoon of lemon juice to the second, and a teaspoon of sugar to the third—these are the adaptation stimuli. Be sure each is well stirred. Begin by taking a sip of the distilled water, just to remind yourself what "no taste" tastes like.

Now take a mouthful of the salty solution and roll it around in your mouth for about 30 seconds. At the end of this adaptation period, spit out the salty water and take a sip of the distilled water. The previously tasteless liquid will now have a noticeable sour/bitter taste. Once this aftertaste has worn off, such that distilled water again has no taste, adapt to the sour (lemon) solution for 30 seconds. Now you will find that the same distilled water tastes faintly sweet. After this taste aftereffect has worn off, adapt to the sweet solution. This time distilled water will take on a sour taste.

Can you see the similarity between this taste aftereffect and the negative color afterimages you experienced from Color Plate 10? In the case of color, a white surface took on the hue that was dependent on the adaptation color. In the case of taste, the distilled water plays the same role as the white surface—both represent a neutral stimulus that becomes temporarily "shaded" by adaptation. There is, however, a real difference between colored afterimages and water taste aftereffects. With color, adaptation obeys

an opponent rule: adapting to red makes white look green, whereas adapting to green makes white look red; blue and yellow are comparably related. With taste, adaptation is not reciprocal: adaptation to salty makes water taste sour, but adaptation to sour makes water taste sweet, not salty. Similar nonreciprocal aftereffects are found in the case of bitter (which you can most easily produce using unsweetened quinine water). Bitter makes distilled water taste sweet, but as you experienced, adapting to sweet makes distilled water taste sour, not bitter. All of this implies that taste does not involve opponent process mechanisms such as those implicated in color vision (McBurney, Smith, and Shick, 1972). It also implies that the taste of water must be changing all the time during the course of a meal, since you are constantly adapting your tongue to different taste substances. Even the salt in your own saliva can act as a mild adaptation stimulus. Because you've adapted to your own saliva, when you sip distilled water it may appear to have a slightly sour taste.

porarily reduces the sweetness of sugar while making the acid in the juice taste extra sour (Bartoshuk, 1980).

Taste Mixtures. So far, our discussion has focused on altering one taste by exposure to another. Next let's consider what happens when two or more taste substances are mixed together (which occurs routinely whenever one cooks). Everyone knows that it's possible to tone down the taste of one substance by adding another—this is one reason why people add sugar to coffee, to mask its bitter taste. This reduction of one taste sensation by another is called **taste suppression,** and it seems to be a general property of taste mixtures (Bartoshuk, 1975; Gillan, 1982). But what do taste mixtures actually taste like? Is taste analogous to color vision, where two component hues (for instance red and green) can create an entirely new hue (yellow)? Or is taste more like hearing, where two tones played together still maintain their individuality?

The answer to this interesting and important question is not clear. McBurney (1978) maintains that new qualities are not produced by the mixture of taste components. According to this view, lemon juice with sugar added may taste both sour and sweet; but it won't taste salty or anything else new. This outcome is reminiscent of the situation in hearing, not color vision. Schiffman and Erickson (1980), however, report that sometimes a mixture will produce an unexpected taste, one not usually associated with the taste of any of the components. Such a result would be in line with the behavior of color vision, not hearing. How does one unravel these seemingly contradictory observations? Part of the problem stems from the inherently subjective nature of these perceptual judgments. In effect, people must "introspect" on their taste sensations, decomposing the mixture into constituents. (To see how difficult this is, try analyzing the tastes evoked by each dish in your next meal.) As discussed in Chapter 1, introspection is not a simple task, and it is subject to all sorts of extraneous influences, such as the instructions given to people. As an alternative, people could be asked to "construct" a taste mixture that matches the taste(s) of a solution mixed by the experimenter. Such an experiment would be analogous to the metameric color-matching experiments described in Chapter 6. However, to perform such a taste-matching experiment requires having some idea of what components should be provided for the mixture. And this brings us back to the question raised at the outset—the question

as to the existence of basic taste qualities. At present, this question represents the fundamental issue in taste research, and until it is resolved we'll have to be content enjoying what we eat without knowing exactly what we are tasting.

TASTE PREFERENCES

Liking and disliking are not usually thought of as natural properties of sensory stimulation. There seems to be nothing inherently sad about the color blue, for example. Taste may be an exception, however. People can reliably rate various tastes along a dimension of "pleasant/unpleasant," and one person's ratings are very likely to agree with another's. Bitter is usually judged "unpleasant," while sweet, at least in low concentrations, is rated "pleasant." Such judgments are called **taste hedonics** ("hedonic" is derived from the Greek word meaning "pleasure"). Some taste experts believe that these hedonic qualities stem from biological factors governing food selection. Organisms ranging from insects to primates, man included, crave sweet substances. This may be adaptive, since sweet substances are generally high in calories, meaning that they provide energy. Bitter is typically associated with toxic substances, which would explain why nearly all animals show an aversion to bitter substances. In fact, some plants and animals have capitalized on this universal aversion by evolving a bitter-tasting skin themselves, a characteristic that wards off potential predators (Gittleman and Harvey, 1982).

This natural aversion to bitter can be overcome, however, as evidenced by the almost universal enjoyment of such substances such as beer, coffee, and quinine water. And just as natural aversions can be conquered, unnatural ones can be *acquired* (Garcia and Koelling, 1966; Garb and Stunkard, 1974). Extreme nausea following ingestion of some food is a sure bet to cause an animal to reject that food the next time it is available. This phenomenon, called **conditioned taste aversion,** is an extremely potent method for discouraging predators from disturbing farm animals such as chickens and sheep. One meal of sheep meat laced with lithium chloride (a chemical that induces violent nausea) will dissuade a coyote from going near the source of that meat in the future. By the same token, one night of heavy indulgence in whiskey is enough to discourage a person from ordering whiskey sours in the near future.

Although sweet tastes are usually thought of as pleasant, extremely sweet food or drink can be unpleasant. Howard Moskowitz, a food consultant, has studied how hedonic ratings vary with the concentration of various substances. He finds that for sweet substances, pleasantness increases with concentration up to a point, after which the substance becomes more and more unpleasant. This transition point Moskowitz (1978) calls the *bliss point*—the concentration yielding the highest hedonic rating. As you might expect, young children have a higher bliss point than do adults, which explains why advertisements for highly sweetened breakfast cereals are aimed primarily at the Saturday morning television audience. Contrary to expectation, however, some obese individuals actually have a lower bliss point than do people of normal weight (Grinker and Hirsch, 1972), although this finding does not hold for all sweet substances (Drewnowski, Grinker, and Hirsch, 1982).

Besides concentration, a food's color can also influence how much people like its taste. One clever study (Duncker, 1939) had people rate the taste of white chocolate and brown chocolate, and they did this while either blindfolded or not. With their eyes open, people judged the white chocolate as weak in taste, whereas the blindfolded group liked it just as much as the brown chocolate.

The same pattern of results has been found for fruit-flavored beverages and cake (DuBose, Cardello, and Maller, 1980). The food industry, aware of the influence of color on taste perception, often adds color to products. Margarine, for instance, is naturally very pale but is dyed yellow to mimic the color of real butter. Likewise, orange food coloring is added to many orange juice products, and this strategy improves the flavor scores of these products (see Pangborn, 1960). To convince yourself of the potent effect color has on taste perception, just add green food coloring to milk and see how it tastes.

The general topic of taste preferences is a fascinating one; there is much interesting material that cannot be presented here for lack of space. However, some good articles on the subject have been written (see, for example, Moskowitz, 1978, and Rozin, 1979).

The Interaction Between Taste and Smell

Several times in this chapter we have stressed the role played by odor in what we usually think of as taste. Holding your nostrils closed while you eat dramatically demonstrates this role. One study (Mozel et al., 1969) found that the ability to identify food substances is severely hampered when odor perception is eliminated. In this study, twenty-one familiar substances were individually liquified in a blender and dropped onto a person's tongue from an eye-dropper; the person's task was to name the food. The results are summarized in Figure 11.14, which shows the percentages of people tested who could identify each of the twenty-one substances. The shaded bars give the results when the odor of the solution could be smelled; the unshaded bars give the results when odors were blocked from reaching the olfactory epithelium. Obviously, smell improved performance greatly. In fact, for several very familiar substances, including coffee, garlic, and chocolate, correct identification was impossible without smell.

There is something paradoxical about odor's contribution to taste: when odor is added to a substance that is being tasted, people do not report that its smell has increased in strength, they say instead that its *taste* has increased (Murphy, Cain, and Bartoshuk, 1977). Demonstrate this for yourself—begin eating with your nostrils held closed, then release them. Opening your nostrils means that odor will be added; but instead of experiencing this addition as smell, you will find that it is taste that has become stronger. In other words, taste and smell blend into a single experience, and this combined experience is typically referred to as "taste." One of the skills that "taste" experts develop is the knack of attending to the odors of the food or drink they are sampling. If you've ever watched a serious wine taster at work you know what we mean. First of all, wine tasters prefer to evaluate wine when it is close to room temperature, so that the odorous vapors are more abundant. To further promote the release of vapors, a taster will swirl the liquid around in the glass and will then deeply inhale the vapors with the nose placed right at the mouth of the glass. This odor information alone is often sufficient to identify the particular wine being sampled. Because wines vary along several dimensions, wine discrimination has become a popular vehicle for studying perceptual learning, the enhancement in perception brought about by practice (see, for example, Owen and Machamer, 1979). In fact, entire books have been written on the sensory evaluation of wine (Amerine and Roessler, 1983).

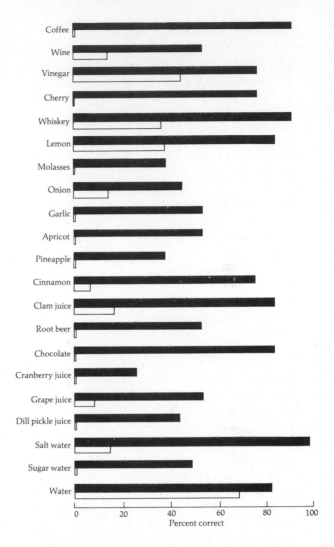

FIGURE 11.14
The percentages of subjects who could identify a substance dropped onto their tongues when they could smell the solution (shaded bars) and when they were prevented from smelling the solution (unshaded bars). (Adapted from Mozel et al., 1969.)

Summary and Preview

This examination of the "minor senses," olfaction and gustation, brings us to the end of our survey of seeing, hearing, taste, and smell. You should now have a more complete appreciation of how marvelously sensitive human beings are to the noisy, odorous, light-reflecting, tasty objects that make up their world. And you should likewise appreciate that this world is defined by the human sensory nervous system—other species with different nervous systems live in a world different from ours. The environment offers an abundance of opportunities for perception; whether one capitalizes on those opportunities depends on having receptors and brain mechanisms to register and process sensory information. Understanding perception requires studying *what* there is to be perceived (the environment as a source of stimulation) and *how* the process is implemented (the mechanisms of perception).

As stressed throughout these chapters, perception serves to guide thought and action. This means, therefore, that your perceptions of the world can be influenced by what you intend to do or what you are thinking. You've seen in this chapter and others that the evidence from your senses is often supplemented by evidence from other sources, including what you have learned about the world during previous encounters with it. In the final chapter, then, we shall consider the role of knowledge in perception and the role of perception in such complex activities as reading.

Chapter 12

Knowledge and Perception

The Greek philosopher Aristotle had many insightful things to say about perception, including the following:

Under the influence of strong feeling we are easily deceived regarding our sensations . . . for example the coward under the influence of fear and the lover under that of love have such illusions that the former owing to a trifling resemblance thinks he sees an enemy, the latter his beloved . . . men sick of a fever sometimes think they see animals on the walls owing to some slight resemblance in the figures drawn there . . . in cases where the patient is not very sick, he is still conscious of the deceptions, but where his condition is more aggravated, he even rushes upon these animals. (Parva Naturalia, *quoted in Davidoff, 1975)*

Aristotle's comments capture a very important idea: though perception does originate in the responses of the sense organs, perception can go beyond those responses. This phenomenon occurs because perception is influenced by additional information about the world,

information which supplements that provided by the senses themselves. In this chapter we shall examine various supplementary sources of information and their impact on perception.

Of the supplementary information that has an impact on perception, none is more important than the perceiver's knowledge of the world. Such knowledge arises from several different sources. One form of knowledge is the memories that come from a lifetime of experiences with objects and events in your environment. For example, by lifting objects of various sizes, you've learned that an object's size and weight are related. This information allows you to gauge, without thinking, how much effort will be needed to lift an object, even one that you have never seen before. A second form of knowledge comes from specific cues, or prompts, that immediately precede some event. To illustrate, the knowledge that a visitor is coming helps you recognize that the muffled tapping sound you hear is not the thumping of your own heart but the visitor knocking timidly on your door.* A third form of knowledge comes from the very act of perceiving. Here, perceptual information derived at one moment can help to guide and clarify subsequent perceptual judgments. For instance, once an initial sip of the dark liquid in your glass tells you that you're drinking cola, not coffee, you can use subsequent sips to determine what sort of cola it is.

All these forms of knowledge enable the perceiver to make predictions about objects and events that are likely to be encountered. Though you aren't aware of these predictions, they have a powerful influence. Generally that influence is a helpful one, since the "more we know about what is to come, the easier it is to perceive what is at hand" (Lindsay and Norman, 1977, p. 227). But knowledge, though usually helpful, can impair perception in some instances. Since perception relies on expectations about "what is to come," it will be misled whenever those expectations are wrong. To appreciate the important and intimate connection between perception and knowledge we shall have to examine both the good and the bad aspects of that connection. Though knowledge is usually subsidiary to perception, under some conditions knowledge is powerful enough to override completely what your senses tell you. Knowledge has its most powerful influence when sensory information is weak, ambiguous, or unclear. But even when sensory information is strong, unambiguous, and clear, knowledge still has an impact. In this chapter we shall discuss the ways in which various forms of knowledge influence perception.

*This seemingly impossible confusion was actually made not once but several times in rapid succession, by the noted Scottish philosopher, Thomas Reid (James, 1890, vol. 2, p. 100).

Top-Down Versus Bottom-Up

Before we discuss how and when knowledge influences perception, it will be useful to develop a framework for understanding these influences. Earlier chapters described perception as the product of a chain of events that begins with things happening in the environment and culminates in your perception of those happenings. As you saw, that view gave a satisfactory account of the phenomena discussed previously. According to this view, perception results from a one-way flow of information from the receptors upward to higher and higher stages of processing. Such a view has been characterized as **bottom-up.** As you will learn in this chapter, however, that bottom-up view must be modified in order to account for knowledge's role in perception. In effect, information from higher stages (knowledge) exerts an influence downward on earlier stages of processing. This influence is described as **top-down,** and it implies that perception is not simply the result of a one-way flow of information.

An example of the top-down influence on perception is the so-called **phonemic restoration effect.** Richard Warren (University of Wisconsin at Milwaukee) tape-recorded spoken sentences and then carefully excised one brief speech sound from each, replacing it with a nonspeech sound, such as a cough. Listeners claimed to hear not only the cough but also the excised sound (Warren, 1970; see also Samuel, 1983). In a similar vein, George Miller (1962) presented various words to listeners and asked them to identify what they heard. To make the task difficult, the words were presented in the midst of noise (such as the sound made by static on the radio). Miller presented the words either in random order or in a sentence. He found

423

UNCERTAINTY AND PERCEPTION

that in a sentence, the words were much easier to identify. To illustrate, suppose listeners heard the words "who," "some," "red," and "socks." Suppose further that another word ("bought") was presented between "who" and "some" but the listener heard only the first consonant of that word, "b." Because the words formed a sentence, information from the other words made it easier to identify the incomplete word (Lindsay and Norman, 1977, pp. 276–277). In other words, knowledge of the structure of the English language (top) helped listeners know what to expect and how best to interpret what they were hearing (bottom).

In most situations, your perceptual experience is shaped by both top-down and bottom-up influences. Sometimes the two work together, supplementing each other; at other times they are in conflict, and information of one type must be weighed against information of the other type. Let's consider first what happens when knowledge's top-down influence is minimized.

Uncertainty and Perception

One way to discover knowledge's importance in perception is to examine perception under conditions in which knowledge is minimized—that is, when people are uncertain about what to expect. Box 12.1 provides one example of uncertainty. Here are a few more everyday examples, starting with one from the sense of touch. When a person knows what part of his or her body is going to be touched, the person can feel a much more delicate touch than if he or she had no prior knowledge as to what part of the body was about to be touched (Meyer, Gross, and Teuber, 1963). Studies of hearing have produced analogous results. When a lis-

tener does not know what frequency to expect, a faint tone is harder to hear (Green, 1961). Similarly, when a stationary target begins to move, observers are slower in responding to that movement when they do not know ahead of time in what direction the target will move (Ball and Sekuler, 1980).

In the cases just considered the perceiver's lack of knowledge can be overcome very easily. For example, in the case of vision, the effects of uncertainty can be reduced if, just prior to the onset of movement, the observer gets a cue as to the direction in which the target will move (Ball and Sekuler, 1981). But presenting a misleading cue makes detection of the movement even harder. Similarly, cuing a listener about the frequency to be presented makes detection of the sound easier, while a misleading cue makes the sound harder to hear (Johnson and Hafter, 1980).

In the examples just described, the cue that eliminated uncertainty was distinct from the stimulus that had to be detected. Sometimes, however, helpful cues are provided by the very stimulus you are trying to perceive. Suppose, for example, a stranger begins talking to you but you can't understand a thing he is saying. Suddenly you realize that he's speaking English, only with a strong Eastern European accent. Realizing that you are hearing accented English helps you to understand what's being said. In other words, exposure to a brief sample of speech makes you a more capable listener.

These effects are not limited to *spoken* language; they occur just as readily with language in *written* form, as the following example illustrates. When you receive a letter from a friend whose handwriting is particularly hard to read, the letter is at first difficult to decipher; but after a while you learn the "code," making the scrawl easier to read. This common experience has also been studied systematically. In one study (Cor-

BOX 12.1
"Doctor, Is It Broken?"

The x-ray, or radiograph, is one of medicine's most important diagnostic tools. Besides detecting breaks in bones, radiographs are used to visualize tumors, benign and malignant. The interpretation of an x-ray requires not only good vision but also considerable practice. A skilled x-ray interpreter works with amazing speed and accuracy, even without knowing precisely *what* to look for or *where* to look. However, a significant number of abnormalities get overlooked. Why do such oversights occur?

To answer this question, Harold Kundel, a radiologist, and Calvin Nodine, a psychologist, recorded the eye movements of interpreters who were reading x-rays (Kundel and Nodine, 1983). Because the eye's visual acuity is not uniform over the entire retina, the interpreter must successively fixate different regions of the x-ray; failure to do so can cause her to overlook an abnormality. To guide these fixations, the interpreter draws upon several forms of knowledge (Carmody, Nodine, and Kundel, 1980). First, she must recognize what anatomical structure is depicted in the x-ray. For instance, is it a chest or is it a leg? This initial judgment establishes expectations about that structure's normal appearance. The x-ray interpreter is also guided by knowledge that particular parts of that structure are most likely to be abnormal. These parts should be fixated first and most carefully. Kundel and Nodine found that when interpreters were instructed where to look, a glance as brief as one-third of a second was sufficient for detection of the abnormality.

Still, on occasion the interpreter fixated the right spot but failed to detect the abnormality. You might say that the interpreter was looking *at* the right place but not *for* the right thing. This kind of oversight represents an effect of uncertainty such as the ones described in the text. To perform optimally, then, the interpreter should know where to look and what to look for.

coran and Rouse, 1970) observers were asked to identify words briefly flashed one at a time. Each word was either typewritten or handwritten. When successive words were all typewritten, observers were quite accurate in identifying the words. Likewise, observers were accurate when one word after another was handwritten. However, when handwritten and typewritten words were randomly intermixed, identification was much poorer. A computer metaphor can be used to explain this result: a different perceptual strategy, or "subroutine," is used to analyze typewritten material than is used to analyze handwritten material. Having to select the appropriate subroutine takes some time. Thus if the subroutine is not already in place and the observer must devote some fraction of the word's brief presentation to selecting a subroutine, less time is left for actually analyzing the word, leading to slower identification. Selection of the proper subroutine requires information about the kind of materials that need to be analyzed— handwritten or typewritten. Therefore selecting the proper subroutine requires a top-down process.

As you've seen, uncertainty can impair perception when the object or event to be detected is presented only briefly. Presumably this impairment comes about because it takes time for any top-down influence to work. Note, however, that uncertainty cannot completely override bottom-up information. For example, if you encountered a gorilla in the grocery store, you would surely recognize it quickly, no matter how unexpected the encounter.

Ambiguity and Perception

Besides uncertainty, the ambiguity of some event or object can also lead the top-down process astray, thereby impairing perception. The following dialogue from Shakespeare's *Hamlet* is not of much consequence to the drama itself, but it does provide an interesting example of the interplay between ambiguity and perception. To set the scene, Hamlet has been talking with some courtiers; Polonius enters.

POLONIUS: *My lord, the Queen would speak with you, and presently.*

HAMLET: *Do you see yonder cloud that's almost in the shape of a camel?*

POLONIUS: *By th' mass, and 'tis like a camel indeed.*

HAMLET: *Methinks it is like a weasel.*

POLONIUS: *It is back'd like a weasel.*

HAMLET: *Or like a whale?*

POLONIUS: *Very like a whale.*

HAMLET: *Then I will come to my mother by and by. [Aside] They fool me to the top of my bent.*

(Act III, Scene ii)

At first, you may be tempted to accuse Polonius of being a sycophant—a "yes-man." But look at the situation Polonius is in. With a stimulus as ambiguous as a cloud, any person *could* see a whale, a weasel, or a camel, even if that person were not trying to curry favor with the Prince of Denmark. In fact it is very easy to see many things in an ambiguous stimulus. But there are limits to what can be seen in such a stimulus; ambiguity is not a license to see *anything*. Instead, perception of ambiguous stimuli is constrained by the physical attributes that the perceiver registers. For example, Polonius probably would not have said the cloud looked like a red triangle. Let's see how perceptual processes work in the face of some particular unstructured, ambiguous stimuli.

RESOLVING VISUAL BLUR

Jerome Bruner, of the New School, and Mary Potter, of the Massachusetts Institute of Technology, created ambiguous stimuli by blurring a series of slides (Bruner and Potter, 1964). These slides depicted various scenes and objects, such as a dog standing on some grass, a traffic intersection seen in aerial view, and a fire hydrant. For each slide, Bruner and Potter slowly reduced its blur, gradually bringing it into sharper focus. Starting when the slide was extremely blurred, people kept writing down what they saw. When the slide was badly out of focus, people's descriptions were usually inaccurate; for example, a pile of earth might be mistaken for a dish of chocolate ice cream. But as the slide's focus improved, so did people's accuracy. (Test yourself using the pictures in Figure 12.1.)

Bruner and Potter found that when the initial degree of blur was great, observers often failed to recognize what they were looking at until the image was almost perfectly focused. However when the initial degree of blur was not so great, observers tended to recognize what they were looking at even when it was noticeably blurred. Why should early exposure to a high degree of blur retard later recognition of a picture? One possible explanation became clear when people expressed their thoughts aloud while looking at the pictures. No matter how blurred the picture, people had an interpretation of what some of its parts might be, and this interpretation influenced their perception of the rest of the picture (a top-down influence). When the picture was extremely blurred, visual information contradicting that interpretation did not become available for quite a while. Consequently someone initially seeing a highly blurred picture became locked into a wrong interpretation. In this case, the top-down influence retarded correct perception.

FIGURE 12.1

These four progressively blurred photographs show the same scene. Note that your ability to recognize the contents of the scene is impaired by blur. (Glyn Cloyd.)

There is evidence that the ability to capitalize on top-down information varies among individuals. Potter (1966) showed this by repeating the original experiment but testing observers ranging in age from 4 years to 19 years. For any given age, some observers tended to be rapid recognizers whereas others tended to be slow; but as shown in Figure 12.2, younger observers took about 50 percent longer to recognize the picture than did older observers. Besides differing in speed of recognition, young and old observers seemed to arrive at solutions in different ways. The older observers' descriptions formed a coherent series, with a guess at one moment evolving into another, related guess the next moment. In contrast, younger observers' descriptions consisted of a parade of unconnected guesses, often focusing on a single small detail, rather than on the entire scene. This difference between older and younger individuals suggests that experience may be necessary before top-down information can be used efficiently.

RESOLVING AUDITORY BLUR

We've just made the point that visual perception can be misled when a person is looking at a blurred picture. Likewise, auditory perception can be misled by vague, muffled sounds, as the following experiment shows. B. F. Skinner, of Harvard University, had people listen to a tape recording of low-intensity speech sounds heard against a background of noise (Skinner, 1957). Skinner describes the sound as resembling fragments of "natural speech heard

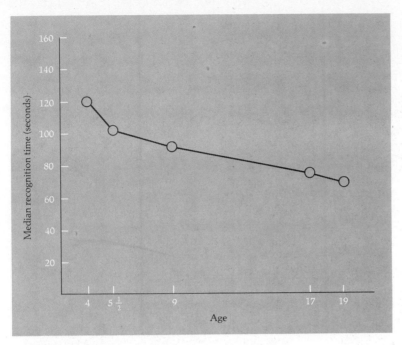

FIGURE 12.2
Median time for recognition of pictures as blur was reduced. (Adapted from Potter, 1966.)

through a wall.'' Listening to these sounds, some listeners heard a different message with each repetition. The following is one set of responses (successive responses are separated by slashes):

Do not do that/ spell the party/ have you pummeled him/ how do you do/ good-night/ you know a part/ cracker/ have you anything/ two four one eight/ call station/ sour pickles/ calm down/ keep out of it/ hobo/ do it again/ you are mine/ I knew her/. (Skinner, 1957, p. 261)

Using a tape recorder and a clean handkerchief, you can repeat Skinner's study. With the handkerchief covering your mouth so as to muffle your voice, tape-record yourself as you read in a monotone three- or four-word fragments from this book. Record a dozen fragments, letting several seconds of silence separate successive fragments. Now have someone listen to the recording played at low volume. During each pause, have the person say what is heard. Repeating this with a number of different people, you'll be surprised at the variety of interpretations you get of the same fragment. The implication is that people attempt to impose structure on ambiguous sounds, and that the structure will vary from one person to the next. But again note that the imposed structure is constrained by the physical attributes of the ambiguous stimulus. For example, the people you test will never report the muffled recording as someone singing a song.

It's commonly thought that a person's interpretation of ambiguous sensory messages reveals something about that person's motivation and interests. The Viennese psychiatrist Sigmund Freud discussed this idea in his book *The Psychopathology of Everyday Life* (Freud, 1910/1938). Although most of the errors Freud dealt with were errors of speech or memory, he did consider some to be perceptual errors. Take two examples. Freud described one woman who was so anxious about having children that she often mistook the word "stock" for the word "stork"—presumably reflecting her unconscious preoccupation with the arrival of a child. The second example pertained to Freud himself. An avid collector of antiques, Freud confessed that he saw the word "antiquities" on every shop sign that bore any resemblance to that word. Despite his sophisticated knowledge about the mind, even Sigmund Freud was apparently not immune to top-down influences.

THE RORSCHACH TEST

Some psychopathologists have exploited ambiguous stimuli to aid them in personality assessment. So-called projective tests are types of psychological tests that use ambiguous pictures and designs to tap a person's private world. Presumably, these ambiguous stimuli provide an outlet for the person's private fantasies and perceptions. The best-known projective test is the one developed in the 1920s by Hermann Rorschach, a Swiss psychiatrist. As you may know, the **Rorschach test** consists of a set of inkblots, which the person is asked to describe. Some psychiatrists believe that they can draw inferences about a person's mental state if that person describes seeing something bizarre—such as a bloody axe buried in a man's head. For our purposes these bizarre responses are less important than the fact that people can give detailed descriptions of these inkblots—proof that even very ambiguous stimuli can provide

enough structure to fuel perception (Wertheimer, 1957).

THE AUTOKINETIC EFFECT

A stimulus even less structured than an inkblot—namely a single point of light in a dark room—can be used as a projective test. Suppose you are seated in a dark room looking at a small, stationary spot of light—such as the glow from a cigarette. Under these conditions, the spot of light will appear to drift about (Matin and MacKinnon, 1964). This illusory motion is called the **autokinetic effect** ("autokinetic" means "self-moving"), and some people believe that it results from involuntary drifting movements of the eye. Certain drugs, such as marijuana or alcohol, increase the autokinetic effect (Sharma and Moskowitz, 1972), perhaps because these drugs increase the eye's tendency to drift.

Rechtschaffen and Mednick (1955) exploited the autokinetic effect as a projective test. Observers sat in a totally dark room, about 2.5 meters from a very small, stationary light. They were told that the experiment would test their ability to see the words that would be written by the movements of the small light. Though the light never actually moved, the autokinetic effect did produce considerable illusory movement. Every one of the nine observers reported that the light had written at least two words, and one observer reported seeing forty-three words. Some of the words were innocuous (such as "the" or "and"), others were highly personal. In fact, after "reading" the words, one observer became very upset and demanded to know where Rechtschaffen and Mednick had gotten all that information about him. We don't mean to encourage prying into other people's business, but you may wish to try this fascinating projective test on your friends. They may find it hard to believe that the light didn't really "write" all that stuff about them.

Autokinetic "writing" demonstrates how important suggestion can be when perceiving impoverished stimuli. Seeing words is not an inevitable consequence of autokinetic motion. In fact, most people simply see random motions, not words. Rechtschaffen and Mednick's viewers were different though, because they had been told to expect the light to write something. When they experienced illusory motion, the viewers naturally tried to decipher what the light was writing. Under the same circumstances, suggestion could just as well have caused viewers to see outline drawings or the messages on traffic signs. Box 12.2 describes other situations in which suggestion plays a powerful role in perception.

BOX 12.2
Did I See It or Just Imagine It?

A mental image of an object can so strongly resemble the object itself that you may confuse the two. One of the most original demonstrations of this confusion was provided by an early experimental psychologist, Cheves Perky (1910). While seated in a completely dark room, Perky's observers stared steadily at a screen some distance away. On a signal from Perky, the observer conjured up a mental image of some particular object, such as a banana. While the observer generated the requested image, Perky surreptitiously cast on the screen a dim image matching the object that the observer was trying to imagine. For instance, when an observer was told to imagine a banana, a banana-shaped, yellow image was cast on the screen. Prior testing by Perky had indicated that this image would be just barely visible. To further mimic a mental image, the real image on the screen was jiggled slightly, producing a shimmering quality. (If all of this sounds complicated, it's because it was; three people were required to run Perky's apparatus.)

Twenty-seven different observers were asked to describe various "imagined" shapes. Twenty-four observers never realized that they were *seeing* things, not just *imagining* them. (An experimenter's error allowed the other three observers to catch on to Perky's deception.) When the experiment was finished, "the observer was asked if he was 'quite sure that he had imagined all these things.' The question almost always aroused surprise, and other times indignation" (Perky, 1910, p. 431). The observers' descriptions of their "imaginings" are remarkable. One person volunteered, "I can get it (the image) steadily so long as I keep my mind absolutely on it." Another commented, "The banana is up on end; I must have been thinking of it growing." Many observers unwittingly combined what they saw with what they imagined: one reported seeing a lemon (the real image) lying on a table (a mental image); another reported seeing a leaf (a real image) covered with red veins (a mental image). Even after they were shown the entire setup and told about having been fooled, many observers still refused to believe that they had actually seen something real and argued steadfastly that they had imagined it all. More recently, some of Perky's findings have been followed up (Segal and Fusella, 1970; Reeves, 1981).

Confusions are not restricted to mix-ups between mental images and perceptions. Things you know or remember can also be confused with what your senses tell you, and recent studies show how easily such confusions can occur. Elizabeth Loftus, of the University of Washington, has shown that observers cannot discriminate between what they've actually seen and what they're told they've seen (but haven't). Both sources of information—sensory and nonsensory—blend inextricably together. In one study, Loftus showed observers a series of slides depicting various stages of an automobile accident. Afterward, observers answered questions about the accident. Some of the questions were designed to implant incorrect information in the observers' minds. For example,

(*Continued on next page*)

the question "What was the color of the car that sped past the 'yield' sign?" implanted the idea that a traffic sign at the accident site was a "yield" sign, when in fact it was a "stop" sign. Later, the observers were shown two slides and had to select the one that accurately portrayed the accident scene. One slide contained a "stop" sign, the other a "yield" sign. Most observers incorrectly chose the slide showing the "yield" sign.

Moreover, when warned that they might have been exposed to misleading information, the observers denied the possibility and insisted that they had really seen the "yield" sign (Loftus, Miller, and Burns, 1978).

Loftus's research says something important about the credibility of courtroom testimony. An eye witness to an accident or to a crime may end up reporting in court not just what was seen but some combination of what was seen

and what some lawyer was able to plant in the witness's memory (Loftus, 1979). Above and beyond its practical implications, Loftus's research reinforces the point made earlier by Perky: people sometimes cannot distinguish between the products of their senses and the products of nonsensory processes. No wonder, then, that perceptual experience can be so strongly influenced by those other forces.

BORING'S AMBIGUOUS FIGURE

The power of an unambiguous stimulus to bias the perception of an ambiguous one has been vividly demonstrated with varying versions of Edwin Boring's ambiguous figure, which you encountered earlier, in Chapter 4 (Figure 4.19). Recall that the figure could be seen either as a young woman facing away from the viewer or as an old hag facing toward the viewer. That figure is reproduced here as the middle panel of Figure 12.3. On the left is a version of the drawing that makes it more clearly depict a young woman; on the right a version that makes it more clearly depict an old woman.

It has been found that when observers are shown only the ambiguous drawing (middle panel), the majority initially see an old woman (Leeper, 1935). However, this tendency can be dramatically altered by having the observer look first at one of the less ambiguous versions of the drawing. When people are first shown the left panel of Figure 12.3 and then the middle panel, virtually all of them initially see the middle panel (the ambiguous drawing) as depicting a young woman. Conversely, when people are first shown the right panel of Figure 12.3

and then the middle panel, virtually all of them then see the ambiguous drawing as depicting an old woman. In other words, exposure to either unambiguous drawing can "prime" the subsequent perception of the ambiguous drawing. Incidentally, this priming effect requires visual experience; it cannot be produced by verbal descriptions emphasizing either the young woman or the old woman (Leeper, 1935).

FAULTY PERCEPTION FROM STRUCTURED STIMULI

So far, this section has considered how perception deals with stimuli that are inherently unstructured or ambiguous. Sometimes, however, the stimulus contains a good deal of structure, but some defect in the perceiver degrades the stimulus, reducing its perceived structure. For example, an uncorrected myopic eye forces the rest of the visual system to work with a blurred, ill-defined image—a condition resembling the one represented in the top two panels of Figure 12.1. Similarly, a defective ear forces the rest of the auditory system to work with muffled

FIGURE 12.3
An example of the way priming biases perception.

input—a condition resembling that in the Skinner experiment described earlier. Moreover, impaired vision or hearing resulting from defects in the sensory organ can lead to serious psychological disturbance. Let's consider one example.

Paranoia is a mental disorder characterized by delusions of persecution. Although the idea is controversial, some psychiatrists have attributed paranoia to hearing impairment, since these two conditions are sometimes associated (Zimbardo, Andersen, and Kabat, 1981). It is certainly easy to understand why paranoia and hearing loss might be causally linked. People can gradually develop a hearing loss without being aware of it. Suppose that such a person is surrounded by people who are talking to one another at a normal conversational level. The hearing-impaired person will have difficulty understanding what the others are saying and may conclude that they are whispering to keep him from hearing. If he asks them why they are whispering, they deny that they are. After a while, all the "secretive" discussions may be construed as part of a

plot. Note that the situation would be quite different if the person were aware of his impaired hearing. So the irrational condition termed "paranoia" may in some cases result from the rational impulse to explain difficulty in hearing.

Philip Zimbardo, a psychologist at Stanford University, tested this possible link between hearing loss and paranoia by simulating a temporary hearing loss in a dozen college students (Zimbardo, Andersen, and Kabat, 1981). He did this by hypnotizing a group of students and implanting the posthypnotic suggestion that they were partially deaf. After coming out of hypnosis, half of the students *were* told that they would be temporarily losing some of their hearing; the other half *were not* told this. A well-rehearsed conversation was then carried on in the presence of each "hearing-impaired" student. This conversation included laughter and grimaces designed to pique the interest of the "hearing-impaired" listener.

Within a day, those individuals who were unaware of their hearing impairment developed significant paranoid tendencies in their thinking, emotional responses, and social behavior. In contrast, individuals who were aware of their hearing loss showed no such tendency. Incidentally, Zimbardo does not claim that all paranoid delusions spring from an unrecognized loss of hearing. However, his research supports the possibility that paranoid tendencies in some middle-aged and older people may develop out of the gradual hearing impairment that often accompanies aging (recall Chapter 10).

Familiarity and Perception

There's little doubt that familiarity can sharpen perception. The experienced bird watcher, for instance, can distinguish among species of birds that to most people look indistinguishable. Simply being exposed to a variety of interesting stimuli can sharpen one's capacity to discriminate among them. Eleanor Gibson called this process **perceptual differentiation** (Gibson, 1969). Differentiation allows one to detect properties, patterns, and distinctive features previously ignored. For example a novice wine drinker may order "white wine" and be quite content with just about any wine (so long as its color is right). In fact the novice would have difficulty telling one variety from another. A more seasoned wine drinker, however, would specify a particular variety of white wine and would know if the wine had a taste that was unusual for that variety (see Owen, 1984).

Adult humans, incidentally, are not the only group whose perceptions can become differentiated. Recall the preferential looking procedure described in Chapters 5 and 6. There we noted that human infants prefer to look at novel stimuli and tend to ignore stimuli that they have seen many times before. Monkeys exhibit the same behavior. Nicholas Humphrey (1974a) took advantage

of this ability, to determine what animals would be classed as similar by monkeys and what animals would not. When shown a series of pictures of other monkeys, a monkey looked at each picture as though it were novel and interesting. This lack of habituation implies that the monkey distinguished among members of its own species. However, monkeys lumped together members of other species. Once a monkey had initially seen a picture of some domestic animal (such as a pig), the monkey quickly lost interest not only in other pigs, but also in other four-legged species as well (such as cows).

However, several months' exposure to pictures of various animals changed the situation drastically. Following such exposure, the monkeys distinguished not only one species from another, but also among members of each species. Humphrey concludes that in some circumstances "insensitivity to visual detail seems to be simply a consequence of visual inexperience" (Humphrey, 1974a, p. 114). The aphorism claims that "familiarity breeds contempt"; but in Humphrey's study, "familiarity bred perceptual differentiation."

Lester Krueger (1975) has reviewed the many other ways in which familiarity affects perception. While the existence of such effects is beyond question, there are a number of unsettled issues concerning the exact way in which such effects come about. For instance, does familiarity actually alter what you *see*, or does familiarity alter your ability to *use* what you've seen?

REDUNDANCY

As just discussed, repetition of sensory experiences enhances their familiarity. Repetition also makes the sensory input less informative—you know what to expect. Other times, although the information is not repetitive, it still does not add much to what you already know. Such information contains **redundancy.** Here's a simple example. In English, the letter "u" is redundant after a "q." Once you have seen the "q" you know what follows. But information may be redundant even if it is not as perfectly predictable as the "u" after a "q." In fact, there are varying degrees of redundancy, and methods have been developed to quantify them (Garner, 1962). To learn what sorts of redundancy sensory information contains, consider the sense of sight.

You use your eyes to view objects or collections of objects. Like the objects themselves, such collections can be natural, such as a flock of birds, or artificial, such as a group of buildings. Whether natural or artificial, the objects are seldom randomly arranged; instead, they occcur in predictable arrangements. To illustrate, suppose that someone is looking out the window at some object you cannot see. As soon as she tells you that the object has leaves, you know that it probably also has branches and a trunk. You make this educated guess be-

cause certain objects tend to occur together. As the following study shows, perception can capitalize on these regularities.

CONTEXT: WORD AND OBJECT SUPERIORITY

Nearly one hundred years ago, James McKeen Cattell described a strange phenomenon. Cattell was interested in how long it took to perceive letters, words, colors, and pictures of objects. In one study, he pasted letters on a revolving drum (see Figure 12.4) and determined the rate at which the letters could be read aloud as they passed by a slit in a screen. Cattell found that it took about twice as long to read unrelated words as it did to read words that formed a sentence. He also found a similar disadvantage for reading unrelated letters compared to letters that formed a word (Cattell, 1886, p. 64). The relative ease with which letters can be read if they are embedded in a word rather than presented with unrelated letters is known as the **word superiority effect.**

FIGURE 12.4
Cattell's apparatus for testing the word superiority effect.

Since Cattell's original report, dozens of follow-ups have confirmed the original finding. But what causes word superiority? One possibility is that the surrounding letters of a word make it easier to *deduce* the remaining letters. For example, once you've seen the letters "LABE," the chances are good that the next letter will be "L." In this case, the letter recognition might be expedited because the prior letters reduced the need to spend much time on the last letter.

Various studies have used methods more sophisticated than Cattell's to demonstrate that the word superiority effect cannot be chalked up entirely to deduction (Reicher, 1969; Wheeler, 1970). These studies instead suggest that familiarity directly affects the process of extracting visual information. In one study (Johnston and McClelland, 1973), observers were given a brief presentation of either a word or a single letter. In either case, this test stimulus was followed by a patterned masker that obliterated any after-image (see Figure 12.5). After this sequence of events, the observer was given two alter-natives and had to pick the one that corresponded to the test stimulus. For example, if the word "COIN" had been the test stimulus, the observer might have to choose between the alternatives "COIN" and "JOIN." Since either "C" or "J" could form a word with the remaining three letters ("OIN"), the observer could not use the other letters to deduce the correct answer. Instead, a correct answer required actually being able to see the first letter clearly enough to decipher whether it was a "C" or a "J." The letter that distinguished the two alternatives could occupy any position in those words (for example, "BENT" or "BUNT"). Thus the observer could not just attend to one particular position in a test word. When the test stimulus consisted of a single letter, such as "J," the observer again had to choose from two alternatives, such as "C" and "J." Again, the observer could not do better than chance unless he or she had seen the letter.

The results were typical of many word superiority studies. Observers were more accurate in choosing between "COIN" and

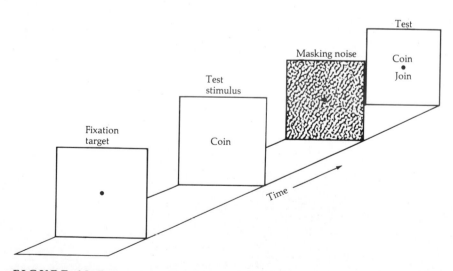

FIGURE 12.5
The sequence of events seen by observers in the study by Johnston and McClelland (1973).

"JOIN" than they were in choosing between "C" and "J." Although trials with single letters presumably required less processing, observers were nonetheless more accurate on trials on which they had to process all four letters (Johnston and McClelland, 1973). This finding demonstrates that when you see a word, you do not process each letter separately and in isolation from the rest. In fact, observers who try to restrict their attention to just one letter of a word are less accurate in perceiving that letter than when they do attend to the word within which the letter was embedded (Johnston and McClelland, 1974). Somehow, a large unit (such as a word) may be perceived more accurately than any of its isolated component parts (such as a letter).

The perceptual advantage enjoyed by some larger units is not restricted to words. In fact, James Pomerantz, of the State University of New York at Buffalo, has reviewed many analogous studies that made use of *figural* units and groupings. To take one example from Pomerantz's research (1981), observers were shown a set of slanted lines such as those in Figure 12.6. The observers had to identify the single item that was perceptually distinct from the other three. For each presentation, Pomerantz measured how long it took to make this judgment. On average, observers took 1.9

seconds to spot the odd element in stimuli such as those shown in panel A (here, the negative diagonal at the lower right). Next Pomerantz created a more complicated stimulus by adding to each diagonal an "L" shaped figure (see panel B). This addition produced the stimuli shown in panel C. When observers had to spot the odd item in this new set, they took only 0.75 seconds—65 percent faster than with the "simpler" stimuli. Pomerantz called this improvement in performance a **configural superiority effect.** A related study (Weisstein and Harris, 1974), found that it is easier to identify a briefly flashed line when that line is part of a drawing of a three-dimensional object. Both results imply that the ease with which some stimulus component is processed depends on the context of that component. You should be able to appreciate the analogy between these configural superiority effects and the word superiority effect discussed earlier.

However, adding elements to a simple figure does not always make discrimination easier. Consider the stimuli shown in Figure 12.7. Again, when Pomerantz's observers selected the odd item from a set of single parentheses such as those in the left panel, response times averaged 2.4 seconds. When a single, horizontal parenthesis was added to each vertical one, the stimulus in the right

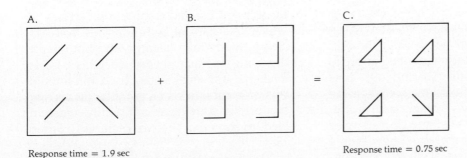

Response time = 1.9 sec   Response time = 0.75 sec

FIGURE 12.6
Displays producing the configural superiority effect.

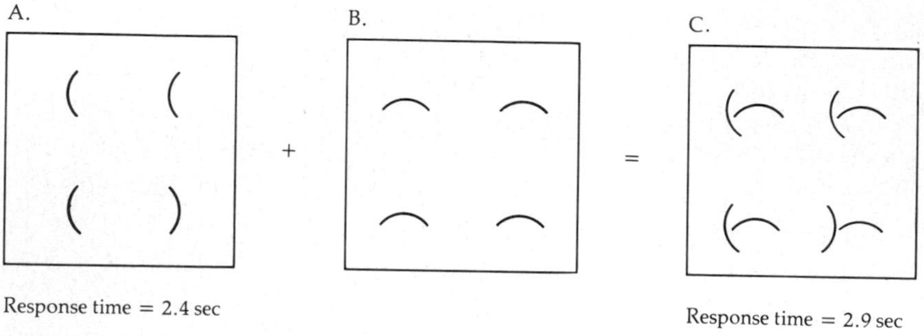

A.

Response time = 2.4 sec

C.

Response time = 2.9 sec

FIGURE 12.7

Displays producing a configural "inferiority" effect.

panel was created. When observers had to select the odd item in this new set, they took 23 percent longer. These conditions, rather than producing a configural superiority effect, produce the opposite. Pomerantz suggests that because the added horizontal elements did not form perceptual groups with the vertical ones, no new features emerged to aid perception.

To summarize, the ability to recognize an object is altered by the object's context. Sometimes context makes an object more recognizable, at other times it makes the object less recognizable. At the moment no one knows how to predict all the effects of various contexts, but Pomerantz (1981) and Julesz and Schumer (1981, pp. 594–599) outline methods for making some predictions.

NATURAL SCENES

Thus far, our examples have focused on relatively simple stimuli. How well, though, do the principles already described apply to more complex stimuli? To find out, let's consider some studies of how scenes of the real world are perceived. In one such study, Irving Biederman, of the State University of New York at Buffalo, measured how long a person took to extract visual information from photographs of various indoor and outdoor scenes (Biederman et al., 1974). The pho-

tographs of scenes were presented for varying durations, followed by a masking stimulus that erased any lingering pictorial information. Observers were queried about the general nature of the scene as well as about the presence of particular objects in that scene.

Even when photographs were presented for as little as one-tenth of a second, observers were able to describe the overall nature of the scene as well as to identify nearly half of the objects contained in the scene. How can so much information be extracted from such a complex stimulus in so short a time? For one thing, real-world scenes are full of the redundancies we mentioned earlier. Consequently, seeing any one object provides a clue about what else is present, particularly in nearby locations. To see how important these redundancies really are, Biederman created real-world scenes in which the natural redundancies were reduced. Biederman began with photographs depicting various scenes such as streets, kitchens, and desk tops. Each photograph was then cut into six rectangular pieces, and the pieces were then randomly reassembled, as shown in the two pictures in Figure 12.8.

Biederman's observers had difficulty describing these random scenes, and they also had difficulty identifying objects contained

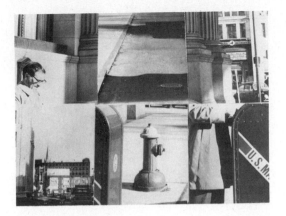

FIGURE 12.8
Scrambled and unscrambled scenes. (From Biederman et al., 1973.)

in them. Though the process of scrambling merely rearranged objects without splitting any of them, disrupting their normal relations nonetheless made the individual objects more difficult to see. Evidently, observers use the normal relations among objects to speed perception of a scene and its components. This conclusion is sup-

ported by another of Biederman's studies (Biederman, 1981). When the natural relations among objects are violated, rather than simply scrambled (see Figure 12.9), observers have difficulty detecting the violation in brief presentations (Biederman, Mezzanotte, and Rabinowitz, 1982). But once the violations have been detected, people spend

FIGURE 12.9
In this picture, the presence of the floating sofa is inconsistent with the natural relations among the rest of the objects. (From Biederman et al., 1982.)

more time examining those unexpected parts of the scene, as a study by Geoffrey Loftus and Norman Mackworth (1978) revealed. They measured how observers fixated various parts of scenes, half without surprises (such as the farm scene in the top panel of Figure 12.10) and half with surprises (such as the modified farm scene in the bottom panel of Figure 12.10, in which an octopus has taken the place of the tractor). Loftus

FIGURE 12.10

Two farm scenes, one without surprises and one with. (Adapted from Loftus and Mackworth, 1978.)

and Mackworth found that viewers tend to fixate surprising elements (such as the octopus) before they fixate nonsurprising elements (such as the tractor). Moreover, viewers fixate the surprising elements for longer periods—in effect doing a "double take." Considered together, these studies show that a person's expectancies about the natural relations among objects make it easier to recognize those objects.

PERSPECTIVE

We've just seen that object recognition is enhanced when objects appear in their normal relation to one another. This means that people have expectancies about the appearance of scenes as a whole. Moreover, people seem to have strong expectancies about individual objects, and these expectancies are reflected in the mental representations they have of particular objects. Stephen Palmer, of the University of California, has studied these representations by showing people pictures of various common objects, such as chairs, houses, grand pianos, teapots, and horses (Palmer, Rosch, and Chase, 1981). Each object was photographed from twelve different perspectives, including front, side, back, and top. A set of perspectives for one object is shown in Figure 12.11. For each object, Palmer found the perspective that was rated most typical for that object. Figure 12.12 shows the most typical perspective for each of the objects studied.

Palmer then tried to test whether or not objects were most easily recognized when seen from their most typical perspective. When observers had to name the objects portrayed in various photographs, they did in fact take much less time when the perspective was typical than when it was not.

FIGURE 12.11
A single object seen from twelve different perspectives. (From Palmer et al., 1981.)

FIGURE 12.12

Twelve different objects seen from their most typical perspectives. (From Palmer et al., 1981.)

Perhaps pictures of an object taken from atypical perspectives are less easily recognized because observers do not anticipate seeing the object from those perspectives. Considered in this way, the effects of perspective on recognition represent another example of how stimulus familiarity/unfamiliarity influences perception.

This section has emphasized how visual information is extracted from natural scenes and artificial displays. The nature of the extraction process varies with the viewer's goals and with the character of the scene or display. When information is to be extracted from displays of visible language, the extraction process is called *reading*. But the term "reading" is not restricted to what you do with words printed on a page; the same term can be used to describe what you do when you examine a map, study someone's facial expression, or interpret a musical score (see Box 12.3). The parallels between reading and other forms of sophisticated visual exploration are not accidental, since reading may have evolved out of those other visual skills. After all, long before members of our species had to cope with visible language, they were using their eyes and brains to wring information out of their visual world.

Perceptual Aspects of Reading

As you read this sentence, your eye movements and fixations control the rate at which you take in information from the printed page. Ordinarily, you vary the movements of your eyes in order to match your comprehension of what you're reading. Thus it's possible to learn a lot about reading by studying readers' eye movements and fixa-

BOX 12.3
Reading Music

Printed words and a musical score use very different symbols and rules for conveying their respective messages. Nonetheless, reading a sentence requires some of the same skills that you'd need in order to read the bars of music shown below.

When you read words, what you have just read provides a context that helps you to anticipate, or infer, what you are about to read. When reading music, a person makes similar inferences, as has been shown by John Sloboda (1976). He took various passages of music and purposely changed some of the notes. Then he asked trained musicians who had never seen these passages before to play them on the piano. Sloboda was interested in whether people would play the notes as written or would restore the passage to its original form. Since any

particular note on its own is neither correct nor incorrect, only the context provided by the unaltered notes could guide any restorations.

Sloboda tested several musicians who were proficient sight readers. Each was given several different baroque and classical pieces for the piano, none of which had been previously seen or heard by the participants. In each piece, Sloboda introduced a number of changes by raising or lowering the pitch of a note within the same musical stave. He found that playing of the unaltered notes was quite accurate: only 2 percent of them were misplayed. However, 40 percent of the altered notes were misplayed. These "errors" were actually corrections, of course, since most of them restored the music to its original, unaltered form. These corrections suggest that the musicians were guided

by inferences derived from the structure of the music.

You probably believe the adage that "practice makes perfect." But Sloboda's study challenges that adage. After the original data were collected, the same musicians got a second chance to play each piece. Though the percentage of errors on the unaltered notes *decreased* somewhat (a result that is consistent with the adage), the percentage of errors on the altered notes *increased*. Evidently, playing the piece a second time established even stronger expectations about what the notes should be. You make similar inferences as you read, which explains why you probably missed many of the typographical errors in this book. In reading as well as in music, then, your expectations of what you *should* see can blind you to what is really there.

tions. Exactly what do your eyes do when you read? Recall from Chapter 8 that your eyes jump, or saccade, whenever your gaze shifts from one object to another, and that your eyes are relatively still between saccades. As just noted, reading words is much like reading a map or reading someone's face. All these varieties of reading require a mix

of saccades and fixations. The number of saccades and the duration of fixations depends on a reader's skill and on the difficulty of the text (Rayner, 1978). We'll confine the discussion to the behavior of a skilled reader (such as yourself) who is reading moderately difficult material (such as this text).

As you read a single line of this paragraph, your eyes make about five saccades. Between saccades, your eyes fixate every word except the smallest ones (such as "the"), which are usually skipped (Rayner, 1978). On average, a fixation lasts one-quarter of a second, although fixations can range from as little as one-tenth of a second to more than half a second. The actual duration of fixation increases when the word is uncommon, complicated, or unexpected. In addition, the distance traveled by a saccade can vary from just two letters to as many as eighteen letters. Finally, the direction of saccades also varies. About 90 percent of the time, a saccade moves your gaze rightward, to a word you haven't already looked at. Occasionally, though, you make a leftward, or regressive, saccade to recheck a word you've already read and perhaps misinterpreted. Of course, you also make a large leftward saccade at the end of each line.

To understand how you acquire information while reading, we need to consider two questions. First, how fast is the textual information taken in while you're reading? And second, what accounts for the variability among saccades while you're reading? As you know, the eyes move very fast during a saccade, so most processing of visual information must occur during the fixations between saccades. But the entire duration of any fixation cannot be devoted exclusively to text processing, since the visual system has more to do than this. Decisions have to be made about where to move the eyes next, and those decisions must be relayed to the saccadic control system. What part of a fixation, then, is devoted to analyzing the fixated word and what part to programming the next saccade?

Keith Rayner, of the University of Massachusetts, answered this question by using a computer to present text on a television screen (Rayner et al., 1981). While a person read the text, the person's eye movements were registered by the computer, which in turn used that information to modify what appeared on the television screen. In particular, whenever the reader's eyes fixated a portion of the text, a masking stimulus covered the letters in that portion. This scheme is depicted in Figure 12.13. When the mask came on immediately after the eyes began fixating (a condition that resembles trying to read without a fovea), reading was difficult. But when the mask was delayed by as little as one-twentieth of a second, people had little trouble reading the text. This shows that only a small fraction of the entire fixa-

FIGURE 12.13

Setup used by Rayner et al. (1981) for studying the ability to read without central vision.

tion duration is required to encode the text. Incidentally, if this seems like a very short time to do so much, recall from Biederman's study that a person gets the gist of a complex scene in a comparably short time. Rayner's results suggest that the bulk of a fixation period is spent programming the next saccade. Recognizing this, other researchers (Biederman et al., 1981) have suggested that reading would be considerably faster if the visual system were relieved of this programming chore. In fact this has been accomplished by using a computer that presents words one after another, all in the same spatial position (Sperling et al., 1971). With this mode of presentation, an observer needs to fixate just one position, eliminating any time spent on saccadic programming.

These findings make it clear that people can process text very rapidly during reading. But what exactly are they processing? While reading this page, you probably have a sense that each line (or perhaps even the entire paragraph) is focused sharply. But this must be an illusion, since only the very center of your retina allows good acuity. For example, without use of the foveas, one observer in Rayner's studies (McConkie and Rayner, 1975; Rayner and Bertera, 1979) misread the sentence "The pretty bracelet attracted much attention" as "The priest brought much ammunition." Such errors are not surprising, since these people were reading with retinal regions that could specify only the overall length and shape of words but could not clearly identify each letter.

When the foveas are available, though, how many letters does a person see clearly at any one moment? To answer this question, one could determine how reading is affected when the number of letters displayed at any moment is reduced. So long as the number of letters being displayed exceeds the number being used by the reader, reading speed should be unaffected. To produce this situation, Rayner programmed the computer to reveal only that portion of the text on which the person fixated, masking all other portions with small *x*'s. Thus as the person's eyes moved, new letters were constantly being revealed. This procedure, illustrated in Figure 12.14, gave people the impression that they were reading through a "window" that moved along in synchrony with their eyes.

When the window was extremely narrow (so that people saw just one letter at a time), they could read correctly about 90 percent of the words. Needless to say, though, reading under these conditions was slowed.

FIGURE 12.14
Setup used by Rayner et al. (1981) for studying the ability to read with only central vision.

As the window widened to include seven or nine letters, entire words could be read at once, enabling error-free performance. However, reading was still slower than normal. Reading did not even reach normal speed until the window was wide enough to reveal about four words. Presumably, readers use words to the right of fixation to guide decisions about the next saccade. Though only dimly perceived, these words furnish a preview of what will be encountered on the next fixation.

You can demonstrate to yourself how important peripheral vision is in reading. Take a 5 × 8 file card and cut a rectangular "window" in it one-half inch wide and one-quarter inch high. Orient the card so that the window's larger dimension is vertical, then place the card over some page in this book. When the window is properly aligned on the page, you will be able to see just about one word at a time through the window. Move the card along the line of text as you try to read. After you've practiced a while, have a friend measure how long it takes you to read a passage of text 100 words long. Now, using new text, repeat this test with a window large enough to expose four words at a time. Comparing your reading speeds with the two windows, you'll discover that peripheral vision does indeed play an important part in reading.

Marcel Just and Patricia Carpenter, of Carnegie Mellon University, have identified the major processes involved in reading and have summarized them in the flow chart shown in Figure 12.15 (Just and Carpenter, 1980). Note that a number of the processes represented are top-down ones of the kind mentioned earlier in this chapter. For example, the right-hand box, "Long-Term Memory," includes rules about letter shape (orthography), the normal structures used in writing (discourse structure), and background information for what is being read (episodic knowledge). As each new word is encountered, these top-down processes guide the reader.

If you are reading an ordinary novel, these top-down influences can be enormously helpful in processing the text. To give a simple example, after reading "John hit the nail with a," there is little uncertainty about the next word, making it easier for you to process "hammer." However, certain books minimize the usefulness of top-down influences, forcing you to deal with each word, one at a time. The following brief passage from James Joyce's *Finnegans Wake* illustrates what we have in mind. First read it silently. Then read it aloud, listening carefully to yourself.

. . . she thawght a knogg came to the dowanstairs dour at that howr to peirce the yare and dowandshe went, schritt be schratt, to see was it Schweep's mingerals or Shuhorn the posth with a tillycramp for Hemself and Co, Esquara, or them four hoarsemen on their apolkaloops, Norreys, Soothbys, Yates and Welks . . . (Joyce, 1939/1967, p. 480)

Reading this passage was difficult because your expectations were of little help.

In other conditions, expectations actually get in the way. Suppose you've just read the words "There were tears in her brown." Usually you'd interpret the word "tears" as referring to liquid produced by the lacrimal gland, rather than as referring to a rip in something. This interpretation leads you to expect the next word to be "eyes." So on encountering the word "dress" you fixate that word longer than you normally would. This kind of sentence has been called a "garden path" sentence (Carpenter and Daneman, 1981) because its early part leads the reader astray—down the proverbial garden path. If a word (such as "tears") has several meanings, the reader selects among them according to rules, or expectations, that maximize the chances of being right. For ex-

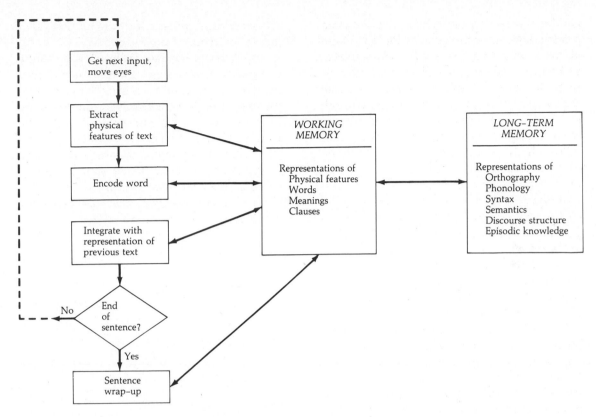

FIGURE 12.15
Schematic diagram of the major processes involved in reading comprehension.
(Adapted from Just and Carpenter, 1980.)

ample, a common meaning is usually selected over a less common one. Or if only one meaning has the grammatical form required by the phrase (say, a noun), that meaning is selected. Presumably the errors revealed by garden path sentences reflect these normally helpful selection factors.

Wayne Shebilske, of the United States National Research Council, suggests that research on reading may help writers produce textbooks that are easier to read and understand (Shebilske, 1980). For one thing, writers need to recognize that spoken language differs in important ways from written language. The difference is illustrated by the

difficulty one encounters in reading transcripts of spoken language—as when taped conversations held in the White House were transcribed and published several years ago. Besides being shocked at what was said, many people were surprised by the poor grammar and incomplete sentences. Ordinarily, speakers can get away with such lapses and still be easily understood. The reason is that spoken language consists not only of the words and phrases spoken but also of gestures and intonations (recall our discussion of speech perception in Chapter 10). These auxiliary dimensions of spoken language cannot be captured in a transcript.

A reader, therefore, is handicapped in comparison to a listener. As a result, the reader needs additional help—such as explicit transitions between one idea and another, and punctuation that parses the sentence into meaningful phrases. By the same token, ungrammatical writing is easy to spot because the reader can go back and reread it; ungrammatical speech, once uttered, is gone forever—unless tape-recorded.

Perception Without Knowledge

One theme running throughout this chapter is that knowledge shapes perceptual experience. Implied, of course, is an interaction between the neural events underlying perception and the neural events underlying knowledge. Up to this point, however, we've made no attempt to speculate about the neural basis of this interaction. Though not much is yet known about that basis, a glimpse into it can be obtained by studying people with certain neurological disorders. Such disorders disrupt knowledge in a way that severely impairs some perceptual functions while leaving many others intact. People with these disorders may perceive normally but be unable to make sense of what they perceive. Generically known as **agnosias** (from the Latin, meaning "without knowledge") these disorders take many different forms, depending on which neural structures have been damaged. To see what perception without knowledge might be like, consider one particularly interesting type of agnosia, known as **prosopagnosia.** In this condition, a patient can see and describe another person's face but cannot recognize whose face it is, even if the person is a close relative. The following case involves a fairly typical patient who suffered from cerebral lesions of uncertain origin:

When her husband or mother visited her, she failed to recognize them immediately, and only when a conversation was begun did she identify her visitors. When she was shown photographs of her two older children of preschool age, she failed to identify them; when she was told that these were indeed her children, she remarked that "they don't look like they should." Her failure in facial recognition extended to public personalities such as television stars. When watching television, she was unable to identify performers who were well-known to her until they spoke or sang. (Benton, 1980, p. 178)

Most patients diagnosed as prosopagnosic can distinguish between faces and other objects, and when looking at two faces side by side they can tell them apart. Their problem seems to be an inability to identify *who* that face belongs to.

Actually, there is reason to believe that patients suffering from prosopagnosia may have more generalized problems. Damasio, Damasio, and van Hoesen (1982) point out that the inability to recognize faces of relatives and friends is so overwhelming that other types of recognition losses are likely to be overlooked. They describe patients who are unable to recognize other familiar things besides faces. For instance, they tell of a bird watcher who could no longer identify birds, and a farmer who could no longer recognize his own cows. The three patients whom they studied in detail had similar kinds of losses. They also describe a patient who could not recognize her own car in a parking lot. She could locate her car only by systematically examining the license plate numbers on every car until she found her license number; the *appearance* of the car was of no help to her. Thus instead of a loss restricted to recognition of faces, prosopagnosia may involve a more general impairment of the ability to recognize complex objects (Damasio, Damasio, and van Hoesen, 1982). Regardless of its precise cause, prosopagnosia, like other agnosias, demonstrates how incomplete perception is without knowledge.

Summary

This chapter has emphasized the important role that knowledge plays in shaping perceptual experience. William James made this point well when he wrote, "Whilst part of what we perceive comes through our senses from the object before us, another part (and it may be the larger part) always comes . . . out of our own head" (James, 1890, vol. 2, p. 103). The knowledge that influences perception takes many forms—including uncertainty, ambiguity, redundancy, context, and familiarity. Taken together, these various forms of knowledge maximize the effectiveness of the actions that are dictated by perception. As stated in the first chapter of this book, perception's chief role is to guide one's actions within the world. Thus knowledge of the world not only shapes perception but also imbues perception with value and utility.

Appendix

Some Behavioral Methods for Studying Perception

Ever since our species first appeared on the scene, *Homo sapiens* has used various behavioral methods for studying perception. Naturally, our early ancestors had to resort to rather informal and haphazard methods, such as asking a companion, "Are those the footprints of a wooly mammoth?" or "Did you hear that terrible roar from the forest?" Though these methods are crude by modern standards and suffer from numerous flaws (see Chapter 1), they are quite adequate for many purposes. Just consider how often you yourself rely on these same methods every day.

The Birth of Psychophysics

As science and commerce became more complex, a need arose for greater reliability and accuracy in sensory judgments. This need, in turn, fostered the development of more formal methods. In 1860, Gustav Theodor Fechner, a German physicist and philosopher, published a book in which he formalized behavioral methods that various people had developed in order to study perception (Fechner, 1860/1966). Formalizing the "rules" of a method allowed people to compare different sets of observations. Fechner's methods continue to be important today, and many of the results described in this book came from application of those methods. This Appendix will outline those methods and some of their modern variants.

Though Fechner proved to be very farsighted, he could not anticipate all the many methods that are currently used. Some of these newer methods are described at various places in the text itself. Such methods include preferential looking (Chapters 5, 6, and 7), multidimensional scaling (Chapter 11), magnitude estimation (Chapters 10 and 11), reaction time (Chapter 5), and the various methods used to study animal perception (Chapter 5). Note that we do not present any method in elaborate detail; instead, we only summarize key features. To develop such detail would require a large volume of its own, and fortunately such a volume has already been published by others (Baird and Noma, 1978). We have an unimpeachable precedent for keeping details to a minimum while emphasizing the major concepts. Fechner himself wrote:

Had I wished . . . to set forth here all the special methods of experimentation and calculation that have to be taken into account in more detailed investigations, or had I wanted to provide a theoretical basis and experimental proof for all the rules that are applicable, I would have disturbed the flow of the argument, interfering with the interests of those who are more concerned with the general understanding of the methods than with their use by themselves. (Fechner, 1860/1966, p. 60)*

When an archaeologist unearths some ancient tool, the archaeologist's understanding of the tool depends on an appreciation of the tool's intended purpose. Similarly, to understand the methods Fechner presented in his book one must inquire first about the purposes Fechner had in mind for those methods. In other words, why did he want to measure perception?

An amateur philosopher with considerable training in physics, Fechner was interested in establishing a new science, which he termed **psychophysics.** Psychophysics, as envisioned by Fechner, was to be "an exact theory of the . . . relations of body and soul or, more generally, of the material and the mental, of the physical and psychological worlds" (1860/1966, p. 7). Appropriately enough, Fechner called his book *Elements of Psychophysics.* Part of Fechner's program de-

pended on an ability to measure the sensations that physical stimuli evoke in human observers. Since these sensations arise from an interaction between the physical and psychological worlds, Fechner believed that if he could quantify the sensations evoked by various stimuli, he would be able to develop equations that would tie the two worlds together.

Suppose that you, like Fechner, wished to write a simple psychophysical equation that would relate the quantity of sensation to the intensity of some stimulus. To portray such an equation, you might produce a graph relating sensation and intensity, with stimulus intensity on the horizontal axis and sensation magnitude on the vertical. For a psychophysical equation that is described by a straight line, you'd need to find out only two things before you could draw such a graph. First, you'd need to determine the minimum stimulus value that evoked any sensation whatever. This value would define the point at which the straight line intersected the horizontal axis. Second, you'd need to determine the rate at which the sensation grew as you increased stimulus intensity. Graphically, this rate of growth would correspond to the slope of the psychophysical equation. The first of these values (the intercept) is known as the **absolute threshold**—the stimulus intensity that an observer can just barely detect. The second of these values is known as the **difference threshold**—the minimum amount by which stimulus intensity must be changed in order to produce a noticeable change in the sensation. With certain assumptions (described below), knowledge of these two values—the absolute threshold and the difference threshold—would enable you to write the desired psychophysical equation. And this is what Fechner tried to do.

One assumption crucial to Fechner's enterprise was that the difference threshold would be constant. If the difference threshold changed in value—say, from when you were working with weak stimuli to when you were working with strong stimuli—there would be no single value that could be used to estimate the slope of the psychophysical equation; instead, the slope itself would change from one part of the line to another, implying that the corresponding equation is more complex than that for a straight line. And in fact the difference threshold is most certainly *not* constant. For example, if you presented an observer with a light of 100 units intensity and then varied its intensity, an observer might not notice the change until the light reached an intensity of 110 units. The difference threshold here would be 110 − 100, or 10 units. If you repeated the process, beginning now with a light of 1,000 units, you would find that the observer did not notice a change of just 10 units, as he or she did before. Instead, a much larger change would be required to produce a just noticeable change—say, a change from 1,000 to 1,100 units. So in this second case, the difference threshold would be 1,100 − 1,000, or 100 units.

From the work of his contemporary Ernst Weber, Fechner knew that although the difference threshold itself was not constant, it tended to be a constant *proportion* of the initial stimulus value. In the hypothetical examples just described, both difference thresholds were 10 percent of the initial stimulus. Using various stimuli, Weber had shown that a fixed-proportion increase in stimulus intensity was sufficient to produce a just noticeable change in sensation. To honor him, Fechner called this constancy **Weber's Law.** As we've just seen, Weber's Law states that

$$\Delta I / I = k$$

where ΔI ("delta *I*") signifies the difference threshold (the amount by which stimulus intensity must be changed in order to produce a just noticeable change), *I* signifies the stimulus intensity with which you start, and *k* signifies that the proportion on the left side of the equation is a constant.

Some of the methods developed by Fechner, which are the focus of this Appendix, were designed to measure just noticeable differences. Using these methods, others have ascertained that Weber's Law holds only approximately, thereby undermining Fechner's aim. However, the methods Fechner systematized continue in use today. Since they play such a key role in the study of perception, it's worth spending some time summarizing them here. But Fechner's methods aren't the only important behavioral methods in use today. So after we've summarized Fechner's major methods, we'll turn to some modern variants of those methods. Finally, we'll consider some methods that represent important new departures in the behavioral methods used to study perception.

In most of the examples given below, we'll pretend that the thresholds you're after are visual thresholds; however, the methods we'll consider are not limited to use in vision—any or all could be adapted for studying hearing, smell, or taste as well. Within our visual framework, the absolute threshold is the minimum intensity of a flash of light that an observer can see; lesser intensities produce no sensation. The difference threshold is the smallest perceivable difference in intensity between two flashes of light; smaller differences cannot be discerned.

Before we turn to the various ways for measuring absolute and difference thresholds, you should know that Fechner himself doubted how well one could measure a threshold that truly merited the description "absolute." He observed (1860/1966, p. 108) that even when no light whatever was present, observers in complete darkness tended to experience a dim, vague light that arose from what he termed an "inner source of light sensation." Today, we call this source of light **intrinsic light** or, more poetically, **dark light.** Fechner realized that intrinsic light would cause problems for an observer who tried to determine whether a stimulus did produce *some* sensation or whether the stimulus produced *no* sensation whatever. He knew that observers were liable to confuse this inner source of light with the real thing. This confusion would prevent the observer from making absolute judgments about the dim light alone; instead, the observer would have to discriminate the effects of a real, dim light from the effects of intrinsic light. Various studies have borne out Fechner's concern about intrinsic light, showing that this intrinsic light affects vision in a number of ways (Barlow and Sparrock, 1964; Rushton, 1965).

Fechner's Three Methods

To measure thresholds, Fechner proposed three different behavioral methods, known today as the **method of limits,** the **method of constant stimuli** and the **method of adjustment** (over the years, they have been known by a variety of names). Since Fechner wanted to measure both absolute thresholds and difference thresholds, he had to formulate two slightly different versions of each method—one version for each type of threshold that he needed to measure. Here, we'll present both versions for the method of limits and for the method of constant stimuli. Since the method of adjustment is used primarily to measure absolute thresholds, we'll describe only that version of the method.

Although the three methods differ in their details, they share some things in common. For example, all the methods require observers to use either of two prescribed categories of responses. Also, in order to measure an absolute threshold, all the methods specify presenting just one stimulus at a time; the observer's task is to report whether that stimulus elicited any sensation at all. In order to measure a difference threshold, all the methods specify presenting two stimuli at a time; here, the observer's task is to compare the sensations elicited by the two and report which is greater. More specifically, to measure the absolute threshold, the stimuli are weak, and the responses are either "Yes, I see it" or "No, I don't see it." To measure difference thresholds, the intensity of one stimulus, the *standard stimulus*, is greater than zero, and the intensity of the other stimuli, the *comparison stimuli*, may be either more intense or less intense than the standard; the response categories are "brighter" and "dimmer." There are many variations on these methods but these three basic formats are recognizable in a great many studies (Woodworth and Schlosberg, 1954, p. 195).

THE METHOD OF LIMITS

In this method, a light is changed in small steps in order to find the step at which the observer's response changes. The threshold is defined as that intensity of light at which the response changes.

Absolute Threshold. A single flash of light is changed in successive, discrete steps, and the observer's response to each is recorded. Suppose the light is initially so weak (or altogether absent) that the observer responds "No, I don't see it." In this case, the light is increased in steps until the observer *can* see it. The light intensity at which the observer's response changes is taken as an estimate of the threshold. Or the light may initially be intense enough that the observer responds "Yes, I see it." In this case, the light is decreased in steps until the observer can*not* see it. Again, the intensity of light at which the response changes provides an estimate of the threshold. A series of light flashes that approaches the threshold from below (starting with very weak stimuli) is called an *ascending series*; a series that approaches the threshold from above is called a *descending series*. Often, ascending and descending series yield systematically different estimates of the threshold, so most experimenters use both types of series in alternation and then average the results.

Difference Threshold. On each trial, two flashes of light are presented—one called the *standard*, the other called the *comparison*—either one after the other or side by side. The intensity of the standard light remains constant, whereas the intensity of the comparison stimulus is changed in a series of steps. After each change, the observer judges the comparison stimulus as "brighter" or "dimmer" than the standard. In an ascending series, the comparison stimulus is initially weaker than the standard and increases; in a descending series, the comparison stimulus is initially stronger than the standard and decreases. A series terminates when the observer's response changes from "dimmer" to "brighter" (in an ascending series), or from "brighter" to "dimmer" (in a descending series). The threshold, then, is the absolute value of the difference between the lights at the time the response changed. As before, ascending and descending series may be alternated and the threshold estimates averaged.

THE METHOD OF CONSTANT STIMULI

In this method, each of a fixed set of stimuli is presented many times in a quasi-random order. The frequency with which each stimulus elicits each of the two responses is tallied. The threshold is the stimulus intensity that evokes a particular proportion of the two responses.

Absolute Threshold. The experimenter begins by selecting a set of light intensities varying from very weak (or zero intensity) to reliably visible (typically, somewhere between four and seven intensities are tested). They are presented one at a time in a quasi-random order that ensures each will occur equally often. After every presentation, the observer reports whether the light was seen or not. Once each light intensity has been presented many times (at least 20 to 25 times) the proportion of "seen" and "not seen" responses is calculated for each light level. Ordinarily, more intense lights evoke greater proportions of "seen" responses. So a graded series of light intensities should evoke a graded series of proportions of "seen" responses. The absolute threshold is the intensity of light that evokes "seen" responses on 50 percent of the trials. Appendix Figure 1 illustrates how the threshold can be estimated by graphic means.

Difference Threshold. Two stimuli are presented on each trial. One of these, the standard stimulus, has a fixed intensity; the

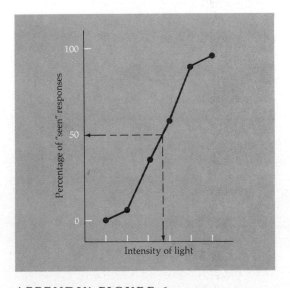

APPENDIX FIGURE 1
The results of an absolute threshold experiment using the method of constant stimuli.

other, the comparison stimulus, is selected randomly from a set of stimuli whose different intensities bracket the standard. On each trial the observer judges whether the intensity of the comparison stimulus was stronger or weaker than that of the standard. Many such judgments are obtained for all pairs of comparison and standard stimuli.

Results are summarized by plotting the proportion of trials on which each comparison stimulus is judged to be stronger than the standard. These proportions are then used to identify comparison stimulus intensities that are just noticeably different from the standard. Two just noticeably different comparison stimuli are identified: one of these is the comparison stimulus that is just noticeably *weaker* than the standard; the other is the comparison stimulus that is just noticeably *stronger* than the standard. By convention, a comparison stimulus that 75 percent of the time is judged weaker than the standard is considered to be just noticeably *weaker* than that standard; also, a comparison stimulus that 75 percent of the time is judged stronger than the standard is considered to be just noticeably *stronger* than that standard. Once these two just noticeably different stimuli are identified, the threshold is calculated by averaging the absolute differences in intensity between the standard and each of the stimuli that are just noticeably different from the standard.

THE METHOD OF ADJUSTMENT

The observer adjusts the light so that it is just visible (absolute threshold) or appears to match some other, standard light (difference threshold).

Absolute Threshold. The experimenter provides the observer with a light and the means of varying the intensity of that light. The observer adjusts the intensity so that the light changes from invisible to just barely visible,

providing one estimate of the absolute threshold. The observer also adjusts the light from visible to just barely invisible, providing another estimate of threshold. Typically, the two kinds of estimates are repeated several times and the results averaged. Observers report that they find this method easier to use than the method of limits, even though the two clearly resemble each other. Probably observers find it easier to judge the stimulus on the basis of continuous trial and error (method of adjustment) than when they see just one stimulus at a fixed value (method of limits).

Modifications of Fechner's Methods

Over the years, researchers have introduced various modifications to each of Fechner's methods as the need arose. Sometimes these modifications were shaped by the apparatus and stimuli that were available to a particular researcher. Other times, the modifications were designed to minimize some deficiency of the method or to promote efficiency. We'll consider two modifications that are particularly important.

THE STAIRCASE METHOD: A MODIFICATION OF THE METHOD OF LIMITS

The method of limits has several limitations that were apparent almost from its inception. As you'll recall, this method requires that a series of stimuli be presented, all of which elicit the same response—such as, "Yes, I see it." Moreover, the method often involves presenting many stimuli that are far from the observer's actual threshold—making the basic method of limits inefficient, since such stimuli contribute little to the estimate of threshold. A newer variant of the method of limits, the so-called **stair-**

case method, offers enhanced efficiency (Cornsweet, 1962). In a typical staircase, the experimenter begins with an intensity well above the threshold and decreases it until the observer declares it invisible. As soon as the response changes, the direction of stimulus change is reversed. Now intensity increases until the response changes again, following which the intensity decreases once more. In a typical staircase, these alternations in the direction of stimulus change continue until six or seven "reversals" have occurred (see Appendix Figure 2). The threshold is then estimated by the average of all the stimulus intensities at which the observer's responses changed. With this staircase procedure, most of the stimulus values are concentrated in the threshold region, making it a more efficient procedure.

There's a problem, though, with this simple staircase procedure. Like the basic method of limits, a simple staircase allows the observer to become aware of the scheme that governs stimulus presentation. The ob-

server's responses are then liable to be influenced by that knowledge. For example, an observer may anticipate that the threshold is being approached and change the response prematurely. To overcome this problem, Tom Cornsweet (1962) introduced a procedure that retains the efficiency of a staircase but minimizes the observer's knowledge of the direction from which the threshold is being approached. Cornsweet's idea was to interleave two or more concurrent staircases.

Appendix Figure 3 illustrates a simple case of two interleaved staircases and *strict alternation* between them. On trial *1*, staircase *A* begins with a stimulus that is expected to be above threshold, and the observer reports seeing it. On trial *2*, staircase *B* starts with a stimulus that is expected to be below threshold, and the observer reports not seeing it. On trial *3*, the next stimulus from staircase *A* is presented—at a lower intensity than before, since the observer saw it the first time. On trial *4*, the next stimulus

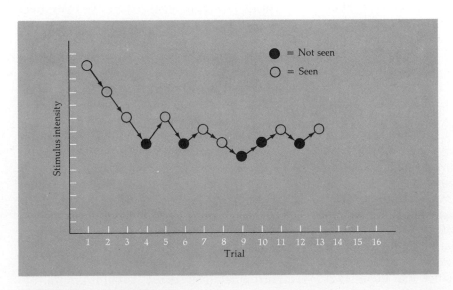

APPENDIX FIGURE 2
The results of a staircase experiment.

SOME BEHAVIORAL METHODS FOR STUDYING PERCEPTION

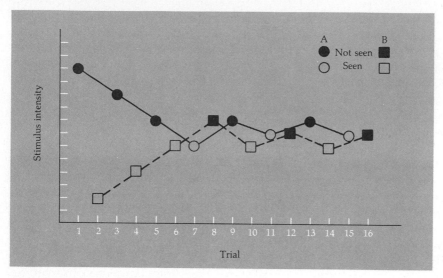

APPENDIX FIGURE 3

The results of an experiment using two interleaved staircases.

from staircase *B* is presented, and so on. As Appendix Figure 3 shows, over the course of trials both staircases converge and the stimulus intensities tend to be concentrated about a single value, the threshold. A further improvement developed by Cornsweet involves *randomly* interleaving the two staircases so that the observer can never figure out which staircase to expect from trial to trial.

MODIFICATIONS OF THE METHOD OF CONSTANT STIMULI

Although constant stimuli's random presentation of stimuli precludes the problems associated with limits's serial ordering of stimuli, constant stimuli, like limits, is inefficient. In particular, many of the stimuli presented are far enough away from the threshold to be of relatively little use. For instance, little information is gained from presenting light intensities that are always detectable or light intensities that can never be detected. This inefficiency can be avoided by pretesting, which allows the stimuli to

be carefully tailored to the capacities of the observer. Alternatively, various methods have been developed to adapt or modify the stimulus set while the experiment itself is in progress (Andrews and Miller, 1978; Watt and Andrews, 1981; Watson and Pelli, 1983). This latter approach is preferable over mere pretesting because the observer's sensitivity fluctuates somewhat during an experiment. As a result, a set of stimuli that pretesting showed to be optimal might not be optimal for the entire experiment. The most sophisticated (and efficient) versions of these adaptive strategies require the use of a computer, but the gain—in efficiency and accuracy—seems well worth the effort.

There is another reason that many researchers consider the method of constant stimuli to be inefficient: ordinarily, the method requires two stimuli per trial—a standard and a comparison—rather than just one. And, naturally, it takes longer to present two stimuli than it does to present just one. Fortunately, in many circumstances, the standard is probably superfluous. Usually, an observer's judgments are just as precise in the absence of a standard as they are in the presence of one (Woodworth and Schlosberg, 1954, pp. 217–218).

To appreciate what omitting the standard entails, consider an experiment by Suzanne McKee, of Smith Kettlewell Institute in San Francisco (1981). To measure the difference threshold for visual velocity—the smallest difference in speed that an observer can discriminate—McKee used the method of constant stimuli but with the standard omitted. On each trial, a computer caused a single vertical line to move across a television display; only one line was presented per trial. The line's velocity on each trial was chosen randomly from a set of seven highly similar velocities. The observer watched a line pass by and judged whether its velocity was faster or slower than the mean of all seven velocities.

Note that McKee never actually had to show the observers which velocity was the mean; instead, by watching a few presentations of all the velocities, the observers built up a highly accurate mental representation of the mean velocity. It should not surprise you that observers can make accurate perceptual comparisons even when there is no explicit standard present. After all, the method merely requires an observer to do what he or she does many times every day: combine separate samples of perceptual information into an accurate overall perceptual impression. (For a quantitative treatment of the integration of separate perceptual samples, see Helson, 1964.)

Forced-Choice, Objective Methods

So far, all of the methods that we've been discussing rely on the observer's own, subjective report of what is or is not seen. These reports are termed "subjective" because you cannot judge whether the observer was correct or incorrect. For instance, when an observer reports "I see it," you must take that report at face value; you can neither dispute it nor verify it. In a moment we'll mention why this may be a problem. But first let's consider an effective solution.

In recent years, an alternative, objective approach—the **forced-choice method**—has gained considerable popularity. In an experiment using a forced-choice method, the observer must *prove* that he or she can see the stimulus, and the observer's claims can be checked. The observer gives proof by identifying some characteristic of the light other than its intensity. For example, the experimenter might arrange to present a dim light either to the right or to the left of a fixation point. The observer does not have to say whether the light was visible; instead the observer merely identifies the light's position—responding either "left" or "right." In modern times, the forced-choice method was introduced by H. Richard Blackwell, of Ohio State University (Blackwell, 1946). However, the method was probably devised by C. Bergmann in 1852, nearly one hundred years before Blackwell (Fechner, 1860/1966, p. 242). In order to measure visual acuity, Bergmann used a forced-choice method with grating stimuli. He devised a way to vary the orientation of a test grating (recall Chapter 5), and instead of asking the observer whether a particular grating was visible, Bergmann forced the observer to identify the grating's orientation.*

But what has been learned from the use of forced-choice methods that wasn't known before? For one thing, these methods show that the nervous system provides a lot more sensory information than you may be aware of. Putting this another way, forced-choice research shows that people can discern lights so dim or sounds so weak that people claim they cannot see or hear them. Here's a typical demonstration of this fact.

---

*Bergmann not only devised the forced-choice method, he also discovered that stimulus uncertainty reduces detectability (see Chapter 5) and that some orientations are easier to see than others—the oblique effect (see Chapter 4).

Suppose that you begin by using one of Fechner's methods, say the method of adjustment, to measure an absolute threshold. After running many trials, you have determined what intensity of light the observer says is just barely visible. You then take that same "threshold" light intensity and present it to the same observer in a forced-choice experiment. The dim light is flashed either to the left or to the right of a fixation point while the observer tries to identify its location. Although such comments are not part of the actual data-collection procedure, the observer may frequently volunteer that his responses are mere guesses and that nothing was actually visible. After many trials, you tally up the number of times the observer was correct. Despite the observer's claims, you find that he was correct 100 percent of the time. Next you decrease the light's intensity to a level *below* the threshold value previously determined by the method of adjustment. When you repeat the forced-choice testing with this new, even dimmer light, the observer protests even more strongly, insisting after every trial that he hadn't seen the light and that he was only guessing about its location. Surprisingly, though, the observer continues to do well—perhaps getting 70 to 75 percent of the choices right. Note that this is well above chance level; if the observer were really just guessing, on average only 50 percent of the responses would be correct. Similar results have been obtained in studies of the other senses. Typically, forced-choice testing confirms that stimuli can be discerned whose intensities are well below the absolute thresholds defined by Fechner's subjective methods.

Forced-choice testing is also useful for eliminating extraneous (nonsensory) differences among observers. In subjective (non–forced-choice) experiments, results can be strongly influenced by the criterion that the observer uses for saying whether or not she sees a light. The **criterion** is the implicit rule that the observer uses to convert sensory information into overt responses. For example, one observer may have a strict criterion; she will not say she sees something unless the sensory evidence is quite strong. Another observer may have a more lax criterion; she is satisfied with even weak sensory evidence. The first observer's responses might lead you to conclude that the observer's threshold was considerably higher than the second observer's when in fact their apparent differences could have been caused by criterion differences alone.

Forced-choice methods, then, should be employed whenever you want to factor out possible criterion differences among observers. The same holds true if you are dealing with groups of observers whose criteria are likely to differ. Since elderly people tend to be reluctant to risk saying that they detect some stimulus unless they are quite sure (Rees and Botwinick, 1971), forced-choice methods are useful in comparing the sensory capacities of older and younger observers. To take another example, hospitalized schizophrenics may be reluctant to admit that they see anything that they are not absolutely sure about. So forced-choice methods are important in comparing the vision of schizophrenic and normal observers. In these comparisons and others, if you cannot factor out possible *criterion* differences, you cannot evaluate possible differences in *sensory* capacities. More commonly, researchers have to worry about the constancy of a single observer's criterion from one test to another. This would be important if you wanted to determine whether some treatment—such as perceptual training—had changed an observer's ability to see, or whether the training had affected only the observer's willingness to *say* he sees something.

Before concluding this outline of forced-choice methods, we should note that some of Fechner's original methods can be converted into forced-choice versions. You can devise a forced-choice method of limits or a forced-choice method of constant stimuli. In fact, forced-choice staircases have become particularly popular (Heinemann, 1961). In this last instance, you would present a light on each trial, as you would normally; but now you would vary its spatial position. In order to be correct, the observer would have to identify the light's location.

Sensory Decision Theory

There's a final topic that we must consider in this brief survey of behavioral methods. That topic is **sensory decision theory (SDT),** a term that covers both a set of procedures as well as a sophisticated psychophysical theory (Green and Swets, 1966). SDT, also sometimes called **signal detection theory** in recognition of its origins in electrical engineering, explicitly recognizes that perceptual measurements are influenced by the motivational state as well as the sensory capacities of the observer. As a result, SDT's procedures can distinguish the two influences, providing separate measures of sensory and nonsensory influences (McNicol, 1972; Pastore and Scheirer, 1974). At the completion of an SDT experiment, you have not one but two measures of the observer's performance. One measure, *d'*, reflects the observer's sensory capacity; the other measure, *beta*, reflects the observer's criterion for acting on the information provided by the senses.*

*One sensory area to which SDT has been applied is the question of whether acupuncture truly reduces the sensation of pain or merely makes a patient less willing to report the presence of pain. Experimental results with SDT are mixed; some data suggest a change only in the patient's criterion for reporting pain (Clark and Yang, 1974), other data suggest a genuine sensory change (Chapman, Chen, and Bonica, 1977).

SDT has also been applied to problems in a wide variety of nonsensory areas. These include the study of memory (Banks, 1970; Swets, 1973), anxiety (Grossberg and Grant, 1978), medical diagnosis (Emmerich and Levine, 1970; Swets, 1979), identification in police lineups (Wells, Lindsay, and Ferguson, 1979), perception of hazards in mine shafts (Blignaut, 1979), and other problems as well. In each, SDT has been useful because of its ability to separate informational and motivational influences on judgments.

As we've said, SDT recognizes that the response "Yes, I see it" depends on two factors—sensory capacity and motivation. To tease the two apart, SDT compares the frequency with which the observer says "yes" when some dim light *has* been presented and the frequency with which the observer says "yes" when *no* light has been presented. Take an example. Suppose some observer says "yes" every single time a very dim light is presented. You might think his eyes are very sensitive. However, you discover that the same observer also says "yes" when no light whatever is presented. Clearly, you should not take every "yes" at face value.

To achieve its goals, SDT must always compare the observer's responses in two different circumstances. When vision is being assessed, SDT determines the observer's responses to a weak light as well as to no light whatever. Typically, these two kinds of trials are randomly intermixed. After each trial, the observer responds "yes" or "no." A "yes" response on a trial *with* a light is termed a "hit" (because the observer was correct, or made a hit); a "yes" response on a trial *without* a light is termed a "false alarm" (because the observer erred, saying he saw something when nothing had been presented). After presenting many trials of each type—light and no-light—the experimenter tallies the proportion of stimulus trials on which the observer responded "yes" and the proportion of *no*-stimulus trials on which the observer responded "yes."

The two proportions, the hit rate and false alarm rate, can be plugged into equations in order to get the sought-after values of *d'* and *beta*. It's not necessary to work through the details of these calculations here; in fact, researchers generally rely on published tables in order to convert their hit and false alarm rates into *d'*.

To make sure that you've got the idea of SDT, consider the outcome of a hypothetical experiment. Suppose that two observers are tested with the same dim light and that both achieve the same hit rate. However, one observer produces a higher false alarm rate than the other. Which observer has the higher sensitivity to the dim light? The answer is, the observer whose false alarm rate is lower—her responses indicate that she was superior in discriminating the presence of light from the absence of light. Sensory decision theory treats all tests of detection as tests of an observer's ability to discriminate the stimulus's presence from its absence (recall Fechner's "inner source of light sensation"). Good discrimination is shown by the combination of a high hit rate and a low false alarm rate. A large difference between an observer's responses when there is a light and when there isn't a light signifies that she can distinguish between the two. Poor discrimination is evidenced when the hit and false alarm rates are equal or nearly equal. In the extreme, when the two rates are equal, you know that the observer has completely failed to distinguish between the absence and presence of a light.

In our discussion of the observer's criterion for reporting sensory information, we've emphasized differences among observers. But you should recognize that any single observer's criterion varies, depending on a number of variables. SDT specifies how an observer's criterion is likely to change along with changes in the relative importance of hitting or missing the stimulus. If an observer is in a situation where it is vital to detect *all* the stimuli and the cost of making a few false alarms is trivial, then SDT predicts the observer will adopt a lax criterion.

This is exemplified in the situation of a radar operator who must monitor the radar for any sign of approach by the enemy. The operator must not miss any possible enemy intrusions whatever. However, if false alarms are costly—in monetary terms or in psychological terms—the observer will adopt a stricter criterion. This is exemplified in the situation of a person who on several successive nights has imagined the sound of a burglar and therefore called the police. He must be very cautious about sounding yet another false alarm.

SDT also specifies how the criterion might change along with changes in the probability that a stimulus will occur. If the observer knows ahead of time that a stimulus is very likely to occur, then an optimal strategy is to adopt a lax criterion for reporting the presence of the stimulus. However, if the observer knows that a stimulus is very unlikely, the optimal strategy is to adopt a strict criterion (that is, to require more powerful evidence before reporting that the very unlikely event has actually occurred.)

This concludes our discussion of psychophysical methods. Though Fechner's goals for psychophysics—an exact science of the relation between mind and body—have not been completely realized, there can be little doubt about the value of his contributions. As a result, today many people all over the world celebrate October 22, called by some "Fechner Day" (Boring, 1961). For on that date, in 1850, Fechner first got the idea for his psychophysics.

References

ABRAHAM, A., and MATHAI, K. V. (1983) The effect of right temporal lobe lesions on matching of smells. *Neuropsychologia, 21,* 277–281.

ADAMS, A. J., ZISMAN, F., RODIC, R., and CAVENDER, J. (1982) Chromaticity and luminosity changes in glaucoma and diabetes. In G. Verriest (ed.), *Colour vision deficiencies, VI. Proceedings of the Sixth Symposium of the International Research Group on Colour Vision Deficiencies.* The Hague: W. Junk, Publishers. Pp. 413–416.

ADDAMS, R. (1834/1964) An account of a peculiar optical phaenomenon. In W. Dember (ed.), *Visual perception: The nineteenth century.* New York: Wiley. Pp. 81–83.

ALBANO, J. E., MISHKIN, M., WESTBROOK, L. E., and WURTZ, R. H. (1982) Visuomotor deficits following ablation of monkey colliculus. *Journal of Neurophysiology, 48,* 338–351.

ALBRECHT, D. G., FARRAR, S. B., and HAMILTON, D. B. (1984) Spatial contrast adaptation characteristics of neurones recorded in the cat's visual cortex. *Journal of Physiology, 347,* 713–739.

ALPERN, M. (1981) Color blind color vision. *Trends in NeuroSciences, 4,* 131–135.

AMERINE, M. A., and ROESSLER, F. B. (1983) *Wines: Their sensory evaluation* (rev. ed.). New York: Freeman.

AMOORE, J. E. (1970) *Molecular basis of odor.* Springfield, Ill.: Thomas.

AMOORE, J. E. (1977) Specific anosmia and the concept of primary odors. *Chemical Senses and Flavor, 2,* 267–281.

ANDREWS, D. P., and MILLER, D. T. (1978) Acuity for spatial separation as a function of stimulus size. *Vision Research, 18,* 615–620.

ANNIS, R. C., and FROST, B. (1973) Human visual ecology and orientation anisotropies in acuity. *Science, 182,* 729–731.

ANSTIS, S. M. (1974) A chart demonstrating variations in acuity with retinal position. *Vision Research, 14,* 589–592.

ANSTIS, S. M. (1978) Apparent movement. In R. Held, H. W. Leibowitz, and H.-L. Teuber (eds.), *Handbook of sensory physiology,* vol. 8. Berlin: Springer Verlag. Pp. 655–673.

APPELLE, S. (1972) Perception and discrimination as a function of stimulus orientation: The oblique effect in man and animals. *Psychological Bulletin, 78,* 266–278.

ARMSTRONG, D. M. (1968) *A materialist theory of mind.* London: Routledge and Kegan Paul.

ASLIN, R. N. (1981) Development of smooth pursuit in human infants. In D. F. Fisher, R. A. Monty, and J. W. Senders (eds.), *Eye movements: Cognition and visual perception.* Hillsdale, N.J.: Erlbaum. Pp. 31–51.

ATKINSON, J., BRADDICK, O., and MOAR, K. (1977) Contrast sensitivity of the human infant for moving and stationary patterns. *Vision Research, 17,* 1045–1047.

AXELSSON, A., and LINDGREN, F. (1978) Hearing in pop musicians. *Acta Otolaryngology, 85,* 225–231.

BAILEY, I. L., and LOVIE, J. E. (1976) New design principles for visual acuity letter charts. *American Journal of Optometry and Physiological Optics, 53,* 740–745.

BAIRD, J. C. (1982) The moon illusion: II. A reference theory. *Journal of Experimental Psychology: General, 111,* 304–315.

BAIRD, J. C., and NOMA, E. (1978) *Fundamentals of scaling and psychophysics.* New York: Wiley.

BAIRD, J. C., and WAGNER, M. (1982) The moon illusion: I. How high is the sky? *Journal of Experimental Psychology: General, 111,* 296–303.

BAKER, C. L., and BRADDICK, O. J. (1982) Does segregation of differently moving areas depend on relative or absolute displacement? *Vision Research, 22,* 851–856.

BALDWIN, W. R. (1981) A review of statistical studies of relations between myopia and ethnic, behavioral, and physiological characteristics. *American Journal of Optometry and Physiological Optics, 58,* 516–527.

BALL, K., and SEKULER, R. (1980) Models of stimulus uncertainty in motion perception. *Psychological Review, 87,* 435–469.

BALL, K., and SEKULER, R. (1981) Cues reduce direction uncertainty and enhance motion detection. *Perception & Psychophysics, 30,* 119–128.

BALLANTYNE, J. C. (1977) *Deafness.* 3rd ed. Edinburgh: Churchill Livingstone.

BANKS, M. S. (1982) The development of spatial and temporal contrast sensitivity. *Current Eye Research, 2,* 191–198.

BANKS, M. S., ASLIN, R. N., and LETSON, R. D. (1975) Sensitive period for the development of human binocular vision. *Science, 190,* 675–677.

BANKS, M. S., and SALAPATEK, P. (1978) Acuity and contrast sensitivity in 1-, 2-, and 3-month-old human infants. *Investigative Ophthalmology and Visual Science, 17,* 361–365.

BANKS, W. P. (1970) Signal detection theory and human memory. *Psychological Bulletin, 74,* 81–99.

BARBUR, J. L. (1981) Subthreshold addition of real and apparent motion. *Vision Research, 21,* 557–564.

BARIBEAU-BRAUN, J., PICTON, T. W., and GOSSELIN, J. (1983) Schizophrenia: A neurophysiological evaluation of abnormal information processing. *Science, 219,* 874–876.

BARLOW, H. B. (1972) Single units and sensation: A neuron doctrine for perceptual psychology? *Perception, 1,* 371–395.

BARLOW, H. B. (1982) What causes trichromacy? A theoretical analysis using comb-filtered spectra. *Vision Research, 22,* 635–644.

BARLOW, H. B., BLAKEMORE, C., and PETTIGREW, J. D. (1967) The neural mechanism of binocular depth discrimination. *Journal of Physiology, 193,* 327–342.

BARLOW, H. B., FITZHUGH, R., and KUFFLER, S. W. (1957) Change of organization in the receptive fields of the cat's retina during dark adaptation. *Journal of Physiology, 137,* 327–337.

BARLOW, H. B., and HILL, R. M. (1963) Evidence for a physiological explanation of the waterfall illusion. *Nature, 200,* 1345–1347.

BARLOW, H. B., and SPARROCK, J. M. B. (1964) The role of afterimages in dark adaptation. *Science, 144,* 1309–1314.

BARTLETT, N. R. (1965) Dark adaptation and light adaptation. In C. H. Graham (ed.), *Vision and visual perception.* New York: Wiley. Pp. 185–207.

BARTOSHUK, L. M. (1974) Taste illusions: Some demonstrations. *Annals of the New York Academy of Sciences, 237,* 279–285.

BARTOSHUK, L. M. (1975) Taste mixtures: Is mixture suppression related to compression? *Physiology & Behavior, 14,* 643–649.

BARTOSHUK, L. M. (1978) History of taste research. In E. C. Carterette and M. P. Friedman (eds.), *Handbook of perception,* vol. 6A. New York: Academic Press. Pp. 3–18.

BARTOSHUK, L. M. (1979) Bitter taste of saccharin related to the genetic ability to taste the bitter substance 6-*n*-propylthiouracil. *Science, 205,* 934–935.

BARTOSHUK, L. M. (1980) Separate worlds of taste. *Psychology Today, 14,* 48–63.

BARTOSHUK, L. M., DATEO, G. P., VANDENBELT, D. J., BUTTRICK, R. L., and LONG, L. (1969) Effects of *Gymnema sylvestra* and *Synsepalum dulcificum* on taste in man. In C. Pfaffmann (ed.), *Olfaction and taste,* vol. 3. New York: Rockefeller University Press. Pp. 436–444.

BATTEAU, D. W. (1967) The role of the pinna in human localization. *Proceedings of the Royal Society of London, Series B, 168,* 158–180.

BAYLOR, D. A., LAMB, T. D., and YAU, K. W. (1979) Responses of retinal rods to single photons. *Journal of Physiology 288,* 613–634.

BEATTIE, G. W., CUTLER, A., and PEARSON, M. (1982) Why is Mrs. Thatcher interrupted so often? *Nature, 300,* 744–747.

BECK, J. (1966) Perceptual grouping produced by changes in orientation and shape. *Science, 154,* 538–540.

BEDICHEK, R. (1960) *The sense of smell.* Garden City, N. Y.: Doubleday.

BEIDLER, L. M. (1978). Biophysics and chemistry of taste. In E. C. Carterette and M. P. Friedman (eds.), *Handbook of perception,* vol. 6A. New York: Academic Press. Pp. 21–49.

BEIDLER, L. M., and SMALLMAN, R. L. (1965) Renewal of cells within taste buds. *Journal of Cell Biology, 27,* 263–272.

BEKESY, G. VON (1960) *Experiments in hearing.* New York: McGraw-Hill.

BEKESY, G. VON (1964) Olfactory analogue to directional hearing. *Journal of Applied Physiology, 19,* 369–373.

BEKESY, G. VON, and ROSENBLITH, W. A. (1951) The mechanical properties of the ear. In S. S. Stevens (ed.), *Handbook of experimental psychology.* New York: Wiley. Pp. 1075–1115.

BELENDIUK, K., and BUTLER, R. A. (1978) Directional hearing under progressive impoverishment of binaural cues. *Sensory Processes, 2,* 58–70.

BELL, H. H., and LAPPIN, J. S. (1973) Sufficient conditions for the discrimination of motion. *Perception & Psychophysics, 14,* 45–50.

BENTON, A. L. (1980) The neuropsychology of facial recognition. *American Psychologist, 35,* 176–186.

BERGER, K. W. (1964) Some factors in the recognition of timbre. *Journal of the Acoustical Society of America, 36,* 1881–1891.

BERGLUND, B., BERGLUND, U., ENGEN, T., and LINDVALL, T. (1971) The effect of adaptation on odor detection. *Perception & Psychophysics, 9,* 435–438.

BERKELEY, G. (1709/1950) *A new theory of vision.* London: Dent.

BERKLEY, M. (1970) Visual discriminations in the cat. In W. Stebbins (ed.), *Animal psychophysics.* New York: Appleton-Century-Crofts. Pp. 231–247.

BERLIN, B., and KAY, P. (1969) *Basic color terms: Their universality and evolution.* Berkeley: University of California Press.

BEXTON, W. H., HERON, W., and SCOTT, T. H. (1954) Effects of decreased variation in the sensory environment. *Canadian Journal of Psychology, 8,* 70–76.

BIEDERMAN, I. (1981) On the semantics of a glance at a scene. In M. Kubovy and J. R. Pomerantz (eds.), *Perceptual organization.* Hillsdale, N.J.: Erlbaum. Pp. 213–253.

BIEDERMAN, I., GLASS, A. L., and STACY, E. W., JR. (1973) Searching for objects in real-world scenes. *Journal of Experimental Psychology, 97,* 22–27.

BIEDERMAN, I., MEZZANOTTE, R. J., and RABINOWITZ, J. C. (1982) Scene perception: Detecting and judging objects undergoing relational violations. *Cognitive Psychology, 14,* 143–177.

BIEDERMAN, I., MEZZANOTTE, R. J., RABINOWITZ, J. C., FRANCOLINI, C. M., and PLUDE, D. (1981) Detecting the unexpected in photointerpretation. *Human Factors, 23,* 153–164.

BIEDERMAN, I., RABINOWITZ, J. C., GLASS, A. L., and STACY, E. W., JR. (1974) On the information extracted from a glance at a scene. *Journal of Experimental Psychology, 103,* 597–600.

BIRCH, J., CHISHOLM, I. A., KINNEAR, P., MARRE, M., PINCKERS, A. J. L. G., POKORNY, J., SMITH, V., and VERRIEST, G. (1979) Acquired color vision defects. In J. Pokorny, V. Smith, G. Verriest, and A. J. L. G. Pinckers (eds.), *Congenital and acquired color vision defects.* New York: Grune and Stratton. Pp. 243–348.

BIRREN, F. (1941) *The story of color: From ancient mysticism to modern science.* Westport, Conn.: Crimson Press.

BIRREN, F. (1978) *Color and human response.* New York: Van Nostrand Reinhold.

BLACKWELL, H. R. (1946) Contrast thresholds of the human eye. *Journal of the Optical Society of America, 36,* 624–643.

BLAKE, R. (1978) Strategies for assessing visual deficits in animals with selective neural deficits. In R. B. Aslin, J. R. Alberts, and M. R. Petersen (eds.), *Development and perception.* New York: Academic Press. Pp. 95–112.

BLAKE, R. (in press) The visual world of the cat. *Scientific American.*

BLAKE, R., and FOX, R. (1972) Interocular transfer of adaptation to spatial frequency during retinal ischaemia. *Nature, 240,* 76–77.

BLAKE, R., and HIRSCH, H. V. B. (1975) Deficits in binocular depth perception in cats after alternating monoculuar deprivation. *Science, 190,* 1114–1116.

BLAKEMORE, C. (1976) The conditions required for the maintenance of binocularity in the kitten's visual cortex. *Journal of Physiology, 261,* 423–444.

BLAKEMORE, C. (1977) *Mechanics of mind.* Cambridge: Cambridge University Press.

BLAKEMORE, C. (1979) Representation of reality in the perceptual world. In *Brain and Mind, CIBA Foundation Symposium,* vol. 69. Amsterdam: Excerpta Medica. Pp. 139–152.

BLAKEMORE, C., and CAMPBELL, F. W. (1969) On the existence of neurones in the human visual system selectively sensitive to the orientation and size of retinal images. *Journal of Physiology, 203,* 237–260.

BLAKEMORE, C., CARPENTER, R. H. S., and GEORGESON, M. A. (1970) Lateral inhibition between orientation detectors in the human visual system. *Nature, 228,* 37–39.

BLAKEMORE, C., MUNCEY, J. P. J., and RIDLEY, R. M. (1973) Stimulus specificity in the human visual system. *Vision Research, 13,* 1915–1931.

BLAKEMORE, C., NACHMIAS, J., and SUTTON, P. (1970) The perceived spatial frequency shift: Evidence for frequency selective neurones in the human brain. *Journal of Physiology, 210,* 727–750.

BLAKEMORE, C., and TOBIN, E. (1972) Lateral inhibition between orientation detectors in the cat's visual cortex. *Experimental Brain Research, 15,* 439–440.

BLIGNAUT, C. J. H. (1979) The perception of hazard. II. The contribution of signal detection to hazard perception. *Ergonomics, 22,* 1177–1183.

BLIVEN, B., JR. (1976) Annals of architecture: A better sound. *The New Yorker,* November 8, pp. 51–135.

BOBROW, N. A., MONEY, J., and LEWIS, V. G. (1971) Delayed puberty, eroticism, and sense of smell: A psychological study of hypogonadotropism, osmatic and anosmatic (Kallmann's syndrome). *Archives of Sexual Behavior, 1,* 329–344.

BODIS-WOLLNER, I. (1972) Visual acuity and contrast sensitivity in patients with cerebral lesions. *Science, 178,* 769–771.

BOLL, F. (1877/1977) On the anatomy and physiology of the retina. *Vision Research, 17,* 1253–1267.

BONNET, C. (1982) Thresholds of motion perception. In A. Wertheim, W. Wagenaar, and H. W. Leibowitz (eds.), *Tutorials in motion perception.* New York: Plenum Press. Pp. 41–79.

BORING, E. G. (1930) A new ambiguous figure. *American Journal of Psychology, 42,* 444.

BORING, E. G. (1942) *Sensation and perception in the history of experimental psychology.* New York: Appleton-Century-Crofts.

BORING, E. G. (1961) Fechner: Inadvertent founder of psychophysics. *Psychometrika, 26,* 3–8.

BORNSTEIN, M. H., KESSEN, W., and WEISKOPF, S. (1976) The categories of hue in infancy. *Science, 191,* 201–202.

BORNSTEIN, W. S. (1940) Cortical representation of taste in man and monkey. II. The localization of the cortical taste area in man and a method of measuring impairment of taste in man. *Yale Journal of Biology and Medicine, 13,* 133–156.

BOUGH, E. W. (1970) Stereoscopic vision in macaque monkey: A behavioural demonstration. *Nature, 225,* 42–44.

BOWMAKER, J. K. (1983) Trichromatic colour vision: Why only three receptor channels? *Trends in NeuroSciences, 6,* 41–43.

BOYCE, P. R. (1981) *Human factors and lighting.* New York: Macmillan.

BOYNTON, R. M. (1974) The visual system: Environmental information. In E. C. Carterette and M. P. Friedman (eds.), *Handbook of perception,* vol. 1. New York: Academic Press. Pp. 285–307.

BOYNTON, R. M. (1980) Design for an eye. In D. McFadden (ed.), *Neural mechanisms in behavior.* New York: Springer Verlag. Pp. 38–72.

BOYNTON, R. M. (1982) Spatial and temporal approaches for studying color vision: A review. In G. Verriest (ed.), *Colour vision deficiencies, VI. Proceedings of the Sixth Symposium of the International Research Group on Colour Vision Deficiencies.* The Hague: W. Junk, Publishers. Pp. 1–14.

BOYNTON, R. M., and GORDON, J. (1965) Bezold-Brücke hue shift measured by color naming technique. *Journal of the Optical Society of America, 55,* 78–86.

BRADLEY, R. M. (1979) Effects of aging on the sense of taste: Anatomical considerations. In S. S. Han and D. H. Coons (eds.), *Special senses in aging: A current biological assessment.* Ann Arbor, Mich.: Institute of Gerontology, University of Michigan. Pp. 3–8.

BRADY, P. T. (1970) Fixed-scale mechanism of absolute pitch. *Journal of the Acoustical Society of America, 48,* 883–887.

BRAUNSTEIN, M. L. (1976) *Depth perception through motion.* New York: Academic Press.

BREGMAN, A. S., and MILLS, M. I. (1982) Perceived movement: The Flintstone constraint. *Perception, 11,* 201–206.

BREGMAN, A. S., and PINKER, S. (1978) Auditory streaming and the building of timbre. *Canadian Journal of Psychology, 31,* 151–159.

BREITMEYER, B. G. (1975) Simple reaction time as a measure of the temporal response properties of transient and sustained channels. *Vision Research, 15,* 1411–1412.

BRIDGEMAN, B., and STAGGS, D. (1982) Plasticity in human blindsight. *Vision Research, 22,* 1199–1203.

BRINDLEY, G. S. (1970) *Physiology of the retina and visual pathway.* Baltimore: Williams & Wilkins.

BRINDLEY, G. S., and LEWIN, W. S. (1968) The sensations produced by electrical stimulation of the visual cortex. *Journal of Physiology, 196,* 479–493.

BROADBENT, D. E. (1977) The hidden preattentive process. *American Psychologist, 32,* 109–118.

BROUWER, J. N., GLASER, D., SEGERSTAD, C. H. A., HELLEKANT, G., NINOMIYA, Y., and VAN DER WEL, H. (1983) The sweetness-inducing effect of miraculin: Behavioral and neurophysiological experiments in the rhesus monkey, *Macaca mulatta. Journal of Physiology, 337,* 221–240.

BROWN, J. F. (1931) The visual perception of velocity. *Psychologische Forschung, 14,* 199–232.

BROWN, J. L., and MUELLER, C. G. (1965) Brightness discrimination and brightness contrast. In C. H. Graham (ed.), *Vision and visual perception.* New York: Wiley. Pp. 208–250.

BRUNER, J. S., and POTTER, M. C. (1964) Interference in visual recognition. *Science, 144,* 424–425.

BUCKALEW, L. W., and COFFIELD, K. E. (1982) An investigation of drug expectancy as a function of capsule color and size and preparation form. *Journal of Clinical Psychopharmacology, 2,* 245–248.

BURGER, J. F. (1958) Front–back discrimination of the hearing system. *Acustica, 8,* 302–310.

BURKE, W., and COLE, A. M. (1978) Extra-retinal influences on the lateral geniculate nucleus. *Review of Physiology, Biochemistry, and Pharmacology, 80,* 105–166.

BURR, D. C., and ROSS, J. (1982) Contrast sensitivity at high velocities. *Vision Research, 22,* 479–484.

BUTTERWORTH, G., and CASTILLO, M. (1976) Coordination of auditory and visual space in newborn infants. *Perception, 5,* 155–160.

CAELLI, T., and DODWELL, P. (1982) The discrimination of structure in vectorgraphs: Local and global effects. *Perception & Psychophysics, 32,* 314–326.

CAIN, W. S. (1975) Odor intensity: Mixtures and masking. *Chemical Senses and Flavor, 1,* 339–352.

CAIN, W. S. (1977) Differential sensitivity for smell: Noise at the nose. *Science, 195,* 796–798.

CAIN, W. S. (1978) The odoriferous environment and the application of olfactory research. In E. C. Carterette and M. P. Friedman (eds.), *Handbook of perception,* vol 7. New York: Academic Press. Pp. 277–304.

CAIN, W. S. (1979) To know with the nose: Keys to odor identification. *Science, 203,* 467–470.

CAIN, W. S. (1982) Odor identification by males and females: Predictions versus performance. *Chemical Senses, 7,* 129–142.

CAIN, W. S., and ENGEN, T. (1969) Olfactory adaptation and the scaling of odor intensity. In C. Pfaffmann (ed.), *Olfaction and taste,* vol. 3. New York: Rockefeller University Press. Pp. 127–157.

CAIN, W. S., and MURPHY, C. L. (1980) Interaction between chemoreceptive modalities of odour irritation. *Nature, 284,* 255–257.

CALIS, G., and LEEUWENBERG, E. (1981) Grounding the figure. *Journal of Experimental Psychology: Human Perception and Performance, 7,* 1386–1397.

CALLAHAN, P. S. (1977) Moth and candle: The candle flame as a sexual mimic of the coded infrared wavelengths from a moth sex scent. *Applied Optics, 16,* 3089–3097.

CAMPBELL, D. T. (1974) Evolutionary epistemology. In P. A. Schlipp (ed.), *The philosophy of Karl Popper.* LaSalle, Ill.: Open Court. Pp. 413–463.

CAMPBELL, F. W., and MAFFEI, L. (1981) The influence of spatial frequency and contrast on the perception of moving patterns. *Vision Research, 21,* 713–721.

CAMPBELL, F. W., and ROBSON, J. G. (1968) Application of Fourier analysis to the visibility of gratings. *Journal of Physiology, 197,* 551–566.

CAMPBELL, F. W., and WURTZ, R. H. (1978) Saccadic omission: Why we do not see a grey-out during a saccadic eye movement. *Vision Research, 18,* 1297–1303.

CAMPION, J., LATTO, R., and SMITH, Y. M. (1983) Is blindsight an effect of scattered light, spared cortex, and near-threshold vision? *The Behavioral and Brain Sciences, 6,* 423–486.

CAREY, S., and DIAMOND, R. (1977) From piecemeal to configurational representation of faces. *Science, 195,* 312–314.

CARLSSON, L., KNAVE, B., LENNERSTRAND, G., and WIBOM, R. (1984) Glare from outdoor high mast lighting: Effects on visual acuity and contrast sensitivity in comparative studies of different floodlighting systems. *Acta Ophthalmologica, 62,* 84–93.

CARMODY, D. P., NODINE, C. F., and KUNDEL, H. L. (1980) An analysis of perceptual and cognitive factors in radiographic interpretation. *Perception, 9,* 339–344.

CARPENTER, P. A., and DANEMAN, M. (1981) Lexical access and error recovery in reading: A model based on eye fixations. *Journal of Verbal Learning and Verbal Behavior, 20,* 137–160.

CARTER, J. H. (1982) The effects of aging upon selected visual functions: Color vision, field of vision, and accommodation. In R. Sekuler, D. Kline, and K. Dismukes (eds.), *Aging and human visual function.* New York: A. R. Liss. Pp. 121–130.

CATTELL, J. M (1886) The inertia of the eye and brain. *Brain, 8,* 295–312.

CAVANAGH, P. (1982) Functional size invariance is not provided by the cortical magnification factor. *Vision Research, 22,* 1409–1412.

CHAPANIS, A. (1965) Color names for color space. *American Scientist, 53,* 327–346.

CHAPMAN, C. R., CHEN, A. C., and BONICA, J. J. (1977) Effects of intrasegmental electrical acupuncture on dental pain: Evaluation by threshold estimation and sensory decision theory. *Pain, 3,* 213–227.

CHEVREUL, M. (1839/1970) *The principles of harmony and contrast of colors.* F. Birren (ed.). New York: Reinhold.

CHURCHLAND, P. M. (1984) *Matter and consciousness.* Cambridge, Mass.: MIT Press.

CLARK, W. C., and YANG, J. C. (1974) Acupunctural analgesia? Evaluation by signal detection theory. *Science, 184,* 1096–1098.

CLAUS, R., HOPPEN, H. O., and KARG, H. (1981) The secret of truffles: A steroidal pheromone? *Experientia, 37,* 1178–1179.

CLELAND, B. G., LEVICK, W. R., and WÄSSLE, H. (1975) Physiological identification of a morphological class of cat retinal ganglion cells. *Journal of Physiology, 248,* 151–171.

COHEN, J. (1969) *Sensation and perception. II. Audition and the minor senses.* Chicago: Rand McNally.

COLLEWIJN, H., MARTINS, A. J., and STEINMAN, R. M. (1983) Compensatory eye movements during active and passive head movements: Fast adaptation to changes in visual magnification. *Journal of Physiology, 340,* 259–286.

COLLINGS, V. B. (1974) Human taste response as a function of locus on the tongue and soft palate. *Perception & Psychophysics, 16,* 169–174.

COLLINS, B. L., and WORTHEY, J. A. (1984) *The role of color in lighting for meat and poultry inspection.* U.S. Department of Commerce, National Bureau of Standards Report No. 84-2829. Washington, D.C.

COMETTO-MUNIZ, J. E., and CAIN, W. S. (1982) Perception of nasal pungency in smokers and nonsmokers. *Physiology & Behavior, 29,* 727–731.

CORCORAN, D. W. J., and ROUSE, R. O. (1970) An aspect of perceptual organization involved in reading typed and handwritten words. *Quarterly Journal of Experimental Psychology, 22,* 526–530.

COREN, S., and GIRGUS, J. S. (1978) Visual illusions. In R. Held, H. W. Leibowitz, and H.-L. Teuber (eds.), *Handbook of sensory physiology,* vol. 8. Berlin: Springer Verlag. Pp. 551–568.

CORNSWEET, T. N. (1962) The staircase-method in psychophysics. *American Journal of Psychology, 75,* 485–491.

CORNSWEET, T. N. (1970) *Visual perception.* New York: Academic Press.

CORSO, J. F. (1981) *Aging sensory systems and perception.* New York: Praeger.

COWART, B. J. (1981) Development of taste perception in humans: Sensitivity and preference throughout the life span. *Psychological Bulletin, 90,* 43–73.

CROCKER, E. C., and HENDERSON, L. F. (1927) Analysis and classification of odors. *American Perfumer and Essential Oil Review, 22,* 325–327.

CROWE, S. J., GUILD, S. R., and POLVOST, L. M. (1934) Observations on the pathology of high-tone deafness. *Bulletin of the Johns Hopkins Hospital, 54,* 315–379.

CUTTING, J. E. (1978) Generation of synthetic male and female walkers through manipulation of a biomechanical invariant. *Perception, 7,* 393–405.

CUTTING, J. E., and PROFFITT, D. R. (1981) Gait perception as an example of how we may perceive events. In R. Walk and H. L. Pick (eds.), *Intersensory perception and sensory integration.* New York: Plenum Press. Pp. 249–273.

DALLOS, P. (1981) Cochlear physiology. *Annual Review of Psychology, 32,* 153–190.

DALLOS P., and CHEATHAM, M. A. (1976) Production of cochlear potentials by inner and outer hair cells. *Journal of the Acoustical Society of America, 60,* 510–512.

DALTON, J. (1798/1948) Extraordinary facts relating to the vision of colour: With observations. In W. Dennis (ed.), *Readings in the history of psychology.* New York: Appleton-Century-Crofts. Pp. 102–111.

DAMASIO, A. R., and BENTON, A. L. (1979) Impairment of hand movements under visual guidance. *Neurology, 29,* 170–178.

DAMASIO, A. R., DAMASIO, H., and VAN HOESEN, G. W. (1982) Prosopagnosia: Anatomic basis and behavioral mechanisms. *Neurology, 32,* 331–341.

DANIEL, P. M., and WHITTERIDGE, D. (1961) The representation of the visual field on the cerebral cortex in monkeys. *Journal of Physiology, 159,* 203–221.

DARTNALL, H. J. A., BOWMAKER, J. K., and MOLLON, J. D. (1983) Human visual pigments: Microspectrophotometric results from the eyes of seven persons. *Proceedings of the Royal Society of London, Series B, 220,* 115–130.

DARWIN, C. J. (1976) The perception of speech. In E. C. Carterette and M. P. Friedman (eds.), *Handbook of perception,* vol. 7. New York: Academic Press. Pp. 175–226.

DAUM, K. M. (1983) Accommodative dysfunction. *Documenta Ophthalmologica, 55,* 177–198.

DAVIDOFF, J. B. (1975) *Differences in visual perception: The individual eye.* New York: Academic Press.

DAVIS, E. T., and GRAHAM, N. (1981) Spatial frequency uncertainty effects in the detection of sinusoidal gratings. *Vision Research, 21,* 705–712.

DAVIS, H., DEATHERAGE, B. H., ROSENBLUT, B., FERNANDEZ, C., KIMURA, R., and SMITH, C. A. (1958) Modification of cochlear potentials produced by streptomycin poisoning and by extensive venous obstructions. *Laryngoscope, 68,* 596–627.

DAVIS, H., and SILVERMAN, S. R. (1960) *Hearing and deafness.* New York: Holt, Rinehart and Winston.

DAVIS, R. G. (1977) Acquisition of verbal associations to olfactory and abstract visual stimuli of varying similarity. *Journal of Experimental Psychology: Human Learning and Memory, 3,* 37–51.

DAVIS, R. G. (1981) The role of nonolfactory context cues in odor identification. *Perception & Psychophysics, 30,* 83–89.

DE BOER, I. (1956) Pitch of inharmonic signals. *Nature, 178,* 535–536.

DE MONASTERIO, F. M., and GOURAS, P. (1975) Functional properties of ganglion cells of the rhesus monkey retina. *Journal of Physiology, 251,* 167–195.

DENTON, G. G. (1980) The influence of visual pattern on perceived speed. *Perception, 9,* 393–402.

DESILVA, H. R. (1926) An experimental investigation of the determinants of apparent visual movement. *American Journal of Psychology, 37,* 469–501.

DESOR, J. A., and BEAUCHAMP, G. K. (1974) The human capacity to transmit olfactory information. *Perception & Psychophysics, 16,* 551–556.

DETWILER, P. B., HODGKIN, A. L., and MCNAUGHTON, P. A. (1980) Temporal and spatial characteristics of the voltage response of rods in the retina of the turtle. *Journal of Physiology, 300,* 213–250.

DEVALOIS, R. L., and DEVALOIS, K. (1975) Neural coding of color. In E. C. Carterette and M. P. Friedman (eds.), *Handbook of perception,* vol. 5. New York: Academic Press. Pp. 117–166.

DEVALOIS, R. L., SMITH, C. J., KITAI, S. T., and KAROLY, A. J. (1958) Responses of single cells in different layers of the primate lateral geniculate nucleus to monochromatic light. *Science, 127,* 238–239.

DEWSON, J., PRIBRAM, K., and LYNCH, J. (1969) Effects of ablations of temporal cortex upon speech sound discrimination in the monkey. *Experimental Neurology, 24,* 579–591.

DICHGANS, J., and BRANDT, T. (1978) Visual–vestibular interaction: Effects on self-motion perception and postural control. In R. M Held, H. W. Leibowitz, and H.-L. Teuber (eds.), *Handbook of sensory physiology,* vol. 8. Berlin: Springer Verlag. Pp. 756–804.

DIRKS, D. D. (1978) Effects of hearing impairment on the auditory system. In E. C. Carterette and M. P. Friedman (eds.), *Handbook of perception,* vol. 4. New York: Academic Press. Pp. 567–608.

DIXON, N. F. (1981) *Preconscious processing.* New York: Wiley.

DOANE, M. G. (1980) Interaction of eyelids and tears in corneal wetting and the dynamics of the normal human eyeblink. *American Journal of Ophthalmology, 89,* 507–516.

DOBELLE, W. H., and MLADEJOVSKY, M. G. (1974) Phosphenes produced by electrical stimulation of human occipital cortex, and their application to the development of a prosthesis for the blind. *Journal of Physiology, 243,* 553–576.

DOBELLE, W. H., MLADEJOVSKY, M. G., EVANS, J. R., ROBERTS, T. S., and GIRVIN, J. P. (1976) "Braille" reading by a blind volunteer by visual cortex stimulation. *Nature, 259,* 111–112.

DODD, B. (1977) The role of vision in the perception of speech. *Perception, 6,* 31–40.

DODGE, R. (1900) Visual perception during eye movement. *Psychological Review, 7,* 454–465.

DOTY, R. L., GREEN, P. A., RAM, C., and YANKELL, S. L. (1982) Communication of gender from human breath odors: Relationship to perceived intensity and pleasantness. *Hormones and Behavior, 16,* 13–22.

DOUEK, E. (1974) *The sense of smell and its abnormalities.* Edinburgh: Churchill Livingstone.

DOWLING, J. E. (1966) Night blindness. *Scientific American, 215,* 78–84.

DOWLING, W. J. (1978) Scale and contour: Two components of a theory of memory for melodies. *Psychological Review, 85,* 341–354.

DOWLING, W. J., and FUJITANI, D. S. (1971) Contour, interval, and pitch recognition in memory for melodies. *Journal of the Acoustical Society of America, 49,* 524–531.

DRASDO, N. (1977) The neural representation of visual space. *Nature, 266,* 554–556.

DREHER, B., FUKADA, Y., and RODIECK, R. W. (1976) Identification, classification, and anatomical segregation of cells with X-like and Y-like properties in the lateral geniculate nucleus of old-world primates. *Journal of Physiology, 29,* 433–452.

DREWNOWSKI, A., GRINKER, J. A., and HIRSCH, J. (1982) Obesity and flavor perception: Multidimensional scaling of soft drinks. *Appetite: Journal of Intake Research, 3,* 361–368.

DUBOSE, C. N., CARDELLO, A., and MALLER, O. (1980) Effects of colorants and flavorants on identification, perceived flavor intensity, and hedonic quality of fruit-flavored beverages and cake. *Journal of Food Science, 45,* 1393–1399, 1415.

DUNCKER, K. (1929/1938) Induced motion. In W. D. Ellis (ed.), *A source book of gestalt psychology.* New York: Humanities Press. Pp. 161–172.

DUNCKER, K. (1939) The influence of past experience upon perceptual properties. *American Journal of Psychology, 52,* 255–267.

DURLACH, I., and COLBURN, H. S. (1978) Binaural phenomena. In E. C. Carterette and M. P. Friedman (eds), *Handbook of perception,* vol. 4. New York: Academic Press. Pp. 365–466.

ECCLES, J. (1979) *The human mystery.* Berlin: Springer Verlag.

EICHENBAUM, H., MORTON, T. H., POTTER, H., and CORKIN, S. (1983) Selective olfactory deficits in case H. M. *Brain, 106,* 459–472.

EIMAS, P. D., and CORBIT, J. D. (1973) Selective adaptation of linguistic feature detectors. *Cognitive Psychology, 4,* 99–109.

EMMERICH, D. S., and LEVINE, F. M. (1970) Differences in auditory sensitivity of chronic schizophrenic patients and normal controls determined by use of a forced-choice procedure. *Diseases of the Nervous System, 31,* 552–557.

ENGEN, T. (1960) Effects of practice and instruction on olfactory thresholds. *Perceptual and Motor Skills, 10,* 195–198.

ENGEN, T. (1982) *The perception of odors.* New York: Academic Press.

ENGEN, T., and PFAFFMANN, C. (1960) Absolute judgments of odor quality. *Journal of Experimental Psychology, 59,* 214–219.

ENROTH-CUGELL, C., HERTZ, B. G., and LENNIE, P. (1977) Convergence of rod and cone signals in the cat's retina. *Journal of Physiology, 269,* 297–318.

ENROTH-CUGELL, C., and ROBSON, J. G. (1966) The contrast sensitivity of retinal ganglion cells of the cat. *Journal of Physiology, 187,* 517–552.

EPSTEIN, W. (1963) The influences of assumed size on apparent distance. *American Journal of Psychology, 76,* 257–265.

ERICKSON, R. P. (1963) Sensory neural patterns and gustation. In Y. Zotterman (ed.), *Olfaction and taste.* Oxford: Pergamon Press. Pp. 205–214.

ERICKSON, R. P. (1968) Stimulus coding in topographic and nontopographic afferent modalities: On the significance of the activity of individual sensory neurons. *Psychological Review, 75,* 447–465.

ERICKSON, R. P. (1982) Studies on the perception of taste: Do primaries exist? *Physiology & Behavior, 28,* 57–62.

ERICKSON, R. P. (1984) On the neural bases of behavior. *American Scientist, 72,* 233–241.

EVANS, E. F. (1974) Neural processes for the detection of acoustic patterns and for sound localization. In F. C. Schmitt and F. G. Worden (eds.), *The neurosciences: Third study program.* Cambridge, Mass.: MIT Press. Pp. 131–145.

EVANS, E. F. (1982a) Functional anatomy of the

auditory system. In H. B. Barlow and J. D. Mollon (eds.), *The senses.* Cambridge: Cambridge University Press. Pp. 251–306.

EVANS, E. F. (1982b) Functions of the auditory system. In H. B. Barlow and J. D. Mollon (eds.), *The senses.* Cambridge: Cambridge University Press. Pp. 307–331.

EXNER, S. (1888) Über optische Bewegungsempfindungen. *Biologisches Centralblatt, 8,* 437–448.

FANTZ, R. L. (1961) The origin of form perception. *Scientific American, 204,* 66–72.

FECHNER, G. T. (1860/1966) *Elements of psychophysics.* D. H. Howes and E. G. Boring (eds.), H. E. Adler (trans.). New York: Holt, Rinehart and Winston.

FEDERAL RAILROAD ADMINISTRATION. (1982) *Rail–highway crossing accident/incident inventory bulletin, calendar year 1981.* Washington, D. C.: U.S. Department of Transportation.

FELSTEN, G., and WASSERMAN, G. S. (1980) Visual masking: Mechanisms and theories. *Psychological Review, 88,* 329–354.

FERSTER, D. (1981) A comparison of binocular depth mechanisms in areas 17 and 18 of the cat visual cortex. *Journal of Physiology, 311,* 623–655.

FINLAY, D. (1982) Motion perception in the peripheral visual field. *Perception, 11,* 457–462.

FLETCHER, H. F., and MUNSON, W. A. (1933) Loudness, its definition, measurement, and calculation. *Journal of the Acoustical Society of America, 5,* 82–108.

FOLEY, J. M. (1980) Binocular distance perception. *Psychological Review, 87,* 411–434.

FOSTER, D. H., THORSON, J., MCILWAIN, J. T., and BIEDERMAN–THORSON, M. (1981) The fine-grain movement illusion: A perceptual probe of neuronal connectivity in the human visual system. *Vision Research, 21,* 1123–1128.

FOX, R. (1978) Visual masking. In R. Held, H. W. Leibowitz, and H.-L. Teuber (eds.), *Handbook of sensory physiology,* vol. 8. Berlin: Springer Verlag. Pp. 629–653.

FOX, R., ASLIN, R. N., SHEA, S. L., and DUMAIS, S. T. (1980) Stereopsis in human infants. *Science, 207,* 323–324.

FOX, R., and CHECK, R. (1968) Detection of motion during binocular suppression. *Journal of Experimental Psychology, 78,* 388–395.

FOX, R., LEHMKUHLE, S. W., and BUSH, R. C. (1977) Stereopsis in the falcon. *Science, 197,* 79–81.

FOX, R., and MCDANIEL, C. (1982) The percep-

tion of biological motion by human infants. *Science, 218,* 486–487.

FRANK, M. (1973) An analysis of hamster afferent taste nerve response functions. *Journal of General Physiology, 61,* 588–618.

FREEMAN, R. D., and PETTIGREW, J. D. (1973) Alteration of visual cortex from environmental asymmetries. *Nature, 246,* 359–360.

FREUD, S. (1910/1938) Psychopathology of everyday life. In A. A. Brill (ed. and trans.), *The basic writings of Sigmund Freud.* New York: Modern Library. Pp. 35–178.

FREYTAG, E., and SACHS, J. S. (1968) Abnormalities of the central visual pathways contributing to traffic accidents. *Journal of the American Medical Association, 204,* 871–873.

FRISBY, J. P. (1972) Real and apparent movement—same or different mechanisms? *Vision Research, 12,* 1051–1055.

FRISBY, J. P. (1980) *Seeing.* Oxford: Oxford University Press.

FRISBY, J. P., and CLATWORTHY, J. L. (1975) Learning to see complex random-dot stereograms. *Perception, 4,* 173–178.

FRISBY, J. P., and MAYHEW, J. E. W. (1976) Rivalrous texture stereograms. *Nature, 264,* 53–56.

FUCHS, A., and BINDER, M. D. (1983) Fatigue resistance of human extraocular muscles. *Journal of Neurophysiology, 49,* 28–34.

FUKADA, Y. (1971) Receptive field organization of cat optic nerve fibers with special reference to conduction velocity. *Vision Research, 11,* 209–226.

FURCHTGOTT, E., and FRIEDMAN, M. P. (1960) The effect of hunger and taste on odor RLs. *Journal of Comparative and Physiological Psychology, 53,* 576–581.

GAMBLE, E. A. M. C. (1921) Review of *Der Geruch* by Hans Henning. *American Journal of Psychology, 32,* 290–295.

GARB, J., and STUNKARD, A. J. (1974) Taste aversions in man. *American Journal of Psychiatry, 131,* 1204–1207.

GARCIA, J., and KOELLING, R. A. (1966) Relation of cue to consequences in avoidance learning. *Psychonomic Science, 4,* 123–124.

GARFIELD, E. (1983) The tyranny of the horn—automobile, that is. *Current Contents, 26,* 5–11.

GARNER, W. R. (1962) *Uncertainty and structure as psychological concepts.* New York: Wiley.

GESCHEIDER, G. A. (1976) *Psychophysics: Method and theory.* Hillsdale, N. J.: Erlbaum.

GESTELAND, R. C. (1978) The neural code: Integrative neural mechanisms. In E. C. Carterette and M. P. Friedman (eds.), *Handbook of perception*, vol. 6A. New York: Academic Press. Pp. 259–276.

GESTELAND, R. C. (1982) The new physiology of odor. *Environmental Progress, 1,* 94–97.

GESTELAND, R. C., YANCEY, R. A., and FARBMAN, A. I. (1982) Development of olfactory receptor neuron selectivity in the rat fetus. *Neuroscience, 7,* 3127–3136.

GEYER, L. H., and DeWALD, C. G. (1973) Feature lists and confusion matrices. *Perception & Psychophysics, 14,* 471–482.

GIBSON, E. J. (1965) Learning to read. *Science, 148,* 1066–1072.

GIBSON, E. J. (1969) *Principles of perceptual learning.* New York: Appleton-Century-Crofts.

GIBSON, J. J. (1950) *The perception of the visual world.* Boston: Houghton Mifflin.

GIBSON, J. J. (1966) *The senses considered as perceptual systems.* Boston: Houghton Mifflin.

GIBSON, J. J. (1979) *The ecological approach to visual perception.* Boston: Houghton Mifflin.

GILCHRIST, A. L. (1977) Perceived lightness depends on perceived spatial arrangement. *Science, 195,* 185–187.

GILINSKY, A. S. (1955) The effect of attitude upon the perception of size. *American Journal of Psychology, 68,* 173–192.

GILLAN, D. J. (1982) Mixture suppression: The effect of spatial separation between sucrose and NaCl. *Perception & Psychophysics, 32,* 504–510.

GILLAN, D. J. (1984) Evidence for peripheral and central processes in taste adaptation. *Perception & Psychophysics, 35,* 1–4.

GINSBURG, A. P., EVANS, D. W., SEKULER, R., and HARP, S. A. (1982) Contrast sensitivity predicts pilots' performance in aircraft simulators. *American Journal of Optometry and Physiological Optics, 59,* 105–108.

GITTLEMAN, J. L., and HARVEY, P. H. (1980) Why are distasteful prey not cryptic? *Nature, 286,* 149–150.

GLISTA, G. G., FRANK, H. G., and TRACY, F. W. (1983) Video games and seizures. *Archives of Neurology, 40,* 588.

GOETHE, J. W. VON. (1840/1970) *Theory of colours.* C. L. Eastlake (trans.). Cambridge, Mass.: MIT Press.

GOGEL, W. C., and MERSHON, D. H. (1969) Depth adjacency in simultaneous contrast. *Perception & Psychophysics, 12,* 13–17.

GOLDBERG, M. E., and WURTZ, R. H. (1972) Activity of superior colliculus in behaving monkey. I. Visual receptive fields of single neurons. *Journal of Neurophysiology, 35,* 542–559.

GOLDMAN, A. I. (1976) Discrimination and perceptual knowledge. *Journal of Philosophy, 73,* 771–791.

GORDON, B. (1972) The superior colliculus of the brain. *Scientific American, 227,* 72–82.

GOURAS, P., and ZRENNER, E. (1981) Color coding in the primate retina. *Vision Research, 21,* 1591–1598.

GRAHAM, C. H. (1965) Visual space perception. In C. H. Graham (ed.), *Vision and visual perception.* New York: Wiley. Pp. 504–547.

GRANT, V. W. (1942) Accommodation and convergence in visual space perception. *Journal of Experimental Psychology, 31,* 89–104.

GRAZIADEI, P. P. C. (1973) Cell dynamics in the olfactory mucosa. *Tissue and Cell, 5,* 113–131.

GREEN, D. G. (1968) The contrast sensitivity of the colour mechanisms of the human eye. *Journal of Physiology, 196,* 415–429.

GREEN, D. M. (1961) Detection of auditory sinusoids of uncertain frequency. *Journal of the Acoustical Society of America, 33,* 897–903.

GREEN, D. M. (1982) Profile analysis: A different view of auditory intensity discrimination. *American Psychologist, 38,* 133–142.

GREEN, D. M., KIDD, G., JR., and PICARDI, M. C. (1983) Successive versus simultaneous comparison in auditory discrimination. *Journal of the Acoustical Society of America, 73,* 639–643.

GREEN, D. M., and SWETS, J. A. (1966) *Signal detection theory and psychophysics.* New York: Wiley.

GREEN, M. (1980) Orientation-specific adaptation: Effects of checkerboards on the detectability of gratings. *Perception, 9,* 369–377.

GREEN, M. (1983) Inhibition and facilitation of apparent motion by real motion. *Vision Research, 23,* 861–865.

GREGORY, R. L. (1970) *The intelligent eye.* New York: McGraw-Hill.

GREGORY, R. L. (1979) The aesthetics of anaesthetics. *Perception, 8,* 123–124.

GREGORY, R. L., and DRYSDALE, A. E. (1976) Squeezing speech into the deaf ear. *Nature, 264,* 748–751.

GRIFFIN, D. (1959) *Echoes of bats and men.* New York: Doubleday/Anchor.

GRINKER, J., and HIRSCH, J. (1972) Metabolic and behavioral correlates of obesity. In K. Porter and J. Knight (eds.), *Physiology, emotion, and psychsomatic illness.* Amsterdam: Elsevier. Pp. 349–374.

GROSSBERG, J. M., and GRANT, B. F. (1978) Clinical psychophysics: Applications of ratio scaling and signal detection methods to research on pain, fear, drugs, and medical decision making. *Psychological Bulletin, 85,* 1154–1176.

GROSSLIGHT, J. H., FLETCHER, H. J., MASTERTON, R. B., and HAGEN, R. (1978) Monocular vision and landing performance in general aviation pilots: Cyclops revisited. *Human Factors, 20,* 27–33.

GRUBER, H. E., and DINNERSTEIN, A. J. (1965) The role of knowledge in distance perception. *American Journal of Psychology, 78,* 575–581.

GULICK, W. L. (1971) *Hearing: Physiology and psychophysics.* New York: Oxford University Press.

GUTH, S. K. (1981) The science of seeing—a search for criteria. *American Journal of Optometry and Physiological Optics, 58,* 870–885.

HALL, M. J., BARTOSHUK, L. M., CAIN, W. S., and STEVENS, J. C. (1975) PTC taste blindness and taste of caffeine. *Nature, 253,* 442–443.

HALPERN, B. P. (1983) Tasting and smelling as active, exploratory sensory processes. *American Journal of Otolaryngology, 4,* 246–249.

HALSEY, R. M., and CHAPANIS, A. (1951) On the number of absolutely identifiable spectral hues. *Journal of the Optical Society of America, 41,* 1057–1058.

HAMMOND, P., and MacKAY, D. M. (1977) Differential responsiveness of simple and complex cells in cat striate cortex to visual texture. *Experimental Brain Research, 30,* 275–296.

HANSON, D. R., and FEARN, R. W. (1975) Hearing acuity in young people exposed to pop music and other noise. *Lancet, 2,* 203–205.

HARMON, L. D. (1973) The recognition of faces. *Scientific American, 229,* 70–82.

HARTLINE, H. K. (1940) The receptive fields of optic nerve fibers. *American Journal of Physiology, 30,* 690–699.

HARVEY, L. O., ROBERTS, J. O., and GERVAIS, M. J. (1983) The spatial frequency basis of internal representations. In H.-G. Geissler, H. F. J. M. Buffart, E. L. J. Leeuwenberg, and V. Sarris (eds.), *Modern issues in perception.* Rotterdam: North Holland. Pp. 217–226.

HEBB, D. O. (1949) *The organization of behavior.* New York: Wiley.

HECHT, S., SHLAER, S., and PIRENNE, M. H. (1942)

Energy, quanta, and vision. *Journal of General Physiology, 25,* 819–840.

HEFNER, R. S., and HEFNER, H. E. (1983) Hearing in large and small dogs: Absolute thresholds and size of the tympanic membrane. *Behavioral Neuroscience, 97,* 310–318.

HEINEMANN, E. G. (1961) The relation of apparent brightness to the threshold for differences in luminance. *Journal of Experimental Psychology, 61,* 389–399.

HEINEMANN, E. G., TULVING, E., and NACHMIAS, J. (1959) The effect of oculomotor adjustments on apparent size. *American Journal of Psychology, 72,* 32–45.

HELD, R. (1979) Development of visual resolution. *Canadian Journal of Psychology, 33,* 213–221.

HELMHOLTZ, H. (1909/1962) *Treatise on physiological optics* (3rd ed.). J. P. C. Southall (ed.). New York: Dover.

HELSON, H. (1964) Current trends and issues in adaptation level theory. *American Psychologist, 19,* 26–38.

HENNING, H. (1916) *Der Geruch.* Leipzig: Barth.

HESS, E. F. (1965) Attitude and pupil size. *Scientific American, 212,* 46–54.

HEYWOOD, S., and RATCLIFF, G. (1975) Long-term oculomotor consequences of unilateral colliculectomy in man. In G. Lennerstrand and P. Bach-y-Rita (eds.), *Basic mechanisms of ocular motility and their clinical implications.* Elmsford, N.Y.: Pergamon Press. Pp. 561–564.

HICKEY, T. (1977) Postnatal development of the human lateral geniculate nucleus: Relationship to a critical period for the visual systems. *Science, 198,* 836–838.

HOCHBERG, J. (1971) Perception. I. Color and shape. In J. W. Kling and L. A. Riggs (eds.), *Woodworth and Schlosberg's experimental psychology* (3rd ed.). New York: Holt, Rinehart and Winston. Pp. 395–474.

HOLLO, A. (1977) Age four. In *Sojourner microcosms: New and selected poems.* Berkeley, Calif: Blue Wind Press. P. 30.

HOLMES, G. (1944) The organization of the visual cortex in man. *Proceedings of the Royal Society of London, 132,* 348–361.

HOLWAY, A. F., and BORING, E. G. (1941). Determinants of apparent visual size with distance variant. *American Journal of Psychology, 54,* 21–37.

HOOD, D. C., and FINKELSTEIN, M.A. (1983) A case for the revision of textbook models of color vision: The detection and appearance of small brief lights. In J. D. Mollon and L. T. Sharpe (eds.), *Colour vision: Physiology and psychophysics.* London: Academic Press. Pp. 385–398.

HORNER, D. G. (1982) Can vision predict baseball players' hitting ability? *American Journal of Optometry and Physiological Optics, 59,* 69P.

HOWARD, M. (1983) The Warner touch. *New Republic, 188,* 9–12.

HUBEL, D. H., and WIESEL, T. N. (1962) Receptive fields, binocular interaction, and functional architecture in the cat's visual cortex. *Journal of Physiology, 160,* 106–154.

HUBEL, D. H., and WIESEL, T. N. (1970) Stereoscopic vision in macaque monkey. *Nature, 225,* 41–42.

HUBEL, D. H., and WIESEL, T. N. (1974a) Uniformity of monkey striate cortex: A parallel relationship between field size, scatter, and magnification factor. *Journal of Comparative Neurology, 158,* 295–306.

HUBEL, D. H., and WIESEL, T. N. (1974b) Sequence regularity and geometry of orientation columns in the monkey striate cortex. *Journal of Comparative Neurology, 158,* 267–294.

HUBEL, D. H., and WIESEL, T. N. (1977) Functional architecture of macaque monkey visual cortex. *Proceedings of the Royal Society of London, 198,* 1–59.

HUBEL, D. H., and WIESEL, T. N. (1979) Brain mechanisms of vision. *Scientific American, 241,* 150–163.

HUBEL, D. H., WIESEL, T. N., and LeVAY, S. (1977) Plasticity of ocular dominance columns in monkey striate cortex. *Philosophical Transactions of the Royal Society of London, Series B, 278,* 377–409.

HUBEL, D. H., WIESEL, T. N., and STRYKER, M. P. (1978) Anatomical demonstration of orientation columns in macaque monkey. *Journal of Comparative Neurology, 177,* 361–80.

HUGHES, A. (1977) The topography of vision in mammals of contrasting life style: Comparative optics and retinal organization. In F. Crescitelli (ed.), *Handbook of sensory physiology,* vol. 7/5. Berlin: Springer Verlag. Pp. 613–756.

HUMPHREY, N. K. (1974a) Species and individuals in the perceptual world of monkeys. *Perception, 3,* 105–114.

HUMPHREY, N. K. (1974b) Vision in a monkey without striate cortex: A case study. *Perception, 3,* 241–255.

HURD, P. D., and BLEVINS, J. (1984) Aging and the color of pills. *New England Journal of Medicine, 310,* 202.

HURVICH, L. M. (1969) Hering and the scientific establishment. *American Psychologist, 24,* 497–514.

HURVICH, L. M. (1981) *Color vision.* Sunderland, Mass.: Sinauer Associates.

HURVICH, L. M., and JAMESON, D. (1966) *The perception of brightness and darkness.* Boston: Allyn and Bacon.

HUYSMAN, J. K. (1884/1931) *Against the grain.* New York: Illustrated Editions.

HYVARINEN, L., and ROVAMO, J. (1981) Acquired blindness for achromatic stimuli. In L. Maffei (ed.), *Colour vision deficiencies, V. Proceedings of the Fifth Symposium of the International Research Group on Colour Vision Deficiencies.* The Hague: W. Junk, Publishers. Pp. 94–99.

IAVECCHIA, J. H., IAVECCHIA, H. P., and ROSCOE, S. N. (1983) The moon illusion revisited. *Aviation, Space, and Environmental Medicine, 54,* 39–46.

IMIG, T. J., and ADRIAN, H. O. (1977) Binaural columns in the primary field (A1) of cat auditory cortex. *Brain Research, 138,* 241–257.

ITTELSON, W. H. (1951) Size as a cue to distance: Static localization. *American Journal of Psychology, 64,* 54–67.

ITTELSON, W. H. (1952/1968) *The Ames demonstrations in perception.* New York: Hafner.

JACOBS, G. H. (1983) Colour vision in animals. *Endeavour, New Series 7,* 137–140.

JACOBSEN, S. G., MOHINDRA, I., and HELD, R. (1983) Monocular form deprivation in human infants. *Documenta Ophthalmologica, 55,* 199–211.

JAMES, W. (1890) *The principles of psychology.* 2 vols. New York: Holt.

JAMES. W. (1892) *Psychology: A briefer course.* New York: Holt.

JAMESON, D., and HURVICH, L. M. (1968) Opponent-response functions related to measured cone photopigments. *Journal of the Optical Society of America, 58,* 429–430.

JAMESON, D., and HURVICH, L. M. (1978) Dichromatic color language: "Reds" and "greens" don't look alike but their colors do. *Sensory Processes, 2,* 146–155.

JEFFRESS, L. A., and TAYLOR, R. W. (1961) Lateralization vs. localization. *Journal of the Acoustical Society of America, 33,* 482–483.

JEGHERS, H. (1937) The degree and prevalence of vitamin A deficiency in adults. *Journal of the American Medical Association, 109,* 756–762.

JOHANSSON, G. (1975) Visual motion perception. *Scientific American, 232,* 76–88.

JOHANSSON, G. (1977) Studies on visual perception of locomotion. *Perception, 6,* 365–376.

JOHANSSON, G., VON HOFSTEN, C., and JANSSON, G. (1980) Event perception. *Annual Review of Psychology, 31,* 27–64.

JOHNSON, D. M., and HAFTER, E. R. (1980) Uncertain-frequency detection: Cuing and condition of observation. *Perception & Psychophysics, 28,* 143–149.

JOHNSTON, J. C., and MCCLELLAND, J. L. (1973) Visual factors in word perception. *Perception & Psychophysics, 14,* 365–370.

JOHNSTON, J. C., and MCCLELLAND, J. L. (1974) Perception of letters in words: Seek not and ye shall find. *Science, 184,* 1192–1194.

JONES, E. E., and BRUNER, J. S. (1954) Expectancy in apparent visual movement. *British Journal of Psychology, 45,* 157–165.

JOYCE, J. (1922/1934) *Ulysses.* New York: Random House.

JOYCE, J. (1939/1967) *Finnegans Wake.* New York: Viking Press.

JUDD, D. B. (1960) Appraisal of Land's work on two-primary color projections. *Journal of the Optical Society of America, 50,* 254–268.

JULESZ, B. (1971) *Foundations of cyclopean perception.* Chicago: University of Chicago Press.

JULESZ, B. (1984) A brief outline of the texton theory of human vision. *Trends in NeuroSciences, 7,* 41–45.

JULESZ, B., and MILLER, J. E. (1975) Independent spatial frequency-tuned channels in binocular fusion and rivalry. *Perception, 4,* 125–143.

JULESZ, B., and SCHUMER, R. A. (1981) Early visual perception. *Annual Review of Psychology, 32,* 575–627.

JUNG, R. (1973) Visual perception and neurophysiology. In R. Jung (ed.), *Handbook of sensory physiology,* vol. 7/3A. Berlin: Springer Verlag. Pp. 1–152.

JUNG, R., and SPILLMANN, L. (1970) Receptive-field estimation and perceptual integration in human vision. In F. A. Young and D. B. Lindsley (eds.), *Early experience and visual information processing in perceptual and reading disorders.* Washington, D.C.: National Academy of Sciences Press. Pp. 181–197.

JUST, M. A., and CARPENTER, P. A. (1980) A theory of reading: From eye fixations to comprehension. *Psychological Review, 87,* 329–354.

KALMUS, H. (1955) The discrimination by the nose of the dog of individual human odours and in particular the odour of twins. *British Journal of Animal Behaviour, 3,* 25–31.

KANIZSA, G. (1976) Subjective contours. *Scientific American, 234,* 48–52.

KAUFMAN, L. (1974) *Sight and mind: An introduction to visual perception.* New York: Oxford University Press.

KAUFMAN, L., and ROCK, I. (1962) The moon illusion. *Scientific American, 207,* 120–132.

KELLER, H. (1908) Sense and sensibility. *Century Magazine, 75,* 566–577, 773–783.

KELLING, S. T., and HALPERN, B. P. (1983) Taste flashes: Reaction times, intensity, and quality. *Science, 219,* 412–414.

KELLY, D. H. (1976) Pattern detection and the two-dimensional Fourier transform: Flickering checkerboards and chromatic mechanisms. *Vision Research, 16,* 277–289.

KEMP, D. T. (1979) Evidence of mechanical non-linearity and frequency-selective wave amplification in the cochlea. *Archives of Otorhinolaryngology, 224,* 37–45.

KERTSA, L. G. (1962) Voice identifications. *Nature, 196,* 1253–1257.

KEVERNE, E. B. (1982) Chemical senses: Taste. In H. B. Barlow and J. D. Mollon (eds.), *The senses.* Cambridge: Cambridge University Press. Pp. 428–447.

KIANG, N. Y. S. (1968) A survey of recent developments in the study of auditory physiology. *Annals of Otology, Rhinology, and Laryngology, 77,* 656–675.

KIANG, N. Y. S. (1975) Stimulus representation in the discharge patterns of auditory neurons. In E. L. Eagles (ed.), *The nervous system,* vol. 3. New York: Raven Press. Pp. 81–96.

KINCHLA, R. A., and WOLFE, J. M. (1979) The order of visual processing: "Top-down," "bottom-up," or "middle-out." *Perception & Psychophysics, 25,* 225–231.

KINNEY, J. A., LURIA, S. M., RYAN, A. P., SCHLICTING, C. L., and PAULSON, H. M. (1980) The vision of submariners and national guardsmen: A longitudinal study. *American Journal of Optometry and Physiological Optics, 57,* 469–478.

KNUDSEN, E. I., and KONISHI, M. (1978) A neural map of auditory space in the owl. *Science, 200,* 795–797.

KNUDSEN, E. I., and KONISHI, M. (1980) Monaural occlusion shifts receptive-field locations of auditory midbrain units in the owl. *Journal of Neurophysiology, 44,* 687–695.

KOELEGA, H. S., and KOSTER, E. P. (1974) Some experiments on sex differences in odor perception. *Annals of the New York Academy of Sciences, 237,* 234–246.

KOENIG, W. (1950) Subjective effects in binaural hearing. *Journal of the Acoustical Society of America, 22,* 61–62.

KÖHLER, W. (1920/1938) Physical Gestalten. In W. D. Ellis (ed.), *A source book of gestalt psychology.* New York: Humanities Press. Pp. 17–54.

KOLERS, P. A. (1972) *Aspects of motion perception.* Elmsford, N.Y.: Pergamon Press.

KOLERS, P. A., and VON GRUNAU, M. (1975) Visual construction of color is digital. *Science, 187,* 757–759.

KOWLER, E., and MARTINS, A. J. (1982) Eye movements of preschool children. *Science, 215,* 997–999.

KRUEGER, L. E. (1975) Familiarity effects in visual information processing. *Psychological Bulletin, 82,* 949–974.

KRUK, R., and REGAN, D. (1983) Visual test results compared with flying performance in telemetry-tracked aircraft. *Aviation, Space, and Environmental Medicine, 54,* 906–911.

KRUK, R., REGAN, D., BEVERLEY, K., and LONGRIDGE, T. (1981) Correlations between visual test results and flying performance on the Advanced Simulator for Pilot Training (ASPT). *Aviation, Space, and Environmental Medicine, 52,* 455–460.

KUHL, P. K., and MELTZOFF, A. N. (1982) The bimodal perception of speech in infancy. *Science, 218,* 1138–1141.

KÜHNE, W. (1879/1977) Chemical processes in the retina. *Vision Research, 17,* 1273–1316.

KUNDEL, H. L., and NODINE, C. F. (1983) A visual concept shapes image perception. *Radiology, 146,* 363–368.

KÜNNAPAS, T. M. (1968) Distance perception as a function of available visual cues. *Journal of Experimental Psychology, 77,* 523–529.

KURTENBACH, W., STERNHEIM, C. E., and SPILL-MANN, L. (1984) Change in hue of spectral colors by dilution with white light (Abney effect). *Journal of the Optical Society of America A, 1,* 365–372.

KURTZ, D., and BUTTER, C. M. (1980) Impairments in visual discrimination performance and

gaze shifts in monkeys with superior colliculus lesions. *Brain Research, 196,* 109–124.

LADD-FRANKLIN, C. (1909/1962) The nature of the colour sensations. In J. P. C. Southall (ed.), *Helmholtz's treatise on physiological optics,* vol. 3. New York: Dover. Pp. 455–468.

LADEFOGED, P., and BROADBENT, D. E. (1957) Information conveyed by vowels. *Journal of the Acoustical Society of America, 29,* 98–104.

LAING, D. G. (1983) Natural sniffing gives optimum odour perception for humans. *Perception, 12,* 99–118.

LANCET, D. (1984) Molecular view of olfactory reception. *Trends in NeuroSciences, 7,* 35–36.

LAND, E. H. (1959) Experiments in color vision. *Scientific American, 200,* 84–94, 96, 99.

LANDIS, C. (1954) Determinants of the critical flicker fusion threshold. *Physiological Review, 34,* 259–286.

LAPPIN, J. S., DONER, J. F., and KOTTAS, B. L. (1979) Minimal conditions for the visual detection of structure and motion in three dimensions. *Science, 209,* 717–719.

LAWLESS, H. T., and ENGEN, T. (1977) Association to odors: Interference, memories, and verbal labeling. *Journal of Experimental Psychology, 3,* 52–59.

LAWRENCE, M. (1967) Hearing. In M. Alpern, M. Lawrence, and D. Wolsk (eds.), *Sensory processes.* Belmont, Calif.: Brooks/Cole. Pp. 65–101.

LEDERMAN, S. J. (1979) Auditory texture perception. *Perception, 9,* 93–103.

LEE, D. N. (1980) The optic flow field: The foundation of vision. *Philosophical Transactions of the Royal Society of London, Series B, 290,* 169–179.

LEE, D. N., and REDDISH, P. E. (1981) Plummeting gannets: A paradigm of ecological optics. *Nature, 293–294.*

LEEHEY, S. C., MOSKOWITZ-COOK, A., BRILL, S., and HELD, R. (1975) Orientational anisotropy in infant vision. *Science, 190,* 900–902.

LEEPER, R. W. (1935) A study of a neglected portion of the field of learning—the development of sensory organization. *Journal of Genetic Psychology, 46,* 41–75.

LEGRAND, Y. (1968) *Light, colour and vision* (2nd ed.). R. W. G. Hunt and F. R. W. Hunt (trans.). London: Chapman and Hall.

LEHMKUHLE, S. W., and FOX, R. (1977) Global stereopsis in the cat. Paper presented at the

Association for Research in Vision and Ophthalmology, Sarasota, Fla.

LEIBOWITZ, H. W. (1983) A behavioral and perceptual analysis of grade crossing accidents. *Operation Lifesaver National Symposium 1982.* Chicago: National Safety Council.

LEIBOWITZ, H. W., and MOORE, D. (1966) Role of changes in accommodation and convergence in the perception of size. *Journal of the Optical Society of America, 56,* 1120–1122.

LEIBOWITZ, H. W., POST, R. B., BRANDT, T., and DICHGANS, J. (1982) Implications of recent developments in dynamic spatial orientation and visual resolution for vehicle guidance. In A. Wertheim, W. Wagenaar, and H. W. Leibowitz (eds.), *Tutorials in motion perception.* New York: Plenum Press. Pp. 231–260.

LENNIE, P. (1980) Parallel visual pathways: A review. *Vision Research, 20,* 561–594.

LENNIE, P. (1984) Recent developments in the physiology of color vision. *Trends in Neuro-Sciences, 7,* 243–248.

LEVINSON, E., and SEKULER, R. (1976) Adaptation alters perceived direction of motion. *Vision Research, 16,* 779–781.

LINDSAY, P. H., and NORMAN, D. A. (1977) *Human information processing* (2nd ed.). New York: Academic Press.

LIVINGSTONE, M. S., and HUBEL, D. H. (1981) Effects of sleep and arousal on the processing of visual information in the cat. *Nature, 291,* 554–561.

LOFTUS, E. F. (1979) *Eyewitness testimony.* Cambridge, Mass.: Harvard University Press.

LOFTUS, E. F., MILLER, D. G., and BURNS, H. J. (1978) Semantic integration of verbal information into a visual memory. *Journal of Experimental Psychology: Human Perception and Performance, 4,* 19–31.

LOFTUS, G. R., and MACKWORTH, N. H. (1978) Cognitive determinants of fixation location during picture viewing. *Journal of Experimental Psychology: Human Perception and Performance, 4,* 565–572.

LUDEL, J. (1978) *Introduction to sensory processes.* New York: Freeman.

LUDVIGH, E., and MILLER, J. W. (1958) Study of visual acuity during ocular pursuit of moving test objects. I. Introduction. *Journal of the Optical Society of America, 48,* 799–802.

LUMSDEN, C. J., and WILSON, E. O. (1983) *Promethean fire: Reflections on the origin of mind.* Cambridge, Mass.: Harvard University Press.

LYTHGOE, J. N. (1979) *The ecology of vision.* Oxford: Clarendon Press.

MCADAMS, S. (1981) Spectral fusion and the creation of auditory images. In M. Clynes (ed.), *Music, mind, and brain: The neuropsychology of music.* New York: Plenum Press. Pp. 279–298.

MCARTHUR, D. J. (1982) Computer vision and perceptual psychology. *Psychological Bulletin, 92,* 283–309.

MCBURNEY, D. H. (1974) Are there primary tastes for man? *Chemical Senses and Flavor, 1,* 17–28.

MCBURNEY, D. H. (1978) Psychological dimensions and perceptual analyses of taste. In E. C. Carterette and M. P. Friedman (eds.), *Handbook of perception,* vol. 6A. New York: Academic Press. Pp. 125–155.

MCBURNEY, D. H., and GENT, J. F. (1979) On the nature of taste qualities. *Psychological Bulletin, 86,* 151–167.

MCBURNEY, D. H., and MOSKAT, L. J. (1975) Taste thresholds in college-age smokers and non-smokers. *Perception & Psychophysics, 18,* 71–73.

MCBURNEY, D. H., SMITH, D. V., and SHICK, T. R. (1972) Gustatory cross adaptation: Sourness and bitterness. *Perception & Psychophysics, 11,* 228–232.

MCCABE, P. A., and DEY, F. L. (1965) The effect of aspirin upon auditory sensitivity. *Annals of Otology, Rhinology, and Laryngology, 74,* 312–325.

MCCONKIE, G. W., and RAYNER, K. (1975) The span of the effective stimulus during a fixation in reading. *Perception & Psychophysics, 17,* 578–586.

MCCUTCHEON, N. B., and SAUNDERS, J. (1972) Human taste papilla stimulation: Stability of quality judgments over time. *Science, 175,* 214–216.

MCFADDEN, D. (1982) *Tinnitus: Facts, theories and treatments.* Washington, D.C.: National Academy of Sciences Press.

MCFADDEN, D., and PLATTSMIER, H. S. (1983) Aspirin can potentiate the temporary hearing loss induced by intense sounds. *Hearing Research, 9,* 295–316.

MCGURK, H., and MACDONALD, J. (1976) Hearing lips and seeing voices. *Nature, 264,* 746–748.

MCKEE, S. P. (1981) A local mechanism for differential velocity detection. *Vision Research, 21,* 491–500.

MCLEOD, R. W., and ROSS, H. E. (1983) Optic-flow and cognitive factors in time-to-collision estimates. *Perception, 12,* 417–423.

MacNichol, E. (1964) Three-pigment color vision. *Scientific American, 211,* 48–56.

McNicol, D. (1972) *A primer of signal detection theory.* London: Allen & Unwin.

Maffei, L., and Fiorentini, A. (1972) Retinogeniculate convergence and analysis of contrast. *Journal of Neurophysiology, 35,* 65–72.

Maffei, L., and Fiorentini, A. (1973) The visual cortex as a spatial frequency analyzer. *Vision Research, 13,* 1255–1267.

Mair, R. G., and Engen, T. (1976) Some effects of aphasic lesions on odor perception. *Sensory Processes, 1,* 33–39.

Mair, R. G., Gesteland, R. C., and Blank, D. L. (1982) Changes in morphology and physiology of olfactory receptor cilia during development. *Neurosciences, 7,* 3091–3103.

Malcolm, R. (1984) Pilot disorientation and the use of a peripheral vision display. *Aviation, Space, and Environmental Medicine, 55,* 231–238.

Malpelli, J. G., and Baker, F. H. (1975) The representation of the visual field in the lateral geniculate nucleus of *Macaca mulatta. Journal of Comparative Neurology, 161,* 569–594.

Mansfield, R. (1974) Neural basis of orientation perception in primate vision. *Science, 186,* 1133–1135.

Marc, R. E. (1982) Chromatic organization of the retina. In D. S. McDevitt (ed.), *Cell biology of the eye.* New York: Academic Press. Pp. 435–471.

Marcel, A. J. (1983) Conscious and unconscious perception: An approach to the relations between phenomenal experience and perceptual processes. *Cognitive Psychology, 15,* 238–300.

Marin, O. S. M. (1976) Neurobiology of language: An overview. *Annals of the New York Academy of Sciences, 280,* 900–912.

Mariotte, E. (1668/1948) The discovery of the blindspot. In W. Dennis (ed.), *Readings in the history of psychology.* New York: Appleton-Century-Crofts. Pp. 42–43.

Mark, L. S., and Todd, J. T. (1983) The perception of growth in three dimensions. *Perception & Psychophysics, 33,* 193–196.

Marr, D. (1976) Early processing of visual information. *Philosophical Transactions of the Royal Society, Series B, 275,* 483–524.

Marr, D. (1982) *Vision.* New York: Freeman.

Marron, J. A., and Bailey, I. L. (1982) Visual factors and orientation-mobility performance. *American Journal of Optometry and Physiological Optics, 59,* 413–426.

Martens, W., and Blake, R. (1980) Uncertainty impairs grating detection performance in the cat. *Perception & Psychophysics, 27,* 229–231.

Massaro, D. W., and Cohen, M. M. (1983) Consonant/vowel ratio: An improbable cue in speech. *Perception & Psychophysics, 33,* 501–505.

Masterton, B., Heffner, H., and Ravizza, R. (1969) The evolution of human hearing. *Journal of the Acoustical Society of America, 45,* 966–985.

Masterton, B., Thompson, G. C., Bechtold, J. K., and Robards, M. J. (1975) Neuroanatomical basis of binaural phase-difference analysis for sound localization: A comparative study. *Journal of Comparative and Physiological Psychology, 89,* 379–386.

Masterton, R. B., and Imig, T. J. (1984) Neural mechanisms of sound localization. *Annual Review of Physiology, 46,* 275–280.

Mather, G., and Moulden, B. (1980) A simultaneous shift in apparent direction: Further evidence for a "distribution-shift" model of direction coding. *Quarterly Journal of Experimental Psychology, 32,* 325–333.

Matin, E. (1974) Saccadic suppression: A review and an analysis. *Psychological Bulletin, 81,* 899–917.

Matin, L., and MacKinnon, G. E. (1964) Autokinetic movement: Selective manipulation of directional components by image stabilization. *Science, 143,* 147–148.

Meiselman, H. L., and Dzendolet, E. (1967) Variability in gustatory quality identification. *Perception & Psychophysics, 2,* 496–498.

Meredith, M. A., and Stein, B. E. (1983) Interactions among converging sensory inputs in the superior colliculus. *Science, 221,* 389–391.

Meyer, V., Gross, C. G., and Teuber, H.-L. (1963) Effect of knowledge of site of stimulation on the threshold for pressure sensitivity. *Perceptual and Motor Skills, 16,* 637–640.

Michaels, C. F., and Carello, C. (1981) *Direct perception.* Englewood Cliffs, N.J.: Prentice-Hall.

Miller, G. (1962) Decision units in the perception of speech. *IRE Transactions on Information Theory, 8,* 81–83.

Miller, J. D. (1978) Effects of noise on people. In E. C. Carterette and M. P. Friedman (eds.), *Handbook of perception,* vol. 4. New York: Academic Press. Pp. 609–640.

Mills, A. W. (1958) On the minimum audible angle. *Journal of the Acoustical Society of America, 30,* 237–246.

MILLS, A. W. (1960) Lateralization of high-frequency tones. *Journal of the Acoustical Society of America, 32,* 132–134.

MISHKIN, M., UNGERLEIDER, L. H., and MACKO, K. A. (1983) Object vision and spatial vision: Two cortical pathways. *Trends in NeuroSciences, 6,* 414–417.

MITCHELL, D. E., FREEMAN, R. D., MILLIDOT, M., and HAEGERSTROM, G. (1973) Meridional amblyopia: Evidence for modification of the human visual system by early visual experience. *Vision Research, 13,* 535–558.

MITCHELL, D. E., and WARE, C. (1974) Interocular transfer of a visual aftereffect in normal and stereoblind humans. *Journal of Physiology, 236,* 707–721.

MØLLER, A. R. (1974) Responses of units in cochlear nucleus to sinusoidally amplitude-modulated tones. *Experimental Neurology, 45,* 104–117.

MOLLON, J. D. (1982) Color vision. *Annual Review of Psychology, 33,* 41–85.

MONCRIEFF, R. W. (1956) Olfactory adaptation and odor likeness. *Journal of Physiology, 133,* 301–316.

MOORE, M. E., LINKER, E., and PURCELL, M. (1965) Taste sensitivity after eating: A signal detection approach. *American Journal of Psychology, 78,* 107–111.

MORAY, N. (1959) Attention in dichotic listening: Affective cues and the influence of instructions. *Quarterly Journal of Experimental Psychology, 11,* 56–60.

MOSKOWITZ, H. R. (1978) Taste and food technology: Acceptability, aesthetics, and preference. In E. C. Carterette and M. P. Friedman (eds.), *Handbook of perception,* vol. 6A. New York: Academic Press. Pp. 157–194.

MOULTON, D. G. (1974) Dynamics of cell populations in the olfactory epithelium. *Annals of the New York Academy of Sciences, 237,* 52–61.

MOULTON, D. G. (1976) Minimum odorant concentrations detectable by the dog and their implications for olfactory receptor sensitivity. In D. Muller-Schwarze and M. M. Mozell (eds.), *Chemical signals in vertebrates.* New York: Plenum Press. Pp. 455–464.

MOUNTCASTLE, V. B. (1975) The view from within: Pathways to the study of perception. *Johns Hopkins Medical Journal, 136,* 109–131.

MOVSHON, J. A. (1975) The velocity tuning of single units in cat striate cortex. *Journal of Physiology, 249,* 445–468.

MOVSHON, J. A., and LENNIE, P. (1979) Pattern-selective adaptation in visual cortical neurones. *Nature, 278,* 850–852.

MOZEL, M. M., SMITH, B., SMITH, P., SULLIVAN, R., and SWENDER, P. (1969) Nasal chemoreception in flavor identification. *Archives of Otolaryngology, 90,* 367–373.

MURPHY, B. J. (1978) Pattern thresholds for moving and stationary gratings during smooth eye movement. *Vision Research, 18,* 521–530.

MURPHY, C., CAIN, W. S., and BARTOSHUK, L. M. (1977) Mutual action of taste and olfaction. *Sensory Processes, 1,* 204–211.

MYERS, E. N., and BERNSTEIN, J. M. (1965) Salicylate ototoxicity: A clinical and experimental study. *Archives of Otolaryngology, 82,* 483–493.

NAGEL, T. (1982) What is it like to be a bat? In D. R. Hofstader and D. C. Dennett (eds.), *The mind's I.* New York: Bantam. Pp. 391–403.

NAKA, K. I., and RUSHTON, W. A. H. (1966) S-potentials from colour units in the retina of fish (*Cyprinidae*). *Journal of Physiology, 185,* 536–555.

NAVON, D. (1977) Forest before trees: The precedence of global features in visual perception. *Cognitive Psychology, 9,* 353–383.

NAVON, D., and NORMAN, J. (1983) Does global precedence really depend on visual angle? *Journal of Experimental Psychology: Human Perception and Performance, 9,* 955–965.

NEGUS, V. (1956) The air-conditioning mechanism of the nose. *British Medical Journal, 1,* 367–371.

NELSON, J. I., KATO, H., and BISHOP, P. O. (1977) Discrimination of orientation and position disparities by binocularly activated neurons in cat striate cortex. *Journal of Neurophysiology, 40,* 260–283.

NEWALL, S. M., BURNHAM, R. W., and CLARK, J. R. (1957) Comparison of successive with simultaneous color matching. *Journal of the Optical Society of America, 47,* 43–56.

NEWTON, I. (1704/1952) *Opticks, or a treatise of the reflections, refractions, inflections & colours of light* (4th ed.). New York: Dover.

NIEMEYER, W., and STARLINGER, I. (1981) Do the blind hear better? Investigations on auditory processing in congenital or early acquired blindness. II. Central functions. *Audiology, 20,* 510–515.

NIKARA, T., BISHOP, P. O., and PETTIGREW, J. D. (1968) Analysis of retinal correspondence by studying receptive fields of binocular single units in cat striate cortex. *Experimental Brain Research, 6,* 353–372.

NILSSON, T. H., and NELSON, T. M. (1981) Delayed monochromatic hue matches indicate characteristics of visual memory. *Journal of Experimental Psychology: Human Perception and Performance, 7,* 141–150.

NISBETT, R., and WILSON, T. D. (1977) Telling more than we can know: Verbal reports on mental processes. *Psychological Review, 84,* 231–259.

NIXON, J. C., and GLORIG, A. (1961) Noise-induced permanent threshold shift at 2000 cps and 4000 cps. *Journal of the Acoustical Society of America, 33,* 904–908.

NOBLE, W. (1983) Hearing, hearing impairment, and the audible world: A theoretical essay. *Audiology, 22,* 325–338.

NOZICK, R. (1981) *Philosophical explanations.* Cambridge, Mass.: Harvard University Press.

OGAWA, H., YAMASHITA, S., and SATO, M. (1974) Variation in gustatory nerve fiber discharge pattern with change in stimulus concentration and quality. *Journal of Neurophysiology, 37,* 443–457.

OLSON, H. F. (1967) *Music, physics, and engineering* (2nd ed.). New York: Dover.

ORBAN, G. A., DE WOLF, J., and MAES, H. (1984) Factors influencing velocity coding in the human visual system. *Vision Research, 24,* 33–39.

ORBAN, G. A., VANDENBUSSCHE, E., and VOGELS, R. (1984) Human orientation discrimination tested with long stimuli. *Vision Research, 24,* 121–128.

OWEN, D. (1980) *Camouflage and mimicry.* Chicago: University of Chicago Press.

OWEN, D. H. (1984) Improvement in wine and cola discrimination: Some support and some problems for the differentiation theory of perceptual learning. *Perception, 13,* in press.

OWEN, D. H., and MACHAMER, P. K. (1979) Bias-free improvement in wine discrimination. *Perception, 8,* 199–209.

OWSLEY, C. J., SEKULER, R., and SIEMSEN, D. (1983) Contrast sensitivity throughout adulthood. *Vision Research, 23,* 689–699.

PACKWOOD, J., and GORDON, B. (1975) Stereopsis in normal domestic cat, Siamese cat, and cat raised with alternating monocular occlusion. *Journal of Neurophysiology, 38,* 1485–1499.

PALMER, S. E. (1975) Visual perception and world knowledge: Notes on a model of sensory-cognitive interaction. In D. A. Norman and D. E. Rumelhart (eds.), *Explorations in cognition.* New York: Freeman. Pp. 279–307.

PALMER, S. E., ROSCH, E., and CHASE, P. (1981) Canonical perspective and the perception of objects. In J. Long and A. Baddeley (eds.), *Attention and performance,* vol. 9. Hillsdale, N. J.: Erlbaum. Pp. 135–151.

PANGBORN, R. M. (1960) Influence of color on the discrimination of sweetness. *American Journal of Psychology, 73,* 229–238.

PANGBORN, R. M., TRABUE, I. M., and BARYLKO-PIKIELNA, N. (1967) Taste, odor, and tactile discrimination before and after smoking. *Perception & Psychophysics, 2,* 529–532.

PANTLE, A., and PETERSIK, J. T. (1979) Factors controlling the competing sensations produced by a bistable stroboscopic motion display. *Vision Research, 19,* 143–154.

PANTLE, A., and PICCIANO, L. (1976) A multistable movement display: Evidence for two separate motion systems in human vision. *Science, 193,* 500–502.

PARKER, D. E. (1980) The vestibular apparatus. *Scientific American, 243,* 118–135.

PASTORE, R. E., and SCHEIRER, C. J. (1974) Signal detection theory: Considerations for general application. *Psychological Bulletin, 81,* 945–958.

PATERSON, C. A. (1979) Crystalline lens. In R. E. Records (ed.), *Physiology of the human eye and visual system.* New York: Harper & Row. Pp. 232–260.

PATTERSON, R. D., and GREEN, D. M. (1978) Auditory masking. In E. C. Carterette and M. P. Friedman (eds.), *Handbook of perception,* vol. 4. New York: Academic Press. Pp. 337–361.

PEARLMAN, A. L., BIRCH, J., and MEADOWS, J. C. (1979) Cerebral color blindness: An acquired defect in hue discrimination. *Annals of Neurology, 5,* 253–261.

PELI, E., and PELI, T. (1984) Image enhancement for the visually impaired. *Optical Engineering, 23,* 47–51.

PENFIELD, W., and PERROT, P. (1963) The brain's record of auditory and visual experience. *Brain, 86,* 595–696.

PERKY, C. W. (1910) An experimental study of imagination. *American Journal of Psychology, 21,* 422–452.

PETERSIK, J. T. (1978) Possible role of transient and sustained visual mechanisms in the determination of similarity judgments. *Perceptual and Motor Skills, 47,* 683–698.

PETTIGREW, J. D. (1972) The neurophysiology of binocular vision. *Scientific American, 227,* 84–95.

PETTIGREW, J. D., and DANIELS, J. D. (1973) Gamma-aminobutyric acid antagonism in visual cortex: Different effects on simple, complex, and hypercomplex neurons. *Science, 182,* 81–83.

PFAFFMANN, C. (1955) Gustatory nerve impulses in rat, cat, and rabbit. *Journal of Neurophysiology, 18,* 429–440.

PICK, A. D. (1979) Listening to melodies: Perceiving events. In A. D. Pick (ed.), *Perception and its development: A tribute to Eleanor J. Gibson.* Hillsdale, N. J.: Erlbaum. Pp. 145–165.

PICK, G. F., EVANS, E. F., and WILSON, J. P. (1977) Frequency resolution in patients with hearing loss of cochlear origin. In E. F. Evans and J. P. Wilson (eds.), *Psychophysics and physiology of hearing.* London: Academic Press. Pp. 273–281.

PIRENNE, M. H. (1967) *Vision and the eye* (2nd ed.). London: Chapman and Hall.

PIRENNE, M. H. (1970) *Optics, painting and photography.* Cambridge: Cambridge University Press.

PITTENGER, J. B., and SHAW, R. E. (1975) Aging faces as viscal-elastic events: Implications for a theory of nonrigid shape perception. *Journal of Experimental Psychology: Human Perception and Performance, 1,* 374–382.

PITTENGER, J. B., SHAW, R. E., and MARK, L. S. (1979) Perceptual information for the age level of faces as a higher-order invariant of growth. *Journal of Experimental Psychology: Human Perception and Performance, 5,* 478–493.

PITTENGER, J. B., and TODD, J. T. (1983) Perception of growth from changes in body proportions. *Journal of Experimental Psychology: Human Perception and Performance, 9,* 945–954.

POGGIO, G. F., and FISCHER, B. (1978) Binocular interaction and depth sensitivity in the striate and prestriate cortex of the behaving monkey. *Journal of Neurophysiology, 40,* 1392–1405.

POGGIO, T. (1984) Vision by man and machine. *Scientific American, 250,* 106–116.

POKORNY, J., GRAHAM, C. H., and LANSON, R. N. (1968) Effect of wavelength on foveal grating acuity. *Journal of the Optical Society of America, 58,* 1410–1414.

POLLACK, I., and ROSE, M. (1967) Effect of head movement on the localization of sounds in the equatorial plane. *Perception & Psychophysics, 2,* 591–596.

POLYAK, S. L. (1941) *The retina.* Chicago: University of Chicago Press.

POMERANTZ, J. R. (1981) Perceptual organization in information processing. In M. Kubovy and J. R. Pomerantz (eds.), *Perceptual organization.* Hillsdale, N J.: Erlbaum. Pp. 141–180.

POMERANTZ, J. R. (1983) The grass is always greener: An ecological analysis of an old aphorism. *Perception, 12,* 501–502.

POSNER, M. I. (1980) Orienting of attention. *Quarterly Journal of Experimental Psychology, 32,* 3–25.

POSNER, M. I., NISSEN, M. J., and OGDEN, W. C. (1978) Attended and unattended processing modes: The role of set for spatial location. In H. L. Pick and I. J. Saltzman (eds.), *Modes of perceiving and processing information.* Hillsdale, N. J.: Erlbaum. Pp. 137–158.

POTTER, M. C. (1966) On perceptual recognition. In J. S. Bruner (ed.), *Studies in cognitive growth.* New York: Wiley. Pp. 103–134.

POWER, R. P. (1981) The dominance of touch by vision: Occurs with familiar objects. *Perception, 10,* 29–33.

PRITCHARD, R. M. (1961) Stabilized images on the retina. *Scientific American, 204,* 72–78.

PRITCHARD, R. M., HERON, W., and HEBB, D. O. (1960) Visual perception approached by the method of stabilized images. *Canadian Journal of Psychology, 14,* 67–77.

PROUST, M. (1928) *Swann's way.* New York: Random House.

PUCCETTI, R., and DYKES, R. W. (1978) Sensory cortex and the mid-brain problem. *Behaviour and Brain, 1,* 337–344.

RAMACHANDRAN, V. S., and ANSTIS, S. M. (1983) Extrapolation of motion path in human visual perception. *Vision Research, 23,* 83–86.

RATLIFF, F. (1965) *Mach bands: Quantitative studies on neural networks in the retina.* San Francisco: Holden-Day.

RATLIFF, F. (1972) Contour and contrast. *Scientific American, 226,* 90–101.

RATLIFF, F. (1984) Why Mach bands are not seen at the edges of a step. *Vision Research, 24,* 163–165.

RAUSCH, R., and SERAFETINIDES, E. A. (1975) Specific alterations of olfactory functions in humans with temporal lobe lesions. *Nature, 225,* 557–558.

RAYNER, K. (1978) Eye movements in reading and information processing. *Psychological Bulletin, 85,* 618–660.

RAYNER, K., and BERTERA, J. H. (1979) Reading without a fovea. *Science, 206,* 468–469.

RAYNER, K., INHOFF, A. W., MORRISON, R. E., SLOWIACZEK, M. L., and BERTERA, J. H. (1981) Masking of foveal and parafoveal vision during eye fixations in reading. *Journal of Experimental Psychology: Human Perception and Performance, 7,* 167–179.

RECHTSCHAFFEN, A., and MEDNICK, S. (1955) The autokinetic word technique. *Journal of Abnormal and Social Psychology, 51,* 346.

RECORDS, R. E. (1979a) Eyebrows and eyelids. In R. E. Records (ed.) , *Physiology of the human eye and visual system.* New York: Harper & Row. Pp. 1–24.

RECORDS, R. E. (1979b) Retina: Metabolism and photochemistry. In R. E. Records (ed.), *Physiology of the human eye and visual system.* New York: Harper & Row. Pp. 296–318.

REES, J., and BOTWINICK, J. (1971) Detection and decision factors in auditory behavior of the elderly. *Journal of Gerontology, 26,* 133–136.

REEVES, A. (1981) Visual imagery lowers sensitivity to hue-varying, but not to luminance-varying, visual stimuli. *Perception & Psychophysics, 29,* 247–250.

REEVES, A. (1982) Untitled letter to the editors. *Vision Research, 22,* 711.

REGAN, D. (1982) Visual information channeling in normal and disordered vision. *Psychological Review, 89,* 407–444.

REGAN, D., and BEVERLEY, K. I. (1978) Looming detectors in the human visual pathway. *Vision Research, 18,* 415–421.

REGAN, D., and BEVERLEY, K. I. (1982) How do we avoid confounding the direction we are looking and the direction we are moving? *Science, 215,* 194–196.

REGAN, D., and BEVERLEY, K. I. (1984) Figure–ground segregation by motion contrast and by luminance contrast. *Journal of the Optical Society of America A, 1,* 433–442.

REGAN, D., BEVERLEY, K. I., and CYNADER, M. (1979) The visual perception of motion in depth. *Scientific American, 241,* 136–151.

REGAN, D., and CYNADER, M. (1979) Neurons in area 18 of cat visual cortex selectively sensitive to changing size: Non-linear interactions between responses to two edges. *Vision Research, 19,* 699–711.

REHN, T. (1978) Perceived odor intensity as a function of airflow through the nose. *Sensory Processes, 2,* 198–205.

REICHER, G. M. (1969) Perceptual recognition as a function of meaningfulness of stimulus material. *Journal of Experimental Psychology, 81,* 275–280.

RICHARDS, W. (1970) Stereopsis and stereoblindness. *Experimental Brain Research, 10,* 380–388.

RICHARDS, W. (1971) The fortification illusions of migraines. *Scientific American, 224,* 88–98.

RIGGS, L. A., RATLIFF, F., CORNSWEET, J. C., and CORNSWEET, T. N. (1953) The disappearance of steadily fixated visual test objects. *Journal of the Optical Society of America, 43,* 495–501.

RIGGS, L. A., VOLKMANN, F. C., and MOORE, R. K. (1981) Suppression of the blackout due to blinks. *Vision Research, 21,* 1075–1079.

RIPPS, H. (1982) Night blindness revisited: From man to molecules. *Investigative Ophthalmology and Visual Sciences, 23,* 588–609.

RISSET, J. C. (1978) Musical acoustics. In E. C. Carterette and M. P. Friedman (eds.), *Handbook of perception,* vol. 4. New York: Academic Press. Pp. 521–564.

RITTER, M. (1984) Size constancy as a function of fixation distance and retinal disparity. In L. Spillmann and B. R. Wooten (eds.), *Sensory experience, adaptation, and perception.* Hillsdale, N. J.: Erlbaum. Pp. 189–200.

ROBINSON, D. A. (1981) The control of eye movements. In V. B. Brooks (ed.), *Handbook of physiology,* sec. 1, vol. 2, part 2. Bethesda, Md.: American Physiological Society. Pp. 1275–1320.

ROBSON, J. G. (1966) Spatial and temporal contrast-sensitivity functions of the visual system. *Journal of the Optical Society of America, 56,* 1141–1142.

ROCK, I., and HARRIS, C. S. (1967) Vision and touch. *Scientific American, 216,* 96–104.

ROGERS, B. J., and GRAHAM, M. E. (1979) Motion parallax as an independent cue for depth perception. *Perception, 8,* 125–134.

ROGERS, B. J., and GRAHAM, M. E. (1984) Aftereffects from motion parallax and stereoscopic depth: Similarities and interactions. In L. Spillmann and B. R. Wooten (eds.), *Sensory experience, adaptation, and perception.* Hillsdale, N. J.: Erlbaum. Pp. 603–619.

ROGOWITZ, B. (1984) The breakdown of size constancy under stroboscopic illumination. In L. Spillmann and B. R. Wooten (eds.), *Sensory experience, adaptation, and perception.* Hillsdale, N. J.: Erlbaum. Pp. 201–214.

RONCHI, V. (1970) *The nature of light: An historical survey.* Cambridge, Mass.: Harvard University Press.

ROSE, J. E., BRUGGE, J. F., ANDERSON, D. J., and

HIND, J. E. (1967) Phase-locked response to low-frequency tones in single auditory nerve fibers of the squirrel monkey. *Journal of Neurophysiology, 30,* 769–793.

ROSE, J. E., GROSS, N. B., GEISLER, C. D., and HIND, J. E. (1966) Some neural mechanisms in the inferior colliculus of the cat which may be relevant to localization of a sound source. *Journal of Neurophysiology, 29,* 288–314.

ROVAMO, J., HYVARINEN, L., and HARI, R. (1982) Human vision without luminance contrast system: Selective recovery of the red-green colour contrast system from acquired blindness. In G. Verriest (ed.), *Colour vision deficiencies, VI. Proceedings of the Sixth Symposium of the International Research Group on Colour Vision Deficiencies.* The Hague: W. Junk, Publishers. Pp. 457–466.

ROZIN, P. (1978) The use of characteristic flavorings in human culinary practice. In C. M. Apt (ed.), *Flavor: Its chemical, behavioral, and commercial aspects. Proceedings of the Arthur D. Little Symposium.* Boulder, Colo.: Westview Press. Pp. 101–128.

ROZIN, P. (1979) Preference and affect in food selection. In J. H. A. Kroeze (ed.), *Preference behavior and chemoreception.* London: Information Retrieval. Pp. 289–302.

ROZIN, P. (1982) "Taste-smell confusions" and the duality of the olfactory sense. *Perception & Psychophysics, 31,* 397–401.

RUBERT, S. L., HOLLENDER, M. H., and MEHRHOF, E. G. (1961) Olfactory hallucinations. *Archives of General Psychiatry, 5,* 121–126.

RUBIN, M. L., and WALLS, G. L. (1969) *Fundamentals of visual science.* Springfield, Ill.: Thomas.

RUCKER, C. W. (1971) *A history of the ophthalmoscope.* Rochester, Minn.: Whiting.

RUNESON, S., and FRYKHOLM, G. (1983) Kinematic specifications of dynamics as an informational basis for person-and-action perception: Expectation, gender recognition, and deceptive intention. *Journal of Experimental Psychology: General, 112,* 585–615.

RUSHTON, W. A. H. (1965) Visual adaptation. The Ferrier Lecture. *Proceedings of the Royal Society of London, Series B, 162,* 20–46.

RUSHTON, W. A. H. (1979) King Charles II and the blind spot. *Vision Research, 19,* 225.

RUSSEL, M. J. (1976) Human olfactory communication. *Nature, 260,* 520–522.

RUSSELL, B. (1959) *My philosophical development.* New York: Simon and Schuster.

RUSSELL, J. A., and WARD, L. M. (1982) Environmental psychology. *Annual Review of Psychology, 33,* 651–688.

RYAN, A., and DALLOS, P. (1975) Absence of cochlear outer hair cells: Effect of behavioral auditory threshold. *Nature, 253,* 44–46.

RYAN, A., DALLOS, P., and MCGEE, T. (1979) Psychophysical tuning curves and auditory thresholds after hair cell damage in the chinchilla. *Journal of the Acoustical Society of America, 66,* 370–378.

RZESZOTARSKI, M. S., ROYER, F. L., and GILMORE, G. C. (1983) An introduction to two-dimensional fast Fourier transforms and their applications. *Behavior Research Methods and Instrumentation, 15,* 308–318.

SAFIRE, W. (1979) Mondegreens: I led the pigeons to the flag. *New York Times Magazine,* May 27, pp. 9–10.

SAMUEL, A. G. (1983) We really is worse than you or them, and so are ma and pa: Reply. *Journal of Experimental Psychology: Human Perception and Performance, 9,* 321–322.

SAWUSCH, J. R., and JUSCZYK, P. (1981) Adaptation and contrast in the perception of voicing. *Journal of Experimental Psychology: Human Perception and Performance, 7,* 408–421.

SCHECHTER, P. J., and HENKIN, R. I. (1974) Abnormalities of taste and smell after head trauma. *Journal of Neurology, Neurosurgery, and Psychiatry, 37,* 802–810.

SCHEMPER, T., VOSS, S., and CAIN, W. S. (1981) Odor identification in young and elderly persons: Sensory and cognitive limitations. *Journal of Gerontology, 36,* 446–452.

SCHIFF, W. (1965) Perception of impending collision. *Psychological Monographs, 79,* 1–26.

SCHIFFMAN, H. R. (1967) Size estimation of familiar objects under informative and reduced conditions of viewing. *American Journal of Psychology, 80,* 229–235.

SCHIFFMAN, S. S. (1974) Physiochemical correlates of olfactory quality. *Science, 185,* 112–117.

SCHIFFMAN, S. S. (1983) Taste and smell in disease. *New England Journal of Medicine, 308,* 1275–1279, 1337–1343.

SCHIFFMAN, S. S., and DACKIS, C. (1975) Taste of nutrients: Amino acids, vitamins, and fatty acids. *Perception & Psychophysics, 17,* 140–146.

SCHIFFMAN, S. S., and ERICKSON, R. P. (1980) The issue of primary tastes versus a taste continuum. *Neuroscience and Biobehavioral Reviews, 4,* 109–117.

SCHIFFMAN, S. S., REYNOLDS, M. L., and YOUNG, F. L. (1981) *Introduction to multidimensional scaling.* New York: Academic Press.

SCHILLER, P. H., and KOERNER, F. (1971) Discharge characteristics of single units in superior colliculus of the alert rhesus monkey. *Journal of Neurophysiology, 34,* 920–936.

SCHNEIDER, G. E. (1969) Two visual systems. *Science, 163,* 895–902.

SCHNEIDER, R. A., and WOLF, S. (1955). Olfactory perception thresholds for citral utilizing a new type of olfactorium. *Journal of Applied Physiology, 8,* 337–342.

SCHWARTZ, E. L. (1980) Computational anatomy and functional architecture of striate cortex: A spatial mapping approach to perceptual coding. *Vision Research, 20,* 645–669.

SCHWARTZ, E. L. (1983) Cortical mapping and perceptual invariance: A reply to Cavanagh. *Vision Research, 23,* 831–835.

SCHWARTZ, E. L., CHRISTMAN, D. R., and WOLF, A. P. (1984) Human primary visual cortex topography imaged via positron tomography. *Brain Research, 294,* 225–230.

SCOTT, A. B. (1979) Ocular motility. In R. E. Records (ed.), *Physiology of the human eye and visual system.* New York: Harper & Row. Pp. 577–642.

SEASHORE, C. E. (1938) *Psychology of music.* New York: McGraw-Hill.

SEGAL, S. J., and FUSELLA, V. (1970) Influence of imaged pictures and sounds on detection of visual and auditory signals. *Journal of Experimental Psychology, 83,* 458–464.

SEKULER, R., and BALL, K. (1977) Mental set alters visibility of moving targets. *Science, 198,* 60–62.

SEKULER, R., and GANZ, L. (1963) A new aftereffect of seen movement with a stabilized retinal image. *Science, 139,* 1146–1148.

SEKULER, R., OWSLEY, C. J., and BERENBERG, R. (unpublished ms.) Contrast sensitivity during provoked visual impairment in multiple sclerosis.

SEYFARTH, R. M., and CHENEY, D. L. (1984) The natural vocalizations of non-human primates. *Trends in NeuroSciences, 7,* 66–73.

SHAPLEY, R., KAPLAN, E., and SOODAK, R. (1981) Spatial summation and contrast sensitivity of X and Y cells in the lateral geniculate nucleus of the macaque. *Nature, 292,* 543–545.

SHARMA, S., and MOSKOWITZ, H. (1972) Effect of marijuana on the visual autokinetic phenomenon. *Perceptual and Motor Skills, 35,* 891–894.

SHARPE, D. T. (1974) *The psychology of color and design.* Chicago: Nelson-Hall.

SHAW, E. A. G. (1974) Transformation of sound pressure level from the free field to the eardrum in the horizontal plane. *Journal of the Acoustical Society of America, 56,* 1848–1861.

SHAW, R., and BRANSFORD, J. (1977) Introduction: Psychological approaches to the problem of knowledge. In R. Shaw and J. Bransford (eds.), *Perceiving, acting, and knowing.* Hillsdale, N. J.: Erlbaum. Pp. 1–39.

SHEBILSKE, W. L. (1980) Structuring an internal representation of text: A basis of literacy. In P. A. Kolers, M. E. Wrolstad, and H. Bouma (eds.), *Processing of visible language,* vol. 2. New York: Plenum Press. Pp. 227–239.

SHEPARD, R. N. (1981) Psychophysical complementarity. In M. Kubovy and J. R. Pomerantz (eds.), *Perceptual organization.* Hillsdale, N. J.: Erlbaum. Pp. 279–341.

SHEPARD, R. N., and ZARE, S. L. (1983) Path-guided apparent motion. *Science, 220,* 632–634.

SIEGEL, J. A., and SIEGEL, W. (1977) Absolute identification of notes and intervals by musicians. *Perception & Psychophysics, 21,* 143–152.

SIEGEL, R. K. (1984) Hostage hallucinations: Visual imagery induced by isolation and life-threatening stress. *Journal of Nervous and Mental Disease, 172,* 264–272.

SIMMONS, F. B., EPLEY, J. M., LUMMIS, R. C., GUTTMAN, N., FRISHKOPF, L. S., HARMON, L. D., and ZWICKER, E. (1965) Auditory nerve: Electrical stimulation in man. *Science, 148,* 104–106.

SINNOTT, J., BEECHER, M., MOODY, D., and STEBBINS, W. (1976) Speech and sound discrimination by monkeys and humans. *Journal of the Acoustical Society of America, 60,* 687–695.

SKINNER, B. F. (1957) *Verbal behavior.* New York: Appleton-Century-Crofts.

SLOAN, L. L. (1980) Need for precise measures of acuity. *Archives of Ophthalmology, 98,* 286–290.

SLOBODA, J. A. (1976) The effect of item position on the likelihood of identification by inference in prose reading and music reading. *Canadian Journal of Psychology, 30,* 228–237.

SMITH, M., SMITH, L. G., and LEVINSON, B. (1982) The use of smell in differential diagnosis. *Lancet, 2,* 1452.

SOUTHALL, J. P. C. (1937/1961) *Introduction to physiological optics.* New York: Dover.

SPERLING, G. (1976) Movement perception in

computer-driven display. *Behavior Research Methods and Instrumentation, 8,* 144–151.

SPERLING, G., BUDIANSKY, J., SPIVAK, J. G., and JOHNSON, M. C. (1971) Extremely rapid visual search: The maximum rate of scanning letters for the presence of a numeral. *Science, 174,* 307–311.

SPERRY, R. W. (1980) Mind–brain interaction: Mentalism, yes; dualism, no. *Neurosciences, 5,* 195–206.

SPERRY, R. W., MINER, N., and MEYERS, R. E. (1955) Visual pattern perception following subpial string and tantalum wire implantations in the visual cortex. *Journal of Comparative and Physiological Psychology, 48,* 50–58.

SPILLMANN, L. (1971) Foveal perceptive fields in the human visual system measured with simultaneous contrast in grids and bars. *Pflügers Archiv Gesamte Physiologie, 326,* 281–299.

STARLINGER, I., and NIEMEYER, W. (1981) Do the blind hear better? Investigations on auditory processing in congenital or early acquired blindness. I. Peripheral functions. *Audiology, 20,* 503–509.

STEINMAN, R. M. (1976) Role of eye movements in maintaining a phenomenally clear and stable world. In R. A. Monty and J. W. Senders (eds.), *Eye movements and psychological processes.* Hillsdale, N. J.: Erlbaum. Pp. 121–154.

STEINMAN, R. M., CUSHMAN, W. B., and MARTINS, A. J. (1982) The precision of gaze. *Human Neurobiology, 1,* 97–109.

STEINSCHNEIDER, M., AREZZO, J., and VAUGHN, H. G. (1982) Speech-evoked activity in the auditory radiations and cortex of the awake monkey. *Brain Research, 252,* 353–365.

STEVENS, J. K., EMERSON, R. C., GERSTEIN, G. L., KALLOS, T., NEUFIELD, G. R., NICHOLS, C. W., and ROSENQUIST, A. C. (1976) Paralysis of the awake human: Visual perception. *Vision Research, 16,* 93–98.

STEVENS, S. S. (1951) Mathematics, measurement, and psychophysics. In S. S. Stevens (ed.), *Handbook of experimental psychology.* New York: Wiley. Pp. 1–49.

STEVENS, S. S. (1956) The direct estimation of sensory magnitude—loudness. *American Journal of Psychology, 69,* 1–25.

STEVENS, S. S. (1960) Psychophysics of sensory function. *American Scientist, 48,* 226–252.

STEVENS, S. S. (1962) The surprising simplicity of sensory metrics. *American Psychologist, 17,* 29–39.

STEVENS, S. S. (1975) *Psychophysics: An introduc-tion to its perceptual, neural, and social prospects.* New York: Wiley.

STEVENS, S. S., and GUIRAO, M. (1967) Loudness functions under inhibition. *Perception & Psychophysics, 2,* 459–465.

STEVENS, S. S., and NEWMAN, E. B. (1934) The localization of pure tones. *Proceedings of the National Academy of Sciences, 20,* 593–596.

STEVENS, S. S., and WARSHOFSKY, F. (1965) *Sound and hearing.* Chicago: Time-Life Books.

STONE, H., and PRYOR, G. (1967) Some properties of the olfactory system of man. *Perception & Psychophysics, 2,* 516–518.

SUMMERFIELD, Q. (1975) How a full account of segmental perception depends on prosody and vice versa. In A. Cohen and S. G. Nooteboom (eds.), *Structure and process in speech perception.* New York: Springer Verlag. Pp. 51–68.

SWETS, J. A. (1973) The relative operating characteristic in psychology. *Science, 182,* 990–1000.

SWETS, J. A. (1979) ROC analysis applied to the evaluation of medical imaging techniques. *Investigative Radiology, 14,* 109–121.

SWETS, J. A., TANNER, W. P., JR., and BIRDSALL, T. G. (1961) Decision processes in perception. *Psychological Review, 68,* 301–340.

SYMONDS, C., and MACKENZIE, I. (1957) Bilateral loss of vision from cerebral infarction. *Brain, 80,* 415–455.

TAYLOR, C. A. (1965) *The physics of musical sounds.* New York: Elsevier.

TAYLOR, M. M., and WILLIAMS, E. (1966) Acoustic trauma in the sports hunter. *Laryngoscope, 76,* 969–979.

TEGHTSOONIAN, R., TEGHTSOONIAN, M., BERGLUND, B., and BERGLUND, U. (1978) Invariance of odor strength with sniff vigor: An olfactory analogue to size constancy. *Journal of Experimental Psychology: Human Perception and Performance, 4,* 144–152.

TELLER, D. Y. (1979) The forced-choice preferential looking procedure: A psychophysical technique for use with human infants. *Infant Behavior and Development, 2,* 135–153.

TERHARDT, E., and WARD, W. D. (1982) Recognition of musical key: Exploratory study. *Journal of the Acoustical Society of America, 72,* 26–33.

THOMAS, J. P., GILLE, J., and BARKER, R. A. (1982) Simultaneous visual detection and identification: Theory and data. *Journal of the Optical Society of America, 72,* 1642–1651.

THOMPSON, P. (1984) The coding of velocity of

motion in the human visual system. *Vision Research, 24,* 41–45.

THOMSON, J. A. (1980) How do we use visual information to control locomotion? *Trends in NeuroSciences, 3,* 247–250.

THORSON, J., LANGE, G. D., BIEDERMAN-THORSON, M. (1969) Objective measure of the dynamics of a visual movement illusion. *Science, 164,* 1087–1088.

TIMNEY, B., and MUIR, D. W. (1976) Orientation anisotropy: Incidence and magnitude in Caucasian and Chinese subjects. *Science, 193,* 699–700.

TITCHENER, E. B. (1915) *A beginner's psychology.* New York: Macmillan.

TYLER, C. W. (1981) Specific deficits of flicker sensitivity in glaucoma and ocular hypertension. *Investigative Ophthalmology and Visual Science, 20,* 204–212.

TYLER, C. W., and NAKAYAMA, K. (1984) Size interactions in the perception of orientation. In L. Spillmann and B. R. Wooten (eds.), *Sensory experience, adaptation, and perception.* Hillsdale, N. J.: Erlbaum. Pp. 529–546.

UHLRICH, D. J., ESSOCK, E. A., and LEHMKUHLE, S. (1981) Cross-species correspondence of spatial contrast sensitivity functions. *Behavioral Brain Research, 2,* 291–299.

ULLMAN, S. (1979) *The interpretation of visual motion.* Cambridge, Mass.: MIT Press.

UNGER, P. (1971) A defense of skepticism. *Philosophical Review, 80,* 198–219.

UTTAL, W. R. (1981) *A taxonomy of visual processes.* Hillsdale, N. J.: Erlbaum.

VAN ESSEN, D. C. (1979) Visual areas of the mammalian cerebral cortex. *Annual Review of Neuroscience, 2,* 227–263.

VAN ESSEN, D. C., and MAUNSELL, J. H. R. (1983) Hierarchical organization and functional streams in the visual cortex. *Trends in NeuroSciences, 6,* 370–375.

VAUTIN, R. G., and BERKLEY, M. A. (1977) Responses of single cells in cat visual cortex to prolonged stimulus movement: Neural correlates of visual aftereffects. *Journal of Neurophysiology, 40,* 1051–1065.

VENABLES, P. (1964) Input dysfunctions in schizophrenia. In B. Maher (ed.), *Progress in experimental personality research,* vol. 1. New York: Academic Press. Pp. 1–47.

VERHEIJEN, F. J. (1963) Apparent relative movement of "unsharp" and "sharp" visual patterns. *Nature, 199,* 160–161.

VERNON, P. E. (1977) Absolute pitch: A case study. *British Journal of Psychology, 68,* 485–489.

VIEMEISTER, N. F. (1983) Auditory intensity discrimination at high frequencies in the presence of noise. *Science, 221,* 1206–1208.

VOLKMANN, F. C., RIGGS, L. A., and MOORE, R. K. (1980) Eyeblinks and visual suppression. *Science, 207,* 900–902.

VON NOORDEN, G. K. (1981) New clinical aspects of stimulus deprivation amblyopia. *American Journal of Ophthalmology, 92,* 416–421.

WADE, N. J. (1983) *Brewster and Wheatstone on vision.* New York: Academic Press.

WALD, G. (1950) Eye and camera. *Scientific American, 183,* 32–41.

WALKER, J. (1984) How to stop a spinning object by humming and perceive curious blue arcs around a light. *Scientific American, 250,* 136–144.

WALLACE, P. (1977) Individual discrimination of humans by odor. *Physiology and Behavior, 19,* 577–579.

WALLACH, H. (1963) The perception of neutral colors. *Scientific American, 208,* 107–116.

WALLACH, H., and FLOOR, L. (1971) The use of size matching to demonstrate the effectiveness of accommodation and convergence as cues for distance. *Perception & Psychophysics, 10,* 423–428.

WALLACH, H., and O'CONNELL, D. N. (1953) The kinetic depth effect. *Journal of Experimental Psychology, 45,* 205–217.

WALLS, G. L. (1942) *The vertebrate eye and its adaptive radiation.* New York: Hafner.

WALLS, G. L. (1960) Land! Land! *Psychological Bulletin, 57,* 29–48.

WARD, W. D. (1966) Temporary threshold shift in males and females. *Journal of the Acoustical Society of America, 40,* 478–485.

WARD, W. D. (1968) Susceptibility to auditory fatigue. In W. D. Neff (ed.), *Contributions to sensory physiology,* vol. 3. New York: Academic Press. Pp. 195–225.

WARD, W. D. (1970) Musical perception. In J. V. Tobias (ed.), *Foundations of modern auditory theory,* vol. 1. New York: Academic Press. Pp. 407–447.

WARD, W. D., and GLORIG, A. (1961) A case of firecracker-induced hearing loss. *Laryngoscope, 71,* 1590–1596.

WARREN, R. M. (1970) Perceptual restoration of missing speech sounds. *Science, 167,* 392–393.

WASSERMAN, G. S. (1978) *Color vision: An historical perspective.* New York: Wiley.

WÄSSLE, H., PEICHL, L., and BOYCOTT, B. B. (1981) Dendritic territories of cat retinal ganglion cells. *Nature, 292,* 344–345.

WATSON, A. B., and PELLI, D. G. (1983) QUEST: A Bayesian adaptive psychometric method. *Perception & Psychophysics, 33,* 113–120.

WATT, R. J., and ANDREWS, D. P. (1981) APE: Adaptive probit estimation of psychometric functions. *Current Psychological Reviews, 1,* 205–214.

WEALE, R. A. (1982) *A biography of the eye.* London: Lewis.

WEISSKOPF, V. F. (1976) Is physics human? *Physics Today, 29,* 23–29.

WEISSTEIN, N. (1980) The joy of Fourier analysis. In C. S. Harris (ed.), *Visual coding and adaptability.* Hillsdale, N. J.: Erlbaum. Pp. 365–380.

WEISSTEIN, N., and HARRIS, C. S. (1974) Visual detection of line segments: An object-superiority effect. *Science, 186,* 752–755.

WELCH, R. B., and WARREN, D. H. (1980) Immediate perceptual response to intersensory discrepancy. *Psychological Bulletin, 88,* 638–667.

WELLS, G. L., LINDSAY, R. C. L., and FERGUSON, T. J. (1979) Accuracy, confidence, and juror perceptions in eyewitness identification. *Journal of Applied Psychology, 64,* 440–448.

WENGER, M. A., JONES, F. N., and JONES, M. H. (1956) *Physiological psychology.* New York: Holt, Rinehart and Winston.

WERTHEIMER, M. (1912/1961) Experimental studies on the seeing of motion. T. Shipley (trans. and ed.), *Classics in psychology.* New York: Philosophical Library. Pp. 1032–1088.

WERTHEIMER, M. (1923/1958) Principles of perceptual organization. In D. C. Beardslee and M. Wertheimer (eds.), *Readings in perception.* Princeton, N. J.: Van Nostrand. Pp. 115–135.

WERTHEIMER, M. (1957) Perception and the Rorschach. *Journal of Projective Techniques, 21,* 209–216.

WERTHEIMER, M. (1961) Psychomotor coordination of auditory and visual space at birth. *Science, 134,* 1692–1693.

WESTFALL, R. S. (1980) *Never at rest: A biography of Isaac Newton.* Cambridge: Cambridge University Press.

WEVER, E. G. (1978) *The reptile ear.* Princeton, N. J.: Princeton University Press.

WEVER, E. G., and BRAY, C. W. (1937) The perception of low tones and the resonance-volley theory. *Journal of Psychology, 3,* 101–114.

WHEATSTONE, C. (1838/1964) Some remarkable phenomena of binocular vision. In W. N. Dember (ed.), *Visual perception: The nineteenth century.* New York: Wiley. Pp. 114–129.

WHEELER, D. D. (1970) Processes in word recognition. *Cognitive Psychology, 1,* 59–85.

WHITE, H. E., and LEVATIN, P. (1962) "Floaters" in the eye. *Scientific American, 206,* 119–127.

WIESEL, T. N., and HUBEL, D. H. (1960) Receptive fields of ganglion cells in the cat's retina. *Journal of Physiology, 153,* 583–594.

WIESEL, T. N., and HUBEL, D. H. (1966) Spatial and chromatic interactions in the lateral geniculate body of the rhesus monkey. *Journal of Neurophysiology, 29,* 1115–1156.

WIGHTMAN, F., and KISTLER, D. J. (1980) A new "look" at auditory space perception. In G. van den Brink and F. A. Bilsen (eds.), *Psychophysical, physiological and behavioral studies in hearing.* Delft: Delft University Press. Pp. 441–448.

WILKINS, A. J., NIMMO-SMITH, I., TAIT, A., McMANUS, I. C., DELLA SALA, S., TILLEY, A., ARNOLD, K., and BARRIE, M. A. (in press) A neurological basis for visual discomfort. *Brain.*

WILKINS, P. A., and ACTON, W. I. (1982) Noise and accidents: A review. *Annals of Occupational Hygiene, 25,* 249–260.

WILSON, J. P., and SUTTON, G. J. (1981) Acoustic correlates of tonal tinnitus. In *Tinnitus, CIBA Foundation Symposium,* vol. 85. London: Pitman. Pp. 82–100.

WINTER, R. (1976) *The smell book: Scents, sex, and society.* Philadelphia: Lippincott.

WOLLBERG, Z., and NEWMAN, J. D. (1972) Auditory cortex of squirrel monkey: Response patterns of single cells to species-specific vocalizations. *Science, 175,* 212–214.

WOODHOUSE, J. M., and BARLOW, H. B. (1982) Spatial and temporal resolution and analysis. In H. B. Barlow and J. D. Mollon (eds.), *The senses.* Cambridge: Cambridge University Press. Pp. 133–164.

WOODWORTH, R. S. (1938) *Experimental psychology.* New York: Holt.

WOODWORTH, R. S., and SCHLOSBERG, H. (1954) *Experimental psychology* (rev. ed.). New York: Holt.

WRIGHT, R. H. (1966) Why is an odour? *Nature, 209,* 551–554.

WUILLEMIN, D., and RICHARDSON, B. (1982) On the failure to recognize the back of one's own hand. *Perception, 11,* 53–56.

WURTZ, R. H., and GOLDBERG, M. E. (1972) Activity of superior colliculus in behaving monkey. *Journal of Physiology, 35,* 587–596.

WURTZ, R. H., GOLDBERG, M. E., and ROBINSON, D. L. (1982) Brain mechanisms of visual attention. *Scientific American, 244,* 124–135.

YODOGAWA, E. (1982) Symmetropy, an entropylike measure of visual symmetry. *Perception & Psychophysics, 32,* 230–240.

YONAS, A. (1984) Reaching as a measure of infant spatial perception. In G. Gottlieb and N. A. Krasnegor (eds.), *Measurement of audition and vision in the first year of postnatal life: A methodological review.* Norwood, N. J.: Ablex.

YOST, W. A., and NIELSEN, D. W. (1977) *Fundamentals of hearing.* New York: Holt, Rinehart and Winston.

YOUNG, F. A. (1981) Primate myopia. *American Journal of Optometry and Physiological Optics, 58,* 560–566.

YOUNG, F. A., SINGER, R. M., and FOSTER, D. (1975) The psychological differentiation of male myopes and nonmyopes. *American Journal of Optometry and Physiological Optics, 52,* 679–686.

YOUNG, P. T. (1928) Auditory localization with acoustical transposition of the ears. *Journal of Experimental Psychology, 11,* 399–429.

YOUNG, T. (1801/1948) Observations on vision. In W. Dennis (ed.), *Readings in the history of psychology.* New York: Appleton-Century-Crofts. Pp. 96–101.

ZACKS, J. (1970) Temporal summation phenomena at threshold: Their relation to visual mechanisms. *Science, 170,* 197–199.

ZAHN, C. T. (1971) Graph-theoretic methods for detecting and describing gestalt clusters. *IEEE Transactions on Computers, C-20,* 68–86.

ZEKI, S. M. (1978) Functional specialization in the visual cortex of the rhesus monkey. *Nature, 274,* 423–428.

ZEKI, S. M. (1980) The representation of colours in the cerebral cortex. *Nature, 284,* 412–418.

ZELMAN, S. (1973) Correlation of smoking history with hearing loss. *Journal of the American Medical Association, 223,* 920.

ZIHL, J., VON CRAMON, D., and MAI, N. (1983) Selective disturbance of movement vision after bilateral brain damage. *Brain, 106,* 313–340.

ZIHL, J., and WERTH, R. (1984) Contributions to the study of blindsight. 2. The role of specific practice for saccadic localization in patients with post-geniculate vision field defects. *Neuropsychologia, 22,* 13–22.

ZIMBARDO, P. G., ANDERSEN, S. M., and KABAT, L. G. (1981) Induced hearing deficit generates experimental paranoia. *Science, 212,* 1529–1531.

ZISMAN, F., and ADAMS, A. J. (1982) Spectral sensitivity of cone mechanisms in juvenile diabetes. In G. Verriest (ed.), *Colour vision deficiencies, VI. Proceedings of the Sixth Symposium of the International Research Group on Colour Vision Deficiencies.* The Hague: W. Junk, Publishers. Pp. 127–131.

ZRENNER, E. (1983) *Neurophysiological aspects of color vision in primates.* Berlin: Springer Verlag.

ZUREK, P. M. (1981) Spontaneous narrowband acoustic signals emitted by human ears. *Journal of the Acoustical Society of America, 69,* 514–523.

ZWICKER, E., and SCHARF, B. (1965) A model of loudness summation. *Psychological Review, 72,* 3–26.

Glossary

The number in parentheses following each term refers to the page number of the text on which that term is introduced.

Abney's law (94)   A principle stating that the visual effectiveness of a light composed of different wavelengths can be predicted from the sum of the responses to the wavelengths considered separately.

absolute distance (217)   The distance from an observer to an object. See **relative distance.**

absolute threshold (450)   The minimum stimulus intensity that a person can detect. See **difference threshold.**

achromatic system (203)   In the opponent-process view of color vision, the pathway that generates and transmits information about an object's lightness. See **chromatic system.**

accommodation (38, 218)   The variation in the eye's optical power brought about by temporary changes in the shape of the lens.

acoustic energy (291)   The variations in air pressure produced by the vibration of an object.

acoustic reflex (304)   Muscular contractions within the middle ear that damp sound vibrations by stiffening the eardrum and restricting the movements of the ossicles.

acoustics (293)   The branch of physics concerned with sound.

action potentials (62)   Brief electrical discharges that are generated by a neuron and that represent the "vocabulary" of communication within the nervous system.

adaptation (131, 191, 323, 414)   A reduction in the responsiveness of neurons, produced by prolonged stimulation.

additive color mixture (190)   A color that results when several component colors are combined in such a way that each component contributes a portion to the spectral composition of the combination. See **subtractive color mixture.**

aerial perspective (238)   The tendency for objects at a distance to appear less distinct, since light reflected from those objects must travel through atmosphere containing particles of dirt and water.

afterimage (29, 203)   A visual sensation that persists after exposure to some intense stimulus; also, an illusory color produced by exposure to an intense stimulus.

agnosias (446)   Neurological conditions in which people cannot recognize objects; depending on the sense involved, an agnosia is said to be visual, auditory, or tactile.

ambient system (275)   The aspect of vision responsible for spatial orientation; uses information from peripheral as well as central vision. See **focal system.**

Ames room (235)   A specially constructed room in which the floor-to-ceiling heights as well as the sizes and shapes of the doors and windows have been distorted to make the room appear rectangular when viewed from one specific vantage point. To an observer looking into the room through a peephole, people of identical heights standing in different parts of the room look dramatically different in height. The Ames room illustrates how perceived distance influences perceived size.

amplitude (295)   The property of sound waves that is related to the magnitude of the change in air pressure produced by a sound source. This property, sometimes referred to as *intensity*, is related to loudness. See **intensity.**

analytic introspection (139)   A method for studying perception in which trained people attend to and describe the experiences evoked by some stimulus.

aneurysm (111)   A balloon-like bulge in an artery that can cause deformation of neighboring nerve fibers, producing visual field losses in the case of the internal carotid arteries.

anosmia (398)   An inability to smell odors.

Anton's syndrome (17)   A rare neurological condition in which a cortically blind person denies his or her blindness.

anvil (incus) (302)   The middle member of the three ossicles within the middle ear; it relays sound vibrations from the hammer to the stirrup.

apparent motion (280)   The illusory impression, created by the rapid alternation of objects presented at different spatial locations, that the objects have moved smoothly from one location to the other. See **element movement, group movement.**

aqueous humor (35)   A watery fluid, produced by the ciliary body, that nourishes structures within the eye's anterior chamber and helps maintain the eye's shape.

astigmatism (51)   An error in refraction caused by variation in optical power along various meridians of the cornea.

audiogram (329)   A graph depicting threshold intensity for hearing pure tones of different frequencies.

auditory canal (301)   The hollow cavity leading from the pinna to the eardrum, which in humans is about 2.5 cm long and 7 mm in diameter.

auditory cortex (326)   A region of the cortex devoted to analysis of complex sound information, including biologically relevant sounds involved in communication.

auditory nerve (319)   The bundle of nerve fibers innervating the cochlea and carrying information from the ear to higher stages of the auditory system. Also known as the *eighth cranial nerve.*

autokinetic effect (428)   The illusory impression of motion created when a small stationary target is seen in a homogeneous dim field.

axon (69)   The portion of a neuron over which action potentials are conducted. A group of axons constitute a *nerve* or a *tract.*

basilar membrane (306)   The thin sheet of tissue separating the tympanic canal and the cochlear duct.

binaural (324)   Listening with two ears. See **monaural.**

binaural cues (324)   Sources of sound information for localizing a sound source by comparing the sounds received by the two ears.

binaural unmasking (369)   A reduction in the ability of masking noise heard with both ears to mask another sound heard by one ear only. See **masking.**

binocular (124)   Seeing with two eyes. See **monocular.**

binocular cell (124)   A visual cortical cell receiving excitatory input from both eyes.

binocular rivalry (226)   The alternation of a percept over time between one eye's view and the other eye's view when the two eyes view very different stimuli.

blindsight (115, 277)   The ability of some cortically blind people to point to the location of a light that they cannot see.

Bloch's law (85)   The principle that all stimuli in which the product of time and intensity is constant will be equally detectable.

blue-yellow cells (207)   Neurons showing a polarized response to spectral lights, which increases over one portion of the spectrum and decreases over another portion; the transition between the two types of responses occurs between the regions of the spectrum called blue and yellow. See **red-green cells.**

bottom-up (422) A tendency for perception to be shaped by the flow of information from the receptors to higher nervous centers. See **top-down.**

bone conduction (333) The transmission of sound wave vibrations through the bones of the skull to the cochlea. A procedure for testing the integrity of the cochlea in the presence of middle ear damage.

brightness (182) The dimension of color experience related to the amount of light emitted by an object. See **hue, saturation.**

Bruch's membrane (42) A layered structure situated between the choroid and pigment epithelium of the eye.

cataract (38) Clouding that reduces the lens's transparency and, hence, degrades the quality of the retinal image.

choroid (35) A dark, spongy structure containing blood vessels that supply nourishment to the retina; because of its heavy pigmentation, the choroid absorbs scattered light.

chromatic system (203) In the opponent-process view of color vision, the pathway that generates and transmits information about an object's color. See **achromatic system.**

cilia (392) A tiny tuft of thin hairs projecting out of each olfactory receptor cell and extending through the mucous layer into the nasal cavity; thought to be the site where odorous molecules trigger electrical changes in the olfactory receptor cell.

ciliary body (35) Located in the eye, a spongy network of tissue that manufactures aqueous humor.

closure (143) The Gestalt principle of organization referring to the tendency of the visual system to obscure small breaks or gaps in objects. See **proximity, similarity.**

cochlea (305) A coiled, fluid-filled chamber in the inner ear containing the specialized organ for hearing, the basilar membrane.

cochlear duct (306) One of the three wedge-shaped chambers of the cochlea.

cochlear emissions (317) Sounds that are generated entirely from within the cochlea.

cochlear nucleus (324) A structure receiving input from the auditory nerve; its cells exhibit a high degree of frequency tuning.

cocktail party effect (368) The ability to attend selectively to the speech of one person in the midst of many other speakers.

collector cells (54) Specialized neurons within the eye that receive and process information from the photoreceptors.

color constancy (189) The tendency of an object's color to remain unchanged despite changes in the spectrum of light falling on—and reflected by—that object.

color contrast (201) A change in color appearance brought about by juxtaposing particular color pairs.

color deficiency (210) In humans, a departure from normal trichromatic color vision; takes various forms, including anomalous trichromacy, dichromacy, and monochromacy.

common chemical sense (397) An aspect of olfaction responsible for the detection of strong concentrations of potentially dangerous substances; responsible for the "feeling" in the nose produced by certain substances.

complementary (184) Describing two colors that can be mixed to form white.

complex cells (120) Visual cortical cells that do not exhibit clearly defined ON and OFF regions within their receptive fields, making it difficult to predict what stimulus will produce the largest response. See **simple cells.**

composite light (184) According to Newton, any light that is made up of several different color components. See **pure light.**

computer vision (177) The ability of machines, notably computers, to perceive and interpret a visual scene.

conditioned taste aversion (418) Learned avoidance of certain taste substances, usually following nausea from ingesting the substance.

conduction loss (332) A form of hearing loss attributable to a disorder in the outer or middle ear; it typically involves an overall loss in sensitivity at all sound frequencies. See **sensory/neural loss.**

cones (54) Photoreceptors that are specialized for daylight and color vision. See **rods.**

configural superiority effect (435) The finding that, under some circumstances, a complex figure, or part of a complex figure, may be seen more readily than one of its parts presented in isolation.

conjunctive (31)   Referring to those movements of the eye in which both eyes move in the same direction. See **vergence.**

contralateral fibers (100)   In the case of vision, those optic nerve fibers that project from one eye to the opposite side of the brain. See **ipsilateral fibers.**

contrast (138, 148)   The difference in light intensity between an object and its immediate surroundings; also, the intensity difference between adjacent bars in a grating.

contrast sensitivity function (CSF) (155)   A graph depicting a person's ability to see targets of various spatial frequency; on the x-axis is the spatial frequency of the test target; on the y-axis is sensitivity, the reciprocal of the minimum contrast needed to see the test target.

contrast threshold (145)   The minimum contrast needed to see some target.

convergence (218)   The ability of the eyes to turn inward, toward each other, in order to fixate a nearby object.

convergence insufficiency (231)   Difficulty with turning the eyes inward to fixate a nearby object.

cornea (34)   The transparent portion of the eye's front surface, which refracts light and allows it to pass into the eyeball.

cortical magnification (112, 248)   The mapping of the retina onto the visual cortex so that the representation of the fovea is exaggerated or magnified.

criterion (458)   The implicit rule used by an observer in order to convert sensory information into overt responses.

critical flicker frequency (CFF) (253)   The highest perceptible rate of temporal variation in light intensity.

cross-adaptation (400)   A temporary loss in sensitivity to one odor following exposure to a different odor.

cross-fiber theory (410)   The idea that taste qualities are represented by the pattern of neural activity among an ensemble of neurons; also has application in vision, hearing, and smell.

cross-modality matching (345)   A psychophysical procedure in which one sort of stimulus (for instance, a light) is adjusted so that the sensation the stimulus produces matches the sensation produced by a different sort of stimulus (for instance, a sound).

crowding effect (89)   The tendency for small letters to be difficult to read when they are in close proximity to one another.

crystalline lens (38)   The elliptical optical element located immediately behind the iris of the eye. Temporary variations in thickness alter the eye's accommodation, or optical power.

cutoff frequency (153)   The spatial frequency at which a lens's transfer function falls to zero; the highest frequency that a lens can image; the highest frequency to which a visual system can respond.

dark adaptation (93)   The increase in visual sensitivity that accompanies time in darkness following exposure to light.

dark light (452)   See **intrinsic light.**

decibel (dB) (297)   A unit for expressing sound amplitude.

depth of field (37)   The range of distances over which the image of a scene remains sharply focused; varies with pupil size.

depth perception (216)   The ability to appreciate distances between objects and distances from the perceiver to objects.

detection (137, 180)   The process by which an object is picked out from its surroundings; also, the process by which the presence of some object is perceived.

dichromatic (195)   Referring to a person whose eye contains two types of cone photopigments.

difference threshold (450)   The minimum amount by which stimulus intensity must be changed in order to produce a just noticeable change in sensation.

diplopia (231)   Double vision, a condition that results when images from the two eyes are seen separately and simultaneously.

direct scaling techniques (344)   A set of psychophysical procedures for measuring subjective sensory experiences such as loudness or brightness; these procedures are based on the assumption that people can rate sensory magnitude.

direction-selective cell (277)   A neuron in the visual cortex that responds most vigorously to a particular direction of target movement.

direction selectivity (120)   A tendency of some neurons in the visual system to respond most strongly to objects that move in a particular direction.

discrimination (137, 180)   The process by which one object is distinguished from another.

discrimination threshold (346)   The minimum physical difference, usually an intensity difference, that allows two objects to be distinguished from each other.

disparity-selective cells (228)   Cells in the visual cortex that receive input from both eyes and that respond only when an object is situated at a particular distance from the two eyes. See **stereoblindness.**

distance senses (6)   See **far senses.**

divergent (44)   Referring to light whose wavefronts spread outward, usually as the light proceeds away from its source.

Doppler shift (355)   A change in the perceived pitch of the sound produced by some object as the object approaches or recedes from the listener.

Dualism (22)   The philosophical view that mental events need not be associated with neural events. See **Mechanism.**

duplex (84)   Referring to the co-existence within the eye of two different systems, scotopic and photopic. The scotopic system provides high sensitivity in dim light; and the photopic system provides high resolution under daylight conditions.

dynamic visual acuity (270)   The finest spatial detail that can be resolved; measured while a target is moving.

eardrum (tympanic membrane) (302)   The thin, oval membrane that covers the end of the auditory canal and separates the outer ear and the middle ear; it vibrates when sound waves strike it.

eccentricity (68)   The distance between the center of the retina and the location of the retinal image cast by an object.

echoes (293)   Reflected sound waves.

electromagnetic radiation (25)   Energy that is produced by oscillation of electrically charged material; light encompasses a small portion of the electromagnetic spectrum.

element movement (284)   In an ambiguous type of apparent movement, the percept that some of the stimulus' components are stationary while one component moves back and forth. See **apparent motion, group movement.**

emmetropic (46)   Referring to an eye whose focal point, in the absence of accommodation, coincides exactly with the retina.

epistemology (10)   The branch of philosophy concerned with the origins and nature of knowledge, particularly knowledge derived from the senses.

equal loudness contours (339)   A set of curves describing the sound intensities at which different frequencies all sound equal in loudness. See **loudness matching.**

Eustachian tube (304)   The opening connecting the middle ear and the throat, which maintains air pressure within the middle ear at nearly the same value as the air pressure in the outside environment.

extraocular muscles (28)   In humans, six large muscles attached to the globe of the eye; by rotating the eyeball within the orbit, the coordinated contractions of these muscles control the direction of gaze. See **rectus muscles.**

far senses (distance senses) (6)   Senses, such as vision, that enable an organism to perceive objects or events some distance away. See **near senses.**

fibrous tunic (33)   The strong, leathery outermost layer of the eyeball.

figure-ground perception (144)   The tendency to see part of a scene (the figure) as a solid, well-defined object standing out against a less distinct background (the ground).

flavor (405)   A complex sensation associated with food, based on the food's taste, temperature, texture, and smell.

flicker (253)   Temporal variation in light intensity; also, the percept of such temporal variation.

floaters (39)   Debris that drifts about within the eye's vitreous casting shadows on the retina and producing dark spots that appear to move along with the eye.

focal system (275)   The aspect of vision that is responsible for object identification and discrimination; predominantly uses central, rather than peripheral, vision. See **ambient system.**

focus of flow (260)   The point in space from which, as a person moves through the environment, all objects seem to shift radially outward; when the person both fixates and moves toward the same point in space, that point is the focus of flow.

forced-choice method (457)   A psychophysical procedure in which a person must identify the interval during which a stimulus occurred; in an alternative version, the person must identify the spatial location at which a stimulus was presented.

Fourier analysis (154)   A method for calculating the frequency content of any temporal or spatial signal; can be used to determine the spatial frequency content of a visual scene or other target.

free nerve endings (392–393)   Nerve cells in the olfactory epithelium that mediate the common chemical sense.

frequency theory (312)   The idea that the basilar membrane vibrates as a unit in response to sound, in synchrony with sound pressure changes. See **place theory.**

frequency tuning curve (322)   A graph describing the sensitivity of an auditory neuron to tones of various frequencies.

fundamental frequency (349, 356)   The lowest frequency among the set of frequencies associated with a complex sound.

Gestalt principles of organization (141)   Certain stimulus properties that control the perceptual grouping of objects. See **closure, proximity, similarity.**

glaucoma (36)   A relatively common ocular disorder in which fluid pressure builds up within the eyeball, eventually causing blindness if not corrected.

grating (145)   A target consisting of alternating darker and lighter bars, used to study spatial vision. See **sinusoidal grating.**

group movement (284)   In an ambiguous type of apparent movement, the percept that all stimulus components move back and forth *en masse* (as a group). See **apparent motion, element movement.**

habituation (209)   The process by which an organism ceases to respond to some stimulus.

hammer (malleus) (302)   The outermost of the three ossicles within the middle ear; one end of the hammer is attached to the eardrum, and the other end relays sound vibrations to the anvil.

hearing acuity (363)   The highest frequency that can be heard by an organism.

Hermann grid (74)   A regular, geometric pattern within which illusory spots are seen; the presence and strength of the illusory spots depend on the spacing of the grid's elements.

hertz (Hz) (297)   A unit for expressing the frequency with which the intensity of a sound or a light varies over time.

horopter (224)   An imaginary plane in visual space that contains objects whose images fall on corresponding points of the retinas of the left and right eyes; any object situated on the horopter will be seen as single.

hue (182)   The dimension of color experience that distinguishes among red, orange, yellow, green, blue, and so on; the dimension of color most strongly determined by light's wavelength; commonly used as synonym for *color*. See **brightness, saturation.**

hypercolumn (122)   An aggregation of columns of cortical cells whose receptive fields overlap on the same restricted region of the retina.

hyperopic (47)   Referring to an abnormally short eyeball, in which the image is blurred because the eye's focal point lies behind the retina.

impedance matching (304)   The process whereby differences in pressure or resistance between two elements are overcome, as in the middle ear, where impedance matching is partially achieved through the amplification of sound vibrations by the three ossicles.

induced motion (279)   The illusory impression, created when moving contours are nearby a stationary object, that the stationary object is moving.

inner hair cells (307)   The approximately 3,500 flask-shaped structures situated along the length of the basilar membrane of the human ear. See **outer hair cells.**

intensity (73)   The physical variable expressing the strength or amplitude of a stimulus, such as light or sound. Intensity can be measured by physical devices such as photometers and sound-level meters. See **amplitude.**

interaural intensity difference (325)   The difference in the intensity of sound arriving at the two ears; one of the sources of information for sound localization. See **interaural time difference.**

interaural time difference (325, 360)   The difference in the time of arrival of a sound wave at the two ears; one of the sources of information for sound localization. See **interaural intensity difference.**

interposition (232)   A monocular depth cue based on occlusion of a distant object by a closer one.

intrinsic light (dark light) (452)   The impression, in complete darkness, of a dim cloud of light.

ipsilateral fibers (100)   In the case of vision, those optic nerve fibers that project from one eye to the same side of the brain. See **contralateral fibers.**

iris (36)   The two-layered ring of tissue that gives the eye its characteristic color.

isomorphism (143, 249)   The Gestalt hypothesis that spatial distribution of brain activity evoked by some object hears a topological resemblance to that object.

lateral geniculate nucleus (102)   A group of nerve cell bodies arranged in layers in the thalamus, each layer receiving input from either the left eye or the right eye; the major relay station between the eye and the visual cortex.

lateral inhibition (66)   Antagonistic neural interaction between adjacent regions of a sensory surface, such as the retina.

lightness (73)   A perceptual variable that is correlated with light intensity.

lightness constancy (80)   The tendency for the perceived lightness of an object to remain constant despite variation in the level of its illumination.

lightness contrast (79)   An effect in which a fixed physical intensity of light produces different perceived lightnesses depending upon the intensity of the light's background.

linear perspective (237)   The convergence of lines that makes a two-dimensional representation of a scene appear to be three-dimensional.

looming detectors (263)   Neurons that are sensitive to a progressive expansion of targets within their receptive fields; also known as *size-change detectors*.

loudness (338)   The subjective experience associated with sound intensity.

loudness matching (339)   A psychophysical procedure in which a listener adjusts the intensity of one tone until it sounds as loud as another tone. See **equal loudness contours.**

Mach bands (72)   Illusory spatial gradations in perceived lightness that occur in the absence of corresponding gradations in the actual spatial distribution of light.

macula (41)   The small, circular central region of the retina where vision is most acute.

malleus (302)   See **hammer.**

magnitude estimation (339)   A psychophysical procedure in which people assign numbers to stimuli in proportion to the perceived intensity of those stimuli.

masking (368)   A reduction in one stimulus' visibility or loudness as a result of the juxtaposition of another, stronger stimulus.

Mechanism (21)   The philosophical view that ascribes all mental experiences to neural events. See **Dualism.**

medial geniculate nucleus (326)   A structure in the thalamus that is part of the auditory system.

melody contour (353)   The rise and fall of successive notes in a musical passage.

meridional amblyopia (118)   A loss in visual acuity for lines of a particular orientation.

metameric (186)   Referring to the relation between two stimuli that appear to be identical despite physical differences.

metamers (171)   Two or more objects that appear identical despite actual physical differences.

method of adjustment (452)   A psychophysical procedure in which a person adjusts a stimulus so that it is just detectable (absolute threshold) or until a just noticeable change is produced (difference threshold).

method of constant stimuli (452)   A psychophysical procedure in which each of a fixed set of stimuli is presented in random order.

method of limits (452)   A psychophysical procedure in which the stimulus intensity changes progressively in small steps until the person's response changes, for example from "No, I don't see it" to "Yes, I do see it."

microelectrode (63)   A thin wire that can be inserted into brain tissue in order to record action potentials.

microspectrophotometry (197)   A technique for measuring, at various wavelengths, the quantity of light reflected or absorbed by a small object; used to measure cone photopigments.

modification (414)   Alteration in the taste of one substance when it is sampled together with another substance.

monaural (325)   Listening with one ear. See **binaural.**

monochromat (193)   A person whose eye contains just one type of cone photopigment.

monocular (324)   Seeing with one eye. See **binocular.**

motion aftereffect (waterfall illusion) (278)   The illusory impression, after prolonged viewing of movement in one direction, that a stationary object is moving in the opposite direction.

motion parallax (242)   A source of potent monocular depth information based on differences in relative motion between images of objects located at different distances from an observer.

multichannel model (147)   The hypothesis that spatial vision is the product, in part, of sets of neurons responsive to different spatial frequencies.

multidimensional scaling (MDS) (386)   A quantitative technique for geometrically representing similarity among stimuli.

myelin (99)   A membrane that insulates a neuron's axon and speeds conduction of nerve impulses along that axon.

myopic (47)   Referring to an abnormally long eye, in which the retinal image is blurred because the eye's focal point lies in front of the retina.

naive realism (11)   The philosophical view that perception accurately portrays all objects and events in the world.

nanometer (57)   A unit of length, in the metric system, corresponding to one-billionth of a meter, used for specifying wavelength of light.

near senses (6)   Senses, such as touch, that require close proximity between the perceiver and the object or event to be perceived. See **distance senses.**

neurogram (372)   A graph depicting variations over time in the neural activity within a large number of frequency-selective neurons in response to a complex sound.

neutral point (195)   In a dichromatic eye, the wavelength of light that appears white (neutral in color).

Newton's color circle (186)   A geometric arrangement of colors summarizing the results of mixing varying amounts of different colors.

noise (299)   A complex sound whose many constituent frequencies combine to produce a random waveform.

nonspectral colors (187)   Colors, such as purple, that are not found in the spectrum.

oblique effect (118)   The tendency for lines oriented vertically or horizontally to be more visible than lines oriented along a diagonal.

ocular dominance (124)   The variation in strength of excitatory input from the two eyes to a binocular cell of the visual cortex.

oculomotor cues (217)   Kinesthetic cues to depth derived from muscular contractions of the extraocular muscles.

odor adaptation (399)   A reduction in odor sensitivity following prolonged exposure to an odorous substance.

odor constancy (397)   The tendency of an odor's perceived intensity to remain constant despite variations in the flow rate of air drawn into the nose.

odor hallucinations (399)   Odors experienced without any physical stimulus; a phenomenon sometimes associated with brain damage.

olfactory brain (394)   A cluster of neural structures that receives projections from the olfactory bulb via the olfactory tract.

olfactory bulb (394)   The brain structure that receives input from the olfactory nerve.

olfactory epithelium (392)   A patch of tissue situated near the top of the nasal cavity and containing the olfactory receptor cells.

olfactory nerve (393)   The bundle of axons from olfactory receptor cells that project to the olfactory bulb, carrying information about odorous substances from the nose to the brain. Also called the *first cranial nerve.*

olfactory receptor cell (392)   One of the specialized structures within the olfactory epithelium that register the presence of odorous substances.

ophthalmoscope (39)   An optical device used to visualize the inside of the eye.

optic ataxia (264)   A neurological disorder characterized by difficulties in the visual guidance of limb movement.

optic chiasm (100)   The point at which nerve fibers from the two eyes are rerouted to higher visual centers, with some fibers from each eye projecting to the same side of the brain (ipsilateral fibers) and the remainder projecting to the opposite side of the brain (contralateral fibers).

optic disk (41)   The region of the eye where the optic nerve penetrates the retina; also, the region where major blood vessels enter and exit the eye's interior.

optic nerve (99)   The bundle of axons of retinal ganglion cells that carries visual information from the eye to the brain. Also known as the *second cranial nerve.*

optic tracts (101)   The two bundles of axons of retinal ganglion cells formed after the nerve fibers exit the optic chiasm.

organ of Corti (307)   The receptor organ for hearing, situated within the cochlear duct.

orientation (148)   The degree of inclination of a contour within a two-dimensional plane.

orientation selectivity (117)   A unique property of visual cortical cells, whereby they respond best to contours of a particular orientation, with the response decreasing as the orientation deviates increasingly from the preferred value.

ossicles (302)   A series of three tiny bones that transmit sound vibrations from the eardrum to the oval window. See **hammer, anvil, stirrup.**

otosclerosis (333)   A disorder of the middle ear involving immobilization of the stirrup.

outer hair cells (307)   The approximately 12,000 cylindrical structures situated along the length of the basilar membrane of the human ear. See **inner hair cells.**

oval window (302)   The small opening into the inner ear, which is covered by a thin membrane and which receives vibrations from the ear drum via the ossicles.

overtones (356)   A set of higher frequencies that, together with the fundamental frequency, defines the timbre of a musical instrument. See **timbre.**

papillae (407)   Little bumps distributed over the tongue's surface, the walls of which are lined with taste buds.

perceived distance (235)   The apparent visual separation between two objects or between an object and the viewer.

perception (1)   The acquisition and processing of sensory information in order to see, hear, taste, smell, or feel objects in the world; also guides an organism's actions with respect to those objects.

Perception may involve conscious awareness of objects and events; this awareness is termed a *percept.*

perceptual differentiation (432)   The tendency of exposure to particular stimuli to sharpen one's ability to distinguish among them.

perfect pitch (351)   The comparatively rare ability to identify any musical note played or to reproduce vocally any named note. See **relative pitch.**

perimetry (110)   A procedure for measuring a visual field, which involves determining the positions in visual space where a person can and cannot see a small spot of light.

pheromones (382)   Odors that serve as sexual signals.

phoneme (370)   A sound difference that affects the meaning of an utterance; widely regarded as the fundamental unit of speech.

phonemic restoration effect (422)   The tendency to hear a sound that has actually been deleted from an utterance.

phosphenes (127)   Visual sensations arising entirely from neural events within the visual pathways, in the absence of light stimulation.

photon (85)   The smallest unit of light energy.

photopic (84)   Referring to vision under daylight levels of illumination. See **scotopic.**

photopigment (57)   Light-sensitive molecules within a photoreceptor; light causes the photopigment to isomerize, releasing energy that alters the photoreceptor's electrical potential.

photoreceptors (53)   Specialized nerve cells (rods and cones) in the eye that contain photopigment; absorption of light by these cells triggers changes in the cells' electrical potential.

pigment epithelium (42)   A layer of the retina that helps to dispose of cellular debris.

pinna (301)   The part of the ear projecting from the side of the head; by influencing the frequency composition of sound waves entering the ear, this prominent structure plays a role in sound localization.

pitch (349)   The subjective counterpart to sound frequency.

place theory (313)   The idea that different portions of the basilar membrane vibrate in response to different sound frequencies. See **frequency theory.**

power law (342)   The psychophysical principle

that sensation magnitude tends to grow as a power function of stimulus intensity.

presbycusis (330)   In hearing, an age-related gradual loss of sensitivity to high-frequency tones.

presbyopia (50)   A significant decline in accommodative ability beginning in middle age.

profile analysis (346)   The process by which the relative activity of various neurons registers some property of a stimulus.

proprioception (264)   The sense that enables one to feel where one's limbs are.

prosopagnosia (446)   An inability to recognize faces. See **agnosias.**

proximity (141)   The Gestalt principle of organization referring to the perceptual tendency to group together objects that are near one another. See **similarity, closure.**

psychophysics (2, 450)   The branch of perception that is concerned with establishing quantitative relations between physical stimulation and perceptual events.

pupil (36)   The aperture in the eye formed by two sets of concentric bands of muscle; the constriction and dilation of these muscles vary the diameter of the pupil.

pure light (183)   According to Newton, any light that cannot be broken down into constituent colors. See **composite light.**

pure tones (297)   Sinusoidal variations in sound pressure, such as those produced by striking a tuning fork.

Purkinje shift (92)   Perceptual variation in the relative lightness of different colors as illumination changes from daylight to twilight.

random-dot stereogram (226)   A pair of pictures composed of black and white dots randomly positioned within the pictures; when such pictures are viewed stereoscopically (one picture seen by each eye), a vivid sensation of depth results, making an object appear to stand out from its surroundings.

receptive field (65)   The area of the retina within which the activity of a neuron can be influenced; sometimes defined in terms of the region of visual space from which a neuron can be influenced.

rectus muscles (28)   Four of the extraocular muscles; largely responsible for moving the eyeball back and forth horizontally (medial rectus and lateral rectus) and up and down vertically (superior rectus and inferior rectus). See **extraocular muscles.**

red-green cells (207)   Neurons showing a polarized response to spectral lights, which increases over one portion of the spectrum and decreases over another portion; the transition between the two types of responses occurs between the regions of the spectrum called green and red. See **blue-yellow cells.**

redundancy (433)   Referring to information that is either repetitive or highly predictable.

refraction (52)   The bending of light by an optical element such as a lens.

relative distance (217)   The distance between two objects. See **absolute distance.**

relative pitch (352)   The comparatively common ability to identify a tonal interval without necessarily knowing the particular tones that make up that interval. See **perfect pitch.**

resolution (83)   The ability to distinguish spatial details of an object.

resonant frequency (301)   The frequency at which a given object vibrates when set into motion.

reticular activating system (107)   A brain stem structure that governs an organism's general level of arousal.

retina (33, 39)   The innermost layer of the eyeball, where light is detected by photoreceptors and transduced into neural signals that are processed by collector cells.

retinal disparity (220)   A slight difference in lateral separation between objects seen by the left eye and by the right eye; makes stereopsis possible. See **stereopsis.**

retinal ganglion cells (62)   The collector cells that are responsible for the last stage of visual processing within the retina; axons of the retinal ganglion cells constitute the optic nerve.

retinal image (41)   The distribution of light falling on the retina; the quality and overall intensity of this image influences visual perception.

retinotopic map (105)   A neural representation within the visual system that preserves the spatial layout of the retina.

Ricco's Law (86)   The principle that stimuli will be equally detectable if the product of their intensity and area is constant.

rods (54)   Photoreceptors that are specialized for vision under dim light. See **cones.**

Rorschach test (428)   A projective psychological test in which people are shown inkblots and asked to describe what they see.

round window (307)   The thin membrane that covers a small opening into the middle ear; displacement of this membrane compensates for pressure variations within the cochlea.

saccades (266)   Rapid, jerky movements of the eyes, which function to change fixation from one location to another.

saturation (182)   The dimension of color experience that distinguishes pale or washed-out colors from vivid colors. See **brightness, hue.**

sclera (33)   The tough, dense material that forms the eye's outermost coat; seen from the front, the sclera is the white of the eye.

sclerosis (38)   The hardening of any living tissue; hardening of the eye's crystalline lens may play a role in presbyopia.

scotoma (110)   A region of blindness within the visual field.

scotopic (84)   Referring to vision under dim levels of illumination. See **photopic.**

selective adaptation (164, 277)   A method of studying mechanisms of perception, in which a person's sensitivity to particular targets is depressed by prolonged exposure to one particular target.

sensory decision theory (SDT) (459)   A quantitative treatment of detection and discrimination performance, in which the observer is characterized as a maker of statistical decisions; the system also prescribes techniques that allow the observer's sensitivity to the stimulus to be estimated independently of the observer's criterion, or preference for particular responses. Also called *signal detection theory.*

sensory/neural loss (332)   A form of hearing loss originating within the inner ear or the auditory pathways; may involve selective loss of sensitivity to a limited range of frequencies. See **conduction loss.**

sensory transduction (1)   The process occurring within sensory receptors, by which physical energy (stimulus) is converted into neural signals.

shape constancy (176)   The tendency for an object's perceived shape to remain constant despite changes in the shape of the retinal image of that object.

signal detection theory (459)   See **sensory decision theory.**

similarity (141)   The Gestalt principle of organization referring to the perceptual tendency to group together objects that are similar to one another in texture, shape, and so. See **closure, proximity.**

simple cells (120)   Visual cortical cells that exhibit clearly defined ON and OFF regions within their receptive fields. See **complex cells.**

single cell recording (63)   The use of a microelectrode to record the neural activity of individual nerve cells as they respond to stimulation.

sinusoidal grating (145)   A target in which the intensity of darker and lighter bars varies sinusoidally over space. See **gratings.**

size aftereffect (174)   A change in the apparent size of an object following inspection of an object of a different size.

size constancy (247)   The tendency for an object's perceived size to remain constant despite changes in the size of the retinal image of that object as viewing distance varies.

sound pressure level (SPL) (298)   A reference level for sound intensity.

spatial frequency (148)   For a grating target, the number of pairs of bars imaged within a given distance on the retina; units of spatial frequency are cycles/mm or, equivalently, cycles/degree of visual angle.

spatial phase (148)   The position of a grating relative to some visual landmark.

spatial summation (83, 85, 204)   The process by which neural signals from neighboring retinal areas are combined, thereby increasing sensitivity. See **temporal summation.**

specific anosmias (398)   Conditions in which people have normal odor sensitivity for some substances but reduced sensitivity for other substances. See **anosmia.**

specific nerve energies (13)   The doctrine that the qualitative nature of a sensation depends on which particular nerve fibers are stimulated.

spectrogram (371)   A graph depicting the frequency composition of a sound as a function of time.

spectral colors (182)   Hues that are present in a spectrum created by diffracting white light as, for example, in a rainbow.

squint (231)   See **strabismus.**

stabilized retinal images (266)   Images whose location on the retina remains fixed despite movements of the eye.

staircase method (454)   A psychophysical procedure in which the stimulus presentations, governed by a person's responses, are made to bracket the threshold; an interactive variant of the method of limits.

stapes (302)   See **stirrup.**

stereoblindness (230)   The inability to see depth using retinal disparity information, a condition thought to result from a reduction in the number of binocular visual cells in the visual cortex. See **disparity-selective cells.**

stereoscope (224)   An optical device for presenting pictures separately to the two eyes.

stereopsis (220)   Binocular depth perception based on retinal disparity. See **retinal disparity.**

stimulus (1)   The pattern of physical energy set up by an object or event in the environment.

stirrup (stapes) (302)   The innermost of the ossicles within the middle eàr; attached to the oval window, it receives sound vibrations from the anvil and sets the oval window into vibration.

strabismus (231)   Squint; a condition in which the two eyes are misaligned, making normal binocular fixation impossible.

subjective color (214)   The experience of color produced by transient stimulation with black and white targets.

subtractive color mixture (190)   A color produced when each of a number of components absorbs a portion of the light's spectrum, thereby subtracting that portion from the reflected spectrum. See **additive color mixture.**

superior colliculus (102)   A subcortical brain structure located in the midbrain; this structure, thought to receive input primarily from W- and Y-type retinal ganglion cells, plays a role in the initiation and guidance of eye movements.

superior olivary nucleus (superior olive) (325)   A structure containing neurons sensitive to differences in the time of arrival of sound at the two ears and to differences in the intensity of sound arriving at the two ears. These neurons presumably play a role in sound localization.

synapse (57)   A tiny gap between adjacent nerve cells. See **transmitter substance.**

taste buds (407)   Garlic-shaped structures lining the walls of the papillae on the tongue and containing chemical-sensitive cells that register the presence of taste solutions.

taste hedonics (417)   Judgments of the pleasantness of taste substances.

taste suppression (416)   The reduction in the strength of one taste sensation by another; for example, sugar suppresses the bitter taste of coffee.

tectorial membrane (307)   An awning-like layer of tissue arching over the hair cells within the inner ear.

temporal summation (85)   The process by which signals from a neuron or neurons are cumulated over time, thereby increasing sensitivity. See **spatial summation.**

temporary threshold shift (334)   A short-lived decrease in hearing sensitivity caused by exposure to noise.

texture gradient (238)   A form of perspective in which the density of a surface's texture increases with distance, providing information about the slant of the surface.

threshold intensity (321, 329)   The minimum sound intensity necessary to elicit a neural response from an auditory neuron.

tilt aftereffect (131)   A temporary change in the perceived orientation of lines following adaptation to lines of a similar, but not identical, orientation.

timbre (356)   The quality of sound that distinguishes different musical instruments. See **overtones.**

tinnitus (319, 335)   An annoying, persistent ringing in the ears.

tonotopic organization (316)   The orderly layout of preferred frequencies over the length of the basilar membrane.

top-down (422)   A tendency for perception to be shaped by a flow of information from higher nervous centers toward lower ones. See **bottom-up.**

transfer function (152)   A graph showing, for various target spatial frequencies, the contrast contained in an image.

transmitter substance (59)   The neurochemicals that flow across synaptic gaps between adjacent nerve cells, allowing cells to communicate with one another. See **synapse.**

traveling wave (315)   The movement of the basilar membrane in response to fluctuations in fluid pressure within the cochlea.

trichromatic (195)   Referring to a person whose eye contains three types of cone photopigments.

tympanic canal (306)   One of the three wedge-shaped chambers of the cochlea.

tympanic membrane (302)   See **eardrum**.

univariance principle (192)   The hypothesis that any photoreceptor's response corresponds to just a single variable, the amount of light absorbed; because photoreceptors obey the univariance principle, the wavelength characteristics of light that stimulate a photoreceptor are not directly represented in the receptor's response.

vascular tunic (33)   The middle layer of the eyeball; responsible for much of the eye's nourishment.

vergence (31)   Referring to eye movements in which the two eyes move in opposite directions. See **conjunctive**.

vestibular canal (306)   One of the three wedge-shaped chambers of the cochlea.

vestibular eye movements (272)   Eye movements that promote the steadiness of gaze by compensating for movements of the head and body.

vestibule (272)   A chamber in the inner ear involved in vestibular eye movements.

visual acuity (158)   A measure of the smallest detail that a person can resolve.

visual cues (217)   Sources of depth information based on monocular and binocular image properties.

visual field (110)   The extent of visual space over which vision is possible with the eyes held in a fixed position.

visual masking (268)   The reduction of one target's visibility by the presentation of another target nearby in time and space.

vitreous (39)   The thick transparent fluid that fills the eye's largest chamber.

waterfall illusion (278)   See **motion aftereffect**.

wavelength (25)   The distance from the peak of one wave to the peak of the next. For electromagnetic radiation, such as light, wavelength is determined by the rate at which the emitting substance oscillates. This physical property of light, specified in nanometers, is related to the perceptual experience of hue.

Weber's Law (451)   The principle that for various stimulus intensities, the difference threshold tends to be a constant fraction of the stimulus.

window of visibility (155)   The range of spatial frequencies that, with sufficient contrast, an observer can see.

word superiority effect (433)   The finding that, under some conditions, an entire word may be read more rapidly (or seen more easily) than just one of the word's letters.

X cells (69)   A class of retinal ganglion cells characterized by small receptive fields, thin axons, and relatively sustained responses to visual stimulation. See **Y cells**.

Y cells (69)   A class of retinal ganglion cells characterized by large receptive fields, thick axons, and relatively transient responses to visual stimulation. See **X cells**.

Young-Helmholtz theory (196)   The theory that human color vision is trichromatic—that is, it depends on the responses of three types of cones.

Name Index

Subject Index

About the Authors

Robert Sekuler is a professor of psychology and neurobiology/physiology at Northwestern University, Evanston, Illinois, and professor of ophthalmology at Northwestern University School of Medicine, Chicago. After undergraduate work at Brandeis University, Sekuler earned a Ph.D. in psychology from Brown University in 1964. Prior to joining the faculty at Northwestern in 1965, he was a postdoctoral fellow at the Massachusetts Institute of Technology. Author or co-author of some 100 scientific papers, he has contributed major chapters to *The Handbook of Perception*, *The Handbook of Sensory Physiology*, and the *Annual Review of Psychology*. An internationally recognized authority on perceptual changes in aging, Sekuler is co-editor (with Don Kline and Key Dismukes) of the highly successful volume *Aging and Human Visual Function* (1982). He is frequently asked to consult on the role of perception in accidents and applied settings, and currently chairs the Committee on Vision of the National Academy of Sciences/National Research Council. In addition to his work on the perceptual consequences of aging, Sekuler's research emphasizes pattern vision and the perception of visual motion.

Randolph Blake is a professor of psychology and neurobiology at Northwestern University, Evanston, Illinois. He received a Ph.D. from Vanderbilt University in 1972 and then spent two years as a postdoctoral fellow in the Sensory Sciences Center at the University of Texas Graduate School of Biomedical Sciences. He joined the faculty at Northwestern in 1974. In recognition of his undergraduate teaching contributions, Blake received the Distinguished Teaching Award at Northwestern. He has published extensively in major psychology and neuroscience journals and has contributed chapters to edited books including *Models of the Visual Cortex*, *Frontiers of Visual Science*, and *Development of Perception*. His research focuses on visual perception, with particular emphasis on binocular vision and the neural correlates of pattern perception. In recognition of his research contributions, Blake received a Career Development Award from the National Institutes of Health and the American Psychological Association's Distinguished Scientific Award for an Early Career Contribution to Psychology.

A Note on the Type

The text of this book was set in Palatino, a type face designed by the noted German typographer Hermann Zapf. Named after Giovanbattista Palatino, a writing master of Renaissance Italy, Palatino was the first of Zapf's type faces to be introduced to America. The first designs for the face were made in 1948, and the fonts for the complete face were issued between 1950 and 1952. Like all Zapf-designed type faces, Palatino is beautifully balanced and exceedingly readable.

This version of Palatino was composed via computer-driven cathode ray tube by Waldman Graphics, Inc., Pennsauken, New Jersey.

Printed and bound by Rand McNally & Co., Taunton, Massachusetts.